BEACON
BIBLE COMMENTARY

BEACON
BIBLE COMMENTARY

In Ten Volumes

Volume IV
The Major Prophets

ISAIAH
> *Ross E. Price, M.A., M.Th., Ph.D.*

JEREMIAH, LAMENTATIONS
> *C. Paul Gray, M.A., Ph.D.*

EZEKIEL
> *J. Kenneth Grider, M.A., Ph.D.*

DANIEL
> *Roy E. Swim, B.D., D.D.*

BEACON HILL PRESS OF KANSAS CITY
Kansas City, Missouri

BEACON BIBLE COMMENTARY

In Ten Volumes

Preface

"All scripture is given by inspiration of God, and is profitable for doctrine, for reproof, for correction, for instruction in righteousness: that the man of God may be perfect, throughly furnished unto all good works" (II Tim. 3:16-17).

We believe in the plenary inspiration of the Bible. God speaks to men through His Word. He hath spoken unto us by His Son. But without the inscripted Word how would we know the Word which was made flesh? He does speak to us by His Spirit, but the Spirit uses the written Word as the vehicle of His revelation, for He is the true Author of the Holy Scriptures. What the Spirit reveals is in agreement with the Word.

The Christian faith derives from the Bible. It is the Foundation for faith, for salvation, and sanctification. It is the Guide for Christian character and conduct. "Thy word is a lamp unto my feet, and a light unto my path" (Ps. 119:105).

The revelation of God and His will for men is adequate and complete in the Bible. The great task of the Church, therefore, is to communicate the knowledge of the Word, to enlighten the eyes of the understanding, and to awaken and to illuminate the conscience that men may learn "to live soberly, righteously, and godly, in this present world." This leads to the possession of that "inheritance [that is] incorruptible, and undefiled, and that fadeth not away, reserved in heaven."

When we consider the translation and interpretation of the Bible, we admit we are guided by men who are not inspired. Human limitation, as well as the plain fact that no scripture is of private or single interpretation, allows variation in the exegesis and exposition of the Bible.

Beacon Bible Commentary is offered in 10 volumes with becoming modesty. It does not supplant others. Neither does it purport to be exhaustive or final. The task is colossal. Assignments have been made to 40 of the ablest writers available. They are trained men with serious purpose, deep dedication, and supreme devotion. The sponsors and publishers, as well as the contributors, earnestly pray that this new offering among Bible commentaries will be helpful to preachers, teachers, and laymen in discovering the deeper meaning of God's Word and in unfolding its message to all who hear them.

—G. B. WILLIAMSON

Acknowledgments

Permission to quote from copyrighted material is gratefully acknowledged as follows:

Abingdon Press: Henry Sloane Coffin and James Muilenberg in Volume V, *The Interpreter's Bible.*

Bible House of Los Angeles: W. C. Stevens, *The Book of Daniel.*

Wm. B. Eerdmans Publishing Co.: E. J. Young, *The Messianic Prophecies of Daniel.*

Fleming H. Revell: G. Campbell Morgan, *Studies in the Prophecy of Jeremiah.*

Westminster Press and Epworth Press (London): James D. Smart, *History and Theology in Second Isaiah.*

Scripture quotations have been made from the following copyrighted sources:

The Amplified Old Testament. Copyright 1964, Zondervan Publishing House.

The Berkeley Version in Modern English. Copyright 1958, 1959, Zondervan Publishing House.

The Bible: A New Translation, James Moffatt. Copyright 1950, 1952, 1953, 1954, by James A. R. Moffatt. Used by permission of Harper and Row.

The Bible: An American Translation, J. M. Powis Smith, Edgar J. Goodspeed. Copyright 1923, 1927, 1948 by The University of Chicago Press.

Revised Standard Version of the Holy Bible. Copyright 1946 and 1952 by the Division of Christian Education of the National Council of Churches.

The Basic Bible: Containing the Old and New Testaments in Basic English. Copyright 1950 by E. P. Dutton and Co., Inc.

Knox Version of the Holy Bible, by Msgr. Ronald Knox. Copyright 1960 by The Macmillan Co.

The Holy Bible from the Peshitta, translated by George M. Lamsa. Copyright 1933, 1939, 1940, by A. J. Holman Co.

Four Prophets: A Modern Translation from the Hebrew, by John B. Phillips. Copyright 1963 by The Macmillan Co.

Quotations and References

Boldface type in the exposition indicates a quotation from the King James Version of the passage under discussion. Readings from other versions are put in quotation marks and the version is indicated.

In scripture references a letter (*a, b,* etc.) indicates a clause within a verse. When no book is named, the book under discussion is understood.

Bibliographical data on a work cited by a writer may be found by consulting the first reference to the work by that writer, or by turning to the bibliography.

The bibliographies are not intended to be exhaustive but are included to provide complete publication data for volumes cited in the text.

References to an author in the text, or inclusion of his books in the bibliography, does not constitute an endorsement of his views. All reading in the field of biblical interpretation should be discriminating and thoughtful.

How to Use "Beacon Bible Commentary"

The Bible is a Book to be read, to be understood, to be obeyed, and to be shared with others. *Beacon Bible Commentary* is planned to help at the points of understanding and sharing.

For the most part, the Bible is its own best interpreter. He who reads it with an open mind and receptive spirit will again and again become aware that through its pages God is speaking *to him.* A commentary serves as a valuable resource when the meaning of a passage is not clear even to the thoughtful reader. Also after one has seen his own meaning in a passage from the Bible, it is rewarding to discover what truth others have found in the same place. Sometimes, too, this will correct possible misconceptions the reader may have formed.

Beacon Bible Commentary has been written to be used with your Bible in hand. Most major commentaries print the text of the Bible at the top of the commentary page. The editors decided against this practice, believing that the average user comes to his commentary from his Bible and hence has in mind the passage in which he is interested. He also has his Bible at his elbow for any necessary reference to the text. To have printed the full text of the Bible in a work of this size would have occupied approximately one-third of the space available. The planners decided to give this space to additional resources for the reader. At the same time, writers have woven into their comments sufficient quotations from the passages under discussion that the reader maintains easy and constant thought contact with the words of the Bible. These quoted words are printed in boldface type for quick identification.

ILLUMINATION FROM RELATED PASSAGES

The Bible is its own best interpreter when a given chapter or a longer section is read to find out what it says. This Book is also its own best interpreter when the reader knows what the Bible says in other places about the subject under consideration. The writers and editors of *Beacon Bible Commentary* have constantly striven to give maximum help at this point. Related and carefully chosen cross-references have been included in order that the reader may thus find the Bible interpreted and illustrated by the Bible itself.

Paragraph Treatment

The truth of the Bible is best understood when we grasp the thought of the writer in its sequence and connections. The verse divisions with which we are familiar came into the Bible late (the sixteenth century for the New Testament and the seventeenth century for the Old). They were done hurriedly and sometimes missed the thought pattern of the inspired writers. The same is true of the chapter divisions. Most translations today arrange the words of the sacred writers under our more familiar paragraph structure.

It is under this paragraph arrangement that our commentary writers have approached their task. They have tried always to answer the question, What was the inspired writer saying in this passage? Verse numbers have been retained for easy identification but basic meanings have been outlined and interpreted in the larger and more complete thought forms.

Introduction to Bible Books

The Bible is an open Book to him who reads it thoughtfully. But it opens wider when we gain increased understanding of its human origins. Who wrote this book? Where was it written? When did the writer live? What were the circumstances that caused him to write? Answers to these questions always throw added light on the words of the Scripture.

These answers are given in the Introductions. There also you will find an outline of each book. The Introduction has been written to give an overview of the whole book; to provide you with a dependable road map before you start your trip—and to give you a place of reference when you are uncertain as to which way to turn. Don't ignore the flagman when he waves his warning sign, "See Introduction." At the close of the commentary on each book you will find a bibliography for further study.

Maps and Charts

The Bible was written about people who lived in lands that are foreign and strange to most English-speaking readers. Often better understanding of the Bible depends on better knowledge of Bible geography. When the flagman waves his other sign, "See map," you should turn to the map for a clearer understanding of the locations, distances, and related timing of the experiences of the men with whom God was dealing.

This knowledge of Bible geography will help you to be a better Bible preacher and teacher. Even in the more formal presentation of the sermon it helps the congregation to know that the flight into Egypt was "a journey on foot, some 200 miles to the southwest." In the less formal and smaller groups such as Sunday school classes and prayer meeting Bible study, a large classroom map enables the group to see the locations as well as to hear them mentioned. When you have seen these places on your commentary maps, you are better prepared to share the information with those whom you lead in Bible study.

Charts which list Bible facts in tabular form often make clear historical relationships in the same way that maps help with understanding geography. To see listed in order the kings of Judah or the Resurrection appearances of Jesus often gives clearer understanding of a particular item in the series. These charts are a part of the resources offered in this set.

Beacon Bible Commentary has been written for the newcomer to Bible study and also for those long familiar with the written Word. The writers and editors have probed each chapter, each verse, every clause, phrase, and word in the familiar King James Version. We have probed with the question, What do these words mean? If the answer is not self-evident we have charged ourselves to give the best explanation known to us. How well we have succeeded the reader must judge, but we invite you to explore the explanation of these words or passages that may puzzle you when you are reading God's written Word.

Exegesis and Exposition

Bible commentators often use these words to describe two ways of making clear the meaning of a passage in the Scriptures. *Exegesis* is a study of the original Greek or Hebrew words to understand what meanings those words had when they were used by men and women in Bible times. To know the meaning of the separate words, as well as their grammatical relationship to each other, is one way to understand more clearly what the inspired writer meant to say. You will often find this kind of enriching help in the commentary. But word studies alone do not always give true meaning.

Exposition is a commentator's effort to point out the meaning of a passage as it is affected by any one of several facts known to the writer but perhaps not familiar to the reader. These facts may be (1) the context (the surrounding verses or chapters), (2) the historical background, (3) the related teachings from other parts of the Bible, (4) the significance of these messages from God as they relate to universal facts of human life, (5) the relevance of these truths to unique contemporary human situations. The commentator thus seeks to explain the full meaning of a Bible passage in the light of his own best understanding of God, man, and the world in which we live.

Some commentaries separate the exegesis from this broader basis of explanation. In *Beacon Bible Commentary* writers have combined the exegesis and exposition. Accurate word studies are indispensable to a correct understanding of the Bible. But such careful studies are today so thoroughly reflected in a number of modern English translations that they are often not necessary except to enhance the understanding of the theological meaning of a passage. The writers and editors seek to reflect a true and accurate exegesis at every point, but specific exegetical discussions are introduced chiefly to throw added light on the meaning of a passage, rather than to engage in scholarly discussion.

The Bible is a practical Book. We believe that God inspired holy men of old to declare these truths in order that the readers might better understand and do the will of God. *Beacon Bible Commentary* has been undertaken only for the purpose of helping men to find more effectively God's will for them as revealed in the Scripture—to find that will and to act upon that knowledge.

Helps for Bible Preaching and Teaching

We have said that the Bible is a Book to be shared. Christian preachers and teachers since the first century have sought to convey the gospel message by reading and explaining selected passages of Scripture. *Beacon Bible Commentary* seeks to encourage this kind of expository preaching and teaching. The set contains more than a thousand brief expository outlines that have been used by outstanding Bible teachers and preachers. Both writers and editors have assisted in contributing or selecting these homiletical suggestions. It is hoped that the outlines will suggest ways in which the reader will want to try to open the Word of God to his class or congregation. Some of these analyses of preachable passages have been contributed by our contemporaries. When the outlines have appeared in print, authors and references are given in order that the reader may go to the original source for further help.

In the commentaries on Isaiah and Jeremiah the authors have indicated many of their expository outlines in ways different from those found elsewhere in this set. Note carefully (1) series of italicized words, (2) numbered or lettered outlines embedded in the body of the text, (3) teachable and preachable outlines in the regularly indicated divisions of the text.

In the Bible we find truth of the highest order. Here is given to us, by divine inspiration, the will of God for our lives. Here we have sure guidance in all things necessary to our relationships to God and under Him to our fellowman. Because these eternal truths come to us in human language and through human minds, they need to be put into fresh words as languages change and as thought patterns are modified. In *Beacon Bible Commentary* we have sought to help make the Bible a more effective Lamp to the paths of men who journey in the twentieth century.

A. F. HARPER

Table of Contents

VOLUME IV

Abbreviations and Explanations

The Books of the Bible

Gen.	Job	Jonah	I or II Cor.
Exod.	Ps.	Mic.	Gal.
Lev.	Prov.	Nah.	Eph.
Num.	Eccles.	Hab.	Phil.
Deut.	Song of Sol.	Zeph.	Col.
Josh.	Isa.	Hag.	I or II Thess.
Judg.	Jer.	Zech.	I or II Tim.
Ruth	Lam.	Mal.	Titus
I or II Sam.	Ezek.	Matt.	Philem.
I or II Kings	Dan.	Mark	Heb.
I or II Chron.	Hos.	Luke	Jas.
Ezra	Joel	John	I or II Pet.
Neh.	Amos	Acts	I, II, or III John
Esther	Obad.	Rom.	Jude
			Rev.

Vulg.	The Vulgate
LXX	The Septuagint
ASV	American Standard Revised Version
RSV	Revised Standard Version
Amp. OT	Amplified Old Testament
NASB	New American Standard Bible
NEB	New English Bible
LP	*Living Prophecies,* by Kenneth N. Taylor
Berk.	The Berkeley Version
Phillips	*Four Prophets,* by John B. Phillips
Basic Bible	The Basic Bible Containing the Old and New Testaments in Basic English
Knox	The Holy Bible: A Translation from the Latin Vulgate in the light of the Hebrew and Greek Originals, trans. by Ronald A. Knox
Von Orelli	*The Prophecies of Isaiah,* by C. von Orelli
IB	Interpreter's Bible
IDB	The Interpreter's Dictionary of the Bible
ISBE	International Standard Bible Encyclopedia
NBC	The New Bible Commentary
NBD	The New Bible Dictionary
BBC	Beacon Bible Commentary
HDB	Hastings' Dictionary of the Bible

c.	chapter	OT	Old Testament
cc.	chapters	NT	New Testament
v.	verse	Heb.	Hebrew
vv.	verses	Gk.	Greek

The Book of the Prophet

ISAIAH

Ross E. Price

Introduction

A. Importance

Isaiah stands foremost among the so-called "Greater Prophets." Of all Israel's celebrated messengers, he is the king. The writings which bear his name are among the profoundest of all literature, and for general excellence and distinction his prophecy has no parallel. Isaiah therefore stands without peer and excels the other prophets by the force of his personality, the wisdom of his statesmanship, the power of his oratory, and the clearness of his insights. His ministry was timely and far-reaching in its influence. The last forty years of the eighth century B.C. produced great men, but the greatest of these was the prophet Isaiah. His name means "the Eternal One is Salvation," and he frequently engages in a play on words using his own name, or one of its cognates, to emphasize his central theme: "Salvation by faith."

B. The World in Isaiah's Day

The historical background of Isaiah is found in II Kings 15—20 and II Chronicles 26—32.

(1) *Politically,* world forces were in conflict for supremacy. Assyria, the colossus to the northeast, dominated the scene. The twenty-third dynasty was in power in Egypt in Isaiah's early days, and the twenty-fourth and twenty-fifth followed before his death. The city of Rome was founded only a few years after his birth. The Mycaean age was closing in Greece with the rise of the famous city-states. At the time of Isaiah's birth, the northern kingdom of Israel, with its capital city at Samaria, was only a quarter-century away from its downfall. Syria met her doom during his later years.

According to the title of his book, Isaiah prophesied in Jerusalem during the reigns of Uzziah, Jotham, Ahaz, and Hezekiah. There is a strong tradition that he met his death at the hands of the wicked king Manasseh. At least we know that his great experience in the Temple (c. 6) came in the year of Uzziah's death, and he was still active as late as the siege of Jerusalem by Sennacherib in 701 B.C.

As a young man Isaiah witnessed the rapid development of Judah into a strong commercial and military state. Under Uzziah, Judah attained a degree of prosperity and strength she had not enjoyed since the days of Solomon. She had walled cities, tower fortresses, a large standing army, and a seaport for commerce on the Red Sea. Her inland trade had increased, tribute was being paid to her by the Ammonites, and successful wars were waged against Philistia and the Arabians. Such was the picture during the long fifty-two years of prosperous reign by Uzziah.

In the reign of Jotham the Assyrians turned their armies westward and southward for world conquest. City after city, including eventually Damascus of Syria, was reduced to rubble or else compelled to pay tribute to Assyria. This led Rezin of Syria and Pekah of Israel to form an alliance to resist the aggressor. They felt it imperative to enlist the aid of Judah in their opposition to the Assyrian advance. Thus King Ahaz was summoned to join their alliance. When he refused to do so, Rezin and Pekah declared war on him, with the view to forcing him into their compact or of dethroning him and placing the son of Tabeel upon the throne of David (II Kings 16: 5; Isa. 7: 6). The struggle which ensued is known as the Syro-Ephraimitic war (734 B.C.)

Hezekiah succeeded Ahaz, and though he inherited a heavy burden of foreign tribute from his father's reign, he instituted reforms by tearing down the groves and removing the high places with their pillars (II Kings 18: 4, 22). He commanded worship before the true altar in Jerusalem, and even invited those left in the Northern Kingdom to celebrate the Passover with Judah in Jerusalem (II Chron. 30: 1).

The fall of the Northern Kingdom came in January of 721 B.C. at the hands of the Assyrian, Sargon II. He carried away more than 27,000 captives and brought colonists from Babylon to settle in their place in the adjacent cities of Samaria (II Kings 17: 6, 24). Judah escaped only by paying heavy tribute.

When Hezekiah died, Manasseh, his son, succeeded him to the throne of Judah. He immediately abandoned his father's reforms, thus encountering the opposition of the prophet. Manasseh shed much blood (II Kings 21:2-16), and according to Epiphanius,[1] had Isaiah sawed in two—not, however, before the prophet had given us some of the greatest Messianic prophecies of Holy Writ.

(2) *Socially* there were the rich and the poor classes in Isaiah's time with the usual chasm between them. Abuses, re-

[1]*The Lives of the Prophets* (C. C. Torrey, trans., Philadelphia: Society of Biblical Literature and Exegesis, 1946), p. 34.

sentments, unrest, profiteering, land-grabbing, extortion, and eviction prevailed. Corrupt city governments and bribe-taking judges made life miserable for the poor. Luxury and idleness coupled with indifference to the suffering of others characterized those who were prosperous. Drunkenness was taking its usual toll and increasing poverty, sorrow, and distress.

(3) *Religious conditions* were anything but ideal. Baalism had infiltrated the worship of the upper and lower classes alike. Superstitious customs from the East and the gruesome worship of Moloch had polluted pure religion. Moral fiber was lacking and ethical standards were low. The ordinary prophets were too busy with strong drink to give attention to the spiritual welfare of the people. And had they wanted to help the people, they lacked any message of truth and power. Women were coarse, sensual, drunken, pampered, and careless.

Temple revenues had been increased, but there was a widening divorce between religion and life. Religious devotion was only a formal thing taken over secondhand from those who were devoid of the true understanding of God and His demands. Soulless service of God was polluted with the actual worship of other gods, and the land was full of idols before which rich and poor alike bowed down. Soothsayers and diviners had many clients. Through all the national life ran a pride and self-complacence which led the people to forget any dependence upon God. Isaiah deplored the mechanism of mere ritual and called for a return to sincere and spontaneous worship.

C. The Man

(1) *His nativity.* Isaiah was born about 760 B.C., though some Bible scholars would say 770 B.C.[2] He was a native of Jerusalem and the Southern Kingdom. He seems to have belonged to a family of some rank, for he had easy access to the king and close intimacy with the high priest. Tradition has it that he was a cousin of King Uzziah. He was familiar with Jerusalem. His imagery is derived from scenes in that city, and his interest seems chiefly confined to the city proper. His urban metaphors are appropriate to him in the same manner as the pastoral similes are to Amos. He was familiar with the Temple and its ritual, and seems to have functioned during most of his long life as court preacher for the city and nation.

[2]R. H. Pfeiffer, *Introduction to the Old Testament* (New York: Harper and Bros., 1941), p. 422.

(2) *His family.* Isaiah was married as early as 735 B.C. and had two sons, to each of whom he gave a symbolical and prophetic name. The eldest was called *Shear-jashub,* "a remnant shall return." He was probably born about 734 B.C., sometime after Isaiah's great vision in the Temple described in c. 6. The younger, *Maher-shalal-hash-baz,* "hastening to the spoils" or "hurrying to the prey," was so named in prediction of the soon-coming plundering of Damascus and Samaria by the Assyrians. Isaiah refers to his wife as "the prophetess" (8:3), but we are not to suppose from this that she shared her husband's gift of prophecy. Rather, the title seems to have been given to her because of her husband's function.

(3) *His sanctification and call.* It is very probable that Isaiah was influenced by contacts with Amos, Hosea, and Micah. His immediate contemporary was Micah. But the greatest spiritual influence in his life was the crisis he experienced in the Temple in the year that King Uzziah died. Some Bible scholars look upon this as his inaugural vision, but it came to him after some years of experience in preaching. It served definitely to deepen his spirituality and clarify his insights about God's character and the nature of his own calling.

We may note that the experience was sudden, visual, and auditory. In it the transcendent God was revealed in majesty and glory to His worshipping creature. Isaiah saw the vision, and heard the song of the holy ones and the voice of the eternal God. In contrast to the holy God he saw his own uncleanness, and as conviction gripped his soul he cried out his confession of it. The result was a cleansing and purification of lip and life that qualified him to carry out the divine commission.

Having heard the call of the Eternal for an ambassador, Isaiah immediately responded. As God's transformed man he now stood ready for his assignment. He was to stand as God's mouthpiece, a political and religious counselor in Jerusalem, until cities were wasted without inhabitants. Right down into the valley of exile and deportation he was to go as the comforter, critic, and counselor of his people. He was thus to minister, knowing all the while that many would not listen to him and that only a remnant would ever be saved to become the nucleus of a new Zion and the substance of a holy seed.

(4) *His personal characteristics.* Isaiah was one of the greatest spirits of all time, a man of faith with an optimistic view of the ultimate outcome of the Lord's cause. He gave God's message to

the men of his time, and the centuries have recognized him as a man of keen political insight and statesmanship.

Isaiah was both a poet and an orator—an artist with words; his brilliancy of expression is unsurpassed. Moreover, he always had his eye upon the future; thus the predictive element is strong in his prophecy. His character and genius have been summarized under the fourfold characterization as statesman, reformer, theologian, and poet.[3] Surely he was all of these. His views were clear, consistent, and sound. He had great concern for social justice and national righteousness. His oracles show that his horizon was worldwide. His was the true missionary outlook. If he was an aristocrat by birth, he was also one in character and spirit.

D. His Ministry

Isaiah's ministry lasted a working lifetime, during which he passed from youth to old age. It was all spent in his own community: a busy life of preaching, predicting, remonstrating with kings, priests, and people, and writing his prophecies. If tradition is correct, he saw the passing of four kings before his own martyrdom. As a statesman he has no equal among the prophets. Not even Elisha faced such grave and trying times. Kings were saved from suicidal policies by his discernment. His faith was the source of encouragement to many in Jerusalem and the salvation of Judah more than once.

As a preacher of social righteousness he has no equal unless it be Amos. Kings, judges, princes, and merchants were all rebuked by him. He spent his life trying to help people see God as he knew Him. He stood out as a spiritual giant in his day—an accurate seer and predictor of destinies.

E. His Message

Outstanding in Isaiah's prophecy is his rich concept of *the eternal God*.[4] For the prophet, God towers above all things earthly. He is "the Lord of hosts," "the high and lofty One that inhabiteth eternity," "the mighty One of Israel," "Maker" of all

---

[3] S. R. Driver, *Isaiah, His Life and Times* ("Men of the Bible" series) (New York: Fleming H. Revell Co., n.d.), Chap. IX.

[4] The great Hebrew term for God, *YAHWEH*, Moffatt translates, "The Eternal." W. F. Albright looks upon it as part of a formula meaning, "He who causes to be what comes into existence" (*From the Stone Age of Christianity* [Baltimore: Johns Hopkins Press, 1940], pp. 197-98). See the explanation of this term in BBC, II. 110, fn. 1.

things, and the Eternal One who doeth all things. God directs the course of history; there is no other God beside Him, and He has no intention of sharing His deity with any man-made rival. He is a God both of wisdom and of might. Moreover He is passionately ethical—the Holy One. Of Him the seraphim sang, "Holy, holy, holy" (6:2-3).

This holiness means more for Isaiah than mere divinity; it also means purity. His God demands repentance and faith, and the Eternal One alone is Salvation. Hence there must be a returning to God and a putting away of evildoing (1:16), plus a quiet waiting upon God in practical faith that He will bring deliverance. If God's people suffer oppression, it is because of their sins. Yet there will come the time of God's forgiveness and comfort. Hence in Isaiah's prophecy God speaks of himself as: "thy Redeemer," "thy God," "the Holy One of Israel," "thy Saviour," "thy Maker," "He that formed thee," and "thine husband."

The people of Israel are precious in His sight above other nations. He has not forgotten them. He pities their sufferings and weaknesses, and is concerned about their needs. Like a Shepherd, He will feed them and lead them in places of blessed abundance. He who carried them from birth will carry them even down to old age. With the Eternal as their God they may be assured of a time of future exaltation and blessing.

Isaiah has much to say about *the righteous remnant*, which he thinks of as God's magnificent minority, the seed of a new and pure beginning arising out of each devastating crisis. Here is the kernel of the doctrine taken up later by Paul; it is this spiritual remnant, rather than political Israel and Judah, which is the kingdom of God. In the light of the fact that a remnant would always survive, Isaiah could never speak of the judgment on the state as total destruction. There will always be this surviving minority which will eventually be the holy nucleus. From this remnant will come the ideal state over which Messiah, the ideal David, will be Lord. The hope of Judah is thus projected beyond the existing nation. There Messiah reigns over a redeemed and spiritual Israel. Its future will be Jerusalem, purified from dross, as the Eternal's "holy mountain." Men will then believe and depend upon God alone. Hence this new and righteous remnant is not only the magnificent minority but a true "fellowship of faith."

Two famous passages give us the kernel of Isaiah's teaching concerning *Messiah*—9:6-7 and 11:1-10. Herein is introduced the person of a wonderful King through whom the new order of things is to come. Out of the root of Jesse, after catastrophe has cut down the tree of the Davidic monarchy (11:1-10), shall sprout a *Branch*. Upon Him the Spirit of the Eternal One will rest in full measure. This will display itself in keenness of discernment, equity of decision, righteous proclamation, and abiding fidelity. Under His discipline and government the wild beasts will lose their predatory natures and grow tame. Peace will then become universal because of the widespread knowledge of the Eternal.

The other passage (9:6-7) ascribes to this coming King superhuman characteristics. Born as a child, the dominion rests upon His shoulder in regal dignity, and the fourfold name He bears is: "Wonderful-Counselor," "Hero-Divine," "Eternal Father," and "Prince of Peace."

Messiah is "God with us," a righteous King, a Hiding Place from the tempest, a Stream in the desert, and a great shade-giving Rock in a weary land. His salvation will have cosmic totality, and redemption shall include restoration of the material and animal orders as well as the social and moral.

Yet Messiah is also the Suffering Servant of the Lord, vicariously suffering for the salvation of the people (52:13—53:12). See the three other "servant songs" preceding, as listed in footnote 10 under comments on Isaiah 53.

In summary, Isaiah's teaching about *salvation* shows that the eternal God himself begins salvation (49:8; 59:16; 61:10; 63:5). Man appropriates it through faith and waiting upon God in reverence (12:2; 33:2, 6). The salvation of God is everlasting (45:17; 51:6, 8). His salvation is universal—it is for Zion and to the ends of the earth, even to the Gentiles (46:13; 49:6; 52:10; 62:11). His salvation is at hand (46:13; 56:1). It is something to rejoice in and to publish abroad (12:2-3; 25:9; 60:18). Furthermore, the world is to be saved through the Suffering Servant.

Finally, Isaiah has something to say about *spiritual worship*. Mere outward ritualism cannot satisfy God. Righteousness is more than mere temple-treading. Both ritualism and sensualism are equally false. Formalism and fleshly living are sheer stupidity. None can escape the bar of conscience before which God arraigns all men. Hence a genuine change of heart is more important than conformity to ritual. Isaiah's vision of God would argue that true worship is first of all a divine-human encounter. It moves from reverent contemplation to revelation and moral insight, and then advances to a state of real communion, which in turn bears fruition in commitment and service.[5] A vision of God always begets a sense of one's own unworthiness, and the first impulse of a cleansed heart is the quest to lead others to God.

Isaiah's contribution to the Judeo-Christian faith is great and lasting. Out of his prophetic insights come to us the seeds carried across many a century from which have sprung the more definitive concepts of atonement and salvation. For truly, all we like sheep had gone astray, and the Lord hath laid upon Christ the iniquity of us all, that with His stripes we might be healed. Only in such confidence may we return to our God, who will have mercy upon us, being assured that He will also abundantly pardon.

F. The Unity and Authenticity of the Book

The question of "how many Isaiahs" has greatly troubled the critics. And, like Manasseh, they have sawed this writer into *Proto, Deutero,* and *Trito* Isaiah, offering their postulates as unquestionable facts. But tradition is unanimously in favor of the unity of the Book of Isaiah. Photographs of the recently discovered Isaiah Scroll from the Qumran community near the Dead Sea show no break in the writing between chapters 39 and 40. No manuscripts nor traditional evidence are known to man where the book has not been together as a unit.

Equally great and learned scholars may be cited on both sides of the controversy over the unity of Isaiah's prophecy and its oneness of authorship. This writer is willing to join such scholars as George L. Robinson, C. W. E. Naegelsbach, Oswald T. Allis, and others in contending for one Isaiah.[6] His argument is

[5]He who leads men in creative Christian worship will profit by a careful study of these four stages as suggested in Isaiah 6. A valuable study of "Creative Worship" is to be found in chapters VII—IX of E. S. Brightman's *Religious Values* (New York: Abingdon Press, 1925), pp. 173-237.

[6]For discussions of the problem of how many Isaiahs, and a history of the critical attacks upon the unity of the book, consult A. B. Davidson, *Old Testament Prophecy* (Edinburgh: T. and T. Clark, 1904); Geo. L. Robinson, "Isaiah," *International Standard Bible Encyclopedia,* edited by James Orr (Chicago: The Howard-Severance Co., 1915), pp. 1504-5; and Carl W. E. Naegelsbach's introduction to his commentary on Isaiah in the *Commentary on the Holy Scriptures,* edited by John Peter Lange (Grand Rapids, Michigan: Zondervan Publishing House, n.d.). A modern writer who seeks to justify the threefold authorship of the book is R. H. Pfeiffer, *op. cit.* The drawing of a bold, black line between chapters 39 and 40 in the Moffatt Bible seems purely arbitrary. To this writer the case presented for the unity of Isaiah by Oswald T. Allis seems convincing. Cf. *The Unity of Isaiah* (Philadelphia: Presbyterian & Reformed Pub. Co., 1950).

that, when one begins to divide the prophecy and ascribe it to various authors, there is no stopping place. Consistent application of the principle that one appeals to for such division would demand, not three Isaiahs, but at least six, and more logically a whole school of Isaiahs. In such a case who is to say just what has been written by the original prophet, if anything? Hence the logic of the principle is self-invalidating. It should therefore become suspect. If one reads with an open mind c. 35 and then turns immediately to c. 40, he will at least admit that both passages could easily have come from the same pen, mind, and hand. It must also be admitted that if one has not decided on *a priori* principles to rule out the supernatural and predictive element from Isaiah's writing, there remains little reason for dividing it among multiple authors. A preview and prediction of the Captivity and Exile is just as possible as a retrospect of a contemporaneous account, if the part of an omniscient God be not excluded. That Isaiah believed his book embodied predictions is evident (30:8), and Isaiah's God challenges the opposers to predict the future and declare the things that are to come hereafter as only He can do (41:21-24). Yet how true it is that when one sly reason fills the heart of an interpreter, many honest ones will take its part!

Outline

ISAIAH: "THE ETERNAL GOD IS SALVATION"

A DIAGRAMMATIC ANALYSIS OF ISAIAH'S PROPHECY

Chapters									
1—6	7—12	13—23	24—27	28—33	34-35	36-39	40—48 FIRST ENNEAD	49—57 SECOND ENNEAD	58—66 THIRD ENNEAD
PROLOGUE / JUDAH AND JERUSALEM / PARABLE / ORACLE	CONSPIRACY VS. ASSURANCE	BURDEN; "MESSAGES", OF SOLEMN "IMPORT"	EPINICION*	WARNING AGAINST UNHOLY ALLIANCES	THE GREAT FINALE AND THE NEW EXODUS	EXIT ASSYRIA / ENTER BABYLON	THE PURPOSE OF PEACE	THE PRINCE OF PEACE	THE PROGRAM OF PEACE
INTRODUCTORY PROPHECIES	THE BOOK OF IMMANUEL	ORACLES AGAINST FOREIGN NATIONS	WORLD JUDGMENT AND ISRAEL'S REDEMPTION	SIX WOES OF WARNING	SALVATION INDIGNATION	ISAIAH'S FAITH VS. HEZEKIAH'S FEARS	COMFORT AND DELIVERANCE FOR THE OPPRESSED	THE SUFFERING SERVANT-REDEEMER	THE FUTURE GLORY OF THE SONS OF GOD
JUDGMENT					PROSPECT AND RETROSPECT	HISTORICAL INTERLUDE	CONSOLATION		

*A song of triumph or choral ode in honor of a victor.

ENNEAD: A group of nine items (here, chapters)

PART ONE

JUDGMENT

Isaiah 1—33

Section **I** *Introductory Prophecies*

Isaiah 1:1—6:13

A. THE GREAT ARRAIGNMENT, 1:1-31

1. *Title* (1:1)

The vision of Isaiah the son of Amoz (1:1) as an opening statement identifies the prophet and tells us the nature of his inspiration. The name **Isaiah** means "the eternal God is Salvation." The word **vision** indicates simply "a divine revelation" or "a vision from God respecting future events." Hence it would be a divinely given insight (cf. II Chron. 32:32; and I Sam. 9:9; also Num. 12:6). This vision involved **Judah and Jerusalem,** the Southern Kingdom and its capital. It was received during the reigns of four of her great kings—**Uzziah, Jotham, Ahaz, and Hezekiah** (see Chart *A*). We know nothing more about the prophet's father. He is not to be confused with the prophet Amos, for the names are spelled differently.

2. *Moral Stupidity* (1:2-9)

Here the eternal God pleads before the whole universe against His stupid and disobedient people. The **heavens** and

earth (2) are called upon to listen as the divine lawsuit is prosecuted. Sin has its cosmic significance; and nature passed under a curse because of it. Hence Isaiah is not the first to call heaven and earth to witness as God remonstrates with sinners (cf. Deut. 30:19; 32:1; Ps. 50:1-6; Mic. 1:2; 6:1-2).

Isaiah pictures God as a father whose **children . . . have rebelled against** their own parent (2). Israel, on the other hand, is contrasted with the dumb beasts of burden who at least know whence comes their food and the way back to their **master's crib** (feeding rack). The people's lack of discernment is such that God complains, **Israel doth not know** (3).[1]

Alas for the **sinful nation** (4)! They, like beasts of burden, are **laden with iniquity** and have become a veritable "sperm of perversity." Designed to be a holy seed, they have not only become sons of lawlessness but corrupters of others. **They have forsaken the Lord,** treated Him with contempt, and become utterly estranged. Men in their decline into evil first *forsake,* then *spurn,* and finally *apostatize* from the truth.

Under the Mosaic system stripes awaited the lawbreaker, but here is pictured a person with no place left on his body to be **stricken** (5), so many are his sins. Full of **wounds, and bruises** (6) unmedicated, there is no place for a new stripe-lash. Yet his rebellion continues.

Isaiah envisions the penalty for sin that eventually comes upon Judah. **Your country is desolate** (7) because of foreign invasions, its **cities . . . burned** and its fields plundered **in your** very **presence.** The permanent city would be reduced to a temporary dwelling, like a shanty **in a vineyard** (8) or a shack in a cucumber patch.[2] Except for the fact that the God of the angelic and starry hosts kept alive a few survivors (9), utter destruction would have been their lot as it was for **Sodom** and **Gomorrah.** Significantly this **very small remnant** makes up God's magnificent minority and becomes the seed of a new beginning (cf. Intro., "His Message").

---

[1]The word "me" appears in the Septuagint (LXX), the Vulgate, and the other ancient versions.

[2]Today in Palestine the tourist may see these temporary shacks, made from a few poles and palm branches, standing in the midst of the cucumber and melon patches to provide shade and temporary lodging for the pickers. But after the fruit season they stand beneath the burning sun in deserted silence.

3. *Pious Hypocrisy* (1:10-17)

Isaiah addresses the leaders and the people of Jerusalem with the epithets **rulers of Sodom** and **people of Gomorrah** (10). He then points out the sacrilege of **sacrifices** unaccompanied by obedience in heart and life (11). The **fat** and **blood** were set apart for the worship of God in such animal sacrifices. But the Eternal declares His satiation and nausea with these forms, coming from insincere worshippers. True worship is more than mere "temple-treading," and to behold God's face requires more than a gift in the **hand** (12). **Iniquity** and **the solemn meeting** are inconsistent with each other (13); **incense** and invocation are abominations when lacking true sincerity. Thus God expresses His loathing for their **new moons** (festivals) and their **appointed** seasonal **feasts** (14).

When we come to worship, God recalls what our hands have been doing at other times than prayer time. He refuses to behold the uplifted palms or listen to the pious petitions of men whose **hands are full of blood** (15). And such were those hands stretched upward in the Temple—red with the blood of the slain who had been sacrificed to the greed for gain, lust, and vindictiveness. Isaiah, like Paul, pleads for the uplift of holy hands in prayer (I Tim. 2:8). And, like the Psalmist, he knows that only the clean hand and the pure heart may stand in God's holy presence (Ps. 24:3-4). For all with such defiled hands the divine command is: "Wash yourselves. Purify yourselves!" (16, Berk.) "Quit your meanness!" (Sam Jones.) This calls for both the Holy Spirit. God's people must **seek judgment** (17), i.e., become the champions of justice and the challengers of all oppression.

4. *Proffered Pardon* (1:18-20)

God presses the divine lawsuit. **Come now, and let us** adjudicate the matter (18; lit.). But the divine ultimatum is one of grace and mercy—"Repent and be forgiven!" **Scarlet** and **crimson** were the colors of the robes worn by the princes to whom Isaiah preached. God's promise is that, even though one's sins be deep-dyed and as irremovable as the stain of blood, grace can restore the character to moral whiteness and purity. Thus John speaks of those whose robes have been washed in the blood of the "washing of regeneration" and the purifying baptism with the Lamb of God (Rev. 3:4-5; 7:14).

"Scarlet Sins White as Snow" is the theme of 1:4-18, where we note: (1) God's condemnation of sin, 4-6; (2) God's invitation to sinners, 18a; and (3) God's promise of salvation, 18b (G. B. Williamson).

The great **if** of 19 makes it plain that God has honored the soul of man by giving him a part in his own salvation. He cannot forgive an unrepentant people. But in the case of true repentance blessing accompanies the spiritual forgiveness. **But if ye refuse . . . ye shall be devoured** (20); Isaiah places before his hearers the alternative of "eating" or being "eaten"—salvation or the sword.

5. *Civic Corruption* (1:21-23)

Isaiah's sad wail: **How** (21), like the opening word in each of the first four chapters of Lamentations, is an expression of sorrow, amazement, and anguish, all in one meaningful sigh. **How is the faithful city become an harlot!** Such is his graphic picture of Jerusalem's unfaithfulness. Once the abode of **judgment** (justice) and **righteousness,** his beloved city has now become the stronghold of oppression and assassins. Actual prostitution also entered largely into the ritual of many of the forms of idolatry to which the Israelites were tempted (Num. 25:1-2). The **silver** (22) of sterling character had been filled with lead alloy, and the **wine** of truth diluted with falsehoods. Rebel **princes** consort with **thieves** (23), and wickedness is rampant in high places. **Every one loveth gifts** (bribes) and the nation's corruption begins with its rulers. In such a state of affairs nothing can be accomplished without the giving of a *baksheesh* (a tip or a bribe). And since everyone asks for it, the case of the **widow** and the orphan receives no hearing, for "peace gifts" are more desired than peace itself.

6. *Redemptive Justice* (1:24-31)

Therefore God, who is known as the **Lord of hosts, the mighty One of Israel** (24), speaks in indignation, "Alas! with vengeance I will relieve my offended sense of justice" (paraphrase). But although patience turns to punishment, it is for the sake of salvation. God punishes that He may save, and He smites in order to heal. The promise of restoration to holiness (25-26) involves a spiritual refining that results in fidelity and **righteousness.** The unfaithful city may then be called a faithful town. **I will turn my hand** (25) indicates a part of the refining process for the sake of sweeping off all the surface impurities.

When the divine Refiner has taken off all such "skimmings," nothing but pure metal remains. God's judgment is never retributive only; it is always redemptive, and it culminates in cleansing. Thus **Zion shall be redeemed with judgment** (justice), **and her converts with righteousness (27).** Yet apostasy brings **destruction (28),** "for our God is a consuming fire" (Heb. 12:29).

Once this refining process has taken its course, God's people will be forever **ashamed** of those sacred **groves of the oaks** where they practiced their lustful idolatries and also of the **gardens** surrounding them (29). Such scenes of impure ceremonies, chosen in preference to the Lord's sanctuary, become a sordid part of one's memories. Let us recall them, not as pleasant places, but as gardens without water, faded leaves, and parched ground (30). Here are fire hazards in times of drought—like **tow**[3] and **spark,** they are highly combustible (31). Sin itself is but the instrument of destruction, and whosoever is deceived thereby is not wise. The mighty and the proud who are foremost in idolatry often perish with the idol that they have made; **they shall both burn together, and none shall quench them.**

B. Prophetic Insights—the Nation and Its Capital, 2:1—4:6

1. *Title* (2:1)

The word that Isaiah . . . saw concerning Judah and Jerusalem (1) should not be thought of as mere repetition of his more general introduction in the opening verse of c. 1. The prophet now sets the theme, not only of his thoughts for the next three chapters, but his chief concern throughout his prophecy, for he looks at every other question from the standpoint of the chosen people. In this section of his book Isaiah puts the situation of Jerusalem and Judah in his own day in bold contrast with the day of God's peace and the day of God's judgments. He describes his vision of the nation and its capital as it really is, and as God's divine interventions of judgment and redemption will surely shape it. Hence his **word** delineates what he **saw**[4] by

---

[3]Tow is that part of the flax which remains after the linen substance has been stripped from it. It is most combustible.

[4]The Hebrew term here may mean "to see or behold," but it is especially appropriate in speaking of those things which are presented to the minds of the prophets (Gesenius), and hence it suggests "to look upon with the mind, to contemplate." Psychologically, Isaiah seems to be both auditory and visionary—he both sees and hears the word of the Lord (cf. 6:8).

37

divinely inspired insights to be true concerning Judah and Jerusalem. The Septuagint says: "The word which came from the Lord to Isaiah . . . concerning Judah and concerning Jerusalem."

2. *Divine-human Contrasts* (2:2-22)

Here Isaiah sets before us the ideal, the actual, and the imminent: the day of righteousness, the day of idolatry, and the day of retribution.

a. *The ideal day of peace and righteousness* (2:2-4). Here the idealism of the young prophet paints for us his vision of hope for **the mountain of the Lord's house** (2; Mt. Zion) as a universal center of worship. Micah had also seen this vision (Mic. 4:1-5).[5] **All nations shall flow unto it** like a constant stream of pilgrims and converts from every region of the earth. He pictures the house of God as a rendezvous for inquirers of the Lord and a stronghold of the word of truth (3). There they may learn the rules for the conduct of life on a higher plane—both the principle and its applications. With God as the sovereign Arbiter for international questions, Isaiah envisages a day when there shall be a universal cessation of hostilities. The instruments of destruction shall be changed into instruments of production (4). Plowshares resemble short **swords,** and **spears** are like **pruninghooks** for both length and sharpness.

b. *The idolatrous day of pride* (2:5-9). Failure to **walk in the light of the Lord** (5) always results in moral and spiritual darkness. When man repudiates the divine ideal, he degenerates to self-seeking and self-exaltation. **Forsaken** (6) of God, one finds himself abandoned to his own puny resources. **The house of Jacob** had yielded to the influence and the corruption of Eastern cults with their mania for divination, striking hands with strangers, and making common cause with foreigners, when the divine ideal was that they should be a peculiar and separate people of God. **Replenished from the east;** "influenced from the east" (Berk.), by pagan rites and practices. In their pride and impiety they worshipped **silver and gold** (7), and **horses and chariots,** as well as **idols . . . the work of their hands** (8), which are "no-gods."[6] So universal had this craze for an easy religion,

[5]The problem of who quotes whom here cannot be definitely settled. Some scholars think both men are quoting an older unknown prophet.

[6]Here Isaiah makes a play on the plural of the word for **idols**, which in Hebrew is *elilim* (vain, false gods), in contrast with the plural for *gods*, which in Hebrew is *elim*.

easy money, military security, and the gadgets of living become that **the mean man ... and the great man** (9)—all classes—were given over to it. Thus does man lower himself to a worship of the creature instead of the Creator, who alone can forgive.

c. *The imminent day of God's power and judgment* (2: 10-22). Man's little day of prowess pales into insignificance in comparison with the great **day of the Lord** (12). Isaiah sees a day coming in which idolaters shall hide themselves in terror before the manifestation of **the Lord** (10), whom they have despised (cf. Rev. 6:15-16). **The holes of the rocks** (10, 19) reflects the fact that Palestine is full of limestone caverns which men have used as asylums in times of terror. **The lofty looks of man shall be humbled** (11) and his arrogance brought low, for the day of God's exaltation is the day of man's humiliation. "The Eternal of hosts hath a day" (12, lit.). This is a day in which proud man finds himself in the hands of a Higher Power. The pride of man is compared to the great **cedars of Lebanon** (13) and **the oaks of Bashan,** symbols of strength and vigor. Also **the high mountains** (14) were places of pagan worship and idolatrous sacrifices.

Not even man's best fortifications, his **high tower** and his **fenced wall** (15), can abide. Neither can those stately **ships of Tarshish** (16). These were vessels capable of the round-trip ocean voyage from Palestine to the famous smelters of Tartessus[7] in Spain. Proud cultures with their works of art and **pleasant pictures** with their lustful imagery (call them "fine arts" if you please) shall crumble away (cf. Rev. 18:11-19). Man's proud attempts at self-deification, his magnificence and self-sufficiency, and his refusal to recognize his own finitude melt away **and the Lord alone shall be exalted in that day** (17). God is the Supreme "Idol Smasher" (Iconoclast). The very things man has rated as superhuman are "no-gods" and come to naught before essential Deity (18; Mic. 1:7).

The dread presence of the Eternal and the splendor of His majesty will send haughty mankind scrambling underground once God strikes this earth with terror (19; Joel 3:16; Hag. 2:6; Heb. 12:26; Rev. 6:15-16). Then man will **cast his idols ... to the moles and to the bats** (20), blind rodents that inhabit the darkness. Those idols will have proved powerless to save their pagan

---

[7]A Phoenician colony located near the Strait of Gibraltar.

human worshippers. In unspeakable panic men will flee into
fissures in the **rocks and clefts** in the hills when God arises **to
shake terribly the earth** (21; Luke 23:30). In this day Isaiah
counsels, **Cease ye from man** (22). Why depend upon man
whose breath is so fleeting and whose prowess so futile? "Of
what account is he?" (22, RSV).

3. *Judgments on Leaders and Proud Ladies* (3:1—4:1)

a. Judah's men of stature replaced (3:1-12). Isaiah warns
that **the Lord of hosts** (1) is about to remove both support and
sustenance **from Judah** (1-4). As our moderns would express it:
"God is going to 'knock the props from under you.'" What a
calamity befalls the state when breadwinners, soldiers, judges,
prophets, wise men and mature leaders, captains, statesmen,
counselors, craftsmen, and eloquent orators are all replaced by
"capricious children" and "insolent novices"! **Captain of fifty**
(3) is a military rank (cf. Num. 31:14; Deut. 1:15). In such an
instance anarchy reigns for lack of responsible leadership; people
are **oppressed** and exploit one another; disrespect is shown for
men of rank; and deference toward the **honourable** (5) is utterly
lacking. Nor can any man of means or even meager ability be
persuaded to become **a ruler of the people** (7) or a **healer** of the
body politic. For when weak hands hold the rudder of state,
utter lawlessness ensues.

The causes of the ruin of **Jerusalem** and the fall of **Judah**
(8) are not far to seek. They defy almighty God with their
speech and conduct, and flaunt **their sins as Sodom**, unashamed
(9). Full-grown vice wears no veil but parades itself openly.
To provoke the eyes of his glory (8) means "defying his glorious presence" (RSV).

But Isaiah would remind us that one must reap the harvest
of his own doing (vv. 10-11). Weal befits the righteous, and woe
betides the wicked. So the prophet laments, **O my people, they
which lead thee cause thee to err** (12).

b. The Eternal's pleadings with Judah's princes (3:13-15).
The heavenly Judge-Advocate remonstrates with **the ancients . . .
and the princes** (14)—the rulers of His people—protesting their
greed and denouncing their oppression as they **grind the faces of
the poor** (15).

c. God's denunciation of the proud ladies of Zion (3:16—

4:1). Isaiah is confident that when the Lord's arm of justice
reaches round to the haughty **daughters of Zion** (16) these
arrogant "state dolls" shall surely be degraded (16-17). In their
haughty . . . walk and proud actions calculated to attract the
attention of men, Isaiah accuses them of a shameless and im-
modest carriage. Their **wanton** glances, delicate steps, anklets
with silver bells **tinkling,** were repulsive to God. Their "look at
me" attitude which said, "Come hither, my love!" filled the
prophet with disgust. He prophesied for them a plague of scurvy
and nakedness (17; Lev. 13:2; 14:56), baldness and barrenness.
They would also suffer the indignities of female captives, stripped
naked with bodies exposed, as they stood in the slave market.

Isaiah promises them "ashes for beauty," when their gaudy
paraphernalia shall be replaced by a captive's garb (18-24). The
prophet's enumeration of their twenty-one articles of vanity
evidences his contempt. He mentions their ankle-bells, **cauls**
(haloes), **tires** (metal half-moons) for headdress (18), ear-pen-
dants, **bracelets,** veils (19), and turbans. He adds **ornaments of
the legs** (20; stepping chains reaching from one foot to the other
like hobbles to enforce shorter steps), glittering girdles, perfume
boxes and toilet waters, and magic **tablets** (formulae suspended
from neck and ears). The list continues with signet **rings, nose
jewels** (still worn in India today; 21), evening gowns (festal
robes), outer petticoats, shawls and stoles, handbags or purses
(22), mirrors of polished bronze, muslin robes, outer veils, and
muffler scarfs (23).[8]

And it shall come to pass, that instead of (24) these items of
finery shall come the adornment of shame and humiliation. Isaiah
sees the **sweet smell** of perfume replaced by the stench of ulcers,
the expensive sash replaced by a bit of twine string (the belt of
poverty). A shaved head replaces the latest hairdo. The **stomach-
er** (a rich robe) is replaced by a burlap garment; instead of a fine
complexion comes sunburn, and instead of a beauty treatment a
barbarian's brand.

The prophet further declares that by wars Jerusalem's male
population will be laid waste **by the sword** (25)—a calamity for
these vain and amorous women. Hence Jerusalem's **gates** (26),
the places of concourse, shall become centers for mourning when

---

[8]Perhaps the list of these items in John B. Phillips, *Four Prophets* (N.Y.:
Macmillan Co., 1963), p. 68, is as precise as any. Some of the Hebrew terms
are now obscure.

the ravaged and desolate captive women **shall sit upon the ground.**

The chapter break is most unfortunate here. To complete the picture the prophet declares the time will come when **seven women** (4:1) will seek the same husband because of the scarcity of men remaining after the war. They promise to support themselves for the sake of being **called by thy name** and being his wife, thus removing the **reproach** of being unwed and childless. Let it be remembered that a woman without a husband and a child in Old Testament times had no hope of being the mother of the Messiah.

4. *The Day of Messianic Mercies* (4:2-6)

a. The divine-human Messiah (4:2). **The branch of the Lord** is set forth here as the Founder of a new and redeemed Israel. He is **beautiful and glorious.** With a redeemed and vitalized people, even **the fruit of the earth** shall become **excellent and comely.** As Plumptre notes: "The prophet turns from the Jerusalem that then was, with the hypocrisies and crimes of the men and the harlot fashions of its women, to the vision of a new Jerusalem, which shall realize the ideal of Ps. 15 and 24. There everyone should be called 'holy' (cf. I Cor. 1:2; II Cor. 1:1), and the name should be no unreal mockery (Isa. 32:5), but should express the self-consecration and purity of its inhabitants."[9]

b. The holy and purified remnant (4:3-4). This concept is expressed by Isaiah's words, **He that is left . . . and he that remaineth** (3). Verse 3 includes those who have escaped the divine judgments upon corruption. They are to be **called holy** (and God does not call people what they are not). These are worthy to be enrolled in the "holiness hall of fame." They constitute "God's magnificent minority" (cf. Intro.) **in Zion** (the kingdom) and **Jerusalem** (the city).

Verse 4 tells of the divine transformation of these people, which is twofold: a washing away of their **filth** (outward cleansing) and a purging of their stains (inward purity; cf. Titus 3:5). The two divine means are: **the spirit of judgment** (bring-

[9]"Isaiah," *Ellicott's Commentary on the Whole Bible*, ed. Charles John Ellicott (Grand Rapids, Michigan: Zondervan Publishing House, n.d.), *ad loc.*

ing justification) and **the spirit of burning** (bringing sanctification). Thus Isaiah intimates that this is a purging blast of the breath of God. (In Heb. "spirit" means also "wind" or "breath.") "Breathe on us, Breath of God," is an appropriate prayer for every man who desires divine endowment.

    c. The manifestation of the divine presence, protection, and pleasure toward His people (4:5-6). Isaiah sees the ancient Shekinah and pillar of God's presence as an overshadowing **cloud . . . by day** and a radiant and fluorescent light **by night** (5; cf. Exod. 13:21; Num. 9:15; 10:34). Likewise **a tabernacle,** or tent—the "canopy of the Eternal's protection"—stretches over all as a **defence** and a **covert** (5-6). We rejoice that God's atonement for our sins is both a canopy and a pavilion of grace. The Shekinah of the divine presence is a shade from the burning **heat,** and a shelter from the pelting sleet (6). This creative miracle of grace shows God's blessing on every aspect of man's life: his sacred **assemblies** (5, the church), each **dwelling place** (the home), and "every one that is written among the living" (3, the individual). Every relationship is under the overarching canopy of divine love.

C. The Song of the Vineyard, 5:1-30

    This beautiful passage is similar to the parable Jesus gave to the leaders of Jerusalem (cf. Matt. 21:33-46). It is followed by a series of "woes," as Jesus followed His parable with such a series also (cf. Matt. 23:13-36). The Psalmist sings a song of similar content (cf. Ps. 80:8-13). The entire chapter is poetry, as may be seen in the modern-speech versions. The following outline treats it as a unit message under three aspects.

1. *The Moral Vineyard* (5:1-7)

    a. Favorable in situation (5:1-2). Isaiah pictures God as the Lover of His people, and His covenant people as God's husbandry. They are situated on **a very fruitful hill** (1) whose soil is fertile with rich minerals (as is the case even today in Palestine). The site is conspicuous for location (as is true of the Holy Land). God places His people on an eminence of blessing, that they may witness conspicuously to His goodness (cf. Matt. 5:14).

    Verse 2 pictures the basic essentials in the preparation of any vineyard. It must be **fenced** by means of **the stones** that are **gathered out** as its soil is spaded up. The larger ones would serve

to build a watch **tower** on its highest point, and a wine vat[10]
where the juice could be trampled from its grapes. This being
done, the vineyard would be **planted . . . with the choicest vine**
(lit., "vine of Sorek") with its luscious, dark purple grapes. All
this the Eternal had done for Judah and Jerusalem, fenced as it
was by the divine laws and providential circumstances. God had
driven out the idolaters before them, made the Davidic dynasty
a tower of strength, and had given them the Temple as a center
from which the fruits of righteousness and joyful worship might
issue.

b. *Disappointing in fruit* (5:2). **It brought forth wild
grapes,** sour, hard, and small. These were typical of the deeds of
injustice and iniquity which Isaiah enumerates in vv. 8-23. Thus
in sharp contrast the prophet notes the divine Husbandman's
care for His vineyard and its failure to produce a proper fruit.

c. *The Lord's grand jury* (5:3). Summoning the **inhabitants
of Jerusalem, and men of Judah,** the divine Husbandman begs:
"Please arbitrate between Me and My vineyard" (Berk.). God
has a way of condemning sinners out of their own mouths.

d. *The divine Plaintiff's pleading* (5:4). There is pathos here
as the Eternal asks: **What** more **could have been done?** Why
should it bring **forth wild grapes?** God's best seems to have elici-
ted only the people's worst (II Kings 17:13-20; II Chron. 36:
15-16).

e. *The divine verdict* (5:5-6). Shifting His role from Plaintiff to that of Judge, God declares: I will remove the vineyard's
protecting providences (5); I will forsake it to the elements of
disintegration and decline (6); I will withdraw My blessings.
To take away the hedge (5) would be to place it at the mercy of
straying goats which delight to crop off the tender branches. To
destroy **the wall** would be to allow any cloven-footed devil to
romp across it at pleasure. But God further declares: And I will
become its Enemy; **I will lay it waste** (6). The desolation resulting from divine neglect is ruinous; for where pruning and

---

[10]A wine vat was made of stone on two levels. The upper and larger
vat was shallower and in it the grapes were thrown and trodden (cf. Isa.
63:3). The lower one was smaller and deeper. Into it the grape juice would
flow by a channel from the upper vat. From thence it was dipped up and
poured into the goatskin bottles (such as are still used for water today in
some parts of Palestine) for carrying and preservation.

cultivation fail, nothing of real value grows. When the divine Vinedresser turns it over to its own devices, **briers and thorns** take over, for not even vineyard soil can remain neutral. Foul growth always comes where fruit-bearing fails. With no rain, only thorny desert plants can survive.

f. God's expectations frustrated (5:7). Like a faithful preacher, Isaiah states specifically what he means. Like Nathan, he can say to **the house of Israel:** "Thou art the man" (II Sam. 12:7). God "looked for justice, but, behold, bloodshed; for righteousness, but, behold, shrieks from the oppressed!" (lit.) Isaiah often makes a play on words, as in this case: God looked for *mishpat*, but, behold, *mispah;* for *sedakah,* but behold, *se'akah!*

2. The Wild Grapes (5:8-25)

Here Isaiah points out six sins in which Judah was guilty of provoking God and predicts certain retributions.

a. Woe to the wealthy "land grabbers" (5:8-10). How much land does a man need? The answer seems to be the same as for money: "Just a little more than he now has!" Hence the greed for joining **house to house** and **field to field** (8). Here is the enlargement of one's estate which crowds out the smaller land-holder. But this selfishness of vast accumulations, even by fair means, was provided against by Jewish law (Num. 27:1-11; 33:54; I Kings 21:3-4). Extensive farming may have some advantages but it depopulates the land. Intensive farming has always been more productive of a thriving rural economy (witness Japan today). Isaiah records overhearing a divine oath to the effect that **many houses** (9) will stand empty, mansions will be uninhabited, and the land will become unproductive. Whereas **ten acres** are capable of producing 4,000 gallons of grape juice, they will produce only **one bath** (8 gallons). As for the small grain, "ten bushels of seed will produce but one bushel" (10, Berk.) in harvest.

In some areas of the West in these days of extensive, mechanized farming, one drives mile after mile past deserted and empty farm buildings on wheat ranches which have been bought up by the land magnates of large-scale farming. But now, as in Isaiah's day, grasping greediness always builds a lonely estate, "and you are made to dwell alone in the midst of the land" (8, RSV).

b. Woe to the devotees of dissipation (5:11-17). The prophet here describes the unreasonable indulgence in appetite and sensual enjoyment that was so prevalent in his homeland. Constant wine sipping from **morning** until late at **night** (11) and blatant music accompanying revellings without reverence or reflection upon **the work of the Lord** (12) beget a voluptuous personality with a dead conscience and spiritual insensibility.

Therefore: result number 1. Exile follows ignorance; **honourable men** (nobles) die of famine; and the **multitude** (commoners) die of **thirst** (13). Death is the great leveler of all pomp of circumstance and pride. The mean and the mighty both are only mortal.

Therefore: result number 2. **Hell** (*sheol*) reaps a bounteous harvest (14-15), and the judgments of a holy God are manifested (16-17). **Strangers** (perhaps Bedouin nomads) shall occupy the landed estates of **fat ones** (the wealthy) while their flocks graze midst the ruins of Israel (17).

c. *Woe to the defiant cynics* (5:18-19). In the case of the contemptuous and presumptuous, the little **cords** of falsehood soon become cart ropes of defiant sins (18; the Rabbis compared sin in its beginning to a fine-hair-string but in its finish to a cart rope). Sin's load may become so great that it requires a **cart rope** to drag it along. Skeptical of any impending judgments, they disregard Heaven's warnings and in their fool's paradise challenge God to **hasten his work, that we may see it** (19).

d. *Woe to those who would pervert moral values* (5:20). Here we have false teachers who use fair-sounding terms to gloss over the real nature of evil. But merely changing the name of a snake will not transform its nature. Sin is sin no matter how dignified its designation. Modern relativism insidiously undermines virtue by painting the charms of license in the poetry of passion.

e. *Woe to the conceited and self-sufficient* (5:21). People who are a law unto themselves see no need for either Isaiah's counsel or the word of God. Fancying themselves both wise and shrewd, they say: "I don't need Christ."

f. *Woe to the judges who are intrepid drinkers* (5:22-25). This woe singles out that class of magistrates who pride themselves on being able to "hold their liquor well" (i.e., drink heavily and not get drunk; 22). Yet for a bribe they pervert justice in the courts, setting aside the just claims of those who have a righteous cause (23).

Therefore: result number 3. The consuming **fire** and the decaying rot will come as judgment against all such forms of wickedness (24). **Root** and **blossom** are vital to fruitfulness. When a plant becomes rotten at the root and the blossoms turn to powder, it is doomed. So when the hidden sources and the outward manifestations of prosperity and productivity are corrupted, the end for both is near. Isaiah traces the reason for this decay to the nation's rejection of **the law of the Lord** (written law) and **the word of the Holy One** (the spoken oracle). When people have no regard for either Scripture or sermon, their stubborn resistance always brings dire consequences.

Therefore: result number 4. **The anger of the Lord** is **kindled against his people** (25). God's anger was revealed in the judgments which had already fallen upon His people. The earthquake in the days of Uzziah (Amos 1:1) was but a portent of heavier judgments to come. **Their carcases** were as refuse in **the streets** in days of pestilence and famine. Despite all this, God's anger had not subsided, for **his hand is stretched out still** to smite. The final sentence of this verse is an oft-repeated refrain in Isaiah's prophecy (cf. 9:12, 17, 21; 10:4; 23:11; cf. Lev. 26:14-39).

3. *The Desolation* (5:26-30)

Isaiah now turns his face northeastward toward the instruments of God's retributions. The hostile Assyrian nation will be summoned and will respond with the most efficient desolation, ravaging the land and its people.

a. A hostile nation summoned (5:26). **An ensign to the nations from far** would be a summons to battle. Sometimes this ensign was simply a flag, sometimes another symbol or emblem. Isaiah says God **will hiss** ("whistle," RSV) **unto them.** Hissing is said to have been used by bee-keepers to call the bees out of the hives or to assemble the swarm. So God will assemble the hostile nations and their response will be immediate.

b. The ravages of the coming invader (5:27-30). Verse 27 pictures a sure, swift attack by an enemy so securely clad that not even a shoelace breaks, and so relentless that he takes no time for repose. Fully prepared and "hastening to the prey" in battle come these Assyrian archers and charioteers (28). Since the ancients did not shoe their horses, those with the hardest hoofs were selected for war duty. The dust-whirl of their onslaught

would resemble the whirlwinds of the desert. **Their roaring (29)**
would be like a lioness (fiercest of the lion family), and like
young lions growling and tearing their prey, or carrying it off
unhindered by any who might rescue.[11] **Like the roaring of the
sea (30)** in the time of tempest with wave after wave roaring to
the attack, so will the enemy come. Both the outlook and the uplook spell darkness and despair for doomed Palestine.

In summary, the divine judgments will be like the devouring
fire, like the terrific earthquake, like the invasion of a desolating
army, like the roaring of a pack of lions leaping upon the prey,
like the raging tide as it breaks over the rocks, and like a land
over which Egyptian darkness has fallen. All this came to Judah
during Isaiah's lifetime.

D. THE TRANSFORMING VISION, 6:1-13

This is not the beginning of Isaiah's work as a prophet. In
1:1 he himself declares that he prophesied during Uzziah's reign.
This transforming vision came to him as something that deepened
his spiritual life and insights. It was a purging experience centered around a crisis of confession and consecration.[12]

The chapter is a good example of the four stages of "Creative
Worship": (1) Contemplation (vision), 1-4; (2) Revelation (self-
evaluation), 5; (3) Communion (divine-human encounter), 6-7;
and (4) Fruition in service (commission and commitment), 8-13.
Or if we think of the chapter as an example of "The Making of
a Prophet," then the following points become apparent: (1) A social crisis, (2) A heavenly vision, (3) A humble confession, (4) A
personal cleansing, (5) A call to service, and (6) An irrevocable
commitment. A number of commentators have called attention

---

[11]The Assyrian inscriptions give Sennacherib's boast of having carried
off 200,150 captives in his first attack against Judah.

[12]"This is not the first . . . of Isaiah's prophecies, but his inauguration
to a higher degree of the prophetic office: verse 9, etc., implies the tone
of one who had already experienced of the people's obstinacy" (Robert
Jamieson, A. R. Fausset, David Brown, *Commentary, Critical and Explanatory, on the Whole Bible* [Grand Rapids, Michigan: Zondervan Publishing
House, n.d.], *ad loc.* Plumptre, Naegelsbach, and Delitzsch agree with this,
and George L. Robinson suggests it. The opening statement in this chapter would also indicate that Uzziah was not yet dead when Isaiah saw this
vision, though the recording of it was probably not made until afterward.
That Isaiah wrote Uzziah's biography is evident from II Chron. 26:22. On
Isaiah's call and sanctification see Introduction.

to: (1) The **Woe** of condemnation and confession, 5; (2) The **Lo** of cleansing, 7; and (3) The **Go** of commission, 9.

1. *The Time of Tragedy* (6:1a)

King Uzziah was under sentence of death from leprosy, which came as a divine judgment upon his presumption (II Chron. 26:16-21). Hence the throne of Judah was vacant though Jotham, the king's son, acted as regent during his father's illness. It was a time of crisis and transition for Judah. Uzziah's death came as a disillusionment to the young prophet concerning his hopes for the nation, and was thus a crisis in his ministry.

Isaiah had lived through the last twenty years of Uzziah's reign. There was an appearance of outward material prosperity, but much inward corruption. The king, having profaned the holiness of the Temple, was dragging out the dregs of his leprous life in seclusion (II Chron. 26:21). The question as to the future of his people must have loomed large in the prophet's thoughts. The earthquake had terrified Jerusalem and left in the mind of young Isaiah an overshadowing sense of impending judgment. And yet, above the wreckage of his earthly hopes, there burst upon his soul the vision of God and the unseen world, where henceforth he could look for the realization of his shattered earthly dreams.

2. *The Vision of Heavenly Glory* (6:1b-4)

a. A vision of exalted beings (6:1b-2). At a time when Judah's throne stood empty by reason of a king's mortality, Isaiah declared; **I saw also the Lord,** the true King Eternal, who alone hath immortality, **sitting upon a throne, high and lifted up, and his train filled the temple** (1). The vision came to Isaiah while participating as an official court prophet in the Temple ceremonies. Standing with the priests "between the porch and the altar," he was gazing through the open doors of the sanctuary as the smoke of incense from the golden altar ascended before the veil of the Temple. The Hebrew word used as the divine title is *Adonai* ("Lord" printed with capital *L* and lower case *ord* to distinguish it from *Yahweh*, also translated "LORD," but printed in capital letters in the KJV and RSV). St. John understood it to specify Jesus Christ (John 12:41). Enthroned and exalted, His robe filled the Temple with the glory of transfiguration radiance.

Around this royal Person hovered the seraphim ("burning ones"; not to be confused or identified with cherubim, "shining ones").[13] Unworthy to look upon Deity, they veiled their faces and their feet before His majestic holiness.

b. *The heavenly pattern of service* (6:3-4). In addition to their reverently veiled faces and feet, the wings and voices of the seraphim were in perfect readiness to run their Lord's errands and chant in antiphonal chorus their threefold ascription of holiness to the Lord of hosts.[14] Their pattern of service is one of reverence, readiness, and rejoicing; which most appropriately befits One whose "majestic splendour fills the whole earth!" (Moffatt) Little wonder that the foundations of the Temple thresholds vibrated as the song of holiness rang out and the Temple began to fill with the **smoke** of the heavenly Shekinah!

3. *The Vision of Human Failure* (6:5)

a. *The vileness of self* (6:5a). Only the holy see God and live (Exod. 33:20; Matt. 5:8); hence it becomes imperative that he who will later say, "Woe!" to Jerusalem must first cry, **Woe is me!** Any man in the presence of the Eternal is deeply conscious of his own nothingness, but man with uncleansed lips in such a Presence can only loathe his vileness. Well, then, might Isaiah exclaim: "I am struck dumb" (as the Hebrew has it), "unworthy to sing God's praise, or to proclaim God's message." **A man of unclean lips** cannot say sincerely: "Holy, holy, holy." Since the lips give expression to the soul, their uncleanness is sure evidence of an uncleansed heart. If Isaiah were a modern, he would warn us that the "gift of gab" may be, not a gift, but a peril. Certainly a foul-mouthed man is no fitting ambassador or messenger for a holy God. Carnality usually concentrates into one characteristic expression in each life. With Isaiah it defiled his lips. Anyone thus unclean is soon to be undone.

b. *The vileness of society* (6:5b). Isaiah realized that those among whom he lived were **a people of unclean lips.** As the disease of a plant usually becomes apparent in its blossom, so any

---

[13]**Seraphims** is used nowhere else in the OT. Here it specifies God's attendants arranged about the throne like hovering courtiers. And according to this reference these creatures had six wings and one face, whereas the *cherubim* in Ezekiel's vision had four faces and four wings (Ezek. 1:6; cf. Gen. 3:24; Exod. 25:18-20; Ezek. 10:14; 20:21).

[14]We do not strain exegesis when we see in this trisagion an intimation of the Holy Trinity. Cf. H. Orton Wiley, *Christian Theology* (Kansas City, Mo.: Nazarene Publishing House, 1940), I, 440.

fault in a man is usually manifest in his speech (Jas. 3:2). Having observed heavenly worship, the prophet was painfully conscious of the defects in the devotion of his own people. The leprous condition of their king was nothing in comparison to their own leprous speech with its bitter and hasty words, its formal and insincere prayers, its hard speeches against divine providence (Jude 15b). Yet even when lips are unclean, one can still rejoice if his spiritual eyesight is capable of seeing God, for the divine Spirit may use this portal of the soul to work a transformation. Eyes that **have seen the King, the Lord of hosts,** must cause the heart to cry for cleansing.

4. *The Coal of Cleansing* (6:6-7)

a. *From the altar of atonement* (6:6). **The altar** from which the **coal** was taken suggests the sacrifice which had just been consumed by the altar fire. And back of the fire and oil stands the shedding of blood with its atonement for the soul (Lev. 17: 11).[15]

b. *For the purging of iniquity* (6:7). "One of the seraphims" with a burning coal touched the prophet at the point of his greatest need. Calvary provided a Pentecost for every uncleansed believer. "Pardon and purity are the conditions alike of the prophet's work and of the completeness of his own spiritual life."[16] The heavenly ministrant called attention to both elements of the great change: **thine iniquity** (vacillation)[17] **is taken away, and thy sin** (wickedness)[18] **purged** (expiated).[19] Thus by the fire of divine love[20] all sinful uncleanness was burned away from the prophet's mouth and heart.

[15]The contention being that the tongs and the live coal were from the brazen altar of sacrifice, not the golden altar of incense. Its fire had been originally kindled by God himself and it was kept burning continually (cf. Lev. 9:24).

[16]Plumptre, *op. cit., loc. cit.*

[17]The Hebrew term here indicates the quality of being "up and down."

[18]The Hebrew term includes sins of weakness as well as wickedness.

[19]The Hebrew word, *Kaphar,* is in the Hebrew *Pual* (passive) verb form here, which Gesenius notes is perhaps best translated "obliterated" or "deleted" since it is both passive and intensive in form. Hence the KJV translation is valid.

[20]It is the contention of Delitzsch that the *seraphim* were the ministrants of the "fire of divine love." Cf. Franz Delitzsch, *Biblical Commentary on the Prophecies of Isaiah,* 2 vols. (Grand Rapids, Michigan: Wm. B. Eerdmans Publishing Company, 1949 [reprint]), I, 197.

51

5. The Call to Service (6:8-9a)

a. The divine program (6:8a). For the Lord to redeem or even to warn mankind, He needs an instrument. Only a man among men will suffice (59:16; Ezek. 22:30). Isaiah was permitted to "listen in" on the deliberative council of the heavenly beings as the voice of the Lord called for a workman and a messenger: **Whom shall I send, and who will go for us?**

b. The divine permission (6:8b-9a). "Isaiah, whose anxiety to serve the Lord was no longer suppressed by the consciousness of his own sinfulness, no sooner heard the voice of the Lord, than he exclaimed, in holy self-consciousness, 'Behold me here; send me.' "[21] The true servant of God goes because his heart prompts him in holy love to the task. In such case the call to service takes on the nature of divine permission. This **Go** of divine commission is not a command but the acceptance of a volunteer. The true call is the cry of a heart that has heard the heavenly message and yearns to go forth to tell the world of God's love.

In 6:1-8 we learn of "The Saving Vision." (1) Isaiah saw God, 1-4; (2) Isaiah saw his own sinfulness, 5; (3) Isaiah saw the grace of God, 7; (4) Isaiah saw the work assigned to him, 8 (G. B. Williamson).

6. The Solemn Commission (6:9-13)

Isaiah's service was accepted, and God said, **Go, and tell this people** (9). The prophet's commission was a difficult one. He was not to be admired and loved, pampered and flattered, but to play the role of a suffering servant of the Eternal. Frustrated with the apparent futility of his task, he must cry: "Who hath believed our report?" (53:1) "I have spread out my hands all the day unto a rebellious people" (65:2). His was to be not only a crucified life, but a crucified ministry, as he watched his beloved nation go down under the divine judgments. Because of its stubborn impenitence, there was to be nothing left but the root of the tree. He was to be the messenger of doom to an obdurate people. Only a remnant would hear and be saved as by fire, mere brands from the burning. And he went, he witnessed, he reproved, he suffered, he died. But the seed he scattered in tears still bears a harvest.

---

[21]Delitzsch, *op. cit., ad loc.*

a. Constant denunciation (6:9-11). Here Delitzsch's translation deserves notice: "He said, Go, and tell this people, Hear on, and understand not; and look on, but perceive not. Make ye the heart of this people greasy, and their ears heavy, and their eyes sticky; that they may not see with their eyes, and hear with their ears, and their heart understand, and they be converted, and one heal them."[22] Isaiah realized that most of his hearers would only be hardened by his preaching, for what one *is* determines what one *sees* and *hears.* In spiritual things we see with the heart and the understanding. Had Isaiah lived in modern times he would have spoken of "fat heads" instead of **fat** hearts (10), but for the Hebrew psychology **the heart** was the most comprehensive term. Divine things must be loved in order to be understood. A lazy heart fails of conversion. A quick eye, an open ear, and a responsive heart beget converting (turning around). God's healing awaits the person who thus exercises responsibility for the spiritual understanding of his sensations. Isaiah's phrase **this people** (9-10) designates a society plagued with spiritual insensibility. But the offers of salvation which a man receives necessarily serve to fill up the measure of his sins. There is a judicial hardening, an insanity of will, that befalls the one who refuses the overtures of God.

Isaiah's protest of an assignment so severe comes in his question: **How long?** (11) But the question of **how long** is God's business; "how faithfully" is the greater question for His ministers. The divine answer is, **Until . . . cities** are razed to the ground, **houses** are empty of inhabitants, and **the land be utterly desolate.** Right down to the very ruin which stubborn rebellion brings upon itself, through a long ministry in Jerusalem—this was to be the duration of Isaiah's commission.

b. Coming exile and deportation (6:12). **And the Lord have removed men far away** is the Hebrew way of looking beyond secondary causes, ascribing the mass deportations by the Assyrians and Babylonians ultimately to God's judgments. Captivity is the reward of insensibility. And if the people of Judah will not hear the lesson spelled out for them in plain Hebrew, then God will be forced to teach it to them in Assyrian (28:9-13).

And there be a great forsaking in the midst of the land (12) refers not to spiritual apostasy but to the deserted spaces

---

[22]*Ibid.,* I, 199.

thus left in Judah (cf. ASV: "And the forsaken places be many in the midst of the land").

c. *Survived only by a very small remnant* (6:13). Should there be as much as **a tenth** of the nation remaining, even this must be burnt out, like the stump of a terebinth or **oak** tree when it is felled (paraphrasing). But notwithstanding, out of that stump will come forth a holy aftergrowth. God's people become **the holy seed,** and the hope of the future.[23] So the door of hope is left ajar.

[23]On the doctrine of the remnant, consult John Bright, *The Kingdom of God* (Nashville: Abingdon-Cokesbury Press, 1953), c. 3. Bright observes: "The reader of Isaiah senses at once that denunciation and doom are balanced there by a glorious hope . . ." (p. 83). Isaiah predicted both the exile and return, as Plumptre states: "From the first hour of Isaiah's call the thought of an exile and a return from exile was the keynote of his teaching, and of that thought thus given in germ, his whole after-work was but a development, the horizon of his vision expanding and taking in the form of another empire than the Assyrian as the instrument of punishment" (*op. cit., loc. cit.*). As to the holy seed, the NT writers think of this as Jesus, the Author of a new humanity, the final One of the remnant, who comes as the true Son of Man (cf. Gal. 3:16). In Isaiah, the idea of the name of his son, *Shear-jashub* (7:3; the remnant) constantly reappears (cf. 1:27; 4:2-3; 10:20; 29:17; 30:15; cf. also Rom. 11:5, 26-27).

Section II The Book of Immanuel

Isaiah 7:1—12:6

A. The Syro-Ephraimitic Conspiracy, 7:1—9:1

1. *The Divine and the Human Alternatives* (7:1-25)

The Syro-Ephraimitic war of 734 B.C. is one of the great crises in Isaiah's ministry. Side by side stood the young prophet of perhaps thirty years and the still younger king of not more than twenty-one, with political principles diametrically opposed. Isaiah, true to his name, insisted that salvation for the nation would be found in trusting God for deliverance and safety. Ahaz sought to play the game of politics on purely human principles by patronizing Assyria, the major nation of his day. See Introduction, "The World in Isaiah's Day," for the historical background.

a. A king's consternation (7:1-2). The league of **Rezin** and **Pekah** had brought them to war against **Jerusalem** (1), but they could not take the city. The quaking **house of David** (2; the king and his advisers) trembled when they heard that these two inveterate enemies had become friends for the purpose of dethroning Ahaz (see Chart *A*) and placing a pro-Syrian on the throne.

b. A king's counselor (7:3-9). (1) *Calm courage counseled* (3-4). God spoke to Isaiah: **Go forth now . . . thou, and . . . thy son** (3). Ahaz was superintending the project of diverting the city's water supply from outside the walls through an aqueduct to the inside of the city to prevent it from being taken by the enemy, a project completed by Hezekiah (II Kings 18:17; II Chron. 32:3-4, 30; Isa. 22:9, 11). Isaiah met him at the broad place used by the men who operated the public laundry as a spot for drying their washings.[1] If the king was frantic about defense, Isaiah would tell him where the real defense of a nation lies. Ahaz must not panic at the approach of these two "fagends of flickering torches" (4, Moffatt). The right temper for such a time is one of calm courage and waiting upon the Lord (30:15).

---

[1] In India and Burma many such places are still in use.

(2) *Scheming sons of men* (5-9a). Rezin of **Syria,** and Pekah, **the son of Remaliah,**[2] from the land of **Ephraim** (5, the chief tribe of north Israel), planned to stage a coup and set up a new government. The Lord assured Ahaz that their plan of "divide and conquer" would not succeed (7). God's decree reverses man's connivings. These kings and their people were mere men, who would soon pass from the scene[3] (8-9a).

(3) *Distrust means distress* (9b). Isaiah makes a play on words here, warning Ahaz that if he will not *affirm* his faith in the true God, his kingdom will not be *confirmed.*[4]

c. *The sign of Immanuel* (7:10-17). (1) *The Eternal's proffered proof* (10-13) came as God offered to let Ahaz choose any kind of **sign** (11) he wanted, in heaven, on earth, or in the unseen world, as a miraculous confirmation of his faith. To have accepted it would have placed him under obligation to the divine program, for God gives us sufficient grounds on which to trust His counsels. *The refusal to test or trust* (12) is couched in the form of feigned piety as (perhaps with a sneer) the king cites Exod. 17:2 and Deut. 6:16. Ahaz had made up his mind to call in Assyrian aid, and did not wish to be persuaded that God and Isaiah were right. What tries the patience of God (13) is man's inveterate unbelief. Ahaz would neither test nor trust Isaiah's God, but he would flaunt, ignore, and **weary** Him.

(2) *No faith? Then no Messiah* (14-17)! Isaiah now declares in the presence of the king and his courtiers ("house of David") that, before the brief years of a childhood pass, the lands of Syria, Ephraim, and even Judah, would all be desolated by the Assyrian

---

[2]Pekah is so called to emphasize his insignificance (II Kings 15:25). Then, as today, the phrase **son of** may express contempt and even a curse. Cf. "sons of Belial." Our taxi driver in Cairo expressed his scorn for the man who pushed his cart across the street in front of us, calling him in Arabic the "son of a donkey." Therefore the phrase **son of Tabeal** (6) indicates the low origin of the man in spite of the fact that in Aramaic Tabe-El means "God is Good."

[3]True to Isaiah's prophecy, at the end of sixty-five years Ashurbanipal had carried off the last remnant of the inhabitants of Samaria and peopled it with an alien race.

[4]George Adam Smith suggests: "If you will not have *faith,* you cannot have *staith*" ("The Book of Isaiah," *The Expositor's Bible,* ed. W. Robertson Nicoll [Hartford, Conn.: The S. S. Scranton Co., 1903]), *ad loc.*

armies. The name **Immanuel** (14) that a maiden[5] would give her firstborn would depict "God's presence." Nevertheless, ere the child's short innocence had passed, they would know God's punishments. Isaiah saw that any realization of the nation's Messianic hopes in his generation had now suffered an indefinite postponement. Refusing a "God with us" program, Judah would now know "God against us." Once again came those inescapable alternatives for Ahaz: Trust God and realize *Isaiah* ("God is salvation") or trust in man and know the meaning of *Shear-jashub* ("only a remnant shall escape").[6]

"Immanuel" in 7:14 reveals (1) God disclosed to man; (2) God identified with man; (3) God companied with man, "the eternal Contemporary" (G. B. Williamson).

[5]"Conservative Christian thought on the proper translation of the Hebrew term here moves between two poles. One is the recognition that the Septuagint (the Greek translation of the OT made some one hundred fifty years before Christ) understood the meaning to be 'virgin,' and Matthew so applied it in reference to the birth of Jesus (Matt. 1:22-23). The other is the necessity of protecting the historical fulfillment of Isa. 7:1-20 in Isaiah's time, and the uniqueness of the virgin birth of Jesus. There was a child born in Isaiah's time, and that child was *not* virgin-born as was our Lord.

"It is possible to see in Isaiah's use of the term *almah* (a young woman of marriageable age) in 7:14 an evidence of divine wisdom, since the Hebrew language also has a word (*bethulah*) which means only virgin. The Bible affirms only *one* Virgin Birth, not *two*, as would be the case if we both accept the historical accuracy of Isaiah 7 and at the same time insist that *almah* here must be translated 'virgin.'

"Therefore there is in Isaiah's prophecy the dual reference that conservative Bible scholars find in many OT Messianic prophecies. The words of the prophet had a clear reference to events then about to happen. At the same time those words had an added meaning for the future that has been seen more clearly in the light of NT revelation" (W. T. PURKISER).

The reader will find many facets of the whole problem explored in the treatment by Dr. Naegelsbach, *op. cit.;* Professor George Rawlinson in "Isaiah" (Exposition and Homiletics), *The Pulpit Commentary,* ed. H. D. M. Spence and Joseph S. Exell (Chicago: Wilcox and Follett, n.d.); E. H. Plumptre, *op. cit.;* two chapters in Edward J. Young, *Studies in Isaiah* (Grand Rapids, Michigan: Wm. B. Eerdmans Publishing Co., 1954), pp. 143-98; and on the meanings of *almah, bethulah,* and *Immanuel* by R. B. Y. Scott "Isaiah 1—39" (Exegesis), and by G. G. D. Kilpatrick, "Isaiah 1—39" (Exposition), *The Interpreter's Bible,* ed. George A. Buttrick, *et al.* (Nashville: Abingdon Press, 1956).

[6]Isaiah therefore has a word for modern rulers: "If you will not *affirm* a faith in Almighty God, God will not *confirm* your little kingdoms in their hoped-for security."

Butter and honey (15), more properly "curds and honey" (RSV), is not only a good formula for the unweaned child, but it is likewise the only available food in a time of devastation and invasion.[7] The expression **before the child shall know to refuse the evil, and choose the good (16)** specifies at least a three-year infancy. By that time **the land that thou abhorrest (16)**—the lands of the two kings who were creating such panic in Judah— would be deserted and Judah herself would be in worse straits than when the ten tribes **departed from Judah (17)**.

d. When God's patience wearies (7:18-25). **In that day (18)** is a phrase of solemn import which Isaiah must have trumpeted into the ears of the young king. He repeated it four times in these eight verses.

The "Egyptian gadfly" and the "Assyrian bumblebee" (18-19) are now to be called in to infest the high hills and deep valleys of Judah. Moreover, Isaiah informs the king: **The razor that is hired (20)** for another shall also shave you smooth. **Head . . . hair of the feet** describes the completeness of the coming disaster. Only the simplest and minimum diet will be possible from pitifully small flocks and herds (21-22). Cultivation will cease. **Where there were a thousand vines (23)**, "worth a thousand shekels of silver" (RSV), there will be only **briers and thorns.** On once-cultivated land only the hunter will roam (24), "And as for all the hills which used to be hoed with a hoe, you will not come there for fear of briers and thorns; but they will become a place where cattle are let loose and where sheep tread" (25; RSV). Thus spoke the Lord through His prophet to the king who had no faith.

2. *The Fear of the Lord Is Wisdom* (8:1—9:1)

Having warned the king, Isaiah turned to the people of Judah. Chapter 8 continues the general subject of c. 7.

[7]Clabbered milk is delightfully satisfying in times of high temperature in arid countries. It is heartily relished by workers in the hot summer as they reap the harvests. Honey is abundant in Palestine and is one of nature's most nourishing and wholesome foods. With no refrigeration, and in times of devastation of the land and crops by foreign invaders, foods movable and spontaneously produced by nature would be the only abundant articles for eating.

Chemically, the modern medical formulae prescribed for the nurture of infants are not too much different from this combination named by Isaiah. "Curds and honey" are chief items in the diet of Bedouin Arabs yet today.

a. The sign of the prophet's unborn son (8:1-4). **A great roll** (1) is better translated "a large tablet," and **a man's pen** more properly designates "common Hebrew characters." Ancient people wrote upon clay tablets, later upon wood, metal, or stone which had been covered with wax. The inscription was to be the name of Isaiah's yet unconceived and unborn son: **Maher-shalal-hash-baz** ("Spoilsoonpreyquick"—Moffatt). In Hebrew characters this would make an impressive sign. The child's name was to be prophetic of the imminent plundering of Syria, Samaria, and even Judah, by the Assyrians.

To prove that the sign was a divine prediction, Isaiah summoned **faithful witnesses** (2). **Uriah** was probably the high priest of that time (II Kings 16:10-16) and thus a collaborator and tool of the king. Hence he would not be likely to favor the prophet. **Zechariah** was probably the father of Ahaz' queen (II Kings 18:2; II Chron. 29:1). The signature of these two notaries as to the date of the prediction would validate it and also gain public attention for it.

The title **the prophetess** (3) for Isaiah's wife is similar to that given to the wives of Salvation Army officers today. The wife takes equal rank with her husband even though she may have ranked above or below him before the marriage.

Isaiah was assured that before the young child learned to say, **My father** (Abi), **and my mother** (Immi), **Damascus** and **Samaria** (4, the two capital cities) should become the spoil of the Assyrians. Tiglath-pileser confirms the fulfillment of this prophecy in his inscriptions relating his conquest.

b. Shiloah versus the Euphrates (8:5-8). **The Lord spake . . . again** (5) suggests the way Isaiah piled divine oracles one upon another. God's instrument of judgment now is pictured as flooding waters, irresistible disaster. The pool of **Shiloah** (6; see Neh. 3:15) is a large reservoir in the Tyropoean valley southeast of Mount Zion at Jerusalem. It is supplied with water by Hezekiah's tunnel, a narrow conduit cut through the limestone rock for a distance of 1,750 feet. This pool in turn is fed by waters which spring from beneath the Temple area. The gentle flow of these **waters** is contrasted with the surging and overflowing of **the river** (Euphrates, 7), which takes its course from the mountains of Turkey and flows down across modern Iraq to the Persian Gulf. (See map 1.)

God declares, through His prophet, that to **rejoice in** (6)

Rezin's policy is to share in his ruin (5-7). **Judah** also shall be overrun by Assyrian armies, and their flood will reach even to her capital city. **Judah** is the land of **Immanuel** (8) and Jerusalem is its **neck** (head).

c. *Fear God above any human conspiracy* (8:9-15). Those who **gird** (9) themselves against the Lord must surely come to consternation. Even the cleverest plans against God's cause **come to nought** (10). The Lord spoke to Isaiah firmly instructing him not to **walk in the way of this people** (11). The ancient command forbade following a multitude to do evil (Exod. 23:2). Therefore the sincere servant of God must beware of the tone and tenor of a sinful society. God counseled Isaiah not to fear their charge of treason (**confederacy**, in v. 12, is better translated "treason"). He who puts the will of God foremost for the nation is the true patriot.[8] Popular opinions may prove to be only a snare in their outcome.

Only when God is present with us are we saved from our enemies (Num. 14:9). The God of Hosts should be man's proper object of dread, not any human conspiracy. Thus Isaiah warned against being swept into panic by popular fears. God will be either our **sanctuary** (14) or our **stone of stumbling**. Israel and Jerusalem will trip and fall because of their misdirected fears. They will then be trapped and taken like an animal in a snare (15).

d. *God's man can wait* (8:16-18). Isaiah ordered **the testimony** (oracle) to be written and deposited with his **disciples** (16). He then expressed his willingness to await God's vindication of his prophecy (17). In 18 he reminded all that he and his family constituted God's **signs** to Israel, each of them with a significant and symbolic name.

e. *Fortune-telling versus God's word* (8:19-22). **Should not a people seek unto their God?** (19) With this question Isaiah warns his disciples against consulting spirit mediums that whisper and **mutter**. To consult the dead for the sake of the living is to forsake the dawn for darkness. Let men consult **the law and . . . the testimony** (20)—the message and counsel of God! Rejec-

[8]The same thing happened to Isaiah as to Amos and Jeremiah. "Whenever the prophets were at all zealous in their opposition to the appeal for foreign aid, they were accused and branded as standing in the service of the enemy, and conspiring for the overthrow of the king" (Delitzsch, *op. cit.*, p. 236).

tion of the divine revelation in preference for fortune-telling brings only famine and blasphemy (raving at self, the government, and God). In this case both the uplook and the outlook are **darkness** (22).

f. God's program not ultimately gloom (9:1). This verse is 8:23 in the Hebrew Bible, and thus part of the preceding passage. Isaiah sounds the hopeful note as he turns his eyes to the future. Though **Zebulun** and **Naphtali** (upper and lower Galilee) would be laid waste by the invader (II Kings 15:29), a time of glory was ahead, exceeding anything Israel had ever known (cf. Moffatt's translation).

The way of the sea was the ancient caravan route from Damascus to the Mediterranean, from the land **beyond Jordan** through **Galilee of the nations.**

B. THE PRINCE WITH THE FOURFOLD NAME, 9:2-7

Isaiah's real hopes were in the God who is Salvation. He therefore expresses the conviction that there is promise for revival through the birth and reign of the Messianic **Prince of Peace.** Here is one of the prophet's finest poems, setting forth the daring vision of a whole nation redeemed and established in peace under a Godlike King. It may have been set to music and sung by his disciples.[9] Here he projects God's great deliverance on the screen of the future. It suggests the new order of salvation which our Saviour introduced in Galilee.

1. *The Dawning Light* (9:2)

Isaiah's expression **the people** now has reference to his nation whittled down to a mere remnant. But the darker the cloud, the brighter the rainbow. This **great light** first streamed forth in Galilee as Jesus began His ministry there. His person and message were like a great dawning upon forlorn and weary wanderers through **the land of the shadow of death** (II Cor. 4:6).

2. *The Increase of Joy* (9:3)

It is characteristic of the Judeo-Christian heritage that the "golden age" is never past, but always future. Isaiah's portrayal of that future declares it exuberant with rejoicing. **Joy in harvest**

---

[9]For a fine poetic translation, see George Buchanan Gray, "A Critical and Exegetical Commentary on the Book of Isaiah," *International Critical Commentary* (New York: Charles Scribner's Sons, 1912), pp. 164-65.

is proverbial for great delight. Men recently victorious in battle are never happier than **when they divide the spoil. Not increased** is better "increased its joy" (Berk.). "Its" and "not" in the original are different in form but identical in sound.

3. *Deliverance from Oppression* (9:4)

The yoke for beasts of burden is symbolical language for tyranny and oppression. Their Egyptian bondage was readily recalled whenever the Hebrews came under the yoke of a foreign tyrant. A workman in the Near East today seeks rest from **the staff of his shoulder.** Two men carry heavy loads swung from a staff resting on their shoulders. **The rod of his oppressor** whipped the slave to his task whenever he was tempted to slacken his pace. In Isaiah's picture, burden and blows are both done away with by great deliverance such as God wrought by "the sword of the Lord, and of Gideon" against **Midian** (Judg. 7:20-21).

4. *From Strife to Peace* (9:5)

Not all the armor is mentioned here, but attention is focused upon the soldier's boots and his outer cloak. Isaiah seems to hear the **confused noise** of the booted feet and see the stained **garments rolled in blood.** His assurance is that, after the battles, even these items will be collected and burned. What a victory it is when peace like a torch kindles fires under the heaped-up implements of war!

5. *The Child with the Miraculous Nature* (9:6)

Here we have Isaiah's characterization of **a child** of miraculous birth, **a son** of marvelous gift, for on **his shoulder** He wears the badge of true authority! Isaiah's prophetic use of the Hebrew perfects (speaking of coming events as if they had already occurred) to express this manifestation of the infant King bespeaks humanity's greatest Child. The long-awaited Messiah is born and is seen growing up amidst the very surroundings which have known the former darkness of Galilee.

The Child's name expresses His marvelous nature. Just as Isaiah had given his own children symbolic names, so he gives this Child four compound titles which are rich with divine symbolism.

Wonderful, Counsellor should be hyphenated.[10] The picture

---

[10]Handel has done Bible readers a disservice by separating the two so forcefully in his oratorio, *The Messiah.* Of course he was following Martin Luther's German translation.

thus becomes one of full and extraordinary prudence, a Wonder of a Counsellor—"an angel of great counsel" (LXX). This becomes more meaningful when we recall that the word "angel" means divine messenger. Jesus was a personal Wonder. He was a wonderful One who gave marvelous counsel, and He was a marvelous One who gave counsel. Isaiah is expressing here the divine attribute of Omniscience, but stated in true Hebrew fashion.

Mighty God suggests the Divine Warrior, or a "Hero divine." He has superhuman prowess, not simply because the Spirit of Almighty God rests upon Him in anointing, but because the nature of essential deity resides within Him. The Hebrew word *El* "always means the Godhead in a specific or absolute sense" (Naegelsbach). Here is the divine attribute of omnipotence. No son of David fulfills this attribute except Jesus of Nazareth (Rom. 1:4).

Everlasting Father is better understood under the concept of "Father of Eternity," or "Father perpetually." He is the Father whose temporal predicate is eternity and whose spatial predicate is ubiquity, since the Father-God is everywhere throughout His universe. To designate one as "the father of" is the Hebrew and Arabic way of saying that he is properly the source of the thing designated as his attribute. Since Christ abides as a Priest forever after the order of Melchisedec, there is no point in time or space where He is not present. Here we see a third attribute, omnipresence.[11]

Prince of Peace is a name which indicates a successful rule in a blessed and true prosperity. Peace belongs to the ideal Kingdom. But R. B. Y. Scott is right in suggesting "Prince Beneficent"[12] as a more accurate rendering. The Hebrew term *shalom* indicates not only absence of war, but a condition of rich, harmonious, and positive well-being. This is what we understand under

[11]The Hebrew term *ad* (meaning "until, even to, up to, as far as, to the point that"), here translated **everlasting**, has a spatial as well as a temporal significance. Coming from *adah* (to pass over, to go on), its primary meaning is passing, or progress in space, and then secondarily, duration of time. Hence *Abi ad* means not only "perpetual Father" but also "ubiquitous Father." He is not only a Father forever but an ever-present Father, existing everywhere at one and the same time and for all time. Cf. Gesenius; and Brown, Driver, and Briggs, Hebrew *Lexicons.*

[12]IB, V, 233.

the fourth great attribute, omnificence—unlimited in creative bounty.

6. *Administrator of Peace and Righteous Government* (9:7)

Such a divine Ruler will experience an ever-widening **government** with an unending **peace.** Under His rule there will be a stable and ordered justice. **The zeal of the Lord of hosts will perform this. With judgment and with justice**—i.e., "in justice and righteousness" (Berk.).

In 9:6-7, "A Son Is Given" as (1) The omniscient Counsellor; (2) The omnipotent Deliverer; (3) The omnipresent Comforter; (4) The beneficent Ruler (G. B. Williamson).

C. The Eternal's Pleadings, 9:8—10:4

Here we have a poem of four stanzas, each concluding with a threatening refrain, **but his hand is stretched out still** (9:12, 17, 21; 10:4)—a refrain which first appeared in 5:25. The poem is directed against the blind optimism and arrogance of the Northern Kingdom with Samaria as its chief city.

1. *Stanza One: Ephraim's Arrogance* (9:8-12)

This stanza expresses God's anger and impending judgment at Israel's pride and iniquity. Isaiah suggests that pride and presumption only hasten doom.

God sent a word . . . it hath lighted upon Israel (8). There is a parallelism of contrast here, a frequent Hebrew idiom. God's word is sent to the Southern Kingdom, but it is focused upon, and spotlights, the Northern Kingdom as the object of His anger and impending judgment.

Since Ephraim represents the ten northern tribes, the declaration is: **All the people shall know, even Ephraim** (9). They shall perceive the word that God has sent and understand that it means them. In pride and arrogance they boast that though **the bricks** of their buildings **are fallen** (10), they will rebuild **with hewn stones;** and though the sycamore pillars of such buildings have been cut down, they shall be replaced with the more expensive and substantial **cedars. Bricks** of adobe and a sycamore-wood framework are the building materials for the simple huts of the peasants in Egypt even today.[13] **Hewn stones** and **cedar**

---

[13]One sees them in the villages of the *fellahin* along the Nile.

framework are the building materials of the wealthy nobles. Thus arrogantly Israel ignored the warnings of invasion. They expressed their determination to rebuild on an even grander scale following the Assyrian devastations.

But, says Isaiah, **the Lord shall set up the adversaries of Rezin** (king of Syria) **against him** (11). And so it was, for after Syria had been conquered by the Assyrian she was compelled to take part in an attack upon Samaria. God controls history. With the **Syrians before, and the Philistines behind** (12; see map 1), Israel would find herself caught in a pincers movement and be compelled to wage a defensive warfare on two fronts. **For all this his anger** has not abated, **but his hand is stretched out still** and raised to smite.

2. *Stanza Two: Fatal Delusions* (9:13-17)

Isaiah tells us that Israel's leaders who seek to guide the people are themselves lost because of their disregard for God's disciplines: **the people turneth not unto him that smiteth them** (13). God's judgments seek to produce repentance and conversion, but arrogance is no sign of either. Correction despised only hardens into perversity. **Therefore the Lord will cut off . . . head and tail, branch and rush, in one day** (14). Verse 15 explains these symbols. The nobility are represented by palm branches, and ordinary men by the cat-**tail** or bulrush. The point is that "great and small in one day shall fall." **The ancient and honourable are the head** but a false **prophet** is contemptible and base— **he is the tail.** The time-serving selfishness of such would-be spiritual guides betrays the people into disaster. **The leaders . . . cause them to err** (16). False guides are a basic contradiction— chosen to lead, they lead only astray. Because the whole nation has done wrong, the Lord has no delight **in their young men** (17) —the flower of the nation—and no mercy even for its **widows** and orphans. That nation has fallen on evil times when **every one is an hypocrite and an evildoer, and every mouth speaketh folly.** The stanza closes with the same warning refrain, as stanzas one, three, and four: **but his hand is stretched out still.**

3. *Stanza Three: Blazing Anarchy* (9:18-21)

Amidst mounting **wickedness,** bitter rivalry had arisen between **Manasseh** and **Ephraim** (21), the two tribes descended from Joseph, and both are turned against **Judah.** Civil strife sets each man against his fellow. Isaiah's picture is one of ungodliness blazing like a brush **fire** up every wooded ravine of Israel (18). **Through the wrath of the Lord of hosts** (19) the land is blackened. The fuel for the fires is none other than the people of the strife, as if a man were to **eat . . . the flesh of his own arm** (20), i.e., destroy his own flesh and blood. The fury of factions leaves no room for pity between man and man when insatiable greed holds sway. Tribal jealousies serve only to devour the unity of a nation.

Sin brings its own punishment (cf. 33:11-12; Heb. 6:8; Jas. 3:5). Chaos and confusion pervade the whole order of society when moral anarchy prevails. Sons of the same parents in civil strife fulfill the prophecy that "a man's foes shall be they of his own household" (Matt. 10:21, 36; Mark 13:12). Under these conditions God's **hand is stretched out still** (21); not in mercy but in judgment.

4. *Stanza Four: Legislated Oppression* (10:1-4)

This stanza denounces the legislators and judges who **write grievousness** (1), i.e., laws and decrees to defraud the weak and the poor. In the day of God's visitation they too shall crouch among the prisoners. Whenever the laws and the courts make **widows . . . their prey** and **rob the fatherless** (2) while all the formalities of justice are being punctiliously observed, jurisprudence has reached an all-time low. Isaiah asks, **What will ye do in the day of visitation** (3), when the Supreme Judge of the universe calls you to account? What ally can protect you from the wrath of the Eternal? **Where will ye leave your glory,** i.e., hide your ill-gotten gain? Without God as an Ally, exile and death become their only expectation. With the fourth refrain, **his hand is stretched out still** (4), Isaiah's "doom-gong" tolls its sad finale.

D. God's Rod of Anger, 10:5-34

Our prophet now turns his attention to the significance and destiny of Assyria (see map 1). His apostrophe to this bloodthirsty and haughty nation is couched in a sevenfold reminder.

1. *Assyria Is Only God's Instrument* (10:5-11)

Woe betide the **Assyrian . . . rod** of God's **indignation** (5). He is but the instrument of the Lord's anger. His passion for conquest will eventually become his own destruction. Sent **against any hypocritical nation** (6; Israel), Assyria's intention is different from the divine purpose. His boasting ignores the fact that he is but God's means of discipline for the nations and the cities he enumerates, and over whose downfall he so vainly gloats. **Carchemish, Arpad,** and **Damascus** (9) were cities overrun or destroyed by the Assyrians. Since their **idols** (10) had proved no defense against the Assyrian armies, these proud pagans expected no effective resistance from the Israelite cities of **Calno, Hamath,** and **Samaria.** They expected also to conquer **Jerusalem and her idols** (11).

2. God Both Proposes and Disposes (10:12-14)

When God is through with him, then punishment is certain for the Assyrian. He foolishly thinks his own hands have gained these victories for him, but once **the Lord hath performed his whole work,** then He **will punish . . . the stout heart of the king of Assyria** (12). The boastfulness of Assyria is vividly described in 13-14.

3. Divine Fires Shall Consume (10:15-19)

Let not **the ax** think itself greater than the woodman or **the saw** greater than the sawyer (15). The tail does not wag the dog. The Lord will send **a burning like the burning of a fire** (16) upon Assyria. **The light of Israel** (17) **shall consume the glory** (fame) **of his forest** (18; the nation itself). So **few** will be the survivors that **a child may** count them (19).

4. God Leaves a Remnant (10:20-23)

Isaiah here turns from Assyria, to speak of **the remnant of Israel, and . . . Jacob** (20). God always has His righteous minority who lean upon the Lord. For the remnant of Assyria there is as yet no word of hope, but for that of Israel the prophet recalls the name of his own son Shear-jashub, whose name means **The remnant shall return** (21; cf. 7:3) and predicts a brighter future. The smiter was the king of Assyria, whose help and protection Ahaz and his counselors had courted instead of trusting in God. When trust in the arm of flesh fails, one realizes (often too late) that faith in God is the truest wisdom. It was so in Israel. Even though the people were then **as the sand of the sea** in number, only **a remnant of them shall return** (22). When God's finished work **shall overflow with righteousness** its character is both punitive and corrective. For **consumption decreed** (22) and a **consumption, even determined** (23) read, "Annihilation is determined . . . a full destruction and that a decisive one" (Berk.).

5. *The Oppressor's Yoke to Be Broken* (10:24-27)

In this apostrophe to His people, God reminds the Assyrian that He has more than one rod. **The Lord of hosts shall stir up a scourge** (26) for the Assyrian. Thus God assures Zion that, when His punishment of her is finished, He will surely deal with Assyria. Therefore the divine consolation is: **Be not afraid** (24). **For yet a very little while** (25) **. . . and the yoke shall be destroyed because of the anointing** (27), which was the seal of the covenant and the assurance of its fulfillment. The destruction of Assyria shall be like **the slaughter of Midian at the rock of Oreb** (26; cf. Judg. 7:25).

6. *The Oppressor Halted* (10:28-32)

As of now the Assyrian has come to the very gates of Jerusalem, plundering the approaching and surrounding environs, but it takes more than threats and a shaking of the fist to defeat and plunder Zion. God's people still stand under the divine protection. The progress of the invader is traced through **Aiath** (28; near Heshbon in Moab); **Migron** was south of **Aiath**. **Michmash** was northeast of Jerusalem. An encircling movement is thus suggested. **Geba** (29), **Ramah, Gibeah of Saul, Gallim** (30), **Laish, Anathoth, Madmenah** (31), and **Gebim,** as far as they can be located, were villages ringing Jerusalem to the north. **Nob** (32) was a village north of the city and within sight of it. "Thus far and no farther" the enemy could come. He could only **shake his hand against . . . Zion, the hill of Jerusalem.**

7. *The Haughty to Be Humbled* (10:33-34)

When God says, "Thus far," He means also, "No farther." No matter how high the tree of pride may grow, the divine Woodman will bring it low. God will cut the arrogant down to size, felling him like a cedar of **Lebanon.** The lesson is that when a tool has served its purpose it may then be tossed aside. History is directed by an all-wise and all-powerful God, who does what seems fit with armies and inhabitants of earth, regardless of the designs of men. This prophecy saw its fulfillment when in a single night under the sword of the destroying angel the Assyrian with his vast army was brought down in defeat. One hundred eighty-five thousand troops fell under the plague, and Sennacherib himself was assassinated by two of his sons (37:36-38; II Kings 19:35-37). Thus does God humble such proud, blaspheming mortals as Sennacherib, Napoleon, and Hitler.

E. The Shoot from the Stump of Jesse, 11:1-10

This is the third Messianic picture in the Book of Isaiah. The first was a prophecy of Immanuel in c. 7; the second, the Wonderful Counselor in c. 9. Now comes the great antitype of Melchisedek, the King of Righteousness and Peace. He stands as God's Rod of Righteousness in contrast to Assyria as the Eternal's rod of anger.

1. *The Personality of Messiah* (11:1-3a)

a. *His origin* (11:1). Isaiah sees the Messiah as a Shoot from **the stem** (stump) **of Jesse,** and **a Branch** from Jesse's family **roots.** He arises as a young sapling with new strength and vigor achieving life out of death. Our Lord sprang not only from the Davidic dynasty, but, more significantly, from a ruined and sinful humanity. He became a Tree of Life for earth's dying millions and the Founder of a new humanity. The word **Branch** comes from the same Hebrew root as one name for our Lord, the "Nazarene."

b. *His endowments* (11:2-3a). Isaiah sees the coming One endowed with a supernatural character and anointed by the sevenfold Spirit of the Lord (cf. Rev. 3:1b). Of this, the seven-branched lampstand in the Tabernacle was a type. These seven operations of the Holy Spirit are manifested in the Messiah.

The spirit of wisdom (2). This is that quality which enables one to use right means for the end in view, giving success and efficiency in life.

The spirit of **understanding** indicates not only knowledge in general, but discrimination in particular. It is the art of distinguishing a difference and approving the excellent.

The spirit of counsel designates the ability to impart wisdom to others and to guide them rightly. **Might** would indicate not only strength of purpose, but an ability to bring things to pass. In the Septuagint the Greek term indicates not only physical strength but also mental and spiritual power. Jesus manifested it in His authority over demons, diseases, nature, and death.

The spirit of knowledge and of the fear of the Lord is one unit, with two aspects—knowledge of and reverence for God. By means of **the spirit of knowledge** divine things and the Divine Being become intensely real. The Holy Spirit is the Medium of fellowship between the Father and the Son. He is likewise the One who brings to redeemed humanity an intimate knowledge of both. **The fear of the Lord** is reverence for the divine commands. It involves true piety, devoutness, and a sensitive regard for God's authority and will.

The seventh quality of Messiah's endowment is referred to as **quick understanding in the fear of the Lord** (3*a*). In the Hebrew a keenness of the sense of smell is suggested. Some have translated it: "He shall draw His breath in the fear of the Lord." Delitzsch translates it, "And fear of Jehovah is fragrance to Him." But the truer concept seems to specify a keenness of insight, an acute discernment of all facts and relationships. Jesus clearly perceived both the thoughts and characters of those about Him and needed no one to tell Him what was in man (John 2:25).

2. *The Principles of Messiah's Reign* (11:3*b*-5)

The King of righteousness does not judge by mere appearances, or reprove on the basis of mere hearsay (3). His decisions are with justice and **equity** even for the poor and the meek. His word is as powerful as **the rod** (4) in bringing judgment upon the merciless and the wicked. **Righteousness** and fidelity are **the girdle** (the encircling principle) of both His compassion and His strength (5).

3. *The Peace of Messiah's Realm* (11:6-9)

Here we see nature's predatoriness transformed into a blessed peaceableness. It is essentially a vision of an idyllic and Edenic age. Whether resting (6), feeding (7), or playing (8), **they shall not hurt nor destroy** (9) each other. The carnivorous animal becomes a vegetarian; the venomous serpent becomes a harmless playmate. Animals heretofore opposites in nature may now be gathered into one group by **a little child**. And the land shall be as **full of the knowledge of the Lord** as the ocean bed is with water. Distrust between man and his fellow creatures is part of the curse which came because of sin, and shall be done away with only by man's final redemption.

4. *The Point of Messianic Rally* (11:10)

In that day the **root of Jesse . . . shall stand** as a flagstaff and point of rendezvous for the multitudes. The nations shall come to Him for consultation and instruction. For **ensign** see comment on 5:26.

5. *The Place of Messiah's Rest* (11:10*d*)

His rest shall be glorious, i.e., He shall abide evermore in the eternal glory. Messiah's dwelling place is with the Eternal. Thus when He comes among men, the prophecy of "God with us" shall be realized. Also His dwelling place shall be famous, as God's abiding point among His people. "Glorious things of thee are spoken, Zion, city of our God."

F. THE REHABILITATED AND REJOICING REMNANT, 11:11—12:6

1. The Recovery of the Remnant (11:11-12)

In that day (11) the **Lord** will again raise His **hand . . . to recover** the survivors of His people in a return from dispersion. These are **the outcasts of Israel** and **the dispersed of Judah** (12). They will return from **Pathros** and **Cush,** two districts of the Nile River valley; from **Elam** and **Shinar,** two districts of the Tigris-Euphrates River basins; from **Hamath,** the valley of the Orontes River; and from the **islands of the sea** (the Mediterranean). These are symbolically representative of **the four corners of the earth:** south, east, north, and west.

2. The Reconciled Remnant (11:13-14)

Envy and strife shall cease between **Ephraim** and **Judah** (13) and they shall unite against their common foes. **The shoulders of the Philistines** (14) probably refers to the foothills (Shephelah) as one descends toward the west plain of Philistia (the Gaza strip); **Edom, Moab,** and **Ammon** are the trans-Jordan highlands south and east of the Jordan River (east of the Dead Sea and the Arabah).

3. The Roadway for the Remnant (11:15-16)

Here the prophet seems to be saying that **the tongue of the Egyptian sea** (15; the Gulf of Suez) shall be dried up and **the river** (the Euphrates or perhaps the Nile) shall be divided into **seven streams** (dry wadies) over which men may cross **dryshod.** Moreover, there is to be a raised **highway** (16) stretching across the great plains of Mesopotamia for the homecoming of Messiah's people. Isaiah sees this return as comparable to God's provision for Israel in the exodus **out of the land of Egypt.**

4. The Rejoicing of the Remnant (12:1-6)

This short chapter gives us two songs of deliverance which were to be sung on the occasion of the new exodus. Each song is introduced with the expression **in that day.** The chapter thus constitutes a great doxology which concludes the Book of Immanuel.

71

a. *The thank-song of deliverance* (12:1-3). This first song
expresses Israel's gratitude. Although the Eternal had been
angry, His anger is now turned away and He has comforted His
people, delivering them and restoring them to their land. Here in
v. 2, Isaiah inserts his own name, which means **Jehovah is my
strength.** As such God is both the Source of one's salvation and
the Theme of one's song. Drawing **water out of the wells of salvation** (3) recalls the ceremony in which the priests descended to
the Pool of Siloam and brought back water to the Temple court,
where it was poured out in libation before the Lord (cf. the
setting of John 7:37-39).

b. *The thank-song of God's doings* (12:4-6). This poem lifts
up a call for praise, prayer, proclamation, and exaltation of the
name of **the Lord** (4). In songs of praise His glorious doings
are to be made known throughout **all the earth** (5). The inhabitants **of Zion** are exhorted to sing and shout the greatness of
the Holy One of Israel (6), whose presence and majesty are
among them. When God's glorious presence is manifested among
His people, shouting and singing often break forth in the congregation of the saints. Too many congregations today are remiss
at this point.

This brief chapter centers around the theme "God in the
Midst." (1) God is great, 6, as Creator, Redeemer, and Conqueror; (2) God is in the midst of His people, 6b, always and
everywhere; therefore (3) Shout the greatness of God, 4, who is
our Strength, 2; our Salvation, 2; and our Song, 2, 5 (G. B. Williamson).

Section **III** *Oracles Against Foreign Nations*

Isaiah 13:1—23:18

A. CONCERNING BABYLON, 13:1—14:27

The title of the section contained in cc. 13—14 is given in v. 1. It is a **burden,** a prophecy of grievous import, clearly seen in a vision by **Isaiah the son of Amoz,** concerning the doom and desolation of **Babylon.** The Hebrew word translated **burden** suggests "an oracle of doom." **Babylon** in Isaiah's day was the chief province of Assyria (see map 1). Sargon, the Assyrian, took for himself the title "vicar of the gods in Babylon."

1. *A Dialogue of Destiny* (13:2-22)

a. The divine announcement (13:2-3). In this divine announcement we have the summons from "signal hill." The foreign invaders were thought of as weapons of God's indignation. Thus when God commanded His **sanctified ones,** the reference is to the fierce tribes of the destroyer, appointed for a special task.

b. The prophet's description (13:4-10). The first scene is the tumult of the mustering multitudes (4-5), in which the **Lord of hosts** is calling an army to battle. The prophet announces, **The day of the Lord is at hand; it shall come as a destruction from the Almighty** (6).[1] The call is therefore to *wail* and *travail* (6, 8). Hands will become feeble and hearts dismayed, while men stare at each other aghast, **their faces . . . as flames,** flushed with excitement (8). Desolation, destruction, and darkness (9-10) shall be characteristics of that day. There shall be desolation for the earth, and destruction of **sinners** from out of it (9). These will be accompanied by astronomical disturbances[2] such as make the stars fade, the sun fail at dawning, and cause the moon . . . not . . . to shine (10).

c. God speaks of retribution (13:11-12). The divine declaration is: "I will punish and put an end to sinners in their pride.

---

[1]The Hebrew is *shodmish-Shaddai. Shaddai* comes from the verb root *shadad,* "to destroy"; hence the phrase may be translated, "destruction from the destroyer."

[2]Astronomical disturbances in the day of the Lord (*Yom Yahweh*) are natural symbols of a time of terror (Joel 2:31; 3:15; Matt. 24:29; Luke 21:25).

Tyrants shall bite the dust, and mortals become more scarce than gold."

d. *The oracle continued* (13:13-16). Isaiah's portrait of that day depicts a trembling **heavens** and a reeling **earth** (13). There will be a frantic flight of the foreigner from Babylon to safety in **his own land** (14). Like hunted animals or shepherdless sheep, foreigners will stampede homeward for safety; yet whoever is overtaken shall **fall by the sword** (15). Infants shall be **dashed to pieces** (16) in the sight of their parents; **houses** will be plundered and **wives** raped. In the midst of such a picture God speaks again.

e. *The role of the Medes* (13:17-18). It is **the Medes** (17) who shall destroy Babylon in Assyria. This terrible nation cannot be bribed with **silver** or **gold**. Their **bows** (18) and sharp arrows will slaughter **the young men**; they have **no pity** for the unborn child, nor do they **spare children** (18). The Medes were skilled archers, and they were destined to destroy both Nineveh and Babylon (cf. Intro. to Daniel, this volume).

f. *Babylon's desolation* (13:19-22). **Babylon**, the pride of all Chaldeans, will resemble **Sodom and Gomorrah** (19) in the day of her overthrow. It shall be uninhabited for generations, and not even the **Arabian** (20) Bedouins will camp there with their flocks.[3] It will be the haunt of wild birds and howling **beasts** (21). **Owls** may be translated "ostriches"; **satyrs** means "shaggy beasts"—perhaps wild goats; **dragons** (22) is better "jackals." Time's up, and Babylon's days are numbered.

2. *Restoration for Israel* (14:1-4a)

The restoration of Israel and Jacob to their homeland is related to the destruction of Babylon. As the Babylonian captivity was a rejection of Israel as God's peculiar people, so the restoration bespeaks God's choice of them once again. The prophecy in summary proclaims **mercy on Jacob** (1), election for **Israel**, with **strangers** (foreigners) for their neighbors and friends. Their former taskmasters shall be their **servants and handmaids** (2); their captors shall now be their **captives**. The **sorrow, fear,**

---

[3]Bedouins shrink in superstitious horror from camping on sites of ruins. According to Herodotus, Babylon was the most famous and the strongest of all the cities of Assyria. It was fabulously adorned. Modern archaeologists have found it a hideous waste. The vast city became a desolated ruins.

and **hard bondage** (3) of captivity will be replaced by the singing of a song of triumph.

3. *Song of the Tyrant's Downfall* (14:4b-23)

The newer translations refer to this passage as "a taunt-song" —a derisive utterance in poetic and figurative speech.

a. The joy of release from terror (14:4b-8). This proverb of peace comprises the first of five stanzas in the song of Babylon's doom. The tyrant and his **golden city** (4) are no more. His **staff** of wickedness is broken and his **sceptre** (5) of authority that rained unceasing blows of unrelenting persecution upon the nations is quiet. The **earth is at rest** and her people are **singing** (7). The Assyrian kings made it a practice to cut down the forests wherever they conquered. Hence even the **trees rejoice** (8) in the fact that since the tyrant has fallen there is respite from the woodsman's ax. **Fir trees** would be the Aleppo pine.

b. The welcoming underworld (14:9-11). **Hell** (here the place of the dead) hastens **to meet** the once proud king of Babylon. Summoning the ghosts of the former **chief ones of the earth,** the underworld bids him welcome with its taunt-song: "So you are as weak as the rest of us, eh? (10) Your pomp descends to the grave to the sound of your funeral harps. A mattress of maggots is beneath you, a blanket of worms covers you, while giant spectres[4] haunt you (11)." Death puts all on the same level, and the proud man is eaten of worms at the end of earth's glory.

c. The end of a false ambition (14:12-15). Since this stanza begins with an apostrophe to **Lucifer,**[5] some have taken it as a description of the fall of Satan. Valid exegesis would hold that at best it is only typically satanic, for the subject of the taunt-song is still the king of Babylon. Summarized, it says:

> *Ah, how you have fallen,*
> *You shining son of the dawn!*
> *You who once laid all nations low*
> *Are now cut down to the ground.*
> *Recall your boasts!*
> *You who would ascend above the stars,*
> *And sit among the gods beyond the northwind,*
> *Are now cut down to the abyss!* (Lit.)

[4]The Hebrew for **the dead** (9) is *Rephaim*, 'shades, or giant spectres."

[5]This Latin term means "light bringing" and indicates the "morning star," Venus. The KJV **son of the morning** translates better "morning star."

Then, as in some cases today, divine names were used for their kings by various nations, but they remained nonetheless human, and pitifully mortal. He who was most illustrious now stands as an object lesson of retribution. One short lifetime suffices to have seen kaisers defeated and dictators die in defeat and disgrace. This present century has witnessed an emperor of a proud nation renounce his deity over a nationwide radio hookup.

d. A king without a grave (14:16-20a). In this stanza the prophetic word declares: Kings have honorable burials but thou shalt be trodden underfoot as **an abominable** thing (19). Your final humiliation is at hand. The onlookers **shall narrowly look upon thee** (16; "stare at you," RSV), pondering your fate. **Is this the man** who made kingdoms quake, turned the earth into a desert, laid its cities in heaps of rubble, and never released **his prisoners** (17)? Unlike other **kings of the nations** (18) who receive an honorable burial, Babylon's king shall lie unburied among the slain, **a carcase trodden under feet** (19), not **joined with** his ancestors in death (20a).

e. The broom sweeps clean (14:20b-23). This final stanza depicts the fate of the king's posterity. One's evil influence never confines itself to him alone. When a great tree is felled in the forest, it brings smaller ones crashing down with it. The wicked king had ruined, not only himself, but his land, his people, and his posterity. The last clause of 20 is more properly rendered as an imprecation: "May the descendants of evildoers not be mentioned forever" (Berk.). The prophet recognizes that the king's **children** (royal heirs) must die, lest they revolt and rebuild **cities,** thus seeking to repossess the earth (21). The Eternal's vow is to wipe out **Babylon** completely, leaving not even a **son, and nephew** (22; grandson). Swamps and **bittern** (23; waterfowl) will take over the territory, the Lord's **besom** (broom) **of destruction** having swept the city away.

4. *The Oath of Assyria's Doom* (14:24-27)

Here follows a second and shorter oracle against Assyria, of which Babylon was the chief province. The **sworn** purpose of **the Lord of hosts** (24) is the utter destruction of **the Assyrian** (25). Thus Isaiah offers fresh assurance to Israel concerning her present enemy. It will be **in my land, and upon my mountains** (the mountains of Palestine) that Assyria shall meet its doom. The burden of Assyrian oppression will be lifted off the back of God's people. The Lord's outstretched **hand** will assure the outcome which none **shall disannul** (26-27).

B. CONCERNING PHILISTIA, 14:28-32

This oracle of warning came to **Palestina** (29, Philistia; the name Palestine comes from Philistine). It was dated **in the year** of the death of **king Ahaz** (28), and warns against false pride. Dates for this period of Old Testament chronology are difficult to determine, and for the death of Ahaz range from 727 to 716 B.C.[6] The historical background is found in II Chron. 28:18-27.

1. *Premature Exultation* (14:28-30)

Isaiah reminds the Philistines that although their chastening rod, the Assyrian king, Tiglath-pileser, has been broken in death, their rejoicing and their invasion of Judah are both premature. The successors of that oppressor will be more destructive than he was. **Out of the serpent's root** (29) shall come one more poisonous. Sargon was worse than Tiglath-pileser, and Sennacherib was like the **flying serpent** of the desert in his attack. Philistia is told that Judah's **firstborn of the poor** (30), those who have inherited a double portion of poverty, will find food and refuge, but Philistia's **root** and **remnant** shall die of **famine** and the sword.

2. *Terror Advances* (14:31)

Shrieking lamentations befit the **city** and its **gate** (government). Away to **the north** are seen the **smoke** of burning towns[7] and the smoke signals for a fresh rendezvous for another attack. **None shall be alone,** i.e., there shall be no stragglers among the enemy. The Philistine city of Ashdod would be the gateway to the nation as an invading army made its approach from the north along the coastal trunk road, down across the plain of Sharon toward the Gaza strip (see map 2).

3. *The Only Sure Refuge* (14:32)

Here Isaiah seems to be pondering his reply to an embassy from the Philistines enquiring about their fate. His answer is that even **the poor of his people** shall fare better than Philistia. The Lord has founded Zion and she stands firm under His protection. In her the afflicted shall find refuge.

---

[6]IB suggests 720 B.C. (*ad loc.*).

[7]There is a remarkably frequent recurrence of the words, "I burnt" (*ashrup*), in the Assyrian inscriptions.

C. Concerning Moab, 15:1—16:14

This oracle of Moab's doom[8] takes chiefly the form of an elegy.[9] Due to the uncertainty of the text and the resulting variety of translations by the scholars,[10] this is a confessedly difficult passage. Here the expositor finds little help from the exegetes. Isaiah may have worked over a former, and now anonymous, elegy which lamented a great calamity suffered by Moab from a northern invader prior to his day. Verse 13 of c. 16 would seem so to indicate. If this be the case, Isaiah sees the elegy as applicable to the fate which he himself prophesies will befall Moab just three years hence (16:14).

1. *The Devastation of Moab* (15:1-9)

a. Moab is undone (15:1-4). Because of the fall of her two chief cities[11] in a single night, **Moab is laid waste, and brought to silence** (1). Consequently Moab wails aloud (2-4) with heads shaved and beards clipped. Clothed **with sackcloth**, the people ascend to the sacred shrines[12] and to **the tops of their houses** for prayer. Even as folk meet in the intersections of **their streets**, they weep. **Heshbon** and **Elealeh** (4) were Moabite towns about

---

[8]**Moab** means "from father" and suggests the descent of the Moabites from the elder daughter of Lot, who gave this name to her son. Cf. Gen. 19:30-37.

[9]The prophet is painfully affected by what he sees. All that he predicts evokes his deepest sympathy as he identifies in true empathy with the unfortunate nation whose woe and desolation he predicts. Jeremiah includes this oracle almost in its entirety in his own oracle on Moab. Cf. Jeremiah 48.

[10]For an understanding of these two chapters see Num. 21:26-30; II Kings 3; Isa. 25:10-12; Jeremiah 48; Ezek. 25:8-11; Amos 2:1-3; Zeph. 2:8-11. The comments of Delitzsch, *op. cit.*, and John Skinner, *The Book of the Prophet Isaiah*, "Cambridge Bible for Schools and Colleges" (Cambridge: University Press, 1915), are superior. For the geographical situation consult map 2. See also Denis Baly, *The Geography of the Bible* (New York: Harper and Brothers, n.d.), Chap. XIX. The articles on "Moab," "Moabite," and "Moabite Stone," in Merrill T. Unger, *Unger's Bible Dictionary* (Chicago: Moody Press, 1957), and in the ISBE should be noted. See also comments on Jeremiah 48 in this volume.

[11]**Ar** (1) is the ancient Hebrew term for "City," and **Kir** is the ancient name for the modern El Kerak. **Dibon, Medeba, Nebo** (2), and **Horonaim** (5) are all mentioned in the inscription on the Moabite stone, which testifies to their antiquity.

[12]**Nebo** was the mountain with the temple of Chemosh, the central sanctuary of Moab, in honor of her chief deity.

two miles apart, between the Jabbok and the Arnon rivers, northeast of the Dead Sea.

b. *The prophet mourns for Moab* (15:5-9). **My heart shall cry out for Moab** (5) is the prophet's way of saying that he too participates in this pain. The calamities which he must announce move him to sorrow and not to exultation.[13] The flight of Moab's **fugitives** (5) and the fate of those who escape the destroyer (9) are no occasion for rejoicing on the prophet's part. From **the waters of Nimrim** (6; the Wady Shaib), near the modern city of Es Salt in the north, to **Zoar** (5), across the torrent **Zered**[14] in the south, the fugitives beheld a once beautiful land turned to utter waste (cf. II Kings 3:19). **An heifer of three years old** (5) is probably the name of a town and should read "Eglath-shelishi-yah" (RSV). Thus their cries rang through the length and breadth of Moab, reaching to **Eglaim** (twin pools, 8) and **Beer-elim** (the well of the princes). Even the streams flow red with the **blood** (9) of the slain, while the destroyer pursues them like a lion after its prey.

2. Moab Seeks Sanctuary (16:1-7)

a. *A plea and a peace offering to Zion* (16:1-5). A tribute of **lambs** (1) seems ever to have been Moab's tax. It was so in the days of Ahab (II Kings 3:4), who collected a heavy tax from his tributary people. The Moabite chieftains having fled to **Sela** (Petra),[15] deliberating in their distress, directed their appeal to **Zion** (1) for sanctuary for their fugitives. The prophetic advice is that submission to the house of David is Moab's real and only hope. Confusion **at the fords of** the river **Arnon** (2; see map 2) would result as the people, driven from their homes by the invader, sought to escape. The steep terrain and the narrow descents would create congestion along these escape routes. The picture is that of fluttering birds that scatter from a rifled **nest.** The plea

---

[13]The Moabites were akin to the Hebrews both racially and linguistically.

[14]The KJV says: **brook of the willows** (7). But these willows are really oleanders. Cf. Denis Baly, *op. cit.*, p. 217. The **Zered** served as a boundary line between Moab and Edom. It is the southernmost of the four main trans-Jordan rivers which flow westward into the rift valley. The Yarmuk and the Jabbok flow into the Jordan River; the Arnon and the Zered make their rapid descent into the Dead Sea itself.

[15]Petra is the Rose-Red fortress of the biblical Edomites. Cf. the *National Geographic Magazine*, CVIII, No. 6, 853-70. It is one of the favorite side trips from Jerusalem in modern Jordanian tourism.

is that the Moabite **outcasts** (3-4*a*) may find in Zion a refuge from the destroyer. In response to this act of mercy, God gives Judah a promise of merciful love (4*b*-5); **the throne shall be established** and it shall be characterized by the trustworthiness and justice of the Davidic dynasty.

    b. But what about Moab's sincerity? (16:6-7) Moab has a reputation for **haughtiness and . . . pride** (6). Can her sincerity be depended upon now? Her pride and false boasts, colored by insolence and sham, demand a retribution of wailing and misery (7). **Kir-hareseth** or "Kirharesh" (11) is probably "Kir of Moab" (15:1), southeast of the Dead Sea.

    3. *The Stricken Condition of Moab* (16:8-12)

    a. Failure of the vine and harvest (16:8). Grapes and small grain were the chief crops of this part of the trans-Jordan highlands. Both would be destroyed.

    b. The battle shout has replaced the shout of vintage (16: 9-10). No longer is heard the song of the vintage gatherers and the reapers, but the cry of the enemy as they trample on the fields and tear up the vines. For **Heshbon, and Elealeh** (9), see comment on 15:4.

    c. The prophet mourns Moab's unavailing prayers (16:11-12). Moab's unavailing petitions at the high place of her Chemosh worship call forth the prophet's feelings of pity. Prayer to false gods is always futile.

    4. *A Past Oracle and Present Fulfillment* (16:13-14)

    The word of **the Lord** (13) was the judgment promised to Moab by Balaam (Num. 24:17) and Moses (Deut. 23:3-4). Moab's glory shall soon turn to mere mockery. Despite her present multitudes, her escapees shall be few and insignificant. **Three years** (14) are but a brief interval, but they seem long to one who hires himself to another. Or **as the years of an hireling** may be intended to indicate the definiteness of the prediction, as a hired hand is careful not to work beyond the time for which he is paid.

    D. Concerning Damascus and Ephraim, 17:1-14

    In this oracle Isaiah spells out the doom of the Syro-Ephraimitic alliance (see Intro.). He presents the inevitable issues of an alliance based on practical rejection of the true God and the adoption of foreign idolatries. The date is prior to the Assyrian conquest of Damascus, perhaps about 735 B.C.[16]

1. The Ruin of Damascus (17:1-3)

Damascus (1) has been destroyed more often than any other city, yet it boasts also of being the oldest continuously inhabited city of the world. It has never permanently ceased to be a city, though it has more than once become a **heap** of ruins. There were two **cities of Aroer** (2) east of the Jordan River, one in the land of Reuben, the other in Gad.[17] The very name signifies "laid bare, or naked," as ominous of utter ruin. And a town *is* in ruins when it becomes only a place **for flocks** (2). **Ephraim** (3) is due to lose her defenses, and **Damascus** her domain. The prophet paints their downfall under the symbol of the departing and transient **glory of the children of Israel.**

2. The Fate of Ephraim (17:4-6)

Isaiah conceives the fate of the Northern Kingdom under the symbol of an emaciated **Jacob** (4). He is sure that Israel is as ripe for judgment as when **the harvestman gathereth the corn** (5). The great Harvestman will leave only so many stalks of wheat as one can gather in **his arm** (5). It shall be as if one were gleaning stalks of wheat in the vale of **Rephaim,**[18] where battles were often fought at harvesttime. Or like an **olive tree** from which the berries have been beaten off, with but a few stray ones left in the topmost and **outmost . . . branches** (6).[19] Only a small remnant would be left of this Northern Kingdom.

[16]George Adam Smith refers to this oracle as "one of the earliest and most crisp of Isaiah's prophecies, of the time of Syria's and Ephraim's league against Judah, somewhere between 736 and 732 B.C." (*op. cit., ad loc.*).

[17]Cf. Deut. 2:36; 3:12 for Aroer in the land of Reuben, which later became the possession of Moab (Jer. 48:19); and Num. 32:34; Josh. 13:25; II Sam. 24:5 for a city with the same name in Gad, near Rabbah of Ammon. The first was Amoritish and the other Ammonitish.

[18]Probably "the valley of the giants" (terrible ones) on the border between Benjamin and Judah (Josh. 15:8). Here David repeatedly defeated the Philistines (II Sam. 5:18, 22; 23:13; I Chron. 11:15; 14:9). Perhaps the modern *el-Bika'*, which slopes away to the southwest from the rim of the Valley of Hinnom, is referred to here.

[19]In the olive harvest the trees are beaten with long sticks (Deut. 24:20). The women and the older girls then gather up the fruit from the ground. The youngsters often climb into the branches to reach the highest fruit, but rarely can one beat every olive from its tree.

3. The Futility of Fabricated Gods (17:7-8)

In that hour of calamity, those few who have been transformed by the bitter disappointments of a futile idolatry will recognize their **Maker** as the true Source of their strength (7). No longer will a man **look to . . . the work of his hands, neither . . . that which his fingers have made** (8). The **groves** and **images** for the practice of idolatry seem fitting only to the soul that has lost its God and must have some visible substitute in the form of an idol.

4. The Fruit of Apostasy (17:9-11)

Israel's **strong** (fortified) **cities** shall be like a **forsaken** tract of forest, deserted now again as they once were by the Canaanites at the time of the invasion of Palestine by **the children of Israel** (9). The nation's abandonment of the **God of . . . salvation** (10) in offering homage to **strange slips** (foreign cults) upon her soil, with their **pleasant** and hedged-in "hothouse" plantings,[20] guarantees a sad harvest. Sin at first looks promising; however its ultimate outcome will not be one of good fortune but of **grief and . . . desperate sorrow** (10-11). Having transplanted heathen gods into their worship, they must reap the Lord's abandonment of the nation to its enemies.[21]

5. The Finale for Assyria (17:12-14)

In this stanza Isaiah pictures the sounds of the mixed multitudes in the Assyrian army as **the noise of the seas** (12). **But God shall rebuke them, and they shall flee . . . as the chaff of the mountains before the wind** (13),[22] and like "whirling dust be-

---

[20]These were probably gardens of the Adonis cult in which pots filled with earth were planted with flowers, small grain, and vegetables, and tended for rapid growth under the sun's heat. These were then regarded as manifestations of the reproductive powers of Adonis, the god of fertility. A prominent and voluptuous part was taken in these rites by women; hence Isaiah addresses Israel here in the second person feminine. The prophet is sure that such devotion to foreign gods will leave the nation helpless in the day of calamity.

[21]Let the preacher consult Alexander Maclaren's sermon on "A Godless Life," in his *Expositions of Holy Scripture* (New York: George H. Doran Co., n.d.), based on verses 10-11 of this passage.

[22]Even today in Jordan and Syria, high, flat prominences are used as threshing floors. There the chaff is winnowed from the wheat on these windy places.

fore the storm" (13, RSV).[23] Thus overnight the situation will change completely with the Assyrian hordes vanquished between **eveningtide** and **morning** (14). Isaiah often adds the reason after describing the event. **This,** then, **is the portion** (14) of Judah's plunderers **and the lot** of those who pillage her wealth. God supplies the terminal point beyond which the instrument of His judgment cannot go. The evening may see him spreading trouble and consternation, but for him **the morning** dawns desolate and serene.

E. CONCERNING ETHIOPIA, 18:1-7

This address seems to have been the prophet's response at the arrival in Jerusalem of ambassadors from Ethiopia to confer with Judah on the Assyrian menace. His people have been cast into excitement because of the news of the Assyrian advance, but Isaiah reminds them that the Lord is quietly watching and biding His time until the Assyrian is ripe for destruction. At that time God will act with His pruning knife of destiny. When the Ethiopians see His sudden miracle they will send tribute to the Lord at Mount Zion. It is difficult to know to which southward march of Assyria to ascribe this prophecy—Sargon's or Sennacherib's— for at the time of both of these an Ethiopian ruled Egypt.

1. *The Apostrophe to Ethiopia* (18:1-2)

The exclamation, **Woe** (1), is used here as an expression of compassion rather than anger; it may also be translated "ah," or "alas." The mighty Ethiopian is terrified by the approaching and perhaps mightier Assyrian. The designation **land shadowing with wings** has been a troubler for the translators. The Septuagint reads "land of winged boats"; and George Adam Smith, "land of many sails."[24] The river craft of Egypt and Ethiopia use sails as well as oars, and a sailboat ride on the Nile is one of the delights of the modern tourist who visits Egypt. **The rivers of Ethiopia**

---

[23]The **rolling thing** is not a tumbleweed in a whirlwind, but those spinning "dust-devils" (as the Arabs call them), little twisters that precede the storm in swift succession. Cf. Denis Baly, *op. cit.,* p. 65.

[24]It has been variously translated as "land of the rustling wings" (ASV), "land of the whirring wings" (Gray in ICC), "land of buzzing insects" (Phillips). The idea of "buzzing insects" is based on the fact that Ethiopia is one home of the dreaded tsetse fly, and the fact that "the fly . . . of Egypt" is spoken of in 7:18. But George Adam Smith's translation seems most plausible.

are the Blue and the White Nile,[25] with their tributaries dividing the land. The Hebrew term is *Cush,* which would include the modern Arab state of Sudan as well as modern Ethiopia. When Isaiah speaks of **ambassadors by the sea** (2), it should be kept in mind that the natives refer to the upper Nile as a "sea" because of its great width. **Vessels of bulrushes** is better translated "vessels of papyrus" (ASV, RSV). These would be light, paper-covered[26] skiffs. **Go, ye,** may very well mean, "Return ye," as Isaiah bids the Ethiopian envoys depart. Judah cannot accept the alliance they have come to proffer. **A nation scattered and peeled** means "very tall and bronzed." Herodotus described the Ethiopians as "the tallest and most handsome of all men." Isaiah seems to have been impressed with the stately comeliness of these bronzed warriors.[27]

A nation meted out and trodden down in the Hebrew is "line, line, and treading down." Probably the reference is to the warriors of Ethiopia, marching line upon line and stamping to the beat of drums as they moved in unison step by step.[28] **Whose land the rivers have spoiled** is better translated "whose land the rivers divide" (RSV).

2. *A Message for Ethiopia* (18:3-6)

Since the brunt of the Assyrian attack must fall upon Jerusalem, **all the inhabitants of the world** may watch for the alarm signal of the battle there. Isaiah says: **All ye . . . see ye . . . hear ye** (3). Two signals, **an ensign** (banner) and a **trumpet** blast, will indicate the decisive moment.

Next Isaiah paints in vivid poetry the calmness and deliberation of the divine judgments. The Lord awaits the issue with quiet strength, watching all the while from the heavenly seat of

---

[25]See the *National Geographic* map, "The Nile Valley: Land of the Pharaohs," Atlas plate number 58, May, 1965, for much valuable information.

[26]Our English word "paper" is from "papyrus," whose broad, reedlike leaves were used for writing material. A boat frame covered with these and then daubed with pitch would be a light canoe and very maneuverable.

[27]People of the Near East are shorter than the average European or American.

[28]A recent visitor observed and photographed the marching army of a Zulu chieftain in Swaziland. Each warrior was over six feet tall, and they came in ranks lined one after another to the beating of Zulu drums, stamping fiercely as they marched in step, until the very earth shook as though they were a passing freight train. Delitzsch thus translates "a people of treading down," i.e., stomping the earth as they march.

His glorious presence, like dazzling **heat** in sunshine, and silent **dew** of the nighttime (4). Serene as a summer cloud, He bides His time, not in negligence, but with well-ordered resolution. Then at the critical moment ere **the harvest** (5) has arrived, when the blossom is over and the flower turns to ripening grape, there comes the knife of destiny. The **pruning hooks** sever the tendrils, and the anticipated vintage never occurs. **The fowls** of the summer and **the beasts** of winter shall forage upon the unripened grapes (6).

This is the prophet's way of saying that man proposes, but God disposes. The Assyrians fell in ruin at the height of their power, and the birds of carrion and the beasts of prey fed upon the dead bodies of their stricken warriors (cf. 37:36).

3. *Ethiopia's Tribute* (18:7)

Here Isaiah sees the Ethiopians offering themselves to the eternal God as a freewill offering by reason of the profound impression made upon them by the mighty acts of divine providence. From these who are tall, tan, and terrible shall come gifts to **Mount Zion, the place of the name of the Lord of hosts** (see comments on v. 2).

F. CONCERNING EGYPT, 19:1—20:6

Isaiah was a statesman with an international outlook based on a knowledge of the ways of God. Here is his diagnosis of the causes of national ruin and his delineation of remedy. In 19:1-17 we see a nation descending step by step from judgment to judgment; in vv. 18-25 we see it ascending step by step from salvation to salvation. In c. 20, Isaiah reminds us that those who are doomed for captivity cannot really save others from it. His acted parable warns against the futility of a pro-Egyptian policy for Judah.

1. *Confounding the Overconfident* (19:1-17)

a. *When morale is lost* (19:1-4). The beginning of the divine visitation upon this self-sufficient nation is the advent of the Lord riding **upon a swift cloud** (1) to institute judgment. Ezekiel also had a vision of this cloud-chariot as God came to deal with men (Ezek. 1:4). At His appearance Isaiah notes that Egypt's **idols** (false gods) will tremble, **and the heart of Egypt shall melt** as courage vanishes. Passing by all secondary causes, the prophet hears God saying, **I will set ... every one against his brother (2).** There is no real unity for a nation that has many gods. Civil strife was rampant in Egypt just prior to 712 B.C. There was no strong central government and the land was filled with internal discord. Lacking a united purpose back of a strong national program, **counsel (3)** was destroyed and the nation became witless and perplexed. "Whom the gods would destroy, they first make mad." When statesmanship fails, magical arts make a poor substitute. But Egypt had (and has) a reputation for these (Exod. 7:22; 8:7). **Idols ... charmers**[29] **... familiar spirits, and ... wizards** make poor counselors in any day of national crisis. Such a time is ripe for dictators, for one of God's judgments upon anarchy is **a cruel lord; and a fierce king (4)**—a despot. Those who will not have responsible government open the door to irresponsible demagoguery.

b. When natural resources fail (19:5-10). Were it not for the waters of the Nile, Egypt would be but a part of the desert. The Nile is the only conqueror of the Sahara. It is the sole source of life and the chief artery of movement for the people of the lands it traverses.

The sea (5) is a native expression for this wide and significant river at flood stage (usually August through October). **The river** specifies its main stream. **The rivers (6)** would refer to the many irrigation canals leading from the Nile, or perhaps to the arms of the Nile at its delta. **The brooks** would likewise indicate smaller water-courses. For **brooks of defence,** see II Kings 19:24. Were the Nile to fail, **every thing sown** would **wither (7),** and **the fishers** would **mourn (8).** Verse 7 may be read, "There will be bare places by the Nile" (RSV). Since much flax is grown in Egypt for the production of linen, **they that work in fine flax** would **be confounded (9). They that weave networks** refers to the production of the cotton fabrics for which Egypt is noted. A better translation for v. 10 is: "And the pillars of Egypt shall be broken in pieces; all they that work for hire shall be grieved in soul" (ASV). Employers will become bankrupt, and therefore all who work for hire will be dismayed because unemployed. The leading classes, or pillars of an economy (entrepreneurs), are the main stays of the state along with its working classes. When management "goes under," labor goes unemployed.

---

[29]"Mutterers," responding with a low, thin voice, like those that "peep" in 8:19, even using some peculiar form of ventriloquism.

c. *When wisdom fails* (19:11-15). **Zoan** (11) is Tanis (the modern San el Hagar) on the northeast corner of the Nile delta. Hence it was one of the nearest of the great cities of Egypt in relation to Judah. It was a residence of the Egyptian kings as early as Rameses II (13th century B.C.) and was probably the residence of the Ethiopian dynasty of Egyptian kings. Whenever **wise counsellors . . . become brutish** they make the silliest plans. Any one of Pharaoh's advisers would claim to be **the son of the wise and ancient kings.** But to all these counsellors Isaiah poses the question: Being devoid of wisdom, how can you lay claim to it by right of family descent? Professions were hereditary among the Egyptians, but heredity is no guarantee of either brains or efficiency. Hence Isaiah's challenge: **Let them tell thee now . . . what the Lord** has planned for **Egypt** (12; cf. I Cor. 1:20).

Noph (13) was the ancient site of Memphis, capital of Lower Egypt, ten miles southeast of Cairo. Her **princes** had joined those of **Zoan** and had **seduced Egypt,** when they should have been her **stay. A perverse spirit** (14) has caused more than Egypt to err. Perverted minds and warped judgments conceive only distortion. Little wonder that they caused Egypt to stagger **as a drunken man staggereth in his vomit.** With no ability to walk straight and think straight, neither high nor low will accomplish anything for Egypt (15). A modern example would be any nation that thinks it can drink, fight, or spend itself into security.

d. *When weakness prevails* (19:16-17). Isaiah's phrase **like unto women** (16) bespeaks a situation of terror and weakness (cf. Jer. 48:41). The judgmental **hand of the Lord of hosts** swings repeatedly over **Egypt** with smiting blows. If the God of Judah proposes to punish Egypt, the mere mention of **Judah** is **a terror** (17) to those who are aware of the divine decree. Yet "the fear of the Lord is the beginning of wisdom" and repentance. Here, then, is the logical transition point to Egypt's conversion.[30]

2. *Colonization for Conversion* (19:18-25)

a. *A spiritual beachhead* (19:18). **Five cities** with a common language, a common Lord, and a capital of righteousness could do much to redeem a country. But has a program of benevolent infiltration really been tried on a national scale? It would require an abundance of lay missionaries of all walks of life. Isaiah seems to have felt that nations as well as individuals could

---

[30]Cf. Skinner and Delitzsch.

be missionaries. The Hebrew prophets were sure that Judah's mission among the nations was one of spiritual leadership rather than imperial conquest.[31] Speaking **the language of Canaan** indicates the use of the Hebrew of Judah either as their native tongue or at least as their sacred language of worship. Swearing **to the Lord of hosts** would be an acknowledgment of God. That one of these should **be called, The city of destruction**[32] hardly makes sense. The Septuagint reads: "City of Righteousness." This would seem to be a better name for the capital of a league of five redemptive cities.

    b. Alternatives to desolation (19:19-22). These alternatives Isaiah lists as: (*a*) **An altar . . . in the midst . . . and a pillar (witness) at the border** (19). **An altar** for the worship of the true God and an obelisk[33] inscribed in His honor would constitute **a witness . . . in the land of Egypt** (20). (*b*) *A calling upon God for a Saviour to deliver* (20*b*), **for they shall cry unto the Lord . . . and he shall deliver them.** This looks forward to a conversion of Egypt to the worship of the true God.[34] If a nation in desperate plight begins to recognize the hand of God in its calamity, it is in position to repent and find mercy. (*c*) *A knowledge of the Lord and a proof of conversion* (21). The eternal God will now make himself **known.** Animal and vegetable offerings become acceptable when vows made to God are kept. (*d*) *Chastisement from*

---

[31]Alfred Lilienthal, a Jew, argues for the spiritual mission of Israel today, in his article, "Israel's Flag Is Not Mine," *Reader's Digest,* 55:329 (Sept., 1949), pp. 49-54. He says: "Judaism, I have felt, was a religious faith which knew no national boundaries, to which a loyal citizen of any country could adhere."

[32]The Greek is *polis asedek; 'ir haccedek* must have been the Hebrew that was being translated. Some have suggested "City of the Sun," which they identify with Heliopolis, the city of the sun-god Ra, situated northeast of Memphis. Others suggest Leontopolis, "the City of the Lion," since there was in later years a Jewish temple there built by the Jewish refugee Onias, who appealed to this very prophecy as sufficient warrant for its being built there (cf. Josephus *Antiquities* xiii. 3. 1 f., and *Jewish Wars,* vii. 10. 2. Cf. also the *Sibyllene Oracles* v. 488-510). Driver, however, suggests: "Isaiah says, that it will be no more *'ir ha-cheres,* the city of the *sun,* but *'ir ha-heres,* the city of *destruction,* the city in which the sun-worship has been destroyed" (*op. cit.,* p. 94).

[33]This can hardly be a reference to the great pyramid of Cheops at Giza, as the British Israelites would contend. Cf. S. R. Driver, *op. cit.,* p. 94.

[34]Egypt was a Christian country from the third to the seventh centuries A.D.

the Lord with its ministry of healing (22). **He shall smite and heal;** for when God smites, it is in order that He may heal (cf. Hos. 6:1).

c. *A neighborhood of nations* (19:23-25). For Isaiah this neighborhood will include (a) *highways for communication and commerce* (23), and (b) *alliances for mutual blessings and benefits* (24-25). This **highway** connecting two ancient enemies and running through Palestine would still be an ideal thing in the Near East. Here the prophet sees **Israel** as the third member of this Messianic league functioning as **a blessing in the midst** (24). Each of them bears one of the endearing titles from the Lord—**Egypt my people . . . Assyria the work of my hands, and Israel** in preeminence as His **inheritance** (25).[35]

3. *The Sign of Coming Captivity* (20:1-6)

Here the prophet challenges the pro-Egyptian party in Jerusalem with the question: **How shall we escape** (6) if the enemy captures our refuge? He is quite certain that Egypt and Ethiopia shall suffer Ashdod's fate at the hands of Assyria. This historical note brings to a conclusion Isaiah's warning message to Egypt and Ethiopia.

a. *Tartan takes Ashdod* (20:1). This occurred in 711 B.C. **Sargon** was one of the greatest of the Assyrian monarchs. The title **Tartan** is Assyrian for "Generalissimo." **Ashdod** was the gate-city of Philistia. Azuri, king of Ashdod, refused to pay tribute and revolted. Sargon deposed him and placed his brother Akhismit on the throne. The people in turn revolted against Akhismit and chose Yaman as their king. Sargon then marched against the city, took it, and carried off its gods and treasures as booty. In the light of this event, Judah pondered an alliance with Egypt for the sake of safety. Isaiah opposed the pro-Egyptian policy.

b. *God's command to Isaiah* (20:2). The command, **Loose the sackcloth . . . put off thy shoe,** called for the removal of the burlap outer garment of the prophetic order (II Kings 1:8) and the removal of his sandals.

---

[35]Kilpatrick is absolutely right: "The alternative is before us, a godless civilization moving to its own doom and damnation, or a race which has found its salvation and its peace in a common faith and obedience to Almighty God." For "peace is not basically a matter of treaties but of a new spirit in human relationships" (IB, V, 283).

c. A sign and a symbol (20:3-4). Walking about the streets of Jerusalem **naked and barefoot,** clad only in the long linen tunic worn next to the skin, for **three years,** Isaiah became a prophecy in action. This acted parable, behaving as if he were already a captive, would speak a silent but solemn message to the people of Jerusalem (cf. Acts 21:11). It would warn them against an Egyptian-Ethiopian alliance.

d. Shame and dismay (20:5). Here is a picture of the treatment of prisoners on their march to captivity. **Expectation, and . . . glory** turn now to fear and shame. Of what value is an alliance with Egypt if this is to be her fate? Not Sargon, or Sennacherib, but Esarhaddon fulfilled this prophecy.

e. The cry of the coastlands (20:6). **This isle** is better translated "coast-land." The term would include Philistia, Phoenicia, and Tyre. The whole seaboard would find no ability to resist the conqueror even with the help of Ethiopia and Egypt.

Isaiah thus preached by his actions that it is best to trust the Lord for deliverance. Captives cannot save one from captivity. Hence an alliance with Egypt is of no value to Judah.

G. CONCERNING "THE WILDERNESS OF THE SEA," 21:1-10

This oracle on the doom of Babylon is best related to the Assyrian reconquest of Babylon following the revolt of Merodach-baladan in 710 B.C.[36] That patriot had sought indefatigably to free his native city from its condition of unwilling subjection to Assyria. As many as twelve years earlier he had sent ambassadors seeking to encourage other nations to join him in revolt. Isaiah was convinced that Babylon, like Egypt, was certain to go down before the Assyrian. If the pro-Egyptian party in Jerusalem thought of joining with Egypt and thus aiding Babylon, the prophet assures them it is of no use. As surely as Sargon's cavalcades marched against Babylon, so surely the report would come back, **Babylon is fallen** (9).

1. *The Terrifying Vision* (21:1-5)

In the cuneiform inscriptions, south Babylonia was called "land of the sea." Xenophon describes the whole plain of the Euphrates, which is intersected by marshes and lakes, as looking like a sea. The words of this oracle seemed to have come to the

---

[36]Cf. Driver, Naegelsbach, and Plumptre.

prophet like **whirlwinds** in the Negeb (desert southland). Desert lands are tempestuous with their updrafts and twisters, as pilots of low-flying small aircraft across desert areas can well testify. But like a sirocco off the desert **from a terrible land** (1), **a grievous vision is declared unto** the prophet (2). Moffatt calls it "a grim revelation." **The treacherous** man still deals in treachery, and **the spoiler** still seeks his spoils. Assyria practiced sudden warfare, falling upon his foes before they were ready for battle. At his words the nations move—**Go up, O Elam: besiege, O Media.**

The agitation of the prophet is graphically set forth as like convulsive pains of childbirth. Writhing with mental anguish, he is stunned at what he hears and **dismayed** (3) at what he sees. Where the modern person would have said, "My mind reels," the Hebrew says, **My heart panted** (4). The twilight, which is a delightful time on the desert, is no longer a time of peace but one of panic. In his vision the prophet sees the banqueting Babylonians with the **table** spread. They **eat** and **drink** (5) when they ought to be watching and preparing to do battle. In the very midst of their reveling comes the summons: **Arise, ye princes, and grease your shields!**[37] The banqueting breaks up in confusion, for the foe is at the very gates.

2. The Prophet as a Watchman (21:6-9)

At this moment God speaks to His messenger to make his own soul **a watchman** (6) and report whatever he sees. He discerned a riding company of **horsemen** in pairs, followed by troops of **asses** and **camels** (8).[38] Sharpening his ears to their keenest intensity, **he hearkened diligently.**[39]

The phrase, **he cried, A lion** (8), has given the translators trouble. Phillips thinks of it as an admonition to "watch closely as a lion watches his prey." Plumptre takes it to indicate a cry, like a lion, of eager impatience during the **daytime** and the **whole**

---

[37]The shields were greased on the side toward the enemy to more effectively ward off his blows with spear or sword.

[38]In place of **chariot** (9) read "troop" or "cavalcade." Both asses and camels were captured in large numbers when Sennacherib defeated Merodach-baladan. His inscription says 11,173 asses and 5,230 camels.

[39]Gesenius tells us that the basic idea of the Hebrew term is to "prick up the ears" and to "listen sharply." The Hebrew idiom says: "Listening, he listened intently."

nights of waiting and watching for the prophetic insight that shall enable him to declare the outcome. At last the vision became vocal and he again saw a cavalcade of horsemen riding two by two, and heard the sounds of a captured city. Thus he was able to announce, **Babylon is fallen . . . and all . . . her gods he hath broken** (9).[40] The idolatrous system was unable to save its devotees.

3. *Apostrophe to the Afflicted* (21:10)

Isaiah now turns toward his own people and speaking for the Lord he cries: **O my threshing, and the corn of my floor.** There is deep pathos in this simile of suffering. The expression "son of a threshing floor" is idiomatic for an afflicted people. Isaiah would have preferred to speak otherwise but everything— even Babylon—must go down before the Assyrian. As surely as Sargon's battalions went against her, so surely must the announcement come, "Babylon is fallen."[41] Judah cannot yet expect respite from the Assyrian menace for which she so constantly longs. The prophet concludes, **That which I have heard . . . have I declared.**

H. CONCERNING DUMAH (EDOM),[42] 21:11-12

The prophet hears someone calling repeatedly to him out of Mount **Seir** in the land of the Edomites: "Guardian,[43] is **the night** almost over?" And the night patrolman answers: "When the morning comes, it will still be night. If you wish to **enquire** further, come back later and ask." The word **Dumah** means "silence." But the Septuagint translator, knowing that **Seir** was located in the land of Edom, used the Greek term for *Idumea.* Isaiah was probably punning in this reference to Edom. At Petra,

---

[40]The destruction of the idols usually accompanied the overthrow of any state of which they were deemed the patrons and the protectors.

[41]This message of doom finds its echo in Rev. 14:8; 18:2, where Babylon is typical of all antichristian influences.

[42]**Dumah** is the modern site of *ej-Jauf* at the southeast end of the *Wadi Sirhan,* located on a line due east from Ezion-geber and *Jebel Ramm.* Consult the *Rand McNally Bible Atlas,* Map XI, p. 245.

[43]The Hebrew for **watchman** does not specify a "lookout" but rather a "guardian." Luther's German is excellent here, and closer to the Hebrew than is the KJV.

capital of Edom, was her rose-red fortress and necropolis.[44] The tombs and treasury were securely carved into the red sandstone. One wonders if Isaiah thought of Edom as "the silent city of the dead" from which a voice broke through the dark night of Assyrian oppression asking, "How much longer?" The answer to Mount **Seir** from Mount Zion is, "A change is coming, but whether it brings any permanent relief is debatable."

Edom had offended Sargon by joining with Ashdod of the Philistines, and now felt that her night of oppression by that tyrant was long. Isaiah answers, "Even if morning dawns, another night soon follows." And history validates the prophecy. The Assyrian conqueror was followed by the Chaldean, the Greek, and the Roman. Isaiah was not a provincial preacher; he was a statesman with an international reputation and an international outlook. He saw history in the hands of the Eternal One. Only one who thus acknowledges God acting within the arena of history has any real hope for eternal dawn.

I. CONCERNING ARABIA, 21:13-17

Shifting his vision a bit farther south and east, the prophet discerns what is in store for Arabia (see map 1). In Isaiah's lifetime north Arabia felt the weight of the Assyrian oppression and paid tribute. Two facts stand out in the prophet's mind, the peril and flight of the commercial caravans and the conquest of Kedar by the Assyrian.

1. *Calamity for the Caravans* (21:13-15)

Some commentators think that Isaiah is punning here again and change the second **Arabia** to *'Ereb,* which would then mean "of the evening." They believe the prophet was warning the Dedanites that they must spend the night in some thicket. Whitehouse, however, makes a good case that the term should be translated "steppe" and calls attention to the fact that this part of Arabia is steppe-land.[45] The **travelling companies of Dedanim**

[44] Cf. David S. Boyer, "Petra, Rose-Red Citadel of Biblical Edom," *National Geographic Magazine,* CVIII, No. 6 (Dec., 1955), 853-70. For an admirable sketch of the history and archaeology of the Edomites see Nelson Glueck, "The Civilization of the Edomites," *Biblical Archaeologist,* X, No. 4 (Dec. 1947), 77-84. For a discussion of the degrading practices of their religion see Geo. L. Robinson, *The Sarcophagus of an Ancient Civilization; Petra, Edom, and the Edomites* (New York: The Macmillan Co., 1930).

[45] "Isaiah," *The Century Bible* (Edinburgh: T. C. and E. C. Jack, 1905), *ad loc.*

(13) indicates caravans. These Dedanites were, for the most part, traveling merchants between the Persian Gulf and Palestine. Due to the Assyrian peril they were forced to leave their regular caravan routes with their oases, and flee for shelter to thickets or rocky outcroppings in the land south of Edom.[46] Thither the prophet exhorts the **inhabitants . . . of Tema**[47] to bring **water to him that** is **thirsty** and **bread for him that fled** (14),[48] from those who pursued him with **drawn sword** and **bent bow** (15).

2. *Cessation of Kedar's Glory* (21:16-17)

Again Isaiah risks his reputation as a prophet by setting a time within which the nomadic tribes of north Arabia will be utterly put to rout. Where KJV reads **within a year** (16) the Dead Sea Scroll of Isaiah reads "within three years" (cf. 16:14); but in either case it becomes a test as to his forecast of the future. By the authority of the eternal God of Israel he declares that the remaining **number** of Kedar's[49] mighty **archers** shall be greatly **diminished** (17). **The years of an hireling** (16); cf. 16:14, comment.

As long as his **mighty men**, armed with their death-dealing bows, could ravage and plunder others at pleasure, "the grievousness of war" was not felt. They sang and shouted from the tops of their mounts (cf. 42:11). But Isaiah prophesied the day when **Kedar** itself would be attacked and plundered. "The drawn sword" and "the bent bow" in the hand of the Assyrian would be turned upon them. They would realize that history often decrees that one shall reap what he has sowed.

---

[46]The land of Dedan lies along the eastern shore of the Red Sea (see map 1) halfway between Petra and Mecca, and centered around *el 'Ela*.

[47]**Tema** (sometimes spelled Teima) is north and east of Dedan (*el-'Ela*) about half the distance to Dumah (*ej-Jauf*). The people were outstanding in their practice of Arab hospitality. One of their own poets has written: "No fire of ours was ever extinguished at night without a guest, and of our guests never did one disparage us." Cf. Albert Barnes, *Notes on the Old Testament*, ed. Robert Frew (Grand Rapids, Michigan: Baker Book House, 1950), *ad loc.*

[48]In 1611, at the time of the KJV translation, the word "prevent" meant "to go out to welcome."

[49]**Kedar** was probably the area north of the *Wadi Sirhan*, due east of the Dead Sea and almost at the center of the north end of the Arabian peninsula. Kedar was a son of Ishmael (Gen. 25:13), as were also Dumah and Tema (Gen. 25:14-15).

J. A SOLEMN UTTERANCE FROM THE VALLEY OF VISION, 22:1-25

Instead of **valley of vision** (1) the Septuagint reads "the valley of Zion." But even this does not help us know which of the valleys next to Mount Zion is meant. Jerusalem's surrounding valleys are the Kidron, the Tyropoean, and Hinnom. Was Isaiah's home in one of these valleys, and is that the reason this oracle has such a name? Both the Tyropoean and the Hinnom valleys have been suggested.

The best vision of Mount Zion is from Hinnom, south of the city; hence Moffatt favors Hinnom and so translates. The greater contrast of depth and the valley with a water supply however is the Tyropoean. It seems more likely that this was the home of the prophet. There he received his revelations and visions. Interpreters have differed as to whether this oracle is a prophecy of the future or a portrayal of a situation contemporaneous with the prophet. The latter seems more probable in this context.

1. *Presumptuous Security* (22:1-14)

a. The city and the prophet (22:1-4). Here we have in bold contrast a lighthearted people giving themselves over to revelry and a sorrowing prophet who sees how inappropriate such exultation is in the light of the present peril. The people are thrilled over what the prophet knows is but a temporary alleviation of peril rather than a permanent relief. On the other hand, there seem to have been some among them who felt the present insecurity and were determined to drown their apprehensions with wine and feasting.

The time for this oracle must have been 701 B.C. when Sennacherib temporarily raised the siege of Jerusalem (II Kings 18: 13-16). Sennacherib defeated the Egyptians at Eltekeh, then returned to complete the siege of Ekron. Instead of ascending to Jerusalem himself, he sent a detachment eastward up the mountain passes to overrun Judah and threaten the capital. He himself advanced southward in hot pursuit of the fleeing Egyptians. This decision on Sennacherib's part may well have been the occasion for celebrations in Jerusalem (cf. Intro.). Isaiah could not believe the present respite to be a time for rejoicing when he knew with how heavy a tribute Hezekiah had purchased it, and how soon the Assyrian Rabshakeh (chief of the officers) would be at the gates demanding unconditional surrender.

House tops (1) would be used not only for observation of the departing enemy, but for festival celebrations. Isaiah is sure that the **slain men** (2) will not have died in valor against the sword but under bad politics. The **rulers** (3) will flee en masse, and be captured before **the archers** can even draw a bow. It is in such a fiasco of cowardice that the prophet refuses any comfort as he weeps **bitterly** over **the spoiling of the daughter of my people** (4).

b. *A day of tumult* (22:5-8a). Here the prophet foresees **a day** (5)—the coming siege of the city. It would be under two important contingents of the Assyrian army, **Elam and Kir** (6). **Elam,** the empire east of Babylonia, was in league with the Assyrians. **Kir** in this context cannot now be located with certainty. The assault would be made with the **shield** unsheathed, their **chariots** racing, and their bows drawn to shoot. They would set **themselves in array** (7) at the very gates of the city, "and the defences of Judah are laid bare" (8a; Smith-Goodspeed).

c. *A false reckoning of defenses* (22:8b-11). **The house of the forest** (8b) was the largest of Solomon's buildings, made with columns of cedar brought from Lebanon and serving as the armory. Hezekiah had repaired the walls of the city (II Chron. 32:5), and had dug his famous tunnel[50] for collecting **the waters of the lowel pool** (Siloam; 9). Certain of **the houses of Jerusalem** (10) built of native stone were torn down to fortify the wall, and a **ditch** (reservoir) **for the water** (11) was dug between the two walls. But no account was taken of the Lord, who had situated their city over such a water supply and **fashioned it long ago.** Isaiah knew that material defenses avail but little if one disregards the divine Source of true security.

d. *National danger calls for national repentance* (22:12-14). "When God calls for a fast, you stage a feast," says the prophet. "Shaved heads, burlap robes, tearful eyes, and mournful groans become a nation on the brink of disaster" (12). But some who heard the prophet's warning flippantly remarked, **Let us eat and drink; for to morrow we shall die** (13). There is a point where impenitent presumption passes the bounds of divine forgiveness: **Surely this iniquity shall not be purged from you till ye die** (14). "For such a state of mind Isaiah will hold out no promise;

---

[50]The waters of the Gihon spring were conveyed to the Pool of Siloam by a subterranean tunnel (II Kings 20:20; II Chron. 32:30). Cf. *Unger's Bible Dictionary,* article "Hezekiah (The Siloam Inscription)," pp. 480-81.

it is the sin against the Holy Ghost, and for it there is no forgiveness."[51]

2. *Perversions of Stewardship* (22:15-25)

a. *A presumptuous prime minister* (22:15-19). This is Isaiah's only personal invective against an individual. **Shebna** (15) was probably a foreigner in the service of the king as steward of the king's palace. At the defeat of the Egyptians by Sennacherib the pro-Egyptian party (which held the reigns of government under Hezekiah in Jerusalem) lost face, and the influence of the king's adviser, **Shebna**, was broken. **Shebna** was an officious administrator. In his desire for status he had a tomb **hewed** out for himself (16) among those of the kings and princes of Judah, though he was neither a citizen nor a venerable patriarch. **The Lord** (17), who covered him with excellent garments and clothed him gorgeously, was about to roll him up in a bundle of **captivity** and toss him into a foreign land to die there. Thither, too, should go his **chariots of . . . glory** (18) which have brought **shame** and contempt to his **lord's house.** Not content to ride on a mule or horse as an ordinary official (Judg. 5:10; 10:4; 12:14; II Sam. 17:23), he must have stately chariots whenever he appeared in public. The verdict of the Lord is, **I will drive thee from thy station** (19).

b. *The elevation and downfall of Eliakim* (22:20-25). Politics had reached such a low state that a change of ministry was the only wise thing for the city. **Eliakim** means "God will establish," and God refers to him as **my servant** (20). To him were to be transferred the **robe** and **girdle** of Shebna, and he would become a **father** (benefactor) **to the inhabitants of Jerusalem** (21). **The key of the house of David** became his symbol of authority (22). He was like a peg **in a sure place** (23), and would have a position of honor among his kindred. But though he brought honor and respect **to his father's house,** the filling of important offices with **vessels of small quantity** (24; worthless and incompetent relatives) ruined him. How much weight can one peg carry? "The fate of the overburdened nail is as grievous as that of the rolling stone."[52] Let the modern man of state (or church) beware of nepotism.

[51]George Adam Smith, *op. cit., ad loc.*
[52]*Ibid.*, p. 319. By the rolling stone Smith understands Shebna, the foreigner, who was eventually tossed into foreign captivity.

In the case of the presumptuous city we have (1) The tragedy of the unaware, 1-14; in Shebna's case, (2) The tragedy of the unashamed, 15-19; and in the case of Eliakim's relatives, (3) The tragedy of the undeserving, 24-25.

When one considers the tumultuous and sensual city, the correctness of Moffatt's title for this oracle as "the vision of the valley of Hinnom" (Gehenna) seems apparent. *Gehenna* symbolizes the destiny of all such base and presumptuous *epicureanism,* whether in ancient or modern times.

K. CONCERNING TYRE, 23:1-18

This chapter has two main sections. Verses 1-14 speak of the fall of Tyre, while vv. 15-18 speak of the city's eventual restoration. Basically there are four strophes dealing with Tyre's calamity (1-5), Tyre's humiliation (6-9), Tyre's empire in disintegration (10-14), and Tyre's renewal and sanctification (15-18).

The oracle is best dated in the days of Sargon (710 B.C.), or Sennacherib (702 B.C.),[53] even though its more complete fulfillment came in the days of Nebuchadnezzar, Alexander the Great (332 B.C.), or even the later conquest of Tyre by the Moslems in the thirteenth century A.D.[54]

1. *The Fall of the Mart of Nations* (23:1-5)

In Isaiah's day "Tyre . . . was the pioneer of commerce, the parent of colonies, the mistress of the Sea."[55] Strategically located, it was 20 miles south of Sidon (see map 2) and 23 miles up the coast from Acre (the plain of Asher). In the days of Isaiah it consisted of two parts, a rocky coast of great strength on the mainland, and a small, well-fortified city upon a rocky offshore island less than a half-mile out to sea. King Hiram had built a breakwater for it 820 yards long and 9 yards thick, making it one

---

[53]Sargon records the fact that he plundered the district of Samaria, the house of Omri, and reigned from Yatnan (Cyprus), "which is in the midst of the sea of the setting sun," from Phoenicia and Syria to remote cities of Media. Sennacherib boasts of the fact that Luti, king of Zidon, fled to Yatnan (Cyprus), "which is in the midst of the sea."

[54]One of the best interpretations of this difficult chapter is by George Adam Smith, *op. cit.* See also Skinner, *op. cit.;* Plumptre, *op. cit.;* and Rawlinson, *op. cit.;* the articles on Tyre in *Unger's Bible Dictionary;* and A. S. Kapelrund, "Tyre," *The Interpreter's Dictionary of the Bible,* ed. George A. Buttrick (Nashville: Abingdon Press, 1962), IV, 721-23; and comments on Ezekiel 27—29 in this volume.

[55]S. R. Driver, *op. cit.,* p. 103.

of the best harbors in the Mediterranean. According to Josephus, the city had been founded about 240 years before the time of Israel's King Solomon.[56]

The famous **ships of Tarshish (1)** were Phoenician vessels sailing the Mediterranean as far west as the colony of Tartessus (Spain). The prophet calls upon them to wail because of the news they have received, as they docked at **Chittim** (Cyprus) on their eastward voyage. The **house** (harbor) to which they were sailing **is laid waste.**

Due to the twofold meaning of the Hebrew, **ye inhabitants of the isle (2)** may refer to those situated on the small island of Tyre or to the "inhabitants of the coast" (RSV). **The merchants of Zidon** were traders from the mother city, whose commerce filled not only Tyre but other daughter cities. They sailed upon **great waters (3;** "many an ocean," Moffatt). **Sihor** means "the dark river," hence the Nile. Its **seed** and **harvest** shippings produced a fine **revenue** for this "merchant of the nations" (RSV).[57]

But now **Zidon (4)** is called upon to lament in shame as a barren woman, since she has been bereft of her colonies and Tyre —the "stronghold of the sea." Surely when news of this is heard in **Egypt,** anguish will prevail **at the report of Tyre (5);** not because the Egyptians bore any great affection for foreigners, but because the fall of Tyre would portend evil for themselves. Any power great enough to capture Tyre would be expected soon to attempt the conquest of the Nile valley. A secondary reason would be the lack of shipping and sale for Egyptian goods.

2. The Failure of Human Glory (23:6-9)

Isaiah exhorts the inhabitants of the Phoenician coastlands to flee as far away as **Tarshish,** the extreme colony of their commerce, to seek safety **(6).** When Alexander the Great laid siege to the city of Tyre in 332 B.C. its old men, women, and children were sent to its colony at Carthage. The prophet next raises the chiding question: **"Is this** heap of ruins **your joyous city, whose antiquity is of ancient days?" (7)** And though it was not as ancient as Sidon, yet it was very old. Herodotus says in

---

[56]*Antiquities* viii. 3. 1.

[57]In addition to the shipping of wheat from Egypt, these Phoenician vessels also carried the linen products of Egypt's flax industry (Ezek. 27:7). The Egyptians had no timber for building large ships. Moreover, they hated the sea, and hence were willing for the Phoenicians to provide the ships to carry their products to the various Mediterranean ports.

450 B.C. that its temple of Melkart (Hercules) had been built 2,300 years previously.[58] Now **her own feet shall carry her afar off to sojourn** in a distant land. Referring to the far-ranging voyages of Tyre's merchantmen and colonists, *The Berkeley Version* translates this clause, "whose feet carried her to settle far away."

Who hath taken this counsel against Tyre (8), the city that dispensed crowns to the rulers of her colonies, and whose traders[59] were **the honourable** men and **princes . . . of the earth?** It is God's edict, **for the Lord of hosts hath purposed it** (9). His program is to desecrate the temples in which the heathen take so much **pride, and to bring into contempt** all that earth so vainly honors.

3. *The Falling Apart of an Empire* (23:10-14)

The colonists of **Tarshish** are now called upon to exert their full independence of Tyre, since "there is no restraint any more" (10, ASV). Cyprus did revolt about this time, and the Phoenician colonies took part in attacking the mother city under Sennacherib, according to Josephus.[60] God has **stretched out his hand over the sea** (11) and hath shaken **the kingdoms,** even the great maritime power and all the cities of her coast and commerce. And the Eternal said, **Thou shalt no more rejoice, O thou oppressed**[61] **. . . daughter of Zidon** (12). Even though you flee **to Chittim** (Cyprus), the usual refuge of Phoenician kings, you will not be safe there. In the days of Esarhaddon, when the king of Sidon fled to Cyprus, the Assyrian monarch pursued him there and cut off his head.

Isaiah next cites the example of the **land of the Chaldeans . . . the Assyrian . . . brought it to ruin** (13). Sargon conquered Babylon in 710 B.C., making himself its king, but in 705 B.C. it rebelled and regained its independence. In 704 B.C., Sennacherib reconquered it, and again in 700 B.C. when his eldest son was made viceroy. Isaiah seems to be saying that, if the Assyrians have their way, Tyre, like Babylon, will be only a ruins and an uninhabited waste. **The towers** are siege-towers erected by the Assyrian against Babylon; **the palaces** were not **raised** but *razed*

[58]ii. 44.
[59]The word is *Canaanite*, connoting "merchant" or "trader."
[60]*Op. cit.*, ix. 14. 2.
[61]The word means "defiled, or raped."

(torn down and demolished) by them as they reduced the city to ruins.[62]

This strophe climaxes with the chiding exhortation, "Cry aloud with pain," **ye ships of Tarshish: for your strength is laid waste (14)**; i.e., your stronghold has been wrecked, your haven is destroyed.

4. *A Future of Sacred Stewardship* (23:15-18)

Seventy years (15) is a symbolic number just as is the number forty. It indicates here an indefinite time span, a conventional period of disaster. **According to the days of one king** would mean without any alteration of policy or hoped-for change. At the end of her time of being **forgotten** of God, Tyre shall **sing as an harlot.** "Tyre will fare as the prostitute in the song" (Berk.). Isaiah had been using this symbol for the commercial city and its international trade. He therefore sees the city after its divine visitation once more welcoming foreigners of all nations as her lovers for the sake of commercial gain. But now as a revived center of commerce her trade is transformed in the sanctified stewardship which is rendered. **Take an harp . . . thou harlot (16)** is reminiscent of the fact that ancient harlots were usually at least amateur musicians, and the harp was the usual instrument.

The promise now is, **The Lord will visit Tyre, and she shall turn to her hire (17)**. By the mercy of God, Tyre will again become a center of commerce and deal once more with all the world's kingdoms.[63] But **her merchandise and her hire shall be holiness to the Lord (18)**; i.e., the proceeds of her trade shall be dedicated to the Lord. "There is nothing intrinsically wrong or debasing in commerce. Rightly pursued, and engaged in with the view of devoting the profits made in it to good and pious ends, the commercial life may be as religious and as acceptable to God as any other. The world has known many merchants who were Christians, in the highest sense of the word. . . . Applied to religious uses . . . such an employment of the gains made sanctifies commerce, and makes it a good and blessed thing."[64]

---

[62]Note *The Berkeley Version,* Moffatt's translation, and that of J. B. Phillips.

[63]This prophecy seems now to be fulfilled in the case of Beirut, the modern successor to Tyre. Yet who knows whether Tyre itself may not become a center of commerce, even though for now Haifa and Beirut serve its ancient functions?

[64]George Rawlinson, *op. cit.,* p. 374.

Section **IV** *World Judgment and*
                Israel's Redemption

("The Little Apocalypse")

Isaiah 24:1—27:13

Bible scholars are not agreed whether we have prophecy in
these chapters or what is called "apocalyptic." Sometimes it is
difficult to distinguish between the two. Prophecy usually fore-
tells a definite future. Apocalyptic directs the mind more ab-
stractly and symbolically to the future, in contrast with the
present. While apocalyptic is usually filled with visions, symbolic figures, numbers, and names, it may be considered most
correctly as an expression of the author's faith and his philosophy
of history. The student of apocalyptic must learn not to literalize
all of the symbolism he finds. To try to apply each item to some
historical specific is to involve oneself in extravagant allegorizing.

In these chapters Isaiah is giving us a statement of his faith
and philosophy (or theology) of history. He tells us in general-
ized pictures what God is doing and will yet do about man's environment, which has become defiled with sin. This section has
a loose unity and takes on the nature of a great eschatological
oratorio. Isaiah deals with such apocalyptic themes as: God's
judgments upon sin and sinners; tribulations such as war, famine,
pestilence; geological convulsions; astronomical disturbances;
moral warfare in the spirit realm; the ultimate triumph of the
divine program; the eschatological banquet in honor of divine
victory; the elimination of death; the resurrection of the righteous from the dead; the birth pangs of a new era. A large place
is given to songs of praise to God for His deliverance of the
redeemed; refuge from the divine wrath for a little time of waiting while great tribulation is upon the earth; the divine winnowing and separation of character types; the final trumpet blast; and
the assembling of the redeemed to worship the Eternal.

Down through history, times of great international crisis have
been characterized by a resurgence of apocalypticism. It was so
in Isaiah's day. Surely there is also predictive prophecy here,
but in the main it is a spiritual commentary on the great Assyrian

crisis which scourged the earth during Isaiah's lifetime. These chapters not only follow immediately after cc. 13—23 but they are closely related to their same general theme.[1]

A. DESOLATIONS IN THE EARTH, 24:1-23

This chapter depicts for us God's judgments upon man's environment, as He proceeds to eliminate sin's contaminations from the cosmos.[2]

1. *The Proclamation of Desolation* (24:1-3)

a. *The "topsy-turvy" earth* (24:1). **Behold,**[3] **the Lord maketh the earth empty . . . and turneth it upside down.** His upturning and scouring of the material universe is like the washing of a dirty dish. "Man cannot escape those judgments which shatter his material habitation," for "man's sin has rendered necessary the destruction of his material circumstances, and the Divine judgment includes a broken and rifled universe."[4] When thirty million men die in a world war and six million Jews are cremated, and when man holds in his power the scientific means of global atomic warfare, with the assured possibility of earth's depopulation, Isaiah's prophecy is more than idle speculation. We may be sure that a sinful civilization is doomed.

b. *No distinction* (24:2). **As with the people, so with the priest . . . servant . . . master,** etc. This judgment involves all ranks and classes of society in a common destruction. "And it is a universal one, not merely throughout the whole of the land of Israel, but in all the earth."[5] Isaiah agrees with Hosea's proverb (4:9) and assures us that natural calamities are no respecters of men's persons. Flood, famine, plague, earthquake instantly abolish all our human and artificial distinctions, for they know no favored class.

[1]Cf. George L. Robinson, *The Book of Isaiah* (New York: Y.M.C.A. Press, 1910), pp. 99-106.
[2]One of the best discussions of this chapter is by George Adam Smith, *op. cit.,* c. XXVIII, "The Effect of Sin on Our Material Circumstance."
[3]"With Isaiah 'hinneh' (behold) always refers to something future" (Delitzsch, *op. cit.,* p. 425).
[4]G. A. Smith, *op. cit.,* p. 417.
[5]Delitzsch, *op. cit.,* p. 426.

c. *A depopulated earth* (24:3). **The land shall be utterly emptied, and utterly spoiled.** For **land** the majority of the more recent versions read "earth."[6] What the prophet envisages here is an imminent world judgment which shall depopulate the earth. The object of judgment is the global world,[7] and thus a cosmic judgment. Isaiah's authority for this prophecy is, **the Lord hath spoken.** "Such is the sentence of the Eternal" (Moffatt).

2. *Symptoms of Chaos* (24:4-12)

a. *The state of man's environment* (24:4-6). (a) **The earth** is smitten and withered up. The world is wasted, and the foremost **people of the earth do languish** (4). (b) **The earth is polluted by its inhabitants** (5); lit., "has become wicked." Profanation of the land by the conduct of its people through the shedding of blood, the practice of idolatry, the committing of adultery, etc., is a common idea of the Old Testament.[8] Sins that desecrate humanity do likewise with man's environment. In Hebrew **the laws** (5) is singular. Hence it indicates something even more basic than the Mosaic code. Man has **transgressed** the Torah of his own basic humanity and conscience. He has "overstepped" the divine **ordinance.** He has **broken the everlasting covenant.** Delitzsch observes: "It was with the whole human race that God concluded a covenant in the person of Noah, at the time when the nations had none of them come into existence at all."[9] What is specified here is the fact that mankind has violated the basic rationale of its own humanity by refusing to live in accordance with its creaturehood under the divine government.[10] (c) With his graphic inferential conjunction **therefore,** Isaiah moves the spotlight of his prophecy from the sin to its punishment. **Therefore hath the curse devoured the earth, and they that dwell therein are desolate** (6), i.e., they bear their punishment and are dealt with as guilty. **The inhabitants of the earth are burned** by the consuming fires of divine wrath. Lit., "are parched up," as God's fiery indignation shrivels them. **And**

---

[6] Cf. ERV, ASV, RSV, and others.

[7] Cf. Gray and Skinner.

[8] Cf. Gen. 4:10; Num. 35:33; Deut. 21:1-9; Job 16:18; Ps. 106:38; Jer. 3:9.

[9] *Op. cit.,* p. 427.

[10] "The sin of the world lies in the violation of these fundamental dictates of morality, especially the law against murder, which is the principal stipulation of the Noahic Covenant (Gen. 9:5-6)"—Skinner, *op. cit.,* pp. 181-82.

few men are left.[11] Modern nuclear warfare shows greater potential for the fulfillment of such a prophecy than did the ancient Assyrian custom of piling burning materials against the walls of a fortified city to decompose its rocks. A scorched and depopulated earth is not beyond the possible today.

b. Cessation of satisfactions (24:7-9). In v. 7, Moffatt correctly suggests the "vine-juice" (sap of the vine) fails, leaving a situation where "the vines are dry" and **the vine languisheth.** In that case there is no vintage; hence **all the merryhearted do sigh** in sorrow.

> *No lilting now of tambourines,*
> *No lilting now of lutes,*
> *No sounds of revelry;*
> *No singing as the wine is drunk,*
> *For any liquor has a bitter taste* (8-9, Moffatt).

Wine made from immature and juiceless grapes is sure to be bitter.[12]

c. The city is rife with confusion (24:10-12). Any city is a chaos with its buildings fallen in, its homes barricaded, its streets echoing with cries for food and drink, mirth gone, and its beautiful gates only battered ruins.

The city of confusion (10)[13] is a phrase in contrast with "strong city" of salvation in 26:1. Man's "city of chaos" (RSV) is always set over against the city of God. The Septuagint says in its Greek: "desolation in every city." Such was the case in Isaiah's day as city after city in Palestine fell before the attack and looting of the plundering Assyrian armies.

Every house is shut up, that no man may come in. "The surviving inhabitants have barred their doors, suspicious of the intrusion of unbidden guests" (Skinner). Where civic lawless-

---

[11]Delitzsch sees here "the genuine mark of Isaiah . . . in the description of the vanishing away of men down to a small remnant." Skinner notes that "desolating and practiced wars have reduced the population of all countries; but the process of extermination is not yet at an end." Cf. their commentaries, *ad loc.*

[12]But Delitzsch suggests: "All the sources of joy and gladness are destroyed . . . the taste of the men themselves turns it to bitterness."

[13]The Hebrew term *tohu,* in the phrase *kiryath tohu,* is the same as in Gen. 1:2, where the primeval earth was *tohu wabochu,* "without form, and void."

ness and looting are prevalent there is reason enough that every
door is barricaded with any surviving inmates in terror.[14]

There is a crying for wine in the streets (11). This is better
translated by Delitzsch, "There is a lamentation for wine in the
fields," i.e., in the open country.[15] **All joy is darkened.** "The
sun of joy has set" (Delitzsch). All rejoicing has ceased, for
"even the factitious merriment, which wine is capable of producing, is denied now to the inhabitants of the earth . . . from whom
all mirth is gone."[16]

In the city is left desolation (12), for it is only a crumbling
ruins. Even the gate, which is usually the pride of any Near or
Far Eastern city, **is smitten with destruction**—a shattered ruins.

3. Only a Remnant Remains (24:13-16a)

a. *Like gleaning grapes* (24:13). **When thus it shall be** is
better translated "for so it will be." Here again is the prophet's
characteristic thought of the "remnant,"[17] for he knows that few
will survive the judgment that is about to affect the whole world.

b. *These sing for joy* (24:14). Out of earth's ruin and
wreckage comes the song of the righteous remnant. Isaiah with
prophetic vision exclaims: "Yonder, men **lift up** their voices; they
sing for joy at the majesty of the Eternal One, they shout more
loudly than the sea."

c. *Praise the God of Israel* (24:15). **Wherefore glorify ye
the Lord in the fires** is a bit misleading. Delitzsch translates it:
"Therefore praise ye Jehovah in the lands of the sun, in the
islands of the sea the name of Jehovah the God of Israel." The
word **fires** (*'urim*) has reference more specifically to "the lands
of light, or of the sun-rising," hence the east. **The name of the
Lord God of Israel**[18] recalls the fact that His name indicates His

[14]This writer recalls the rioting, burning, looting, and even shooting
which characterized the Watts riot in Los Angeles in August, 1965, where
even the most efficient police force was helpless to bring things under
control.

[15]"Men weep in the fields because there is no vintage" (Plumptre, *op.
cit., ad loc.*). The Hebrew bears this meaning.

[16]Rawlinson, *op. cit., ad loc.*

[17]For Isaiah's doctrine of the remnant see Introduction.

[18]"*Yahweh* in its literal grammatical signification, puts emphasis upon
the absolute, underived, and therefore unlimited, unconditional, unchange-
able, eternal being of God" (Alexander Maclaren, *op. cit.,* p. 117).

nature (cf. 30:27) as revealed and made nameable both in judgment and in mercy. **In the isles of the sea** must have reference to the Mediterranean area to the west of the prophet as he looked and spoke from Jerusalem. Hence west calls on the east to sing the Eternal's praises.

d. *Glory to the righteous one* (24:16a). **From the uttermost part of the earth . . . songs.** Delitzsch says, "Praise to the Righteous One!" He thinks "the reference is to the church of righteous men, whose faith has endured the fire of the judgment of wrath." Rawlinson comments: "The righteous remnant perceive that the calamities which have come upon the earth are ushering in a time of honor and glory for themselves; and they console themselves by making this fact the burden of some of their songs. Their honor, it must be remembered, is bound up with God's glory; which will not shine forth fully till their salvation is complete, and they reign with him in glory (II Tim. 2:12)."[19]

Moffatt translates:

> *From earth's far bounds the chorus sounds,*
> *Now glory dawns for upright men.*

4. *Treachery and Terror Fill the Earth* (24:16b-20)

a. *An emaciated prophet surveys the ruins* (24:16b). **But I said, My leanness, my leanness!** The Hebrew is "leanness to me." Many of the modern translations read: "I pine away."

b. *Barbarous plundering* (24:16c). Isaiah's thoughts return to the Assyrian invaders of his own day with their atrocities. **The treacherous . . . have dealt treacherously** ("The robbers run riot in robbery," Smith-Goodspeed).

c. *Pitfall and snare* (24:17). **Fear . . . the pit . . . the snare** is translated, "Panic, pitfall, and plot[20] are upon you, inhabitant of the land!" (Berk.) "Man will be like a hunted animal, flying from pursuit, and in danger at each step of falling into a pit or

---

[19]*Op. cit.,* p. 385. Let the reader consult Jesus' parable of the tares, "gather out the tares *first* . . . then shall the righteous shine forth as the sun in the kingdom of their Father." Neither Jesus nor Isaiah taught a "suppressionist millennium." The wicked will be eradicated from the earth *first,* and then shall the righteous possess it as their own. See Matt. 13:30, 43. Dr. H. Orton Wiley used to emphasize this in his classes.

[20]This is a good English attempt to preserve Isaiah's play on the terms, *pachad, pachoth,* and *pach,* in the Hebrew. Cf. Jer. 48:43 ff.; Amos 5:19.

being caught in a snare."[21] "The words paint the rapid succession of inevitable calamities."[22]

d. *No escape* (24:18a). **He who fleeth . . . shall fall . . . and he that cometh up out . . . shall be taken.** Moffatt's translation is graphic: "He who scurries from the panic steps into a pit, he creeps out and is caught within a snare." Hunters in the jungles pursue their game with shouts and loud cries to stampede the animal into a camouflaged pit. If perchance the unwitting captive tries to jump out, his head and neck thus extended make him easy to lasso.

e. *Cataclysms rend the earth* (24:18b-20). **The windows from on high are open** (18) recalls not only Noah's day and the great Flood but the ancient cosmology which regarded the firmament of heaven as holding back the celestial waters except when the windows were opened to let these flow through upon the earth. **And the foundations of the earth do shake,** as in the case of the earthquake which occurred during Uzziah's reign and of which both Amos (1:1) and Isaiah (2:19) speak. **The earth is utterly broken.**[23] Here Plumptre sees the three stages of an earthquake: "the first, cleavage of the ground; [next] the wide open gaping; [and] the final shattering convulsion. The rhythm of the whole passage is almost an echo of the crashes."[24]

The earth shall reel to and fro like a drunkard (20) in his staggering, and **like a cottage,** or more correctly, "like a hammock."[25] **The transgression** (is) **heavy upon it.** Isaiah traces the cause of such terrestrial convulsions to man's sins and rebellion against God. Thus the world totters under the weight of its iniquity. **It shall fall, and not rise again.** Some fallen drunkards are able to get to their feet again. Not so the earth, that shall stagger to a final fall under the weight of human iniquity.

5. *Judgment Overtakes the Exalted Hosts* (24:21-22)

a. *Angels and rulers* (24:21). **In that day . . . the Lord shall punish the host . . . on high, and the kings . . . upon the earth.**

[21]Rawlinson, *op. cit.*, X, 385.

[22]Plumptre, *op. cit.*, *ad. loc.*

[23]"The earth is . . . broken . . . shattered . . . shaken" (Berk.). "The earth breaks asunder . . . cracks asunder . . . shakes asunder" (Smith-Goodspeed).

[24]*Op. cit.*, *ad. loc.*

[25]Cf. Delitzsch, Moffatt, Plumptre.

Here divine judgment falls upon the "wicked spirits in the heaven-lies" (cf. Matt. 24:29; Eph. 6:12) who are looked upon as the patrons of the kings of the earth and their source of supernatural inspiration and support.

Plumptre thinks that Isaiah is "identifying these spiritual evil powers with the gods whom the nations worshipped, and these again with the stars in the firmament. Isaiah [thus] fore-sees a time when their long protracted rebellion shall come to an end, and all authority and power be put down under the might of Jehovah (I Cor. 15:25)."[26] The same thought is found in a Rabbinical saying: "God never destroys a nation without having first of all destroyed its prince."[27]

b. *Imprisoned and punished* (24:22). **Gathered . . . as pris-oners . . . in the pit** suggests that they will be incarcerated in the abyss of *Tartarus* (II Pet. 2:4, "pits of darkness," ASV; cf. Jude 6; Rev. 20:2-3). **After many days shall they be visited.** Divine visitations in the biblical sense can mean a bestowal of either grace or punishment. Hence the RSV reads: "punished,"[28] which is in keeping with the analogy of Isaiah's eschatological represen-tations here. Released from their confinement in "death row," they now meet their penalty.

6. *The Eternal Reigns on Mount Zion* (24:23)

When God's eternal reign begins, His glory will eclipse both sun and moon. **Then shall the moon be confounded, and the sun ashamed.** One translation reads, "The moon will blush and the sun grow pale" in comparison with the radiant splendor of **the Lord of hosts, who shall reign in mount Zion, and in Jerusalem, and before his ancients gloriously.** When the earth has been destroyed, one gathers that Isaiah, like John, looks for a New Jerusalem. Hoffman holds that **his ancients,** "like the twenty-four *presbuteroi* of the Apocalypse, are the sacred spirits, forming the counsel of God, to whom He makes known His will concern-ing the world, before it is executed by His attendant spirits the angels."[29] But Delitzsch believes that reference is "not to angels but to human elders after God's own heart." In the divine pres-ence they both behold and reflect the Shekinah of the Eternal.

---

[26]*Op. cit., ad loc.*
[27]Quoted by Delitzsch, *op. cit., ad. loc.*
[28]Cf. Gesenius' *Hebrew and Chaldee Lexicon* on the term *Paqad.*
[29]*Schriftbeweis,* i, 320-21.

B. The Songs of the Redeemed, 25:1-12

As in the Johannine Apocalypse, so here in Isaiah, the songs of the redeemed are an important feature. The first song rejoices in the overthrow of the imperial city and is filled with thanksgiving to God. The second is concerned with the Lord's victory banquet, while the third is a hymn of adoration to "our own God" emphasizing His saving presence.

1. The Song of the Supernatural Stronghold (25:1-5)

a. *The divine fidelity* (25:1). Isaiah identifies himself with the redeemed community and utters this hymn in its name, expressing its thankfulness for the mercies of the Lord toward it. He is the covenant-making and covenant-keeping God. He executes gloriously His purposes, proves himself true, and has demonstrated how He can bring to pass that which seems incredible. The RSV translates the last clause, "plans formed of old, faithful and sure."

b. *Pulling down earth's strongholds* (25:2). Under God's power, heights become heaps, ramparts become ruins, and the palaces of aliens become permanent ash heaps. The oppressing city has at length been overthrown.

c. *God's enemies must honor and fear Him* (25:3). Even earth's **strong** and **terrible** ones must acknowledge a greater power. The oppressors now recognize God's might.

d. *God is the Refuge of the poor* (25:4). He was a Shelter **to the needy** when **the blast** threatened to sweep them away. "Storm troopers" have met a **wall** that will not fall. The divine Champion is both a Shelter against **the storm** and a Shade from the sun.

e. *The song of the ruthless is silenced* (25:5). As clouds quench **the heat,** so God quiets the tumult of the enemy aliens. He is a protecting Screen against the consuming violence of **the terrible ones.**

2. The Eternal's Victory Banquet (25:6-8)

The phrase **in this mountain** appears twice in this paragraph and once again in the next. It refers, under the symbol of Mount Zion, to the spiritual stronghold of the redeemed. A rich eschatological banquet of both spiritual and material enjoyments is another chief symbol of apocalyptic literature (Ps. 36:8; 63:5;

Matt. 8:11; 26:29). "God's Future for the Faithful" will bring four significant freedoms:

a. *Freedom from hunger and thirst* (25:6). **Wines on the lees** (aged, and therefore deemed better) and **fat things full of marrow** (rich meat) represent the satisfying luxuries of an Eastern banquet.

b. *Freedom from ignorance* (25:7). **The veil** that now blinds men's eyes to real insights and an intuitive grasp of the truth will be withdrawn (I Cor. 13:12; II Cor. 3:15).

c. *Freedom from death and sorrow* (25:8). **Death** has now been swallowed up **in victory** (I Cor. 15:54-55). Tears have been dried by the divine kerchief, and the taunts of the ungodly hurled against the righteous in their days of suffering are now forever silent (Ps. 79:10). God cares and has not left us orphans (John 14:18).

d. *Freedom from the curse* (25:8). **The rebuke** (reproach or curse) **of his people** is taken **away**. All those sufferings, whose ultimate ground is sin, the Eternal has terminated. The cause is gone and the consequence is no more. Blessed hope! The curse is now annulled and the reproach of man since Eden is removed, **for the Lord hath spoken it.**

3. *The Song of Faith's Vindication* (25:9-12)

a. *Faith's affirmation and reward* (25:9). The redeemed people now declare their faith and gratitude. **Lo, this is our God; we have waited for him, and he will save us: this is the Lord ... we will ... rejoice in his salvation.** Salvation anticipated is now realized. The eternal and living God is no illusion. He is "our own God," says the Hebrew.

b. *Pride's humiliation and debasement* (25:10-12). **The hand of the Lord** (10) brings judgment as well as mercy. The haughty and arrogant will perish in the cesspools of iniquity. **Moab** is their type: born of incest (Gen. 9:30-38), practicing seduction (Num. 25:1), and perishing in corruption. Verse 11 is made more clear in *The Berkeley Version:* "Though Moab stretches out his hands in the middle of it as a swimmer stretches out [his hands] to swim, He shall lay low his pride despite the craftiness of his hands."

Isaiah uses his own Jordan rift valley as a symbol of "the great gulf fixed" (Luke 16:26) between those who trust in the Lord and those who are so arrogantly self-sufficient as not to need

God. For though the land of Moab is so high and exalted, it is on yonder side of that desolate sea in which nothing lives. And God **shall bring down their pride together with the spoils of their hands (11). The high fort (12)** of evil will crumble at last.

C. The Song of Our City of Refuge, 26:1—27:1

Here Isaiah pictures the feeling of God's people as they glory in the strength of "the city of God," a strength, not of material bulwarks, but **salvation** with its attendant peace and blessedness. Here, too, the prophet declares a faith that life is mightier than death. Death is not the final word for the heroes of faith—that word is resurrection.

1. *The Song of Two Cities*[30] (26:1-6)

a. The city of our defense (26:1-4). **We have a strong city;** its **bulwarks** are **salvation (1)**; its **gates** are open to the loyal **(2)**. There the steadfast soul finds true **peace (3)**, and **the Lord Jehovah is** the Rock of Ages **(4)**.[31] A thorough commitment to God secures both stability and peace.

The city is one of strength because of its impregnable offense as well as defense. Its walls and fortifications are not dead stone but dynamic and inexhaustible salvation. Its gates are opened to a righteous nation (*Goi tzaddik*), one that keeps troth and is characterized by fidelity. The one who is steadfast in disposition God guards with constant peace; for when the inmost nature is free from all equivocation, then a **perfect peace** (*shalom*) that is deep and constant abides.

In 26:1-4, we are shown "The Strong City." (1) It is fortified by **walls and bulwarks** of **salvation**, 1; (2) Its **gates** are open to the **righteous**, 2; (3) Its inhabitants are kept in **perfect peace**, 3-4, trusting in the Lord in a troubled world (G. B. Williamson).

b. The city razed to dust (26:5-6). **The lofty city** God lays

---

[30]Alexander Maclaren's sermon on "The Song of Two Cities," based on Isa. 26:1-10, is worthy of notice. Cf. *op. cit.* The same may be said for his sermons "Our Strong City" (on 26:12) and "The Inhabitant of the Rock" (26:3-4).

[31]The name for God in v. 4 is *Yah Yahweh* (only here and at 12:2 in the OT); it reads in the Septuagint, "God, the great, the Eternal." It is a superlative expression for the Absolute Deity, "the Rock of Ages," as the added Hebrew phrase should be translated. God is a certain Refuge for all eternity, inasmuch as He is the dynamic and eternal Cause of all being.

low (5). **The poor** and **needy** may now walk there (6). The
oppressive city is so leveled to the ground that those it formerly
oppressed may now travel unhindered across its precincts. The
people of God shall one day judge the world.

2. *The Song of the Soul's Desire* (26:7-10)

a. *"For the just the way is level"* (26:7, Berk.). It is free
from the obstacles that bring about the downfall of the wicked
(Jer. 31:9; Prov. 3:6, margin; 11:5).

b. *God's presence, the soul's desire* (26:8). During a time
of trial the loyal soul does not relax any of its love and piety
toward God. **Thy name** is that which reveals God's character and
will. It is also His memorial (Exod. 3:15). "Father, glorify thy
name" (John 12:28).

c. *Longing for God's justice* (26:9). It is by divine **judgments** that men learn what is right. It is also true that men make
greater advances in virtue and piety in days of affliction than in
the time of great external prosperity. The discipline of divine
guidance does not guarantee our creaturely comforts, but if followed, it assures spiritual progress. "Before I was afflicted I went
astray; but now I observe thy word" (Ps. 119:67, ASV).

d. *Evil men never learn* (26:10). Wicked men, even in a
good land, never learn to be good or to see God's majesty. God's
judgments are calculated to bring sinners to their senses, but men
do not always respond in this way. It is a perversity of the man
who prospers to think of himself, I must be living right. Yet
prosperity is no sign of rectitude. One's good fortune may be
due to the piety and industry of those among whom he dwells.

3. *Prayer to Our Living Lord* (26:11-15)

a. *Let the heedless see* (26:11). Unbelievers are loath to
recognize the divine providences. But God's jealousies over His
people burn like a consuming **fire.** The original Hebrew is
graphic! "Lord, Thy hand is lifted up, but they see not. They
shall see to their shame Thy jealousy for Thy people; yea, fire
shall devour Thine adversaries."

b. *Maintain our welfare* (26:12). The plea is that the **Lord**
will **ordain peace** for His own, since what they have done is
ultimately the divine accomplishment.

c. *Other lords have ruled us, but only You deserve remembrance* (26:13). It is a terrible thing when God's people descend

so low as to say, "We have no king but Caesar" (John 19:15). For
Caesar, by whatever name he is known, is never the kind of ruler
that inspires praise. No other lord compares with the true God,
before whom the humblest commoner may plead his case. Moreover, the rule of any other king over the people of Israel was
inconsistent with the ideal theocracy and thwarted the realization
of the divine will in the national life of His people.

d. *Death of world rulers* (26:14). The verse makes better
sense if the italics are omitted from the KJV: **Dead, they shall not
live; deceased, they shall not rise.** Earthly kings are now but
dead ghosts[32] which return no more, and the Eternal wipes out
all remembrance of them.

e. *The nation increased* (26:15). "Thou hast increased our
nation, extending its frontiers afar." Some such statement is more
true to the Hebrew of this verse. **The nation is increased** in
numbers and its borders are advanced. God is glorified only
when His people win new converts and extend the boundaries of
Christ's kingdom.

4. *The Song of the Chastened Sufferers* (26:16-19)

a. *Under the Lord's chastenings we whispered our petition*
(26:16). Here the word **prayer** has reference to "secret speech,"
hence a "whisper" as in the ASV margin. "In distress they
sought Thee, they poured forth a whispered prayer" (Berk.).

b. *Our travail availed us nothing toward deliverance or conquest* (26:17-18). The symbol of birth pangs is frequent in
Scripture for times of great sufferings. Here we have a picture
of the fruitlessness of mere human strivings. "The issue of all
their painful toil was like the result of a false pregnancy, a
delivery of wind" (Delitzsch).

c. *Only God can raise the dead to songs of joy and life* (26:
19). Here Moffatt's translation makes better sense:

> O thou Eternal, thy dead shall live again,
>   awakening from the dust with songs of joy;
> for thy dew falls with light and life,
>   till dead spirits arise.

Dust is the natural symbol of death—that captivity from which
there is no return. **The dew of herbs** is the moisture by which

---

[32]*Rephaim*, sometimes translated "shades," is technical Hebrew for the
inhabitants of the underworld.

God gives life to plants. God, who sent death as a penalty for man's sin, is our only Resource for its removal. The assurance of eternal life must rest upon a simple faith in God, who alone is the Author and Giver of it. "The Old Testament doctrine of the resurrection is but the conviction of the sufficiency of God Himself, a conviction which Christ turned upon Himself when He said, *I am the Resurrection and the Life. Because I live, ye shall live also.*"[33]

5. *The Song of Faith's Hiding Place* (26:20-21)

a. *The summons to safety* (26:20). **Come, my people . . . hide . . . for a little moment, until the indignation be overpast.** Thus with tender solicitude the eternal God calls His little flock. As in the night when the avenging angel passed through Egypt, so now the Lord warns that there will be a moment during which His anger will be abroad in the earth. He will exact from its inhabitants the penalty for their deeds of blood which the earth will now reveal. During this moment of wrath and world punishment let the faithful keep to their chambers with closed doors in trustful waiting.

b. *When God departs* (26:21). Here God is represented as a Monarch leaving His capital and going forth to take vengeance on His foes. Uncovered **blood** cries for vengeance (Gen. 4:11; Ezek. 24:7-8). Even **the earth** now refuses to conspire with the guilty by drinking in innocent blood; rather it exposes the dead bodies as evidence against the killers. When God's wrath explodes, it is imperative to keep out of the way.

6. *Song of the Sword of the Lord* (27:1)

a. *A keen and relentless sword* (27:1a). The Hebrew term here may refer to **sword** or any other cutting instrument. The Septuagint term *machaira* refers to the short sword of the heavily armed Greek soldier which he drew for use in close and mortal combat. The three characterizations of this instrument of divine punishment are **sore**[34] (more probably "well-tempered"), **great** (swift), **and strong.** Moffatt says: "great, grim, sweeping sword."

b. *Two snakes and a dragon* (27:1b). Commentators have offered many suggestions for the application of these terms, rang-

[33]George Adam Smith, *op. cit.,* p. 451. Italics are Smith's.
[34]The Greek of the Septuagint for this term is "holy." Whitehouse, *op. cit., ad loc.,* suggests "ruthless" as a translation of the Hebrew.

ing from mythological and astronomical to political and national figures. The simplest explanation of Isaiah's reference would specify the "darting" **serpent** (desert adder), the "coiled" **serpent**, and the Nile **dragon** or crocodile. These have been made to apply to Assyria (on the swift Tigris River), Babylon (on the winding Euphrates), and Egypt (whose river was called the sea). Apocalyptic figures are meant to be somewhat obscure. Suffice it here to let the reference indicate three types of godless world powers: the raider, the besieger, and the deporter. Allegorically, Satan and his kingdom are intended.

D. The Lord's Redemptive Concern for His People, 27:2-13

The great eschatological oratorio now moves to its conclusion. A song about God's care for His vineyard is followed by an interpretation of Israel's sufferings, and the closing scene is the final harvest and the last trumpet, which calls the dispersed to their homeland.

1. *The Lord's Song to His Pleasant Vineyard* (27:2-6)

Contrasted with 5:1-7, here is a jubilation set over against that dirge.

a. *The eternal Guardian* (27:2-3). **I the Lord do keep it . . . night and day** (3). Here is a distinct reversal of the sentence of condemnation passed upon the vineyard in 5:1-7. Instead of abandonment there is constant care. Instead of the clouds being commanded not to give rain, the vineyard is watered whenever water is needed. Lest any spoilers molest it, the Lord guards it day and night.

b. *The eternal Gardener* (27:4). There is no **fury** in the heart of the divine Gardener toward His vineyard now. His zeal and consuming fire are now for the **briers and thorns**. God hates nothing but sin. Where His vineyard is fruitful, His one concern is its cleansing, that it may bear fruit more abundantly (John 15:2).

c. *The eternal Protector of the penitent* (27:5). **Let him . . . make peace with me** and he shall know My protection. Unconditional surrender to God is the condition of His peace. God prefers to consume the sin rather than the sinner. Hence His constant invitation to make peace is graciously extended to His enemies.

d. The promise of productivity (27:6). **He shall cause them
... to take root ... blossom and bud, and fill the face of the
world with fruit.** God's spiritual Israel like a great vine will
spread through all the earth, bringing blessings to mankind.

2. *The Expiating Chastisements* (27:7-11)

The prophet now addresses himself to the meaning of Israel's
sufferings. The sufferings of God's people are not to the same
degree or for the same purpose as those of their oppressors. When
God's people are attacked by the ungodly, the rod of the smiter
is ruthless with hatred. Not so the rod of God. There is a redemptive ministry in its smiting.

a. When mercy tempers judgment (27:7-8). God's judgments upon the enemies of His people are more to be feared than
the attack of such enemies upon God's people. Whenever God's
chastisements fall upon His people, they are in careful **measure**
(8) and not to exceed their power of enduring. The Lord even
tempers the sirocco (**the east wind,** 8) with its blistering desert
heat. In short, God was angry with His people at times, but not
without love. God's punishment is a way to salvation.

b. The conditions for expiation (27:9). **By this ... shall the
iniquity of Jacob be purged, and this** is what is required **to take
away his sin:** let him beat **the stones** of his idolatrous altars fine
as chalkstones, and let him make sure there are no idol **groves** or
images left standing. God cannot cure a man from sinning who
will not utterly repudiate his sin.

c. The desolated fortress city (27:10-11). The man who
builds up his defenses against the divine dealings shall know only
the divine destruction suited to His enemies. His soul shall be like
a deserted and forsaken ... **wilderness** where Satan's calves can
feed, and there ... lie down, and consume the branches (10).
Or where women will **come** and gather its withered **boughs** for
firewood (as they still do in Palestine today). The soul that
refuses to become repentant under the divine chastisements is
**of no understanding: therefore he that made them will not have
mercy on them, and he that formed them will shew them no
favour** (11). God's chastisements are calculated to cure us of
our idolatry and sin; but if like a stubborn and **defenced city** we
hold out against the divine siege, redemptive chastisement can
become only punitive judgment, leaving nothing but desolation.

In that case we are "not a people of discernment" (as the Hebrew has it).

3. *The Diaspora's Return* (27:12-13)

Here God promises to gather the dispersed (*the Diaspora,* as they were called) of Israel back to their homeland.[35] This divine ingathering of His people focuses upon Mount Zion.

a. *The Lord's winnowing time* (12a). **Beat off** is better translated "beat out" as with the threshing flail; hence *The Berkeley Version* says: "The Lord shall thresh out grain." God will thus carefully separate the wheat from the straw and chaff. Instead of the gleaning of a few olives from the topmost boughs, there will be a full and abundant gathering, and yet each single olive will be inspected "one by one."

b. *Individual ingathering* (27:12b). **Ye shall be gathered one by one, O ye children of Israel.** Isaiah sees here a selection on the basis of individual character by the divine Harvester. He is not speaking here of mass immigration to the Holy Land, but of a spiritual selection ("election," if you please) on the basis of individual qualifications. Such is the case with God's saving grace, and such is the care with which the Lord will gather His people.

c. *A trumpeted recall from exile* (27:13). **The great trumpet shall be blown** (cf. 18:3; Zech. 9:14; Matt. 24:31; I Cor. 15:52; I Thess. 4:16), **and they . . . which were ready to perish** (the lost ones) **in the land of Assyria** (the east), **and the outcasts in the land of Egypt** (the west), shall come and **worship the Lord in the holy mount at Jerusalem.** It is a blessed prospect, this prophecy of homecoming. It must be cherished in every age. Among the hopes of the human heart none is dearer than the prospect of returning from the far country to the love and bounty of the Father's presence. Though the present finds us captive in a distant land, we await the glorious homecoming of the saints.

---

[35]Delitzsch violently disagrees with this and says: "I regard every exposition of verse 12 which supposes it to refer to the return of the captives as altogether false. The Euphrates and the brook of Egypt, i.e., the *Wady el-Arish,* were the north-eastern and south-western boundaries of the land of Israel, according to the original promise (Gen. 15:18; I Kings 8:65), and it is not stated that Jehovah will beat on the outside of the boundaries, but within them" (*op. cit.,* p. 460). The *Wady el-Arish* is fifty miles southwest of Gaza.

> *Though exiled from home, yet still I may sing:*
> *"All glory to God, I'm a child of the King!"*

It is not certain that Isaiah intended v. 13 to be taken literally, for a trumpet sounded in Jerusalem could hardly be heard in Babylon. Yet years later those in Babylonian lands must have been inspired by the prospect of its fulfillment which took place as the Jews were permitted to return to their own country under the decree of Cyrus.

There are many striking elements in this apocalyptic prophecy. Isaiah impresses us with a wealth of imagination and a variety of symbols. The proclamations of judgment are interspersed with songs that reveal a deep and delicate vein of feeling and faith. Sustained by a lively faith, the eye of the prophet reaches beyond the dark days of the Assyrian scourge and future Babylonian captivity to the bright vision of hope and the blessed fulfillment of the eternal purpose. He was a true pastor-prophet.

Section **V** Six Woes of Warning

Our study of Isaiah's prophecies now brings us to what has been called "The Book of Woes."[1] Just as cc. 7—12 reflected the relation of the nation to Assyria in the time of Ahaz, so now do cc. 28—33 reflect the relation of the nation to Assyria as it stood in the time of Hezekiah. The policy of looking toward Egypt is traced a step at a time. In his denunciations of this policy Isaiah begins with Israel and its capital city of Samaria, but he concentrates upon Judah and Jerusalem, and finally concludes with a woe against the Assyrian destroyer.

Hezekiah was a pious king but he seems to have been weak enough to yield to the influence of his nobles, the corrupt priests, and the false prophets who infested his court. Thus we find him permitting, if not sanctioning, the nefarious league with Egypt which Isaiah assails as being contrary to the will of God.

A. WOE TO THE POLITICIANS, 28:1-29

This prophecy must have been given before the downfall of the Northern Kingdom, which came in January, 721 B.C. Samaria, flourishing in all her pride and evil passions, is ripe for judgment. We may date this speech before the actual siege of Samaria, which lasted about three years. This would place it about the time Hezekiah began his reign.

1. *When Drunkenness Prevails* (28:1-13)

A prophecy of **woe** befits a dissolute people. No nation has ever built an enduring society by means of drunken dissipation. A nation enslaved by wine is unfit to govern itself.

a. The crown of shame (28:1-4). Isaiah here sounds a warning to Samaria's dissolute nobility. Samaria's hill surrounded by its wall was shaped like a **crown** (1) and gave this impression to one observing it from a distance. Also banqueting revellers were often crowned with a chaplet wreath of greenery and flowers, especially if they were nobles. Isaiah now sees such **glorious beauty** as only a **fading flower**. With her nobles thus **overcome with wine**, Isaiah sees that the city itself will soon be

---

[1]Cf. Delitzsch, *op. cit.*, II, 1.

overcome by the Assyrian invader. There are many **fat** (fertile and flourishing) **valleys** as one journeys from Jerusalem to the hill of Samaria.

God's instrument of judgment upon Ephraim will be a **mighty and strong one** (2), the "storm troopers" of destruction and violence which shall cast down to the earth with the hand. The trampled **crown** (3), once the symbol of Ephraim's glory, shall then become the symbol of his shame. The first to be devoured as the Assyrian moves southward will be this Northern Kingdom—swallowed down like the first ripe fig (**hasty fruit,** 4) of the **summer.**[2]

b. *The "crown of glory"* (28:5-6). Isaiah draws a sharp contrast. The **diadem of beauty** for God's righteous minority is **the Lord of hosts.** He is their adorning **Crown** (5). The **spirit of judgment** (justice) and valor is God himself (6), guiding those who must sit on the judgment seat and render important decisions. He will give **strength to them** who must **turn** back the tide of **battle** at their very gates. The Lord is an inspiring Spirit, while wine is an intoxicating and degrading one (Eph. 5:18).

c. *The destiny of debauchery* (28:7-13). Turning his attention to the south and focusing it upon the leaders of his own nation, Isaiah describes a revolting scene of drunken debauchery. The actors are: (*a*) polluted politicians (vv. 7-8). A group of staggering priests and some stupefied prophets (7*a*), **erring in vision** and stumbling in decision (7*b*), complete the company. Surrounding their conference **tables,** they are so overcome with wine that **all tables are full** of their filthy **vomit** (8). In the very moments when they should have been under the influence of the Spirit of God, they are under the influence of the spirit of alcohol.

(*b*) Mockers of admonition (9-10). The revellers mock the prophet, and he replies to their derision. Isaiah styles them as a group of scoffers (9) who react to his rebukes with the haughty response: "Whom does he think he's teaching? Infants barely weaned? Why this stammering **precept upon precept;** this **line upon line,** with **here a little, and there a little?**" (10) With this

---

[2]The early fig is a special delicacy (Hos. 9:10; Mic. 7:1) for any passer-by. Figs usually ripen in early August. If then one sees a ripe fig in June, his eye is attracted by it and it scarcely touches his hand before he has eaten it. Isaiah predicts that luxurious Samaria will vanish like such a dainty morsel.

series of monosyllables[3] they make light of the prophet's precepts, rating him as an intolerable moralist. As for themselves, they are full-grown and free, and do not need him to teach them **knowledge.**

(c) God's judgments in a foreign tongue (11-13). To those who would reject his ethical monosyllables Isaiah predicts a time when they will come under God's chastisements by means of the Assyrian monosyllables.[4] Commands given in a barbarous and babbling speech will then interpret for them God's will. Having rejected their true Refuge (12), they shall now listen to God's judgment (13). Thus will their heathen conquerors utter the Lord's precepts to a people who would not listen to the prophet's preachments. Fallen, **broken . . . snared, and taken**—such will be the outcome of their debacle of drunkenness.

2. *When Rulers Scoff* (28:14-22)

"No one can bargain successfully with death," Isaiah insists, "so stop your mockery and face up to reality!"

a. *Falsehood is no foundation* (28:14-15). Hezekiah's chief princes are now addressed as **scornful men, that rule this people** (14). Isaiah is sure that **death** (15) and **hell** (*sheol,* place of the dead) make no agreements. Men cannot save themselves from either by bargaining. **Lies** constitute no hiding place, and deceit is no repose, though these men were trusting in them.

b. *Faith alone is salvation* (28:16-17). Just as certainly as a covenant with death is a delusion, so it is certain that the only true element of permanency **in Zion** is the **sure foundation** stone of faith (16). The literal Hebrew reads, "Behold, I am He that hath laid the foundation stone of Zion." Hence the **precious** and **sure foundation** is the divine and indestructible purpose of God. He whose house is built on rock fears not the fiercest storm. For on the stone is this inscription: "The believer is not anxious" (16b).

Judgment (justice) is God's measuring **line, and righteousness** is His plumb line (17; cf. Peter's application in I Pet. 2:6). God's elect cornerstone measures up to any architectural standard of perfection. On any other foundation disaster overwhelms either **the refuge of lies** or **the hiding place** of deceit.

---

[3]V. 10 is all monosyllables in the Hebrew.
[4]The Assyrian language is composed mainly of monosyllables and three fundamental vowels.

From 28:14-18, Phineas F. Bresee preached a temperance message entitled "Holiness and Civic Righteousness." (1) The liquor interests **have made a covenant with death, and with hell,** 15; (2) The nation has not yet seen the full **overflowing scourge** that will follow an unrestricted liquor traffic, 15; (3) Our duty is to recognize the awful curse with which we have to deal, but preach Jesus Christ—the **precious corner stone, the sure foundation,** 16 (*Sermons on Isaiah*).

c. *Calamity cancels compacts with doom* (28:18-19). The underworld cannot thwart divine retribution. The overwhelming **scourge** (18) will be a daily terror (19). "As often as the Assyrian invasion sweeps through Palestine, it shall thin the population by death and captivity."[5] An alliance with Egypt, artfully planned and secretly instituted, regardless of its seeming diplomatic value, would not prove a safeguard against this constant death. For concealed within this friendly alliance with Egypt was a repudiation of the obligations entered into previously with Assyria. It was not **a covenant with death** and **hell** but a courtship with them. Isaiah declares, "It will be sheer terror to understand the message" (19c, RSV).

d. *Human cleverness is inadequate* (28:20). He who "makes his bed" without God finds neither rest nor comfort. Isaiah quotes a familiar proverb. He is sure that Hezekiah's counselors will find their **bed** too short and **the covering** too narrow.

e. *The "strange work" of the Lord* (28:21-22). These scoffers cause God to join ranks with foreigners to fight against His own people (21). They aggravate their own bondage and insure their own destruction (22). They will fare like the Philistines when David destroyed their army like a flood at Baal-**perazim** (II Sam. 5:20; I Chron. 14:11), and when at another time he chased the Philistines before him from **Gibeon** to Gezer (I Chron. 14:13-17). Any attempt to free themselves from the Assyrian bond by a breach of faith in courting the help of Egypt will mean even more stringent bondage. Let them not disregard the warning, for doom is inevitable. God's prophet has heard from heaven.

3. *A Parable of Plowing and Threshing* (28:23-29)

The Almighty suits His method to His purpose, and His chastenings to the person. The prophet now offers comfort while at the same time he answers the question: "So what?"

[5]Rawlinson, *op. cit., ad loc.*

In v. 23, Isaiah, like a faithful teacher, calls for the full attention of his hearers. In 24-25 he reminds the reader that plowing is for sowing. It has its proper time and purpose. The method suits each seed. "When he has leveled its surface, does he not scatter dill, sow cummin, and put in wheat in rows and barley in its proper place, and spelt as the border?" (25, RSV) God-given common sense ordains it so (26).

In 27-29 we see that threshing instruments must be suitable and well-timed. That which is suitable to one kind of seed is ruinous to another. Even the harsher methods are used within the limits of reason. The fact that the thresher knows how to use the flail, the hoof, the stoneboat, and the wagon wheel in his threshing of the various types of grain also argues for that **wonderful . . . counsel, and excellent** wisdom of **the Lord of hosts** (29).

Judah is God's farm (cf. I Cor. 3:9). Jehovah neither plows, harrows, nor threshes perpetually. Nor does He punish all with equal severity. Whatever He does is for a purpose, for the divine judgments are not arbitrary but disciplinary. This is the solemn teaching and gracious message of comfort couched here in the form of a parable.

B. Woe to the Proud Formalists, 29:1-14

From the politicians and nobles Isaiah now turns to the populace of his own city, addressing his second woe to the proud formalists with their empty human commandments learned by rote. He sets forth his theme in the first two verses, announcing to "the city of God" (*'ir-el*),[6] Jerusalem, that notwithstanding the fact that she is **Ariel** (*'Ari-El*), "the lion of God," in the coming distress she shall be reduced to **Ariel** (*'Ariel*), "the altar-hearth of God."[7] Hence the city known symbolically as God's lion shall

---

[6]The Greek of the Septuagint reads, *Ouai polis Ariel.* I am taking the position that Isaiah had also the Hebrew *'ir-el* in mind as he used the term *'Ariel.* Jerusalem was for the prophet at once the "lion of God," "the city of God," and "the altar-hearth of God." **Ariel** is clearly a mystic name for Jerusalem. It is generally explained as equivalent to *'Ari-El,* "lion of God." But Delitzsch suggests that the meaning should be "hearth of God" or "altar of God" as in Ezek. 43:15-16.

[7]Adam Clarke is no doubt correct in saying that "the first Ari-el [*sic*] here seems to mean Jerusalem, which should be distressed by the Assyrians; the second Ari-el seems to mean the altar of burnt offerings" (*A Commentary and Critical Notes: The Old Testament* [New York: Abingdon-Cokesbury Press, n.d.], *ad. loc.*).

now become the place of the Lord's consuming fires (God's furnace).

1. *Formal Sacrifices Call for Devouring Fires* (29:1-8)

a. Rote sacrifices shall become real and retributive burnings (29:1-4). C. von Orelli offers the following translation of these verses:

> 1. Alas, Ariel, Ariel, fortress where David encamped! Add year to year; let the feasts go round. 2. Then I will afflict Ariel, so that there shall be mourning and sighing, and it shall become to me a true Ariel. 3. And I encamp about thee in a circle, and plant stations closely round thee, and set up siege-works against thee. 4. And thou shalt speak deep below the ground, and thy speech shall sound muffled out of the dust; and thy voice shall be like that of a ghost out of the earth, and thy speech shall whisper out of the dust.[8]

Add ye year to year (1) or, "Let the feasts move through their yearly rounds, O Judah, the lion of God, and Jerusalem, city of God, where David erected an altar" (II Sam. 24:25; cf. BBC, Vol. I, comments on Lev. 16:1-34; 23:26-32). God himself proposes a sacrifice that will turn the city of God into the altar-hearth of God (2), where the dying moans of slain victims are heard.[9]

The Lord will besiege Jerusalem (3), heaping a mound against her walls and placing the battering rams. Isaiah declares that "judgment must begin at the house of God" (I Pet. 4:17). Begin at Jerusalem with the gospel (Luke 24:47); begin also at Jerusalem with judgment. Isaiah's lesson seems to say: "If ye lack the fires of true spiritual ardor, ye shall suffer the fires of God's judgments."

The result will be abject humiliation, "From low in the dust your words shall come" (4).[10] Commentators here, including

---

[8] *The Prophecies of Isaiah* (Edinburgh: T. & T. Clark, 1889), p. 164.

[9] "Go on year after year, keep your solemn feasts; yet know that God will punish you for your hypocritical worship, consisting of mere form destitute of true piety! Probably delivered at the time of some great feast, when they were thus employed."—Adam Clarke, *ad loc.*

"Isaiah's second woe is pronounced upon Ariel, the altar-hearth of God, i.e., Jerusalem, the sacrificial center of Israel's worship. David had first inaugurated the true worship of Jehovah in Zion. But now Zion's worship had become so formal and heartless Jehovah determines within another full year to allow Jerusalem to be besieged and fall (vs. 1-4)." G. L. Robinson, *op. cit.*, p. 110.

[10] Adam Clarke, *op. cit.*, *ad loc.*

Clarke, see a reference to some form of spiritism or soothsaying. But Isaiah is probably thinking of the voice of the dying victim as it bleeds slowly to death alongside the brazen altar. Its mournful voice becomes weaker and sharper as it finally falls with crumpled legs to utter its dying moan from **the dust**. Isaiah seems to think of God as the slaying priest and of His people as the first sacrificial victim, followed by their besieging enemies. Jerusalem shall not only be the focal point of an endless yearly round of animal sacrifices but the altar of God upon which nations shall be burned in sacrifice.

b. The destruction of Jerusalem's foes (29:5-8). The fires of the Eternal One will suddenly consume the sacrifice (5-6). The distress of Jerusalem will be severe but it will not last long. **The multitude of thy strangers** (foes, 5) will be ground to powder-like **dust,** and blown away like whirling **chaff. It shall be at an instant suddenly,** like a clap of **thunder, an earthquake,** a whirlwind, or a **tempest (6).**

Ariel's (Jerusalem's) enemies shall vanish like **a dream** (7-8). The sudden disappearance of Sennacherib's army is to be like the fading of a nightmare when the dreamer awakes from his tortured sleep. One night sufficed for the desolation of 185,000 troops (37:35-38; II Kings 19:32-37). God has plenty of time, but He also has abundant power. His deliverances are often sudden though silent.[11] **Her munition** (7) would be her stronghold or defenses.

2. *Sensual Feasts Culminate in Spiritual Ignorance* (29:9-12)

Isaiah's prediction of the manner in which God's deliverance would come did not seem to be either credible or pleasing to his hearers. Hence his challenge to them: "Tarry ye and wonder; take your pleasure and be blind" (9, ASV). Isaiah's Hebrew verbs denote amazement at what is said and an unwillingness to receive it. Blind stupor is the outcome of a long hypocrisy. God's punishment for such offenses is often judicial blindness (10; cf. Rom. 1:24, 26, 28). Hence Isaiah continues: "Your prophets should have been your eyes, but they behold no vision. Your seers should have been your heads, but they lack clear and valid insight" (paraphrase).

---

[11]Isaiah "makes it abundantly clear . . . that the deliverance will be unexpected and unexplainable by the natural circumstances of the Jews themselves, that it will be evident as the immediate deed of God" (George Adam Smith, *op. cit.,* p. 215).

The prophet sees them as a crowd of spiritual illiterates, with an incapacity on the part of their ruling class to understand God's revelations. **Read this** (11) . . . **I cannot; for it is sealed . . . Read this** (12). "But I can't even read." Mentally drunk (9), they see and comprehend nothing of true import.

3. *Rote Religion Ruins True Understanding* (29:13-14)

Empty formality becomes only a mouthing of words with no heart and no soul in its worship. Mere lip homage evidences an estranged heart. God speaks to us in facts, not empty forms. God seems to say, Their worship of Me is but a human maxim without any meaning. "Their fear of me is [but] a commandment of men learned by rote" (13, RSV).

Divine judgments upon human substitutes for piety are what constitute the Lord's **marvellous work** (14; cf. 28:21; Deut. 28: 58-59). When spiritual or political counselors lead the people astray, wisdom has indeed perished.

C. WOE TO THE PERVERSE AND INSUBORDINATE, 29:15-24

1. *Secret Plans* (29:15-16)

Taking **counsel** in secret, the leaders supposed the Lord could not see them (15). In this they forgot the sovereignty of God. "Oh, your perversity," shouts Isaiah, "supposing the creature to be of more significance than the Creator!" Should a man say to his Maker, **He made me not** (16), or criticize the One who formed him as being devoid of **understanding?** This was exactly what Isaiah called it, a **turning of things upside down.** Perverse indeed is that person who sets men above his Maker. "The image of the potter does not suggest to Isaiah the thought of an arbitrary sovereignty, but of a love which in the long run will fulfill itself."[12]

2. *Divine Restoration Brings True Illumination* (29:17-24).

If you wish to reform the politics of any nation you must first regenerate its people.

a. God's reversals are redemptive (29:17-21). Lebanon (the name means "white mountain"), now a forest, **shall be turned into a fruitful field, and the fruitful field** shall become a "forest of fruit trees" (17; Berk., fn.). **The deaf** now **hear . . . the blind** now **see** (18). The open **book** and the open vision are joined with

---

[12]Plumptre, *op. cit., ad loc.*

enlightened receptivity. The **meek . . . and the poor . . . rejoice**
(19) in a holy God. The ruthless, the **scorner,** the unscrupulous
materialists, and those who seek to pervert justice and equity
shall be removed from God's commonwealth (20-21). Those who
watch for iniquity (20) are men "intent on doing evil" (Berk.).

b. God's redeemed have no cause for shame (29:22-24). God,
who redeemed Abraham (22) from idolatry and gave him promises for a holy posterity, will grant **understanding** to the erring,
and instruction to the questioning (24). He will also discipline
them **that murmured,** making them a godly and reverent people.
When they see the divine workmanship in human personalities,
they will hallow the divine **name, and sanctify the Holy One of
Jacob** (23), standing in awe of the God of Israel.

From 29:13-23, Dr. P. F. Bresee preached on "The Verities
of Salvation." He pointed out (1) Reality rather than ritual is
the essence of religion, 13; (2) God does **a marvellous work** in
the spirits of His people in order to make himself real to them,
14; (3) God shows His power in human history, 17; (4) God
shows His power in the transformed lives of other persons, 23
(*Sermons on Isaiah*).

D. WOE TO THE PRO-EGYPTIAN PARTY, 30:1-33

Isaiah uses cc. 30—31 for a denunciation of Judah's pro-
Egyptian policy. He traces Judah's bad politics to their source
in bad religion.

1. *Woe to Those Who Set Egypt Ahead of God* (30:1-17)

Judah's leaders are like **rebellious children** (1) who would
rather listen to the advice of the neighbors than to follow a
parent's counsel.

a. They weave an alliance without God's blessing (30:1-5).
The sin of self-will is manifest in this carrying out of a design
that does not originate within the divine purpose. The net result
is the heaping of **sin** upon **sin**—the sin of concealment upon the
previous sin of trusting in secular alliance. **Cover with a covering**
(1) means to weave a treaty or make an alliance. A **shadow** is
no shelter (2), even though that shadow be cast by the whole
kingdom **of Egypt.** Pharaoh's protection is a poor exchange for
divine aid. To **trust in the shadow of Egypt** (3) was to put
Egypt in the place of God.

Notwithstanding the courtesy of Pharaoh's reception, Judah's
trust in his support will only result in disillusionment and disgrace

(4-5). Zoan (4) is undoubtedly Tanis, which is now a heap of ruins just south of the present *San el Hagar* in the northeast corner of the Nile delta. **Hanes** has been identified with Heracleopolis Magna (the present *Ihnasya el Madina*) by von Orelli, Delitzsch, and Whitehouse (see map 3). Isaiah sees Judah's messengers making their way into the heart of Egypt via these two cities.

b. The useless caravan (30:6-7). Isaiah thinks of this mission to Egypt as a foolhardy enterprise. Hence his oracle on **the beasts of the south** (the Negeb; 6). That desert southland is the lair of lioness and young lion, **the viper** and the swift-darting desert adder. He insists that tribute sent through a **land of trouble** cannot net a **profit** in return. Yet no danger deters them and no sacrifice seems too great in the carrying out of their unworthy plan. Their **asses** and **camels** are laden with the **treasures** with which they hope to purchase the Egyptian alliance. Verse 7b is better translated, "Therefore I have called her 'Rahab [fn., seadragon] who sits still' " (Berk.; cf. also ASV, RSV). "Dragon do-nothing" is the name Isaiah gives to Egypt. The "Rahab" symbol for Egypt seems to specify the Nile "river-horse" (*hippopotamus amphibius*). This huge, sluggish beast constitutes a fitting symbol in Isaiah's mind for the empire on the Nile which brags and boasts, but does not stir from its place to help another.[13]

c. A record for all times (30:8-11). Isaiah now resorts to documentary evidence (8) to prove to posterity that "instruction rejected" was the attitude of a **rebellious people** (9). Their response was "pleasant platitudes preferred" (10). Write it **in a table** (8) would be "on a tablet" (Berk.). They said even worse: "Take your God and go!" Isaiah's continually confronting them with **the Holy One of Israel** (11) seems only to have aroused their antagonism. They stood face-to-face with an infinite holiness which they would not hear, and therefore could not bear.

d. The collapse of human bulwarks (30:12-14). Isaiah's **wherefore, because,** and **therefore** are significant expressions of the law of relationships. (a) Confidence in cunning crookedness (12) expressed by their trust in "fraud" (margin) and **perverseness** seemed to Isaiah to be sheer political folly. To **stay thereon** is to rely upon. (b) To depend upon it would be like putting con-

---

[13]Cf. Delitzsch and Von Orelli. Skinner observes: "This proud boastful monster—its proper name is 'Inaction' " (*op. cit., ad loc.*).

fidence in a broken, bulging **wall** all **ready to fall.** (c) The crash of the weakened **wall** (13) comes like a sudden calamity. It brings with it ruin beyond remedy (14), for it breaks into many **pieces,** like a piece of shattered pottery. "Among the fragments there shall not be found a piece with which to carry a coal of fire from the hearth or to dip water from a cistern" (Berk.).

e. *The alternatives* (30:15-17). The alternatives are either reliance on the eternal God or flight in panic from the Assyrian. Isaiah declares that only **returning** (repentance)[14] and faith spell salvation (15). C. von Orelli translates this verse: "By repenting and remaining quiet you shall be saved, in stillness and in confidence your strength shall lie."[15] Moffatt says:

> *Your safety lies in ceasing to make leagues,*
> *your strength is quiet faith.*

Plumptre observes: "In this case it was the turning from the trust in man, with all its restless excitement, to a trust in God, full of calmness and peace."[16] Hence Isaiah would urge the immediate recall of the Judean embassy now on its way to Egypt. He counsels rather a dignified neutrality as the best policy.

Horses in full retreat (16) is the prophet's next picture. Isaiah quotes his opposers as saying, "No! we want some horses waiting if we have to flee." His rejoinder is, "You'll flee, all right!" They reply, "If so, we want something that has speed." Isaiah retorts: "Your pursuers ride swiftly too." **One** shall chase a **thousand** of you (17), and only one of you shall escape. To **rebuke** would be to threaten. Left like **a beacon upon the top of a mountain,** a lone pole (or pine) atop the **hill,** there Judah will stand as a true image of isolation, a tiny remnant in a wide land devastated by war.

2. *God Waits to Show Favor* (30:18-26)

Verse 18 pictures God's solicitude and His righteousness. Isaiah sees Him withdrawn to His throne on high until such time as He can interpose effectively. **A God of judgment** is a God of justice.

---

[14]The Hebrew term *shubah* occurs only here in the OT. According to Gesenius it indicates not only "returning" but "conversion." The Greek of the Septuagint is *apostrapheis,* meaning "to turn oneself away." Hence Von Orelli suggests that the Greek term *metanoia* would have been a better translation from the Hebrew, since it is the term for repentance.

[15]*Op. cit.,* p. 172.

[16]*Op. cit., ad loc.*

Verses 19-22 are filled with encouragement and promise. (*a*) A **people** shall continue in **Zion** and weeping shall be removed (19). (*b*) Even though hunger prevails, God's presence will be real: "Your Teacher will not hide himself any more, but your eyes shall see your Teacher" (20, RSV). (*c*) His voice will direct their **way** (21). (*d*) They, in turn, will throw away idols and **images** (22).

Nature will regain its beauty and productivity. (*a*) Sufficient **rain** will guarantee an ample yield in both the pasture and the field (23). (*b*) Work animals shall eat a savory silage (24) of "mixed provender with salt."[17] To **ear the ground** probably means to plow. (*c*) Rivulets shall course through the highlands (25), while the forts of the foe are falling. (*d*) Moonlight will be as sunlight, and sunlight will seem to increase **sevenfold** (26).

3. *The Music of the World's Judgment* (30:27-33)

At every stroke of divine judgment upon evil God's people will raise their song of triumph.

a. The Lord's judgment (30:27-28). "The Lord comes to judge the nations with the mighty manifestation of His incensed majesty."[18] Isaiah sees Him with **lips** of fury, **tongue** of flame (27), and **breath** like a torrent that reaches to **the neck** (28). The prophet also sees God as a **sieve of vanity** (destruction) and a **lasso**[19] of doom. Thus under the constraints of a Higher Power, Judah's enemies rush blindly on to destruction.

b. The music of deliverance (30:29-30). The **song** of a festive **night** (29*a*) probably has reference to that holy solemnity known as the Feast of Tabernacles, or ingathering. Of all the Jewish festivals it was the most abounding in joy. It had a night of solemn ritual, the Temple court being lighted with great candelabra. It came to be known as "the feast" (I Kings 8:2, 65; 12:32; II Chron. 7:8-9; Ezek. 45:25).

The flute of ascent to the rock (29*b*) was the daylight ritual which followed. The pilgrims in procession from the country came bringing their firstfruits and playing on their flutes as

---

[17]*B'lil khamitz* is probably a kind of mash of barley, oats, and vetches, made from savory with salt and sour vegetables, and having the chaff removed from the grain by being **winnowed with the shovel.**

[18]Von Orelli, *op. cit.*, p. 177.

[19]Some translators say "leading bridle," others "halter," others "lasso." This last, if applied to wild horses, is the most appropriate.

they ascended through the eastern gate to the rock dome of Mount Moriah (cf. I Sam. 10:5). Amidst it all is heard the majestic **voice** of the Eternal (30*a*), as **his arm** descends in fury (30*b*), scattering His foes with **fire** and **tempest.**

c. *The baton of destiny* (30:31-33). God's **voice** annihilates the Assyrians (31) and leads the music of the attack (32). The sound of drums and the notes of stringed instruments (**tabrets and harps**) symbolize the joy of those redeemed by God's action. **Tophet . . . ordained of old** (33) means literally "place of burning." It was also the name given to the Valley of Hinnom outside Jerusalem and southwest of Mount Zion, where refuse was dumped and the fires kept burning. There wicked King Ahaz offered his son as a burnt offering to Moloch (II Kings 16:3). Since the Hebrew term for king is *melek*, Isaiah makes a play on it, indicating that the Assyrian *melek* will be sacrificed to the heathen god *Moloch.* Although the Assyrian king himself did not die in Jerusalem, undoubtedly many of his soldiers who died on that fateful night of Jerusalem's deliverance were cremated there in this Valley of Hinnom.[20]

Moffatt's rendering of 31-33 is clear and vivid:

> At the Eternal's voice of thunder,
>   the Assyrians are appalled;
> he fights them to the death and clubs them down,
>   to peals of music;
> the pyre to burn them is prepared,
>   both deep and wide,
> piled high with logs set blazing by the breath
>   of the Eternal like a fiery tide.

E. Woe to Those Who Trust in the Flesh, 31:1-9

The princes of Judah sought to strengthen their defenses against the Assyrian menace with horses from Egypt, for Judah lacked a good cavalry. Isaiah's words have a ring of sarcasm in them as he condemns their trusting in an "arm of flesh" rather than **the Holy One of Israel** (1).

1. *The Futility of the Flesh* (31:1-3)

Horses and **chariots** (1), regardless of their number, cannot equal **the Holy One of Israel.** To **stay on horses** was to depend on them.

---

[20]Thus we are made to understand some of the connotation of the term *Gehenna*, as Jesus used it.

Judah's princes were not the only wise ones in the universe. There was wisdom beyond that of Hezekiah's counselors. He who sits on the throne of this universe is no fool. God in His wisdom was bringing disaster, and He never has to "eat" his words. He was taking the offensive against **evildoers** (Judah) and against **the help of them** (Egypt). He would meet them with their own weapons, and outsmart their human cleverness. **The Egyptians are men, and not God; and their horses are flesh, and not spirit** (3). It is God who routs the allies of evil. When He stretches **out his hand,** "the protector totters and the protected one falls, and both perish together."[21] **He that is holpen** means helped.

2. *The Lord Descends to Do Battle* (31:4-5)

God is like that **lion** "against whom the whole body of shepherds is called out without his being alarmed at their noise and crouching at their turmoil."[22] Mere human noise does not stampede Him. He takes His stance on **mount Zion.** And whether He fights *for, on,* or *against*[23] it, one had better not arouse His hostility.

As birds flying (5) is meant to suggest the parent eagle hovering over the nest when its little ones are in peril, and swooping down with fury upon any who would molest them. Not only protection but deliverance is indicated. **Passing over** is the root of *pesah,* from which the word "passover" is derived.

3. *The Lord Has a Sword for Assyria* (31:6-9)

The prophet cries, "Reverse your revolt, O Israel! **Turn ye** (6) **to the Lord.**" Repentance must always be toward God (Acts 3:19; 20:21) if it is to be effective. Thus Isaiah calls upon Judah's leaders to renounce that deep apostasy of which they have been guilty. He continues, **Cast away** your **idols** (7) as a proof of your decision!

Even the famous Damascus steel blade has been known to break. Not so **the sword** (8) of the Lord. Isaiah prophesies that "the Assyrian shall fall by the sword of no man; no human's sword shall devour him" (8, Berk.). **He shall flee from** this

---

[21]Von Orelli, *op. cit.,* p. 178.

[22]*Ibid.*

[23]Interpreters have taken all three translations of the Hebrew preposition.

sword and there will be forced labor for their **young men.**[24] The picture of 9 is of Assyrian soldiers and officers utterly put to rout. "Their very god flies in panic, their princes scatter in sheer terror" (Moffatt). Or, as Von Orelli has it, "His princes retire panic stricken from the banner."[25] Jerusalem has indeed become God's **furnace;** His **fire** both illuminates and consumes.

Thus the Assyrian was to be put to rout, not by the sword of any human hero but by the divine intervention. It was more like a holocaust than a battle, and the power of Assyria was broken forever. Flesh cannot avail in conflict with Spirit.

F. Three Homilies for Jerusalem, 32:1-20

Some commentators treat this chapter as an appendix to the foregoing woe. Isaiah gives a picture of the ideal commonwealth (1-8), rebukes and admonishes the complacent ladies of Jerusalem (9-14), and delineates the blessing resulting from God's outpoured Spirit (15-20).

1. *The True and the False Nobility* (32:1-8)

The noble versus the knave is Isaiah's contrast here.

a. *True nobility of character* (32:1-2). Here Isaiah looks forward to a time when the aristocracy of birth and wealth will be replaced by an aristocracy of character. Both Moffatt and *The Berkeley Version* capitalize **king** indicating that these blessings are to follow the reign of Messiah. Isaiah is sure that true kingliness is an achievement of character, and true discernment a quality of wisdom. He would therefore reprove the knavish nobility of Jerusalem as he holds up before them a portrait of the ideal of character in either king or commoner. In government the **king** is righteous, and the **princes** are just. In character (2) **a man**[26] is **an hiding place** (a refuge), **a covert** (shield),

---

[24]Delitzsch observes: "The power of Assyria is broken forever; even its young men are forthwith subjected to tribute or slavery" (*op. cit., ad loc.*).

[25]*Op. cit.,* p. 179.

[26]The KJV reads, **And a man shall be as an hiding place,** as does also the ASV. Many commentators see here a specific reference to the ONE MAN, Christ Jesus, whom they see as the fulfillment of Isaiah's prophecy. Cf., for example, P. F. Bresee's sermon, "Jesus, Our Sheltering Rock," *Sermons on Isaiah* (Kansas City, Mo.: Nazarene Publishing House, n.d.), pp. 111-19. The majority of the more recent translations and commentators read "each man." In this case Isaiah is picturing a future Messianic commonwealth in which all the men of government will be men of ideal character and true nobles in their administration of the affairs of state.

a stream of fresh **water** (satisfaction), and a great shade (comfort) to the people of his nation. Instead of being an oppressor of the common man, he is a protection against calamity and a source of beneficent activity.

b. True discernment of character (32:3-8). Isaiah sees that a day will come when the moral perceptions of the people will be so spiritually quickened that discernment of character will be without confusion.

In intelligent understanding (3-4) the prophet will **see** clearly (3*a*—here is insight); the people will **hear** willingly (3*b*—here is response). The formerly **rash** person will now have good judgment (4*a*—here is prudence), and **the stammerers** will now **speak** advisedly (4*b*—here is communication). That their speech will not be precipitate, or unthinking, is the idea in the Hebrew, rather than the ability to articulate distinctly. Sound judgment and fluent speech are the combined qualities of the true orator.

In character there will be no mistaken identity and a man will be recognized for just what he is.[27] The character of the fool (6) is manifest in his speech, his mentality, his practice, his doctrine, and his politics. Isaiah anticipated the teaching of Jesus, "Ye shall know them by their fruits" (Matt. 7:16). The character of the knave **(the churl,** 7) cannot be mistaken since he plans wickedness and perverts equity—he is both crafty and fraudulent. Finally, the character of the true noble is readily noted (8). His plans are noble, he stands for what is right, and he manifests a true magnanimity. "When men's eyes are opened

---

[27]**The vile person shall no more be called liberal** is another of Isaiah's plays on words; the *nabal* shall no more be called *nadib*.

The churl is *kilai* in Hebrew. Adam Clarke defines this as "the avaricious man; he who starves himself amidst his plenty, and will not take the necessaries of life for fear of lessening his stock." Such a person gives up interest in both worlds, starved in this one, and damned in the next" (*op. cit.*).

The word for **bountiful** is *shoa,* which Clarke defines as "he who is abundantly rich; who rejoices in his plenty, and deals out to the distressed with a liberal hand" (*ibid.*)

Liberal is translated "noble" in the ASV and RSV. The Greek of the Septuagint is *kalokagathos,* meaning "beautiful and good."

The vile person will speak villany (6) is better translated, "The fool will still utter folly." Cf. ASV. Such a person is guilty of heresy, a hollow profession, and even scoffing at sacred things, for he will utter error against the Lord.

they will no longer confound the essential distinctions of moral character. Things will then be called by their right names."[28]

2. *A Warning to Complacent Women* (32:9-14)

Here we have a threatening oration to the complacent women of Jerusalem.[29] What aroused the prophet's ire was their careless unconcern in the face of the oncoming peril and his oft repeated warnings.

"Listen, you ladies of leisure!" is Isaiah's exhortation. Pay attention, O **careless daughters** (9). These represent that aspect of the public mind characteristic of the luxurious and ease-loving. "In little more than a year" (10, Berk.) your trouble begins, **for the vintage** and harvest **shall fail.**

In times like these, mourning should be the order of the days. Shudder, you careless creatures, and don the robes of sorrow, is the prophetic call. "Strip bare for a girdle of burlap" (11). It is not uncommon for Arab women to strip half naked as a sign of grief when announcing a death, following which their fellow tribesmen join in cries of lamentation. Isaiah calls upon the women of Jerusalem to do so because of the coming desolation of their wealthy estates. Verse 12 is interpreted, "Beat your breasts in mourning" (Berk.) at the coming food shortage.

Only desolation and emptiness await their places of festivity. The gardens of the stately villas will soon be **briers and thorns** (13). Even the king's palace and **city** shall be deserted, and the hill[30] **and towers** become a place for **wild asses** (14).

3. *The Effects of the Outpoured Spirit* (32:15-20)

The prophet Isaiah is not only a witness to the Messiah, but also to the Holy Spirit. This outpouring is to usher in a newness of life and power by which the will of God shall be made to prevail in human society. Isaiah looks for the outpouring of the Spirit (cf. Joel 2:28-32) to sweep away the frivolities of a profli-

---

[28]J. A. Alexander, *Commentary on the Prophecies of Isaiah* (Grand Rapids: Zondervan Publishing House, 1953 [reprint], 2 vols. in 1), II, 2.

[29]Adam Clarke is not sure that the passage is addressed to actual women. The Targums read "ye provinces" and "ye cities." He thinks therefore that verses 9-14 deal with the desolation of Judea.

[30]The Hebrew is *ephel* and no doubt indicates the ground swell at the southern extremity of the eastern hill (Mount Moriah) of Jerusalem. Beneath this the tourist to Jerusalem now sees the huge excavations known as "Solomon's stables," where a large number of horses could be housed.

gate and luxuriant life, instituting in its place something more noble and spiritual. This is to be reflected even in nature until "the downs grow like an orchard and the orchard like a forest" (15, Moffatt).

When God's Spirit is supreme, **judgment** (justice) shall reach from **the wilderness to the fruitful field** (16), i.e., **righteousness** will filter down to the very grass-roots of human society. Here is a picture of a smiling land and a God-fearing, contented people. In 17 we see that holiness begets **peace** and **assurance.** Soul rest and the witness of the Spirit are the treasures of the sanctified. "Righteousness cultivated by peace, produces tranquility of mind and permanent security."[31] These **quiet resting places** (18) are in contrast to the false and carnal security denounced in 9 and 11. **Hail . . . on the forest** (19) refers to God's judgments. The security of His people continues when God brings calamity on their foes. **The city** probably means Nineveh, the capital of the Assyrians.

The people of God shall sow in happiness by unfailing streams where abundant pastures are free. **To sow beside all waters** (20) may be translated "who sow your seed in every well-watered place." Reference to **the ox and the ass** does not justify the supposition that they are yoked together contrary to the ancient commandment. **The ox** is the animal for plowing and **the ass** is the animal for transportation. Isaiah sees a time when one may let his ox or his ass range free without fear of its being stolen by an invading army.

G. Woe to the Assyrian Destroyer, 33:1-24

This discourse presupposes a considerable advance in historical events from c. 31. Its date is suggested by v. 7. The Jewish nobles had been sent to Lachish with tribute for the Assyrian conqueror in hopes that, because of this gift, he would not besiege Jerusalem. They received an answer which filled them with dismay. Sennacherib accepted the treasures but refused to spare the city except on the basis of its unconditional surrender. He thus showed himself faithless (8) and treacherous (1), disregarding conditions of peace which he himself had fixed (II Kings 18:14). Hence this discourse falls between II Kings 18:16 and 17. The embassy referred to in 7 was not the one sent first (II Kings

---

[31]Adam Clarke, *op. cit., ad loc.*

18:14) to make an offer of submission, but the later one that brought tribute to Sennacherib in virtue of this agreement.

The chapter shows how this sudden turn of events was revealed to the prophet beforehand with divine certainty. It also vindicates the preaching of Isaiah as he contended that in God alone is deliverance and that a quiet and devout neutrality was the best political policy for little Judah.

1. The Destroyer and the Divine Deliverer (33:1-9)

a. *Woe to the treacherous one* (33:1). **Woe to thee that spoilest ... and dealest treacherously ... when thou shalt cease to spoil, thou shalt be spoiled.** Thus Isaiah is saying, Not yet have you reaped as you have sown; but when you've finished, then your treachery shall return upon your own head.

b. *Judah's pleading and Palestine's plight* (33:2-9). Isaiah here sympathizes with Jerusalem and joins with the people in intercession. The prophet vocalizes Judah's prayer: **O Lord, be gracious, strengthen us, save us** (2). When God stirs, **nations** are **scattered** (3) and their abandoned **spoil shall be gathered** up (4). Hence he who came to spoil shall find himself spoiled. All the plunder the Assyrian has collected in his march southward will make good booty for the inhabitants of Jerusalem. Moffatt clarifies 4 thus: "We [shall] loot them like locusts, and swarm like grasshoppers over their spoil." The **exalted** Eternal One is Zion's storehouse of **righteousness** (5), stability, wisdom, and salvation; reverence **is his treasure,** (6).

Judah's **ambassadors of peace** (7) cry out angrily in sorrow and disappointment because of the shameless breaking of **the covenant** by the Assyrian (8). None dares venture onto **the highways.** The Assyrian despises **the cities** and has no regard for mortal **man,** trampling down just rights, and refusing any friendly agreement. **Lebanon, Bashan, Carmel,** and **Sharon** (see map 1), all famous for fertility and beauty, have suffered the withering blight of the Assyrian invasion (9). Hezekiah had complied with Sennacherib's conditions of subjection and yet there was no suspension of hostilities.

2. God Will Act (33:10-14a)

Now will I be exalted ... saith the Lord (10). Man's extremity is God's opportunity. Note the emphatic repetition of **now.** Isaiah makes bold to declare that the judgment long threatened against the Assyrian is now immediately pending. His violence becomes kindling for the Lord's fires. The hot, panting rage of the Assyrian shall kindle his own funeral pyre (11-12). In **lime** kilns as in fires of thorns the flame is intense and consumes quickly.

Let the fate of Assyria come as a warning to **ye that are far off** (13; other nations) and to **ye that are near** (Israel herself). For **the sinners in Zion** (14a) there is also the furnace of fire heated with the wrath of the Eternal. The signal deliverance of Jerusalem has demonstrated to them, and all the world, the omnipotence of the Holy One of Israel.

3. *What Kind of Character Stands the Test?* (33:14b-16)

Isaiah asks, **Who among us** can sojourn as a protected guest amidst the fires of God's holiness? The divine wrath against sin is inexhaustible (cf. Ps. 24:3-4). The prophet is certain that there is but one thing that can survive the universal flame; that is a holy character.

"The Life of the Truly Righteous" may be seen in verses 15-16. (1) He walks justly, he speaks honestly, he despises extortion, he refuses **bribes**, he will not listen to **blood** (violence) or look upon **evil**, 15. (2) The security of the righteous is spelled out by the prophet as safe dwelling, sure **defence** ("the fortress of rocks"), and guaranteed sustenance (**bread** and **water** are certain), 16.

4. *Zion and the Eternal One* (33:17-24)

a. The changed outlook (33:17-19). Once more the inhabitant of Jerusalem may **see the king in his beauty** (17), and **the land** in its breadth. The people had been sore at **heart** (18) because of the sight of their king in sackcloth, mourning the loss of city after city, and unable to look across the Judean hills without the sight of Assyrian soldiers. The Rabshakeh with his loud voice hurled insults; **the scribe** to whom the money was handed counted it slowly in the sight of all; military strategists counted **the towers** of Jerusalem's walled defenses. But the people may now relax. The **terror** is gone. "Your heart will meditate on the terrors" (18, Berk.), which are now past. Now recollection of it leaves only thankful awareness of the divine mercy. The old, familiar tongue replaces **a deeper speech** (19)—the barbarous and unintelligible Assyrian language.

b. The theocratic city (33:20-24). Now the rejoicing inhabitant of Jerusalem may speak of: (*a*) **the city of our solemnities,** i.e., our worship, and our immovable **tabernacle** (20). (*b*) Our God is a River of grace (21) where no enemy **galley** can come. (*c*) **The Lord is** our Ruler, Deliverer, and **king** (22). (*d*) Old "Zion" (Judah's then current "ship of state"), whose tackle and sails hung limply, will see better days (23*a*). Spoils will be shared in abundance by all, including **the lame.** All will rejoice that none are sin-sick, for all are now **forgiven** (24; cf. Mic. 7:18). George L. Robinson writes: "Isaiah never pronounced a woe without adding a corresponding promise."[32]

In the promise to Jerusalem, 17-22, Dr. Bresee saw "The Defense of the Sanctified." (1) God's righteousness surrounds every life that is fully surrendered to Him; (2) **The glorious Lord** gives His people pleasant places and ample protection, 21; (3) **The Lord . . . will save us,** and His saving work is an uttermost salvation, 22 (*Sermons on Isaiah*).

[32]*Op. cit.,* pp. 115-16.

INTERLUDE
Isaiah 34—39

Section VI Retrospect and Prospect: Indignation and Salvation

Isaiah 34:1—35:10

Chapters 34 and 35 are two sides of one prophecy.[1] They form a logical transition from the preceding judgmental section of Isaiah's prophecies to the consolation section which follows after the historical interlude of cc. 36—39. In retrospect, c. 34 speaks of final judgment upon the wicked, and in prospect c. 35 turns our attention to a final redemption for the righteous. Here, then, is the literary bond uniting the two hemispheres of Isaiah's prophecy and picturing for us the spiritual destiny of the enemies of God as contrasted with that of His righteous remnant.

A. WHEN GOD BRINGS JUDGMENT, 34:1-17

Sin carries within itself not only a state of corruption and bondage, but the germs of its own destruction. Ungodliness guarantees chaos. Our prophet here emphasizes this fact in a somber chapter on the great finale of judgment.

---

[1]C. C. Torrey insists that these chapters are inseparable, like two sides of a coin, expressing the twin themes of judgment on God's enemies and blessedness for the righteous. Cf. *The Second Isaiah* (New York: Chas. Scribner's Sons, 1928).

141

1. *The Summons and the Sentence* (34:1-4)

This international proclamation comes as an address to the nations. It announces the fact that God has doomed all His enemies for slaughter. Here is the lesson which Isaiah seeks to teach us for all time and for all nations. **Come near, ye nations, to hear** (1) resembles that dramatic moment when the judge in court asks the prisoner to rise and receive his sentence. **Let the earth** "and the fulness thereof" (ASV), **the world,** and all that proceeds from it, **hearken.**

The indignation of the Lord (2) in a final outburst of wrath dooms[2] all His enemies to judgmental destruction. It is eternally true that "they that take the sword shall perish with the sword" (Matt. 26:52). The stench of the corpses and the streams of **blood** (3) depict a day of slaughter such as the world has never seen. Even the elements of the universe shall be involved (cf. Joel 2:30-31; II Pet. 3:10-12). Isaiah contrasts the transitory sun, moon, and stars with the permanence of the Creator God. He likens the falling of the most permanent things in the physical universe to the fall of the early unripened and semi-withered figs. They drop suddenly like rain when the strong winds strike the tree; so also do its leaves in the late autumn.

2. *The Sword and the Slaughter* (34:5-7)

The Lord's great **sword** (5) is turned against **Idumea** (Edom) in vengeance that shall leave that land a desolation. The phrase **bathed in heaven** seems to carry the idea of tempering steel by plunging it into water until its resilience is just right. So God has **bathed** His **sword** in the heavenly waters until it is properly tempered for judgments suited to the sin.

The avenging **sword of the Lord** (6) is greased with **the fat** of its victims and red **with the blood** of the slain.

The sacrificial slaughter takes place **in Bozrah,** about twenty miles southeast of the Dead Sea (see map 2). **Bozrah** was the chief stronghold of the northern part of the country, and a symbol of the uncleanness of Edom. The fall of the mighty ones is depicted as Isaiah names fierce wild beasts to symbolize the rulers of darkness—**unicorns**[3] ... **bullocks** ... **bulls** (7). The RSV

---

[2]**Utterly destroyed** (*cherem*) is a technical word for that which has been irrevocably devoted to Deity and must therefore be destroyed. Cf. Josh. 6:18; 7:12.

[3]**Unicorns** in the KJV margin is rhinoceros. Other commentators have suggested everything from "wild bulls" to "antelope."

142

translates "wild oxen . . . young steers . . . mighty bulls." Moffatt
reads "leaders . . . nobles and notables." All **shall come down**
in judgment. The **land** shall be so drenched with **blood** that the
soil will be enriched with their **fat.**

3. *No Kingdom Save Chaos* (34:8-12)

These verses spell out God's **day of . . . vengeance** and **year
of recompences.** Long-delayed retribution comes at last. **The
controversy of Zion** (8) is "their wrongs to Sion" (Moffatt).

a. The smoke of eternal retribution (34:8-10a). **Streams**
of **pitch,** dust of **brimstone,** and **land** of **burning** (9) seem to
point to the volcanic craters, the lava and basalt outflows, which
characterize portions of this land otherwise noted for its wide
areas of sandstone.[4] When the breath of God comes in judgment
it is a veritable stream of **brimstone.** When **the streams** are flowing **pitch,** and **the dust** of the land is sulphur, the whole territory
will become a fearful place of conflagration. **It shall not be
quenched night nor day . . . for ever and ever** (10).

b. The chaos of eternal emptiness (34:10b-12). Edom's refusal to let Israel pass through her territory at the time of its
trek toward Canaan has now brought judgment. It brings to
Edom the retribution that **none shall pass through it for ever**
(10b). "The day of the Lord" will be terrible for Edom,[5] but a
vindication for Zion (cf. 8). A land which rejects a holy inhabitant shall know unholy inhabitants. Edom is now to be haunted
by loathsome birds and beasts that love darkness and shun the
abode of men. **The cormorant and the bittern** (11) are probably the pelican and the porcupine. The **owl** and the **raven**—
scavangers of the night and of the day—are also there. God has
stretched out over these abandoned wastes His **line of confusion,
and the stones of emptiness** ("plummet of chaos," RSV). This
specifies a return to the primeval chaos as in the time before God's
Spirit brooded over the face of it. So "they shall name it No
Kingdom There" (12, RSV). **The nobles** and **princes shall be**

[4]Cf. Baly, *op. cit.,* pp. 239-51.

[5]As c. 13 singled out Babylon for special doom, so c. 34 singles out
Edom. Edom stands as a symbol of the profane and godless oppressor of
God's people. In the quarrel of Zion with the nations of the world, Edom
has persistently taken the side of Israel's enemies. His profane and earthly
nature renders him incapable of understanding his brother's spiritual claims.
Filled with envy and malice, he is likewise glad to assist in disappointing
such claims. (Cf. G. A. Smith, *op. cit.,* pp. 438-39).

nothing (12). The Edomite nobles were called "dukes" (Gen. 36:15-19). From them a ruler was chosen by the vote of his fellows. But Isaiah suggests there will be no electors and none to elect.

4. *The Denizens of Desolation* (34:13-15)

Here the cosmic curse seems to reach its full progression. The wild growth of the desert covers **her palaces** and **fortresses**. **Thorns** like the *Spina Christi*, **nettles and brambles** (13) have a way of springing up in the area of deserted ruins. The haunting inhabitants of darkness (34:13b-15) range freely where the land is uninhabited by humans. Jackals, hyenas, bats, **owls**, snakes, and **vultures**, along with wild goats and porcupine, now have taken over poor Edom.[6]

5. *The Document of Destiny* (34:16-17)

Isaiah now flings forth his challenge that when fulfillment and prophecy shall one day be compared they will be found to tally with each other. On this he stakes both God's honor and his own. Men are invited to compare Isaiah's picture with its future fulfillment as he urges: **Seek ye out of the book of the Lord** (16). These truths are as sure as the laws of nature in the animal kingdom.

In the Lord's **book** of decrees, each seeks out its own kind. "These creatures are all summoned by the Eternal, and not one fails to come; the Eternal has himself commanded them, and at his impulse have they gathered" (Moffatt). Although the jackals and wolves go in packs, and the lion and the eagle are solitaires, yet none of these lacks **her mate**. God "has allotted them the land, He has assigned it as their home, theirs for all time, their haunt from age to age" (Moffatt).

[6]**The screech owl** (14) is translated "night monster" in the margin of the KJV. The idea of either ghosts or demons is out of place in a list of wild and solitary birds and animals. It must refer to some sort of "nocturnal bird," or perhaps the vampire bat with its screeching and built-in radar system. The satyr of 14 is translated "shaggy monster" by J. A. Alexander. Its Hebrew term is *sa'ir*, "he-goat," so why try to make a demon out of it, as many of the commentators are wont to do? We ought not to read Greek and Roman mythologies back into Isaiah, when "a wild goat" will suffice. **Wild beasts of the desert . . . meet with the wild beasts of the island.** Isaiah makes a play on the terms *Ziim* and *Ijim*. Perhaps they are best translated "desert wolves and jackals" (C. von Orelli). For **vultures** in 15, RSV has "kites." On the flora and fauna of Palestine, cf. Denis Baly, *op. cit.*, Chap. VII, or *Unger's Bible Dictionary*, article "Animal Kingdom."

B. PROMISES FOR HOLY PEOPLE, 35:1-10

Here we have the picture of a glorious future which breaks for the righteous in the day of the Lord. Throughout Hebrew prophecy "the day of the Lord" carries the twofold aspect of judgment and salvation. Isaiah used his highest poetic talent to give us an idea of the glory and happiness that characterize a ransomed people returning to the city of their God.

These happy pilgrims sing of beauty (vv. 1-2), courage (vv. 3-4), healing (vv. 5-7), holiness (v. 8), security (v. 9), and homecoming (v. 10).[7] It is a song of godliness and its fruitage. For godliness redeems its environment (1-2); it encourages those who are incompetent (3-4); it reverses the tide of corruption (5-7); and it charts its course in holiness and happiness (8-10).

1. *The Gladness and the Glory* (35:1-2)

Isaiah sings of the blossoming desert following the first good rainy season, as once again the dry bulbs of the desert narcissus or perhaps the roots of the autumn crocus awaken to new life. That Isaiah's viewpoint is still Jerusalem is evident from the order of his description. East and south from Jerusalem is **the wilderness** (*Jeshimon,* 1). South and again east from this is **the solitary place** (Arabah, for which the RSV reads "the dry land"). **The desert,** the parched trans-Jordan highlands, stretches away to the east of these into the desert steppeland of Saudi Arabia.

All this shall be adorned by **the glory of the Lord** (2) to suit the occasion of the saints' homecoming. **It shall blossom abundantly** as the prophet had seen it do when the rich blooms of the narcissi, the beauty of the Moab lilies, the irises, and the tulips had transformed the desert into a paradise of God. 'Tis then that all nature rings with delight. **The glory of Lebanon** is the rich fragrance of its cedars. **The excellency of Carmel** is its shrubland with its maquis, its rockrose taller than a man, its carob trees, dwarf oaks, and arbutus. Among all these grows a carpet of flowers magnificent in color and variety. **Sharon** is the coastal plain famed for its fertility. What is it other than the splendor **of our God?** It is a time for **joy and singing.**

2. *The Comfort of the Counsel* (35:3-4)

The dispersed of God's people need strength and consolation for the homeward trek; hence the command: **Strengthen ye the**

---

[7]Cf. Naegelsbach, *op. cit.,* pp. 369-70.

weak hands, and confirm the feeble knees (3). Put heart into
the discouraged; brace up the tottering pilgrims (cf. Heb. 12:12).
Say to those with despondent hearts, **Be strong, fear not: behold,
your God** (4). "How can Israel fear since the Lord their God
hastens to them to visit vengeance on the enemy and to redeem
His people?"[8] It is good advice in any age—get your eyes on the
eternal, almighty One! Vengeance is His prerogative, recompense is His retribution, and salvation is His deliverance. 'Tis
he who will come and save you.[9]

3. *The Reality of Deliverance* (35:5-7)

The prophet now begins his enumeration of the specific results of God's salvation. **Eyes . . . shall be opened** (5). There is
a large amount of blindness yet today among the people of the
Near East. The brilliant sun and the blowing sand induce much
of it and the infection thus caused is contagious. **Ears . . . shall be
unstopped.** No doubt the Holy Spirit through Isaiah was predicting the miracles of our Lord at a later date. But also the ear is a
spiritual portal to the will. For hearing involves heeding. Eyes
and ears shall now serve their true spiritual function, to see the
truth and to hear the voice of God speaking to the inner man.

The lame shall **leap** (6) like the bounding antelope. God's
redeemed ones are enabled to run through a troop and jump
over a wall. **The tongue of the dumb** shall raise a shout of praise
and lift a song of thanksgiving. Water will redeem the wasteland.
The desert *wadis* will flow with brooks of water. **The parched
ground** (shimmering sand) **shall become a pool** (7). The mirage[10]
shall become a reality. The blinding mirage, presenting the appearance of water, is hated by the travelers of the Near East, not
only because of the deceptive illusion it presents, but also because
of its intolerable glare. **The thirsty land,** which usually drinks
up any water, will now give forth **water** after the manner of a
gushing spring. Isaiah knew that the grace of God transforming
human personality makes one fundamentally a "giver" rather
than a "getter." It is of interest to know that artesian wells have
been brought in by modern drilling with gushing fountains to
water the banana plantations of the Jordon rift area near Jericho.

---

[8]Naegelsbach, *ad loc.*

[9]The pronoun is emphatic in the Hebrew.

[10]"Mirage" appears in the ASV margin. The Hebrew is *sharab* and
occurs only again in 49:10. It has been translated "burning sand" (RSV),
"scorching sand" (Berk.), "the mirage" (Von Orelli and Delitzsch).

The habitation of dragons is better translated "the lair, of jackals," or of hyenas. The habitat of wild animals is now turned into a pasture for flocks and a place for encampment. Hence peril turns to plenty. **Grass with reeds and rushes** indicates a place of moisture and fertility that is capable of producing such water-loving plants. Hence even nature will participate in the glory streaming from this manifestation of the grace of God. The progression from **grass** to **reeds and rushes** can only symbolize that growth to greatness which grace has a tendency to produce. There is nothing stingy or limited in the potential of the divine deliverance.

4. *The Highway of Holiness* (35:8)

This verse is the sparkling point of the entire chapter. **And an highway shall be there.** Translated freely from the Greek of the Septuagint it reads: "There shall be a clean way and it shall be called a holy way, and there shall by no means pass over there anything unclean, neither shall be there an unclean way. But the dispersed ones shall proceed upon it, and they shall in no wise be deceived [i.e., caused to err]." Paraphrasing from the Hebrew we may read it:

> *A stainless highroad shall appear,*
> *Its name "the Holy Way";*
> *No unclean soul shall travel here,*
> *Nor godless foot e'er stray.*

The Hebrew term for **highway** is *maslul,* indicating an embanked way and a public road, one that has been raised and leveled. But the Greek Old Testament calls it "a clean way." Reference to this highway appears in 11:6; 19:23; 40:3; 43:19; 49:11. Here is presumptive evidence for the unity of authorship for the book.

And a way (Heb., *derek,* a path in which one goes) makes the concept emphatic with special reference to one's walk or conduct. Its name is **The way of holiness** (*evderek hakadosh*), for it is destined alone for the members of God's sanctified Church marching homeward to the city of God—a true *via sacra* (cf. Rev. 21:27). **The unclean** (polluted) has been translated, by Delitzsch, "no impure man." **The wayfaring** one may be the traveling pilgrim. **Fools, shall not err therein** hardly means, "Even simpletons cannot miss it." The Hebrew seems to indicate that no impious heathen will travel this road. Hence Phillips translates: "No rogue to lead men astray." *The Berkeley Version* says: "Fools shall not wander about on it."

Of this holy way Naegelsbach has written: "The Lord built it and destined it to lead to His house. It is a pilgrim way. Hence nothing unclean, neither unclean person or thing, may come up on it . . . Whoever goes on it is a sanctified one, under God's protection and care."[11] This is God's highway. Hence it is for the redeemed and cleansed one, not for the profane, the polluted, or the hypocrite. Nor is it intended for those who live for the world and love selfish pleasures more than this heavenly, homeward way. Isaiah sets forth here the true moral quality of God's people.

It is not a mere roadway to return from exile, but the road by which the pilgrims of all nations shall journey to the mountain of the Lord's house (2:1). Isaiah makes three things crystal-clear: (1) It is unmistakably plain; (2) It is perfectly secure; and (3) It brings one to a safe arrival.

"The Higher Way of Holiness" is the theme of the chapter. Pilgrims enter this way through the tollgate called dedication. (1) They pursue the way with a dependable sense of direction, 8c; (2) They have assurance of protection from contamination by the unclean, 8b, and from ravenous beasts, 9; (3) Travelers on this holy way are compelled by a conviction of mission, 1, 5-7; (4) They shall reach their destination triumphantly, 10 (G. B. Williamson).

5. *The Security of the Pilgrim* (35:9)

Violence and terror have vanished from this highway. **No lion** (king of beasts and king of terrors) **shall be there, nor any ravenous beast** (the Gk. of the LXX uses the same term as we find in Rev. 19:19 for the "wild beast") **shall go up thereon. But the redeemed shall walk there**—those whom the eternal God has ransomed by His grace. There they shall walk released and free.

6. *The Happiness of the Homecoming* (35:10)

The ransomed . . . shall return. The Greek OT reads here: "Those who have been drawn together (assembled) by the Lord shall return." They shall come to Zion with songs.

> *Singing I go along life's road,*
> *Praising the Lord, praising the Lord;*
> *Singing I go along life's road,*
> *For Jesus has lifted my load.*[12]

---

[11]*Op. cit.,* p. 371.
[12]E. E. Hewitt, "Jesus Has Lifted the Load."

C. von Orelli reads it: "And the ransomed . . . shall . . . come
to Zion with shouting, and everlasting joy shall be upon their
head."[13] Isaiah's concept here is that God's garland-wreath of
joy is on their heads. They have been crowned with eternal
gladness. **Joy and gladness** have now replaced **sorrow and
sadness.** The Greek of the Septuagint reads: "Cheerfulness
shall lay hold of them, and grief and pain and sighing flee away"
(cf. Rev. 7:17). The Dead Sea Scroll reads: "For sorrow and
sighing are no more."

This is the "song of the open road" and of the holy people on
their homecoming day. Let the desert rejoice! Let the faint-
hearted take courage! Let the ailing ones be healed! They may
travel through beauty and blessing, pitch their tents by nature's
luscious growth, travel the holiness highway assured of sanctity,
safety, security, and singing. They are the pilgrims whom the
Lord has set free indeed, all homeward bound from earth's threescore years and ten of captive sojourn! "Lord, I want to be in
that number, when those saints come marching home."

[13]*Op. cit.*, p. 192.

Isaiah and Hezekiah

Isaiah 36:1—39:8

A. SENNACHERIB'S INVASION, 36:1—37:38

Chronologically, cc. 38—39 precede cc. 36—37. The biblical order is probably due to the fact that cc. 36—37, which describe the siege of Jerusalem by Sennacherib in 701 B.C., explain and appropriately conclude cc. 1—35. On the other hand cc. 38—39, which record Hezekiah's sickness and Merodach-baladan's embassy of congratulation upon his recovery, quite fittingly introduce cc. 40—66. The parallel passages are to be found in II Kings 18:13—20:18 and II Chronicles 32.[1]

The most glorious work of Isaiah's prophetic ministry during the life of Hezekiah concerns these chief epochs. The most critical year in the prophet's life was 701 B.C. In this time of the nation's supreme peril Isaiah stepped forth in his greatness as a man of God. Knowing that the very national existence of Judah would shortly be at stake, he no longer sought to alarm and dishearten the people. His words became vibrant with encouragement and hope. The unchronological arrangement of these chapters argues for their Isaianic authorship. It is evident from the fact that they conclude with reference to the Babylonish captivity that Isaiah not only knew of that coming event, but so arranged these chapters as to conclude with an index finger pointing in that direction.[2]

According to the Assyrian accounts, Sennacherib came to the throne in 705 B.C. and the campaign against Palestine and Egypt occurred in the year 701 B.C. The fourteenth year of Hezekiah's reign has reference more particularly to the time of his sickness than it does to the siege by Sennacherib.[3] At that time the great deliverance is spoken of as yet future (Isa. 38:6). Hezekiah did not yet have a son and heir,[4] and his song of re-

---

[1]Cf. BBC, II, 476-89.　　　　　　[2]Cf. Delitzsch, *op. cit.*, p. 78.

[3]Cf. Von Orelli, and others.

[4]Manasseh was only twelve years old when his father died.

covery says nothing about the miraculous departure of the Assyrian menace.

Chapters 36—37 are concerned with the contrast between Sennacherib, "the great king," and "the Holy One of Israel," the Eternal King. In c. 36, Sennacherib invades Judah, and his Rabshakeh tries to persuade Jerusalem to capitulate. In c. 37, Isaiah counsels confidence in the face of the Rabshakeh's ultimatum and the angel of God brings a miraculous deliverance.

1. The Encounter: The Rabshakeh's Ultimatum (36:1-20)

a. The contingent from Lachish (36:1-3). **Sennacherib** had three reasons for his attack on Judah. (*a*) Its king had refused to pay the tribute which had been customary since the days of Ahaz; (*b*) he had opened negotiations with Babylon and Egypt for the sake of an alliance against Assyria; and (*c*) he had helped the Philistines of Ekron to rise against their king (who supported Assyria) and had kept that king in prison at Jerusalem.

The term **Rabshakeh** (2) means simply "chief of the officers." Since Sennacherib was busy with the siege of **Lachish**, the largest walled city of the Shephelah, the logical person to send against Jerusalem was the officer next in command, "the staff-commander" (Moffatt). Accompanied by his **great army** he took his stand **by the conduit of the upper pool in the highway of the fuller's field.** This would be to the west of Jerusalem and west of what was later known as the Jaffa gate (see Diagram *D*). "Then went out to him Eliakim, son of Hilkiah, the house-steward, and Shebna, the secretary, and Joah, son of Asaph, the analist" (3).[5]

b. The summons to surrender (36:4-10). The **Rabshakeh** gave, in the name of his king, a message to be relayed **to Hezekiah** (4). Its cleverly worded contents were calculated to undermine Jerusalem's confidence in her allies (4-5), her God (7), her own military strength (8-9), and her destiny (10). Verse 7 shows that the Assyrian officer wrongly interpreted Hezekiah's reformation (II Chron. 30:14) as directed against Jehovah, rather than purging His worship of idolatrous associations. To **give pledges** (8) would be to "make a bargain" (Berk.).

---

[5]Von Orelli's translation. Note that **Shebna** has now been replaced by **Eliakim** and serves only in the secondary office as secretary. Modern terminology would make **Eliakim** the prime minister, and **Shebna** the secretary of state.

c. *The language of commerce and diplomacy preferred* (36: 11-12). The king's committee felt the sting of the Assyrian's sarcasm and urged him to use a language not familiar to the common people. Aramaic was **the language** for international discourse; let him use it, for they understood it. But such was not the purpose of this clever demagogue. If he could, he would undermine the loyalty and patriotism of the people, inciting them to revolt against Hezekiah. To the commoner who must suffer the siege he would address his remarks in plain Hebrew in such clear and vulgar terms that none could miss his meaning.

d. *The plea for mutiny* (36:13-20). The **Rabshakeh** (13) offered the populace plenty of food and drink until such time as they should be deported **to a land** as good as their **own** (17), if they would but surrender (13-17). He urged them not to suppose their God more mighty than the many national gods who had fallen before the conquering march of the Assyrians (18-20).

2. *Isaiah Counsels Courage* (36:21—37:7)

What could the committee answer such a propagandist? Silence had been commanded and their one vocal response had only made matters worse. Their grief was manifested by their **rent** clothing (36:22) as they reported to the king. On hearing the report, **Hezekiah** humbled himself in garments of mourning as he sought the place of prayer (37:1).

"In that supreme hour of calamity the prophet, who had been despised and derided, was their one resource."[6] Hezekiah's plea to **Isaiah** (2) seems to mean, Now, if ever, faith needs not only power to conceive (3) but to realize its full strength to meet a crisis. The plea came as a confession of the failure of human resources and diplomacy. The one hope was that God would take note of the insults to His name. Since the prophet stood nearest to God, his intercession was the only assurance for the **remnant that is left** (4).

Isaiah (6) counseled courage and prophesied Sennacherib's retreat. Let not Hezekiah be afraid of words spoken by the Assyrian "houseboys,"[7] for a sudden impulse will seize Sennacherib and a mere **rumour** (7) will send him home, there to die **by the sword in his own land.**

---

[6]Plumptre, *op. cit., ad. loc.*

[7]The Hebrew word is equivalent to the French *garcon,* "boy" or "waiter."

3. *Faith's Trial and Vindication* (37:8-38)

a. *A strategist in straits* (37:8-9). The **Rabshakeh** returned (8) to report to his master, whom he found, not at **Lachish,** but **Libnah** (see map 1). There news of the movement of the **king of Ethiopia** (9) against him made it impractical to undertake an immediate siege of Jerusalem. Moreover, in the event of a prolonged siege he might find himself in a pincers movement between the Ethiopians and the Jews. In this dilemma he sought to check any triumph by **Hezekiah** with another visit from his **messengers** and another ultimatum.

b. *The trial of faith* (37:10-13). Verses 10-13 are virtually a repetition of 36:18-20, except that now the message was directed to **Hezekiah.** The Assyrian king warned Hezekiah not to be deceived by any promises that **Jerusalem** would not fall. A look at the record would show that it had not been so for other nations attacked by the Assyrian rulers. Sennacherib's jibe seemed thus to fling down the challenge that Nisroch (his god) was greater than the Holy One of Israel, the God of the Hebrews. **Hamath, Arphad,** and **Sepharvaim** (13) were located north of Damascus and west of the Euphrates River (see map 2). Others of these cities named remain yet unidentified as to location, but they were probably somewhere between the Tigris and Euphrates.

c. *The refuge of faith* (37:14). Having read the **letter, Hezekiah . . . spread it before the Lord,** in mute appeal to the Supreme Arbiter.

d. *The pleading of faith* (37:15-20). **Hezekiah prayed** (15). What else can a king do when human resources are inadequate? Sennacherib's challenge called for a showdown, but it was between the real and the sham. There is but one eternal Creator —**Thou art the God . . . thou alone** (16). Here the absolute monotheism of Israel's faith stands in sharp contrast to the polytheism of the Assyrians. Hezekiah was certain that Sennacherib could not reproach the living God with impunity. Other nations and their gods may have perished, since those gods were only **the work of men's hands** (19). Now all nations needed to see who really is God alone. He cannot be consumed by any man-kindled fires, for of Him there is no graven image, and He is Eternal Spirit. On **God of Israel, that dwellest between the cherubims** (16), cf. Exod. 25:21-22.

e. *The answer to faith* (37:21-35). God's reply is always given through His chosen messenger. Because you **prayed to me**

(21), is the explanation for many a divine intervention. The "Song of Faith" (22-29) reflects Jerusalem mocking her proud assailant. This taunt-song of the trusting **daughter of Zion** (22) would remind Sennacherib that it was no mere human person against whom he had dared to raise his **voice** (23). His boasted prowess over great forest and water supplies did not make him master of nature. He could have done none of this without the Lord's permission and there is a limit to his liberties. His Master will now put a leading **hook** (29) through the ring in his **nose** and, as with a bull that has reached the end of his tether, will pull him back home. Or like a snorting stallion, God's **bridle . . . will turn** him round to retrace his steps.

A sign of sure survival is now given by the prophet (30-32). In twelve months' time the land will be clear of its invaders and agriculture will resume its natural course. The Jews were then reaping only a volunteer harvest, and this would continue another year. By then sowing would be unmolested by foreign armies. **Out** from **Jerusalem** and **mount Zion** (32) the escapees shall come as a nucleus for the nation's new beginning, "thanks to the jealous care of the Eternal" (Moffatt). The promise of protection (33-35) is based upon God's concern for His **own** honor and His regard for His covenant with David (35). Therefore, not **an arrow** (33) will fall inside Jerusalem's wall; the arrogant Assyrian shall not place foot inside her nor cast up any earthworks against her. The Lord will send him back by **the way that he came** (34).

f. The deliverance by faith (37:36-38). At last, in a single night, the deliverance came miraculously. When God's **angel** smites (36a; cf. Acts 12:7, 23), it means both death and deliverance. The Hebrew phrase here usually indicates the Second Person of the Trinity,[8] hence the preincarnate Christ. Death and departure followed (36b-37). The histories of both Egypt and Judah contain independent reminiscences of such a sudden and miraculous disaster to the Assyrian army. Herodotus tells of a plague of mice that gnawed the saddle-straps and shield-straps of the Assyrians until they were useless in battle. Rodents are also carriers of plague. But do we need an intermediate, naturalistic explanation of the divine disposals? Yet 185,000 soldiers felled

---

[8]The Hebrew is *Malek Yahweh,* which many OT scholars recognize as referring to a Christophany, or an appearance of Christ.

by malaria, dysentery, or bubonic plague are done fighting, to be sure.

False gods cannot deliver from **sons** one cannot trust (38), much less give victory over a people whom the Lord defends. This verse may have been added by one of Isaiah's disciples, since historical sources indicate that Sennacherib lived sixteen years after this campaign. But Isaiah had prophesied Sennacherib's death by the sword in his own land and here was that prophecy's fulfillment. How slow God's people are to learn how to fight with supernatural weapons!

B. HEZEKIAH'S SICKNESS, 38:1—39:8

As noted above, these chapters are placed here because they serve to introduce cc. 40—66. Parallel passages are II Kings 20: 1-21 and II Chron. 32:24-33. It can no longer be a matter of doubt that the time of Hezekiah's sickness preceded the overthrow of Sennacherib. Likewise the congratulatory delegation from Babylon was in Jerusalem not more than two years subsequent to that sickness.

1. *Hezekiah's Rendezvous with Death* (38:1-22)

a. *Sickness unto death* (38:1). **In those days** (cf. 36:1 with the Assyrian siege impending) **was Hezekiah sick unto death.** The king was about thirty-eight years of age when Isaiah was sent to him saying: **Set thine house in order: for thou shalt die, and not live.** We may very well have here one of those conditional types of prophecy given in order that it might not need to be fulfilled, as in the case of Jonah's proclamation to Nineveh (Jonah 3:4). **Isaiah** may have been consulted as both prophet and physician in this case (cf. 21). His prognosis seemed to regard the case as fatal. Preparation for death would thus be the course of wisdom. Hezekiah at that time had no son; hence the dynasty of David, in which centered so many Messianic hopes, was threatened.

b. *When integrity is an asset* (38:2-6). Godliness is no liability as one faces the end of his earthly sojourn. Yet one who knows of death's approach must surely use his remaining time in preparation of both his outward affairs and his soul. Hezekiah's prayer (2-3) has in it a tone of assurance. With **face turned to the wall** (2) he reminded God that his heart had been without equivocation[9] in his pursuit of that which was good. There is no suggestion in the passage that Hezekiah's illness was a punishment for wrongdoing. The favorable response to his prayer implies that his claim to have served the Lord well was accepted. There is nothing wrong with testifying to perfection provided God's grace is given all the credit for it. Adam Clarke thought Hezekiah lacked humility, to boast of things which only the grace of God makes possible. If Hezekiah was boasting, Clarke would be correct, for goodness comes only by the grace of God. But the king, like Job, must hold to his integrity even in the face of death. **Hezekiah wept** (3) aloud, and God had respect unto his tears.

God's response came through His prophet **Isaiah (4). Go . . . say to Hezekiah, I have heard thy prayer, I have seen thy tears . . . I will add . . . fifteen years (5). And I will deliver thee and this city (6).** Also God intimated that He would bless Hezekiah as He had blessed **David.** The promise of fifteen more years meant that Hezekiah's reign would thus be doubled.

c. *The sign of the sundial* (38:7-8). Asking and giving signs is not unusual in the Old Testament, and especially in the life of Isaiah. Though Jesus would give no sign on demand (Matt. 12:39; 16:1-4; Luke 11:16; etc.), we do find Isaiah offering **a sign** (7) for the confirmation of weak faith at different times. An instrument for measuring time was chosen since the promise was for an extension of time (cf. v. 22). Ingenious sun-clocks may be seen yet today in the Far East at places like New Delhi and Jaipur. **Ahaz** had been fond of importing new devices.

The prophet offered Hezekiah the choice of letting **the shadow** rise or fall **ten degrees** (8; see II Kings 20:9-11). The natural phenomenon would be for it to fall as the day wore on. Hence the supernatural sign would involve a reversal of this process. Thus came the assurance from God that He who could reverse the sundial could as easily replenish the sands of life which had almost run out for Hezekiah. Likewise the retreating shadow with its miraculous lengthening of the day was a pledge of the postponement of that "night" in which "no man can work," which had almost overtaken the king.

[9]*Shalem,* perfect, comes from the adjective *shalam,* "whole, entire." C. von Orelli translates it "with undivided heart." Hezekiah thus testified that there was no double-mindedness about his relationship with God.

d. *The song of the survivor* (38:9-20). This psalm does not appear in the parallel passage in II Kings. (*a*) "Departure at noontime" (9-13) is a good caption of Hezekiah's thought. As he was not yet forty years old, death would have come in his prime, depriving him of the **residue of** his **years** (10). Death also cuts off communication and worship in this world (11). Life for him would thus be rolled up like a shepherd boy's **tent** or a weaver's finished web (12). Hezekiah's weeping continued unto daybreak with pain that was like **a lion** crushing the **bones** of its victim (13).

(*b*) "The song of the mourning **dove**" (14-15) ascends from the king's sleepless soul. "I am in anguish; be Thou my surety" (14, Berk.). In spite of his suffering and **bitterness of . . . soul** (15), Hezekiah believed that if God became surety for him, then death, which is like a dunning creditor, must depart from him.

(*c*) "God's praise among the living" (16-20) arises from those who have learned that "sweet are the uses of adversity." It is a most loving deliverance which casts **all** one's **sins behind** God's **back** (17). And only the living can pass on from generation to generation the account of the eternal goodness. God's readiness to save is a cause for rejoicing and worship. **By these things men live** (16) suggests that Hezekiah had come "to see that the Lord's discipline was a pledge of forgiveness [cf. Heb. 12:11]" (Berk., fn.).

e. *Providential remedies for recovery are not to be rejected* (38:21-22). Isaiah's medical prescription was for **a lump of figs,** i.e., a poultice, on the carbuncle. The prayer of faith for the healing of the sick is not one that rejects the God-given means for recovery made known to medical science. The motto over the door to the French College of Surgeons reads: "I bound up his wounds, God healed him."

2. *The Babylonian Subversion* (39:1-8)

Hezekiah has been called "the man that lived too long."[10] Though he had snatched from death added years for his life, he did not keep them untarnished. Character gained from the agony of some great trial must not be weakened by the subsequent self-indulgence or vanity. We must ever beware of "the moment after!"

---

[10]For the man who died too soon, see I Kings 13.

a. *The flattering delegation* (39:1-4). This embassy from **Merodach-baladan** (1), a prince of Babylon, had two apparent objectives: (*a*) the congratulations and the gift celebrating Hezekiah's recovery; and (*b*) the inquiry about the phenomenon of the sundial (cf. "the wonder . . . done in the land," II Chron. 32:31). But the delegation probably had more serious business than either congratulations or scientific inquiry. If perchance Judah could be induced to join Babylon in an alliance against Assyria, it would be a political maneuver worthwhile.

Hezekiah was glad of them (2), thinking that he had found an ally that might render important aid. Thus he **shewed them the house of his precious things.** The display was something more than ostentation. It was probably a revealing of the resources of his kingdom, intended to impress the Babylonian ambassadors with a sense of Judah's importance as an ally. However, instead they must have formed the idea that Jerusalem would be a grand city to plunder. **Then came Isaiah** (3), and his appearance on the scene betrayed his suspicions that the king might be toying with a foreign alliance. Against such the prophet fought incessantly.

b. *The Babylonian captivity predicted* (39:5-8). **Then said Isaiah** (5), **Behold, the days come, that all . . . shall be carried to Babylon** (6). Hezekiah's strange words in v. 8 are in keeping with the idea that the postponement of a calamity involves also its mitigation. One can almost hear him saying: "So what, as long as I escape?" But such an interpretation seems foreign to Hezekiah's spirit. Some commentators do not see here an indifference toward posterity. Perhaps his comment that **the word of the Lord** is **good** (8) was focused upon the promise of sons to sit upon his throne after him in spite of the prospect of Jerusalem being carried into captivity. But his folly had mortgaged their future. And such folly is being repeated in our times. "After me, the deluge." "Let the future generations pay for it; I'll not be here."

As noted above, this concluding prophecy in the earlier portion of Isaiah's message turns attention to the coming historical situation of Babylonian oppression for which the messages of comfort in cc. 40—66 were intended.

PART TWO

CONSOLATION

Isaiah 40—66

Isaiah's artistry as a prophet and writer is evident in this second part of his great work in what may be called its architectonic arrangement, or structural pattern. This second half has three divisions,[1] each composed of nine (3 x 3) parts. That this entire second half of Isaiah's book forms one complete unit is the contention of such eminent scholars as Franz Delitzsch, C. W. E. Naegelsbach, C. von Orelli, George L. Robinson, George Rawlinson, James Muilenberg,[2] James D. Smart,[3] and Gleason L. Archer, Jr.[4] Others, like J. Skinner and George A. F. Knight,[5]

---

[1]In each of these three divisions the grand themes of future salvation find expression in a distinctive way. In the first part, the glorious God triumphs over powerless idols. From the Christian viewpoint it is the rule of God the Father and the coming of His kingdom which this part celebrates. In the second part, the seer is absorbed in the suffering of the Holy and Just One, which will bring the salvation of the many, and to himself be the path to glory. In NT language, here is the atoning work of the Son of God, clothed in OT garb. Finally, in the third part, the cleansed, glorified, and blessed Church of the future is depicted as a nation of worshippers of the true God of all peoples. Here is the work of the Holy Spirit.—cf. Von Orelli, *op. cit.*, p. 217.

[2]"Isaiah 40—66" (Exegesis), IB, V, 384 ff.

[3]*History and Theology in Second Isaiah* (Philadelphia: Westminster Press, 1965), p. 30.

[4]*A Survey of Old Testament Introduction* (Chicago: Moody Press, 1964). Cf. his chapters on Isaiah.

[5]*Deutro-Isaiah, a Theological Commentary on Isaiah 40—55* (New York: Abingdon Press, 1965), p. 12.

are convinced only of the unity of the sixteen chapters from 40 through 55.

Of this second part of Isaiah's book, Delitzsch observes: "There is nothing in the Old Testament more finished, nothing more splendid than this trilogy of prophetic discourses."[6] The great theme of these chapters is the same as that so often enunciated previously by Isaiah, namely, Israel's redemption. The immediate historical background is the devastation wrought by Sennacherib in 701 b.c.[7] Babylon was chosen by the prophet as the symbol of "the city of the godless," just as Jerusalem and Zion so often in his thinking symbolize "the city of God."

(1) Chapters 40—48 are concerned with *theology*. They set forth the incomparable Deity—the Eternal One—in contrast with the vain and impotent idols of the heathen. Deliverance from the Babylonian captivity is predicted through the Eternal's political servant with the significant and symbolic name Cyrus.[8]

(2) Chapters 49—57 are given to *soteriology*, the doctrine of redemption. They place in contrast the sufferings of God's Servant in the present situation and His glory that shall be revealed in the future. They thus predict a deliverance from a spiritual captivity through the Suffering Personal Servant of the Lord. Each of these first two enneads[9] concludes with the refrain, "No peace . . . to the wicked."

(3) Chapters 58—66 set forth the prophet's *eschatology*, his doctrine of the last days. They place in contrast the hypocrites, the immoral, and the apostates, on the one hand, with the faithful, the mourners, and the persecuted, on the other. Here deliv-

[6]*Op. cit.*, p. 121.

[7]It is not necessary to suppose that 150 years elapsed between cc. 39 and 40. Sennacherib had stripped Judah bare and had almost captured Jerusalem in 701 b.c.

Postulate a prophet, therefore, who was constantly looking for comfort to the future (1:27-28; 2:2-4; 6:13; 7:16; 8:4; 10:20-23; 11:6-16; 17:14; 18:7; 19:19-25; 26:20; 29:5, 17-24; 30:31; 31:8; 32:16-20; 33:17-24; 35:10; 37:26-29, 33-35; 38:5-6), and cc. 40 ff. find a most satisfactory setting at the close of the eighth century b.c. The problem of prime importance before the prophet's mind would naturally be to explain why Jehovah allowed His own chosen people to be thus humiliated (Geo. L. Robinson, *op. cit.*, p. 131).

[8]The rich symbolism of this name applies to much more than a Persian conqueror, as the commentary where this name appears will seek to show.

[9]"Ennead" refers to the ninefold arrangement within each of these three major sections.

160

erance is in the form of a new creature and a new creation, involving, as it does, the future glory of the sons of God and the fate of the wicked. This section concludes with the prediction of "peace . . . like a river" (66:12) to the redeemed in contrast with the destiny of the reprobates in a death where "their worm shall not die, neither shall their fire be quenched" (66:24).

Of the setting and mood of the second major section, Delitzsch observes:

> The prophet lives among the exiles, but not in such tangible reality as Ezekiel, but like a spirit without visible form. We learn nothing directly about the time and place of his appearance. He floats along through the exile like a being of a higher order, like an angel of God; and one must needs confess that this distinction may be used to support the view that the life and action of the Deutro-Isaiah in the exile is an ideal one, not like Ezekiel's corporeal.[10]

A good case can be made from the allusions to place, history, idolatry, and the like, that these point, not to an author living during the exile in Babylon, but to one living in the Holy Land. And though Delitzsch accepts a different author for chapters 40—66, still he further admits:

> And yet much seems to be better explained when chaps. xl—lxvi are regarded as testamentary discourses of the one Isaiah, and the entire prophetic collection as the progressive development of his incomparable charism. For the deliverance predicted, with its attendant circumstances, appears in these discourses as something beyond the range of creaturely foreknowledge, and known to Jehovah alone, and, when it takes place, proclaiming Him the God of gods. Jehovah, the God of prophecy, knows the name of Cyrus before he does himself, and by predicting the name and work of Israel's deliverer proves His Godhead to the whole world, xlv. 4—7. And if chaps. xl—lxvi are not cut off from chaps. i—xxxix and taken by themselves, the entire first half of the collection forms, as it were, a staircase leading up to these discourses to the exiles.[11]

The two hemispheres of Isaiah's book lift up for us a significant contrast. In the first the road that leads into captivity and exile is ever before the prophet's mind. But in the second that which leads back from exile to the city of God is ever uppermost in his thinking. In both, however, he stands as the herald of divine revelation to the nations.

Space does not permit further arguments for the unity of

---

[10]*Op. cit.,* p. 124.
[11]*Ibid.,* pp. 125-26.

these chapters with the thirty-nine that precede them, but the following observation from C. von Orelli is correct:

> The only view known to Jewish tradition (apart from gently hinted doubts of Ibn Ezra) is that the entire book of Isaiah has the prophet of this name for its author, to whose fame as a great, or the greatest, prophet the Second Part (xl—lxvi) contributed not a little.[12]

He further observes the fact that if this tradition be rejected then "one thing remains utterly unexplained—the anonymity of so glorious a book, carefully arranged by the author himself." He then states: "But that the prophet was one anointed with God's Spirit in rare degree, is proved by the unique matter of his treatise."[13]

This embarrassing speculation about an anonymous prophet is removed if one holds that both hemispheres of this great prophecy are from the pen of the prophet and statesman of Jerusalem, the one Isaiah. We believe, as does George L. Robinson, that "Isaiah's message of comfort in chapters 40—66 . . . was addressed to the remnant of Judah in Judah, and to Jerusalem, which survived the disaster of 701 B.C."[14] It is quite probable that Isaiah survived the crisis by at least another decade.

[12]*Op. cit.*, p. 210.

[13]*Ibid.*, p. 215.

[14]*The Bearing of Archaeology on the Old Testament* (New York: The American Tract Society, 1941), p. 102.

Section **VIII** *The First Ennead:*
The Incomparable Deity

Isaiah 40:1—48:22

A. THE COMFORT AND THE MAJESTY OF GOD, 40:1-31

Here the gospel of redemption is announced and assured. The prophet returns to the theme he had introduced at the climax of c. 35 prior to the interlude and amplifies for us its fuller implications throughout the carefully organized chapters that follow.

1. *The Eternal One's Unfailing Consolations* (40:1-11)

Verses 1-11 comprise the introduction to all of the twenty-seven chapters that follow. God commands that a message of comfort and pardon shall be given to His people, while herald voices are raised to prepare for the advent of incomparable Deity.

a. The voice of God with a message of grace (40:1-2). The divine announcement is that servitude is ended, iniquity is pardoned, and sin is expiated. The command, **Comfort . . . comfort** (1), expressed in a double imperative, is characteristic of Isaiah's style. The Greek OT uses the very verb from which we get our noun "Comforter" (cf. John 14:16, 26). The phrase **my people** recalls the covenant relationship in which God declared Israel to be His own possession (Exod. 19:5-6; Lev. 20:26; Deut. 7:6; 14:2). Hosea had found it necessary to say, "Ye are not my people" (Hos. 1:9), but now Isaiah sees approaching the time of grace promised by him (Hos. 2:23). Furthermore, the divine command is, "Speak to the heart" (KJV margin) of **Jerusalem** (2), in a consoling manner. **Her warfare is accomplished** is better translated, "Her forced labor is ended." **Her iniquity is pardoned** bespeaks the fact that payment has been made in full and her punishment has been accepted. **Double for all her sins** is simply an Oriental hyperbole. "Jerusalem has not suffered more than it deserved; but God's compassion now regards what His justice was forced to inflict on Jerusalem as super abundant."[1]

---

[1]Delitzsch, *op. cit.*, p. 135.

"How full of pity God is, to take so much account of the sufferings sinners have brought upon themselves! How full of grace to reckon those sufferings double the sins that had earned them."[2]

b. *The voice of prophecy with a message of righteousness* (40:3-5). **The voice . . . in the wilderness** (3) sounds from a personality that vanishes in the splendor of his calling. **The way of the Lord** has frequent mention in Isaiah. "Level a highroad for our God across the desert" (Moffatt).

The figure in v. 4 is drawn from the engineering operations of the roadmakers for kings of the East. The command continues: Let **every valley . . . be exalted,** and let **the crooked . . . be made straight.** Isaiah's reference is to the basalt outcroppings. Lava rock is difficult terrain over which to build roadway. **The rough places** (the rocky heights) must be leveled. Thus, "on the back of the voice which sets our heart right with God, comes the voice to set the world right, and no man is godly who has not heard both."[3] The downcast must be encouraged, the self-righteous and the carnally secure must be humbled, dishonesty must give way to sincerity, and pride of status must be given up. All this is involved in preparing a highway for our own God through the desolations of our society to the hearts of men.

The glory of the Lord (5; *kebod Yahweh*) involves a visible manifestation of the invisible God, whose coming marks the unveiling of His glory (I Pet. 4:13). The Greek of the Septuagint reads, "The salvation of God." Note that this salvation is for all men. **All flesh shall see it,** since Christ is a universal Saviour and God's summons is to all mankind. Isaiah is sure that this is God's command. **The mouth of the Lord** is the prophet's usual confirmation appended to his inspired proclamations (cf. 1:20).

c. *The voice of faith with a message of reassurance* (40:6-8). **The voice said, Cry,** means, in our modern speech, that Isaiah heard a voice out of the unseen saying, "Preach!" The prophet responded, "What shall I preach?" Isaiah knew that if any man is to speak a life-giving message it must be God-given (cf. 6:8).

The reply from the heavenlies told Isaiah to proclaim the fact of human frailty and transiency: **All flesh is as grass, and all the goodliness thereof** (6). Any claims man has to grace and beauty are only temporary, like **the flower of the field.** Man's

---

[2]George Adam Smith, *op. cit.*, p. 79-80.
[3]*Ibid.*, p. 81.

little demonstrations of prowess are all short-lived. Isaiah's contrast is between the transitoriness of man and the eternity of God and His word.

In the expression, **The spirit of the Lord bloweth upon it** (7), Isaiah has reference to that hot wind from the east known in Palestine as the sirocco.[4] "When in May the sirocco begins to blow, the spring flora acquires at a stroke an autumn look."[5] Homer wrote, "As are the generations of leaves, so are those of men" (cf. 37:27; Job 8:12; 14:2; Ps. 90:5-6). **Surely the people is grass** in comparison with the transcendent majesty of God. Man is both transient and ephemeral. In a perishing world, only God endures.

But the word of our God shall stand for ever (8). Above the change and decay that we see all around us, the Word of God abides. It is more permanent than nature. It is dynamic and outgoing, since it partakes of the nature of God himself (I John 2:17). The Word of our own God[6] stands as a mighty, transforming force within human history, accomplishing that whereunto it was sent.

d. The voice of evangelism with a message of restoration (40:9-11). In this passage the prophet expresses the confident faith that the Lord comes to rule, and to shepherd His own. **O Zion, that bringest good tidings** (9), has been alternately translated in the margin: "O thou that tellest good tidings to Zion." This is the well-known version of it in Handel's *Messiah*. C. von Orelli renders it: "Zion, thou messenger of joy."[7] Delitzsch would prefer, "Evangelist Zion."[8] Since the word for **bringest good tidings** is feminine in the Hebrew, George Adam Smith suggests: "Heraldess of good news." He says it is "the feminine participle of a verb meaning to thrill, or give joy, by means of good news."[9] The Greek term in the Septuagint (*euangelion*) is the one from which we get our word evangelist.

Get thee up into the high mountain recalls the fact that Jerusalem sits atop a height overlooking the Jordan rift and the wilderness of Judea. The command is to mount the heights and

---

[4]The Hebrew is *Ruach Yahweh*, "breath of the Lord." The Hebrew term for *breath, wind,* and *spirit* is in each case *ruach*.
[5]Delitzsch, *op. cit.,* p. 138.
[6]The literal Hebrew meaning of *Dabar Elohenu*.
[7]*Op. cit.,* p. 221.   [8]*Op. cit.,* p. 139.
[9]*Op. cit.,* p. 84.

shout aloud the message of salvation. Zion dare not keep it to herself.

Yet the command is not simply to tell the good news, but to do it with full-throated vehemence. **Lift up thy voice with strength; lift it up, be not afraid.** Modern speech would say, "Speak up! and speak out! do not be ashamed!" The title, **O Zion . . . O Jerusalem,** in its twofold nature, is frequent in Isaiah's prophecies (2:3; 10:12, 32; 24:23; 31:9; 37:22, 32; 41:27; 52:1-2; 62:1; 64:10). This argues for a unity of authorship for the entire book.

Zion's immediate task is one of "home missions," for the command is: **Say unto the cities of Judah,** this notwithstanding the correlative emphasis by Isaiah upon "world missions." Israel's missionary task at home and to the nations is one of Isaiah's major themes. God's people must become ambassadors of salvation.

Behold your God is a dramatic expression equivalent to "Look, here comes your God!"[10] Isaiah's reassurance is that, in spite of all appearances to the contrary, the Eternal One is still active within the arena of history and is still the Keeper of His covenant. God is not dead! He isn't even sick!

Behold, the Lord God will come with strong hand (10) is Isaiah's way of saying that He will come "as a mighty one" (ASV). He will come not only to *be* strong but to show himself strong in the manner of a conqueror. **His arm shall rule for him,** subduing all resistance and winning for himself the Kingdom.

Behold, his reward is with him is in keeping with the fact that "an Arab sheikh, after conquering some rival tribe, usually comes back driving his plunder of livestock before him [cf. Isa. 62:11; Rev. 22:12]" (Berk., fn.). This is an eschatological note indicating that God has for friend and foe the reward prepared that is fitting to each. **And his work before him** simply indicates divine retribution upon the ungodly. Hence Delitzsch translates it: "Behold His reward is with Him and His retribution before Him."[11]

The final picture of God is that of the Divine Shepherd. **He shall feed his flock like a shepherd** (11) is known to all Chris-

---

[10]There should be a comma following **behold,** as is the case in most of the more recent translations.

[11]*Op. cit.,* p. 140.

tians through the oft hearing of Handel's *Messiah.* Isaiah beheld God in both aspects of His infinite sovereignty: with strength to subdue His enemies and a compassionate gentleness for all the members of His flock. Verse 10 sees Him strong; v. 11 sees Him tender and gentle. Meekness is simply strength grown tender. **The lambs** newborn and the ewes giving suck[12] need special care. A mother sheep with a heavy udder of milk should not be overdriven, and some newborn lambs are yet too weak to travel. In that case they must be carried by the shepherd. This prophecy reminds us of another which describes the compassion of Christ: "A bruised reed shall he not break, and the smoking flax shall he not quench" (42:3; cf. Matt. 12:20). Hence this prologue to the second hemisphere of Isaiah's prophecies concludes, as it began, with a note of comfort. Isaiah sees that God has not abandoned this world to chaos; He rules and still shepherds all.

2. *The Eternal One's Unique Character* (40:12-31)

Isaiah now preaches a homily on the immeasurable greatness of the Creator as it is displayed in the works of nature and His government of the world. It expands the idea of vv. 6-8. Isaiah could make use of sharp and penetrating argument. He illustrates the greatness of God by an appeal to the magnitude of His operations as Creator (12), the perfect sufficiency of His knowledge (13-14), the insignificance of all that exists in comparison with Him (15-17), and the fact that no finite representation can be made of Him (18-31).

a. *Lord of creation* (40:12-17). (a) Isaiah speaks of God as Ultimate Creativity (12). **Who hath** should be read, "Who ever measured the waters in the hollow of his hand?" (Moffatt) No idol can survive comparison with the Creator in the magnitude of His operations. The utter futility of measuring the divine works by the palm, the **span,**[13] the **measure,** the **scales,** and the **balance,** is set forth in strong words. God has given dimensions even to His space world which are beyond man's comprehension.

(b) Underived wisdom (13-14) on the part of God is next

---

[12]The Hebrew *luth* is from *ul,* "to suckle, to give milk." Hence those that are with young are those with lambs at their sides. The sheep are not taken to the heights for the summer pasture until after the lambing season is finished.

[13]A **span** is the distance between the point of the little finger and the thumbnail when the hand is widened as far as possible. A **measure** is about one-half of a bushel.

extolled. **Who hath directed the Spirit of the Lord?** (13) No one has the Spirit of God under his private direction. That Spirit who brooded over the primeval chaos and shaped it into a cosmos hardly needs an earthly counselor. **With whom took he counsel?** (14) Whoever was called in to give God advice about justice, knowledge, or prudence?

(c) Unlimited power is another characteristic of true Deity (15-16). The greatest of **the nations** is but **a drop of a bucket** or **the small dust of the balance** (15). Recent studies would change the translation from "bucket" to "rain cloud." Hence the nations in comparison to God's greatness are no more than one drop of rain in a whole storm. They are no weightier than one grain of sand on the scales. Even the isles are like a speck of dust. God handles the islands as easily as a handful of earth. **Lebanon is not sufficient** (16) with all its mighty forests to furnish the necessary wood for a sacrifice to such a God, nor could all its wild beasts constitute an appropriate offering to Him. Like other Old Testament writers, Isaiah is certain that the only acceptable offering for God is the humble and responsive spirit (58:5; 66:2; cf. Mic. 6:6-8).

(d) Unchallenged superiority is the theme of v. 17. **All nations . . . are . . . less than nothing.** This being the case, those commentators who think that God built His hopes on the power and worldly success of a Persian king[14] have missed the true interpretation. The exploits of an earthly Cyrus cannot be the main facet of Isaiah's hopes either. Here the nations are compared to that primeval chaos (cf. *tohu* of Gen. 1:2) which was much weightier than they are. The **nations** and the **nothing** are contrasted in the prophet's mind, and the latter is the more significant. **Vanity** would here be "worthlessness" (Berk.).

b. *Incomparable Deity* (40:18-31). (1) No human craftsman can fashion God's likeness (18-20). **To whom then will ye liken God?** (18) is the question addressed to that universal error of thinking that the Deity can be represented by the works of human hands (cf. Acts 17:29). God allows no imaginary representations of His person, for there is not His like in all the universe. But Isaiah's question is a good one for our day—"What do you think God is like?" **The workman** and **the goldsmith** (19) may cooperate with the smith casting the image and the smelter over-

---

[14]Cf. James D. Smart, *op. cit.,* p. 58.

laying it **with gold** and soldering onto it **silver chains.** These would be for wealthy idolaters. The poverty-stricken would select a piece of mulberry wood that **will not rot** (20) and from it carve an idol. Or he would seek out a clever carpenter to set it up so that it **shall not be moved** (totter). The fact that it might fall over would be a bad omen (cf. Judg. 6:25-31) and suggests its finite impotence. Isaiah's God, on the other hand, is not subject to either tumbling or termites. **Oblation** (20) would be an offering.

(2) No earthly inhabitant can equal God (21-24). **Have ye not known . . . heard . . . understood?** (21) The prophet appeals to the primary intuitions of mankind (cf. Rom. 1:20) for the arguments from natural theology, i.e., creation reveals God's eternal power and deity. Once a person takes into consideration the infinite variety of the universe, only a fool would think he could manufacture a copy of God. **He sitteth upon the circle of the earth** (22). "He sits enthroned on the canopy of the earth, so its inhabitants seem like grasshoppers, he stretches out the heavens like fine cloth, and spreads them out like a tent to dwell in."[15] Likewise it is He **that bringeth the princes to nothing** (23). Before Him dictators come to nought and earthly rulers are mere negation (cf. Job 12:21; Ps. 107:40).[16] It is God's prerogative to remove monarchs from their thrones and consign them to oblivion. "Scarcely planted, scarcely sown, scarcely rooted in the earth, when at a puff from him they wither, the storm sweeps them off like straw" (24, Moffatt).

(3) The stars in the heavens are subject to the Creator (25-26). **To whom then . . . shall I be equal?** (25) is the divine question for which there is no human answer. The challenge is, "Find Me an equal if you can!" Thus speaks the **Holy One.**[17] **Lift up your eyes . . . and behold . . . he calleth them all by names** (26). Some may worship stars as gods, but Isaiah's God is the Great Shepherd of the stars. He calls their names and leads their courses in such precision that **not one faileth.** "He who leaves out of sight no single star in the host of heaven will not forget or neglect the weakest of His flock upon earth."[18] Schiller writes:

[15]Von Orelli, *op. cit.,* p. 224; cf. Moffatt's translation.

[16]Cf. George A. F. Knight, *op. cit.,* p. 39.

[17]This name for God is used in Isaiah 1—39 twelve times, and in 40—66 thirteen times, a fact which argues for identity of authorship.

[18]Von Orelli, *op. cit.,* p. 228.

> *By golden gates He leads them forth;*
> *He counts them over every night;*
> *However oft He takes the path,*
> *His lambs ne'er wander from His sight.*

(4) Such a God is unfailing in His comfort (27-31). (a) His is a solicitude unquestioned and unbounded (27-28a). **Why sayest thou . . . My way is hid?** (27) If God knows and shepherds the stars, He is not unmindful of man, nor unconcerned about the vindication of His own. God's people are not subjects of unheeding fate, nor are their rights disregarded. Again the question, **Hast thou not known?** (28) The Lord is an **everlasting God** who never tires and never lacks insight (cf. Job 5:9; 9:10; Rom. 11:33). (b) His is a strength unfailing (28b-29). **He giveth power to the faint . . . he increaseth strength** (29). He who is never weary strengthens those who are tired, "and upon him that is of no might, He lavisheth power."[19] (c) God has insight unsearchable (28), since there is no plumbing of the depths of **his understanding.** (d) God offers a sustenance unwearying (30-31). Though age and vigor be at their prime, **even . . . youths** and **young men shall . . . fall** (30). Natural strength at its best can be exhausted, but not so the supernatural.[20] Hence **they that wait upon the Lord** in the expectancy of faith rise above the mundane, have stamina for endurance, and find grace for dogged persistence. "For the faithful there is no failure, and faith knows no weariness."[21]

In 28-30 we have the promise of "Strength for Holy Living." (1) God provides strength, 29; (2) Strength is renewed by waiting on the Lord, 31a; (3) God adjusts the supply of strength to the present need, 31b; (G. B. Williamson).

B. Israel Assured of Help, 41:1-29

In this chapter God challenges the reality of heathen gods. Power to predict future events pertains only to Deity. Hence there is an appeal made both to the past fulfillment and to the future predictions which Isaiah's God has achieved. The Lord's

---

[19]George Adam Smith, *op. cit.,* p. 99.

[20]George Rawlinson translates it: "Should even the youths faint and be weary, and should the young men utterly fail, yet they that wait upon the Lord shall renew their strength."

[21]Plumptre, *op. cit., ad. loc.*

prediction of Israel's deliverance is proof of His divinity, and the inability of idols to do anything is proof of their nothingness. The contest between Israel's God and the heathen is given in vv. 1-7. The comforting declaration of God's help and love for His people follows in 8-20. The challenge of the gods of the nations climaxes the chapter in 21-29.

1. *Only God Can Both Predict and Perform* (41:1-7)

a. Summoning the nations (41:1). The argument begun in the previous chapter now continues. God invites **islands** (heathen nations) into a disputation with Him respecting the comparative power of himself and their idols. "Let the islands cease their clamor and come to me, let the peoples of the world take heart afresh; so let them come and plead their cause; we will submit the question to an arbiter, they and I" (Knox).

b. Summoning their conqueror (41:2-4). Here is an argument from history. **Who raised up the righteous man from the east?**[22] i.e., Who raised up Abraham and called him, giving him the power to conquer nations and kings? (Genesis 14) It was the Eternal One. Therefore what God has begun in Abraham, He will carry to its fulfillment in the transformed Israel of the future. He is the Alpha and Omega of destiny (cf. 43:10, 13; 46:4; 48:12; Rev. 1:8, 17-18 with John 8:58). The Lord God brings both creation and history into existence; He governs His universe and directs the course of history.

c. The heathen coalition (41:5-7). These verses are a description of the fearful scurrying of the assembled nations at the divine portrayal of their destiny. They **saw it, and feared** (5), then sought to bolster each other's courage. It may be that a new god is needed to oppose the activities of Israel's God. The **carpenter . . . goldsmith** (7) and other workmen cooperate, and when their production is finished they fasten it securely **with nails** so that it will not totter. It is a supreme touch of irony. Thus is seen the approaching twilight of the pagan gods.

[22]To whom does the prophet have reference? Modern critics almost unanimously decide in favor of Cyrus. Yet such commentators as Torrey, Kissane, Adam Clarke, Calvin, and the Jewish exegetes see a great argument being developed on the basis of Israel's history. Hence the person referred to is Abraham, raised up from the east (Ur of the Chaldees), and from the north (Haran).

2. *Israel's Assurance of God's Help* (41:8-20)

a. *Israel can depend on God* (41:8-10). The election of **Israel** in the person of **Abraham** is the pledge of her deliverance in the coming crisis. She is assured of God's protection. This is the lesson from the call of Abraham. **But thou** (8) stands in apposition to the preceding and hence is emphatic. Nor is the title **my servant** to be read "My petted" or "pampered" one. It is an honorable predicate. **The seed of Abraham** is a significant concept for later New Testament writers,[23] and **Abraham my friend** has taken on rich meaning for all of his descendants (cf. Jas. 2:23).

From the ends of the earth (9) would thus indicate Ur of the Chaldees, on the extreme edge of the prophet's horizon, provided he lived in Palestine. Neither Ur nor Haran could be called the end of the earth from the standpoint of Babylon. **Chief men** is better translated "the corners thereof" (ASV). **I have chosen thee** would indicate that Israel had not made its own God (as in the case of the pagans) but, conversely, God had called and created Israel. **Thou . . . my servant** would indicate that this election was not to be an unconditional salvation but to a special service. If it is to mean Israel's salvation, she too must make her "calling and election sure" (II Pet. 1:10).

The persistent emphasis upon the personal pronoun **I** is calculated to signify the Divine Presence. God promises to **uphold** His servant with **the right hand of my righteousness** (10), "with my victorious right hand" (Heb.). **I will strengthen thee**—equip you for conflict; **I will help thee**—in the actual strain of the conflict; **I will uphold thee**—sustain you to the point of actual victory.

b. *Israel's opposers shall be confounded* (41:11-13). All who burn with enmity against God's people **shall be ashamed and confounded** (11). People who attack them **shall be as nothing** (12). The divine promise is, **I . . . will hold thy right hand** (13). Here is the uplift of Omnipotence!

c. *God's help assures victory* (41:14-16). God can take a worm and thresh a mountain, but first He must find the worm. **Thou worm Jacob** (14) describes vividly human weakness and

---

[23]Cf. Heb. 2:16. Paul used it in three different senses: (1) the seed of Abraham according to the flesh—Jew; (2) heirs of the faith of Abraham; and (3) "the Seed," which is Christ. Hence the election of Israel in the OT must be understood in the light of the NT idea of the calling and election of the Church. But (1) the visible Church falls short; (2) the invisible Church approximates it; and (3) only the person of Christ fulfills it.

helplessness. **Ye men** is better translated "thou insect." Hence Knight states it: "Do not be afraid, thou worm Jacob, thou louse Israel"![24] God does not choose us because we are great but because we yield to His love and purpose (Deut. 7:7). In the expression **thy redeemer** may be seen the influence of the Book of Job (Job 19:25). The concept of the kinsman-redeemer is conveyed by the great Hebrew term *Go'el* (Lev. 25:47-49). Abraham had served as such in the rescue of his kinsman Lot (Genesis 14). **The Holy One of Israel** is Isaiah's familiar name for God (Isa. 1:4).

The idea of a **sharp threshing instrument** (15) depicts invincibility. The prophecy, **Thou shalt thresh the mountains . . . and . . . make the hills as chaff,** would indicate a crushing victory. The threshing sledges with sharp prongs protruding on their underside are still used in Palestine and drawn round and round over the flat, stone threshing floors upon which the grain in the stalk has been piled. Restored to the divine favor, Israel becomes a terrible instrument of judgment to the nations, especially her enemies. "Before God's people the proudest peaks of the world of foreign nations must stoop and be trodden to dust."[25] And after threshing comes the winnowing (16).

From 13-16, Dr. P. F. Bresee preached on "The Agency and Instrumentalities of Holy Victory." (1) God can use unpromising instruments—**thou worm Jacob,** 14; (2) Through yielded lives God can win astounding victories, 15; (3) The instrument of spiritual victory is divine truth—"the word of God . . . quick and powerful," 15-16.

d. God will do exploits on behalf of Israel (41:17-20). The nation will be changed from a state of misery to one of happiness; the land now desolate will become luxuriant and fertile. In a land where a frequent occurrence is the **tongue** parched with **thirst** (17), God promises **rivers in high places . . . fountains in . . . valleys . . . the wilderness** shall become **a pool . . . and the dry land springs of water** (18). Here again is evidence that the terrain in full view of the prophet is not Babylon but Palestine. **I will plant** (19) **the cedar, the shittah tree** (acacia), **the myrtle** (which grows only in the state of Oregon and in Palestine), **the oil tree** (olive), **the fir, the pine,** and **the box tree** (cypress),

---

[24]*Op. cit.,* p. 57.
[25]Von Orelli, *op. cit.,* p. 231.

bespeaks a *land* transformed as well as the *people*. All this is to
the intent that they may **see ... know ... consider, and understand** (20) that the eternal God hath done it. He alone is the
Source of all good.

3. *The Lord Challenges False Gods* (41:21-29)

The question raised here is, Can the nations and their gods
frustrate the plans of the living God? Let the gods give proof
of their power! Let them point out some event in the past which
they have foretold and duly performed, or let them foretell the
future. God had foretold the growth and triumph of the family of
Abraham and He had brought it to pass. This is the guarantee
that the prophecy now made will likewise be fulfilled (25-28).

Produce your cause (21), i.e., "Let your idols come forward
which you consider to be so very strong."[26] Bring forward your
lawsuit, produce your case if you have any. "The false gods are
called upon to come forth and appear in person; and to give evident demonstration of their foreknowledge and power by foretelling future events, and exerting their power in doing good or
evil."[27] **Strong reasons** would mean impregnable proofs. The
challenge continues: **Shew us what shall happen** (22). Let's
see whether event corresponds to prediction. Israel's God can
show such fulfillment of former prophecies, and He is ready to
declare further things still to come. **Shew the things that are to
come hereafter** (23) is the challenge to prophesy. **Do good, or
do evil**; either activity might prove their gods had life. But the
gods of the pagans are "worse than nothing" (24, margin). Their
origin and being are essentially from nothingness (cf. I Cor. 8:40),
and they inspire false hopes in their worshippers. It is only the
true God who is known to have **raised up one from the north**
(25), who also came from the **rising of the sun,** "one that calleth
upon" (ASV) His **name,** even Abraham. Who is the One who has
predicted with such accuracy that we might say, "That's right!"?
(26) Who is the One faithful to His pledged word with power to
effect it? No one like this may be found among the false gods.
It was I who first told it to Zion; I will give her a messenger of
good tidings (27). "As for your idols, I see no one, not a prophet
in their midst, to answer my inquiries!" (28, Moffatt) Idols are
vain; their makers are confused; metal **images** are only an empty

---

[26]Adam Clarke, *op. cit., ad loc.*
[27]*Ibid.*

negation (29). Such, then, is the Eternal One's indictment of the false gods of pagan nations.

C. God Introduces His Chosen "Servant," 42:1-25

In this chapter Isaiah brings us another step forward in his portrait of the Holy One of Israel. Chapter 40 sets forth His uniqueness and His incomparable deity; c. 41 places Him in bold contrast with the nonexistent gods of the heathen. Now, in c. 42, God's divinely redemptive purpose is set before us in the person and characteristics of His Servant. "Next to Jehovah Himself, the Servant of Jehovah is by far the most important personage within our prophet's gaze. He is named, described, commissioned and encouraged over and over again throughout the prophecy."[28] The Servant appears as a human figure of lofty character and unfailing perseverance, a reflection of the very nature of God, who makes God's work of redemption His own, and partakes of the divine compassion. The divine purpose in history is the establishing of God's rule in the hearts of men that thereby they may realize justice, peace, and freedom.

This chapter is full of contrasts. Verses 1-4 are in contrast with vv. 10-17, and vv. 5-9 are in contrast with vv. 18-21. But even within some of its verses there is contrast, as seen in v. 9, for example, between the former things and the new things. Likewise, herein we see righteousness as both meek and militant.

1. *The Ideal Servant and His Work* (42:1-9)

In this section God is speaking, first, to introduce His Servant[29] Messiah; and second, to announce through Him the institution of an entirely new covenant with His people.

a. The meek but majestic servant of Jehovah (42:1-4). This, the first of the so-called "Servant Songs" of Isaiah's prophecy, is concerned with *the character* of the Servant. The second (49:1-6) is concerned with *the calling* of the Servant. The third (50:4-9) depicts *the work* of the Servant. The fourth, and longest (52:

---

[28]George Adam Smith, *op. cit.*, p. 132.

[29]Delitzsch sees the Isaianic concept of the Servant beginning with all Israel, decreasing to the remnant, and culminating in the one suffering Mediator; who, as the Second David, calls forth a second Israel made up of the partakers of salvation, who in turn become the second Adam or the new race of the redeemed. This he thinks of as a rising pyramid at whose apex is the Saviour, who becomes the Seed of a transformed, spiritual, and expanding Israel (*op. cit.*, p. 174).

13—53:12), spells out *the fate* of the Servant. Here the Servant is characterized as sustained, elect, pleasing, anointed, and just (1); unassuming and unostentatious (2); gentle and truthful (3); faithful, courageous, and promoting true religious faith throughout the earth (4).

Behold my servant . . . mine elect (1). We must agree with Plumptre that the characterization here points to more than the visible or even the ideal Israel, but rather to One who is the center of both, with attributes which are reproduced in His people only to the extent that they fulfill the divine ideal. At least we must recognize here a type of our Lord Jesus Christ, since what is affirmed of this **servant** goes infinitely beyond anything to which a prophet was ever called, or of which man has ever been capable. It must therefore refer to the future Messiah (the Anointed). This is also the view of the Jewish exegetes in their Targum (cf. also Matt. 12:17-21).

"He will not be contentious or a lover of faction" (2, Knox). He will rather be the exact opposite of those lying teachers who endeavored to exalt themselves by noisy demonstrations. He brings that which commends itself in character and therefore it requires no forced trumpeting.

"A broken reed he will not crush, and glimmering flax he will not quench; he will bring forth right with faithfulness" (3, Von Orelli). Tender pastoral care will be His course of action toward a bruised and battered humanity, burdened to the point of discouragement and death amidst life's injustices. All such He will seek to save and not destroy. He will bring justice **(judgment)** [30] to reality.

His zeal will not be extinguished till He shall have secured for right a firm standing in the earth. This means He will also be welcomed by a Gentile world that is already conscious of its need (4). The cry for redemption is a universal yearning of the human race.

[30]The Hebrew term for "justice" is *Mishpat.* Its four main meanings are presented and discussed in a footnote by George Adam Smith, *op. cit.,* p. 229. q.v.: (1) In a general sense it has reference to a legal process (cf. 41:1) which culminates in justice for all concerned. (2) It has reference to a person's cause or rights (40:27; 49:4). (3) It may specify an ordinance instituted by Jehovah for the life and worship of His people (58). (4) In general it has reference also to the sum of the laws given by Jehovah to Israel (51:5; 58:2). It thus runs parallel to righteousness, truth, and uprightness. Let the Hebrew student also consult the term in Gesenius' *Lexicon.*

The challenge of 1-4 is "Behold My Servant." (1) The person of the Servant, upheld by God, who delights in Him and puts His Spirit upon Him, 1; (2) The work of the Servant is without display, 2; with infinite patience, 3; with the assurance of victory, 4 (G. B. Williamson).

b. *The medium of a new covenant* (42:5-9). The Servant is now addressed by the eternal and creative God (5). **Thus saith the Almighty and Eternal One**—"craftsman of the world and all the world affords, he who gives being and breath to all that lives and moves on it" (Knox). The idea of Servant is here elevated to the personal apex.[31]

The divine summons is to a universally redemptive mission (6-7). **In righteousness** (6)—"The righteousness of God is the stringency with which He acts in accordance with the will of His holiness."[32] The mission of the Servant is to produce a "covenant people" (Heb., *'am berith*) and a spiritually renewed race (cf. Jer. 31:31-34). To achieve this He will **bring out the prisoners** (7) from their bondage to selfishness and sin, so that their **eyes** may behold what their hope has embraced (Zech. 9:11).

"I am the Eternal One, jealous of My glory, scorning fabricated images, and successful in My predictions. I am *Yahweh,* that is My name, and it means the self-existent, eternal, self-sufficing, independent, omnipotent, living, and life-giving One, whose glory cannot be shared with any sham gods which are mere vanities and nothingness. My former predictions have come to pass, and now I tell you of new things before ever they come to light" (8-9, paraphrasing).

2. *The Servant, a Strong God and Mighty Hero* (42:10-17)

a. *His advent is an occasion for a new song* (42:10-12; cf. Rev. 5:9). No old song will suffice. "Praise him from the sea, all

[31]Delitzsch declares: "An unprejudiced commentator must admit that the 'servant of Jehovah' is pointed out here, as He in Whom and through Whom Jehovah concludes a new covenant with His people, in the place of the old covenant that was broken. . . ." (*op. cit.,* p. 179). He continues: "All that Cyrus did, was simply to throw idolatrous nations into a state of alarm, and set exiles free. But the Servant of Jehovah opens blind eyes; and therefore the deliverance which He brings is not only redemption from bodily captivity, but from spiritual bondage also" (*ibid.,* p. 180).

[32]Delitzsch is commenting here on the Hebrew term *tsedeq,* about which his further comment is: "The action of God in accordance with His purposes of love and His plan of salvation" (*ibid.,* p. 178).

men that sail on it, and all creatures the sea contains; the islands and the island dwellers" (10, Knox). Here, then, is another indication that the prophet's locale is Palestine and not Babylon. "The fulness of the Sea, whose unsearchable depths hide multitudes of silent inhabitants, is to join aloud in the jubilant chorus."[33] Moreover the prophet calls upon the desert with its encampments to raise a shout, and even such ancient enemies as the marauding Arabs of Kedar and the Edomite inhabitants of Petra are to join in the jubilation, shouting it from their highest **mountains** (11). Here again the prophet's locale is Palestine, not Babylon. "All shall give God His praise, till the renown of Him reaches the islands far away" (12, Knox).

b. *He is the Great Avenger* (42:13-17). (*a*) He strides forth to conquer (13). He is like a warrior that stirs up his own rage for the attack and with battle cry flouts His enemies. (*b*) He will no longer forbear to speak and act (14-16). "For an eternity I have kept silent and restrained My speech, but now I will gasp and pant like a woman in birth pangs, and now I will have My say" (14, paraphrasing). "I will turn mountain and hill into a waste, withering all their verdure, make barren islands of the rivers, dry up the marshes" (15, Knox). Thus does the fiery breath of God turn the mountains and hills into heaps of ruins, scorching their vegetation, drying up streams and lakes, and turning the land into a desert. **And I will bring the blind . . . I will make the darkness light before them . . . and not forsake them** (16). When the eyes once blinded by sin are opened to the possibilities of grace for them, then indeed they have discovered new ways of deliverance. These are the things I have just begun to do, says He, and I shall not abandon them. (*c*) Hence those who make idols their gods will surely be put to shame (17). The Lord's glorious acts of judgment and salvation unmask the false gods, to the utter confusion of their worshippers.

3. *The Actual Servant and His Unfitness* (42:18-25)

Isaiah now turns to a contrast of the nation with the Ideal Servant he has to this point been describing.[34]

---

[33]Von Orelli, *op. cit.*, p. 237.

[34]Here we follow the majority of the commentators, but Naegelsbach makes a good case for the position that continues to see here in vv. 18-21 further explications of the picture of the Ideal Servant, even Christ. In that case we have portrayed for us the problem of One so devoted to His task that it is impossible for anything to get His attention.

a. *Blindness has happened unto Israel* (42:18-21; cf. Rom. 11:25). **Hear, ye deaf; and look, ye blind** (18) recalls the prophet's original commission recorded at 6:9. Adam Clarke contends that the question of verse 19 should be changed to read, "Who is [so] blind . . . deaf . . . as he to whom I have sent my messengers?" And further, "Who is so blind as he that is perfectly instructed?" Here is Israel, the servant of God, blind and deaf in a singular and unparalleled way. Those who had been commissioned to be a light to the blind, pathetically enough, were afflicted with the illness which they were supposed to cure in others. **Seeing many things** (20), such as the great acts of God, had been Israel's privilege, but intelligent reception of their intended meaning was lacking. The majority of the Israelites had by contempt quenched the light of God's revelation. Moreover it **pleased** the Lord **for his righteousness' sake to magnify the law, and make it honourable** (21), setting forth its greatness and its glory before His people; but they did not profit by its instruction.

b. *Israel is the prisoner of unbelief* (42:22-25). In spite of Israel's God, she is a plundered and imprisoned people (22). **Who among you will give ear . . . for the time to come?** (23) Surely there must be some among you who will take heed at the divine warnings and repent of your ways! An Israel that has not correct understanding of her past will surely have no right anticipation of her future. **Israel** must realize that her plight is a punishment from her own God, against whom she has sinned and rebelled (24). "Burnt children usually shun the fire; but this nation has learnt no wisdom, although the flames of war have encircled and scorched it."[35] Even the severest chastisements were not taken to heart (25), nor did Israel recognize that the **fire** was kindled by the white heat of God's judgmental love. Hence poor Israel knows "no king but Caesar" (cf. John 19:15).

D. YE ARE MINE: I AM YOUR "HOLY ONE," 43:1—44:5

From a theological standpoint this is a highly significant passage. Now the poet sings of deliverance, having spoken in cc. 41 and 42 of the Deliverer. The mutual reciprocity of the divine-human relationship is stated in the theme for this section of our outline. If God be the Author of His people's punishments (42:25), He is also the Author of their redemption, ingathering,

---

[35]Von Orelli, *op. cit.*, p. 239.

and transformation. They in turn are His witnesses among all nations to the fact that He is the living God. He has chosen them and made them His historical "showcase" to prove that He alone is God and Saviour.

1. The Assurance of Redemption (43:1-8)

a. Preservation promised (43:1-2). The comforting message from the eternal God to the creature He has fashioned is to the effect that Israel is His "purchased possession" and is named for Him alone (1). Adam Clarke contends that the translation should read: "I have called thee by *My* name." To call by name denotes individual choice and appropriation. **Waters . . . river . . . fire** (2) are all symbols of danger. But in the presence of the Great Companion, Israel has nothing to fear. Bridges were lacking in the ancient Near East. Biblical Hebrew has no word for them. But God's promise is that the swollen river shall not wash His people away, nor shall fires passed through **kindle upon** them.

b. Ransom price paid (43:3). Israel's God reminds His people that He already gave **Egypt,** the Sudan, and **Ethiopia** as the price of their **ransom.** The Hebrew tense is perfect; hence it does not refer to a future ransom to be paid to Cyrus for letting the captives return from Babylon. The three nations mentioned were the object of Sennacherib's fury. Bypassing little Jerusalem he never did conquer it. Thus **the Holy One of Israel** had bartered away these three nations to deliver little Judah.

c. A prized possession (43:4). In redemption the love of God achieves its greatest work. "So prized, so honored, so dearly loved, that I am ready to give up mankind in thy place, a world to save thee" (Knox). God is willing to sacrifice all the world for this little people since this little people are to be for all the world. What an "I—thou" relationship this is!

d. A promised rehabilitation (43:5-8). The eternal God will claim His **sons** and **daughters** (6) from the four corners of the compass. By Isaiah's time a fairly wide dispersion of the Hebrews had taken place, as archaeologists now recognize. But as God commanded Pharaoh once to let His people go, so He promises here to so command all nations. "I will restore. . . . Whoever owns my name is my creature, made and fashioned for my glory" (7, Knox).

In 43:1-7, we find "God's Fearless People" described. (1) They are His possession by creation, 1; and by redemption, 2;

(2) They are protected by His presence, 2; (3) Their posterity shall know God's salvation, 5 (G. B. Williamson).

"Bring them out, then, into the light of day, this people of mine that have eyes and still cannot see, have ears, and cannot hear" (8, Knox). "Verse 8 is the climax of the transformation that makes the servant ready for the task."[36] This probably has reference to Israel still unconverted, though Clarke would make it apply to Gentiles.

2. *The Promise of Performance* (43:9-13)

Only the eternal God can both promise and perform it. Hence once again comes Isaiah's procedure of taking **the nations** into court with his three *dramatis personae:* God, the nations, and Israel.

a. Calling the witnesses (43:9-10). **Who among them can declare** (9) that they have gods who are the lords of history? Not these dead idols but the living God has given the interpretation of past events even before they happened. Let the nations call any **witnesses** they can on behalf of their pagan gods! The Eternal One also has testimonials; and He declares to Israel, **Ye are my witnesses** (10). Here the pronouns are emphatic. **Ye** and **my** would indicate that God's people do not exist for themselves alone. They must be God's **witnesses** in order that they may **know . . . believe . . . understand** the real purpose and meaning of their election. **Before me . . . after me . . . no God** would indicate that the Lord has neither predecessor nor successor. The temporal adverbs must not be so construed that the result would be a temporal Deity. God is not a space-time creature. Hence His name—The Eternal One.

b. God takes the witness stand (43:11-13). **I . . . I,** the Eternal One, am the one and only **Saviour** (11). **I . . . declared . . . saved . . . shewed** (12), and it was no alien god that did these things among you; **therefore ye are my witnesses . . . that I am God.** Pagan gods proffer no revelation, and it was no pagan deity that planned and executed the exodus from Egypt. But as day succeeds day, **I remain he,** with power undiminished and holding the destinies of all in **my hand. I will work, and who** (13) can hinder it? (Cf. Job 9:12; 11:10.)

[36]James D. Smart, *op. cit.,* p. 98.

3. *A New Exodus Predicted* (43:14-21)

Isaiah now moves into a section which emphasizes the fact that redemption is by grace (43:14—44:5). **The Holy One of Israel** (14) is the Speaker. The approaching work of redemption is predicted (43:14-21), the sole motive for which is free grace (43:22-28); and the full outcome thereof is the outpoured Spirit of God, producing loyal recruits in abundance (44:1-5).

a. Babylon's frustration (43:14-15). "Thus says the Lord, your Saviour, the Holy One of Israel: For your sake I have sent to Babylon and have brought back all the fugitives and the Chaldeans who glory in their ships. I am the Lord, your Holy One, the Creator of Israel, your King" (*Peshitta* [Lamsa] Version).[37]

b. God of the Exodus speaking (43:16-17). The same God who overwhelmed Pharaoh with his army and chariots in the Red Sea promises deliverance now. The God who can turn **the sea** (16) into a highway, and sink **chariot and horse, the army and the power** (17) like lead beneath its waters, is also able to

---

[37]The Hebrew text of this passage is obscure. The versions evidently did not understand it and any attempt to reconstruct it is largely guesswork. Many of the translations therefore follow the Greek Old Testament (LXX) here. The above quotation from the *Peshitta* makes as good sense as any of them.

There is much to be said in favor of James D. Smart's suggestion that the words **Babylon** and **Chaldeans** be omitted from the verse. It would then read: "For your sakes I will send and cause all the fugitives to embark with rejoicing in their ships" (*op. cit.*, p. 105). See his entire "Excursus on the Babylon-Chaldea Passages" (*ibid.*, pp. 102-6).

The reference here to ships would have been significant in Isaiah's day but not in the time of Cyrus. Chaldean navigation was immense then, according to *Herodotus* 1, 184; and *Strabo* Bk. xvi. That Merodach-baladan, after his defeat by Sennacherib, took flight downstream on Babylonian ships is recorded in an ancient cylindrical inscription of his day. "The ships of Ur" are celebrated at a very remote period in the history of lower Mesopotamia.

Cyrus diverted the Euphrates, and the Persian monarchs built dams and cataracts to prevent upstream navigation against their kingdoms. Hence Clarke and others would insist that this reference is preexilic.

The Chaldeans were a Semitic people who settled in the lower Euphrates valley, and after a long struggle wrested Babylon from the Assyrians, by whom it had been conquered, and established the Chaldean (Babylonian) empire after the fall of Nineveh in 612 B.C. Notice that there is no mention of Cyrus here, and this is the first mention of **Babylon** in this hemisphere of Isaiah's book.

make Israel's enemies **extinct** so that they **are quenched as tow**—
i.e., "out like a light."

c. *Something new in the offing* (43:18-21). The God who
dried up the waters has the ability to supply water in abundance
in the coming deliverance (18). Let God's people therefore turn
from memory to hope, for those epochal events in the past bespeak
decisive events in the future (19). He who makes paths through
the sea will also make a pathway through **the desert** and cause
rivers to spring forth in the howling waste. So the very denizens
of the desert will honor the eternal God because of this change
in their habitat. For the God who once gave drink to Israel in
her desert wanderings can repeat the miracle for the sake of His
chosen ones (20), whereupon **they shall shew forth** His **praise**
(21). Just as the Exodus has significance for Old Testament
saints, so the Resurrection and the new birth have such for those
of us who hold the New Testament faith. The greater intimation
of Isaiah's prophecy is a deliverance from sin's captivity and
bondage, and a new exodus from the Babylon of the godless.

4. *Unworthy Israel and the Forgiving God* (43:22-28)

The Eternal One now speaks His sad indictment of indifferent
Israel. For all My provision and promises your response has not
been worship but rather indifference and sin.

a. *Tired of God* (43:22). **Thou hast not called upon me** . . .
thou hast been weary of me. In each instance the pronoun **me**
is emphatic. A nation tired of its God does but one thing; it
turns to other gods, for man is incurably religious. Such was the
case with **Jacob** and **Israel.** Tiring of God, they turned to a new
faith in pagan allies and their deities. Here we catch a glimpse
of the pain in the heart of the Eternal. Worship offered grudging-
ly is no worship at all.

b. *God is no religious tyrant* (43:23). **Neither hast thou
honoured me with thy sacrifices.**[38] The many **small cattle** of the
morning and evening **burnt offerings,** the oblation of the meal
offering, and the **incense** from the golden altar would not delight
the heart of God so long as Israel had no "heart" in them. "What

---

[38]Many commentators see here a cessation of sacrifices and thus
argue that this was written during the Babylonish captivity, but a similar
cessation of sacrifice must surely have occurred during the rigors of the
Assyrian invasion and the siege of Sennacherib.

the Lord requires is not lavish and expensive offerings, but filial trust in Him and submission to His will."[39]

c. *Israel's offering was not sincerity but sins* (43:24; cf. 1:11, 14). "You have burdened me with your sins" (RSV). "It was I that was burdened, burdened with thy sins; it was I that was troubled, troubled with thy faithlessness" (Knox).

d. *Grace and judgment* (43:25-28). God forgives because He is God. **I . . . I, am he** (25) who alone grants forgiveness and blots out **transgressions** (cf. 1:18).[40] **For mine own sake,** says God. No reason is given but that of His own infinite goodness. "It was I, ever I, that must be blotting out thy offences, for my own honor's sake, effacing the memory of thy sins" (Knox).

Israel has nothing to plead but her guilt (26-28). **Put me in remembrance** (26)—Come, let us settle the matter by frank discussion! If I have missed anything in your favor, remind Me of it! What can you offer by way of argument in self-justification? **Thy first father . . . sinned** (27). This could be either Abraham or Jacob (since Adam is the father not merely of Israel but of all mankind). Archer is perhaps right in saying: "From the standpoint of the laws of justice the Jews had no case to defend, for even their covenant forefather was guilty of sin (in lying to Pharaoh and Abimelech about his wife's status), and their spiritual leaders had turned against the Lord."[41] Both the people and their rulers were guilty, hence both must bear their penalty. "For the guilt of thy first father, for the rebellion of thy own spokesmen against me, I brought thy inviolable princes to dishonour, gave up Jacob to destruction, Israel to the scorn of his enemies" (27-28, Knox). Clarke, however, translates it, as do the *Peshitta* and many modern translations, "Thy princes have profaned my sanctuary," whereas the Greek (LXX) says: "The rulers have defiled my holy things."[42] Sin, therefore, is the

---

[39]Gleason L. Archer, "Isaiah," *The Wycliffe Bible Commentary*, ed. Charles F. Pfeiffer and Everett F. Harrison (Chicago: Moody Press, 1963), p. 640.

[40]This analogy appears in both hemispheres of Isaiah's book and argues for their unity of authorship.

[41]*Op. cit.*, p. 640.

[42]George Adam Smith would translate it: "Therefore I let my holy cities be profaned," citing Hos. 3:4 as warrant for doing so (*op. cit., ad loc.*).

reason for the destruction and reproach of God's people, for sin is a reproach to any nation (Prov. 14:34).

5. *The Outpouring of the Spirit* (44:1-5)

Real salvation is a work of divine grace and the fruit of God's outpoured Spirit. Isaiah now envisages the future glory of Israel because of the refreshing of both the land and its people under the ministry of God's renewing Holy Spirit. It is a promise of spiritual recruits in abundance.

a. *Fear not, O Jacob* (44:1-2). The unfailing love of God returns after judgment like a shower of redeeming grace. **Yet now hear ... my servant ... whom I have chosen** (1). Formerly the Lord turned them over to judgment; now He has become their Helper. **I ... will help thee ... Jesurun** (2). This is a term coined by Isaiah that is a diminutive of endearment, meaning "the upright one." Israel has been chosen for a special mission, and it is because of this that God now promises consolation.

b. *Water and the Spirit* (44:3-4). **Water ... floods ... my spirit ... my blessing** (3) all seem to indicate the invincible, dynamic energy surging from the creative Source of life. Two things are promised: the transformation of nature—man's environment; and the transformation of human nature—man's being. First the symbol, then the reality. **As willows by the water courses** (4) could well mean: like oleanders along the irrigation channels. It is a figure of lush vegetation. James Smart's admonition is timely:

> The parallel in ch. 44:3 between "I will pour water on the thirsty land" and "I will pour my Spirit upon your descendants" is highly important in confirming the impression that in all passages where streams flow in the desert, the desert represents Israel in its barrenness and hopelessness and that the coming of water is the coming of God to transform all things. Thirsty land and men thirsty for God both represent the same reality. The outpouring of the Spirit is the outpouring of God and not just the conferring of certain spiritual benefits upon Israel. This must be kept clearly in mind because the references to the desert have so frequently been assumed to signify the desert between Babylon and Palestine.[48]

c. *New recruits to the covenant* (44:5). The reference here is probably not to the reclamation of defaulting Jews but to new converts from among the heathen. New accessions to the King-

---

[48]*Op. cit.*, p. 110.

dom always follow upon every genuine outpouring of the Holy
Spirit for the Lord adds to the Church those that are being saved
(Acts 2:47). **One shall say, I am the Lord's; and another shall**
make his boast of Jacob's **name; and another shall** inscribe on
his hand the motto: **Unto the Lord,**[44] while still another will lay
claim to the title of Israelite. There is something attractive about
men and women who are genuinely filled with the Spirit. Here
is the secret both of the missionary's motivation and of his
success.

E. "BESIDE ME THERE IS NO GOD," 44: 6-23

This passage places in sharp contrast the only God and the
gods manufactured by human arts and crafts.

1. *No Rock but the Eternal One* (44: 6-8)

The King of Israel is no less than her **redeemer the Lord of
hosts . . . the first, and . . . the last,** and there is none beside Him
(6). **Who** then can predict the future like Him? (7) He it is that
appointed the ancient people Israel. And as a people, Israel has
a far-off past and a distant future. Thus she takes on the nature
of an everlasting people. Only Israel's God is able to **declare . . .
the things that are coming, and shall come.** Let any of the
pagan deities equal this if they can! "Do not be afraid, or bewildered; you can bear me witness that from the first I proclaimed
it in your hearing, there is no other God but I, no other Powers
to rival me" (8, Knox).

2. *The Stupidity of Idolatry* (44: 9-20)[45]

Here we have Isaiah's exposé of the idol factory and its folly.
It takes on the nature of a forthright analysis of the whole process
of producing handmade gods. Isaiah's satire is at its best as he
denounces human attempts to portray God.

a. Self-deception a witness to its own folly (44: 9-11). The
fact is that the works of men can only be less than men—never
greater. So the wretched folly of idolatry is best seen by exposing the base origin of its objects of worship. The makers of

[44]The Code of Hammurabi (226-27) bears evidence of the ancient custom of branding or tattooing the name of the owner on the hand of his slave.

[45]See George Adam Smith's commendable translation of this passage,
op. cit., pp. 153-55.

graven images are all of them vanity (9). Here Isaiah uses again the Hebrew term *tohu*, which specifies primeval chaos. But the vain one is the fabricator, even more so than that which is made. Fashioning images is a futile enterprise. **Their delectable things . . . see not, nor know** and of this their makers and worshippers are themselves **witnesses**. Which is the most inane, the lifeless idol that has neither sight nor knowledge or the stupid one who admires it? Whoever forms **a god,** or casts an **image,** is making a worthless thing—**profitable for nothing** (10). Shame likewise awaits **all his fellows**—whether they be members of his religious fraternity or the partners in his guild of craftsmen (11). They are only **men,** and a man cannot make a God. Even if they stand **together,** each must blush with embarrassment as he looks abashed at his neighbor.

    b. An inanimate object no Saviour and no God (44:12-17). **The smith** works in iron and uses a chisel for iron "cutouts" as he **worketh in the coals,** stooped over the charcoal furnace, **and fashioneth it with hammers** (12). But ere long this god-maker is exhausted **and his strength faileth. He is hungry,** thirsty, and **faint.** But can a tired workman produce an untiring God?

    And **the carpenter** fares no better as a maker of wooden gods (13). He must make rough measurement with the **rule,** then outline it with red chalk. Then comes fitting with **planes, and . . . compass.** And when **after the figure of a man** it takes on some human likeness, it is still only a god in man's own image, though he adds a final touch of **beauty.** So it is made ready for **the house** or temple shrine. Preposterous procedure! Out of crude timber a man? Since certain trees were sacred to different pagan gods, this very carpenter **heweth . . . down cedars . . . cypress . . . oak,** selected in **the forest** (14). And if he cannot find one suitable, **he planteth an ash** for **the rain** to **nourish.** Feature, if you please, this planting of a god! When grown it serves a multiple function. **Then it shall be . . . to burn** and with it **a man** shall **warm himself** and bake **bread** on its glowing embers (15). Or it may be that **he maketh it a graven image, and falleth down thereto.** But it is purely accidental whether the wood serves for fire or for worship. Of course utility and comfort must come first. **Part** for **fire, part** for fuel, **part** for warmth **(16), and the residue thereof he maketh a god** (17), since "leftovers" are sufficient for deity. Real food, real heat, but a man-made "do-nothing" deity is that to which an idolatrous heart

falleth down . . . worshippeth . . . prayeth—that which cannot even hear his cry, **Deliver me . . . my god.**

c. *Idolatry bespeaks a deluded mind* (44:18-20). Such worshippers are like their idols, with **eyes** bedaubed past seeing, **hearts** benumbed past thinking, until they cannot **understand** (18). The heart is the seat of the intellect and will, the central organ of man's being in Hebrew Old Testament psychology. Self-inflicted blindness is the worst form of torture and surpasses Assyrian and Philistine atrocities. Such a one lacks the sense to question, **Shall I make . . . an abomination** and bow **down to the stock of a tree?** (19) Here Isaiah makes even the worshipper "call a spade a spade." "Stump-worshippers" need to be reminded that any such person **feedeth on ashes; a deceived heart** has sent him astray (20). Yet the pity of it all is this: **He cannot deliver his soul** nor admit the **lie in** his **right hand.** Such is the case with a soul too blind and deluded to evaluate his own work, incapable of facing reality, with his critical faculties asleep (I John 5:20-21).

In this passage, with v. 20 as the text, Alexander Maclaren finds "Feeding on Ashes." (1) A life that ignores God is empty of all true satisfaction; (2) Such a man is tragically unaware of his own emptiness; (3) This man needs a power from without to set him free.

3. *The Eternal God Has Fashioned Israel* (44:21-23)

a. *Remember* (44:21). **Remember . . . thou shalt not be forgotten of me**—what comforting words! The whole process involved in the fashioning of idols gives occasion to remind Israel of Him who has been her Fashioner. This is another of Isaiah's vivid contrasts. Twice comes the assuring reminder, **Thou art my servant.** Again these pronouns are emphatic. Pagans fashion their gods, but the Eternal One fashions Israel (cf. 44:12 and 21).

b. *Return* (44:22). "The cloud of thy guilt, the haze of thy sinfulness, I have swept away; come back to me, thy ransomer" (Knox). As the rising sun dispels the fogs that are so frequent in Palestine, so the Sun of heaven dispels Israel's sins. God sweeps them all away as a brisk wind does the clouds.

c. *Rejoice* (44:23). This is the grand conclusion to the whole matter. "For the Lord has redeemed Jacob, and is revealing his glory in Israel" (Smith-Goodspeed). 'Tis the Lord's doing; therefore burst forth into jubilant song, O **heavens** above and **earth** below! The heavenly luminaries were thought by the ancients to sing. We moderns have heard music transmitted on beams of light by modern science. Earth's canyons and **mountains** are to be heard echoing the jubilation of the redeemed. Even the whispering pine tree must add its plaintive note, while the tremolo is to be supplied by the quaking aspen leaves. **Heavens** ... **earth** ... **mountains** ... **forest**—man's environment —all seem to **sing** once **Jacob** is reconciled to his God.

F. GOD COMMISSIONS CYRUS AND ASSURES ISRAEL, 44:24—45:25

1. *The Eternal Redeemer's Message* (44:24-28)

This direct discourse is from the transcendent Deity who declares himself to be the Creator of nature, the Confounder of knaves, the Confirmer of His servants, the Constructor of Jerusalem, and the Caller of Cyrus.[46] Isaiah introduces the speaker as the Eternal Redeemer who has fashioned Israel from birth. Whereupon the One so named proclaims His message.

a. *Deity in action* (44:24-26a). God is the Maker of **all things** (note how the Hebrew speaks of **all things** rather than cosmos, as would the Greeks).[47] By himself **alone** He **stretcheth forth the heavens** and **spreadeth abroad the earth**. None other was with Him as helper or counselor (24). As such a unique Deity, the Lord takes delight in frustrating the omens of pretenders to deity. These flippantly uttered signs of the false prophets, defeated by the true God's power, prove them to be but **liars** (25). So **diviners** go **mad** and the so-called wisdom of the **wise men** appears foolish. On the contrary, God verifies **the word of his servant** and fulfills the predictions of **his messengers** (26a). It is Israel as the depository of God's word that has the true prophetic vocation.

b. *Deity in declaration* (44:26b-28). God alone can say **to Jerusalem**, "Be populated," and to Judah's towns, "Be rebuilt, for **I will raise** their ruins" (26b). Only such a God controls the sea to the extent that He can say, "**Be dry, for I will** drain your

[46]Consult Oswald T. Allis, *op. cit.*, Chap. V, and his chart on the attached flyer, which admirably analyzes this prophetical poem. Cf. pp. 62-80.

[47]Hence St. Paul's term for "the universe" is Hebrew in its concept, though it is expressed in the Greek as *ta panta*, "all things."

rivers" (27).[48] Only He is qualified to declare **of Cyrus** (cf. 45:1, fn.), "He is my shepherd, and he shall fulfill all my purpose" (28, RSV). It is likewise only this God who says **to Jerusalem, Thou shalt be built,**[49] or promises to the Temple, **Thy foundation shall be laid.**

2. *Cyrus Is the Lord's Anointed* (45:1-8)

a. The salutation (45:1). **Thus saith the Lord to his anointed, to Cyrus**[50]—and if the Hebrew be taken seriously, then how

[48]Some commentators see here a reference to the fact that Cyrus and his army diverted the Euphrates River from its usual course through the city of Babylon, using its bed as an entrance to the city. But the reference in this passage is evidently to the wonders wrought by God in the deliverance of Israel at the crossing of the Red Sea (cf. 43:16; 51:10).

[49]Here God is talking, not Cyrus. "The fact is, only the foundation of the temple was laid in the days of Cyrus, the Ammonites having prevented the building; nor was it resumed till the second year of Darius, one of his successors" (Clarke, *op. cit., ad loc.*). The Temple was actually built in the days of Haggai and Zechariah.

[50]The term **Cyrus** is *Koresh* in the Hebrew. In the Elamite language, according to A. B. Davidson, "the name Cyrus is said to mean shepherd." In the Persian the word *Kuru* was used to indicate "the sun." The specific name *Kuros* (**Cyrus**) in Greek would indicate "supreme power, authority, validity, security." Hence it appears as a general term suitable for any ruler to adopt who regarded himself as the supreme authority or as "the Sun" of his people's hopes. And, according to Strabo, the Persian King, Cyrus was at first called Agradates; hence the name Cyrus was later assumed by him. Isaiah seems to use the term as a symbol of deliverance and salvation.

Conservative scholars, such as George L. Robinson, Oswald T. Allis, and C. W. E. Naegelsbach, have insisted that the chapters containing these references to Cyrus were purely prediction used by the prophet to indicate the divine foreknowledge. The one Isaiah of Jerusalem thus projected himself into the future in this instance as also we have seen him doing in chapters 24—27. For, as Robinson says, "Scarcely would a contemporary have spoken in such terms [as Isaiah does] of the real Cyrus of 538 B.C. since . . . in one and the same context, Cyrus is both predicted and treated as proof that a prediction is in him being fulfilled (44:24-28; 45:21)" (cf. his *Book of Isaiah,* p. 136).

It must not be overlooked that the human agent here is "the anointed one" (Messiah) in whom God "fulfills *all* his purpose." Moreover, we see in these references the identification of God with His Servant, who is His Witness, so much so that the victory of the Witness is the manifestation of God's own glory (Smart, *op. cit.,* p. 121). Furthermore, how can the prophet at one moment expect redemption through the power of God's transforming Spirit in Israel, and at another moment transfer the same hope of redemption to a Persian king? It is inconsistent also to think that a prophet who

can this name refer to the king of Persia in the sixth century B.C.?
But even that Cyrus was a king by the grace of God. Yet all
things said about this personage make sense only if they be
applied to the Christ (Messiah), the Son of God, and not to the
Persian king. (Cf. Ps. 2:2, where "anointed" [*messiah*] refers to
the ideal King of the future. The Greek of the Septuagint on this
passage in Isaiah reads *To Christo mou—"My Christ."*)

so emphatically spoke of the nothingness of earthly rulers should now make
an exception to this in the case of the Persian. Moreover, the victories of
45:1-3 are significantly in keeping with Isaiah's theme of salvation and redemption if they are looked upon, not as military conquests in the mid-
sixth century, but as a subduing of the nations before God's Messiah in
preparation for the establishment of God's universal kingdom. Again, God
grasps the right hand of this Cyrus in such a manner that His acts are the
acts of God. At 49:3 the "servant" is assigned a mission to Israel, and at
49:1 He is called from the womb and given His name by God. Hence Smart
insists that it is from within Israel that must come the One who will
recall Israel to its destiny. Smart also insists that the modern scholars are
unable to show how the triumphs of Cyrus were to convince the whole of
humanity of the fact that the God of Israel was the one and only true God
(cf. 45:3 and 6).

It therefore seems quite evident to this writer that, all things considered,
including the unity of Isaiah's prophecy and its frequent element of prediction, plus the spelled-out character and qualities of the individual deliverer, that Cyrus, in Isaiah's prophecy, has primary reference to the one
and only KORESH, the Lord Jesus Christ, who surely in a spiritual sense
fulfills *all* that is predicted of the Cyrus whom Isaiah names and upon whom
he places unlimited hopes as the Servant of God and Redeemer of exiles
and the foreign nations. This contention, we hope, will become more evident
as the items of the commentary progress, as we work through the scriptures
about to come before us. Our contention is that Cyrus can be a world
saviour only if he is really "The World's Saviour," called from the womb
as God's true Messiah and Redeemer.

The advantage of this view is simply stated: it allows us to affirm the
unity of Isaiah's prophecy, which is objected to by critics chiefly on the
basis of the Cyrus passages; and it allows us also to keep the name Cyrus
as the intended name for a prophetically envisaged person. Thus we avoid
the position taken by Smart and Torrey that it is a later interpolation
for sheer political reasons.

Isaiah was truly predicting God's one and only Messiah, the Incarnation
of righteousness, salvation, and deliverance. He is the One who supervises
the new exodus of the spiritual exiles out from the "city of the godless"
(Babylon), and back again to the rebuilding of "the city of God" (the New
Jerusalem). Only such a transformed and spiritual Israel would also serve
to convince the world that the living God is the Eternal One, besides whom
there is none else.

Cf. T. G. Pinches, "Cyrus," ISBE, pp. 773-76. Also M. J. Dresden,
"Cyrus," IDB, Vol. A-D, pp. 754-55.

b. The promises (45:1b-3). To **loose the loins of kings** (1) would be to make them unfit for battle. **Two leaved gates** were typical for kings' palaces. Open gates would be the only way of entrance for most of the walled cities of Isaiah's day (cf. Matt. 16:18; Rev. 21:25). God also promises to go before His anointed to fight and win His battles, making **the crooked places straight** (2), or more specifically, "smooth" (ASV). **Gates of brass** were characteristic of the more wealthy cities. We are informed by Herodotus (i. 179) that Babylon had 100 bronze gates. Iron bars would serve to keep such gates firmly closed and locked. **The treasures of darkness** (3) would have reference primarily to the heaped-up wealth in dark dungeons. This was often the wealth of conquered people, though taxes paid the monarch were included. **Hidden riches** in the Hebrew is *matmon*, from which came later the term mammon (Luke 16:13). Spiritually, **treasures of darkness** would seem to indicate Satan's subjects bound in the darkness of sin and unbelief.

c. The purpose (45:4). God's leaders are not chosen for their own sake, but for the sake of His people. They are but human instruments for the accomplishment of the Lord's purposes, which have His honor and His people as their objects. **For Jacob my servant's sake, and Israel mine elect** has reference to "the ideal Israel, the true Ecclesia rather than the nation as such outwardly" (Plumptre). If this reference is to an ideal Israel, is not the Cyrus reference also to an ideal Cyrus? To surname anyone was, in ancient times, to honor him (Mark 3:16; John 1:42). Such surnames were in most cases intended to be prophetic of future possibilities (or innate potentialities) (cf. Mark 3:17).

d. The preeminent Deity (45:5-8). **There is no God beside me** (5) is the theme of these verses. God's promise is, "I will gird thee, though thou hast not known me" (5c, ASV). The twice spoken **though thou hast not known me** (vv. 4-5) could well emphasize here Isaiah's familiar theme of Israel's blindness to God (so thinks Smart). It may further intimate the dawning Messianic consciousness of Jesus.[51] "That thou mayest know" in 3 is

[51]**Though thou hast not known me** would be a troubling clause for the suggested reference of the term Cyrus. But see the footnote above on 42:18-21, where again Jesus is the suggested Referent. "I have surnamed thee," is translated by Knox to read, "I have found a title for thee." Literally the Hebrew says, "a comparison for thee," as Kissane has pointed out.

now expanded in 6 to read, **That they may know from** east to
west that . . . I am the Eternal One, and there is none else. But
Isaiah would hardly expect a pagan king like Cyrus to make
known to the world the preeminence of Israel's God. Yet the
God of creation, who separated light from darkness, who brings
weal for His friends and woe for His enemies, now proposes that
knowledge of Him shall cover the earth (7). To this end the
psalm of joyful prayer is given which anticipates a time when
the opened **heavens** will **pour down righteousness,** and the
opened **earth** shall see those once dead resurrected to **salvation.**[52]
Then the rich fruitage of the earth will be both **righteousness**
and **salvation,** all as the result of the creative activity of the
eternal and living God (8; cf. Ps. 85:10-13).

The Hebrew terms **righteousness** (*sedeq*) and **salvation**
(*sedaqah*) have specific reference to spiritual well-being which
prevails as a quality in human personality. Note Isaiah's play on
words. It is pertinent to ask how these great spiritual blessings
can be attributed to the activity of Cyrus, the Persian king.
Only God's true Messiah brings salvation. He is the One who
truly fulfills the promises of God to His servant Israel.

3. *The Eternal's Unchallenged Sovereignty* (45:9-13)

a. *God is not accountable to His creatures* (45:9-12). None
can thwart God's plan for Israel. How improper it is for the
pottery to shout at the potter impertinently, "What are you doing?" (9; cf. St. Paul's use of this in Rom. 9:20-21)! **Potsherd**
would indicate a frail mortal. Man was formed of the clay, according to Gen. 2:7. "Strange, if a man should be asked by his
son, why he begot him, or a woman, why she gave birth!" (10,
Knox) Does a newborn child demand of its parents an explanation of its being brought into existence? He who murmurs against
divine providence is guilty of such nonsense. Dare a man question
or sit in judgment on **his Maker** (11)? Isaiah would remind
Israel that the future is entirely in the hands of God, and that it
is of Him one must inquire concerning it. "Do ye question me

---

[52]The Targum of Jonathan so regards this as having reference to a
resurrection. Ronald Knox puts verse 8 in parentheses and translates it as
follows: "You heavens, send dew from above, you skies, pour down upon
us the rain we long for, him, the Just One; may he, the Savior, spring from
the closed womb of earth, and with him let right order take its being."

concerning my children? And do ye give me directions concerning the works of my hands?"[53] The Eternal is both the Ruler and the Creator, supreme both in history and in nature (12). "It was I framed the earth, and created man to dwell in it; it was my hands that spread out the heavens, my voice marshalled the starry host" (Knox).

b. God has raised up a Deliverer for His people (45:13). "I, too, have summoned this man to perform my designs faithfully; go where he will, my guidance shall be his. He shall build up my own city, he shall let my captives go free, without bribe or ransom, says the Lord of hosts" (Knox). **Righteousness** is that aspect of God's activity which has for its object the salvation of His people. The historical Cyrus of Persia never did rebuild literal Jerusalem. Hence we should suspect any interpretation that sees only Cyrus as the referent of this verse. A Greater than Cyrus is here. Let it also be noted that the actual building of the Temple took place, not in the time of Cyrus of Persia, but in the following generation in the days of Haggai and Zechariah.

4. *The Triumph of Israel* (45:14-17)

The promises concerning the future of restored Israel now take an even higher flight. We noted, in 18:7, God's promise that the African nations should bring tribute to Israel's God. The word **thee** in v. 14 is feminine, thus plainly referring to the community of Israel (cf. Von Orelli). **Egypt, Ethiopia,** and **the Sabeans, men of** tall **stature,** shall bow and pray to the **God** of redeemed Israel, acknowledging His transcendent and unique deity. Isaiah now interrupts his vision of the future to offer a prayer of his own to God. "Truly, God of Israel, our Savior, thou art a God of hidden ways! All the makers of false gods must needs be disappointed, must go away ashamed and abashed" (15-16, Knox). "Verily thou art a mysterious God, O God of Israel, Deliverer!" (15, Von Orelli) Any valid doctrine of revelation must admit that ultimately God is unknown and unknowable except as He chooses to reveal himself to man (Job. 11:7). Thus transformed, **Israel** has found not only deliverance **in the Lord,** but an eternal salvation without shame or disappointment forever (17).

[53]Edward J. Kissane, *The Book of Isaiah* (Dublin: Browne and Nolan, Ltd., 1941), *ad loc.*

5. *God Is Not the Author of Chaos* (45:18-19)

Isaiah is quite sure that God has planned the destiny of Israel. He who made **the heavens** and framed and fashioned **the earth** (18) to His will did not create it to lie idle, but to be man's home. Creation was therefore a victory over chaos. Chaos was the dark and formless condition which preceded the summoning forth of light at God's command, heralding the creative activities. Such a God is able to declare, **There is none else.** Therefore we are to seek the Eternal, not in chaos, but in a world of order, for the prophetic word of God was uttered in broad, clear daylight. Isaiah is thus expressing his scorn for the mutterings and double meanings of the heathen oracles spoken in some **dark** cave of the earth. "It was not in secret, not in some dark recess of earth, that my word was spoken. Not in vain I bade the sons of Jacob search for me; I am the Lord, faithful to my promises, truthful in all I proclaim" (19, Knox). "I make known honest things" (Von Orelli).

6. *God Challenges the Nations* (45:20-21)

Once again comes the oft repeated summons as the eternal God flings forth His challenge. Here He addresses the fugitives of the **nations,** reminding them that wooden idols carried to the field of battle are powerless to save (20). Hold a conference! Then show us your proofs! Who announced it at first and foretold it long ago? Was it not I, the Eternal One? I, the faithful God? There is no other that can save! (21)

7. *The Lord Alone Is Saviour and God* (45:22-23)

Each time Isaiah opens a bright prospect for Israel he extends it to take in the rest of mankind. "Turn back to me and win deliverance, all you that dwell in the remotest corners of the earth; I am God, there is no other" (22, Knox). Thus will the nations one day be humbled, for the word of the Lord is endowed with divine energy to accomplish His will (10:7; 55:11; Jer. 23:29). God's solemn oath is that **every knee shall bow** before Him, and **every tongue** confess His name (23). Conversion is not a mass movement but an experience into which one must enter as an individual.

8. *In God Are Righteousness and Strength* (45:24-25)

"Then shall men say of the Lord, that redress and dominion come from him; all those who rebelled against him shall appear

in his presence abashed. Through the Lord, the whole race of
Israel shall be righted and brought to honour" (Knox). The
prophetic ideal is a world in which all men become God's covenant
people, giving Him true allegiance, including believers incorporated from the Gentile nations. "The completeness of God's
rule on earth is the measure of man's fullness of joy."[54] Thy kingdom come on earth! Amen!

G. Israel's God Is Able, 46: 1-13

Isaiah now turns to a contrast between Babylon's idols and
the eternal God's salvation. The satire in his comparison emphasizes the fact that idolaters must carry their idols whereas the
eternal and creative God carries and delivers those who are His
people.

1. Heathen Gods Cannot Save from Captivity, 46:1-2

Bel and Nebo (1), the two Assyro-Babylonian gods, are
singled out by the prophet. **Bel** is the equivalent for the Canaanite
god Baal. **Bel** or Belus means "lord." It was often used in compounds such as Belshazzar. Daniel at a date later than Isaiah
was surnamed by the king and called Belteshazzar (Dan. 1:7).
Nebo or *Nabu* means "the revealer or speaker" and was the
equivalent of the Hebrew word *Nabi'*, meaning prophet. He
served the same function in the Assyro-Babylonian hierarchy of
gods as did Hermes for the Greeks or Mercury for the Romans
(Acts 14:12). Hence he was considered to be the revealing god.
He was also thought to be "the bearer of the tablets of destiny
of the gods." Nebo's temple stood at Borsippa and the temple of
Bel was at Babylon. Such compounds as Nabopolassar, Nebuchadnezzar, and Nabonidus were the names taken by Babylonian
kings using the prefix *Nabu* or **Nebo.**

The idols were carried **upon the beasts, and . . . cattle.** They
thus became **carriages,** i.e., "things carried." As such they were
a burden to the weary, a heavy load on the backs of weary beasts
of burden (pack animals).

Sennacherib's *prism inscription,* column 3:55, tells how
Merodach-baladan, on the approach of Sennacherib, carried off
the patron deities of his land in flight and placed them with
their shrines on shipboard for his flight down the Euphrates.

[54]James D. Smart, *op. cit.,* p. 133.

But these were overtaken and captured. It all happened in the days of Isaiah of Jerusalem, and not in the time of the later Babylonish captivity. Smart is thus right in challenging the Babylonian captivity date for this and the following chapter. The gods were Assyrian as well as Babylonian.

They stoop, they bow down together (2); Isaiah's sarcasm here speaks of "tottering gods and stumbling men." Picture also a god loaded face downward on the back of a pack animal. **They could not deliver the burden,** for the god represented by the man-made image was unable to save its own image from capture. **Themselves are gone into captivity;** having no existence independent of their images, they thus become "captive deities," a strange anomaly indeed. Well then might the people shout, "King save the god!" rather than, "God save the king!" "The fact that these events did not happen when Babylon fell indicates that the oracle was earlier than 539 B.C."[55] Cyrus sought to restore the respective deities to their own localities. Hence this did not take place at his conquest of Babylon.

2. *The Lord Alone Is a God Who Can Sustain* (46:3-4)

Here Isaiah separates in his thinking the **house of Jacob** from **the remnant of the house of Israel** (3). The latter were those of the Northern Kingdom who remained in Palestine. There were Ephraimites still in Palestine, or "what is yet left of the house of Israel" (Von Orelli). **Borne by me** stands in contrast with the heathen burdened with their gods. The living God burdens himself with His people and carries them. The true God carries, whereas the false gods have to be carried. **From the belly . . . from the womb** seems to indicate the divine concern, not only from birth, but from the time of conception (cf. Moses' remonstrance with God at Num. 11:12). **And even to your old age I am he** (4). Though the care of a mother ceases when the child becomes grown, not so with God's solicitude for His own; this endures to the end of life. As George Keith expressed it:

> *E'en down to old age all My people shall prove*
> *My sovereign, eternal, unchangeable love;*
> *And when hoary hairs shall their temples adorn,*
> *Like lambs they shall still in My bosom be borne.*

[55]*Ibid.,* p. 136.

Note here also the emphatic pronoun I. The words **made . . . bear . . . carry . . . deliver** all indicate the God who is able, as contrasted with impotent Bel and Nebo.

3. *God Brooks No Comparison and Has No Peers* (46:5-11)

To whom will ye liken me? (5) is the challenge of incomparable Deity which we have met before in this writing. The living God has no material facsimile. The logic of Isaiah argues that, if images fail their heathen worshipers, why try to fashion a likeness for the Eternal? Isaiah also scorns the procedure of pouring **gold out of** (6) one's purse, and weighing up **silver in the** scales, then hiring **a goldsmith** to smelt it into a mold, thereafter falling **down to worship.** Why bow the head to the earth in adoration, or why **bear him upon the shoulder** (7) since he is a dead god and must be carried as a burden? **From his place shall he not remove,** for stationary gods are not going anywhere. He cannot **answer, nor save,** since a dumb idol makes no response, and cannot come to the rescue of his devotee. Only the Lord is the God of saving might. **Remember this, and shew yourselves men** (8)—at least you are alive. Then why vacillate between the worship of dead idols and the living God? Be of firm mind. "Consider this and make up your mind; lay it to heart, ye rebellious ones" (Von Orelli).

Remember . . . I am God (9). The Hebrew says, "I am *El*," "the Most High." This is followed by the amplification, "I am God," *Elohim.* Hence Von Orelli translates, "I am God, and there is none else; the Godhead, and there is none to be compared to me." **Declaring the end from the beginning** (10) is omniscience. **My counsel shall stand, and I will do all my pleasure** is omnipotence (cf. 40:26-30).

As to the title **a ravenous bird from the east** (11) we may ask, Does this have reference to the symbol of the golden eagle on the flags of Persia? But the symbol is an ancient one, as is that of the falcon. Either "bird of prey" is an apt figure for an invader, and more than one foreigner fulfilled it in Judah's history. The Hebrew term is *ayit,* which is transliterated into the Greek as *aetos,* eagle (LXX). But Smart questions how this could be Cyrus in the word that God had declared **from the beginning** (10) and yet take the place of Israel, who is to fulfill "all God's purpose." He therefore insists that " 'bird of prey' and 'man of my counsel' depict perfectly the double function of the future Servant Israel."[56] Of course **the man that executeth my counsel from a far country** could also refer to Sennacherib. Yet Smart has shown what a dilemma the critics involve themselves in when they apply this **bird** to Cyrus. **I have spoken . . . purposed . . . will also do it.** "When I have said it, I will cause it to happen; when I have prepared it, I will carry it out" (Von Orelli). God's word, unlike the oracle of false gods, passes into certain and immediate action.

4. *God Is the Only Source of Deliverance* (46:12-13)

Ye stouthearted (12) in the Hebrew implies obduracy, trusting in one's own strength and despising God's word (cf. Ezek. 2:4; 3:7). Hence it is a stubborn ignorance. It applies to those who are full of self-sufficiency and think to find strength and righteousness in themselves. These fail of a receptive mind toward the promises of God.[57]

I will place salvation in Zion for Israel my glory, or as Von Orelli has it, "Salvation in Zion my mark of honor to Israel."

H. BABYLON FALLS, 47:1-15

This chapter takes the form of a dirge over the downfall of **Babylon** (1). It bears a close resemblance to the taunt-song against the king of Babylon in 14:4-21. It has its later counterpart in the great cosmic oratorio which appears in Rev. 18:1— 19:10 (cf. 18:1-24). It is an example of God's wrath set to music. Babylon, "the city of the godless,"[58] is addressed as a **tender and delicate** queen, the mistress of kingdoms, who because of her boastfulness and cruelty will be dethroned, disrobed, led into captivity in a distant land, and there be made to grind as a slave behind **the millstones** (2).

1. *Her Fall* (47:1-4)

Isaiah's prediction is that this luxury-loving lady shall be degraded to the status of the meanest slave. **Sit on the ground**

---

[56] *Op. cit.,* pp. 137-38.

[57] However the Septuagint renders it, "Ye who have lost heart."

[58] "Throughout the extent of Bible history, from Genesis to Revelation, One City remains, which in fact and symbol is execrated as the enemy of God and the stronghold of evil. . . . Babylon is the Atheist of the Old Testament, as she is the Antichrist of the New" (George Adam Smith, *op. cit.,* p. 189).

(1) without a throne, is a summons to forlorn captivity, and is a degrading humiliation for one who has heretofore been a queen. Grinding **meal** with **the millstones** (2) was always the most servile form of female labor. **Uncovered** (3), i.e., the female slave has to walk, unveiled and bare-legged with all sense of shame outraged, to the scene of her labors. Thus does God promise to "take vengeance and spare no one" (Von Orelli). The **redeemer** and Vindicator of God's people is lauded by the oppressed (4; cf. Rev. 18:20).

2. *Her Cruelty* (47:5-6)

The empress **of kingdoms** is reduced to loneliness and widowhood (5). Babylon's sin was that she had gone beyond her commission as the chastiser of God's people. Casting off all reverence for the aged, she made the old men perform the hard tasks of bondslaves (6).

3. *Her Haughtiness* (47:7)

History has proved how futile it is for any city to say, **"I shall be empress for ever."** Babylon lies in ruins. Let modern nations take this fact to heart and have due regard for **the latter end** of destiny. There is a divine law that makes of pride its own Nemesis.

4. *Her Self-worship* (47:8)

Self-deification is the acme of pride. This has been the case with many a power state. But mere pretension to deity never makes it so. Babylon, like Nineveh (Zeph. 2:15), has presumed to set herself up in the place of God, saying, **I am, and there is none else beside me.** Regardless, then, of her modern name, "the city of the godless" is destined for military disaster in full measure, despite "the multitude" of her "sorceries." For security in wickedness is the greatest insecurity.

5. *Her Frustration* (47:9-11)

The full bitterness of **widowhood** and bereavement awaits the power-mad city despite the elaborate system of her technocracy or the awesomeness and wealth of her worship. **Thy wisdom and thy knowledge, it hath perverted thee** (10) with a false and overweening self-confidence.

> "Yet there shall come on thee *Evil*,
>   Thou know'st not to charm it.
> And there shall fall on thee *Havoc*,
>   Thou canst not avert it.
> And there shall come on thee suddenly,
>   Unawares, *Ruin*."[59]

Thus will her destruction be both unforeseen and irretrievable.

6. Her Desolation (47:12-15)

a. Salvation is not by magic (47:12-13). Isaiah now challenges all of Babylon's **enchantments** (12), reminding her that her wise counselors, **star gazers** (13). These "future-peekers" cannot really predict or save or heal her maladies. It will take more than a set of almanac editors to save her from her calamities. **Monthly prognosticators** are the ancient counterparts of today's astrologers.

b. Judgment is by fire (47:14-15). The destroying **flame** . . . **shall not be a coal to warm at, nor fire to sit before** (14), but a mighty conflagration and consuming flame. At the sight of it those fickle paramours for whom she has **laboured** will retreat each one to **his** own **quarter,** leaving her abandoned, and **none shall save** (15) or come to her help.

Such, then, is the outcome of forgetfulness of God, cruelty, vanity of knowledge, superficial credulity, pride of wealth—all of which spring from an idolatry of self. Let any modern Babylon be warned.

I. Summons to the New Exodus, 48:1-22

There is little in c. 48 that is new. The themes that are interwoven have all been introduced in earlier chapters. So familiar are they that it is amazing that anyone should be suspicious of the chapter's genuineness. What we actually have here is a powerful sermon pleading with a rebellious people to open their eyes to the destiny that God has planned for them, to recognize God's hand in their history in past and present, and to believe that the future will also come from His hand.

---

[59]*Ibid.*, p. 196. Italics are mine.

1. *The Eternal's Remonstrance with Israel* (48:1-11)

a. *Pride of status* (48:1-2). There is a bit of sarcasm in Isaiah's tone as he addresses this nation that prides itself on having been surnamed **Israel**, as a descendant of **Judah**, and comprising the **house of Jacob** (1). He would remind them that true piety is more than swearing **by the name of the Lord**, or confessing **the God of Israel**, or claiming a **holy** nativity, or even trusting an incomparable Deity. There are such simple matters as **truth** and **righteousness** for which **the Lord of hosts** (2) has a greater concern.

b. *Perversity of stubbornness* (48:3-5). Because of Israel's obstinacy, the eternal God has predicted her future, lest her blessings and adversities should be credited to pagan idols. Divine prediction and performance were necessary to counteract the arched **neck** and the brazen **brow** of an **obstinate** people (4). "What happened in times past, I had foretold long before; warning was uttered, and in the public ear; then, suddenly I would set to work, and the prophecy was fulfilled. I knew well what an untamed creature thou art, neck stubborn as an iron hawser, forehead intractable as bronze" (3-4, Knox).

c. *Prejudice of sophistication* (48:6-8). Isaiah further reminds his nation that God used **new** (6) announcements and surprise performances to outwit a people who were born rebels. God's plea is to the effect that, having heard that which is now fulfilled, they will at least acknowledge His prediction. But, since they still persist in willful ignorance, unheard-of events will surprise them, so that they cannot say, "We knew it ahead of time." These are things they have neither heard nor known, for their ears have been closed to them. What else could God expect from a traitor but sheer treason? "I knew that you would surely lie and that you were called a wicked one from the womb" (8b, *Peshitta*). So God himself foretold, fulfilled, and surprised, as to their destiny, an incredulous and rebellious people. No prophet ever spoke a more severe denunciation of his nation or passed sharper judgment upon its pride and prejudices.

d. *Punishment restrained* (48:9-11). Notwithstanding their sinful stubbornness God's **anger** (9) has been deferred, the crucible has been tempered with mercy, and the demonstration of the divine majesty has been retained. "If I reprieve thee from my vengeance, it is my own honour demands it; yet curb thee I must, for my own sake, or thou wouldst rush to thy doom" (Knox). Hence **I have refined thee, but not, as silver** (10) is refined; for when it is purified, no dross of any kind is left behind. Had I done this with you, I should have consumed you altogether; rather have I put you into the crucible **of affliction,** in order that you may acknowledge your sins and turn to Me. God further reminds Israel that He is doing this for His **own sake** (11), for He will not suffer His **name** to be reviled, or surrender to any other the worship that belongs to Him (11). Salvation is by grace. Hence God's long-suffering with Israel and her deliverance from affliction are not merited, but are graciously given for the sake of His own honor and **glory.**

2. *Had Israel But Hearkened* (48:12-19)

a. Productive creativity (48:12-13). The Eternal is the **first** and **last** and *only* Creator (12). He is still the same God who fashioned **the heavens** (13), founded **the earth,** and holds them in their respective places. He is the Alpha and Omega, the Creator and Preserver of the universe.

b. Prophetic inspiration (48:14-16). Israel's prophetic God is not like the dumb (speechless) idols of the nations. God has demonstrated His love by His prophets. He has worked effectively through His servants whom He has called and commissioned. God's predictions have been an open proclamation, and His Commissioned One advances by the authority and inspiration of the eternal God and His Holy **Spirit** (16).[60] Israel may therefore be certain that God will **do his pleasure on Babylon, and . . . the Chaldeans** (14).

c. The peace that might have been (48:17-19). It is important that Israel ponder what might have been the possibilities of grace for her. God's precepts are those that **profit** (17). His peace is plenteous, and her posterity might have been like the sands of the seashore in number. "I am the Lord thy God, ever ready to teach thee what it concerns thee to know, guide thee on the path thou treadest. If thou hadst but heeded my warnings! Then had a flowing stream of peace been with thee, a full tide of the Lord's favour; thy own race, thy own stock, should have been number-

---

[60]"In verse 16 the pre-incarnate Christ identifies himself as the one sent by the Father and the Spirit to convey God's prophetic message to the inspired prophet" (Gleason L. Archer, *op. cit.,* p. 643).

less as the sand or the pebbles on the sea-beach; the remembrance of thee should never have been cut off from my merciful regard" (17b-19, Knox). Such, then, would have been the fruits of true obedience, which alone brings **peace** (18) and security.

3. *The Summons to Flee from Babylon* (48:20-22)

Here the prophet points the way to action and answers the important question, "So what?" God's message then, as now, is always, "Come out of her, my people" (Rev. 18:4). "Away from Babylon, have done with Chaldea, let this be your triumphant watchword; make it heard everywhere, publish it to the ends of the earth, tell them the Lord has ransomed his servant Jacob" (20, Knox). The same God that **led them through the deserts** (21), and brought them clear, cold **waters** from **the rock,** guarantees abundant satisfaction and spiritual prosperity to any who will break with the old crowd and the idolatrous environment.

There is no peace (22) or salvation for the godless! Here Isaiah reaches the end of his first ennead and sounds the significant refrain: **There is no** *shalom* **(peace,** prosperity, friendship, completion, soundness, safety), **saith the Lord, unto the wicked.** Isaiah had no offer of comfort or peace to the godless, the stubborn and faithless, even though they were Israelites. The day of salvation will come in spite of their sins, but the faithless will not participate in that salvation. Rather, for them it will be a day of recompense (*shelem*).

Section IX The Second Ennead:

The Servant of the Eternal One

Isaiah 49:1—57:21

These nine chapters comprise the most significant portion of Isaiah's entire prophecy. Here he predicts the glorious future deliverance from spiritual captivity through the ministry of the personal Servant of the eternal God. Once again the divisions do not come precisely at each of the chapter breaks, though they are nine in number.

A. THE ETERNAL'S REASSURANCE TO ZION, 49:1—50:3

The argument against idolatry has been concluded. Isaiah now turns our attention to the personal portrait of the ideal Israel, the true Servant of the Lord.

1. The Advent of a Redeemer (49:1-13)

Here the Messiah is introduced as himself speaking, stating the object of His mission with its loving labors lost, His sense of failure keen, and His confidence in the ultimate divine reward.

a. The speaking Servant (49:1-4). **Listen . . . ye people, from far** (1). The whole world is called upon to hear what this Individual says about His mission and destiny. Thus He speaks as a Missionary of the eternal God, **called** in conception (1), made like a **sword** of truth and a sharp arrow of conviction (2), named **Israel, my servant,** and designated God's source of glory (3). With His life completely under the rule of God, He is assured that, though His labor seems useless, His **strength** spent **in vain,** yet **God** will see to His reward and can be trusted with its issues (4).

The portrait of Jesus could scarcely have been anticipated in sharper detail. Isaiah speaks of Him as **called . . . from the womb** (1), thus indicating His miraculous birth as the Son of God, named before birth just as the angelic messenger commanded His earthly parents. His **mouth** was **like a sharp sword** (2) with speech that both wounds and heals, and words that the Holy Spirit inspired. He was hidden away in Egypt **under the shadow**

of the divine **hand,** where He was safe from Herod's wrath. He was **made** like **a polished** arrow in His effective and talented insight (the Heb. uses the same consonants as those for the word meaning "pure or clean"). God kept Him close **in his quiver** at Nazareth during that period of quiet and undisturbed training in preparation for the divine presentation at the Jordan. Whereupon He was introduced as the One well-pleasing to God, His ideal **servant . . . Israel, in whom** God **will be glorified** (3). Yet His labor seemed **in vain** (4), as though He were spending His **strength for nought.** However, He commended His work to **God** in His final high priestly prayer in the Upper Room (John 17).

    b. The speaking Sovereign (49:5-6). The Servant's commission is now spoken of as an honor from the God who chose Him ere ever He was born (5) to be the Restorer of Jacob and the Redeemer of Israel. Yet His commission is not limited to but one nation, for it would be too slight a service to redeem the tribes of Jacob only. Hence the Eternal's promise is, **I will also give thee for a light to the Gentiles, that thou mayest be my salvation unto the end of the earth** (6). God's program of salvation includes a lost world and involves a universal atonement.

    c. Consolation amid contempt (49:7). Here we have the Eternal's word of encouragement to His despised Servant. He who was regarded as a despicable soul, abhorred by His nation, a slave of despots, yet shall be given the homage of kings. No one was ever rejected by any people as was Jesus of Nazareth. He was condemned by the supreme court of His day; publicly denounced by the leaders of His nation; and at the instigation of an assembled mob He was executed as a common criminal in the most shameful and ignominious manner known (Luke 23:18-23). The common name by which He is designated in Jewish writings is *Tolvi*—"the crucified," and among both Jewish and Gentile sinners alike, nothing excites more contempt than the thought that they and all others can be saved only through the merits of "the crucified" One. But God, who is faithful in the fulfillment provided salvation (Acts 4:12).
of His promises, has chosen this **very** Servant and through Him

    d. Commissioned as Saviour (49:8-12). Here a time of pardon is promised through the travail of the soul of the Servant whom God has prepared as a covenant Mediator with the people. It will be **a day of salvation** (8) to be sure. The ruined country will be revived and the forfeited lands parceled out anew. Men that are bound in darkness will be restored to freedom and light as the Servant proclaims for them "a new exodus" (9a). It was from an assurance such as this that the divine Servant gained confidence and strength.

Thus does the merciful shepherd read the promises of God for them that are homeward bound. They shall find highland **pastures** with grass a plenty. Theirs shall be safety from both **sun** and sirocco. Guidance to founts of refreshment will be theirs. **Mountains** shall be to them as **highways,** as they come gathering home from **north** and south, distant **west** and as far east as China (9b-12).[1]

e. *Exultation because of consolation* (49:13). "Here again the glorious liberty of the children of God appears as the center and focus from which the whole world is glorified."[2] Such interludes of exultation are characteristic of Isaiah as we have previously noted.

> *Shout for joy, O heavens, rejoice,*
> *O earth!*
> *O hills, burst into song!*
> *For the Eternal has consoled his people*
> *and pitied his forlorn folk* (Moffatt)

2. *The Assurance of Redemption* (49:14-26)

Isaiah is quite sure that God has not **forgotten** Zion, so let her not lament that she is a wife **forsaken by** her husband and a mother bereaved of her children.

a. *Zion is not forsaken* (49:14-18). No more can **a mother forget her** infant still unweaned (15) than can God **forget** Zion's image engraved in **the palms** of His **hands** (16). Surely the time is now when her builders will outstrip her **destroyers** (17). She shall be adorned with new recruits like **a bride** with her ornaments (18). God never forgets! Zion's complaint has called forth the Lord's loving remonstrance. Peradventure a mother might forget her own, but God has Zion's **walls** tatooed on His

---

[1]Through insight given by the Holy Spirit, Isaiah foresaw that his nation would be scattered as far east as China. Chinese Jews have returned to Palestine in this age of Israel's rebirth. Missionaries even to Japan have become convinced that sometime in the distant past there have been contacts with Hebrew practices.

[2]Delitzsch, *op. cit.,* p. 246.

palms (16). Hence the time of reconstruction is at hand, and the plan for her walls is complete.

b. *The desolate land shall be replenished* (49:19-21). In fact, God's blessings will be Zion's embarrassment. For they will be such that she can neither contain nor explain. **The land** (19) reborn will soon be overpopulated with children born in the time of her bereavement. No longer will she be barren or alone.

This prophecy is now fulfilled, for already the inhabitants of modern Israel are sure that the land is too narrow for them (twelve miles at its narrowest **strait,** 20), while the influx of immigrants has been the little nation's constant embarrassment.

c. *Fosterlings of royalty* (49:22-23). Isaiah assures his depopulated land that the Eternal will signal for newborn generations to take the place of those irretrievably lost. They shall return under the homage and protection of their royal fosters, who now kiss **the feet** of their onetime slaves (disregarding the dust which covers them), as certain evidence of the Lord's fidelity. God fosters for spiritual Israel a countless posterity. At the divine signal they will be nurtured in reverence and assembled in devotion—many children from many lands. For none who look to the Lord are ever disappointed.

d. *The prey of the tyrant rescued* (49:24-26). God is stronger than the captor and knows how to set His **captive** ones free. The divine strategy simply involves setting their foes against each other, and snatching His own people from the tyrant. This will vindicate Him as the eternal Saviour and mighty Redeemer of mankind. There will be no arguing the miraculous deliverance wrought by the divine intervention.

3. *The Almighty in Rebuttal* (50:1-3)

The divine rebuttal appears in the form of questions addressed to individual Israelites who supposed either that God had formally divorced their mother (Zion) according to the law (cf. Deut. 24:1), or had **sold** (1) them to some creditor in payment of some outstanding debt. Neither supposition is correct. Here God takes up this question of estrangement, and lets it be known that *only sin* separates from His presence and favor. Hence the divine remonstrance runs somewhat as follows: Did I ever divorce your mother? Did I ever sell you to My creditor's service in payment of My debts? No, you sold yourselves into sin's bondage! Why did My summons awaken no response? Do I lack the power to deliver? Remember, 'tis I who dry up the water-courses, and I who darken the heavens, causing the eclipse of their luminaries. Or, if I withdraw My light, this leaves all nature in absolute darkness.

Sin alone separates from God. The problem was not with God; the trouble was with the individual members of His Zion. God's power over nature is omnipotent. So His ability to redeem and to restore is unimpeachable. Faith, then, along with a ready response to the Lord's call (cf. v. 2) is the solution of Zion's problem.

B. THE ETERNAL VINDICATES HIS OWN, 50: 4-11

In this section we have *The Servant's Soliloquy* concerning His own perfection through suffering. This is the third of the so-called "Servant Songs."

1. *A Lesson Well Learned* (50: 4-6)

Few men, even ministers, have learned this lesson, yet the Divine Servant declares: "I know how to speak helpfully, to listen wisely, and to obey completely." His are a trained tongue,[3] a listening ear (4), an obedient will, and a silent endurance of suffering. This is an important lesson seldom learned by those who would be the ambassadors of the Eternal. Speaking advisedly to the ungodly, acting spontaneously upon hearing the divine voice, and suffering silently under undeserved abuse are specific qualities of Jesus Christ. No earthly exponent of Deity ever achieves this without "the grace of our Lord Jesus Christ." Full well may Knight refer to this as an "extraordinary new approach to the problem of man's inhumanity to man."[4] It was Isaiah who prophesied it, but it was Jesus who practiced it.

---

[3]**The tongue of the learned** is the KJV reading, but the ASV margin gives the term "disciples" as an alternate reading. The substantive of this in Hebrew (*limmudhim*) seems to have been coined by Isaiah, and occurs substantivally only in the Book of Isaiah at 8:16-17; here at 50:4; and again at 54:13. Hence we have another intimation of the unity of Isaiah's entire book from the standpoint of its vocabulary. An argument for its unity is strongly advanced by Dr. Naegelsbach. Consult his vocabulary for Isaiah as given at the conclusion of his book in the *Lange Commentary*.

[4]*Op. cit.*, p. 202.

2. *A Faith Well-founded* (50:7-9)

The reason the Servant can now face such pain and abusive treatment in His humiliation is because of His faith. His soliloquy may be summarized as follows: My Helper and Vindicator is at hand—**God will help me** (7); hence My unflinching purpose. God will vindicate Me; hence, also, My determined stand. God will justify Me (8); hence, My eventual triumph (9).

With God's help, this suffering Servant is never confounded. With God's help He is never caused to blush for shame. With God as His Advocate no man can condemn Him (Rom. 8:31, 33-34). It would take His accusers so long to make a case against Him that their very garments would become **old** and **moth**-eaten (9). He can trust God for the unknown future since He has learned the fact of God's unchanging loyalty in the present.

3. *A Future Most Fitting* (50:10-11)

Here counsel is offered for those who walk **in darkness** but are seeking for the **light** (10). It is the Servant's assurance to those who **trust in** God. In the Old Testament, he **that feareth the Lord** is the synonym for "being religious" in our modern terminology. Such a person, "though he walketh in darkness" (ASV, margin), is facing toward the **light**. Let him have faith in the fidelity of **God** (I John 1:7).

Here warning is given to those who kindle strife and torture and are playing with **fire** (11). C. von Orelli's translation of this verse is an improvement upon the KJV rendering: "Behold, you are all firebrands, and you gird yourselves with fiery darts—go into the flame of your fire, and you shall be burnt with your own fiery darts. From my hand this has befallen you; you shall lie down to torture." The simple point is, "Whatsoever a man soweth, that shall he also reap." Hearken and hope! Persecute and perish! The last sentence in this chapter is God speaking in judgment. Knight has translated the clause following the semicolon in KJV to read: "Depart into the furnace of your own fire."[5] This would parallel Jesus' words in Matt. 25:41. In the end, evil consumes those who give themselves to it, just as God vindicates those who commit themselves to Him (I Pet. 4:19).

---

[5]*Op. cit.*, p. 205. Knight also says: "The doctrine of hell is just as integral to the Old Testament revelation as it is to the New" (*ibid.*, p. 206).

This passage can refer only to the Ideal Israel as the Servant of Jehovah. Hence it speaks not of the nation but an Individual, and that Individual was Christ.[6]

C. The Eternal's Promised Deliverance, 51:1-23

In this chapter and the next we have a group of more loosely connected dialogues about the divine deliverance. They depict for us the breaking forth of salvation and the taking away of the divine cup of wrath from those who eagerly long for salvation. The clarion call to hearken is threefold, as is the similar call to awaken. The two chapters are therefore closely related, though the discourses are more loosely connected.

1. Hearken I: The Value of Retrospection (51:1-3)

Here the prophet seems to teach that the wonder involved in the origin of Israel is a ground of faith for its restoration and perpetuity. To the loyal nucleus he therefore says: "You who seek redress by way of the Eternal's aid, look again to your providential beginnings (1). Think of **Abraham,** the **rock** from which you were quarried, and of **Sarah, the pit** from which you were **digged!** Abraham, the aged, and Sarah, the barren, whom God blessed and multiplied (2)!" God called Abraham when he was but a single individual and increased him from "the one" to "the many." By God's grace the **desert** becomes **the garden of the Lord** (3), and a **melody** of song now delights the former **wilderness.** It is through faith that the **wilderness** becomes a watered garden like unto **Eden** itself. So the message of the prophet is: "Recollect and rejoice!"

2. Hearken II: The Immediate Prospect (51:4-6)

Here the eternal God declares His possessions in such terms as **my people, my nation,** and promises His blessings in such terms as "My deliverance," **my salvation.** Thus we have the assurance that the divine deliverance is immanent and the divine **salvation**

---

[6]Let the sermonizer consult Maclaren's five sermons dealing with the various aspects of the Servant's ministry and character:

  I. The Servant's Words to the Weary, 50:4
 II. The Servant's Filial Obedience, 50:5
III. The Servant's Voluntary Suffering, 50:6
IV. The Servant's Inflexible Resolve, 50:7
 V. The Servant's Confidence in Ultimate Triumph, 50:8-9
     —*Expositions of Holy Scripture, ad loc.*

is eternal. "The rules of my religion I send forth to light up every nation" (4, Moffatt). "Henceforth, my law shall be promulgated, my decrees be ratified, for a whole world's enlightening" (4b, Knox). This is the promise of a new law with some new listeners, resulting in a new liberty. "Soon, now, my faithful servant will come, even now he is on his way to deliver you; these arms of mine shall execute judgment upon the nations; the remote islands are waiting for me, are looking for my aid" (5, Knox; cf. also Moffatt).

Heaven and earth may vanish, but the Eternal One's triumph knows no end. "Look up, then look down," says the prophet. "The skies shall vanish like smoke, and the earth shall wear out like a garment; its dwellers shall die in swarms; but My salvation shall abide forever, and My victory shall never be annulled" (6, Berk.). With such an "up look" and "down look," the "outlook" is very promising. Thus does Isaiah bring the immediate prospect into faith's perspective.

3. Hearken III: Persecution Calls for Persistence (51:7-8)

Here the divine message advances with the declaration: "Though you know righteousness and keep the law, you are tempted to fear . . . the reproach of men (7). Put aside the fear of men! (a) Men are human and subject to decay, like a moth-eaten garment; but (b) God's salvation is for ever" (8). Another Oriental has expressed it in lines that are similar:

> Think, in this battered Caravanserai
> Whose Portals are alternate Night and Day,
> How Sultan after Sultan with his Pomp
> Abode his destined Hour and went his way.[7]

The premise of the prophet here is that persecution is only a passing thing compared to God's faithfulness.

4. Awake I: The Strong Arm of the Lord (51:9-11)

Again, in this fervent call for God's intervention we have Isaiah's characteristic use of double imperatives in an invocation of God's conquering arm. "Put on strength, as when You dealt defeat to the Egyptian crocodile and wounded the dragon of the Nile (9), or dried up the waters and made a path through the sea ['made the sea's caravans a highway'—Knox; 10]. Then Thy

---

[7]Omar Khayyam, The Rubaiyat, st. xvii.

ransomed ones **shall return** with shouting and exultation" (11; cf. 35:10 here; see also Knox's translation).

5. *The Lord's Response to His People* (51:12-16)

The message of this passage may be summarized in the premise: Forgetfulness of God is what begets the fear of man. The divine message of consolation here is: "I am your Comforter, then why fear frail **man**? (12) Forget not your **maker**, and fear not **the oppressor** (13). Release comes speedily (14). **I am** your own **God**, whose name is **The Lord of hosts** (15). You have My message, My protection, and My covenant, back of which are all of the Creator's resources (16)! I am the One who says to Zion, 'You are **my people**'" (cf. Hos. 1:10).

The enemies of God are mortal and weak; the Protector of the faithful is the Eternal and the Strong One. If God be for us, what matters then who may be against us? (Cf. Knox's translation of this passage.)

6. **Awake II**: *The Prophet Exhorts Jerusalem* (51:17-23)

"Up, up, Jerusalem, bestir thyself!" (Knox).

a. The cup of retribution is empty (51:17-20). The prophet recalls how Jerusalem had become but a drunken and desperate castaway, with no one to give her support and none to take her by the hand and steady her in her stupor. In her ruin by famine and sword, her **sons** (18; princes) had fainted under the divine rebuke. They were left lying at every street corner like an antelope caught **in a net** (20),[8] brought down by the Lord's anger. The ruin is twice twofold. The land is ruined by devastation and **destruction**. The people have fallen by **famine** and **sword** (19). Thus had the cup of divine judgment numbed her senses as she drained it to the dregs.

b. The tormentor's turn to drink (51:21-23). A major feature of the entire Book of Isaiah is this motif in his eschatology which prophesies the reversal of the fortunes of the oppressor and the oppressed. Jerusalem is assured that **the cup** (22) of divine wrath has now been passed to her tormentors who have so thor-

[8]This is the preferred translation of the more recent versions. However, the *Peshitta* version in Lamsa's translation reads: "faded like a wilted beet," which is surely different. The picture explains v. 17. The sons cannot help their mother, for they too have drunk the cup of divine fury and lie like corpses in the intersections (cf. Lam. 2:12).

oughly humbled her. "Cruel oppressors that bade thee lie down and let them walk over thee, dust under their feet, a pathway for them to tread . . ." (23, Knox). Judgment always begins at the house of God, but let us not forget that the God who punishes us is on our side of the issue.

D. RANSOM OF THE "CAPTIVE DAUGHTER OF ZION," 52:1-12

This portion of Isaiah continues the prophet's dialogues about deliverance and completes the theme of chapter 51.

1. **Awake III: The Hymn of Redemption** (52:1-6)

a. The call (52:1-2). Here the call is to attention, strength, beauty, separation, purity, and liberty. The summons quite resembles the initial command of a modern drill sergeant, "Attention!" "Up, up, array thyself, Sion [sic], in all thy strength; clothe thyself as befits thy new glory, Jerusalem, city of the Holy One!" (1abc, Knox) "For pagans and profane men never more shall enter you" (1d, Moffatt). "Shake off the dust, stand erect, then sit down [upon thy royal throne], Jerusalem; free yourself from the bonds about your neck, captive daughter of Zion" (2, Berk.). **Zion** is no more to be a castaway or captive. The call summons her to her highest glory as the priestly queen of cities. Her sitting in **the dust** (2) as a captive is to be exchanged for sitting on a throne as a queen (cf. the contrast here with Babylon's destiny in 47:1). Captives were often bound together by ropes tied from **neck to neck.** Such bands are now to be removed from **Zion,** and she shall no more be a **captive** queen.

b. The condition (52:3-5). Here we have God's soliloquy on Israel's history. The dark strains of the picture are as follows: **sold . . . for nought, oppressed without** a **cause,** ruled over in tyranny, and tortured into blasphemy. But God's musing begins with the promise: "You were bartered away for nothing, and you shall be ransomed without cost" (3, Knox). The Hebrews were enslaved in Egypt and plundered and oppressed beyond all reason by the Assyrians (which might include the Babylonians). They were wantonly carried off into exile, all because they sold themselves by rebellion and disobedience. He who sins always sells himself into bondage, but sin's rewards turn to ashes in his hands. On the other hand, God's atonement is no commercial affair. God owes nothing to the devil, and grace is free to the truly penitent.

c. The promise (52:3, 6). This involves redemption without ransom, as we have already suggested. God owes nothing to any nation. The fact that He uses one as His instrument of judgment upon another is no source of merit to the oppressor. The Assyro-Babylonian captivities brought no glory to the Lord from those nations; hence when His divine purpose was fulfilled, He could wrest their captives from their hands and owe them nothing. But as surely as God predicted His people's captivity, so did He promise their return. By this shall God's people learn His true **name** and nature. "Therefore shall my people learn my name: therefore on the same day (shall they learn) that I am he who says: "Here am I" (6, Von Orelli).

2. *Gospel Tidings for Zion* (52:7-10)

a. *The messengers* (52:7-8). These are the beautiful exponents of **peace**, united in voice and vision. Here is God's characterization of all true evangelists. St. Paul quotes this passage and applies it to the heralds of the gospel, as he catalogues for us his five great missionary "hows"—four questions, followed by this exclamation (Rom. 10:14-15). James Moffatt seems to have caught the beauty of this passage in the following translation:

> *Look! 'tis the feet of a herald*
> *hastening over the hills,*
> *with glad, good news,*
> *with tidings of relief,*
> *calling aloud to Sion,*
> *"Your God reigns!"*
> *All your sentinels are shouting,*
> *in a triumph-song,*
> *for they see the Eternal face to face*
> *as he returns to Sion.*

b. *The message* (52:9-10). Its keynote was sounded in 7, "Thy God reigneth!" Such good news calls for singing about comfort, redemption, and vindication. God bares **his holy arm** (10) for action,[9] so let **all . . . nations** and **all . . . earth** take note of His **salvation.**

3. *The Summons to a New Exodus* (52:11-12)

Here the command is for separation, sanctification, and deliberate action, with the guarantee of the divine protection. Isaiah

[9]The bare right arm, unhampered by any of their flowing garments, is characteristic of the costumes worn by people of the Near and Far East yet today.

is again speaking from Jerusalem and summoning the exiles. He warns them not to seek the spoils of an ungodly environment. A later prophet will hear a voice saying, "Come out of her, my people" (Rev. 18:4), and an apostle will recall this passage as he enjoins the sanctified separation befitting holiness (II Cor. 6:17—7:1). "Get ye out of Sodom!" The city of the godless is no place for the godly. But their departure is to be no rout or night flight or clandestine escape. It is to take on the nature of a deliberate march as in a former exodus under the divine protection with the Divine Presence "fore and aft." There are safety and sure arrival so long as God is both our Vanguard and our Rear Guard.

> *Nor need you hurry forth,*
> *flying like fugitives,*
> *for the Eternal goes in front of you,*
> *and your rear-guard is Israel's God* (Moffatt).

E. "THE SUFFERING SERVANT OF THE LORD," 52:13—53:12

This passage holds first place among all of the Messianic prophecies of the Old Testament. Who but Isaiah could have composed such a literary miracle? And who but the Holy Spirit could have inspired its details? Polycarp called it the golden passional of the Old Testament.

The previous "servant songs"[10] have depicted the prophetic ministry of this Servant of the Lord. In this one He is pictured

---

[10]The four "servant songs" and their major themes are as follows:
  I. The Character of the Servant, 42:1-4
  II. The Calling of the Servant, 49:1-6
  III. The Work of the Servant, 50:4-9
  IV. The Fate of the Servant, 52:13—53:12
According to George L. Robinson, this "servant song" has fifteen verses divided into five strophes of three verses each as follows:
  I. The Servant's Destiny, 52:13-15
  II. The Servant's Career, 53:1-3
  III. The Servant's Sufferings, 53:4-6
  IV. The Servant's Submission, 53:7-9
  V. The Servant's Reward, 53:10-12
                    (*The Book of Isaiah*, p. 146)
This Servant concept is woven throughout the Gospel of Mark (in which we have preserved for us the memoirs and the preaching of Peter). Let the interested reader consult H. C. Thiessen's *Introduction to the New Testament*, pp. 139-49, for valuable insights. See especially his outline of Mark on p. 147.

as Priest vicariously suffering for the sins of others. He is a sin-bearing Martyr, and because of this great high-priestly act as both Offerer and Sacrifice we henceforth hear no more in Isaiah of "the servant of Jehovah" but of "the servants of Jehovah" (54: 17; 56:6; 63:17; 65:8-9, 13-15; and 66:14—although at 61:1-3 the great single "Servant" himself speaks).[11]

Now comes the question of identity. What have we here? Who is described here? Is this a person, or only a personification? Even though it may not be certain of the three previous "servant songs," this fourth one pictures the Servant of Jehovah as an individual Sufferer.[12] He is as plainly announced and de-

[11]"The remnant becomes a redemptive priesthood and not merely a selected strain, a transforming and not merely a destroying ferment."—John Oman, *Grace and Personality*, p. 236.

[12]We have already noted Delitzsch's "pyramid" as a graphic portrayal of the decreasing number of the "righteous remnant" culminating in the one Mediator, "the Servant of Jehovah" (*supra.*, p. 175), but the decreasing remnant culminates in the one Mediator and the expanding Christianity begins with that same Mediator.

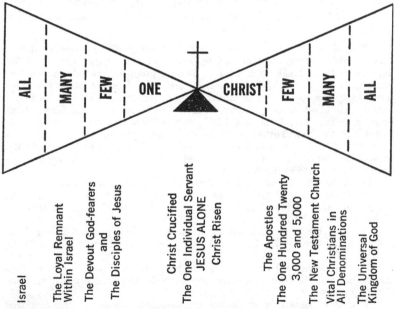

Turning the page sideways and viewing from the right-hand margin, we have the inverted and upright pyramids depicting "The Servant of Jehovah" in history and prophecy.

scribed as if the prophet were standing beneath the Cross beholding the Crucifixion. These predictions find their ultimate fulfillment in Jesus Christ. Hence this Servant of the Lord is none other than the Son of Man. This is how the New Testament regards Him (cf. 53: 7-8 with Acts 8: 26-35; cf. also Luke 24: 25-27, 44-47).[13] St. Paul's commentary on Isaiah 53 is Phil. 2: 5-11. Dr. Fausset declares: "The correspondence with the life and death of Jesus Christ is so minute, that it could not have resulted from conjecture or accident."[14]

In this significant passage four voices speak: First, God speaks (52: 13-15) introducing His Servant. The divine imperative is, **Behold, my servant** (52:13), and the divine message is that suffering is fruitful and sacrifice is practical. Second, the conscience of awakened mankind answers, **Who hath believed . . . ?** (53: 1-3), acknowledging that it has been letting the eye cheat the heart of understanding, admitting that all men have been indifferent to this divinely ordained Sufferer, and confessing the common consciousness of guilt. Thus awakened, it further states: **Surely he hath borne our** sicknesses . . . (53: 4-6), as it recognizes that the hand of God was indeed upon the

---

[13]The New Testament writers definitely apply this passage to Jesus. This is evident from the fact that they use the same Septuagint term for Servant in their Greek as is used in Isaiah's prophecy, namely, *pais*. This has been translated "child" in the KJV and thus does not carry the same force as in the Greek. It is equivalent to *Garcon* in the French, which means "boy" and, more properly, "waiter" or "servant." This Greek term appears in Isa. 42:1; 52:13; and 53:11; and is there translated "servant." It appears in the New Testament in several places such as Matt. 12:18; Acts 3: 13, 26; 4: 27, 30; and is applied specifically to Jesus. In each of these instances it should have been translated "servant," as it has been more properly translated in the ASV.

The New Testament references to this passage prove that:

(1) Prior to Jesus' time it was part of the Old Testament terminology.

(2) It refers to the Messiah (Matt. 8:17; Mark 15:28; Luke 22:37; John 12:38; Acts 8:28-35; Rom. 10:16; I Pet. 2:21-25).

(3) It is taken for granted as applicable to the passion of our Lord (Mark 9:12; Rom. 4:25; I Cor. 15:3; II Cor. 5:21; I Pet. 1:19; 2:21-25; I John 3:5).

That Jesus himself called the attention of His disciples to this passage as prophetic of His own sufferings may be undoubtedly inferred from Luke 24: 25-27 and 44-46.

That this passage is truly Isaianic is substantiated by the fact that rhetorical questions abound in Isaiah's book throughout all its parts just as they do here in this passage. Cf. also Smart, *op. cit.*, p. 200.

[14]Cf. Jamieson, Fausset, and Brown, *op. cit., ad loc.*

Servant, and the reason was sin—but the sin was ours, not His. Third, the prophet enumerates the circumstances of His death (53:7-10), which may be briefly summarized in the observation that, when oppressed, the Divine Servant humbled himself even unto death (Phil. 2:8). Fourth, God again speaks, giving the final verdict (53:11-12) and corroborating the divine purpose announced in 10. Thus the passage begins and ends with the speaking God. Isaiah was well aware that ours is a communicative God, unlike the deaf and dumb pagan deities. Archer is correct in saying that the "profoundest remarks upon the meaning of Calvary are not to be found in the New Testament."[15]

1. The Divine Introduction and Proclamation (52:13-15)

As we consider the passage verse by verse, the modern translations become exceedingly helpful.[16] The expression **my servant** (13) indicates that God himself is speaking. At this point the Servant is actually described in terms of divinity—**he shall be exalted and extolled, and be very high.** But these are immediately coupled with terms that can be used only of a man, and that one a man whose face is **marred** (14) by suffering. At the very outset, then, we have introduced here a divine-human Personage.

Shall deal prudently (13; "shall prosper," RSV; "shall deal wisely," ASV) involves a verb here that has been a troubler to the translators and the various interpreters. Lamsa's translation of the *Peshitta* reads "shall understand," while Knight translates the Hebrew here to say simply "will succeed," and Von Orelli's translation is "shall deal excellently." Knox translates: "See, here is my servant, one who will be prudent in all his dealings." *The Berkeley Version* reads "shall work wisely." Thus the task of the divine-human Servant is to accomplish the purposes of the eternal God. Hence at the very beginning of this so-called "servant song" we have the announcement of the exalted nature and destiny of this Martyr-Figure, whose insight enables Him to deal wisely with the greatest problem—that of human hatred and sin.

---

[15]*The Shadow of the Cross:* Insights into the meaning of Calvary drawn from the Hebrew text of Isaiah 53 (Grand Rapids: Zondervan Publishing House, 1957). The quotation appears on page 3. Another very fine study is that of Edward J. Young, *Isaiah Fifty-three, a Devotional and Expository Study* (Grand Rapids: Wm. B. Eerdmans Pub. Co., 1953).

[16]We especially commend the translations of Knight, Alex R. Gordon (Smith-Goodspeed), and C. von Orelli.

As many were astonied at thee (14) is still spoken by the voice of Deity. It begins a contrast in this verse that is completed in the next (note the **As . . . so,** used to state it), after a descriptive intervening parenthesis. Just as the **many** (the masses) were amazed at Him, so also shall He purify **many nations.** The reason for the amazement of the masses is the fact that in His sufferings He was so disfigured by violence that He no longer looked like a man,[17] since He was "marred, beyond human semblance" (RSV).

Marred more than any man . . . more than the sons of men. "Disfigured till he seemed a man no more, deformed out of the semblance of a man" (Moffatt). "Was ever human form so mishandled, human beauty ever so defaced?" (Knox) The prophet thus indicates that, once the masses of humanity behold this inhumanely marred Servant, they will be appalled. Suffering has ever been the astonishment and the stumbling block of humanity.

So shall he sprinkle many nations (15) has been emended by many commentators in favor of an alternate which would make it read "startle." But interpreters' emendations can be deceptive. Hence Muilenberg says, "It is best to retain 'sprinkle' here, and this interpretation is supported by the Manual of Discipline (iv. 21; cf. iii. 10)"[18] in the recently discovered Dead Sea Scriptures. The idea of **sprinkle** has in it the intimation of purification; hence "he will purify many people from their sins" is the predication here (note that Lamsa's translation of the *Peshitta* uses the term "purify"). This is in keeping with the motif of the great reversal which we noted in the preceding chapter and it fits into Isaiah's eschatology. Hence Knox translates: "He will purify a multitude of nations."

Even **kings shall shut their mouths at him** and marvel in silent awe as they see what was never told them, and ponder what they have never learned. For, as Knight observes, "the Servant's task is to give *the masses* a wholly new view of life . . . for the average man reveals himself as a bully at heart."[19] Hence the meek acceptance of undeserved cruelty will call for reverential

[17]We may recall here Pilate's attempt to secure the pity of the mob which called for the death of Jesus as he presented the disfigured Galilean, saying, "Behold the man!" (John 19:5)

[18]"Isaiah 40—66" (Exegesis), *The Interpreter's Bible*, ed. George A. Buttrick, *et al.*, V (Nashville: Abingdon Press, 1956), 618.

[19]*Op. cit.*, p. 229.

silence even on the part of kings. This is just as Jesus taught it in Mark 10: 45, where again Isaiah's term "the many" reappears.

The Christian way to exaltation via lowly humiliation is thus anticipated by the prophet in this divine announcement and introduction of the Servant. "For that which had not been told them shall they see; and that which they had not heard shall they understand" (*The Peshitta*, Lamsa's translation). As Coffin pertinently observes:

> We do well to emphasize the wisdom of the Lord's servant (cf. Matt. 12:42). Calvary was derided as weakness and folly, but to Paul it was "the wisdom of God" (I Cor. 1:24). The reversals of history, like Israel's restoration from exile, and the Son of God's exaltation from a gibbet to a throne, display divine sagacity which makes human cleverness seem absurd.[20]

2. The Superficial Human Estimation (53:1-3)

Men from Isaiah's day until now have looked upon this prophetic idea of a suffering Messiah as something incredible. **Who hath believed our report?** (1) More specifically, "Who could have believed that which we have heard?" Or, "Who has given any credence to our story?" It is not humanly possible to reconcile greatness with suffering. When people are fortunate we say, "You must be living right." But when reverses come we say, "You must have sinned!" Neither evaluation is wholly or always correct.

Here is the conscience of an awakened and penitent humanity speaking. The prophet has worded it well for any such (cf. John 12:37-43, Amp. NT commentary on this point). The words spoken by the prophet are those of the Holy Spirit interpreting the scandal of the scene.

To whom is the arm of the Lord revealed? The word for **arm** is *zeroa'* and indicates the strong right arm of God intervening in the affairs of men. Hence the expression indicates the decisive action of God. The arm of the Eternal works both deliverance and salvation.

If v. 1 is comprised of exclamation, v. 2 is given to explanation. The phrase, **He shall grow up** (2) is better translated, "He grew up," for this gives the full force of the historical tense. It is prophetically spoken of a future event as accomplished fact.

[20]"Isaiah 40—66" (Exposition), *The Interpreter's Bible*, ed. George A. Buttrick, *et al.*, V (Nashville: Abingdon Press, 1956), 618.

God grasps history in any of its developments as fact, though the event may have stood about seven hundred years future for the prophet Isaiah. **Before him** means, "before Jehovah, under the eye of God, and in conformity to His will and purpose."

As a tender plant would indicate a sapling. The Hebrew term is *yoneq* and comes from the verb *yanaq,* meaning "to suck." Thus the specification is "suckling," for which the English term "sucker" is more commonly applied to anything of the flora species. Thus the prophet is again thinking of the "sucker" or "shoot" from the stump of a tree hewn down. Earlier he had spoken of the Messiah as a "shoot" from the stump of Jesse (11:1). Thus He is to grow up like a "sucker" from a dead tree stump. (Note here again the evidence of unity of authorship for Isaiah's prophecy).

> *Hid are the saints of God,*
> *Uncertified by high angelic sign;*
> *Nor raiment soft, nor empire's golden rod,*
> *Marks them divine.*
> —J. H. Newman, *Lyra Apostolica*[21]

As a root out of a dry ground recalls the fact that God's plants spring up and grow in unlikely places. The Hebrew term here is *shoresh* (root). Isaiah's concept of the Messiah under the aspect of the "suffering servant" sees Him as both the Shoot and the Root of a theanthropic personality. He grows from the "parched earth" (Heb., *'eres siyah*). Isaiah was no doubt aware of the fact that church leaders usually come from the most out-of-the-way and insignificant places of human habitation. Palestine was an unpromising little land from which Messiah came, and little Bethlehem in little Judea was most insignificant. At Nazareth, He grew up in God's sight in humble and lowly circumstances.

He hath no form nor comeliness. There was about Him no majestic kingliness to attract human admiration. The question in Jesus' day was: "Can anything good come out of Nazareth?" He was simply the glamourless Nazarene. There is a difference between "glamour" and "glory." **There is no beauty that we should desire him.** The Servant lacks that "fair appearance"

(Heb., *mar'eh*) that makes for external allurement. He is shunned because He has been disfigured by human malignity.

He is despised and rejected (3). The Hebrew terms are *nibhzeh,* "looked upon with disdain," and *hadhel,* "forsaken" (cf. Matt. 26:31, 56; John 16:32). Loneliness is often the crown of sorrow and suffering. **Despised and rejected of men**—first by the rulers, second by the throngs, and third by the disciples. Thus the Christ trod the lonely *via dolorosa.*

A man of sorrows, i.e., a man of pains. The Hebrew is *'ish makh' oboth.* Jesus' body was indeed sensitive to pain. Men have sometimes raised the idle question whether this were so. But if not, then He was not thoroughly human, as Isaiah seems to indicate. **Acquainted with grief,** *yedhia holi,* "familiar with sickness" —"touched with the feeling of our infirmities" (Heb. 4:15; cf. Heb. 2:18).

We hid ... our faces from him, i.e., we turned our faces from Him in horror, that we might not look upon Him. **We esteemed him not;** we did not reckon Him to be of any significance (cf. John 1:10-11). We took no account of Him, for we regarded Him as an isolated fanatic; hence no one sympathized with Him. Such are some legitimate implications of the Hebrew.

Leaving now the human estimation, we may turn to consider some of the divine realities involved.

3. *The Vicarious Suffering for Our Salvation* (53:4-6)

The opening word, **surely** (4), in this strophe is intended to focus our attention upon the key to the riddle of the suffering Just One. It is better translated "assuredly." G. F. Handel has based one of his most significant songs upon it in his famous oratorio, *The Messiah.* **He hath borne our griefs**—it is important to note that the pronoun **our** is emphatic in this instance. *Ours* were the sicknesses *He* carried; *ours* were the pains *He* bore. *We* supposed *Him* **stricken, smitten ... afflicted.** And it was by means of *His* stripes that there is healing for *us.* The Hebrew term for **carried,** *nasa,* means "to take up and carry away." Thus the Christian beholding Calvary exclaims: "He carried my sins with Him there" (cf. Matt. 8:17; Col. 2:14). But the Hebrew *holayim* (**sorrows**) seems to indicate more specifically "sicknesses," and the Greek of the Septuagint indicates not only our infirmities but also our diseases.

Yet we did esteem him stricken—here is man's false estimate of pain. **Smitten of God,** i.e., under the plague of God. We thought

223

He was under the stroke of a divine penalty. **Afflicted,** *me'unneh,* humiliated, degraded, and humbled.

We made our estimation, but the facts of the case are: **He was wounded for our transgressions** (5). This involves vicarious expiation. The Hebrew term *meholal* really means pierced, transfixed, or bored through, hence nailed. Nailed for our *pesha',* **transgressions,** which were really rebellions. Hence, "He was pierced on account of our rebellions." The pain was *His,* in consequence of the sin that was *ours.* Rebellion is the primary element in all human sin. **Bruised for our iniquities** indicates that the Redeemer was shattered for our "inborn crookedness." The Hebrew, *medhukkah,* means utterly crushed or shattered, and *awonoth* means not only "iniquities" but "twisted and perverted crookedness." The sin principle is basically an incorrigible perversity.

The chastisement of our peace was upon him, i.e., the punishment leading to our peace. Chastisement has reference to disciplinary sufferings. The Hebrew term for **peace** is rich in varied meanings. It would indicate not only peace, but soundness, well-being, prosperity, and completeness. **With his stripes we are healed,** literally, "it has been healed for us." The idea is that by means of His stripes there is healing for us. The Servant's sufferings are not only vicarious but redemptive and curative. The doctrine of divine healing in both Testaments has been too often neglected by the churches, and left for the perversion of fanatics.

All we like sheep have gone astray (6). *Kullanu* would indicate "all of us," "the masses" of mankind, the whole world of men. *Ta'ah* (**gone astray**) means "wandered off course so as to get into trouble." This is Isaiah's vivid description of the manner in which humanity as such behaves. Sheep unattended are always straying, and as wanderers they are both defenseless and lost. This clause is also the confession of a repentant Israel (Ps. 119:176), of a repentant humanity (I Pet. 2:25), confirmed by the mind of our Saviour (Matt. 9:36; John 10:11).

We have turned every one to his own way. Man prefers his own way to God's way. He has transferred his allegiance to the idol of his own will and desires, his own intellect and innate tendencies to be wholly selfish. Sinful man attempts to live a self-contained life. This is humanity's common guilt. **And the Lord hath laid on him the iniquity of us all.** God became the Suffering Servant, provided the vicarious atonement, and bore, in His Son, the iniquities of the world. Since then, vicarious pain has been life's highest decoration. God does not punish the righteous with the wicked (Gen. 18:25). He accepts the suffering of the righteous *for* the wicked (Mark 10:45).

4. *The Patient Endurance of Humiliation* (53:7-9)

Here the prophet speaks, describing the events of Good Friday. **He was oppressed** (7), "harshly treated, mishandled," **He was afflicted,** "humilated." He was humbling himself. He let himself be afflicted. It was therefore a voluntary acceptance that characterized the gentle Christ, who bowed before the maltreatment of the servants of Caiaphas and the soldiers of Pilate. **He opened not his mouth.** This observation of the prophet about the patient Sufferer is spoken twice in this verse. He would not open His mouth. First of all, He did not need to defend himself since no valid accusation was made against Him. Secondly, His trial was only a judicial farce conducted by low-principled hypocrites asserting pious motives, while at that moment they were violating the Jewish laws of jurisprudence; therefore no defense would have made any difference. He spoke to the Sanhedrin only when silence would have been a renunciation of His deity and His messiahship (Matt. 26:63-64). Before Pilate, He spoke only when silence would have renounced His kingship. But before incestuous Herod the Tetrarch, He said nothing at all. **He is brought as a lamb to the slaughter.** The Hebrew term *yubhal* would indicate that He was led to the altar of sacrifice (cf. John 1:36; Rev. 5:12). It was a predetermined death sentence that had been settled upon before ever they gave Him a hearing or trial. Hence He suffered the fate of the sacrificial lamb. **As a sheep before her shearers is dumb,** so this divine Sufferer endured in silence.

He was taken from prison and from judgment (8). The Hebrew suggests that it was by judicial crime that He was taken and by tyranny He was cut off. Books have been written about the illegality of the trial and death of Jesus. Moffatt's translation is valid—"They did away with him unjustly." Gordon renders it: "Through violence in judgment was he taken away" (Smith-Goodspeed).

Who shall declare his generation? The indifference of public opinion and the apathetic attitude of the masses are often appalling. No one seemed concerned about His fate. His judges were not interested in ascertaining the truth about their Prisoner, but only in being rid of Him. **For the transgression of my people**

was he stricken, says the prophet; "struck down for sins of ours" (Moffatt).

He made his grave with the wicked (9). The Hebrew term *resha'im* means "the ungodly, or guilty men." Men assigned the Servant, not the burial of a saint, with reverence and honor, but that of an unjust oppressor for whom no man lamented. In other words, dishonor pursued Him to the very grave. His death was an official execution. **And with the rich in his death** means, more fully, "and with a rich man in his tragic death." Joseph of Arimathaea was a wealthy man. His newly hewn sepulcher became Jesus' burying place. Some interpreters read "felon" here instead of rich, but *'ashir* does mean a man of wealth. **Because he had done no violence** (cf. Job 16:17) means He had done nothing to deserve such a death. **Neither was any deceit in his mouth.** He was an innocent Man. Humanity vented its spleen in vicious treatment of God's Holy One. But "when selfish evil tries to masquerade as justice it prepares its own unmasking."[22]

5. *The Divine Reversal in Exaltation* (53:10-12)

Yet it pleased the Lord to bruise him (10). The Dead Sea Scroll reads: "But Yahweh was pleased to crush him and he pierced him." In short, God permitted the outrage. Moffatt however has caught the intimation of the Resurrection in this verse as he translates it to read: "But the Eternal chose to vindicate his servant, rescuing his life from anguish; he let him prosper to the full, in a posterity with life prolonged."

Thou shalt make his soul an offering for sin—here the Hebrew term *nephesh* (soul) means more fully "person." Lamsa translates the *Peshitta* to read: "He laid down his life as an offering for sin." The Hebrew would seem also to substantiate some such reading as, "Truly He gave himself as an Offering for sin." *Asham* really indicates a "guilt offering" (cf. Lev. 5:14—6:7; 7:1-7). **He shall see his seed,** a spiritual posterity. **He shall prolong his days,** for He lives by dying (John 12:24). **The pleasure of the Lord shall prosper in his hand.** The Hebrew, *hephes,* may mean not only "the good pleasure" but also the purpose. At this Sufferer's hand the purpose of the eternal God is promoted. "His noblest satisfaction will be, that he will be the living witness of the saving work he has accomplished. . . . Enough for him, that the Lord's purpose will be certainly and happily realized by His almighty hand."[23]

Now again God speaks the final verdict, at vv. 11-12.

> *After his travail of soul he shall see light;*
> *He shall be satisfied with his knowledge.*
> *My servant shall justify many,*
> *And he shall bear their iniquities.*[24]

He shall see of the travail of his soul (11). Through all His troublesome toil He shall not spend himself in vain, for travail is for a purpose. **And shall.be satisfied,** for henceforth His cross shall be His throne, and by reason of His death He shall rule the ages. He will find satisfaction in the fact that His death is effective for salvation. **By his knowledge** is a phrase that may be misunderstood unless we are careful to note that the Hebrew, *bedha'to,* indicates "by the knowledge of or about Him." It is by knowing the Redeemer personally that men are saved. Christ does not save sinners by *their* enlightenment but by *His* deed of atoning sacrifice. Yet none are saved who do not *know* Him as a personal Saviour by faith. Thus by His wise submission to His Father's will He imparts to many His own righteousness. **My righteous servant** is a phrase spoken by God. The Ideal Servant is also the Ideal King. God will eventually vindicate His Servant. Christ thus becomes the mighty Victor. Here the Servant's service for God and man reaches its crowning point. Righteous himself, He wins righteousness for many, and makes their iniquities His burden of concern. **Justify many** means "make the masses righteous." Hence there is included in this plan the "whosoever will" (cf. I Pet. 3:18). It is through Him that they attain that new quality of life on a higher plane. For **he shall bear their iniquities,** or, as Moffatt has it, since " 'twas their guilt he bore." Lamsa's translation reads: "He shall justify the righteous; for he is a servant of the many, and he shall bear their sins."

Therefore will I divide him a portion with the great (12). It was Jesus who told us how to become great (Mark 10:43-45). No doubt He had in mind this very promise of God concerning His reward. "Therefore will I give him *the many* for his portion." **And he shall divide the spoil with the strong** (the numerous).

[23]Von Orelli, *op. cit.,* p. 293.
[24]North, *op. cit.,* p. 140.

The Berkeley Version reads: "Therefore I will give to Him His portion among the great, and beside mighty ones shall He apportion gain." St. Paul no doubt has grasped the full meaning of this as he declares: "Wherefore God also hath highly exalted him, and given him a name which is above every name" (Phil. 2:9). God himself states the reason for this: **because he hath poured out his soul** (life) **unto death.** He performed the very highest sacrifice for man of which man can conceive, thus binding all mankind to himself in gratitude and adoration. **He was numbered with the transgressors.** "He let himself be numbered among rebels" (Moffatt). The Sanhedrin condemned Jesus for blasphemy because He asserted His messiahship and His unique sonship to God (Mark 14:61-64; Luke 22:37). **He bare the sin of many.** *Nasa'* **(bare)** means "lifted up and carried off." **Many,** *rabbim,* means "the whole number, the masses." He interposed himself for the sin of the world. There is an integral solidarity to this human race, and this great Son of the Race "endured in His death the precise racial penalty for human sin; and . . . so expressed God's hatred of sin as to render possible the immediate foundation and gradual formation of a new race of men which shall at last perfectly manifest the moral love of God."[25]

He **made intercession for the transgressors** when He cried, "Father, forgive them." He did not die a protesting and indignant victim, invoking the vengeance of God upon His murderers. Instead He prayed for their forgiveness.

This Servant was still future to the prophet but in Jesus Christ of Nazareth this prophetic dream becomes a reality, incarnate in flesh and blood. He is its striking fulfillment in detail.

F. THE LORD'S COVENANT LOVE FOR ZION, 54:1-17

This poem fulfills the command of 40:2 to speak with comfort to God's people. In this message of consolation we have the twofold symbolism of the bride and the city. The bride is rewooed and rewed; the city is rebuilt and resplendent. Thus we have the metaphor of marriage in the first instance and that of the New Jerusalem in the second. At 53:11 the fruit of Messiah's travail was many sons in righteousness. Here the Eternal One summons His spouse to singing and fruitfulness, peace and prosperity. It is a radiant preview of the coming happiness of Zion.

---

[25]Olin A. Curtis, *The Christian Faith*, p. 329.

1. *The Bride, Re-wooed and Rewed* (54: 1-10)

Here the prophet gives us a glimpse of the blessedness of the new people of God. The posterity of the Suffering Servant comprises a host of servants.

   a. The fruitful bride (54: 1-3). **Sing, O barren** (1) are words that carry forward the theme of 51:1—52:12. **The children of the desolate** are essentially the members of the new exodus, comprising those souls redeemed from sin's captivity. Thus Zion's adopted children will far exceed those of her early marriage (cf. I Sam. 2:5b). As the family increases, the **tent** must be enlarged (2). Here the prophet has in mind the old nomadic life with the tent as its dwelling place. The larger tent must have longer **cords** and stronger and more deeply driven **stakes,** if the extended curtains of the tent are to be stretched and sustained. Hence the command, **Lengthen thy cords, and strengthen** thy tent-pegs. The overflowing increase of her population will expand her borders **right** and **left** to re-inhabit the **cities** left **desolate,** and possess the neighboring nations (3). Applied to the Church of today, the call is to lengthen the cords of her affection and strengthen the stakes of her purposes. Churches must not be allowed to become private chapels for a closed society. Nor is the Church an imperial aggressor. She expands by her evangelism that makes her sons into soul winners.

   b. The faithful husband (54:4-8). No longer need Zion blush for **the shame** (4) of her maidenhood (her bondage in Egypt) or the **reproach** of her **widowhood** (her Assyrian invasions or Babylonish captivity). All this may now be forgotten. **Thy Maker is thine husband** (5), whose **name** is **the Lord of hosts;** and **thy** Kinsman, **Redeemer,** is **the Holy One of Israel.** His real name, however, is **The God of the whole earth.** The Church is the chosen bride of the Creator-Governor of the universe. The **wife of youth** (6), the Lord's first love, was only temporarily rejected. Like Hosea with Gomer, God had not divorced Zion, though He punished her with temporary rejection, that He might receive her back again to His yearning heart of love. One wooed and loved in youth is the more regretfully repudiated and the more joyfully restored when found to be truly penitent. The Hebrew of vv. 7-8 suggests the paraphrase: "If I abandoned you, it was but for a moment; but now I hug you to myself right tenderly. In a burst of wrath I did hide My face from you for a moment, but with everlasting kindness will I have mercy on you,

says the Eternal One, your Redeemer." Marriage vows are too
sacred for the alienation of divorce. True love seeks reconciliation. God's **wrath** is but **for a moment,** but His love and pity are
eternal.

c. *The covenant of peace* (54:9-10). (1) Sure as the promise made to **Noah,** 9. "As never again will the earth be destroyed
by water, so I will rebuke thee in wrath no more" (paraphrase).
(2) More enduring than **the hills,** 10. God is wedded to the
faithful to all eternity.

2. *The City, Rebuilt and Resplendent* (54:11-17)

In this picture of the New Jerusalem it is worthy of note
that there is no mention of any temple therein (cf. Rev. 21:22).
The prophet speaks of physical splendor and spiritual life, of
external beauty and inner security, for this new city of God.

a. *The firm foundation* (54:11). Following a tender apostrophe to the disconsolate, God promises: "I will mortice **thy stones**
with lead ore,[26] and make thy foundations of **sapphires**" (paraphrase). Expensive mortar is fitting for precious stones. Sapphire
is the hue of the heavens.

b. *The splendid ramparts* (54:12). "I am going to make thy
minarets like rubies, and thy gates of sparkling jewels. Thy whole
city wall will be of precious stones."[27] John the Revelator saw
similar characteristics for the New Jerusalem (cf. Rev. 21:9-27).

c. *The prosperous sons* (54:13). **All thy children shall be
taught of the Lord.** Jesus applies this verse to His own disciples
in John 6:45. The idea here seems to be that every inhabitant
will likewise be a disciple. God's people are not only informed
but they are disciplined. Here, then, is the inward glory.

d. *The civic righteousness* (54:14). **In righteousness shalt
thou be established . . . far from oppression . . . fear: and . . .
terror . . . shall not come near thee.** This, too, is a miracle of

---

[26]*The Berkeley Version* and Von Orelli are followed by Knight, who
reads: "I am going to inlay thy stones in antimony" (*op. cit.,* p. 250). Antimony is a "lead-ore used for blackening the eyelids, to make the eyes shine
out more lustrously. It is to be the mortar with which the new stones of
Jerusalem will be set, that they may shine forth like dazzling eyes; for they
are brilliant gems. We may also refer to the excellent joining of the wall-
stones used formerly in Palestine. The foundation-stones will be sky-blue
sapphires (Exod. 28:18)" (Von Orelli, *op. cit.,* p. 297).

[27]Translation by George A. F. Knight, *op. cit.,* p. 250.

grace, but it is a consummation devoutly to be wished and sought after. Justice makes a sure foundation for any civilization.

e. *The heritage of the faithful* (54:15-17). "Let men strive against thee as they will, it is with no sanction of mine; whoever strives against thee shall fall because of thee (or perhaps, shall be compelled to fall in with thee)" (15, Knox). The heritage of the faithful is the alchemy of love which turns one's foes into friends.

The achievements of technology are subject also to the divine sovereignty (16). God is still the Arbiter of the instruments of war. The man who builds them and the man who works destruction by means of them still owe their lives to God, and must surrender them when He wills. God's servants may now be exposed to the attacks and the false accusations of evil men, but there is coming a time when they will be invulnerable. **This is the heritage of the servants of the Lord** (17). "Their vindication is from me" (RSV). The New Jerusalem will be invulnerable to attack without and to calumny within. But with our confidence in God's unshakable control of life's affairs, this promise may also find fulfillment even in the inner security which floods the heart of the faithful.

G. THE SUMMONS TO GOD'S PROFFERED MERCY, 55:1-13

Here we have the universal invitation to divine blessing. This chapter begins with the third **Ho** or "Oh" of God's promised redemption based upon the vicarious sacrifice of His Suffering Servant. It is the third portion of the grand passage comprising cc. 54—55.

We noted two important words in the concluding verses of c. 53: "seed" (10), and "the many" (12). These thoughts found enlargement in Isaiah's emphasis upon the bride and the city in c. 54. She who heretofore was barren now finds her seed abundantly multiplied through the graciousness of the eternal God, her Husband. The city, once desolate, is rebuilt with all manner of jewels and precious stones, and shall no more be overpowered by her enemies.

Isaiah now turns his thought to "the many" for whom a universal atonement was made, and heralds to them the universal call—the blessed threefold invitation. Like the cry of the Oriental water seller comes this gracious and eternal invitation.

1. The Call to Satisfaction (55:1-5)

Man without God is an aching void, for his heart is made for God.

a. The true satisfaction versus the false (55:1-2). In these two verses the divine imperative is, **Come ye** (1). (*a*) First of all, God's provision is *free.* Such are the paradoxes set forth here that one buys with **no money,** and purchases **without price.** The humble seeker comes in self-renunciation, saying: "Nothing in my hand I bring; simply to Thy cross I cling." In simple self-surrender he accepts the blessing. The best gifts of life cannot be earned by labor nor purchased with money. The simple requirement is a hungering and a thirsting after righteousness (Matt. 5:6). The invitation reads: "Come along, even you who have no money! Buy wheat and eat!"[28] Or, as Moffatt has it: "Come, eat, O fainting souls!"

(*b*) It is *universal.* The gracious invitation reads: **Ho, every one.** It is that grand word "Whosoever," sounded centuries later by the Saviour of the world (John 3:16).

(*c*) It is *nourishing.* **Water** in Isaiah's prophecy is always a symbol of God's presence in the world. **Water** is for thirst (Ps. 42:2). **Milk** is for strengthening and growth (I Pet. 2:2). **Wine** is for rejoicing and happiness (Zech. 10:7; Matt. 26:29).

(*d*) It is *genuine,* as compared to **that which is not bread** (2). Too many now attempt to satisfy their hunger with "the bread of deceit" rather than "the bread of life." Too many labor for **that which satisfieth not.** "Always spending, and no bread to eat; always toiling, and never a full belly" (Knox). Smart has stated it for our day and time as follows:

> Men are always willing to spend some time and money on religion if they think that through it they can secure the things they want. But the water of life and the bread of life cannot be purchased or earned by any human effort. They have to be accepted as gifts that put one evermore in debt to God, gifts that one can never deserve, because in giving them God gives himself, and in receiving them man receives God himself, the sovereign God, to be the center of his life.[29]

What George Adam Smith says about the Jew is true of many a modern Christian: "Born to be priests, the Jews drew down

[28]George A. F. Knight, *op. cit.,* p. 254.
[29]*Op. cit.,* p. 221.

their splendid powers of attention, pertinacity, and imagination, from God upon the world, till they equally appear to have been born traders."[30] Selling our souls for material gains, we have too often become "traffickers in trivia," forgetting as we do so that there is that which money can never buy.

(e) It is *spiritual.* This divine satisfaction is conditioned upon the hearing of faith, the receptivity of the heart. At this point the divine imperative becomes, "Hear ye!" "Hearing, ye shall give heed and eat the good, and let your soul delight in fatness" (paraphrasing 2b). **Fatness** has reference to delicacies which symbolize the exuberance of spiritual joy. Hearing of this kind is not something done with the ear alone; it involves the will to believe. To the hungry heart of man, there is no real answer save the call of God's own voice to obedience and surrender.

b. *The covenant relationship* (55:3-5). (a) God's **everlasting** compact with the redeemed (3) is set forth in the exhortations: "Lend an ear and come!" "Listen and you shall live!" The thirsty man must come to the waters, or they flow in vain for him. To hear is to respond with heart and life. To **live** is to revive and awaken to a whole new life. The gracious promise is, "I'll cut an eternal covenant with you!"[31]—a **covenant** that is both gracious, and, though ancient, is also new.

(b) God's Messianic mercies involve the unfailing lovingkindnesses which were vouchsafed to **David** (3c-4; cf. II Sam. 7:4-17; and Ps. 89:34-35). Here the divine imperative is simply, **Behold** (4). Just as David was commissioned as a **witness** and a **leader,** so the Ideal David was a Prophet and a King, a Martyr and a **commander,** on the basis of whose person and work God's mercies are sure. Likewise God's people become the Lord's missionaries. They shall sound the call to foreigners, and strangers shall come hurrying to them because of their God (5). God's true (spiritual) Israel includes also converts from among the Gentiles. God's people become attractive when **the Holy One** honors them with His presence and blessing. "Peoples that never heard of thee shall hasten to thy call" (Knox).

---

[30]*Op. cit.,* p. 402.

[31]The ancient ritual for cutting a covenant involved the slaying of a mutually selected ox whose carcass was divided in two halves by splitting its spinal column. Between these two halves of beef the parties to the covenant stood while taking their vows. When these were completed, each man took his half home with him as a token of the agreement.

"Salvation is God's Gift" is the subject of 1-3. (1) Salvation is free, 1; (2) Salvation is full, satisfying the thirsty, hungry soul, 2; (3) Salvation is final, unto life everlasting, 3 (G. B. Williamson).

2. The Call to Repentance (55:6-7)

a. The time for repentance (55:6). God's time is always now. This is the moment of greatest opportunity. Hence these two verses (6-7) comprise the best advice in the entire Bible. Again we have Isaiah's typical use of double imperatives. **Seek ye . . . call ye** (6). God is not always providentially available, not because He is unwilling and unconcerned, but simply because the hinges on the door of salvation are providential circumstances. We may as well recognize the fact that at some times it is easier to find the Lord than it is at others. **While he may be found** is spoken to remind us that divine grace is no excuse for human complacency (Ps. 95:7-9; Rom. 6:1; Heb. 3:7-19). **While he is near** is the time when the human soul is psychologically sensing His presence, and hearing the summons to salvation.

The exhortation is interpreted by Smart as follows:

> *Now* is the moment of greatest opportunity. *Now* God's word is living and powerful and sounds into the midst of the community like a trumpet note. *Now* God offers food and drink to the hungry and thirsty. He is near. He is ready to be found. But there is no response, no one to answer when he calls (ch. 50:2); tomorrow he may hide himself again (ch. 45:15). Today he is waiting to forgive. But if his forgiving love is spurned, tomorrow there may be only his wrath that can be known, and this is what makes it so urgent that men should seek and call upon God and turn about in repentance at once.[32]

Adam Clarke gives the passage a different turn and reads it as follows: "Seek ye the Lord, *because* he may be found: call upon him, *because* he is near. Repent before ye die, for after death there is no conversion of the soul."[33] Plumptre notes that "the appeal shows that the promised blessings are not unconditional. There may come a time (as in Matt. 25:11) when 'too late' will be written on all efforts to gain the inheritance which has been forfeited by neglect (II Cor. 6:2)."[34]

[32]*Op. cit.,* p. 255. His italics.
[33]*Op. cit., ad loc.*   [34]*Op. cit., ad loc.*

b. The scope of repentance (55:7). Again the double imperative is sounded: **Forsake . . . return.** (a) **The wicked** (the scoundrel) must **forsake his** guilty **way.** This is conversion. (b) **The unrighteous man** (Heb., "the man of iniquity") must forsake his unclean **thoughts** ("schemings," Berk.) or purposes. This involves cleansing. There is therefore suggested here a repentance for the sinner, **Let him return unto the Lord.** But there is also suggested a repentance for sins of the spirit (Wesley called it "repentance in believers"). Let such a one return to **our** own **God.** Only a radical repentance can really save, for there must be a revolution of the whole order of one's life.

c. The promise for the penitent (55:7). The promised reward of sincere repentance is **mercy** and abundant **pardon** (the Heb. says: "He will multiply pardon"). One who comes to God in an attitude of sincere repentance may be sure of realizing full restoration. Forgiveness and cleansing are thorough works.

3. *The Call to Transformation* (55:8-13)

The transformation of human nature is a task for Deity based upon the divine ideal. It is likewise an imperative necessity if there is to be any divine-human fellowship worthy of the name.

a. The superiority of the divine ideal (55:8-9). God's people must have His mind dwelling in them in all its holiness and fullness. This is what makes them His people—"zealots for good works" (see Titus 2:14). (a) The divine ways versus the human (8). Here there is a great abyss which separates the two. It was recognized by Isaiah in his Temple vision in c. 6. It reappears here in his thought about the mere human manner of life in contrast with that which is divinely ordained. (b) The heavenly ways versus the earthly (9). Heaven's ways and thoughts are full of godliness and grace. As Smart observes: "Heaven comes to earth when a people on earth responds truly to the word that God speaks from heaven."[35]

Plumptre's observation is: "Men think that the gifts of God can be purchased with money (Acts 8:20). They think that the market in which they are sold is always open, and that they can have them when and how they please (Matt. 25:9-13)."[36]

One's **way** is his established practices. One's **thoughts** are

[35]*Op. cit.*, p. 226.
[36]*Op. cit., ad loc.*

his concepts and ideas—his patterns of thinking. God's thoughts are not so low, common, impure, and trivial as are those of men.

b. *The surety of the divine promise* (55:10-11). Nothing grows on earth without **rain** (10) from above. This verse includes almost every element in Jesus' parables of agriculture (especially that of the soils). Plumptre's observation is again pertinent: "The 'rain' and the 'dew' are the gracious influences that *prepare* the heart; the *'seed'* is the Divine Word, the *'sower'* is the Servant of the Lord, i.e., the Son of Man (Matt. 13:37); the 'bread' the *fruits* of holiness that in their turn sustain the life of others."[37]

The divine **word** (11) achieves its purpose. There is no word that man can say that will melt the stony heart. Therefore let the preacher strive to be in the goodly fellowship of the prophets and let his message be, "Thus saith the Lord." Let the word he utters be the very word of God. It alone controls the future. Its fulfillment is beyond question, for what God says carries in itself a life-giving and fertilizing energy. "It will not come back an empty echo" (Knox).

c. *The signs of the divine revelation* (55:12-13). These are: (a) A joyful spiritual exodus from the land of spiritual captivity and bondage (12a). (b) The peaceful bliss of divine guidance (12b). (c) All nature joining in the paean of praise (12c). The joy of salvation is felt by redeemed mankind, but the imprisoned creation also awaits its liberation as the transformed environment of a saved and happy race. The entire creation is to share in the freedom and glory of the children of God. **Thorn** and **brier** are transformed into God's evergreens, for such are **the fir tree** and **the myrtle tree** (13). A transformed earth, community, and humanity will thus bear witness to the reality of God. Spiritually, this means: Instead of the sot the saint, and instead of the rascal the righteous. Such is the living monument (**name**) of the Lord; the perpetual memorial to the glory of the eternal God is nothing less than a transformed humanity in the midst of a transformed environment. Praise God!

H. Sabbath Keeping and Worship, 56:1-8

Isaiah was no narrow-minded nationalist. He believed that the Lord's redemption was without respect of persons. Hence the great invitation sounded in the previous chapter must be made to

[37]*Ibid.* Italics added.

include the "others" that are to be gathered unto Him. God's house is open to all true worshippers. This poem begins and ends like an oracle, but between its termini is an exhortation followed by a beatitude, which in turn is followed by special promises to two types of proselytes, the foreigner and the unfortunate. Isaiah's God is not only **the Lord God which gathereth the outcasts of Israel,** but He is also One who **saith, Yet will I gather others . . . beside those** (8). Such was Isaiah's worldwide view of God's people.

1. *Salvation's Imminence Makes Righteousness Imperative* (56:1-2)

Centuries later the Prophet of all prophets began His ministry with a similar text: "Repent: for the kingdom of heaven is at hand" (Matt. 4:17). Thus God's reign is always at hand throughout history (Mark 1:15) and expectation is a part of faith. Furthermore, Isaiah would have no one suppose that moral uncleanness is compatible with participation in the promised salvation. God's grace is designed not only to make men blessed but to sanctify them (cf. I Cor. 6:9-11; Eph. 5:5; Heb. 12:14). In true Isaianic fashion come again the double imperatives, **Keep ye judgment, and do justice** (1)—keep the law and do what is right—preserve equity and practice ethics!—attend to justice and produce righteousness! **Justice** is what is lawful, and **righteousness** is conduct in conformity to divine truth.

Blessed is the man that doeth this (2). This has specific reference to the individual **son of man** (person). Keeping the Sabbath and refraining from doing any evil cover both tablets of the law—man's responsibility to God and his responsibility to man. The urgency of living according to the divine precepts is a note which needs to be recovered in modern preaching. The Hebrew word for **blessed** means "happy," as does the Greek word in each of our Lord's beatitudes (Matt. 5:3-10; cf. Ps. 1:1).

2. *Salvation's Inclusiveness Welcomes Outsiders* (56:3-8)

Isaiah is aware that the new covenant of grace will include both the foreigner and **the eunuch** (3). **Son of the stranger** (*benhannekhar*) is one who does not make his home within the borders of Palestine as does the resident alien—*ger*. The foreigner must not say: "The Eternal will excommunicate me" (Moffatt). For God will not deny him citizenship in the Kingdom of grace.

Nor should the eunuch complain that he is barren and worthless. For not fleshly descent, but receptivity for God's word and a willingness to receive of His grace, is the basis of the new covenant. Everlasting life thereunder is not dependent upon fleshly conditions. Ancient Israel had been an exclusive nation and church, but now the door is thrown wide-open to all who will join ranks with the faithful.

a. A monument for the mutilated (56:4-5). **The eunuchs** were excluded from the Old Testament church (Deut. 23:1). This would include not only Israelites who were compelled to submit to such mutilation by their foreign captors, but also many such unhappy victims among the heathen, who had suffered in like manner under the despotism of Oriental courts where polygamy prevailed. Intentional mutilation of the body is a widespread practice among heathen people, but it is a defacing of God's holy creation.

God's promise is that those who keep the Sabbath rest, **choose** what God approves, and abide faithful to the **covenant** will be given a memorial, better than posterity, which time cannot efface (4-5). Stewardship of time for rest and religion, commitment to a way of life that pleases God, and fidelity to one's vows to Him make one a welcome member of the company of the redeemed. Within God's house such will be given both **a place and a name.** The Hebrew word for **place** is better translated "memorial" or "monument," but the term *yadh* really means "hand." On ancient Phoenician and Punic stones the figure of a hand is often found. Can it be that God's promise is not only to preserve the hand print of such a devout person within his **walls** but also to give him a new name typical of a transformed nature? (Cf. Rev. 3:12.) Often a spiritual son or daughter perpetuates one's work and memory better than those of the flesh.

b. Favor for the foreigner (56:6-8). Isaiah has a word of encouragement for the pious proselyte whose life is characterized by (*a*) service, (*b*) reverence, and (*c*) fidelity. Such will find favor from the Lord and their worship will be accepted. They will be allowed to join in the religious festivals, their sacrifices will be accepted, and their prayers heard (7). The promise pertains to **every one that keepeth the sabbath from polluting it** (6). This was the distinguishing mark of the true Israelite, just as the keeping of "the Lord's Day" is the distinguishing mark of a true Christian.

God's **holy mountain** was Mount Moriah, where the Temple was located and a portion of which was the Court of the Gentiles. Solomon had anticipated the possibility of foreign participants in Jewish worship (I Kings 8:41-43). Jesus' anger with the Jewish leaders of His day was due to the fact that this portion of the Temple had been turned into a common bazaar, when Isaiah had indicated that God's **house** should **be called an house of prayer for all people** (7; cf. Matt. 21:13; Mark 11:17). Every privilege of the Israelite worshipper is to belong also to the devout proselyte. Thus Isaiah anticipates Jesus (John 10:16) and Paul (Eph. 2:14).

The oracle concludes with its final and beautiful promise, **The Lord God,** who gathers the scattered sheep **of Israel,** will **gather** still **others** from among the heathen (8). Gordon's translation makes it even stronger:

> *This is the oracle of the Lord God,*
> *Who gathers the outcasts of Israel:*
> *"I will yet gather to them*
> *Those who were gathered against them"*
>   (Smith-Goodspeed)

Racial prejudice and social snobbery are sins which should be rejected by the Christian. For like his Master, he too believes that "there shall be one fold, and one shepherd" (John 10:16). We shall all be brothers there regardless of our skin pigmentation or social status, if and when we arrive in the city of God.

I. The Bane of Apostasy and Idolatry, 56:9—57:21

This passage gives evidence that it was written before the actual Babylonian exile. Its geography is that of Palestine. Its moral picture is Judah in the days of the wicked King Manasseh just prior to Isaiah's death. It also stands as evidence against the "two Isaiahs" theory.

The message of this section is God's moral indictment of an evil generation. The sketch of the national character shows a people with a gnawing conscience but a lost God (quite contemporary to be sure). Their idolatry reacts into weariness. Finally the lost God speaks of His nature and His will. Though He always punishes sin, yet a contrite sinner is never abandoned. But impenitence is destined only for gloomy restlessness.

Its four major sections reveal the faithfulness of the prophet, even in the face of advancing age and increasing antagonism, to proclaim in full strength the diagnosis God had revealed of the moral situation.

1. The Beastliness of Judah's Leaders (56:9-12)

Isaiah could engage in biting and fierce denunciation when the occasion called for it. Yet we have here not so much the voice of the prophet as the voice of God speaking through His prophet to the people.

a. *A call to the beasts of prey* (56:9). Isaiah's characteristic style utters a twofold call, as he summons the enemies of the nation to do their work of judgmental punishment. Recall the ravages of Judah's territory by Assyria and other foreign invaders that were evident in Isaiah's earlier chapters.

b. *Sleeping sentinels* (56:10). Isaiah's paradoxes here are most graphic: blind **watchmen.** Good eyesight is imperative to a watchman, but Judah's leaders do not see impending perils. Self-styled prophets who are **ignorant** of the real dangers have no real insight. Theirs is but an intellectual and moral fuzziness. Mute **dogs** that are unable to **bark** are a peril to safety. Isaiah makes a play on words here indicating that though these men ought to be *khozim* (seers), they are actually only *hozim* (dreamers). Thus they talk only delirious nonsense. Yet given the men who are described in 5:22; 28:7-8; 30:10, plus the circumstances of Manasseh's reign, no other result could be expected. Isaiah pictures them as sentinels who cannot see, nor comprehend, nor warn, nor even stay awake.

c. *"Greedy dogs" and hireling shepherds* (56:11). Isaiah sees them as **dogs** with a ravenous appetite and **shepherds** without sense, insatiable for their own advantage. Prophets who could not even qualify as watchdogs were assuming the office of shepherd. They were unable even to handle a shepherd's crook, much less carry back to the fold a sick and ailing sheep.

d. *Singing the song of drunkards* (56:12)

> "Come, fetch the wine,
>   Let's swill our fill!" they say;
> "And to-morrow will be a rare time too,
>   A royal day!"   (Moffatt)

Such is the attitude of these heedless and dissolute revelers. But who can be sure of **to morrow?** Four things that disqualify the minister of any congregation or the ruler of any nation are: blindness, cowardice, indolence, and greed.

2. The Untimely Fate of the Righteous (57:1-2)

a. *The demise of the men of piety* (57:1). Pity the nation when the few devout souls it still has are taken by death, for they are not succeeded by others of like precious faith. Pity the nation when among its statesmen it has left only a few survivors of a more devout past generation and there are none of like caliber among the younger to replace them. Their death leaves a spiritual and moral vacuum.

b. *Rest in the grave* (57:2). Their souls are vexed by the sodomy and godlessness about them while they live. Mourning over the fact that the nation is being "sold down the river of no return," it becomes a mercy to them when death claims them before calamity falls. Life behind the veil is better far than this.

3. Debauchery of the Idolatrous Degenerates (57:3-13)

a. *Summoning the reprobates* (57:3-5). "But *you*, . . . [come] to me, children of the sorceress, seed of the adulterer and of her who played the whore!" (Von Orelli) "But *you*" is an expression of indignant scorn. Note the prophet's threefold characterization: (*a*) Degenerate parentage (3). Nothing is more cutting and insulting than to revile a person's parents. But the severity of the prophet's invectives arises from the factual nature of their contents. They were, indeed, children of apostasy. (*b*) Insolent mockers (4). "What are you but sons of shame, a bastard race?" (Knox) Don't you realize that what one mocks is an index of his own character and of his own sense of values? (*c*) Passionate perverts practicing infanticide (5). Inflamed with sexual passion under every green tree, slaughtering children in the ravines between the rocky cliffs—what a picture of an idolatrous and sexmad age! Child-sacrifice was condemned by most of the Hebrew prophets, yet Ahaz had practiced it, and his grandson followed in his footsteps. Here Isaiah is scorning the orgiastic rites of heathenized worship.

b. *Lascivious, idolatrous worship* (57:6-10). Here Isaiah depicts the utter profligacy of his countrymen. C. C. Torrey offers the following classification of their gods: gods of the valleys (6),

241

gods of the mountains (7), gods of the house (8), and gods of the foreign shrines (9-10).[38]

Moffatt translates v. 6 as follows: "You choose the slippery gods of the glen, you settle to have them! To them you pour out your libations and offer cereals! Am I to leave all that unpunished?"

Mountain sanctuaries were, and are, common in the Near East. The prophet's indictment now is that Judah, in the persons of her leaders, has set up on these heights her lascivious **bed** (7) and there climbed up to sacrifice. Again he scorns the practices of the immoral sex cult.

Venerating the genital organs was common in pagan worship. Gordon translates v. 8 as follows: "Behind the door and the side posts you have set up your phallic symbol; and apart from me you have stripped and gone up, you have distended your parts; you have bargained for those whose embraces you love; and with them you have multiplied your harlotries, while gazing on the phallus" (Smith-Goodspeed). Carvings of the sexual organs were prominent in the Asherah worship, which led to the exposing of the worshipers' secret organs themselves. One is tempted to ask how much better we moderns are with our multitudinous peddlers of pornography and our sex cinemas, patronized by our worshipers of sex and seduction.

Molech worship, with its perfumed debauchery, was characteristic of the Ammonites, whose god he was (9). Moffatt translates: "For Molek you perfumed yourself, with scent on scent; you made your messengers go far, even to the gods below." Unguents played a great part in the cults of the Semites. Exhausted with lust, when your strength revived you betook yourself to it again, and had not the sense to realize the futility of it all (10).

c. *The Lord's remonstrance* (57:11-13). Divine forbearance must now give way to intervention and exposé. The three items here are as follows: Why such craven fear? (11) Men should not be led by the fear of men to forget and forsake the fear of the Lord. We must not mistake God's patience for apathy.

The Lord now calls for a showdown among the deities. "But I will expose your doings, this 'religion' of yours" (12, Moffatt). The word **righteousness** in KJV is used sarcastically, for such religion is far from it. So Gordon reads: "I will expose this righteousness of yours, these doings of yours" (Smith-Goodspeed).

[38]*Op. cit., ad loc.*

The fate of false gods and their worshipers is set in contrast with the faith of the meek (13). Heaped-up divinities all shall vanish before one gust of the Eternal's breath. **But he that putteth his trust in me shall possess the land, and shall inherit my holy mountain.** "The meek . . . shall inherit the earth" (Matt. 5:5).

4. *Removing the Obstacles to Reconciliation* (57:14-21)

a. *Preparing the way* (57:14). This involves the removal of every hindrance, i.e., the sins heretofore denounced. It should be noted that this motif of exhortation appears in all three enneads of Isaiah's second main division—at 40:3; here; and at 62:10. We may recall that the Church has something to do about revival.

b. *Transcendent but condescending Deity* (57:15-16). Here God's immeasurable greatness meets man's frailty and need. God, as a faithful Creator, has a deep concern for the works of His own hands. He not only dwells on high, but in the hearts of the **humble** and **contrite**—the crushed and lonely spirits.

c. *God's hiding and His healing* (57:17-18). God smites men in their sin and rebellion, that He might heal their mourning and restore their consolations. Because of man's wicked avarice, God smote the sinner and hid himself, but man **went on** in rebellion (17). All sin is self-assertion against the will of God. But now, God says, **I . . . will heal . . . I will lead . . . and restore** (18). This means full consolation to the **mourners,** those touched and filled with godly sorrow for sin.

d. *God is the Author of peace* (57:19-21). The fruit of the **lips** (19) is joyous confession and thankful praise. Here God offers the Near Eastern greeting to all: **Peace, peace to him,** both **far . . . and . . . near.** This means everyone, everywhere. But the wicked continue restless and roiled, like the tossing **sea** (20). Their lives betray their inner unrest and uncleanness. For their thoughts are restlessly seething with evil, which is constantly ripening into acts. Godlessness knows no peace. A rage of passion ferments the inner man; past guilt casts up its **mire** in memory; fear for what the future holds torments and blights one's hope. All such, like the uptossed sea, **cannot rest,** since life's **waters** toss up **mire** and filth.

So concludes, with the same refrain, Isaiah's second ennead of his second division, as did the first, with the eternal contrast of **peace and no peace** (21)—**There is no peace . . . to the wicked.**

Section **X** *The Third Ennead: Future Glory*

Isaiah 58:1—66:24

We come now to the third and final section of the second major division of Isaiah's great book. Chapters 49—57 presented us with the prophet's view of the spiritual agent of our salvation; these chapters now present to us the spiritual conditions of our salvation. It should also be noted that this section opens with the familiar Isaianic double imperative such as we have at 40:1 and 49:1.

This last part of Isaiah begins with a severe reproof meant to purify false concepts of the way to receive the favor and salvation of the Lord. The prophet makes several comparisons and presents several contrasts. True and false piety are contrasted, vengeance and redemption, the wicked nation and the glorified Zion. The drama of salvation and the Lord's covenant are contrasted with the drama of divine vengeance. The book culminates with a prayer of confession from God's people followed by His response, and then climaxes with a notation concerning God's recompense and reward.

A. TRUE AND FALSE PIETY, 58:1-14

Here the prophet is not dealing with utterly godless people but with those who besiege him, as God's seer, with questions about the future. At the same time they pride themselves on their religious usages and customs, especially their fasting. They wonder why the Eternal One takes no notice of their asceticism and does not hasten to their help.

The prophet proceeds to expose the hollowness and falsity of this mere outward piety. He reminds them that on their fast days they combine a false humility with the pursuit of their business, turning even this observance to their own advantage. For though they have ceased from their regular tasks, they avoid loss by driving their employees the harder. The prophet objects that fasting and such hard dealing are inconsistent. Moreover their fast days include violent treatment for those who fail to conform to their empty ostentation. In their self-righteous pretense they seek to place God under obligation to them. Isaiah thus faithfully

244

and forcefully reminds them that true fasting involves one, first, in a genuine humility and, second, in a ministry of mercy. Moreover the true keeping of the Sabbath does not mean a tiresome indolence but an abstinence from secular pursuits for the sake of delighting oneself in the Lord. The chapter is quite carefully and logically organized.

1. *The Herald's Great Commission* (58:1-2)

a. Passionate preaching (58:1). **Cry aloud.** "Without timidity or sparing, the prophet must hold up to the people their sins."[1] "Those who have never heard an angry Oriental [Arab] speak, have no idea of what power of denunciation lies in the human throat."[2] The preacher of repentance is not to mouth smooth syllables and pleasant platitudes. **Spare not.** Unceasingly and without restraint must come this loud call that penetrates marrow and bone as it were. Intrenched perversity calls for dynamic and radical exposure if men are to be convicted and repent. **Like a trumpet** involves the Hebrew word *shophar,* meaning "ram's-horn," the instrument for trumpeting in Isaiah's time.

Shew my people their transgression. *Pasha',* in Hebrew, has reference to trespasses and acts of rebellion, covenant breaking, and the like. Hence deeds are specified and not abstractions. **Their sins** (*chatta'*), in the Hebrew, means "to miss the mark," "to make a false step, to stumble."

b. Rebuke scrupulous formalism (58:2). Religiosity may become a substitute for spirituality. Isaiah hears God speaking somewhat as follows: "Day after day they besiege me . . . [challenge] my dealings with them, a nation, you would think, ever dutiful, one that never swerved from the divine will. Proof they ask of my faithfulness, would fain bring a plea against their God" (Knox). **They seek the Lord;** hence they think they deserve praise and not blame, and cannot understand how God can deal with them as He does. **They ask . . . the ordinances of justice** when what they really need is mercy. They go so far as to think they can call God to account for His doings, but really theirs is an incongruous union of formal recognition of God coupled with an apostate life. Many a modern religionist engages in very proper but thoroughly empty ceremonies.

[1]Naegelsbach, *op. cit.,* p. 630.
[2]George Adam Smith, *op. cit.,* p. 416.

2. *True and False Fasting* (58: 3-7)

a. *Why? Look!* (58: 3-5) Does man serve God for nothing? "They say, 'Why have we fasted, and Thou seest it not? Why do we afflict ourselves, and Thou takest no notice of our humility?' " (3, Berk.) God lets them produce their own complaint: "Why doesn't God acknowledge our piety?" Then He says, in effect, "Look! It's because you seek your own honor and advantage by it, that's why!" "Because on your fast days you seek your own pleasure and oppress all your employees" (Berk.). Such is the complaint of these unconscious hypocrites who are amazed that their service is not accepted as sincere. But the true reason for fasting is prayer, meditation, and penitence. "A person who enjoys confessing his sins is not coming before God with an honest confession, but rather, is giving a performance before men (or perhaps merely before himself) that is intended to demonstrate religiousness."[3]

Ye fast for strife and debate (4). What a distortion of piety is worship that culminates in quarreling and quibbling! Fretful fasting is futile. Fasting and prayer should go together, but God hears not the prayer of the petulant. **Is it such a fast that I have chosen?** (5), asks the Lord. Do you call this a fast? "Fasting like yours today will never bear your prayers on high" (Moffatt). "Is it enough that a man should bow down to earth, make his bed on sackcloth and ashes? Think you, by such a fasting-day, to win the Lord's favour?" (Knox) Such bodily affliction may still miss the spirit of true mourning. Soul-sorrow is the true ideal of fasting (Matt. 5: 20; 6: 16).

b. *God's true fast* (58:6-7). **Is not this the fast that I have chosen?** Not mere self-denial but also loving service. Here the prophet says nothing about bodily mortification. His concern is for works of righteousness toward the oppressed, and benevolence toward the needy. Lift the burden from the **oppressed** (6), show true benevolence to the poor, feed **the hungry**, and clothe **the naked** (7). Liberate the bankrupt person from prison. Fasting and almsgiving were to be closely joined (Matt. 6:1, 16). Service to suffering humanity involved loosing the thongs of their heavy yokes (cf. Matt. 23:4). Housing the homeless, providing for the needy (even those of the household of faith), involves sacrifice. "No man can know God and close his heart against his brother."[4]

[3]James D. Smart, *op. cit.*, p. 248-49.
[4]*Ibid.*, p. 247.

3. *God's Promises* (58: 8-12)

Then . . . thy light . . . thine health . . . thy righteousness . . . shall be thy rereward (8). Here is a series of promises strung together like a necklace of pearls. These four are followed later by six. They all pertain to the righteous man's course of life. **Righteousness** walks before him, and **the glory of the Lord** marches after. Light, health, righteousness, protection, and answered prayer are the attendant blessings of devout people, as promised here.

Then shalt thou call, and the Lord shall answer; thou shalt cry, and he shall say, Here I am (9). Here mankind's two great needs are met: the need for a response and recognition, and the need for the sense of a Presence. Silence and aloneness are thus removed. God himself is the real answer to prayer and the true evidence of sanctification (Luke 11:13). God's best gift is himself.

But God's promises are conditional; God says, "If . . . then." "If you will banish from your midst all oppression, the finger of scorn and slanderous speech, if you will open your heart to the hungry and satisfy the desire of the afflicted, then . . ." (9-10, Berk.). The call is to forego every sort of lovelessness. **Take away . . . the yoke**—remove the rule of tyranny. **Putting forth . . . the finger** is a gesture of contempt and a symbol of scorn. **Speaking vanity** has reference not only to malicious speech and gossip but also to sacrilegious discourse. **Draw out thy soul to the hungry** would mean, simply, forego the satisfaction of your own hunger that the hungry might be fed. Self-denial may be necessary if we are to **satisfy the afflicted soul.**

Then shall thy light rise in obscurity, and thy darkness be as the noon day (10). Here is the idea of a life-career that begins with the morning and advances to the full blaze of noontime radiance. The first promise is personal liberation from the chains of darkness. The second is for an increase of light in such measure that even the obscurest parts are bright as midday. God's children are "sons of light."

The Lord shall guide thee continually (11), for He never withdraws His hand from the devout soul. **And satisfy thy soul in drought,** or as the Hebrew indicates, "through many a drought," since Christ can give you water that is not in the well. **And make fat thy bones;** supple bones are symbolic of vigor and power and bodily health. **Thou shalt be like a watered garden,** an oasis in the desert, a place of blessed refreshment. **Like a**

spring of water, whose waters fail not—this has reference to the very opening or mouth of the fountain "whose waters deceive not" (Heb.), for they are sweet and refreshing.

And they . . . of thee shall build the old waste places (12). "Your sons shall build the ruins of former years and shall revive the foundations of old, and you shall be called the repairer of the breach, the restorer of streets in which to dwell" (Berk.). Judah, in Manasseh's time following the ravages of the Assyrian armies, needed the fulfillment of a promise such as this. What a joy to know that God can make one a blessing beyond his own little life-span! The ancient wastes will be rebuilt because of your influence; children of your spirit will carry on your work.

4. *The Sanctification of the Sabbaths* (58:13-14)

Here is the Lord's second conditional proposition. It pertains to the grandest institution of Hebrew religion. Isaiah's contemporaries were as lax about keeping the Sabbath as they were strict about their fasting. Hence the prophet in the name of God demands a right sanctification of the Sabbath. If thou turn away thy foot from the sabbath indicates that in the prophet's thinking the Sabbath was holy ground. In modern slang we would say: "Stop your kicking about the Sabbath!" Restrain the foot whose step desecrates the holy ground of God's holy day. "To observe the day cheerfully is a test of the people's fidelity to the Lord. The Sabbath is as a sanctuary, not to be trodden upon with irreverent feet" (Berk., fn.).

From doing *thy* pleasure on *my* holy day is a clause in which the pronouns are emphatic. Even in Amos' day the businessmen were impatient with the day because its keeping interfered with their commerce (cf. Amos 8:5). When one recalls what disregard of the day of worship characterizes a modern London, New York, Los Angeles, or Tokyo, he realizes how contemporary is Isaiah's problem. The desertion of worship for places of amusement, beaches, mountains, lakes, theatres, racetracks, gambling halls, etc., gives evidence of our modern lack of piety.

Call the sabbath a delight. Actually the Sabbath was given for man's sake, that he might find worship, rest, and refreshment. One day in seven for the concerns of the soul would be a joy to him who uses it to draw nearer to the Lord. Jesus did not approve the rigid legalism of the Pharisees but He did make the Sabbath a delight (Mark 2:23-27). It is to be regarded as the holy of the Lord, and honourable. "The Lord's holy day" is still part of the

Christian name for it. And a part of any true Sabbath is corporate worship and instruction in the Word of God.

Not doing thine own ways, nor finding thine own pleasure, nor speaking thine own words—not doing your own business, nor seeking mere worldly amusements, nor holding business conversations. For the Oriental, bargaining hassles can become quite loud and heated. For the Occidental, idle talk may involve speaking with malice or gossiping, which is not only unspiritual but displeasing to the Lord.

Then shalt thou delight thyself in the Lord (thou on thy part); **and I** (on My part) **will cause thee to ride upon the high places of the earth** (exaltation—Jerusalem and Judah are on an elevated location), **and feed thee with the heritage of Jacob thy father** (14). Here is God's promise of a victorious march to occupy all the commanding positions, connected with the full enjoyment of the satisfying blessings promised to God's people.

For the mouth of the Lord hath spoken it is the Isaianic formula for a divine (oracle) pronouncement. This clause occurs also in 1: 20 and 40: 5, but nowhere else in the Old Testament.

B. REALIZATION AND REDEMPTION, 59: 1-21

This chapter is a very moving sermon-poem. Its great themes are (1) Corruption, (2) Complaint, (3) Confession, (4) Consolation, and (5) Covenant. Here the faithful prophet uncovers the sins of his people. Then he joins ranks with them and makes confession for them. Whereupon he is able to present his vision of the coming divine intervention. This is followed by God's promise of a new covenant in which the Divine Spirit indwells God's people and the Word of God exerts its living power from generation to generation. The three major sections of the chapter proclaim the nation's corruption, the nation's confession, and the nation's consolation.

1. *The Nation's Corruption* (59: 1-8)

The aftermath of war is very devastating and corroding. The early days of Manasseh were like the postwar periods of this century. Men had learned scientific brutality and the use of that knowledge had proven both corrupting and damning. The chapter continued the divine answer to the question of Judah noted in the previous chapter. Why are we so God-forsaken? Is God indifferent or is He impotent?

a. *Sin separates from God* (59:1-2). When God seems far away, there is often a dark and guilty reason for it. Sin erects barriers to the warm consciousness of the Divine Presence. God-forsakenness is not due to either divine indifference or divine impotence. But he who turns his back to the sun stands facing his own shadow. And, as Coffin so well says: "Sin-dwarfed men lack the capacity to discern God's presence."[5] Why this cold and cheerless distance between yourself and Deity? **Behold—** "Look!" says the prophet. **The Lord's hand is not shortened, that it cannot save; neither is his ear heavy, that it cannot hear** (1). God is just as able and just as sensitive as ever. "It is your own iniquities that interfere between your God and you; your sins have made him veil his face from you, until he will not listen" (2, Moffatt). Hence the murmurers are told that the barrier is one *they* have set up. God's **face** is the symbol of the Divine Presence.

b. *Sin multiplies depravity* (59:3-8). (a) Sin perverts the use of all things. **Hands . . . fingers . . . lips . . . tongue** (3) all become corrupted. For what does a man use as his instruments for sinning except these and the **feet** mentioned in 7? Deeds and words are always revelations of character. "Your fists are soiled with blood, and your fingers with iniquity; your lips have uttered deceit, your tongue murmurs villainy" (Von Orelli).

(b) Truth likewise is perverted (4). "In court no one sues honestly, no plea is just" (Moffatt). The guilt of unrighteous prosecutions was not limited to Isaiah's day. In modern courts men sue each other (even through their respective insurance companies) for more than just and equitable settlements. **They trust in vanity**—chaos (here is Isaiah's characteristic term, *tohu*, cf. Gen. 1:2, which is found in both sections of his book—cf. 24: 10; 29:21; 40:17, 23); **they conceive mischief, and give birth to iniquity.** "They carry mischief in the womb, and bring shame to birth" (Knox).

(c) The springs of human action are poisoned (5). Sin is a cunning entangler. **They hatch cockatrice' eggs, and weave the spider's web.** "What they hatch is deadly; what they do is futile."[6] **He that eateth of their eggs** is one who falls in with their wicked schemes. And he that crushes their eggs (opposes

---

[5] *Op. cit.*, p. 688.
[6] Von Orelli, *op. cit.*, p. 315.

their schemes) arouses even a more venomous opposition. Their projects are fatal to others, and useless to themselves.

(*d*) Violence is advanced (6). "Their threads never become a garment nor can one cover himself in their handiwork: their works are those of mischief, and violent doing is in their fists" (Von Orelli). "Deftly the spider weaves, yet web of hers will never make cloth, none will be the warmer for her toil; so it is with these, all unprofitable their schemes, their doing all undoing" (Knox). Did the prophet have his eye on twentieth-century subversive movements? The mystery of iniquity increases.

(*e*) Murders and evil intentions abound (7). **Their feet run to do evil.** As Von Orelli comments: "They hurry to do evil. Their feet are swift bearers and executors of their thoughts"[7] (cf. Rom. 3:15). Moffatt translates: "Rapine and ruin are the track they follow." Jesus himself had something to say about the source of evil intentions and deeds (cf. Mark 7:14-23). Isaiah notes that the **blood** they shed is **innocent blood,** which could be nothing else than the blood of the faithful who refuse to go along with the evil programs of a depraved community.

(*f*) Ignorance, perversity, and unrest are everywhere (8). Isaiah characterizes their wicked course of action by means of four different Hebrew words for roadways or paths. Violence and **destruction** are on their highways (7*c*); they have missed and are ignorant of **the way of peace** (8*a*); there is no justice **in their goings** (8*b*; *ma'geloth*, course of action, or rut in which wheels revolve); their trodden ways (8*c*) are perverse, and "for him who is brought by chance into contact with them, whose path crosses theirs, peace is over"[8] (8*d*). "The way" (cf. Acts 9:2; 19:9, 23; 22:4; 24:14, 22; etc.) is the central symbol of biblical ethics. Highways of violence, paths of unrest, ruts of injustice, and trails of perversity—none of these guarantee peace.

2. *The National Confession* (59:9-15)

The prophet now moves from his position as accuser and takes his stance among the accused.

a. The complaint (59:9-11). No doubt here we recognize the voices of the oppressed righteous ones in the days of Manasseh's

---

[7]*Ibid.*, p. 316.
[8]*Ibid.*

reign while he was yet a boy king surrounded by corrupt counselors.

Injustice prevails (9a). **Therefore is judgment far from us, neither does justice overtake us.** "So we are far from having our wrongs righted, we come by no redress" (Moffatt). Spiritual **darkness** abounds (9b-10). **We wait for light, but behold obscurity; for brightness, but we walk in darkness.** "We look for light, but all is dark, we look for gleams, and walk in gloom" (Moffatt). "Because of universal sinfulness, the desired state of order and righteousness, in which God would make known His favor, will not begin."[9] Verse 10 describes a state of uncertain groping after support and direction coupled with a vain searching after even a glimmer of light. **We grope for the wall like the blind . . . as if we had no eyes.** The going is indeed slow when hand, not eyes, must show the way. **We stumble at noon day as if it were night.** We are like "dead men in a world of shadows" (Knox). "We grope like a blind man along a wall, we feel our way like one without eyes; we stumble at midday as in the night. In the prime of our life we resemble the dead" (Berk.). A nation that has lost its God soon loses its moorings.

Complaints bring us no relief (11). **We growl like bears, and mourn . . . like doves.** "By comparing themselves to the growling of the bear and to the sighing of the dove, the Israelites let it be understood that both the strong and the weak, each in his way, make audible complaint concerning the prevailing distress."[10] "We long to be righted, all in vain, no rescue is in sight for us" (Moffatt). Any nation is in a perilous state when the minority party cannot even get a hearing.

b. *The confession* (59:12-15). Sin mocks and multiplies (12). "Fools make a mock at sin" (Prov. 14:9), but in the end sin mocks the fool, for **our sins testify against us** (12). Sin in its second edition is always larger than the first. Both Daniel and Ezra find occasion to quote this passage from Isaiah (cf. Dan. 9:5-15 and Ezra 9:6-15). "Out guilt mounts up before thee, our sins accuse us; shame is ever at our side, we confess the wrong done" (Knox).

Apostasy and false doctrine abound (13). "Transgressing, and denying the Lord, and turning away from following our God" (RSV); "Talking perversely and defiantly, telling lies from our

---

[9]*Ibid.*
[10]Naegelsbach, *op. cit.,* p. 639.

heart" (Moffatt). "The clauses point respectively (1) to false and hypocritical worship; (2) to open apostasy; (3) to sins against man, and these subdivided into (a) sins against truth, and (b) sins against justice."[11]

Morality in government is gone (14). **Truth is fallen in the street,** i.e., the *agora,* or broad, open place which made up the public market area and where also court sessions were conducted as public hearings. "Truth in our assemblies has no footing, honesty cannot enter there" (Moffatt). It is a pitiful day in any government when justice, righteousness, truth, and integrity are absent. "Where personal integrity cannot be depended upon, law loses its force, judicial proceedings lose their purpose, and communal life loses its stability."[12]

Truthfulness has become a liability (15). "Truth is so lacking, that if anyone turns from evil, he becomes a victim of plunder" (Berk.). Society has reached an all-time low whenever dishonesty is the best policy, and **he that departeth from evil maketh himself a prey.** Is it any wonder that God, beholding such a state of affairs, is **displeased?**

3. *The Nation's Consolation* (59:16-21)

There are times when even God is shocked. One of these is when there remains no one to intercede for His lost ones.

a. *The divine intercessor* (59:16-19). "And he saw that there was no one, and he was shocked that no one interposed" (Von Orelli). God's amazement at man's unconcern (16a) arises from the fact that no one seems willing to risk involvement. "Was there no champion to come forward?" (Knox). God's intervention in human affairs becomes imperative (16b). "And so his own arm must bring the deliverance he intended, his own faithfulness held him to it" (Knox). God is still the Sovereign of this universe and He will interfere in person to help the downtrodden and oppressed, since they cannot help themselves. Isaiah saw that when the time came for the Incarnation, God would (and, as we Christians know, did) raise up a true Intercessor.

He put on righteousness ... salvation ... garments of vengeance ... and ... zeal (17). Here and in the following verse is the fullest description of the Lord as a Warrior to be found in the Old Testament (cf. Exod. 15:3; see also Eph. 6:14-17; I Thess.

[11]Plumptre, *op. cit., ad loc.*
[12]Muilenberg, *op. cit.,* p. 693.

5:8). The divine armor is made up of spiritual qualities: **righteousness** of heart, **salvation** as His purpose, recompense as His concern, and **zeal** as His manner and mood. There is a jealous love which the eternal God manifests for His sheep that are fleeced and abandoned. "Then he put on might as armour, and victory as a helmet, and vengeance as his clothing, and zeal to be his mantle" (Moffatt).

God's rewards are suited to the deed (18). **Fury** awaits His adversaries, requital is meted out to His enemies, and **recompence** to the heathen. "No island so far off but it shall have its punishment" (Knox). Wrath, recompense, and retribution—all are part of the dark side of "the day of the Lord."

So shall they fear (19) "till the name of the Lord strikes terror into western lands, and the east stands in awe of his fame" (Knox). The intervention of God is a joy to His friends, but it is the terror of His foes, for the living God is both a Redeemer and an Avenger. This is a difficult verse and all modern translations vary widely from the KJV. But Plumptre holds that the KJV translation is at least as tenable as any other rendering. If we accept it, then the promise is filled with splendid imagery; for when the enemy comes to overwhelm us, we have the assurance that **the Spirit of the Lord shall lift up a standard against him.** And a standard is the banner at the head of a marching army. The modern translations find here rather the vehemence of the divine vengeance. "For his vengeance pours out like a pent-up stream, driven by a blast of wind," is Moffatt's rendering. "Here is a river coming upon them in full flood, driven on by the Lord's breath," says Knox.

b. The promised Redeemer and covenant (59:20-21). **And the Redeemer shall come to Zion** (20)—here the Hebrew term is *go'el,* "kinsman redeemer," as we had in 41:14 and 43:1. It appears in the famous passage in Job 19:25 (cf. Rom. 11:26). Lamsa translates it from the *Peshitta* to read: "And a Savior shall come to Zion, and to those who turn from transgression in Jacob, says the Lord."

With these repentant and redeemed ones, God makes a new and eternal covenant: **My spirit . . . and my words . . . shall not depart . . . for ever** (21). The divine anointing and the divine message shall not fail. "The new covenant is to involve the gift of the Spirit, that writes the law of God inwardly in the heart, as distinct from the Law, which is thought of as outside the con-

science, doing its work as an accuser and a judge."[13] Isaiah's basis
for hope lies not in man's faith, virtue, or ability, but in God's
faithfulness and the living power of His Word generation after
generation.

C. A DESCRIPTION OF GLORIFIED ZION, 60:1-22

This chapter carries on the theme of 40:5. The picture is
that of Zion radiant in the glory of the Palestinian morning with
the sun bursting suddenly over the trans-Jordanian highlands and
lighting first upon the high promontory where sits the golden
city of Jerusalem. Darkness still lingers in the deep valleys
around it, but Jerusalem stands scintillating in the sunlight. In
the Near East one does not find the long and slowly breaking
dawning that characterizes the area toward the earth's polar
regions. The sun bursts over the horizon and one knows that
the day has suddenly come.

After the prophet has patiently performed his weary task of
painting the darkness and misery of the sins of his people and
brought them to a hope and assurance of divine forgiveness, he
turns to a portrait of the possibilities of grace concerning the new
city of God wherein all are transformed by grace and made righteous. The triumphs of grace have glorified the city of God, which
now becomes the acknowledged center of the world. The inhabitants of this city are a society of justified and sanctified souls
among whom peace reigns and grace is abundant. To it are
streaming the nations of the world to worship there and to enjoy
its blessings.

The chapter opens with the summons of the dawning. This
is followed by the outward look both east and west, landward
and seaward. Then our attention is focused upon the city in its
rebuilding and adornment with righteousness and peace. Into it
are built the most precious materials in keeping with its internal
moral glory. It has the divine protection and the universal
renown befitting its situation.

1. *The Summons of the Dawning* (60:1-3)[14]

a. The call to radiance (60:1). This prophetic presentation
of the New Jerusalem opens with Isaiah's characteristic double

[13]Plumptre, *op. cit., ad loc.*
[14]The sermonizer will find help and insight in Maclaren's sermon on
these verses entitled "The Sunlit Church" (*Expositions of Holy Scripture*).

imperative followed by the announcement that the long-looked-for "light" has come. **Arise.** Stand up! **Shine.** Become radiant! **Light has come,** and the splendor of the eternal God has arisen upon you! Zion, pictured as a female captive slave lying in mourning on the ground, hears now the divine summons to transformed radiance. The Hebrew term for **glory,** *kabhodh,* has reference to God's own self-manifestation. God has come in His transforming grace, and with Him come beauty and blessing.

b. The contrast revealed (60:2). **Darkness** may be upon the surrounding nations but the Eternal's glory rests upon you. Light at dawning breaks first upon the heights. Zion now becomes the mistress of the nations and the spiritual center of the world.

c. The convergence resulting (60:3). Just as the winged insects of the night converge upon a globe of light, so will the nations gather to Zion's **light, and kings** shall be attracted by her splendor. The function of light is to shine, and when it shines it attracts. God's people are to manifest God's presence to the world. Where this is achieved, those languishing in darkness will converge in hope and expectation. This was part of an earlier promise made by Isaiah himself (cf. 2:2-4).

2. The Outlook East and West (60:4-9)

Here the prophetic message speaks about the promise that the day holds for Zion.

a. The happy "homecoming" (60:4-5). Again with his double imperative Isaiah urges Zion to look around her **and see** how all are flocking in—**sons . . . from afar, and . . . daughters** (4) carried at one's **side.** Furthermore, the prophet promises that with radiant face Zion shall behold them, and with a heart that overflows with wonder and gratitude she shall see the riches of the distant seaports and the treasures of the nations pouring in upon her (5).

b. Caravans from the east (60:6-7). This is the landward look. Under the blazing sun they come from across the Jordan's tide up the steep slopes to Zion, bringing rich treasures of **gold** and perfumes and **flocks** in abundance. The Arabian tradesmen on their young male camels come from **Midian, Ephah,** and even **Sheba,** that land of gold whence came the queen who brought gold, precious stones, and spices to Solomon (I Kings 10:10). The Arabian herdsmen will come from **Kedar** highlands (east of the Dead Sea) and from the country of the Nabataeans (south-ward), bringing flocks for acceptable and inexhaustible sacrifice upon the Lord's **altar,** whose glorious house shall be beautified.

c. *White-sailed ships from the west* (60: 8-9). This is the seaward look. Over the western horizon of the sea and its sandy beach, here come the sea-borne caravans like white **doves** (8) flocking home, bringing **thy sons** from the distant islands with treasures of **silver** and **gold;** all in the **name** of the eternal **God** (cf. Hos. 11:11). **Ships of Tarshish** (9) were the first-class trading ships that plied the Mediterranean waters as far west as Spain.

3. *Rebuilding and Embellishment* (60: 10-18)

This picture of Zion's restoration is very graphic. It even transcends that of Isaiah's youthful ministry (cf. 11: 9; 25: 8).

a. *Reconstruction in wealth and splendor* (60: 10-14). As once foreigners had destroyed the city, so now shall foreigners rebuild it. In graphic details God's promise speaks of a day when **mercy** replaces **wrath** (10), the city **gates** are **open continually** to commerce (11), homage comes from every nation (12) and splendor fills the **sanctuary** of God, as His glorious footstool (13). Men that once despised her shall do obeisance to Zion, acclaiming her the Eternal's City, the beloved **Zion of the Holy One of Israel** (14).

b. *An eternal pride and joy* (60: 15-16). The city once **forsaken** and unvisited shall now be shunned no longer, for it has been made the pride of the ages (15), sustained by royalty and graced by the Redeemer's power (16). Commerce supplies her wants and redemption makes her majestic.

c. *City of peace and righteousness* (60: 17-18). Thus does the city fulfill its name. Under the divine alchemy, bronze becomes **gold, iron** turns to **silver, wood** to **brass,** and **stones** to **iron** (17). Instead of poverty comes wealth, and instead of injustice and oppression, **peace** is appointed governor and **righteousness** is made taskmaster. **Violence** and crime are unknown in this city whose ramparts are named **Salvation** and every gate called **Praise** (18). "No tidings of wreck and ruin within those frontiers; all thy walls shall be deliverance, and all thy gates renown" (Knox). The city's splendor rests on its moral excellence.

4. *New Lustre and Enlargement* (60:19-22)

a. God its glory (60:19-20). No longer is there need for **sun** or **moon**, for God shall be her splendor (19), and the Eternal One her **everlasting light.** Thus **mourning** has an end (20). It is not expressly said here that there will be no more sun and moon. But in any case the city will receive its light more directly from the Lord, and thus it will be no longer subject to the variation of day and night (cf. Rev. 21:23).

b. A people of God's own planting (60:21-22). These verses may be expressed in the following poetic paraphrase:

> *The people shall all be pious,*
> *Secure within their land;*
> *The vine of God's own planting,*
> *The work of His glorious hand.*

> *The least one becomes a thousand,*
> *The smallest a nation strong;*
> *Jehovah the time will hasten*
> *Of that promise cherished long.*

The inhabitants of this New Jerusalem will **all** be **righteous** (cf. Rev. 21:27), and as such **they shall inherit the land for ever** (21), "planted there by the Eternal's hand, his own work, for his own glory" (Moffatt). And because of the divine multiplication the "little flock" has now become **a strong nation.** "I, the Eternal, who have promised this, will hasten its due consummation" (22, Moffatt). "Swift and sudden shall be the doing of it, when once the hour is come" (Knox).

D. THE HERALD AND THE PROGRAM OF SALVATION, 61:1-11

This beautiful poem transcends the limits of any age and stands contemporary in all. It speaks to us of the gospel of God's Anointed One as it records for us His soliloquy about divine grace and the promises of God for the city of God. The Christian may discern in its opening verse an intimation of the Holy Trinity in the persons referred to as **the Spirit, the Lord God,** and **me.** It is not the prophet who speaks here but rather the Servant of the Eternal One—the Herald of Grace once more. The words of our Lord Jesus in Luke 4:21, "This day is this scripture fulfilled in your ears," preclude the application of this passage to any other than the Lord Jesus himself. It would have been sheer presumption on the part of the prophet to glorify himself by ascribing to his life those very attributes which he had already set forth as salient features of the predicted One (cf. 42:1-8; 49:1-12; 50:4-9; 52:13—53:12). We therefore conclude that the speaker in this chapter is not the prophet, for in the dramatic style of his book the same person appears here as in 42:1 ff. and in 48:16.

1. Good News for Wretched Men (61:1-4)

Here in this intensely personal monologue we have the true evangel. It is the gospel from and about the Lord God (cf. Mark 1:1, 14).

a. Messiah's message (61:1-3). In this soliloquy we recognize the utterance of the ideal Servant of the Lord, whose anointing makes Him at once our Prophet, Priest, and King. He opens with the express declaration: **The Spirit of the Lord God** (1) **rests upon me; because** the Eternal has **anointed me** to announce **good tidings** to the lowly (cf. 11:2; and note that the two passages argue for a unity of authorship for Isaiah's book). We may especially note the two words **anointed** and **sent,** as we recall that every true minister of Christ must be both sanctified and commissioned. It is of interest to note that Luke 4:18 includes (since it follows the LXX) "the recovering of sight to the blind." The same promise with the same verb occurs at 35:5 and again at 42:7. Hence this addition is not a contradiction to the Isaianic concern that the people might have their blind eyes opened.

The proclamation includes the **year of the Lord, and the day of vengeance of our God** (2). Here the year of jubilee is set in contrast with the day of vengeance. "Since it will not pass off without violence, the day of redemption is called also God's day of vengeance."[15] Perhaps **year** and **day** are not to be pressed as to their temporal significance. The preaching of Jesus lasted more than a year and the "day of the Lord" will surely last more than one year. **Comfort** is to be proclaimed to **all that mourn** their sins and transgressions.

But a second class of mourners are **them that mourn in Zion** (3)[16] and to such He is appointed **to give** a coronet in the place of **ashes, joy** in the place of gloom, **praise** instead of plaintiveness,

---

[15]Von Orelli, *op. cit.,* p. 325.
[16]John Wesley taught an experience of repentance for believers.

and a new name significant of a new nature—"oaks of Righteousness," and "vines of The Eternal." Moffatt's translation is graphic: "To give them coronals for coronachs [garland crowns instead of funeral dirges], oil of joy for mourning robes, praise for plaintiveness; they shall be sturdy oaks of goodness, planted by the Eternal in his honor." "Heads shall be garlanded, that once were strewn with ashes; bright with oil, the faces that were marred with grief; gaily they shall be clad that went sorrowing" (Knox). Hence Messiah is sent to give to this type of mourners: (*a*) **beauty for ashes;**[17] i.e., a crown in the place of the customary ashes of repentance sprinkled upon the head; (*b*) **the oil of joy for mourning**—the anointing of the Holy Spirit in lieu of their abundant tears; and (*c*) **the garment of praise for the spirit of heaviness** —a glad heart full of praise to God in exchange for a heavy one that moves one to despair. **The planting of the Lord** depicts enduring plants in the garden of God. Nothing gives glory to God like the personal and proven righteousness of His own which is received from Him through faith.

    b. The promise of repair (61:4). **They shall build the old wastes . . . the desolations of many generations.** Restoration of the cities of Judah that had been laid waste by the Assyrians would be a chief concern in the days of Manasseh, the king. But spiritually speaking, God's sanctified ones stand to reverse the desolations wrought by many generations of a depraved heredity and sin. These are the Lord's anointed who build the city of God.

    2. Ministers of Our God (61:5-7)

    Our thoughts are now turned to the spiritual function of these men of Zion attended by material glory.

    a. The priests of the Lord (61:5-6). "While aliens attend to your menial tasks, you shall once more rise to the original ideal as ministers of God supported by the munificence of the nations and boasting of their goodness" (paraphrase). Too often it has been the case that the Jew has become the profiteer instead of the priest. Nor have Christian ministers always escaped this descent. Strangers shall tend your flocks and farm, but "for you, a higher name, a greater calling, priests and chosen ministers of the Lord our God" (Knox).

---

[17]Isaiah makes a play on the two Hebrew words here *'epher* and *pa'er*. Hence Moffatt's happy use of the English terms *coronals* and *coronachs*.

b. Double glory for double shame (61:7). The promise here
is a double portion, which was the inheritance of the elder brother
in each Jewish household. **For your shame ye shall have double**
compensation for the sufferings of former years (cf. 40:2; Zech.
9:12). "They suffered shame in double measure, abuse and insult
were their lot; so now in their own land they shall get double—
theirs is a lasting joy" (Moffatt).

3. *The People Whom God Has Blessed* (61:8-9)

Here the redeemed are promised universal recognition as the
blessed of the Eternal One.

a. The Lord's covenant of love and justice (61:8). As surely
as there are things which God loves, there are also things which
He hates (cf. Prov. 6:16-19). The verse should read, **I hate
robbery** with violence (as Plumptre suggests). C. von Orelli has
it: "For I, Yahweh, love right, I hate villainous robbery." This
is just what Israel and Judah had suffered at the hands of the
Assyrians. The transplantation of whole populations was a gross
abuse of the rights of conquest, and God regarded it as such. Thus
He promises a recompense and reward, in a compact of truth and
judgment.

b. Illustrious offspring (61:9). **Their seed shall be re-**
nowned. And even today respect for their ability attaches to men
of Jewish descent. But the promise becomes more general to
include the seed of all who are sincerely devout. The world must
acknowledge them to be a blessed race.

4. *The Magnificat of the Redeemed* (61:10-11)

It is characteristic of Isaiah at a juncture such as this to
include a song of praise. Here is a beautiful expression of gratitude for the great salvation.

a. The garments of salvation (61:10). We have previously
noted 59:17, where God clothes himself in **righteousness** and
salvation. He now so equips His Servant that He may communicate both. Thus He comes forward festively adorned, like an oriental **bridegroom**, wearing a coronet[18] in the manner of a priest,
or like a **bride** with her jewelry.

[18]"It would appear from Song of Solomon 3:11 that bridegrooms wore a
special head-dress on the day of their espousal, and this is here compared
to the priestly 'bonnet,' or 'mitre' (Exod. 28:4; 39:28; Ezek. 44:18)" (Plumptre, *op. cit., ad loc.*).

The beautiful picture here is one of God's people rejoicing in salvation, clothed with victory, robed in triumph, and wearing the crown jewels of true holiness.

b. The garden of the Lord (61:11). Here is set forth the attractiveness of a fruitful people, whom God brings forth in triumph and renown. Just as surely "as the earth brings forth its shoots, and as a garden causes what is sown in it to spring up, so the Lord God will cause righteousness and praise to spring forth before all the nations" (RSV). The Church's supreme attraction is the happy, holy lives of her people. Holiness and evangelism are very closely joined. The essential result of salvation is **righteousness**, and its incidental result is **praise**. But both are required if God's people are to commend His grace to sinners.

E. The Eternal's Covenant, 62:1-12

This chapter continues the soliloquy of the Unique Servant of the eternal God which began in the previous chapter. It sets before us the passionate zeal of His solicitude for Zion. Whereas the previous chapter spoke of a message to proclaim, this one evidences a determination to proclaim it, and promote its realization.

The chapter is concerned with the building of a holy race[19] of people bearing both a new name and a new nature. It promises to God's people a transfiguration radiance; it pleads for importunate intercessors; it vows the preservation of the fruits of labor; and it proclaims to the marching citizens of Zion's causeway an uttermost salvation that makes the city of God with its sanctified populace both rich and attractive.

1. Demonstration of Zion's Splendor (62:1-3)

Here the speaker professes his zealous solicitude for Zion's radiance. In the sixtieth chapter the command was for Zion to

[19]We may think of this chapter as "God's Covenant with the Holy People." It was so designated by Dr. P. F. Bresee when he preached from it to the students and graduating classes of Pasadena College, and named it "the college chapter." From it Dr. H. Orton Wiley delivered thirty-five Investiture Day addresses to seniors and their fellow students at Pasadena College and Northwest Nazarene College. His last time to do so was in 1960, at which time he repeated his very first sermon on the chapter. That sermon is now in print in a book of sermons by Pasadena College professors entitled *Faith in These Times* (Kansas City: Beacon Hill Press, 1961).

become radiant; now we have Messiah's vow that His own zeal shall make it so.

a. *The zealous servant* (62:1). **For Zion's sake will I not hold my peace, and for Jerusalem's sake I will not rest.** Commentators have suggested three possible identifications for this speaker: God, His Unique Servant, and the prophet. The second possibility seems to be most in harmony with what follows. Thus the Speaker is the same in this as in the preceding chapter.

Brightness . . . a lamp that burneth suggests the fact that for the daytime there is no clearer light than that which comes from the sun; and for the nighttime (in Isaiah's day) no light shines more brightly than a blazing torch. True **righteousness** is all pure light, and **salvation** is a burning flame.

b. *The conspicuous church* (62:2). Here cf. Matt. 5:14. The vindication of Zion's **righteousness** serves specially to radiate her brilliance. **Gentiles** (nations) **shall see** her triumph and every king behold her splendor. Furthermore, this new **glory** calls for **a new name** in keeping with her transformed nature. But this can be announced only by the eternal God, since the name is mysterious and known only to God (65:15; Rev. 2:17; 3:12). It is symbolic of Zion's holiness and closer intimacy with Deity.

c. *The royal diadem* (62:3). The promise here is that Zion shall become **a crown** of jewels **in the hand of the Lord** her God (cf. 28:5). **A crown** suggests that which is distinctly kingly, but a **diadem** implies a tiara like the mitre of the high priest. Two different Hebrew terms for **hand** are used here. The picture is that **the crown of glory** is clasped by **the hand** of the Eternal, whereas the **royal diadem** lies in the open palm **of God.** Thus He holds forth His resplendent Zion for all nations to behold.

2. *Delight with Zion's Betrothal* (62:4-5)

Here the plainly spoken promise is that Zion shall no more be named **Forsaken** (49:14) with her land a desolation.

a. *The delightful bride* (62:4). Under the desolations of the Assyrian invaders the land was **desolate** (*Sh'marnah*), but now the promise is that it shall be called *Be'ulah*, which means **married.** Isaiah, true to his background, considered the married state not only to be fruitful but one in which a lord or "husband" is found and acknowledged. Hence the land is to be occupied and cultivated.

b. The rejoicing bridegroom (62:5). The people of the rural areas are sometimes said to be "married to the land" even in modern times. In this sense the country of Zion may be said to be married to its **sons** who cherish and protect the land. But in another sense God's true bride is made up of the people of Zion; hence we read: **So shall thy God rejoice over thee.** The message of this double use of the figure of marriage suggests that the Holy Land shall not be an unchosen virgin, nor a repudiated wife, nor a widow, but a wife living in conjugal happiness— whether land or people. Hence Zion shall be called "Hephzi-bah," "delightful" (II Kings 21:1).

3. The Diligence of Zion's Watchmen (62:6-7)

To help achieve His goal the Speaker announces that He will choose **watchmen,** who, like himself, shall neither rest nor be quiet until their aim is achieved.

a. The speaking sentinels (62:6). **I have set watchmen upon thy walls, O Jerusalem, which shall never hold their peace day nor night.** The question at once arises concerning the identity of these sentinels, or "lookouts." The conclusion that they are the faithful prophets appointed by the Anointed of the Lord seems most warranted. That Isaiah thought of himself as such is evident from the little oracle concerning Dumah (21:11-12). These are the men who are to constantly **make mention** of the eternal God. But the Hebrew seems to indicate a special officer at the court of ancient kings whose duty was to remind the king of the day's appointments and any special promises he had made. Hence a better rendering would be "ye that are the remembrancers of the Eternal." And this brings to mind the second major function of these **watchmen.** The true prophet must not only discern the present situation and be aware and give warning about approaching peril, but he must mediate between God and the people. He must remind God of His promises and he must intercede for the people.

b. The incessant intercessors (62:7). **"Keep not silence," and give him no rest, till he establish, and till he make Jerusalem a praise in the earth.** God's ministers must know how to claim the promises of God on behalf of the people of God. They are to pray without ceasing for protection and help upon the congregation. They stand in direct contrast with those scorned by Isaiah in 56:10. They are commanded to importune the Eternal until He fulfills His promise of glorifying Jerusalem. Jesus taught His disciples to engage in importunate prayer (cf. Luke 11:1-13), and gave specific and significant promises to such pray-ers. Intercession has an important place in both the Old and the New Testaments.

4. The Decree for Zion's Conservation (62:8-9)

Closely tied to the appointment and responsibility of the "watchers" is this promise in the form of a divine oath, that the fruits of the land shall no more be plundered at harvesttime by the invasions of Zion's enemies.

a. What God swears by (62:8a). **The Lord hath sworn by his right hand** (the symbol of His power), **and by the arm of his strength** (the symbol of His own greatness). Divine oaths usually appeal to two witnesses for their guarantee (cf. Heb. 6:14-20). God swore in His oath to Abraham by two immutable things, himself and His own word (cf. Gen. 22:14-18). What God swears by has to be as great and as eternal as himself.

b. What God swears to—"The Oath of Conservation" (62:8b-9). **Surely I will no more give thy corn to be meat for thine enemies; and the sons of the stranger shall not drink thy wine** (8). This promise calls to remembrance the desolating attacks of the Midianites (Judg. 6:4, 11), the Philistines (II Chron. 28:18), and the Assyrians (16:9), in which the harvests were taken by foreigners and the peasants were left without their hard-earned food. It recalls also the curse pronounced upon spiritual apostasy (Deut. 28:33, 51). Now comes the declaration that hostile invaders shall no more reap the crops that Judah has sown, nor quaff the wine from the grapes she has gathered. Freedom from economic deprivation is more closely attached to freedom from depravation than this world cares to recognize. Hence the promise is that **they that have gathered it shall eat it, and praise the Lord; and . . . shall drink it in the courts of my holiness** (9). Partaking of the produce of the harvest will be consecrated by religious feasts. The enjoyment of the blessing unimpaired will be attended with grateful acknowledgment of the Giver. Thus sanctified with thanksgiving, all eating should be a simple sacrament of joy.

5. The Deliverer with Zion's Reward (62:10-12)

Here is the call to prepare the way for returning exiles, to give the signal and proclamation of salvation on all sides, with a reminder of the coming rewards and recompense, followed by symbolic names which set the divine ideal for the people of God.

a. *The returning exiles* (62:10a). **Go through the gates** may well be a double-sided command. Exit from the lands of captivity is surely enjoined. Similarly the inhabitants of Zion are to form a welcoming committee and a crew of road builders who shall make the return of exiles to Zion as welcome and as easy as possible. Isaiah's double imperatives expose the sense of urgency in the heart of the Speaker.

b. *Zion's causeway* (62:10bcd). **Prepare the way of the people; cast up, cast up the highway; gather out the stones.** Spiritual highways must be prepared so that they lead from the locale of every guilty sinner right up to the heart of God. They must not be "dead-end" roads. Revivals may be more or less spontaneous, but consistent programs of evangelism must involve much preparation. If men are to travel on a higher plane of living, a **highway** must be **cast up.** All hindrances must be removed by a tender solicitude which gathers **out the stones.** If Christ's ambassadors are to make the way straight and plain, they must not clutter divine revelations with the stumbling stones of human prejudices or private opinions. The message must be simple and authentic. If the Church today is to be successful, some of us must needs clear away the obstacles of the charted route, others must bring materials and construct a highway along which the stream of converts may march, others must remove such stones as might cause stumbling (cf. Isa. 57:14), and still others (perhaps the leaders) must **lift up a standard** to direct the march.

c. *The rallying banner* (62:10e). "Raise a signal for all the nations to see" (Knox). "Lift up a banner for the people" (Berk.). The **standard** thus becomes a flag that symbolizes Zion's ideals under which **the people** (the Heb. is plural—"peoples") may assemble, and following which they may march in triumph and loyalty.

d. *The worldwide proclamation* (62:11). **The Lord hath proclaimed unto the end of the world** the advent of **salvation.** This should be good news to any **daughter of Zion** who is such by either birth or adoption. The masculine pronouns, which refer back to the term **salvation** as their antecedent, show that **salvation** itself is a Person. There is a sense in which history is itself a voice of God proclaiming His will to mankind. The question may also be raised whether **the end of the world** (earth) has reference to time or space. Of this we now are sure:

> Christ first came from above down to earth visible to all in the form of a servant. Secondly, He comes continually from above invisibly, by His Spirit and Word and Sacrament that He may sanctify us. Thirdly, He will come again from above visible to all, not in the form of a servant, but in glory (Matt. 25).[20]

And when that moment comes, **his reward** for the righteous **and his** recompense for the wicked will be **with him,** "to render to each man according as his work is" (Rev. 22:12, ASV; cf. Isa. 40:10).

e. Surnamed and not forsaken (62:12). This is the destiny of the city of God's special concern and care. **They shall call them, The holy people, The redeemed of the Lord,** for God's people are lovers of holiness, and they are zealous for good works (Titus 2:14). "None are to be called the redeemed of the Lord but those that are the holy people; the people of God's purchase is a holy nation."[21] The redeemed of the Lord are the ones He has ransomed (Isa. 35:10; 51:10) "out of every nation and of all tribes and peoples and tongues" (Rev. 7:9, ASV). Hence this new Jerusalem, this transformed Zion, shall **be called, Sought out, A city not forsaken** (versus Jer. 30:17). "It is good to associate with the holy people, that we may learn their ways, and with the redeemed of the Lord, that we may share in the blessings of redemption."[22] For, as George Adam Smith has written:

> The Supreme force in the Universe is on man's side, and for man has won victory and achieved freedom. God has proclaimed pardon. A Saviour has overcome sin and death. We are free to break from evil. The struggle after holiness is not a struggle of a weakly plant in an alien soil and beneath a wintry sky, counting only upon the precarious aids of human cultivation; but summer has come, the acceptable year of the Lord has begun, and all the favour of the Almighty is on His people's side. These are the *good tidings* and *proclamation* of God, and to every man who believes them they must make an incalculable difference in life.[23]

F. The Drama of Divine Vengeance, 63:1-6

Interpretations of this chapter have been varied and often are very perverse. All attempted literalizations must surely fail.

---

[20]Naegelsbach, *op. cit.,* p. 669.
[21]Matthew Henry, *op. cit., ad loc.*
[22]*Ibid.*   [23]*Op. cit.,* p. 440.

It is a picture of the Hero-Warrior coming back from the conflict with Edom, Israel's perpetual foe. But it is the Conqueror, not the embattled Warrior, that we see here. The carnage, the struggle, the horrors of the battle are all behind Him. We see only the Victor as He appears marching in splendid majesty and triumphant strength. The poem takes the form of a lyrico-dramatic dialogue, with question and answer alternating. In the previous chapter our attention was focused upon the covenant with the holy people. Here we catch a brief but sobering glimpse of God's dealing with the unholy. Zion's enemies will all be vanquished. The picture here is that of the Eternal's conquering Servant returning as a victorious Warrior from furious encounter with, and conquest over, the foe. The poem briefly depicts the drama of divine vengeance. The central Personage is the divine Saviour-Champion.

1. *The Call for Identification* (63:1)

The question, **Who is this?** elicits the response, It is I. Thus does the prophet's question, like an index finger, point out the radiant Victor in gory garments. **Cometh from Edom** is a dramatic phrase intended to specify not only the locale of the conflict but the nature of the enemy. **Edom** was the land of Esau, the secularist (Heb. 12:16, "profane" in the sense of "unhallowed, common, worldly, or godless"), and **Bozrah** was its capital. The Edomites were typically modern "go-getters" for everything but grace. Their part in history had been one of persistent hostility to the Hebrews. They are therefore representative of the world that hates the people of God.

Bozrah is a rhyming word with the Hebrew term *Bosser,* "vinedresser." In biblical symbolism grapes are connected with the divine wrath in many instances (Rev. 14:18-20). **Dyed garments** would recall the fact that the one treading the grapes in the wine vat often found his garments bespattered with the juice of the grapes. But here the color is that of blood just shed, making the garments a bright red. To say that he was **glorious in his apparel** would mean that this blood-stained vesture of the Conqueror was a glory to Him (cf. Nah. 2:3 and Rev. 19:13).

Travelling in the greatness of his strength pictures this Conqueror walking with chest out and head thrown back and erect, as in the manner of one exulting in his victory. "Tossing back his head in the greatness of his strength," is Von Orelli's translation.

I that speak in righteousness, mighty to save, is His answer
2. *The Call for Explanation* (63:2)
to the question, **Who is this?** "I am he that utters righteousness,
rich in help" (Von Orelli). This recalls 45:19-24, and serves to
identify this important Person as none other than the Ideal
Servant of the Lord of Hosts, who shares the divine attributes.

Here recurs that ancient question, Why? **Wherefore art
thou red in thine apparel, and thy garments like him that
treadeth in the winefat?** Why the blood-stained vesture, or wine-
spattered garments? The color is not that of a warrior's usual
dress. The Hebrew word *adom,* meaning "red" (cf. Adam), is
closely related to the word Edom (cf. Gen. 25:30). The land of
the Edomites has an abundance of red soils and red sandstone
rock. **Winefat** in the Hebrew carries the syllable *Geth,* which
has reference to the idea of "press," and is the first syllable of our
other significant term "Gethsemane," which means "the oil
press."

3. *The Lonely Hero* (63:3)

Accepting the suggested metaphor of the prophet, this Conqueror replies: **I have trodden the winepress alone . . . none
with me.** This solitary One is none other than our Saviour,
confessing His lonely battle in His passion for our vindication
and salvation. **None of the people** (nations) were fit to be the
Eternal's instrument of judgment. But here is One who can
now say: "The prince of this world is judged" (John 16:11;
cf. Rev. 19:15).

**I will tread them in mine anger, and trample them in my
fury.** Alone and single-handed, without allies, stands this one
great Figure in the strength of one great emotion, to trample
down His enemies. The RSV more correctly makes the verbs
past tense rather than future, and reads: "I trod . . . and trampled." " 'Twas their blood splashed my robes, till all my clothes
are stained" (Moffatt).

4. *The Fury of World Judgment* (63:4-6)

**For the day of vengeance is in mine heart, and the year of
my redeemed is come** (4; cf. 61:2). A **day** is time enough for
God to take **vengeance,** to kill, and to destroy, but this **day of
vengeance** ushers in the **year** of redemption. Here we have the
motive for the action of which the blood-stained garments were
the result.

The search for an ally ends in disappointment and amazement at human indifference and inability. **And I looked, and there was none to help; and I wondered that there was none to uphold** (5; cf. 59:16). No man has any part in making the atonement for our sins. The battle was fought by Him single-handed. He had no human allies, for they all forsook Him and fled. **Therefore mine own arm brought salvation unto me; and my fury, it upheld me.**

> The meaning is that no one, in conscious willingness to assist the God of judgment and salvation in His purpose, associated himself with Him. The church devoted to Him was the object of redemption; the mass of those alienated from God was the object of judgment. He saw Himself alone; neither human cooperation, nor the natural course of things aided the execution of His design; therefore He renounced human assistance, and interrupted the natural course of things by a wonderful deed of His own.[24]

I will tread down . . . and make them drunk (6) is suggestive of what Scripture has to say about the cup of divine wrath (51:17; Ps. 75:8; Jer. 25:15). Here again the Hebrew would indicate the use of past tenses in the English translation: "I trod down . . . made drunk . . . brought down" (cf. the RSV). People drunk on the divine wrath may also be thought of as staggering under the divine judgments. **I will bring down their strength to the earth** is better translated, as in the RSV, "I poured out their lifeblood on the earth." Hence their destruction was utter, overwhelming, and absolute. The Hebrew Targums read: "I shattered them to fragments."

This entire picture is an apocalyptic one, and as such it has influenced Rev. 19:11-16, where it has reference to the general judgment of the wicked multitudes. Christ's agony and His cross were indeed a conflict with the powers of evil (John 12:31:32; Col. 2:15), and believers may well shout, "Hallelujah!" for now we are fighting a defeated foe (I Pet. 5:8-11).

G. God's People at Prayer, 63:7—64:12

This passage lets us feel the intercessory heartthrob of the prophet. Isaiah identifies himself with the life and fate of his people, while at the same time he assumes the role of one of the Lord's "remembrancers" (62:6, mar.) and recounts the historical relationships of his people and their God. The prayer,

[24]Delitzsch, *op. cit., ad loc.*

though voiced by the prophet, may also vocalize the concern of
the holy minority still remaining in Judah. Yet God's people at
prayer involves, first of all, God's prophet in prayer. Here, as
George Adam Smith aptly observes:

> We have one of the noblest passages of our prophet's great
> work. How like he is to the Servant he pictured for us! How his
> great heart fills the loftiest ideal of service: not only to be the
> prophet and the judge of his people, but to make himself one with
> them in all their sin and sorrow, to carry them all in his heart.[25]

Isaiah had a strong sense of the nation's guilt. He sees the
people sunk in idolatry and wickedness, incapable of realizing the
Divine Presence or of appreciating God's great promises. Yet
he will make one more effort to save them all by means of intercessory prayer.

Smith further observes: "There is nothing in the prayer to
show that the author lived in the exile . . . the prayer, therefore,
must come from pretty much the same date as the rest of our
prophecy . . . nor is there any reason against attributing it to the
same writer."[26] He then goes on to note that there recur in this
passage some of the prophet's most characteristic thoughts.

Of this passage Muilenberg has written:

> Perhaps there is no utterance of similar scope in the Bible which
> portrays so profoundly and elaborately the nature of the relation-
> ship between Israel and God. The words are born in the agony and
> travail of the prophet for his people and in the great historical
> tradition in which God had made himself known to Israel. They are
> Israel's autobiography in man's loftiest and deepest language.[27]

He analyzes it into seven strophes in the Hebrew, as follows:
historical retrospect (two strophes, 63:7-10 and 11-14), the petition (three strophes, 63:15-16, 17-19; 64:1-5b), the confession
(64:5c-7), and the closing appeal (64:8-12). Plumptre's suggestion is also valid that herein we have praise, narrative, and supplication.[28] That Isaiah composed the prayer for one of the times
of fasting and prayer in Judah is quite probable. There are in it
the consciousness of the corporate personality of the nation, the
recollection of the nation's heritage, and the confession of the

---

[25]*Op. cit.*, p. 449.   [26]*Ibid.*, p. 447.
[27]*Op. cit.*, p. 729.   [28]*Op. cit., ad loc.*

nation's guilt. It is a Kipling *Recessional* from the pen and mind of the greatest Hebrew prophet.

1. *Thanksgiving for Mercies Shown* (63:7-10)

According to Ps. 50:23, this is the proper way to begin any address to God, and especially for those who have forgotten Him.

a. The song of God's loving-kindness (63:7). **I will mention the lovingkindness of the Lord.** Recounting the merciful acts of God according to all that the Eternal has done for us will revive our appreciation of His goodness, mercy, and love. Ronald Knox translates this passage beautifully in the following lines: "Listen while I tell again the story of the Lord's mercies, what renown the Lord has won; all the Lord has done for us, all the wealth of blessings his pardoning love, his abounding pity has lavished on the race of Israel."

The key word here in the Hebrew is *chesed,* which has been variously translated as "steadfast love" "loving-kindness," "loyal love," or "mercy." Moffatt translates it "acts of love" in this passage. These are the things about God that the prophet wishes to celebrate and commemorate. Hence the verse begins and ends with an emphasis upon this significant term. There is also the repetition of **hath bestowed** (the Hebrew term *gāmal*), the threefold use of the name of God, and a threefold use of the phrase **according to.**

b. The adopting, saving, eternal Father (63:8). **Surely they are my people, children that will not lie.** Here is God's adoption of Israel as His children in Egypt, risking everything on His confidence in their basic fidelity. In this hope He became their Saviour and Deliverer, speaking of them as "sons that will never play me false" (Moffatt). Here we have God's faith in man. We may trust Him because He first trusted us. **So he was their Saviour.** "So he became a deliverer to them" (Von Orelli).

c. The pitying Redeemer (63:9). **In all their affliction he was afflicted.** Their afflictions began in Egypt as soon as there arose another Pharaoh who knew not Joseph (Gen. 15:13; Exod. 1:8). Some commentators would translate the Hebrew to read: "In all their afflictions He was not an adversary to them,"[29] or as Naegelsbach in *Lange's Commentary* has it: "In all their

---

[29]Cf. Rawlinson in the *Pulpit Commentary, ad. loc.*

oppression He was not an oppressor."[30] But Von Orelli's translation is preferable:

> As often as they were afflicted, he himself felt affliction, and the angel of his face delivered them; in his love and his forbearance he redeemed them, and he lifted them up and bore them all the days of the foretime.

Now the mystery of God sharing the sorrows of men is made plain to us in Christ. This is intimated when the prophet says: **The angel of his presence saved them.** This expression occurs nowhere else in the entire Old Testament (but cf. Exod. 14:19; Judg. 13:6; and Acts 27:23). We may ask, "What and who is this 'angel of his face'?" Surely it can be no less than "the angel of the Lord" (*mal'akh Yahweh;* cf. Gen. 16:7; Num. 22:23; Judg. 13:3). This is therefore not an angel or an archangel (remember the word "angel" means messenger), but the very personification of the Divine Presence. God sent no substitute. He did not save them through the medium of envoy or messenger. It was His own presence that brought them deliverance. Thus we have here an instance of the preincarnate activity of the Second Person of the Trinity (cf. Exod. 23:20-23; 32:34; 33:2).[31] The mystery of the Holy Trinity is revealed in the New Testament, but light of this relationship breaks through even in the Old. He who is called God's face (*panim*) can be no less than He by whom God both sees and is seen.

In his love and in his pity he redeemed them. According to Delitzsch, a better term for **pity** is "forgiving gentleness." We are told in Exodus that God came down to deliver His people out of Egypt (Exod. 3:6-8*a*). Thus He purchased them to be His own private possession (Deut. 32:9). **And he bare them, and carried them all the days of old,** just as a father does his child. "I bore you on eagles' wings" (Exod. 19:4, RSV) recalls the mother eagle teaching its little ones to fly (cf. the ASV margin). So God brought them safely through the wilderness (Deut. 32:10-12).

d. The grieved Holy Spirit (63:10). But—here is that terrible adversative which introduces the actual in contrast to what should have and might have been. **They rebelled, and vexed his**

---

[30]*Op. cit.,* p. 676.

[31]Space does not permit a full exposition of this position here. The reader is referred to the very splendid exposition of Gen. 12:1 ff. by Lange, and C. W. E. Naegelsbach's exposition of this present verse, both in *Lange's Commentary.* Cf. also Delitzsch's commentary here.

holy Spirit; lit., "His Spirit of holiness." The word **holy** should be capitalized as well as **Spirit.** Here is another intimation of the Trinity, for as *The Berkeley Version* footnote observes: "His 'Holy Spirit' is grieved, which shows the prophet conceived of Him as a person." Plumptre calls this "a foreshadowing of the truth of the trinal personality of the unity of the Godhead."[32] (Cf. Ps. 78:40-41 and 106:43.) "They were rebellious against, and grieved the Holy Spirit by resisting the drawings of His grace and by offending His holy nature with doing evil."[33] **Therefore he was turned to be their enemy** (Lam. 2:3-5), **and he fought against them.** How much better it is to be found on God's side in life's issues than to have Him who should have been our Advocate become our Adversary! "The necessary consequence of resisting the Holy Spirit is that the Lord too is changed into an adversary of him who resists Him. The word, He, stands emphatically before the phrase, fought against them. How dreadful it is to have Him as an adversary!"[34] (Cf. Heb. 10:31.) As Plumptre says: "That which 'vexed' the Holy Spirit was . . . the unholiness of the people, and this involved a change in the manifestation of the Divine Love, which was now compelled to show itself as wrath."[35]

2. Recollection of Deliverances Known (63:11-14)

Then he (better translated, "they") **remembered the days of old.** 'Tis a hopeful day for the backslider who amidst his difficulties remembers that time of grace and God's former deliverance.

Release from bondage and the gift of the Holy Spirit is and ever has been God's twofold work. Notice that the question, **Where is he?** (11), focuses attention upon each of these. First the baptism "unto Moses in the cloud and in the sea" (I Cor. 10:2), then the Holy Spirit within them (the **him** of this passage undoubtedly refers to "the people"[36]). If we analyze vv. 11-12 we have (1) Deliverance—**out of the sea,** (2) Dynamic—the **holy**

---

[32]*Op. cit., ad loc.*

[33]Naegelsbach in *Lange's Commentary,* p. 677. [34]*Ibid.*

[35]*Op. cit., ad loc.*

[36]So contend Delitzsch, Rawlinson, and Plumptre (who says, "not Moses only, but Israel collectively"). C. von Orelli says: "In bestowing Him on these leaders, He made Him dwell in the heart, in the bosom of the nation, which of course gave rise to the possibility of grieving and rebelling against Him, verse 10" (*op. cit.,* p. 333).

Spirit within, (3) Defense—**the divided waters,** and (4) Distinction—**the everlasting name.**

Where is he that brought them up . . . with the shepherd of his flock? Many manuscripts have the word **shepherd** in the plural. This would probably include with Moses such others as Aaron and Miriam. **For he that put his holy Spirit within him,** the RSV reads: "Where is he who put in the midst of them his holy Spirit?" **That led them by the right hand of Moses with his glorious arm** (12) has been rendered, "Who caused his glorious arm to go at the right hand of Moses" (Von Orelli). But here also the arm of the Eternal is personified as One who was ready to grasp Moses if he should stumble. God's comradeship in our struggles is ours if we trust Him. He divided **the water before them, to make himself an everlasting name.** God's mighty deeds give knowledge of His nature (Exod. 9:16). Still today, it is the supernatural that advertises the Supreme Being.

In 13-14 is expressed a wonderful security as God led His people out of bondage, "as confident as sheep in the meadow" (Moffatt). Note the *eternal* name in v. 12, and the *glorious* name in v. 14. Knox's translation of the Vulgate reads: "Through its waters they passed, sure of their foothold as a horse that is led through the desert; carefully as a driver on some treacherous hillside, the Lord's spirit guided his people. Thus didst thou bring them home, and win thyself honour."

On the expression, **as an horse in the wilderness** (13) Moffat reads, "like horses on a level plain." The Hebrew indicates a wide, grassy pastureland, not a sandy desert such as the term **wilderness** suggests. Naegelsbach comments on such imagery as follows:

> One might suppose that Israel would have trodden with trembling, uncertain steps the strange way over the bottom of the sea on which human foot was never set, with the walls of the standing waters on the right hand and on the left. But it was not so. Rapidly and surely, as the desert horse goes over the flat smooth desert, without tottering, so did they march over that strange, perilous road.[37]

As a beast goeth down into the valley (14) is paraphrased by Plumptre to say, "as a herd of cattle descends from the hills to the rich pasturage of the valleys."[38] **The Spirit of the Lord caused**

[37]*Op. cit.,* p. 677.
[38]*Op. cit., ad loc.*

him to rest—"Yahweh's spirit led them to rest" (Von Orelli). **So didst thou lead thy people** suggests the discipline of divine guidance. **To make thyself a glorious name** carries the idea of a sweet memorial and may be read: "To win thyself renown and glory" (Moffatt).

3. *Importunity for God to Acknowledge His Own* (63:15-19)

Here the prophet recounts the tragic conditions of the present and urges the Lord to do something about it.

a. A plea for divine condescension (63:15-16). **Look down** (cf. II Chron. 6:21) . . . **and behold** (15; cf. Ps. 33:13-14). Contemplation of the past has inspired urgency in prayer. **From the habitation of thy holiness and of thy glory** suggests the distance between the height of God's holiness and the inglorious and unholy habitation of the people, who, though they live on the high promontory of Jerusalem's location, are plunged into the depths of sin and iniquity. **Where is thy zeal and thy strength?** Where are the ancient divine solicitude and the former mighty acts? **The sounding of thy bowels and of thy mercies toward me** might read in modern speech: "the sighs of Thy heart," or as *The Berkeley Version* reads: "thy yearning pity and compassion." "Where now is thy jealous love, where is thy warrior's strength? Where is thy yearning heart, thy compassion?" (Knox) **Are they restrained** should rather read: "They are restrained," indicating that they are no longer manifest.

Earthly and fleshly fathers may forget or disown us, but surely the Eternal One cannot. **Doubtless thou art our father** (16) would seem to declare that Jehovah alone is the true Father of Israel. Yet the fatherhood of God extends further than to a single nation (cf. Matt. 3:9). Perhaps the prophet is taking the child's attitude here which says: "Father, I cannot see your face within this darkness, but let me hear your voice and sense your presence."

Though Abraham be ignorant of us, and Israel (i.e., Jacob) **acknowledge us not** suggests that Abraham might disclaim his descendants, but the Lord would still recognize them. Smart thinks that the prophet may have in mind here the fact that the major part of the nation, whom he styles **Abraham** and **Israel**, has repudiated the prophet and his faithful and holy minority. Yet the faithful remnant makes intercession for the whole nation.[39] This would also raise the question as to who are really Abraham's children (cf. 51:1-2; Matt. 8:11-12; John 8: 39-42; Rom. 2:28-29). **Thou, O Lord, art our father, our redeemer.** We must remember here that the redeemer is the nearest relative and has the right of purchase back or redemption from servitude.

Thy name is from everlasting is better rendered in the margin, "Our redeemer from everlasting is thy name." "Our Redeemer has been thy name from of old."[40] **Redeemer** first appears as a name for God in Job 19:25; and in Ps. 19:14 and 78:35. But it occurs at least thirteen times in the later portion of Isaiah's prophecy. This, then, is the Eternal One's unique and immemorial name.

b. *The mystery of the divine abandonment to sinning* (63: 17-19). The query of the wayward ones here would seem almost to criticize and condemn God. Why leave us to wandering? And why abandon us to hardness of character in irreverence? Why do You let Your sheep go astray?

O Lord, why hast thou made us to err from thy ways, and hardened our heart from thy fear? (17) "And hardened our heart so as not to reverence thee?" (Lamsa, *Peshitta*) This smacks of the Near Eastern fatalism which makes everything to be the will of *Allah.* So Jerome (writing years later at Bethlehem) insists that God is not the cause of error and hardness of heart, but that error and obduracy are only mediately occasioned by His patience, while He does not chastise the offenders.[41] Likewise Delitzsch comments: "When men have scornfully and obstinately rejected the grace of God, God withdraws it from them judicially, gives them up to their wanderings, and makes their hearts incapable of faith."[42] This much we know, the effect of sin is more sin. Acts turn into habits which in turn become confirmed patterns of response.

Return for thy servants' sake, the tribes of thine inheritance. "For the love of thy own servants, relent, for the love of the land that by right is thine" (Knox). "Cease, for thy servants' sake" (Moffatt). God always has a remnant that has not bowed its knees to Baal. If God relents, all will be well. How ardently, therefore, does God's holy minority long for only God himself!

---

[39]*Op. cit.,* pp. 269-70.   [40]Rawlinson, *op. cit., ad loc.*

[41]Cf. Naegelsbach, *op. cit.,* p. 679.   [42]*Op. cit., ad loc.*

The divine sanctuary was only a brief possession of the holy people. "The people of thy holiness have possessed the land but a little while; our oppressors have trodden down thy sanctuary" (18; Lamsa, *Peshitta*). Isaiah and the "holiness minority" held the leadership under the later years of Hezekiah, but now that Manasseh has ascended the throne all this has been reversed. **People of thy holiness** we take to mean the righteous remnant of Isaiah's day. Their question seems to ask: "Why should the godless tread the holy mountain?"

We (they) **are** like foreigners to the divine government, or like strangers whom Thou hast never claimed; no better than the heathen, **they were not called by thy name** (19). (The italics show that the word **thine** in the beginning phrase of this verse is not in the Hebrew.) Moffatt translates: "We fare like those who never knew thy rule, whom thou hast never claimed as thine." Our privileges and blessings are all lost. No one would recognize us as God's people.

4. Supplication That God's Power May Be Shown (64:1-5b)

The prayer now takes on the nature of desperation, insisting that the terror of the Lord is better than His silence.

a. Longing for the appearance of God (64:1-3). The prayer is for a visible divine intervention (a theophany), until the world trembles at the awesomeness of the Divine Presence. **Oh that thou wouldest rend the heavens, that thou wouldest come down** (1). The intercessor, now in desperation, asks for another Sinai ablaze with God. "O God, split the heavens that seem as brass and answer from on high!" God in His heavenly palace seemed veiled and silent. **That the mountains might flow down at thy presence** ("quake," RSV).

As when the melting fire burneth (2). Fire is an element in almost all of the biblical theophanies (Heb. 12:18-29). "The manifestation of God's holiness was necessarily a violent one, as fire kindles brushwood, i.e., with huge crackling, or flame making water boil."[43] **To make thy name known to thine adversaries** is in keeping with the fact that revelation is the purpose of all theophanies. **That the nations may tremble at thy presence**, since God's revelation involves judgment upon sinners. "So should the fame of thee go abroad among thy enemies; a world should tremble at thy presence" (Knox).

[43]Von Orelli, *op. cit.,* p. 334.

Terrible things which we looked not for (3) recalls the momentous events between Egypt and Canaan which were beyond Israel's expectation. **Thou camest down, the mountains flowed down** (quaked) **at thy presence.** So these verses begin and end with the same phenomenon in nature. We may recall the great earthquake that is prophesied in the Apocalypse (Rev. 16:18).

b. *The divine incomparability* (64:4-5b). "No **ear** has **heard** nor **eye** has **seen** (4) a God like Thee, who mightily works for those who wait in faith, and who meets with him who delights in righteousness" (paraphrase). Note this passage in St. Paul's usage (I Cor. 2:9). "From ancient times men have not heard or perceived, nor has human eye seen a God besides Thee who works for him who waits for Him. Thou dost meet him who is joyful, who works righteously and who in Thy ways remembers Thee" (Berk.).

5. *Confession That the Trouble Is Sin Alone* (64:5c-7)

When sins of long standing are coupled with self-righteous pollution, the people of Judah are like fading and falling leaves.

a. *The contrasting uncleanness of the people* (64:5c-6). **Behold, thou art wroth** (5) signalizes the shift of the man at prayer from the mood of faith and hope to one of penitence and confession. "But thou hast been wroth at our sins, wroth at our breach of faith" (Moffatt). **For we have sinned.** When a keen sense of God's presence wanes, men often become guilty of sins of presumption, and these are soon followed by deeds of iniquity. **In those is continuance** is translated in the RSV to read: "In our sins we have been a long time." Growing corruption marks the course of evil, so Hosea must say: "And now they sin more and more" (Hos. 13:2, ASV; cf. 57:17). **And we shall be saved** should be more properly read as a question, "And shall we be saved?" (RSV)

We are all as an unclean thing should more properly be read: "We have all become like one who is unclean" (RSV). Sin is a deadly infection. **All our righteousnesses are as filthy rags.** The Hebrew suggests Lev. 15:19-24, and the menstruous cloth. **We all do fade as a leaf.** Sin takes away vitality and the soul's powers of resistance. It dissipates the physical as well as the spiritual manhood. **Our iniquities, like the wind, have taken us away.** The picture is that of withered autumn leaves driven before the wind.

b. The curse of God-forsakenness (7). **None . . . calleth upon thy name.** That people's condition is indeed desperate where no one seeks to avail himself of God's help. **That stirreth up himself to take hold of thee.** "When God hides His face, men lack the impulse to venture toward Him."[44] **For thou hast hid thy face from us** would indicate that the reality of God's presence is completely lost. So far as they are concerned, God is dead. **And hast consumed us, because of our iniquities;** "hast melted us" (in the heat of His divine wrath). *The Berkeley Version* says: "hast delivered us to the control of our iniquities." God save us from ourselves!

6. *Appeal That God Shall Not Abandon His Own* (64:8-12)

This final appeal to God is based upon the Lord's fatherhood. It urges Him to remember His handiwork. It pleads that in wrath He will remember kinship. Then comes the wail of desolation, followed by the pointed question: How can the Eternal One refrain from action?

a. In wrath remember kinship (64:8-9). **But now, O Lord (8)** is an impassioned expostulation which opens this appeal. **Thou art our father,** declares the prophet, though he hardly dares to add, "and we are thy sons," in the light of all such sin and uncleanness just confessed. Note here the emphasis is upon the Father-Creator relationship, whereas at 63:16 it was upon the Father-Redeemer aspect. **We are the clay, and thou our potter; and we all are the work of thy hand** (cf. Job 10:9). Will God destroy His own works? All mankind must, of course, recognize a common creaturehood. We may try to live like gods, but we all die like men (Ps. 82:6-7).

Be not wroth very sore, O Lord (9) in more modern speech means simply, "Be not exceedingly angry" (RSV). **Neither remember iniquity for ever;** God's memory evinces Israel's historical mentality. **Behold, see, we beseech thee, we are all thy people** (cf. 63:8). The prophet was a great advocate and pleader.

b. The wail of desolation (64:10-11). Jesus probably had this passage in mind as He spoke His own great "Apostrophe to Jerusalem" (Matt. 23:37-39). Here the complaint reminds the Eternal that the holy cities are laid waste and the holy . . . **house** consumed by flames while all the old former resorts are ruins. That Isaiah speaks prophetically of the destruction of the

---

[44]Henry Sloan Coffin, *op. cit.,* p. 742.

Temple here is the position of those who hold that **our beautiful house** means Temple, and still contend for Isaianic authorship of this passage.

c. *How can God refrain from forthright action?* (64:12) Man's impatience has often cried: "Why doesn't God do something about it?" **Wilt thou refrain thyself for these . . . O Lord?** Omit the italicized word, *things*. "Wilt thou keep silent still, and overwhelm us with calamity?" (Knox) It would seem that natural tenderness and natural indignation both should find a vent in the divine nature. Such, then, is the mystery of the divine silence which hangs like an oppressive burden over the soul of the prophet.

H. God's Answer to His People's Supplications, 65:1-25

This chapter follows as the sequence and completion of the preceding prayer, while at the same time it is so similar to the chapter which follows that a common authorship and background must be assumed. But here we see the dividing of the ways for the apostates within Judah from the righteous and faithful minority. The chapter makes it quite plain that not all Israel shall be saved; to each shall be dealt his own deserts from God. The faithful God will bring to His faithful remnant a new name and a new blessing.

1. *The Double Aspect of the Divine Recompense* (65:1-16)

That God does make distinctions as to character and practices is the prophet's profound conviction. When God acts in history, it is for both retribution and redemption.

a. *The guilt of distance* (65:1-7). The picture here is that of the Eternal's futile pleading with a persistently rebellious people.

(a) Unavailing accessibility (1-2). **I am sought . . . I am found** (1) are phrases which introduce the fact of God's readiness and eagerness to let himself be found. This is the beginning of the divine response to the prayer of His prophet and His people. Plumptre's paraphrase reads: "I was ready to answer those who did not enquire, was nigh at hand to be discovered by those who did not seek."[45] In fact, God has always taken the initiative toward repairing the broken comradeship between himself and

---

[45]*Op. cit., ad loc.*

man. **I said, Behold me** ("Here am I," RSV), **unto a nation that
was not** calling upon **my name. I have spread out my hands . . .
unto a rebellious people** (2). God, like a Father, had stretched
out both hands to a child that would not come to Him (cf. Matt.
11:28-30). So yet again God must refer to them as **a rebellious
people** (*'am sorer*). The guilt for the seeming distance between
Israel and the Lord rests with an Israel which **walketh in a
way . . . not good.** Like the Son of God centuries later, God must
say: "You search the scriptures, because you think that in them
you have eternal life; and it is they that bear witness to me;
yet you refuse to come to me that you may have life" (John
5:39-40, RSV). The situation is, as Moffatt translated: "I have
stretched my hands, all day, to unruly rebels, who lead a life
corrupt, pleasing themselves."

(*b*) Unwarranted aggravation (3-5). Here the accusation is
that Judah has behaved presumptuously, in a manner both abominable and self-righteous. How then can God adopt anything but
a standoffish attitude toward such people and their practices? It
is difficult to express the divine disgust here in the English of
three hundred fifty years ago, so Moffatt's translation reads as
follows:

> . . . *a people who provoke me to my face continually,*
>   *by sacrificing in their groves,*
>   *and burning incense under the white poplars* [birch, or
>   aspen?]—
> *people who sit on graves and pass the night in vaults,*
> *who eat the flesh of swine and cook them carrion broth,*
> *who say, "Keep far away from me, lest I make you tabu!"*
>
> *Such men are like smoke from a blaze,*
>   *that irritates me all the day.*

Sacrificing **in gardens** (3) was a common practice in Judah
in the days of Ahaz (cf. 1:29; 57:5; and Ezek. 20:28). The nature
goddess was thought to be best worshipped among the groves, or
in gardens, by rites into which sensualism entered as an essential
element. **Altars of brick** (contra. Moffatt) may have been the
tiled roofs of the homes. At least altars made of brick were forbidden by Jewish law (Deut. 27:6; Josh. 8:31).

To **remain among the graves** (4) would also be an unclean
practice for Jews, but quite acceptable for those who sought to
communicate with the spirits of the dead. "Whenever religion

deteriorates to conventional worship, the door opens wide for the entrance of superstition."[46]

To **lodge in the monuments** (secret places) would involve the practices of the mystery cults. This probably took on the form of seeking messages from the other world by sleeping in a so-called "holy place." St. Jerome, in commenting on this passage, calls attention to the fact that men went to sleep in the crypts of the temple of Aesculapius, in the hope of gaining visions of the future. The use of **swine's flesh** had been forbidden since the days of Moses (Lev. 11:7), not only on sanitary grounds but because young hogs were sacrificed in the Tammuz festivals (Ezek. 8:14), or in connection with the Adonis cult (cf. 66:17). This argues that the writer's locale was not Babylon. **Broth of abominable things** (15) would indicate a sacrificial feast of unclean meats. The expression really means "fragments of uncleanness."

Verse 5 indicates that, "although stained with every heathen abomination, they put on sanctimonious airs as members of a secret order, and even avoided contact with their countrymen."[47] As a result of the supposedly sacred rites through which he had gone, the communicant was reckoned "holy" and must not be profaned by any contact with one who was unholy. Each was taboo to the other. So the one who had been initiated into the mystery cult could say, **I am holier than thou.** But all this God calls **a smoke in my nose** ("a stench in My nostrils"). "In Hebraic psycho-physical anthropology, the nose was the seat of anger. The word for 'anger' and nose, or nostrils, is the same in Hebrew."[48]

(c) **Unrestrained accumulation (6-7).** Sins and their consequences form a mighty avalanche in the divine displeasure, which comes pouring into the sinner's bosom with damnation. Here the Lord calls attention to His written declaration of sure recompense: **Behold, it is written before me (6).** He has sworn, **I will not keep silence, but will recompense.** Therefore let not impious man treat the long-suffering of God as though He were forgetful. For He will **even recompense into their bosom** (cf. Jer. 16:18).

---

[46]Henry Sloan Coffin, *op. cit.*, p. 747.

[47]Von Orelli, *op. cit.*, p. 338.

[48]James Muilenberg, *op. cit.*, p. 748.

b. The gulf of distinction (65:8-12). But not all Israel shall be cast off, for a remnant shall be spared even though apostates shall surely taste the divine wrath.

(a) The fortunate future remnant (8-10). **The new wine (8)** specifies the unfermented juice of the grape (cf. the Hebrew term, *tirosh*). God has faithful servants in the midst of an unfaithful nation, and for their sakes He will not destroy utterly. **A blessing is in it.** Only the faithful and the spiritual can rightly claim to be such an element in the cluster of Judah's grapes. How much some communities owe to the few righteous among them!

My mountains (9) refers to the fact that Palestine is really a cluster of mountains. **Sharon . . . and . . . Achor (10)** are symbols for "from west to east," just as "from Dan to Beer-sheba" means "from north to south." **Sharon** is that rich coastal plain extending north along the seacoast from Tel Aviv almost to Mount Carmel. **The valley of Achor** is probably the *Wadi-Kelt* near Jericho (Josh. 7:24; 15:7; Hos. 2:15). Hence the whole land is to be a garden of the Lord, reserved for His "little flock," **for my people that have sought me.**

(b) The fate of those failing to respond (11-12). Those who spread a feast for Fate shall be destined **to the slaughter (12)**, because they have not heeded the call or the wishes of the Lord. **But ye (11)** is emphatic and has reference to the apostates who **forsake** and **forget** true worship for pagan rites. **A table for that troop** may be translated as by the RSV, "a table for Fortune, and fill cups of mixed wine for Destiny." Worshipping the gods of fate is popular in this twentieth century too. Some people trust more to luck than they do in God. And some believe more in horoscopes than they do in the Word of God.

Therefore will I number you to the sword (12) indicates the destruction of the disloyal. **When I called, ye did not answer.** These people did not respond to the divine call to turn and repent, but chose evil instead.

c. The gracious difference (65:13-16). Four times comes that radical contrast **my servants . . . but ye.**

(a) The tables turned (13-15; cf. Berk. and footnotes). Here are predicted blessings for the servants of the Eternal Lord (*Adonai Yahweh*, in Hebrew), but hunger, thirst, pain, and anguish—plus a name that is used only in a curse, and final slaughter—is proclaimed for the ungodly. The dramatic phrase

thus saith the Lord God (13) introduces the oracle of eschatological judgment. The word **Behold** is used four times here. **Hungry . . . thirsty** would indicate economic disaster; **ashamed . . . sorrow** (14) would specify psychological distresses.

Your name . . . a curse (15; cf. Num. 5:21; Jer. 29:22; Zech. 8:13) indicates that they will become a representative example of the penalty of divine wrath. Jewish imprecations often took the form: "May the Lord make thee like unto ———." Even the old, familiar name for God's servants will be changed, for He shall **call his servants by another name** (cf. 62:2; Acts 11:26). The new name and the new blessing came centuries later than Isaiah's time.

(b) The "Amen" of truth (16). God is the real Source of security and blessing. He is the God of fidelity, "the God of the Amen" (cf. Deut. 27:15-26; Ps. 41:13; Rev. 3:14). So now the name of God is changed too. No longer is He "the God of Israel." He is now **the God of truth.**

2. The New Era of Idyllic Peace (65:17-25)

The final answer of God to the complaint and prayer of His people is now given. The entire existing state of things is to pass away. Man's complete environment is also to be made new, in keeping with his new and transformed nature. The old conditions being changed, the old complaints will not arise.

a. The great "De Novo" (65:17-20). God's continuous activity guarantees a new beginning.

(a) The new creation (17-19) insures **new heavens and a new earth** (17; life perhaps on a totally different planet), new memories, new joys, and a new focal point of living, which is the New Jerusalem. **Jerusalem** (18) of the new age will be a delight instead of a distress, both to God and to man. All has been given a universal new beginning. Here the key term is, **I create.** It is the very word which appears in Genesis (1:1, 21, 27) to specify the divine act of bringing into existence.[49] We have met the promise of a new heaven and a new earth already in Isaiah's thought (cf. 34:4; 51:6), at least by implication. Now it becomes explicit. The thought reappears in many forms in the New Testament. It is repeated verbally in II Pet. 3:13; Rev. 21:1; and

---

[49]*Bara* is the Hebrew, and it is to be distinguished from *'ashah,* "to form or shape or fabricate from that which already exists."

substantially in "the restitution of all things" (Acts 3:21). It is implied in Paul's phrase, "the manifestation of the sons of God" (Rom. 8:19). **The former** things (17) are the sin and sorrow of the age just past, which shall fade from the memory of God's people, who are now absorbed in the new delights of their new environment. The redemptive acts of God do, therefore, include man's total environment.

Be ye glad and rejoice . . . for . . . I create Jerusalem a rejoicing, and her people a joy (18). This glorious center of the new creation will be a scene of perpetual gladness. **And I will rejoice . . . and joy in my people** (19). Mankind's one talent is the privilege of making glad the heart of God because we love Him. **The voice of weeping shall no more be heard.** Orientals wail loudly when they mourn (cf. Rev. 21:4).

(b) The nation of centenarians (20). **There shall be no more . . . an infant of days.** This promises a return of the prediluvian longevity of life. The absence of both pestilence and war would be a contributing factor.

> And there shall no more pass from her young or old,
> Without completing his full length of life;
> But the youngest shall die a hundred years old,
> While he who falls short of a hundred shall be
>   counted accursed (Smith-Goodspeed).

Premature death was looked upon as a sign of the divine displeasure. Isaiah's new Jerusalem is not without death and sin. One wonders, then, how it can be free from pain and sorrow. Hence Delitzsch contends that what is pictured here is the millennium and not the final state.

b. *The grand desideratum* (21-25). The one great desire of all ages is herewith promised. Construction is of no delight without its conservation.

(a) The conservation of industry (21-22). **Build . . . plant . . . and eat** (21) all speak as proverbial types of national security. That men will enjoy the fruits of their labors is something which our war-scarred and produce-plundered age can appreciate. Homes will no more be made into rubble by bombs. **They . . . shall long enjoy the work of their hands** (22) carries further this thought of conservation. The Hebrew for **long enjoy** means, lit., "to wear out." Men will have time to wear out the things they have made and use up the things they have earned. Length of life will be **as the days of a tree.**[50] The cedars of Lebanon, the oaks of Bashan, and the olives of Gethsemane live through many generations.

(b) The conservation of progeny (23). The promise that **they shall not . . . bring forth for trouble** specifically indicates that no longer shall they bear children for the sword. Having **their offspring with them** would bespeak the accumulation of many successive generations. The Mosaic law promised long life and a numerous posterity to the godly.

(c) The consolations of piety (24). The silence of God is now ended. **Before they call, I will answer** would mean a removal of the long interval between prayer and the answer thereto. For in this case the answer anticipates the prayer. God knows our needs before we ask.

(d) The consummation of peace (25). **The wolf and the lamb shall feed together** recalls 11:6-9. **The lion** eating **straw like the bullock** would mean that his nature is so changed that he is now herbivorous instead of carnivorous in his appetites. This could be symbolical of changed tastes for all of heaven's inhabitants. At least it suggests the removal of the discords in the harmony of nature itself. **Dust shall be the serpent's meat** (cf. Mic. 7:17) is intended to say that serpents have now become harmless (but cf. Gen. 3:14). **They shall not hurt nor destroy in all my holy mountain, saith the Lord,** is the final solemn assertion that violence is ended and the universe is at rest. "Even so, come, Lord Jesus."

I. THE LORD'S RECOMPENSE AND HIS REWARD, 66:1-24

This final chapter of Isaiah's prophecy is concerned with God's judgments and Zion's jubilation. It speaks of the final siftings and rewards that shall be meted out as the great world harvest of both the wheat and the tares is reaped. The chapter as a whole continues the distinctions and the separation made evident in c. 65, but it carries them down to a last emphatic contrast. Thus George Adam Smith observes: "So we are left by the prophecy, —not with the new heavens and the new earth which it promised: not with the holy mountain on which none shall hurt nor destroy, saith the Lord; not with a Jerusalem full of glory and a people all holy, the centre of a gathered humanity,—but with

---

[50]Here the Septuagint reads "tree of life"; cf. Rev. 22:2.

the city like to a judgment floor, and upon its narrow surface a people divided between worship and a horrible woe."[51] But this final thought and twofold emphasis is in keeping with the thematic emphasis of the entire prophecy, for as Coffin so aptly observes: "This final chapter gives unity to the entire book of Isaiah. The book begins with a people sedulous for ceremonies and lacking in social conscience (1:10-17); it concludes with a plea for the service of God in obedience to his word."[52] Muilenberg insists upon its affinity with the previous chapter and regards it as comprising seven strophes in the Hebrew. He considers it under the general theme of "The New Birth of Zion and the Fire of Judgment."[53] Our sevenfold analysis does not exactly coincide with his.

1. *He Whom God Respects and Whom He Rejects* (66:1-4)

a. The Eternal One's habitat (66:1-2a). With **the heaven as His throne, and the earth** as His **footstool** (1), Isaiah's God is really "too big to house." He therefore disdains man-made temples and seeks rather to dwell in the hearts of the poor and contrite. **Where, then, is the house that** one might **build** for the Lord that would be adequate as **the place of His rest?** The God who fills heaven and earth does not need a temple (I Kings 8:27; II Chron. 6:18).[54]

b. The man whom God respects (66:2b). **But to this man will I look** who **is poor and of a contrite spirit, and trembleth at my word.** *The Berkeley Version* offers this translation of 2b-3a: "I will look favorably upon that man who is humble, feels crushed in spirit, and trembles at My word; rather than on him, who slays an ox as though he slew a man; who sacrifices a sheep as he would break a dog's neck; who brings a cereal oblation as if it were the blood of swine; who presents frankincense as though he were worshiping idols." All men are not equally regarded by God. He accepts only that class of men who are **poor, contrite,** and God-fearing in their attitudes (Ps. 51:17). And here is the true house of God—the soul-temple of the repentant one whose spiritual life answers to that of God him-

---

[51]*Op. cit.*, pp. 465-66.   [52]*Op. cit.*, p. 758.

[53]*Op. cit.*, pp. 757 ff.

[54]V. 6 of this chapter would indicate a temple then standing in Jerusalem at the time of this chapter's writing.

self (1:11-18; 57:15). He declares: "What I care for are humble, broken creatures, who stand in awe of all I say" (Moffatt).

c. *The man whom God rejects* (66:3-4). God rejects the man who will not learn that worship without love for God turns our solemnities into sins. Spiritual security and safety is not to be had by a mixture of paganism and piety. Salvation comes only from the eternal and living God, who shows His mercy and grace only toward the believing penitent. In matters of salvation, therefore, all roads do not lead to Rome!

> *Oxen some sacrifice and also human lives,*
> *they offer lambs and also dogs in worship,*
> *oblations due and swine's blood in their rites,*
> *incense, and yet they reverence an idol!* (3, Moffatt)

What is condemned is not sacrifice as such, but a sacrificial practice which has been debased with corrupt pagan practices.

Isaiah is quite certain that each act of a hypocrite's worship is an idolatrous abomination. This He sought to make plain to those of his day who had **chosen their own ways** to salvation and whose souls delighted **in their abominations** (3b). (For **abominations** the *Peshitta* reads "idols.") Here was a group whose glorying was in their shame (Phil. 3:19). Of all such the eternal God declares: **I also will choose their delusions** (4; devices, torments, afflictions; "childish follies," says the LXX). Little wonder that the Apostle Paul says, "God shall send them strong delusion, that they should believe a lie" (II Thess. 2:11). Ronald Knox seeks to bring out Isaiah's play on words here: "In all this, it is but caprice guides their choice, in all manner of abominations; trust me, at my own caprice I will choose the terrors I bring down upon them." Here the divine vow is to bring upon these pagans the very things they sought to avert by means of their pagan practices. We are free as mortals to choose our ways, but the destination or outcome of such ways cannot be changed. Isaiah seems to enunciate the fact that, as they have chosen their ways, so will God choose their wages, **and will bring their fears (terrors) upon them** ("will recompense them according to their works"—the *Peshitta*). This is the ironic thing in a moral universe: God suits the penalty to the practice.

d. *The divine recompense is in kind* (66:4). **I called, none did answer** would mean that those who turn away from God's call will find that God has turned away from theirs. How long

can a man ignore God and still expect His reply? **I spake, they
did not hear.** Rather **they did evil before mine eyes, and chose
that in which I delighted not** (i.e., "chose what I abhorred").
Headstrong, deliberate deafness arises from delusion. Its penalty
is further delusion in "the deceitfulness of sin" (Heb. 3:13).

2. God's Vindication of the Faithful (66:5-6)

a. The word of the Lord (66:5). Apostates are inclined to
mock those who remain faithful to God. **Hear the word of the
Lord . . . Your brethren . . . hated you . . . cast you out for my
name's sake.** Here we have two sharply separate groups: one
lives by faith, hope, and trust in the word of the Lord; the
other relies on a material Temple and its worship, plus a syn-
cretistic, sacrificial system. For the first there is consolation
(Matt. 5:11); for the last there is sure and sudden recompense.
Moffatt's translation is interpretation also:

> *But ye who stand in awe of the Eternal's word,*
>   *listen to what he promises:*
> *"Your kinsmen, who hate you for your faith in me,*
>   *sneer thus, 'Let the Eternal show his might,*
> *that we may see this joy of yours!'*
>   *They shall be taken aback!"*

Whether the key sentence be a sneer from those who mock or a
happy and sweet response from the persecuted, God's promise in
either case is that the oppressors and persecutors shall be put to
shame. **He shall appear to your joy, and they shall be ashamed.**
Often unbelievers manifest a craze for the spectacle rather than
that which is spiritual. Let them sneer and make light of the
faith of the pious, but already the prophet hears the thunders of
judgment sounding from the city.

b. The threefold voice of recompense (66:6). "Hark! the
city is in uproar! It is coming from the temple! 'Tis the Eternal
dealing vengeance to the full upon his foes!" (Moffatt). **A voice
of noise from the city** was actually "a thunderous voice" (Berk.).
It comes now **from the city** where the mockers had called for a
manifestation of God's glory. It is **a voice from the temple,** the
focal point of their corrupted worship. If Isaiah's home was in
the Tyropoean valley (as we have noted earlier), then the Temple
sounds would be quite audible to him below. This is written
from the standpoint of one outside the city. No doubt Isaiah and

his holiness party had been excluded or expelled from the sacred precincts.

3. Can a Land Be Born in One Day? (66:7-9)

The prophet now turns his attention to Mother Zion as the eternal God continues to speak, promising the miracle of the birth of an entirely new people and their country.

a. The birth pangs of a new nation (66:7). **Before she travailed, she brought forth; before her pain came, she was delivered of a man child.** Birth without travail? So it would seem, for the prophet now sees a whole nation born at once and not growing up by the slow degrees of social increase. Christianity, following Pentecost, became a world force in one generation.

b. The incredible can happen (66:8). **Who hath heard such a thing? who hath seen such things? Shall the earth be made to bring forth in one day?** Can Rome be built in a day? Can a whole country come into being so suddenly? **Shall a nation be born at once?** Yet it did happen in the case of modern Israel in the great crisis of 1948. That little nation declared her identity and has been able to maintain her independence as a nation against great odds. Some commentators, however, make the man child refer to the Messiah. Still others see here the advent of a purely spiritual Israel in the followers of the Suffering Servant.

As soon as Zion travailed, she brought forth her children. But *The Berkeley Version* says: "Yet Zion had hardly travailed, when she gave birth to her children." This reading is more in keeping with what precedes. The Jewish Targum has a much more suggestive reading: "Before distress cometh upon her, she shall be redeemed: and before trembling cometh upon her, as travail upon a woman with child, her king shall be revealed." In the ordinary course of nature, travail must precede birth, and tribulation must be the forerunner of triumph. But each is a sign of a certain and coming event.

c. God doesn't start something He cannot finish (66:9). **Shall I bring to the birth, and not cause to bring forth? saith the Lord.**

> *But why should I not help her to bring forth*
> *what I bring to the birth? says the Eternal.*
> *Why should I close the womb, when I have brought the*
> *babe to birth? so says your God* (Moffatt).

Here let us recall the lament of Hezekiah about this very situation (37:3). Our prophet however is quite sure that midwifery knows something about proper timing for both travail and birth. **Shall I cause to bring forth, and shut the womb? saith thy God.** "The Lord has begun to restore His people; He will not leave their salvation incomplete" (Berk., fn.). The point of it all seems to be: God doesn't start something He cannot finish, nor does He stop with merely preliminary circumstances.

4. *Peace like a River* (66:10-14)

a. Rejoice with Jerusalem (66:10-11). Here is the note of joy and plenty. "Jerusalem is thought of as a mother, and the rich consolation . . . which she receives (51:3) as the milk which comes into her breasts . . . with which she now nourishes her children abundantly."[55]

"Lovers of Jerusalem, rejoice with her, be glad for her sake; make holiday with her, you that mourned for her till now. So shall you be her foster-children, suckled plentifully with her consolations, drinking in, to your heart's content, the abundant glory that is hers" (Knox).

b. Rivers of peace (66:12). **For thus saith the Lord, Behold, I will extend peace** (prosperity) **to her** (the city of peace) **like a river.** Modern translators believe that the great Hebrew term *shalom* should indicate prosperity in this instance. But it is to be such at its full flood tide. **Peace to her,** but no peace to the wicked, is the conclusion of each of Isaiah's previous enneads (48:22 and 57:21). **The glory of the Gentiles like a flowing stream** suggests that the nations shall minister to her prosperity. "Then shall the children of her love be carried astride her hip and fondled upon her lap" (paraphrase).

c. Comforts like a mother's caresses (66:13). "I will console you then, like a mother caressing her son, and all your consolation shall be in Jerusalem" (Knox). "But now in speaking of God's dealing with the nation, it is no baby but an oldster, experienced in wounds and sorrow, returning for consolation."[56]

d. God's hand upon His servants (66:14). Here is an answer to that apparent God-forsakenness so evident in the prayer of c. 64. Clearly now the community of Judah is divided

[55]Delitzsch, *op. cit., ad loc.*
[56]Coffin, *op. cit.,* p. 767.

into two distinct camps—servants of God and the enemies of
God.

> *And when you see it your heart shall rejoice,*
> *And your limbs shall flourish like young grass.*
> *So shall the power of the Lord be revealed toward his*
> *   servants,*
> *And his indignation toward his enemies* (Smith-Good-
> speed).

5. *Judgments by Fire* (66:15-17)

Now come the judgments and the gathering out of the tares.

a. The Eternal's chariots of fire (66:15). **Behold, the Lord
will come with fire, and with his chariots like a whirlwind.** The
final destructive element for this age is fire, just as the final
destructive element for the antediluvian age was water (Genesis
7). Fire is the usual accompaniment of a theophany. Thus God
comes **to render his anger with fury, and his rebuke with flames
of fire.** Here also is an answer to the prayer of 64:1-3 for a great
theophany of fire.

b. The Eternal's sword of fire (66:16). **For by his fire and
by his sword will the Lord plead with all flesh.** Fires had been
used against the cities of Judah in the Sennacherib sieges, and
the sword had been the Assyrian's instrument of slaughter. The
judgment will be like this, and it will be universal upon all flesh.
The slain of the Lord shall be many, because within Judah and
Jerusalem there are many apostates and idolaters.

c. The Eternal's sentence of doom (66:17). The KJV translators had trouble here. **They that sanctify themselves, and
purify themselves in the gardens behind one tree** (the margin
reads: "one after another") **in the midst,** no doubt has reference
to the pagan ritual dances as the devotees in their heathen performances sought holiness of soul. Leave out the word **tree** and
read "one in the midst" and in doing so recognize that "the one"
was their master of ceremonies, who, standing in the middle,
was imitated by the rest of the worshippers.[57] "Vainly they
sought holiness, that would purify themselves in secret gardens,
behind shut doors, and all the while ate flesh of swine and field-

[57]So explains George Adam Smith, *op. cit.*, p. 463, note.

mouse and other meats abominable; one end there shall be
for all of them, the Lord says" (Knox).

6. *The Eternal's Glorious Oblation* (66:18-21)

a. *The gathering of the nations* (66:18). **I know their works
and their thoughts,** and their works proceed from their thoughts
(Mark 7:30-23; cf. Rev. 2:2, 19; 3:1, 8, 15). **It shall come, that
I will gather all nations and tongues**—the hour for the summons
is at hand. **And they shall come, and see my glory.**

b. *The sign of the Eternal's glory* (66:19). **And I will set a
sign among them** is a clause variously interpreted by the commentators. Is this **sign** a mark or a miracle? Some commentators
think that Messiah is that **sign** (cf. Alexander). Others think it a
mighty act of judgment. Knox translates: "All must come and
see my glory revealed, and I will set a mark upon each of them."
**And I will send those that escape of them unto the nations,
to Tarshish, Pul, and Lud.** "What of those that find deliverance?
I have an errand for them, to be my messengers across the sea;
to Africa, and to Lydia where men draw the bow, to Italy, and
to Greece, and to Islands far away" (Knox). **To Tubal, and
Javan, to the isles afar off, that have not heard my fame, neither
have seen my glory.** Escapees from judgment are turned into
missionaries and become the Lord's ambassadors, to Spain and
the western Mediterranean, to the south of Egypt, perhaps So-
maliland, to Lydia in Asia Minor, and the region southeast of
the Black Sea, to Greece, and the islands far away (perhaps
Britain). They thus become a Messianic band of missionaries.
And they shall declare (proclaim) **my glory among the Gentiles**
(heathen).

c. *Converts as an offering to God* (66:20). **And they shall
bring all your brethren for an offering unto the Lord out of all
nations.** The Apostle Paul's holy oblation was his converts he
had won to Christ. Isaiah's vision seems to behold the evangelists
returning with their trophies "as their due offering" (Moffatt).
Some will come **upon horses,** others **in chariots,** still others in
covered wagons (**litters,** coaches), and some **upon mules,** and
the rest upon the **swift** dromedaries—"For an offering to the
Lord on my holy mountain Jerusalem, says the Lord" (Smith-
Goodspeed). Note that it is to resemble the **clean** offering
brought in **a clean vessel** to the Lord. Moral cleanness is the
divine ideal for the people of God.

d. Spiritual leaders shall be selected from them (66:21).
**And I will also take of them for priests and for Levites, saith the
Lord.** This is beyond the prescription of Deut. 17:9 ff. These
newcomers as converts from heathenism are to become ministers
and churchmen, for the wall of separation has now been removed.

7. *The Permanence of Piety and of Punishment* (66:22-24)

"He that is filthy, let him be made filthy still: and he that is
righteous, let him do righteousness still" (Rev. 22:11, ASV).
Here are the enduring destinies. Perpetual worship will characterize one class, eternal torment the other. Permanent and
unchanging is the final state of both the redeemed and the
damned.

a. Your seed shall remain (66:22). **As the new heavens and
the new earth ... remain ... so shall your seed** (race) **and your
name remain** (endure). Here is a destiny as stable and permanent as the new creation.

b. Your worship sustain (66:23). From month to month,
and from week to week, **shall all flesh come to worship before
me, saith the Lord.** As regularly as one succeeds the other, pil-
grimages of worship will arrive. But the true realization of this
is found only in the New Jerusalem of Rev. 21:22-27, and in the
form of the perpetual sabbatism of Heb. 4:9, both of which are
symbols of great spiritual realities.

c. Your triumph be plain (66:24). **And they shall go forth,
and look upon the carcases of the men that have transgressed
against me.** This surely is not intended to be taken literally.
"The corpses of the people who fell away from me" (Von Orelli)
is the prophet's way of speaking of the future state in figures
drawn from the present world. The fate of the guilty must surely
stand as an eternal memorial to sinning. **For their worm shall
not die, neither shall their fire be quenched.** The Jewish Talmud
made the Valley of Hinnom (Gehenna) to be the "mouth of hell."
Jesus himself appropriated this figure to symbolize the state of
those who fail to enter into life (Mark 9:48). The gnawing
worms of sordid memories and the consuming fires of perverted
passions comprise the agonies of the finally impenitent. Thus
the inescapable alternatives are still the holy, purging, cleansing
fire (Matt. 3:11) or the fire unquenchable with its tormenting
flame. How utterly foolish are they who judge themselves un-

worthy of eternal life (Acts 13:46)! **And they shall be an ab-
horring unto all flesh.** Ruined personalities, life's greatest ship-
wrecks, are strewn along the shores of history as a warning to all.

And so the final note is sounded in words more graphic than
those with which his two previous enneads have concluded, and
with a picture Isaiah would have none forget: "There is no peace,
saith the Lord, unto the wicked" (48:22; 57:21). "It is a terrible
ending, but one only too conceivable. For though God is love,
man is free—free to turn from that love; free to be as though he
had never felt it; free to put away from himself the highest,
clearest, most urgent grace that God can show, but to do this
is the judgment."[58]

How soon after preaching like this and drawing the lines so
clearly did Isaiah meet his martyr's death (as tradition says he
did) we cannot say. But Manasseh and his evil counselors
would hardly let the matter drop before they had exterminated
the prophet. Perhaps his final apostrophe to the city was something like that of his Greatest Successor seven centuries later.
Yet it could have sounded much like this one from the pen of
George Adam Smith:

> O Jerusalem, City of the Lord, Mother eagerly desired of her
> children, radiant light to them that sit in darkness and are far
> off, home after exile, haven after storm,—expected as the Lord's gar-
> ner, thou art still to be only His threshing-floor, and heaven and
> hell as of old shall, from new moon to new moon, through the re-
> volving years, lie side by side within thy narrow walls! For from
> the day that Araunah the Jebusite threshed out his sheaves upon
> thy high windswept rock, to the day when the Son of Man standing
> over against thee divided in His last discourse the sheep from the
> goats, the wise from foolish, and the loving from the selfish, thou
> hast been appointed of God for trial and separation and Judg-
> ment.[59]

But Jerusalem is still divided, not only politically, but spiritually,
by a line that disregards the one set by the armistice. That line
is moral and not geographical, and that windswept height is
still God's threshing floor. And men on whose ears this great
prophecy has fallen, with all its music and its gospel, who should
have become partakers of the Lord's deliverance, do yet continue

[58]George Adam Smith, *op. cit.*, p. 467.
[59]*Ibid.*, p. 466.

to prefer their idols, their swine's flesh, and their mice, their broth of abominations—and war instead of peace.

> Almighty and most merciful God, who hast sent this book to be the revelation of Thy great love to man, and of Thy power and will to save him, grant that our study of it may not have been in vain by the callousness or carelessness of our hearts, but that by it we may be confirmed in penitence, lifted to hope, made strong for service, and above all filled with the true knowledge of Thee and of Thy Son Jesus Christ. Amen.[60]

[60]*Ibid.*, p. 467.

Bibliography

I. COMMENTARIES

ALEXANDER, J. A. *Commentary on the Prophecies of Isaiah*. 2 vols. Grand Rapids, Michigan: Zondervan Publishing House, 1953, reprint.

ARCHER, GLEASON L. "Isaiah." *The Wycliffe Bible Commentary*. Edited by CHARLES PFEIFFER and EVERETT F. HARRISON. Chicago: Moody Press, 1962.

——. "Isaiah." *The Biblical Expositor*. Edited by CARL F. H. HENRY. Philadelphia: A. J. Holman Co., 1960.

BARNES, ALBERT. *Notes on the Old Testament*. Grand Rapids, Michigan: Baker Book House, 1950, reprint.

CALVIN, JOHN. *Commentary on the Book of the Prophet Isaiah*. 4 vols. Grand Rapids, Michigan: Wm. B. Eerdmans Publishing Co., 1948, reprint.

CLARKE, ADAM. *The Holy Bible with a Commentary and Critical Notes*, Vol. IV. New York: Abingdon Press, n.d.

COFFIN, HENRY SLOANE. "The Book of Isaiah, 40—66" (Exposition). *The Interpreter's Bible*. Edited by GEORGE A. BUTTRICK, et al., Vol. V. New York: Abingdon Press, 1956.

DELITZSCH, FRANZ. *Biblical Commentary on the Prophecies of Isaiah*. 2 vols. "Keil and Delitzsch Commentaries on the Old Testament." Translated by JAMES MARTIN. Grand Rapids, Michigan: Wm. B. Eerdmans Publishing Co., 1949, reprint.

FAUSSET, A. R. "Isaiah." *Jamieson, Fausset, and Brown Commentary, Critical and Explanatory, on the Whole Bible*. Abridged. Grand Rapids, Michigan: Wm. B. Eerdmans Publishing Co., 1935.

GRAY, GEORGE BUCHANAN. *The Book of Isaiah the Prophet, I—XXXIX*. "The International Critical Commentary." New York: Charles Scribner's Sons, 1912.

HENRY, MATTHEW. *Commentary on the Whole Bible*, Vol. IV. New York: Fleming H. Revell Company, n.d.

KILPATRICK, G. G. D. "The Book of Isaiah, 1—39" (Exposition). *The Interpreter's Bible*. Edited by GEORGE A. BUTTRICK, et al., Vol. V. New York: Abingdon Press, 1956.

KISSANE, EDWARD J. *The Book of Isaiah*. Translated from critically revised Hebrew text with commentary. 2 vols. Dublin: Brown and Nolan, Ltd., The Richview Press, 1943.

MUILENBERG, JAMES. "The Book of Isaiah, 40—66" (Introduction and Exegesis). *The Interpreter's Bible*. Edited by GEORGE A. BUTTRICK, et al., Vol. V. New York: Abingdon Press, 1956.

NAEGELSBACH, CARL W. E. *The Prophet Isaiah*. "Lange's Commentary on the Holy Scriptures." Edited by PHILIP SCHAFF. Grand Rapids, Michigan: Zondervan Publishing House, n.d., reprint.

NORTH, CHRISTOPHER R. *Isaiah 40—55*. "Torch Bible Commentaries." London: S. C. M. Press, Ltd., 1952.

ORELLI, C. VON. *The Prophecies of Isaiah.* Translated by J. S. BANKS. Edinburgh: T. and T. Clark, 1889.

PLUMPTRE, E. H. "The Book of the Prophet Isaiah." *Ellicott's Commentary on the Whole Bible.* Edited by C. J. ELLICOTT. Grand Rapids, Michigan: Zondervan Publishing House, n.d., reprint.

RAWLINSON, GEORGE. "Isaiah" (Exposition and Homiletics). 2 vols. *The Pulpit Commentary.* Edited by H. D. M. SPENCE and JOSEPH S. EXELL. Grand Rapids, Michigan: Wm. B. Eerdmans Publishing Co., 1950, reprint.

SCOTT, R. B. Y. "The Book of Isaiah, 1—39" (Introduction and Exegesis). *The Interpreter's Bible.* Edited by GEORGE A. BUTTRICK, et al., Vol. V. New York: Abingdon Press, 1956.

SKINNER, JOHN. *The Book of the Prophet Isaiah.* 2 vols. "Cambridge Bible for Schools and Colleges." General editor, J. J. S. PEROWNE. Cambridge: University Press, 1905.

SMITH, GEORGE ADAM. *The Book of Isaiah.* 2 vols. "The Expositor's Bible." Edited by W. ROBERTSON NICOLL. New York: A. C. Armstrong and Son, 1900.

WHITEHOUSE, OWEN C. *Isaiah.* 2 vols. "The New Century Bible." General editor, WALTER F. ADENEY. Edinburgh: T. and T. Clark, 1905.

II. OTHER BOOKS

ALBRIGHT, W. F. *From the Stone Age to Christianity.* Baltimore: The Johns Hopkins Press, 1940.

ALLIS, OSWALD T. *The Unity of Isaiah: A Study in Prophecy.* Philadelphia Presbyterian and Reformed Publishing Co., 1950.

ARCHER, GLEASON L., JR. *A Survey of Old Testament Introduction.* Chicago: Moody Press, 1964.

————. *In the Shadow of the Cross* (Insights into the Meaning of Calvary Drawn from the Hebrew Text of Isaiah 53). Grand Rapids, Michigan: Zondervan Publishing House, 1957.

BALY, DENIS. *The Geography of the Bible.* New York: Harper and Brothers, 1957.

BLANK, SHELDON H. *Prophetic Faith in Isaiah.* New York: Harper and Brothers, n.d.

BRIGHT, JOHN. *The Kingdom of God.* New York: Abingdon-Cokesbury Press, 1953.

BRIGHTMAN, EDGAR SHEFFIELD. *Religious Values.* New York: Abingdon-Cokesbury Press, 1925.

CURTIS, OLIN A. *The Christian Faith.* New York: Methodist Book Concern, 1903.

DAVIDSON, A. B. *Old Testament Prophecy.* Edinburgh: T. and T. Clark, 1903.

DRIVER, S. R. *Isaiah: His Life and Times.* "Men of the Bible Series." New York: Fleming H. Revell Co., n.d.

EPIPHANIUS. *Lives of the Prophets.* Greek text and translation by C. C. TORREY. Philadelphia: Society of Biblical Literature and Exegesis, 1946.

KNIGHT, GEORGE A. F. *Deutero-Isaiah: A Theological Commentary on Isaiah 40—55.* New York: Abingdon Press, 1965.

MACLAREN, ALEXANDER. *Expositions of the Holy Scriptures.* Nashville: Sunday School Board of the Southern Baptist Convention, n.d.

OMAN, JOHN. *Grace and Personality.* New York: Association Press, 1961.

PATERSON, JOHN. *The Goodly Fellowship of the Prophets.* New York: Charles Scribner's Sons, 1950.

PFEIFFER, R. H. *Introduction to the Old Testament.* New York: Harper and Brothers, 1941.

ROBINSON, GEORGE LIVINGSTON. *The Bearing of Archaeology on the Old Testament.* New York: American Tract Society, 1944.

———. *The Book of Isaiah* (Revised). Grand Rapids, Michigan: Baker Book House, 1954.

———. *Sarcophagus of an Ancient Civilization: Petra, Edom, and the Edomites.* New York: Macmillan Co., 1930.

SMART, JAMES D. *History and Theology in Second Isaiah.* Philadelphia: The Westminster Press, 1965.

UNGER, MERRILL F. *Unger's Dictionary of the Bible.* Chicago: Moody Press, 1957.

WILEY, H. ORTON. *Christian Theology.* 3 vols. Kansas City, Missouri: Nazarene Publishing House, 1940, 1941, 1943.

YOUNG, EDWARD J. *Studies in Isaiah.* Grand Rapids, Michigan: Wm. B. Eerdmans Publishing Co., 1954.

———. *Isaiah 53.* Grand Rapids, Michigan: Wm. B. Eerdmans Publishing Co., 1953.

III. ARTICLES

BOYER, DAVID S. "Petra, Rose-Red Citadel of Biblical Edom." *National Geographic,* CVIII, No. 6 (December, 1955), 853-70.

DRESDEN, M. J. "Cyrus." IDB, Vol. *A-D,* pp. 754-55.

GLUECK, NELSON. "Civilization of the Edomites." *Biblical Archaeologist,* X, No. 4 (December, 1947), 77-84.

KAPELRUDE, A. S. "Tyre." IDB, Vol. *R-Z,* pp. 721-23.

NORTH, C. R. "Isaiah." IDB, Vol. *E-J,* pp. 731-44.

PINCHES, T. G. "Cyrus." ISBE, 2:773-76

ROBINSON, GEORGE LIVINGSTON. "Isaiah." ISBE, 3:1495-1508.

The Book of the Prophet

JEREMIAH

C. Paul Gray

Introduction

No prophet in the Old Testament has been so widely misunderstood as Jeremiah. For centuries he has been known as the man with the despondent face and weeping eyes. He has been thought of as a temperamental, neurotic individual, a misfit for his times, a bungling preacher who should have developed a better psychological approach to the problems of his day. But this view of the prophet can come only from a superficial reading of the book,[1] and an inadequate understanding of the life and times of Jeremiah. On the contrary, when this so-called "weeping prophet" is seen in true perspective, he turns out to be a great prophet of hope.

In fact, Jeremiah had a genius for hoping beyond that of any Old Testament prophet. Although he had the unpleasant task of gathering up into a new whole the warnings of all his predecessors and pronouncing a sure and final doom on his beloved nation, he saw beyond a horrifying judgment to a new and better day. When everything about him was as black as midnight, he was convinced that there was light ahead. Even when in the depths of excruciating grief, his eyes beheld distant horizons where there would be a new covenant and a new age.

It is true that with his dark and gloomy message and his own inner conflicts, he does not make a pretty figure. People who are highly confident of themselves, and who worship "the god of immediate success," can only despise Jeremiah. In this, however, they only indict themselves as shallow and immature, for the centuries have vindicated Jeremiah. He stands today as the greatest figure of his age. He may have been late in coming into his own, "but the final recognition is ample and full."[2]

A. The Personality of the Prophet

From the standpoint of temperament and disposition, no man was more ill-fitted for his task than Jeremiah. Only a God who "looketh upon the heart" would have selected this strange, sensitive, timid, introspective youth to fill the gigantic task of being "a prophet to the nations." This would be especially true in the

[1] Charles Edward Jefferson, *Cardinal Ideas of Jeremiah* (New York: The Macmillan Company, 1928), pp. 194, 197.

[2] John Paterson, "Jeremiah," *Peake's Commentary on the Bible* (New York: Thomas Nelson and Sons, 1962), p. 539.

closing decades of the seventh and the opening years of the sixth centuries before Christ. This was a period of dislocation, upheaval, and change for the nations of the Near East. Gentle, kindhearted Jeremiah, who loved the simple things of life, was thrown into the vortex of these national and international events very much against his own personal inclinations and desires. He was by disposition much more of a follower than a leader, and his tender, affectionate nature was poorly equipped for the thoroughgoing and ruthless denunciation of sin that his commission required.

It is precisely at these points that an almost unbearable tension developed in his inner life. He was so utterly human and loving by nature, and the demands of his calling were so inflexible, that "his emotions were in constant conflict with his vocation, his heart struggled with his head."[3] This produced an inner conflict that went on for years. The intensity of his sufferings is reflected in a group of passages known as the "Confessions of Jeremiah" (11:18-23; 12:1-6; 15:10-21; 17:14-18; 18:18-23; 20:7-18).

One of the greatest values of the book is that Jeremiah permits us to see the inner struggle of his mind, the vast sweep of his emotions, as he attempted to carry out a heartbreaking task. To his enemies and to the public generally he must have appeared inflexible and unreasonably stubborn. But he shares with us his most intimate thoughts and feelings. We know more about him than about any other Old Testament prophet. We see him in the saddest and most despairing moments of his life, but we also see him in his moments of exultation and hope. The fluctuations of his emotional life can be painful to the reader, as well as exhilarating, since he does not hesitate to express every thought as it arises to the surface. But it is the uninhibited expression of his feelings that intrigues us. He is entirely himself. We are therefore given the privilege of seeing an immature youth develop into a spiritual giant.

His dislike for bearing evil tidings is evident everywhere, but his sense of vocation compels him to keep prophesying even against his will (20:9). Although he had been "set apart" for sacred office in unusual fashion, and was promised by God that he would be like an iron pillar and a bronze wall against his enemies, his tender heart was still so unprepared for what came out of the "unknown bundle" that he was brought to the breaking point more than once. Although mightily used and blessed of

[3]Ibid., p. 537.

God, he was still human enough that he had to wrestle over the issues and pray until he found rest of soul. His sensitive spirit cried out in the blinding intensity of his grief, and he did not hesitate to protest to God the hopeless predicament into which He had led him. There is no pretense or camouflage in this man. He is unashamedly himself: pain is pain, grief is grief, perplexity and pressure are terrifyingly real, and he does not hesitate to say that it is so. It can be said of him as of Another, although in a different way, "Yet learned he obedience by the things which he suffered."

However, it is these inner struggles that cause many people to turn away from Jeremiah. They want a hero who never doubts himself, has no inner conflicts, is always confident, and is constantly successful. But even our Lord could not measure up to these requirements, for He found it necessary to spend entire nights in prayer, was tortured with a thousand pangs in Gethsemane, and was deemed a bungling failure as far as earthly success is concerned. But if "courage is fear that has said its prayers," Jeremiah was one of the most courageous men that ever lived. He deserves our highest admiration. Certainly he also was "a man of sorrows, and acquainted with grief." He is an interesting reflection of the Suffering Servant of the Lord (Isaiah 53), whose ministry and mission are so perfectly portrayed in the life of our Lord. It is no wonder that when men became acquainted with Jesus they thought of Jeremiah (Matt. 16:14).

B. The Life and Times of Jeremiah

Concerning Jeremiah's home and family background we know but little. The preface of the book (1:1-3) tells us that he was born at Anathoth and that his father's name was Hilkiah. Anathoth is a village that lies about three miles northeast of Jerusalem (modern Anata), just inside the territory of Benjamin. It seems to have been a Levitical city from the time of Joshua (Josh. 21:18) and appears to have been the home of Abiathar, the high priest in the time of David (see comments on 1:1-3; also I Kings 2:26). Since the preface plainly states that Jeremiah was "of the priests of Anathoth," we may safely assume that he was of the family of Abiathar. We cannot be certain as to the exact date of Jeremiah's birth, but he must have been born somewhere between 650 and 645 b.c., in the later years of the reign of Manasseh (697-42 b.c.). He received his call in the thirteenth year of the reign of Josiah (*cir.* 626), and since that king came to the throne when he was eight years of age, Josiah and Jeremiah must have been near the same age.

Great events were taking place on the international scene during the lifetime of Jeremiah. The empire of Assyria reached its zenith and declined in his earlier years. Ashurbanipal, the last great king of Assyria, died in 626 B.C. (the year Jeremiah received his call) and after that the empire rapidly deteriorated. Weakened by wars and internal trouble, Assyria was unable to withstand the fierce raids of the Cimmerians and Scythians who attacked her northern and western borders, nor the sledgehammer blows of the Chaldeans and Medes on her southern and eastern flank. When a combined army of Medes and Chaldeans led by Nabopolassar, king of Babylon, laid siege to the capital city, Nineveh, in 612 B.C., that proud city fell with terrible slaughter.[4]

When Nineveh fell, some of the Assyrian leaders fled westward to Haran and sought to reorganize the remnants of the Assyrian army. At the same time these leaders sought an alliance with Pharaoh-Necho of Egypt. Necho responded to their call for help and marched his army up the coast of Palestine (defeating Josiah, king of Judah, at Megiddo on the way) to join the Assyrians.

In the meantime, Nabopolassar's Chaldean kingdom had continued to grow in strength in the east. He began to move slowly westward, taking all that had once been under the control of Assyria. It was inevitable that the Assyro-Egyptian alliance would meet the Chaldean armies to decide who would be master of Asia. By this time Nebuchadnezzar, the young crown prince of Babylon, had replaced his ailing father at the head of the Chaldean forces. After months of maneuvering on the upper Euphrates, one of the most decisive battles of the ancient world was fought at Carchemish (606-605). The Assyro-Egyptian alliance was shattered beyond hope of recovery. Pharaoh-Necho staggered back to Egypt in shameful defeat, and Assyria fell to rise no more. Babylon was now master of the Near East. The repercussions of Carchemish were felt throughout the Fertile Crescent, and especially in the small kingdom of Judah, where Jeremiah was prophesying.

In Judah, Josiah came to the throne in 639 B.C. His reign had followed the long and wicked rule (fifty-five years) of Manasseh, his grandfather, and the two years of his father, Amon. During

[4]C. A. Robinson, *Ancient History* (New York: The Macmillan Company, 1951), p. 103.

the almost sixty years that had preceded Josiah, idolatry and pagan worship had flourished in Judah. Manasseh had brought in many of the religious practices of Assyria and the neighboring nations. Fertility cults with their practice of sacred prostitution were tolerated in the Temple precincts (II Kings 23:4-7; Zeph. 1:4-6); offerings to astral deities were made on the streets of Jerusalem (7:17-18). Even human sacrifice was practiced in the capital of Judah (7:31-32). Religious decay was evident everywhere in Judah, and paganism became so mixed with the worship of the Lord that the common people did not know the difference. The lines of true religion had become blurred, the Temple had fallen into disrepair, and the masses of Judah had become polytheists—worshipping Yahweh along with the gods of their overlords, the kings of Assyria. This is the situation that faced Josiah when he came to the throne of Judah. It was into this kind of environment that Jeremiah was thrust when he was called to prophesy in the thirteenth year of Josiah's reign (*cir.* 626 B.C.).

Although nominally under the rule of Assyria, Josiah seems to have had a larger measure of freedom from Assyrian control than the kings that preceded him. This was possibly due to the fact that the empire was breaking under the strain of debilitating wars, overextended supply lines, and a series of internal troubles. At any rate, Josiah felt free to remove some of the shrines that Manasseh had erected to the Assyrian gods,[5] and to emphasize the worship of the Lord (II Chron. 34:3-7). And because the Temple had fallen into great disrepair, he ordered that it be renovated and refurbished. It was thus in connection with the renovation of the Temple that the greatest event of Josiah's career took place. In the eighteenth year of his reign, while workmen were repairing the house of the Lord, a copy of the book of the law was discovered (II Kings 22:3-8). The book was read in the ears of the king. When Josiah heard of the curses that were pronounced on the nation that failed to keep this law, he rent his clothes in great distress, for he saw how miserably Judah had failed at this point. The king sought to remedy matters immediately. The Josianic reform was the result (see BBC, Vol. 2, on II Kings 22).

Jeremiah had been prophesying for five years when the reform was instituted. Just what part Jeremiah played in this effort at revival, if any, we are not told. This seems rather strange, for Jeremiah was certainly in favor of correcting the

[5]John Bright, "Jeremiah," *The Anchor Bible* (New York: Doubleday and Company, Inc., 1965), p. xxxix.

social injustices, the corrupt business dealings, and the idolatrous practices that the reform espoused. Yet there is no indication that he played any prominent part in the reform. Paterson suggests that it may have been due to his youth, or that he had not as yet been recognized as a prophet.[6] Scholarly opinion is quite divided upon the matter. Whatever the answer, we may be sure that Jeremiah was not indifferent to the reform. If he did at first become involved, and 11:1-8; 12:6 seem to indicate that he might have, he soon saw its inadequacies. His spiritual insight pierced to the heart of Judah's trouble. He saw that outward religious conformity was not equivalent to regeneration of spirit. Superficial repentance could only heal the hurt of the nation lightly. Therefore deep and drastic heart surgery[7] was necessary to national spiritual health (see comments on 4:3-4). It is here that he laid his emphasis.

Apparently the nation outwardly conformed to the commands of Josiah, and for a time pagan worship was halted in Judah. Yet all the evidence points toward the fact that the people, the priests, and the professional prophets loved the corrupt ways to which they had become accustomed in the time of Manasseh and Amon, and were just waiting for a change of administration to go back to their old ways. That opportunity was given when the good king Josiah was killed in the battle of Megiddo by Pharaoh-Necho of Egypt.

The people of Judah quickly selected Jehoahaz, a son of Josiah, to succeed his father. He had ruled only three months in Jerusalem when Pharaoh-Necho demanded that he appear before him in Syria. Jehoahaz dared not refuse. In the interview Necho apparently became strongly displeased with the young king, for he deposed him and sent him in chains to Egypt (II Kings 23:33). In his place he installed Jehoiakim (Eliakim), another son of Josiah, and made him swear allegiance to Egypt. Jehoiakim ruled eleven years in Jerusalem. He seems to have conceived himself to be another Solomon, and he made grandiose plans to enlarge his kingdom, erect great buildings, and enhance his own prestige. He was pagan in his sympathies, and despised Jeremiah and all that he stood for.

It was in the fourth year of Jehoiakim that the battle of Carchemish was fought. This marked a turning point in the affairs of the Near East. Nebuchadnezzar now acquired for Babylon all the lands previously ruled by Assyria and Egypt

[6]*Op. cit.*, p. 538.
[7]*Ibid.*

308

(II Kings 24:7). Although it is not absolutely clear, there are indications that, after the battle of Carchemish, Nebuchadnezzar pursued Necho to the "gates of Egypt." While in the vicinity he seems to have demanded tribute and hostages of Jehoiakim as proof of that king's submission to Babylon.[8]

Shortly after the battle of Carchemish, Nebuchadnezzar was compelled to return to his own land because of the death of his father, Nabopolassar, whom he succeeded upon the throne of Babylon. For a number of years he was unable to return to the west. During this period Jehoiakim broke his oath and sought to throw off the Babylonian yoke. After getting his rule established in Babylon, Nebuchadnezzar in 599-598 gave attention to his possessions in the west. He sought to punish Jehoiakim for his rebellious spirit by marching against Jerusalem. Again the facts are obscure. We do not know if Jehoiakim died within the city during the siege or died in the camp of the Babylonians. II Chron. 36:6 speaks of him being put in fetters of iron for transportation to Babylon, but there is no indication that he ever reached there. II Kings 24:6 speaks as though he died in Jerusalem. It is the opinion of this writer that he died in the camp of the Babylonians from ill treatment and exposure, and they dishonored his body and threw it on a rubbish heap outside Jerusalem (see footnote on 22:18-19).

During the siege Jehoiachin, the son of Jehoiakim, succeeded his father on the throne of Judah, but he ruled only three months. He surrendered the city of Jerusalem to Nebuchadnezzar, and was carried captive to Babylon with his mother, Nehushta, his wives, many of his nobles, and ten thousand of his people (II Kings 24:6-16; II Chron. 36:9-10; Jer. 22:24-30; 37:1). He languished there many years (Jer. 52:31-34; II Kings 25:27-30).

Nebuchadnezzar put Mattaniah, another son of Josiah, on the throne of Judah and changed his name to Zedekiah (II Kings 24:17-20; II Chron. 36:10-13; Jer. 37:1). Zedekiah reigned eleven years. He was of a different disposition from Jehoiakim, and treated Jeremiah with more consideration. He kept his oath of allegiance to Babylon for almost ten years. He finally succumbed to the pro-Egyptian party among his nobles and refused to send tribute to Babylon. This brought the return of the Babylonian armies to Judah. This time the cities of Judah were systematically reduced and Jerusalem was long under siege. The celebrated Lachish Letters throw a great deal of light on the events of this period. These Letters (twenty-one in number),

[8]See II Kings 24:1; also Dan. 1:1.

309

recovered during the excavation of the site of ancient Lachish during the years 1932-38, reflect the conditions that prevailed during the final days of the kingdom of Judah.[9]

After an eighteen-month siege, the city of Jerusalem fell in 587-586 B.C. Zedekiah and many of his people were carried to Babylon. The king's palace and the Temple were totally demolished. Judah became a province of the Babylonian Empire, and Gedaliah, a member of a highly respected Jewish family, was appointed governor over the devastated land. However Gedaliah was cruelly murdered a short time after taking office, and the remnant of the people fled to Egypt for fear of Babylonian reprisals. Little is known of Judah's history in the period immediately following the death of Gedaliah.

Jeremiah was living in Jerusalem during all the foregoing events. He sought to help the various kings that came to the throne of Judah during these turbulent years. They constantly refused his advice and counsel. He was present at the fall of Jerusalem, and chose to remain in Judah with Gedaliah, the governor, after the fall of the city. When Gedaliah was murdered, the remnant of Judah compelled Jeremiah and Baruch, his secretary and disciple, to go with them to Egypt. Tradition tells us that he was stoned to death in Egypt by these same Jews because he preached against their idolatrous practices. He was faithful to his call to the very end.

C. The Composition of the Book

One does not read far into the Book of Jeremiah without discovering that much of the material is not in chronological order. To be sure, chapters 1—6 seem to be in sequence, but from chapter 7 on the material is such that no systematic pattern can be discerned. One finds materials that are dated from

[9]It would appear that the Babylonian army took the smaller cities of Judah before it pressed the siege against Jerusalem. Lachish, a fortress city, lying in the foothills southwest of Jerusalem, served to keep the lines of communication open toward Egypt. Lachish had to be destroyed before Jerusalem could be taken. The language of these Letters reminds one of the Book of Jeremiah. They are written in ancient Hebrew script on pieces of pottery, and many of them deal with the problems of a military officer in an outpost some distance from Lachish. They reveal the frustrations of this officer in those harrowing days just before the fortress of Lachish fell. For a translation of these letters see *Lachish Letters,* ed. Harry Torczyner (London: Oxford University Press, 1938); also W. F. Albright's "A Supplement to Jeremiah: The Lachish Ostraca," *Bulletin of the American Schools of Oriental Research,* No. 61 (Feb., 1936), pp. 15-16; "A Re-examination of the Lachish Letters," *ibid.,* No. 73 (Feb., 1939), p. 16.

widely different periods in Jeremiah's life lying side by side (36 and 37). Other materials are not dated at all, and the reader is hard put to know where they fit in chronologically. Thus to get any sort of orderly picture of Jeremiah's life, one has to jump from one passage to another. At best the situation is confusing. Since the book is sometimes chronological (37—44) and sometimes topical (46—51) but without any discernible underlying motif, one wonders what principle, if any, governed its present organization. Many conjectures have been made, but to this day scholars are not in agreement as to how the book reached its present form.

Kuist suggests that part of the explanation may lie in the convulsive times in which the book was written.[10] Certainly when one looks at the turmoil that prevailed throughout Jeremiah's public ministry, ending as it did in "the siege and fall of Jerusalem, the deportation of the people to Babylon, and the flight of the remnant to Egypt, it is a marvel that any records written within this period survived at all."[11] The times were so chaotic and the dangers suffered by Jeremiah and Baruch after the fall of Jerusalem were so great (41—44) that there was no time to organize and refine the written documents. Although later editors may have attempted to rearrange certain sections, and delete some repetitions, the book as it stands in the Hebrew Bible is essentially the work of Jeremiah and his secretary, Baruch. It is a miracle of God's providence that we even have a Book of Jeremiah.

Chapter 36 reveals how the book came to be written in the first place. Right from the start it seems to have had a turbulent history. The first edition was destroyed by Jehoiakim (36:23), but an expanded second edition appeared a short time later (36:32). This took place in the fourth and fifth years of Jehoiakim's reign (605-604) and would mark the middle point of Jeremiah's career (see 25:3). He prophesied for more than forty years. It is not hard to see that there must have been a third edition, for a large portion of the book must have been added to the second edition subsequent to the events that took place in chapter 36. The events recorded in chapters 21, 23—24, 27—29, 30—34, 37—44 show that they happened later than the fifth year of Jehoiakim.

---

[10]"Jeremiah," *Layman's Bible Commentaries* (London: SCM Press, Ltd., 1961), pp. 12 ff.

[11]*Ibid.*, p. 13.

That the book has passed through very hectic days is further seen when the Septuagint (Greek) edition is placed alongside the Masoretic (Hebrew) text. The Greek text is one-eighth shorter than the Hebrew, and the arrangement is different, especially the oracles against foreign nations. "These oracles are found in the Hebrew text (and so in our English Bible) in chapters 46—51. In the Greek text they are introduced at 25:13."[12] Why these differences between the Hebrew and Greek texts exist has never been conclusively explained. Could it be that there were two main editions of Jeremiah in Hebrew, and the translation into the Greek was made from the shorter one? Whatever the answer, the leaders of the Jewish community who formulated the Hebrew canon apparently considered the longer one to be more representative of Jeremiah.

[12]Kuist, op. cit., p 14

Outline

I. The Preface, 1:1-3
   A. Identification, 1:1
   B. Initiation, 1:2
   C. Certification, 1:3

II. Jeremiah's Induction, 1:4-19
   A. Jeremiah's Call, 1:4-6
   B. Jeremiah's Consecration, 1:5, 9
   C. Jeremiah's Commission, 1:4-10
   D. Jeremiah's Confirmation, 1:11-19

III. Arraignment of the House of Jacob, 2:1—10:25
   A. The Infidelity of Israel, 2:1—3:5
   B. A Plaintive Call to Repentance, 3:6—4:4
   C. Enemy from the North and from Within, 4:5—6:30
   D. The Temple Sermon, 7:1—8:3
   E. Miscellaneous Oracles, 8:4—10:25

IV. Confessions and Predictions, 11:1—20:18
   A. Jeremiah and the Covenant, 11:1—12:17
   B. Parables and Pronouncements, 13:1-27
   C. The Drouth and Its Moral Implications, 14:1—15:9
   D. Confessions of Jeremiah, 15:10-21
   E. Miscellaneous Materials, 16:1—17:18
   F. Symbolic Actions: Meaning and Results, 17:19—20:18

V. A Forecast of the End, 21:1—29:32
   A. Beginning of the Final Siege, 21:1-10
   B. The Fortunes of the House of David, 21:11—23:8
   C. Oracles Against False Prophets, 23:9-40
   D. The Parable of the Figs, 24:1-10
   E. A Preview of the End, 25:1-38
   F. Opposition to Predictions of Doom, 26:1—29:32

VI. The Book of Consolation, 30:1—33:26
   A. The Preface, 30:1-3
   B. From Tragedy to Triumph, 30:4—31:1
   C. Restoration Assured, 31:2-40
   D. Restoration Dramatized, 32:1-44
   E. Further Assurance of Restoration, 33:1-26

VII. Counsel for Kings, 34:1—36:32
   A. Counsel Concerning Babylon, 34:1-7
   B. Counsel Concerning Slaves, 34:8-22
   C. The Example of the Rechabites, 35:1-19

Section **I** *The Preface*

Jeremiah 1:1-3

The first three verses of c. 1 form the title or preface to a Hebrew scroll containing what is known today as the Book of Jeremiah. It was not uncommon for the prophetic books of the Old Testament to have such a title. The words here are designed to identify the contents of the book and to introduce the reader to that which is to follow. As we study these verses, they seem to fall into three parts.

A. IDENTIFICATION, 1:1

The contents of this book are identified and distinguished from all other writings of Scripture as **the words of Jeremiah** (1). Authorship of the book is hereby established. Verse 1 identifies the prophet as to name, family, and birthplace. Several ideas have been advanced by scholars as to the meaning of **Jeremiah** (Heb., *Yirmeyahu* or *Yirmeyah*).[1] The most probable meaning is "the Lord shoots, or hurls." It may be that the prophet's name refers to the thunderbolts of divine truth Jeremiah was to deliver to a wicked and sinful nation. The term could also be thought of as describing the career of the prophet, for he was hurled into the vortex of one of the most catastrophic periods in the history of the ancient world. But perhaps every age is a catastrophic age, and every true spokesman of God is hurled into the midst of political, moral, and spiritual tensions, in somewhat the same way Jeremiah was. The least that the name can teach is that God is active in the affairs of men.

Son of Hilkiah, of the priests that were in Anathoth (see map 2) gives us the prophet's birthplace and something concerning his family. His father, **Hilkiah,** has sometimes been identified as "Hilkiah the priest" who figured so prominently in the discovery of the book of the law in the Temple during the reign of Josiah (II Kings 22). While there is a slight possibility that this

---

[1]See George Adam Smith, *Jeremiah* (New York: George H. Doran Co., 1922), p. 66.

might be true, the weight of the evidence is against it. It seems
clear, however, that Jeremiah's family were **priests. Anathoth,**
his birthplace, was a priestly city as far back as the time of
Joshua (Josh. 21:18). It is the city to which Abiathar, the high
priest in David's reign, retired when dismissed by Solomon because he supported Adonijah for the kingship (I Kings 2:26-27).
It is probable that Jeremiah was a member of the family of
Abiathar, and if so, he could trace his ancestry back to Eli, who
was high priest in the time of Samuel (I Sam. 2:27-36). With this
kind of heritage, the prophet must have been steeped in all the
traditions of the Hebrew religion.

Although it appears that Jeremiah came from a family of
priests, he does not seem to follow in the priestly tradition. His
perspective, bearing, and deportment fall clearly in the prophetic
pattern. There is no indication that he ever filled the priestly
office; in fact this is the only place where his priestly connections
are mentioned in the book. He is embued with the prophetic
spirit, and follows the prophetic tradition completely.

B. INITIATION, 1:2

Jeremiah's career begins with the initiative of God—**to
whom the word of the Lord came** (2). That God always takes
the initiative in man's redemption is one of the singular features
of Sacred Writ. Prevenient grace generates every movement for
good in the world. The "grace that goes before" initiates the
career of every man of God, be he prophet in the Old Testament,
apostle in the New Testament, or a modern-day spokesman of
God. It meant for Jeremiah, as it means for us today, that he
was summoned to speak for God, and that his message was not
his own. It meant that he had been chosen to stand in the inner
councils of Deity, and to serve as the mouthpiece of the Eternal.[2]
God, then, was the Prime Mover behind the life and work of
Jeremiah.

C. CERTIFICATION, 1:3

The contents of the Book of Jeremiah are solidly based in
history. The message of the prophet is not a nebulous theory, the
figment of a deranged mind, but rather the truth of the eternal
God, enacted and set forth in the actual affairs of life. Jeremiah

[2]J. P. Hyatt, *Prophetic Religion* (New York: Abingdon Press, 1947),
pp. 31 ff.

was a flesh-and-blood person whose life and ministry can be dated. His prophetic ministry began "in the days of Josiah . . . king of Judah, in the thirteenth year of his reign" (2)—probably 626 B.C. The word of the Lord continued to come to him **in the days of Jehoiakim . . . unto the end of the eleventh year of Zedekiah (3).** This was 586 B.C., the year that Jerusalem fell by the hand of the Chaldeans. Even after this we find Jeremiah still preaching. Other portions of scripture, as well as secular history, serve to corroborate what he wrote. The contents of the book are certified by the events of history, and indicate that God plays a part in the affairs of earth.

Section **II** *Jeremiah's Induction*

Jeremiah 1:4-19

In v. 4 there is a change from the third person to the first person, indicating that the following verses are autobiographical. Here we find Jeremiah relating the simple facts of his initial encounter with God. His experience at this point is similar to other Old Testament prophets. In Hebrew religion it was expected that any true spokesman of God would come to that "special moment" when he was inducted into divine office.[1] This moment was more dramatic with some than with others.

A. Jeremiah's Call, 1:4-7

The prophet's call did not have all the transcendant features and apocalyptic detail of Isaiah's or Ezekiel's summons to the prophetic office. Yet there is a definiteness and clarity to his call that is a fundamental characteristic of Hebrew religion: **The word of the Lord came unto me, saying** (4). There is a divine-human *confrontation* depicted here. Jeremiah does not say that he saw God, but God came very near, so near that at one point the hand of the Lord was laid upon the mouth of the prophet. The manifest nearness of God is stressed here in contrast to the transcendence of God in the call of Isaiah (Isa. 6:1-8). Here we find God in close personal conversation with a man. A dialogue ensues between Deity and humanity. Here is seen the intimacy that can exist between God and men. But there is no absorption of one's personality into God as some mystics teach. In this encounter God is God and man is man. Jeremiah here, as elsewhere in the book, maintains his own identity in relation to God.

The vividness of this confrontation is revealed by the transitive verbs with which God lays claim to the service of His man. **I formed thee ... I knew thee ... I sanctified thee ... I ordained thee a prophet unto the nations** (5). One can almost see the words sink into the consciousness of the young prophet. Jeremiah is face-to-face with divine demands upon his life. Also, in this

[1]Hyatt, *op. cit.*, pp. 311 ff.

dramatic moment, we can see the decisiveness of God in contrast with the *hesitation* of Jeremiah. He is staggered by the responsibility that faces him. In surprise and consternation, he cries, **Behold, I cannot speak: for I am a child (6)**.[2] His hesitation at this point is to be characteristic of him throughout his career. By nature he is timid and retiring. His sensitive nature is ill-fitted for the superhuman task that is to be his. The awful presence of God was overpowering; the terror of "complete abandonment" of self and future to God could not but shake the bravest of hearts.[3] His natural reaction was to protest; this he did vehemently. Yet his protestations only reveal the humility of his mind, his feelings of unworthiness, and the knowledge of his own limitations. While Jeremiah shrank from a most unpleasant task, we do not find him refusing. There is no element of rebellion in his hesitation.

God brushed aside the young man's objections, saying, **I ordained thee a prophet unto the nations. . . . thou shalt go to all that I shall send thee, and whatsoever I command thee thou shalt speak (5, 7)**. The word translated "ordain" means literally "to give"; consequently, there is in it the idea of being "chosen" or "sent." Jeremiah is, therefore, appointed a prophet to the nations. He is no longer his own; the call of God is inescapable. Jeremiah's *ordination* had taken place in the mind of God before the prophet was born, but at this point the long-range purposes of God have become actual in flesh and blood. With the ordination of Jeremiah the plan of God for His coming kingdom is one step closer to realization.

B. Jeremiah's Consecration, 1: 5, 9

This aspect of Jeremiah's induction into prophetic office can be described under two heads.

---

[2]The Hebrew word for **child** (*na'ar*) is used in the OT to refer to an infant (Exod. 2:6; Isa. 7:16; 8:4; etc.), a small boy (Gen. 21:12; 22:5; 37:2; 43:8), or a young man of marriageable age (Gen. 34:19; II Sam. 18:5, 12, etc.). We therefore cannot determine the age of Jeremiah from this passage. It is quite likely that he was at least seventeen years of age at this time. He may have been older.

[3]Stanley R. Hopper, "Jeremiah" (Exposition), *The Interpreter's Bible*, ed. George A. Buttrick, *et al.* (New York: Abingdon-Cokesbury Press, 1951), V, 802.

1. Sanctification (1:5)

God declared, **before thou camest forth out of the womb I sanctified thee** (5). In this expression we see the fundamental meaning of sanctification in the Old Testament. In the foreknowledge of God, Jeremiah was set apart for service to the holy God, who alone is holy *per se*. To be holy in the Old Testament is primarily to belong to the holy God by His redemptive action. For a person or a nation to be holy meant that they were to be exclusively devoted[4] to God for His purposes or His service.

Jeremiah's experience might be described as the sanctification of a holy calling—"vocational sanctification." The question may be asked, Does such sanctification have any ethical qualities? The answer is that the ethical content depends upon the nature of the God with whom an individual (or nation) stands in dynamic personal relation. A holy calling is the primary emphasis in Jeremiah's case, but ethical sanctification naturally follows. It is impossible for a person to belong to a holy God without that relationship being reflected in holy living. This is the essence of the biblical idea of holiness. Thus vocational sanctification and ethical sanctification are two sides of the same coin. You cannot have one without the other.

2. Implementation (1:9)

God always implements His own plans. Jeremiah was not left alone to perform the command of God in merely human power. **Then the Lord put forth his hand, and touched my mouth.** God's purpose to set Jeremiah apart for a special service is now implemented by the divine touch. It was at this point that he was officially inducted into the prophetic office. From this time forward the divine anointing would impel him to speak forth the word of God: **Behold, I have put my words in thy mouth.** Jeremiah is now qualified to carry out his prophetic task. God thus implements His purposes by the power of His Spirit.

C. JEREMIAH'S COMMISSION, 1:4-10

In the Old Testament when a prophet received a call he was also given a commission. God always calls people from something to something.

---

[4]Cf. John Wesley's view of Christian perfection as being a state of *entire devotement* to God.

1. *To Serve as a Mouthpiece* (1:5, 7, 9)

Jeremiah was appointed a prophet not only to Judah but also to **the nations** (5). The Hebrew word *nabi* is translated "prophet" some three hundred times in the Old Testament. Apparently the word originally meant "to announce" or "to speak."[5] Gradually it came to mean, in Old Testament usage, one who is "qualified, called, and commissioned to speak God's truth to men."[6] The *nabi* of the Old Testament was primarily a preacher, a proclaimer of sacred truth. Under divine compulsion he spoke words to men, but words filled with divine authority. It is in this tradition that Jeremiah finds himself commissioned of God. It was to be his task to stand in the divine inner council and then to go forth and speak of what he had seen and heard. He was commissioned with these words, **Whatsoever I command thee thou shalt speak** (7); **Behold, I have put my words in thy mouth** (9). Jeremiah's faithfulness to this task brought against him the fierce opposition of his own family, his neighbors, his king, and his friends. Although he faltered at times, he never once failed his divine commission.

2. *To Deliver a Message* (1:4-5, 8, 10)

The idea of serving as a mouthpiece presupposes a message. Jeremiah states several times in this chapter, **The word of the Lord came unto me** (4). The outline of a message to Judah and **the nations** (5) is gradually taking shape. The writers of the Bible believed that God's **word** was full of divine power. They were confident that His word would not return unto Him void, but would accomplish His purpose (Isa. 55:11).

What then is the message that is being given to Jeremiah for the people? Even in c. 1 some of the basic elements can be seen. There is strong inference that all men are guilty and stand accountable before God (5, 10). Judah is accountable because she has forsaken the Lord to serve false gods (10, 15-16). **The nations** stand under judgment because their conduct falls below the standard of ordinary human justice. Destruction and trouble await guilty men (10, 15-16), for God is surely coming in

[5]Hyatt, *op. cit.*, p. 48. See also *Hebrew-English Lexicon* by Brown, Driver & Briggs (Oxford: Clarendon Press, 1955), p. 611.

[6]Kyle M. Yates, *Preaching from the Prophets* (Nashville: Broadman Press, 1942), p. 2.

judgment. When He comes, kingdoms and peoples will be rooted up and thrown down (10). God is not asleep as men suppose, but is watching and alert to carry out His **word** (11-12). Finally, this timely warning is followed by a word of hope: God's punishment and judgment are redemptive; that is, He afflicts to heal (10). Beyond judgment there is hope of a restoration—a redeemed people and a new day.

3. *To Execute a Master Plan* (1:10)

In communicating His message to Jeremiah, God revealed His plan of operation. In the process the prophet was given an insight into both the past and the future. God, who had made plans for the redemption of His prodigal world, had seen His plans broken on the rocks of man's freedom.[7] The children of Israel, a chosen instrument, were to have been "a light to the nations" (Isa. 49:6, RSV). Instead they had rebelled against their Deliverer, and had become like the heathen nations around them. The Northern Kingdom had sustained its punishment and had been gone from the pages of history for one hundred years.

Now Judah, which had known the patience and long-suffering of God, had passed "the point of no return" in her stubbornness and sin. The hour of judgment had come. Jeremiah is now commissioned as an overseer (**set** means "to be made") to put God's plan into operation. Judah and other nations are to be shaken to their foundations and overthrown. Perhaps through the refining fires of suffering and sorrow they will find the way of obedience and peace. God said to Jeremiah, **See, I have this day set thee over the nations and over the kingdoms, to root out, and to pull down, and to destroy, and to throw down, to build, and to plant.** It may seem strange that God's plan involves such negative measures. But there seems to be a law in the universe that some things must die in order for others to live and grow. Evil must go in order for good to flourish. Our hands must turn loose of that which is evil, so that they may be free to receive that which is good. The "old, evil, wicked Judah" must be swept away so that a "purified remnant shall return to build the new Jerusalem."[8] But God ends on a positive note: **to build, and to**

---

[7]C. A. McConnell used to say, "God changes His plans to suit man's changing choices, but God's purposes never change; they are eternal."

[8]IB, V (expos.), 805.

plant. There is hope of a better day. When the negative element is eliminated, the positive can flourish with vigor.

D. JEREMIAH'S CONFIRMATION, 1:11-19

After commissioning the prophet, God confirmed His word to Jeremiah by two visions, a command, and a promise. What Jeremiah was shown have been called "inaugural visions"[9] by some scholars; however, we cannot be certain that they followed immediately upon his call. If, however, they did not come immediately, they were given very early in Jeremiah's prophetic career, for God seems to use them to assure him of his prophetic call.

The first vision is that of the **rod of an almond** (wake-up) **tree** (11). God explains the meaning of the vision: "I am watching [wakeful] over my word to perform it" (12, RSV). There seems to be a pun on the Hebrew word for "almond tree" (*shaqed*) and the verb (*shoqed*) "to watch" or "to wake" (a change of one vowel point makes the difference). The almond tree was well ahead of all the other trees to "wake up" in the spring. God was saying to Jeremiah by this vision, "I am wide-awake, alertly watching over My word to see that it is promptly executed." Apparently Judah had been acting as though God was asleep and did not know about her sin.

In Jeremiah's experience we see some of God's ways of dealing with men. (1) God's concern about man's sin, 11-12; (2) God's condemnation for wrongdoing, 14-16; (3) God's command to His prophets, 17a; (4) The divine consolation, 17b-19.

The vision speaks of *God's concern.* Its purpose is to assure Jeremiah that God is keenly alert to the situation, that He is watching with persistent care to see that His word is performed. It also speaks of God's assistance in carrying out His plans. He is "wakefully determined" that His judgments will be accomplished in the earth. Men can always work with the assurance that God is watching with unfaltering vigilance to see that His plans are carried out, whether they are works of judgment or of mercy.

The second vision speaks of *God's condemnation* of Judah and the other nations of that day. He asks: **What seest thou?**

---

[9]J. P. Hyatt, "The Book of Jeremiah" (Exegesis), *The Interpreter's Bible,* ed. George A. Buttrick, *et al.* (New York: Abingdon-Cokesbury Press, 1951), V, 798 f.

And I said, I see a seething pot; and the face thereof is toward (or "from," marg.) **the north (13).**[10] Judah may expect trouble and judgment: **Out of the north an evil shall break forth upon all the inhabitants of the land (14).**

In 626 B.C., Ashurbanipal, the last strong king of Assyria (see map 1), died. With his death the forces of decline set in, and before long the whole Fertile Crescent was seething with plans for revolt. The Assyrian Empire was soon tottering. "The times indeed were ominous."[11] The Neo-Babylonian Empire was rising like a threatening cloud on the horizon. God gave Jeremiah insight into the international situation of his day; and his prophetic intuition saw the approach of the Babylonian hordes against his beloved land. **I will call all the families** (clans) **of the kingdoms of the north, saith the Lord (15).** The armies of the Babylonian king were to be made up of mercenary soldiers of all the kingdoms of the north country which Babylon had conquered. **Jerusalem** would be besieged as well as **all the cities of Judah. They shall set every one his throne** means that the kings would camp there. The hand behind this was the hand of God, and His reason was plain. **I will utter my judgments against** those **who have forsaken me, and have burned incense unto other gods (16).** Judah's idolatry and sin had sealed her doom.

Jeremiah was painfully conscious of how his own people would react when he delivered this message. He knew that he would be personally attacked and hated. His sensitive soul recoiled in horror, but God fortified him for what he must face. "But you! You shall gird up your loins! You shall arise, and you shall speak to them" (17, lit.). Although the verbs can be translated as the Hebrew imperfect, they have here the force of the imperative. **Be not dismayed** (terrified) **at their faces.** God's *command* came as a powerful stimulant to the timid and apprehensive prophet. Jeremiah faced up to his task with new faith and courage. There are times when every man of God needs to hear the "ring of iron" in the voice of the Eternal. It enables one, as it did Jeremiah, to regain the divine perspective.

When dealing with His timid and brokenhearted ones, divine severity is always followed by *God's consolation;* His commands are followed by His promises. He makes a definite promise to the

---

[10]KJV margin has given the literal sense of the Hebrew here.
[11]Kuist, *op. cit.*, p. 29.

young and inexperienced prophet: **Behold, I have made thee this day a defenced city, and an iron pillar . . . against the whole land . . . they shall fight against thee; but they shall not prevail . . . for I am with thee . . . to deliver thee (18-19).** Courage and inspiration flowed into the soul of Jeremiah; God's word could be trusted. Divine inspiration gripped him. His induction into the prophetic office was complete. He was the bearer of the word of the Lord—a spokesman of God—a full-fledged prophet. He turned to his task under the power of the Spirit.

Section III Arraignment of the House of Jacob

Jeremiah 2:1—10:25

This section is made up of several discourses perhaps uttered at different times in the earlier years of Jeremiah's ministry. Chapters 2—6 can almost certainly be said to come from the reign of Josiah; c. 7, with its famous Temple sermon, is quite clearly from the first year of Jehoiakim; while cc. 8—10 could come either from Josiah's reign or from the early years of Jehoiakim. They are grouped together here apparently because they have a common theme—an indictment of the whole house of Israel. These prophecies reveal the dominant concern of the prophet in his earlier years. Some of them seem to be addressed to the people of the Northern Kingdom, others to Judah, but all to the house of Jacob. Many of the thoughts expressed in this section remind us of Hosea, whose life and ministry seem to have had a decided influence on Jeremiah. Over and over again the prophet reminds the people that he is speaking for God.

We can be fairly sure that the prophecies as we have them here are not identical with the prophecies as they were first written. This section, no doubt, was included in the scroll that was destroyed by Jehoiakim (cf. c. 36). What we have is the second edition, for the prophecies were dictated again to Baruch by Jeremiah, "and there were added besides unto them many like words" (36:32). This additional material and the topical arrangement of the writings may explain why some of the passages do not seem to fit well together.

A. The Infidelity of Israel, 2:1—3:5

1. Haunting Memories (2:1-3)

God speaks here of a better day when Israel was a young bride, I remember . . . the love of thine espousals (2). The entire section is cast in poetic form (cf. RSV, Moffatt, et al.). During

326

those early years of privation in the wilderness, when Israel lived a nomadic life, she was completely dependent on God, and He had no rivals for her affection. In those days (symbolic of a life of utter reliance on God) Israel had nowhere else to look for her sustenance and she was completely devoted to the Lord. That was **in a land that was not sown,** meaning that as yet they were not an agricultural people. But later on, in the security of a settled civilization, i.e., after reaching Canaan, they began to put their dependence in material things and forgot the simplicity of an earlier time. Relying on "secondary securities,"[1] Israel had lost her first love.

In those bygone days under the hand of Moses, **Israel was holiness unto the Lord** (3). This meant that she was holy because she belonged to Him unreservedly. It was a holiness based on Israel being "separated" to God for a sacred purpose, yet holy conduct was expected of her precisely because of that relationship. The Lord was always grieved when such conduct was not forthcoming.

All the while that God is speaking about those early love-lit days, the ugly word that is lurking in the background is *unfaithfulness.* The nation had become unfaithful to the marriage (covenant) vows made with the Lord at Sinai. With increasing force and in a hundred different ways this truth will be driven home by Jeremiah.

2. *Ingratitude for Great Deliverances* (2:4-8)

Jeremiah next takes the people to task because they have forgotten the "pit from whence they were digged." God had marvelously delivered them from bondage in Egypt; He had led them **through the wilderness, through a land of deserts and of pits, through a land of drought, and of the shadow of death** (6); He had given them Canaan, **a plentiful country** (7). But instead of being appreciative of the goodness of God, they forgot His mercies, defiled the land, and made His **heritage an abomination.**

The leaders of the nation had been the prime transgressors at this point. **The priests . . . and they that handle the law knew me not** (8).[2] History teaches us that a nation always dies at the top first. So it was with Israel. **The pastors** (lit., shepherds, but

---

[1]IB, V (expos.), 813.

[2]**They that handle the law** seems to indicate that already in Israel there were scribes, or teachers who explained the Law (the Torah).

meaning rulers), **and the prophets**[3] were guilty as well as the priests. Instead of turning to the Lord, who had been their great Benefactor on so many occasions, these religious leaders clung to such false gods as the Baals and prophesied by them. This strange conduct caused God to ask, **What iniquity have your fathers found in me, that they . . . have walked after vanity?** (5) (**Vanity** here means nothingness, and is applied to idols as having no existence at all.) The answer to the above question is that no iniquity could be found in God, but a wretched spirit of ungratefulness characterized Israel. It was this ungrateful attitude that had opened the floodgates of iniquity in the nation.

3. *The Unnaturalness of Israel's Ingratitude* (2:9-13)

Despite Israel's ingratitude, God did not give up the delinquent nation. **I will yet plead** (lit., strive or contend) **with you** (9), i.e., to get you to return. Israel's backslidings are, indeed, a puzzling thing. In the light of all the past actions of God in her behalf, it seems so *unnatural* that they should forsake the Lord and serve idols. God chides them, **Pass over the isles of Chittim, and see; and send unto Kedar**[4] . . . **and see if . . . a nation has changed their gods?** . . . **but my people have . . .** (10-11). Israel has treated the Lord worse than the heathen nations treat their gods, **which are yet no gods** (11). How could a nation do a thing like this? The only answer is that sin introduces into men strange and unnatural passions. **Be astonished, O ye heavens** (12), at the things people do who have once known the riches of God's mercy and love! But the sins of *unfaithfulness* and *ingratitude* are twin evils that open the soul to all kinds of madness and folly.

God goes on to say, **My people have committed two evils; they have forsaken me the fountain of living waters, and hewed them out . . . broken cisterns, that can hold no water** (13). The metaphor is all the more meaningful when one realizes that Palestine is an arid land. To leave a flowing **fountain** with its

---

[3]Reference to **the prophets** here would mean members of the prophetic guild or the school of the prophets. These professional prophets had been present in Israel since the time of Samuel.

[4]The terms **Chittim** and **Kedar** are actually expressions for the extremities of west and east. **Chittim** is Cyprus and the islands thereabout, while **Kedar** is the name of a tribe of Arabs to the east of Judah. These are heathen peoples who serve false gods.

cool, sparkling water for the stagnant, putrid waters of a **cistern is unreasonable.** And to turn to one that is **broken** and **can hold no water** is unthinkable. But the gods to whom Israel has turned are just as worthless and void of help.

4. Unable to Learn from History (2:14-19)

In these verses God seems to be questioning the men of Jeremiah's day, **Why is he** (Israel, the Northern Kingdom) **spoiled? The . . . lions** (strong warriors) **roared upon him . . . his cities are burned without inhabitant** (14-15). Is it because the Northern Kingdom had so many disadvantages? Was he only a poor **slave** born into the household of God? The expected answer is, No. Israel had had every advantage. The Lord had done many wonderful things for him. Therefore the reason for his destruction must be found elsewhere.

God now injects into His argument something much closer home to the men of Judah. **The children of Noph** (Memphis) **and Tahapanes[5] have broken the crown of thy head. Hast thou not procured this unto thyself?** (16-17) One can almost see the men of Jerusalem wince. The reference here is to the shameful defeat of the armies of Judah by Neco (Nechο), king of Egypt, at the battle of Megiddo when Josiah was slain (II Kings 23: 29-30). Why did this happen to Judah? And what is the reason that Israel is gone into captivity? God's answer is the same for both nations, **Thou hast forsaken the Lord thy God** (17).

Despite these humiliations there was still a pro-Egyptian party in Judah, just as there was a pro-Assyrian party. Both were active in the politics of Jeremiah's time. Verse 18 is a divine reprimand, **And now what hast thou to do in the way of Egypt, to drink the waters of Sihor** (the Nile)? **or . . . in the way of Assyria? . . . Thine own wickedness shall correct thee** (19a). **The river** (18) would be the Euphrates (see map 1). Dependence on foreign powers rather than on the Lord had always been a snare to the God-believing nations. Both Hosea and Isaiah had opposed foreign alliances. The real accusation behind these words is that Judah has been *unable to learn* from Israel's fate, or from her own misfortunes. It is tragic when men and nations cannot see by observation the devastating power of sin. Even

---

[5]Memphis was the capital of lower Egypt, and Tahpanhes (**Tahapanes,** KJV) was the site of one of the Egyptian king's favorite palaces (see map 3).

today each generation seems compelled to suffer untold agony because it has learned nothing from God's actions in history.

5. *Unrestrained Sin Leaves One Deeply Stained* (2:20-25)

Jeremiah now speaks of the length to which the house of Jacob had gone in her sin. Several figures are used to describe her condition: a vineyard, a harlot, an object deeply stained, a young she-camel, and a female ass in heat. But first God reminds Israel of His many deliverances **from of old,** and how she had promised, **I will not transgress** (20) again. But she went right on **playing the harlot—upon every high hill and under every green tree,** i.e., worshipping false gods at the many country shrines. The nation had had a most excellent start at Sinai under Moses; she had been planted a **noble vine, wholly a right** (lit., true) **seed** (21). Yet she had degenerated into the worst sort of wild vine. This degenerated condition had become so deeply ingrained that the most powerful cleansing agents known to the ancient world (**nitre,** or lye, and **sope,** 22) were unavailing to purge the stain.

To make matters worse, Israel is apparently blind to her real condition, for she says, **I am not polluted** (23). The truth of the matter is, in her love for strange gods she has become as wanton and unrestrained as a young female camel of the desert, or a **wild ass** of the **wilderness** (24) when they are in heat. So utterly impetuous is Israel that no amount of restraint will avail. She plunges on in her stubbornness. The first half of 25 is God's exhortation to salvation: "Do not let your foot be without shoes, or your throat dry from need of water" (*Basic Bible*). To all the pleading for change, she gives the reply of those who are confirmed in their sin, **There is no hope . . . I have loved strangers, and after them will I go** (25). Thus does *unrestrained sin* sweep one on to a settled and eternal despair. Not that God would not forgive, but that man has deliberately chosen, in full awareness of the implications involved, the gratification of the carnal self.

6. *The Shamelessness of Judah* (2:26—3:5)

Unrestrained transgression eventually leads to a state of shamelessness where the individual is *unable to care.* This is now seen to be the fate of Judah. Although caught in her sin like a **thief** and shamed for her conduct, yet her **kings . . . princes . . . priests, and . . . prophets** (26) go on practicing spiritual whoredom. They say **to a stock** (a tree or idol of wood), **Thou art my father; and to a stone** (idol), **Thou hast brought me forth** (27). They contemptuously turned their back on the Lord to do as they pleased, yet when trouble came, they just as shamelessly turned again and begged Him for help. This reveals the utter unreasonableness of sin, and God chides them, **But where are thy gods that thou hast made thee? let them arise, if they can save thee** (28). There was no lack of these gods, for every city had one or more. When punishment continues unabated, they turn in their wretchedness and **plead** ("complain," 29, RSV) against God as though they had committed no sin whatever, and had every right to expect His help.

Despite the fact that God allows suffering to come in order to turn them from their sin, they learn nothing from their experience. **They received no correction** (30), but killed the true prophets with the **sword** in their madness to serve other gods. God again appeals to reason, **Wherefore say my people, We are lords** (better, "we are free," RSV); **we will come no more unto thee?** (31) These people had a lawless spirit; they had no regard for the rules of God or men. Immature and fickle as children, they insisted on coming to God only when they pleased. **Can a maid forget her ornaments? . . . yet my people have forgotten me** (32). Judah's practice of her religion was a mere matter of convenience. The Lord was someone who could be used if needed, or **forgotten . . . days without number,** if it suited Judah's fancy.

Moffatt interprets the first part of 33, "Your course you have directed to intrigues of love." Judah had become so adroit in the matter of sin that she could teach even the experts in immorality a thing or two. The last part of 34 is obscure. It apparently means that Judah has further added to her guilt by staining her garments with the blood of the poor whom God had found innocent of any act of wrongdoing. At the same time Judah is saying, **I am innocent** (35). Things are pretty hopeless when men reach the place where they believe their own lies. It is nothing less than moral insanity.

God again announces the coming of judgment upon the nation. **Behold, I will plead** ("enter into judgment," ASV) **with thee, because thou sayest, I have not sinned** (35). Judah was a responsible nation; she would be judged accordingly. The Lord seems to say, "Because you take your wickedness so lightly, changing this way and that, you shall be brought to shame by Egypt as you have been already by the Assyrian" (36), a reference to the futility of trust in Egypt (cf. 46:1-28). In the coming day of judgment Judah will weep in shame with **thine hands upon thine head** (37)—in utter grief and despair. God has **rejected** all the things in which Judah has placed her confidence. In none of her ways will she **prosper.** Thus the word is one of doom and judgment. Judah will awake to her shameful condition only when it is too late. Playing with sin, changing from one foreign alliance to another, refusing to heed the warnings of God, indicate an instability that equals her shamelessness. What then does Judah have to look forward to? (1) Judgment is certain; (2) Consternation and desolation await her; (3) Those upon whom she has depended will fail her in the crucial hour; (4) She will have to confess that this need not have been her fate.

The shamelessness of Judah is further illustrated by a return to the figure of marriage in the opening verse of c. 2. The language is reminiscent of Hosea (Hos. 2:1-5; 9:1). Jeremiah refutes the idea of easy repentance. Religiously, Judah had **played the harlot with many lovers** (3:1), yet she seemed to think that she could return to God anytime she chose. She drifted along, casual and unconcerned about her sin. Apparently she had reached the place where she was unable to care. This is verified by the next statement, **Thou hast polluted the land with thy whoredoms . . . thou hadst a whore's forehead** ("as brazen as a harlot," Moffatt), **thou refusedst to be ashamed** (2-3). Judah had now become set in her sin.

That she had reached this point in her shamelessness is confirmed by the fact that she could use such endearing language to God as, **My father, thou art the guide of my youth** (4), yet be ardently devoted to other gods at the same time. This was a pretty mixed-up nation, but no more so than individuals and nations today. With their lips they made a great show of devotion to the Lord, but at the same time had done all the **evil** that they were capable of doing (5). The words of v. 4 may refer to Josiah's reform that took place in the early years of Jeremiah's ministry.[6] Apparently the people conformed outwardly to the edict of the king of Judah, but in their hearts they remained unchanged. They merely combined the worship of the Lord with that of the other gods which they served. Thus they corrupted and made a travesty of serving God.

---

[6]II Kings 22—23.

B. A PLAINTIVE CALL TO REPENTANCE, 3: 6—4: 4

The previous discourses are cast in dark colors. Perhaps they were planned that way to stab awake the conscience of the nation. They reveal to Judah what its condition really is, as over against what it blithely supposed itself to be. They show that the only hope of salvation lies in a complete reversal of the policies that had hitherto been pursued.[7] But the prophet's final words in that section startle one, for they seem to say that any reversal of those policies is now impossible. The fate of the nation is sealed. Thus the previous section closes on a note of doom.

This section, however, is different. Although the prophet continues to paint the nation's sinfulness in somber hues, there is a change of tone. A ray of hope pierces through the darkness. The house of Jacob is invited to repent. There is a plaintiveness in the call that gives a glimpse of the hurt at the heart of God over the condition of His people. While the messages are directed to the children of Israel as a whole, yet the prophet often distinguishes the Northern Kingdom from Judah by the term Israel; at other times the same term is used to denote the two together. Jeremiah compares and contrasts the two nations in their attitudes toward God, and their practice of the religion of the covenant.

1. *The Payoff on Superficial Repentance* (3: 6-11)

In these verses the prophet contrasts Judah with Israel, showing that the former is more guilty than the latter, because Judah had failed to take to heart or learn anything from Israel's fate.

The Lord said also unto me in the days of Josiah the king, Hast thou seen that which backsliding Israel hath done? (6) The Lord goes on to describe the spiritual promiscuity of the Northern Kingdom before its fall, and how He had grieved with a lover's heart for her return. For **high mountain** and **green tree** cf. comment on 2: 20. In spite of His long-suffering and patience, He had been compelled to give her **a bill of divorce** and **put her away** (8). "The Northern Kingdom had sinned away her day of grace and was now in captivity."[8] **Her treacherous sister Judah**

[7]C. J. Ball, "The Prophecies of Jeremiah," *The Expositor's Bible* (New York: George H. Doran Co.), pp. 114 ff.

[8]Kuist, *op. cit.*, p. 31.

saw it (7) . . . **but went and played the harlot also** (8). The people of Jeremiah's time were well aware of the fact that earlier prophets had predicted Israel's fall because she had forsaken the Lord and gone after other gods. **Adultery with stones and with stocks** (9) refers to idol worship of images of stone and wood. Those same prophets had also warned the Southern Kingdom of a like fate, **yet for all this her** (Israel's) **treacherous sister Judah hath not turned unto me with her whole heart, but feignedly** (10). Judah did not learn her lesson very well, although she had every opportunity.

There is a strong implication in 10 that Judah may have made some effort to return to the Lord at one time, but apparently the effort had proved to be a superficial affair. Many scholars think that the reference is to the reform that took place in the eighteenth year of Josiah's reign (II Kings 22—23). After finding the book of the law in the Temple, the king had made a genuine effort to lead the nation back to the worship of God. Despite Josiah's earnest efforts, the people were loath to leave their old ways. Although they conformed outwardly to the edict of the king, it seems their hearts were not in it. At Josiah's untimely death they turned back to their former practices, never to be aroused again from their sinful stupor. Judah's repentance, then, had been a superficial thing. She had turned only in "pretence" (10, RSV), which was no turning at all. In comparing her with the Northern Kingdom, Jeremiah says, **Backsliding Israel hath justified herself more** (is "less guilty," RSV) **than treacherous Judah** (11).

We see from Judah's example how devastating is superficial repentance to an enlightened people. Such repentance is outward, not inward; it is only in semblance, not in deed and in truth. It aggravates guilt instead of reducing it. The person is more treacherous, more guilty, more set to do evil, and more difficult to turn, than if he had never pretended to repent.

2. *The Promptness of God to Forgive the Repentant* (3:12-13)

Grieved with the people of Judah, God now turns His full attention to the exiles of the Northern Kingdom. He commands the prophet, **Go and proclaim these words toward the north. and say, Return, thou backsliding Israel . . . I am merciful . . . I will not keep anger for ever** (12). Though Israel's sin has been very grievous to Him, yet He is ready—even eager—to forgive, if the nation will but turn. These two verses give us an insight into the very heart of God, and what we see there is forgiveness and great mercy.

While the forgiveness of God is ever available to all who come to Him, yet persons and nations must respond to His call. **Only acknowledge thine iniquity, that thou hast transgressed . . . and . . . have not obeyed my voice (13).** We see here that a thoroughgoing confession is a vital element in true repentance. There must be no hedging or qualifying, but a complete and sincere acknowledgment of sin. Such promptness and completeness in man's confession are answered by the promptness and completeness of God's forgiveness.

There was also a message in these words for the men of Judah as well as for the exiles of Israel. With one so forgiving as the Lord, catastrophe and ruin could be averted for Judah—although the hour was late. This seems to be the earnest hope and undying faith of the prophet. By the same token there is also hope for sinful men today—but the condition is the same as it was for Israel and Judah—**only acknowledge thine iniquity (13).** "He that covereth his sins shall not prosper: but whoso confesseth and forsaketh them shall have mercy" (Prov. 28:13).

3. *The Plans of God for Those Who Repent* (3:14-20)

Here the prophet seems to be addressing both Judah and Israel as he sets forth God's future plans for His people. The passage presupposes that both nations have learned their lesson well, and are now ready to follow Him in singleness of heart. It is good to know that God has plans for His people, and that they are thoughts of good and not of evil (29:11).

God makes His familiar call for repentance by declaring His relation to the people, **I am married unto you (14).** He then promises that there shall be a return from exile. **I will bring you to Zion . . . Judah shall walk with . . . Israel, and they shall come together out of . . . the north (14, 18).** It is the righteous remnant which will return—**I will take you one of a city, and two of a family (14)**—and make a new beginning.

There is coming a better day for those who return to the Lord. In that day **I will give you pastors** (rulers) **according to mine heart, which shall feed you with knowledge and understanding (15).** In the past, both Israel and Judah had had some very poor leaders. This will be changed. Further, a new order

335

of spiritual living will exist in that day, and a new relationship with God will come into being. The **ark of the covenant (16)** and the Temple, which had been the proud possession of the Southern Kingdom, and which had been claimed by Judah as a sign of her superiority over Israel, will no longer be a bone of contention between the two nations. God will dwell among His people in a new way, and His presence will abolish the need for symbols of this sort. "It [the ark] shall not come to mind, or be remembered, or missed; it shall not be made again" (RSV).[9]

In that future day **Jerusalem** will be the site of the **throne of the Lord; and all the nations shall be gathered unto it (17)**, and the peoples of the earth will no longer follow the **evil** inclinations of their hearts, but will follow that which is good. **Judah** and **Israel (18)** will be reunited and the things that had divided them in former days will be gone.

We have in these verses one of the recurring facts of prophetic literature: an intermingling of the near and the far. The predictions of a return from exile are mingled with the predictions of the gospel age and the age to come, and they are thoroughly interwoven. There is a hint here of Jeremiah's idea of the new covenant (31:31 ff.). Under this covenant everyone may have a firsthand knowledge of the Lord. A new and more spiritual conception of God will exist among the people.

Despite all these good purposes God has for His people, He still has a problem. **How shall I put thee among the children, and give thee a pleasant land? (19)** The Hebrew here is obscure, but apparently God is saying, "How can I do these good things for you, when you are so far from Me now?" The answer is suggested in the latter part of the verse. He will give them **a pleasant land, a goodly heritage,** when they call Him, **My father; and shalt not turn away from me.**

4. *The Pathway to Genuine Repentance* (3:20—4:4)

God declares, **As a wife treacherously departeth from her husband, so ye have dealt treacherously with me, O house of**

---

[9]There is a good deal of conjecture among scholars concerning the ark of the covenant. Some think that it disappeared during the wicked reign of Manasseh, and if so, it was gone at this writing. Others think it was destroyed with the Temple in 586 B.C., but it does not appear in the list of treasures taken by Nebuchadnezzar in c. 52. No one really knows. Jeremiah, however, is saying that the old order of which it was a symbol will be replaced by the new, and the mere symbol will not be desired or missed.

Israel (20). Yet the suffering, yearning, loving heart of God seeks a way to cure the sin of His people. He proceeds to show how His plans for their welfare can be brought about. The remainder of this section is taken up with pointing out the pathway that leads to genuine repentance.

a. Confession (3:21-25). A sort of dialogue now seems to take place between God and a penitent people. **A voice was heard upon the high places, weeping and supplications of the children of Israel: for they have perverted their way, and they have forgotten the Lord** (21). Then God is heard saying, **Return . . . and I will heal your backslidings** (22). The people reply, **Behold, we come unto thee . . .** "In vain is the sound from the hills, the tumult from the mountains" (23*a*, Driver's trans.); i.e., the people were confessing that "the wild ecstatic religion practiced in the popular nature-worship could bring no real satisfaction and peace."[10] **Truly in the Lord our God is the salvation of Israel.** The confession of the people continues, **Shame hath devoured . . . We lie down in our shame . . . we have sinned against the Lord . . . we and our fathers . . . unto this day** (24-25). Confession means that a person has begun to face himself honestly. It is an acknowledgment that man is not wise enough to direct his own life. God has no way of meeting our needs until a man reaches this point. But when confession is sincere and complete, He immediately begins His work of healing in the soul.

b. Conversion (4:1). "The idea of repentance in the Old Testament is most often expressed by a Hebrew word, *shub*, which literally means 'to turn' or 'to return.' "[11] It is a strong word, and involves the whole man: mind, heart, and actions. It means a conversion of the entire person—a complete turning from that which is evil to face God in utter obedience and reverence. The Hebrew is constructed here so as to emphasize **unto me**, and it means that there must be a clean break with corrupt forms of idolatrous worship, and a wholehearted return to the Lord. "If you will return, O Israel," says the Lord, "to Me you shall return!" (4:1, lit.)

Necessarily involved in "turning" is the idea of forsaking that which is evil—**Put away thine abominations out of my**

---

[10]A. S. Peake, "Jeremiah," *The New Century Bible* (Edinburgh: T. C. and E. C. Jack, 1910), p. 114.

[11]Hyatt, *Prophetic Religion*, p. 167.

sight (1). Repentance includes not only a change of attitude but a change of actions as well. One must rid himself of all objects that occasioned his transgressions (in this case, idols), as well as practices and habits of sin. He must bring forth fruit worthy of repentance (Matt. 3:8). Old Testament repentance and New Testament repentance are at one here.

God now says in the case of Israel, If these things are done, **then thou shalt not remove** (1). This is usually taken to mean that in Judah's case she would not go into exile. But the word translated **remove** can also mean wander (as a fugitive or exile) or "waver" (RSV). If it is taken to mean wander it could mean that the Northern Kingdom would return from exile and no longer wander among the nations. If "waver" is chosen, it means they will be steadfast in their faith. However, the KJV rendering goes well with the context and is to be preferred.

c. Concession (4:2). The next step Israel should take is to concede that there is no help outside of God. This is indicated in 2, where the prophet says, **Thou shalt swear, The Lord liveth.** "Among the Hebrews an oath was a very powerful thing; to swear by a deity was to recognize its existence and to invoke its power."[12] If a Hebrew could really say **in truth, in judgment, and in righteousness** that **the Lord liveth,** it was an acknowledgment that the Lord was the *living* One, that He alone had existence, and all other gods had no reality at all. The prophet knew that if the nation could say these words in sincerity, the problem of idolatry could be disposed of quickly. If Israel would make this concession she would become "a light to the nations," and **the nations** in turn would **glory,** i.e., "make their boast" (lit.), in the living God.

d. Complete Renovation (4:3). A. S. Peake says that vv. 3 and 4 "are among the grandest in prophetic literature and comprise Jeremiah's whole round of theology."[13] Stanley R. Hopper says that these two verses are "a call to a deeper repentance than the peoples of the world, let alone Judah, are prone to."[14] They strike at the root of sin in our lives. No halfway measures will do here. It is likely that in the background of Jeremiah's mind is the reform attempted by Josiah. That effort at revival, which ended only as a surface reformation, must have been bitterly disappointing to a true prophet. It is not hard to believe that this

---

[12]IB, V (exeg.), 831.   [13]*Op. cit.,* p. 115.
[14]IB, V (expos.), 832.

bitter experience drove Jeremiah to a deeper insight into the nature of Hebrew religion. He saw that nothing short of a complete renovation of the hearts of his people would enable the nation to find its way back to God and avert the calamity that was rapidly approaching.

Surface religion would not do; religion must be inward and individual if the national situation was to get better. The prophet therefore cries, **Break up your fallow ground, and sow not among thorns** (3). The national life had become so hardened by years of idolatrous practices and gross injustice that the truth of God could not grow in it. As ground that is not properly cultivated is soon filled with weeds and thorns, so was the ground of the national life of Judah and Israel. And the thorns that were growing there "were the spontaneous product of unregenerate human nature."[15] Among other things, they included thorns of careless living, of social injustice, of past grievances, of hypocrisy, and of unforgiveness. It is impossible for righteousness and true holiness to flourish where these abound.

It may be that Josiah's reform had cut these thorns down but had failed to get them out by the roots. Soon they grew again stronger and wilder than ever. The religion of the living God demanded a radical renovation of the heart life of both the individual and the nation. This is the beginning of Jeremiah's emphasis on inward religion that is so characteristic of his ministry. This concept of complete renovation of the heart is one of the basic tenets of the New Testament: "The ax is laid unto the root of the trees" (Matt. 3:10; etc.).

e. Circumcision of the heart (4:4). Jeremiah next presses for an even deeper truth than in his fallow ground pronouncement. Changing the figure of speech, he cries to the **men of Judah and inhabitants of Jerusalem: Circumcise yourselves to the Lord, and take away the foreskins of your heart** (4). What did Jeremiah mean by this figure of speech? The idea of circumcision was certainly not new to his hearers. Since the time of Abraham it was the initiatory rite by which a man entered the Hebrew religion. It was obligatory upon every male of every family in Israel.

From the beginning (Gen. 17:10-12) circumcision must have signified something more than cutting off a small portion of skin.

[15]John Skinner, *Prophecy and Religion* (Cambridge: University Press, 1951), p. 151.

It must have had a high spiritual implication.[16] Likewise there must be a strong spiritual significance in Jeremiah's words here. (Cf. Deut. 30:6; Jer. 9:26; 33:7-9; Rom. 2:25-29; Gal. 5:6; Col. 2:11.)

Taken in its context the statement, **Circumcise yourselves to the Lord,** teaches that there must take place in the hearts of men a thoroughgoing transformation in order for them to be acceptable to God. A revolutionary change was needed in the lives of the people of Judah at this time. Certainly a cleansing, i.e., a removal of impurity, is pictured here by the prophet's figure of speech. This passage and others like it caused George Adam Smith to say of Jeremiah, "He had a profound sense of the engrained quality of evil, the deep saturation of sin, the enormity of the guilt of those who sinned against the light and love of God."[17] Nothing short of purity of heart is stressed in this passage (cf. Ps. 24:4; Matt. 5:8).

To summarize the meaning of verse 4: (1) Circumcision of the heart refers to an inward work of God in the soul that manifests itself in outward conduct; (2) It has to do with the removal of impurity from the spiritual faculties of man; (3) It is a radical change that goes to the deep of man's moral nature; (4) The operation performed is central to man's basic spiritual needs; (5) It is a demand on the part of God for ethical holiness in man. According to Jeremiah, if men do not comply with God's requirements for this inner purification nothing but judgment and destruction await them (4).[18]

C. ENEMY FROM THE NORTH AND FROM WITHIN,[19] 4:5—6:30

In these chapters Jeremiah sees with prophetic vision the calamity that is coming upon his people. But he perceives also that the situation has a double aspect. There are actually two

[16]John Calvin, "The Book of the Prophet Jeremiah," *Calvin's Commentaries,* trans. by John Owen (Grand Rapids: Wm. B. Eerdmans Publishing Co., 1950), p. 205. John Skinner says, "Circumcision . . . was . . . an act of dedication signifying the removal of the impurity inherent in the state of nature, through which the individual becomes a member of the religious community" (*op. cit.,* pp. 151-52).

[17]*Op. cit.,* p. 246.

[18]See John Wesley's sermon "The Circumcision of the Heart," *Wesley's Works* (Kansas City: Beacon Hill Press, 1958), V, 203.

[19]See Kuist, *op. cit.,* p. 31.

enemies. "One is an unidentified enemy from the north"; the other is Judah's "stubborn and rebellious heart."[20] Each is to play its part in bringing about the downfall of Judah. With great concern Jeremiah describes the coming destruction and the reasons for its coming. He intersperses these pronouncements with exhortations to repentance in hope that the approaching calamity might be averted. It must be remembered that many prophecies in the Old Testament were made in order that they might not be fulfilled.[21] Apparently Jeremiah was hoping that this would be the case here.

The mention of the **evil from the north** indicates that this prophecy has some connection with the vision of the boiling pot in c. 1. As to the identity of the foe from the north (Babylonia), see Introduction. The basic purpose of the prophet, however, is not to identify the foe but to stir the souls of his countrymen to their need for repentance. He is not concerned with all the trifling minutiae that trouble the literalist, because he sees in large outline the gathering storm, and what it will mean to his country.

1. *The Day of Reckoning* (4:5-31)

To the eye of the prophet this enemy from the north is plainly visible on the horizon of time. What he sees in prophetic contemplation fills him with consternation. He lifts up his voice and sends forth a cry of warning!

a. *The trumpet of alarm* (4:5-13). **Blow ye the trumpet in the land** (5). This was the usual way of warning the people of approaching danger. The magnitude of the danger is indicated by the implication that the whole **land** should be aroused, and by the choice of the words he uses to spread the alarm. **Cry, gather . . . into the defenced cities** of Judah and prepare for battle, **for I will bring evil from the north** (5-6). The expression **Set up the standard toward Zion** means "mark out a route for those seeking shelter in Jerusalem" (Berk., fn.). Already the **lion . . . is on his way** (7). This description of a **lion** may well refer to Nebuchadnezzar, **the destroyer of the Gentiles,** who later came with ferocity against Judah. **And thy cities shall be**

---

[20]*Ibid.*

[21]Jonah's prophecy concerning Nineveh is a case in point. See Paterson's *Goodly Fellowship of the Prophets* (New York: Charles Scribner and Sons, 1948), p. 6.

laid waste, without an inhabitant. The enemy is coming! The danger is imminent!

The prophet now describes the cringing victims of this avalanche of divine judgment: **The heart of the king shall perish, and the heart of the princes** (9), i.e., faint from fear and dread. **And the priests . . . and the prophets** shall be appalled and confounded. You may well **lament and howl** (8), says Jeremiah, **for the fierce anger of the Lord is not turned back from us.** In the emergencies of life the unrighteous collapse, for they have no inner braces to give them strength.

On the surface, in v. 10 it seems as though the prophet is reproaching God for misleading the people with false promises. The Targums paraphrase this verse to mean that false prophets have been misleading the people by crying **peace** when there was no peace.[22] But the verse may represent a sob of consternation on the part of the prophet, who cannot reconcile the wonderful promises made to Israel in former days with the terrible judgment he now sees approaching: **the sword reacheth unto the soul** (life; 10).

After this momentary interruption, Jeremiah continues to sound the alarm. The approaching calamity is likened to one of the winds that were accustomed to sweep from the desert into Judah. If they were mild, they were useful for winnowing the grain, but if they were **full** and fierce they were called the dreaded sirocco. This **wind** (12) was so deadly that it blighted and ruined everything it touched. Just so would the enemy from the north be destructive to the people of Judah.

A similar metaphor is used in 13 to further enforce the message. He depicts the **evil from the north** (6) as moving toward Jerusalem as a terrible tornado of doom. **He shall come up as clouds, and his chariots shall be as a whirlwind: his horses are swifter than eagles. Woe unto us! for we are spoiled** (13).

b. The plea for repentance (4:14-18). Jeremiah is so moved by what he sees that he lets forth a lamenting cry, **O Jerusalem, wash thine heart from wickedness, that thou mayest be saved** (14). **How long** will you harbor vile and wicked thoughts in your heart? He seems to be saying, "Be warned! Already the news has been announced in **Dan** [15, the most northern point in Israel], and has also been proclaimed in **mount Ephraim** [prob-

---

[22]See Adam Clarke, *A Commentary and Critical Notes,* IV (New York: The Methodist Book Concern, n.d.), 264.

ably not more than ten miles away], that the enemy from the north is coming." In fact, **the nations** (16) may as well know that Jerusalem is marked for destruction, for **watchers** (apparently "besiegers") **come from a far country.** They are at hand to lay siege to **the cities of Judah.**

The prophet pleads with his people to repent, pointing out the reasons for the coming judgment. **Thy way and thy doings have procured** (18) this fate for you. You have no one to blame but yourselves, for you have been most **rebellious against me, saith the Lord** (17). Your doom is a **bitter** (18) one, but your **wickedness** has gone so deeply into your character that you are rotten at the very heart.

c. The groaning heart (4:19-22). By this time the prophet discerns with unmistakable clearness the calamity and doom that await his beloved people. His own sorrow over the sins of Judah is so great that he can restrain himself no longer, and he laments with a bitter cry. **My bowels, my bowels! I am pained at my very heart** (19; better, with RSV, "My anguish, my anguish! I writhe in pain!"). In aching words, the prophet describes his heartbreak over the vision he sees. His emotion seems too deep for words, but speak he must, **I cannot hold my peace . . .** (19). **The whole land is spoiled** (20). **Tents** and **curtains** is a poetical expression for "dwellings." **How long shall I see the standard** ("war signals," Berk.), **and hear the sound of the trumpet?** (21) It seems more than human feelings and emotions can bear.

But the real reason for the bitterness and pain is found in 22: **My people is foolish . . . they are sottish** (stupid) **children . . . they are wise to do evil, but to do good they have no knowledge.** One can sense the grinding disappointment and feel that the prophet's suffering arises from his identification with his people. Their punishment is his punishment; their fate is his fate. No better picture of a true prophet (shepherd, pastor) can be found in all the range of religious writings.

d. The cosmic catastrophe (4:23-26). Here is one of the most moving eschatological passages in Sacred Writ. It is almost as though the prophet is looking at a picture, on the surface of which a scene is formed at a glance, but which upon closer scrutiny has depths that a superficial look did not reveal. Amazing depths! Jeremiah seems to see through, and beyond, the moment of Judah's destruction to a more distant scene. While contemplating Judah's end, it seems for a moment that the prophet has seen beyond, to the consummation of all things. His "awareness of the 'end' is radical and absolute."[23]

I beheld the earth, and, lo, it was without form, and void (23)—things are back to primeval times, the chaos of Gen. 1:2— **the heavens . . . had no light . . . the mountains . . . trembled (24) . . . there was no man, and all the birds of the heavens were fled (25).** Moffatt translated the last part of 24, "All the hills are swaying." Jeremiah finds himself alone in the universe. The end has become as was the beginning. Where there had been fruit and flowers, there is now nothing but desolation and waste— a veritable **wilderness (26), and all the cities** were gone where flourishing cities once stood.

The **fierce anger** of the **Lord (26)** has brought this about. The implications are that the sin of man has been so great that the earth has been swept clean. The divine judgment has done its cleansing work. The earth's cycle has been completed. A cataclysmic ending has come to the cosmos. This idea is not new among the prophets, but Jeremiah had seen in a flash of inspiration what others had talked about. He transmits to us his vision.

For Jeremiah the moment soon passes and he is back with the weight of Judah's situation on his heart.

e. The game is up!" (4:27-31). **For thus hath the Lord said, The whole land shall be desolate (27);** the impact of Judah's plight strikes him again, and he realizes that "the game is up" for her! What he recognizes concerning her fate is clear enough, but he perceives that God's judgment is tempered with mercy, **yet will I not make a full end.** How characteristic of the Old Testament prophets is this word of mercy! They are incorrigibly hopeful! They see judgment, and they are convinced that it will come, but they also see that the purposes of an intelligent God will be brought to fruition! Beyond judgment is redemption.

But this glimpse of the loving-kindness of God does not make the present any less real. **For this shall the earth mourn . . . I have purposed it . . . neither will I turn back from it (28).** The execution of God's plan of judgment will be carried out. Sin will be punished! **The whole city shall flee . . . every city** (i.e., of Judah) **shall be forsaken (29).** The enemy will

[23]IB, V (expos.), 840.

have done his work of destruction. The whole land will be desolate.

But what about the capital city, Jerusalem? Attention is now focused on her. **And when thou art spoiled, what wilt thou do** (30)? Jerusalem is pictured as an immoral woman who had tried to avoid her fate by decking herself **with crimson** raiment and **ornaments of gold,** by **painting** her eyes with a black powder known as antimony. She had played the harlot but all in vain. **Thy lovers will despise thee . . . seek thy life.** Cajolery and charms will not suffice. "The game is up!"

The prophet has seen the end of the city. He knows that sin, when it has run its course, brings death (Jas. 1:15). So it is with the city that has played the harlot. **I have heard a voice as of a woman in travail** (31), and the cry is of one whose agony is unbearable. It is "the cry of the daughter of Zion gasping for breath" (RSV). She **spreadeth her hands, saying, Woe is me now!** (31) Jerusalem is in her death throes.

2. *The Blistering Indictment* (5:1-31)

The emphasis of c. 4 was on the enemy from the north; in c. 5 we see the enemy within. Here is a terrible indictment of the people of Jerusalem. It may be that the prophet is vindicating God in the eyes of the people for the horrible punishment that has been described in c. 4.

a. The hopeless search (5:1-6). God sends Jeremiah on a search throughout the city to find a righteous man, **if there be any that executeth judgment, that seeketh truth . . . I will pardon it** (1), i.e., the city. This incident is reminiscent of Abraham's prayer for Sodom (Gen. 18:20 ff.). Although the men of Jerusalem speak such pious words as **The Lord liveth** (2), which on the surface would seem to recognize the sovereignty of God, yet in reality **they swear falsely,** for their actions give the lie to their words. Jeremiah's search is in vain.

After his investigation the prophet answers the Lord, **Thou hast stricken them, but they have not grieved . . . they have refused to receive correction** (3). They had not returned from their evil ways, but had continued in their sin **and made their faces harder than a rock.** Then Jeremiah seems to have remembered that the people whom he had seen on his search were the **poor** (4). These were ignorant and **foolish;** perhaps they could be excused. He then goes to the **great men** (5), the upper classes, for surely they will know **the way of the Lord.** He finds that,

345

although they know the way, because of the wickedness of their hearts they too have **broken the yoke, and burst the bonds.** No righteous man could be found. Consequently the city cannot be spared its judgment.

Jeremiah affirms that, since moral conditions are in such a state, there is nothing that can stop the onslaught of the enemy. The people are as helpless as domestic beasts of burden, who having **broken** their **yoke** find themselves in the midst of a forest of wild animals, **a lion . . . shall slay them, and a wolf** and a **leopard . . . Their transgressions are many, and their backslidings are increased** (6). The truth is that when people are out of contact with God they have no inner defenses, and they fall a prey to every evil influence of the enemy. **A wolf of the evenings** is better "a wolf from the desert" (Berk.).

b. The provocative question (5:7-9). God now asks these people a question, **How shall I pardon thee?** (7) It was God who had prospered them and **fed them to the full;** but instead of being grateful, they forsook God and gave allegiance to idols that were **no gods** at all. In their perverseness and rebellion **they assembled themselves by troops in the harlots' houses.** This certainly has reference to their faithlessness to God and represents spiritual adultery, but it could also refer to the impure rites of the Canaanite religions which practiced sacred prostitution as a part of their ritual.

It would seem from Jeremiah's indictment that actually the people were grossly immoral among themselves. He likened them to "lusty stallions" (RSV) neighing for their neighbors' wives (8). Their wickedness knew no limits. With conditions like this prevailing, the people had given God no grounds on which to pardon them. Therefore He cries, **Shall not my soul be avenged on such a nation as this?** (9) He has no alternative but to punish.

c. The stern retribution (5:10-14). God now gives the command for His people's sin to be turned back upon their own heads, "Go up through her vine-rows and destroy . . . strip away her branches" (10, RSV). The Hebrew here is difficult, but the above seems to fit the context. The enemy is "bidden to ravage the vineyard, i.e., Judah,"[24] **but make not a full end** (10). Apparently the nation is to be cut back to the ground, where only

---

[24]Peake, *op. cit.*, p. 130.

the stem remains. Later, new life can begin again from the root. But for the present, full punishment must be exacted, **For the house of Israel and . . . Judah have dealt very treacherously against me** (11).

In fact they deliberately refused to believe the warnings of the true prophets of God, but **belied** (denied) (12) **the Lord** by saying, "He will do nothing" (RSV), **neither shall evil come . . . sword nor famine.** The people had believed the words of the false prophets who had said there was no cause for alarm. But said Jeremiah, **The prophets shall become wind, and the word of God is not in them** (13). Their false predictions will but fall upon their own heads.

God speaks again to Jeremiah, **I will make my words in thy mouth fire, and this people wood, and it shall devour them** (14). The "word of God" is thought to be full of divine energy and accomplishes great things; here it is a **fire** which consumes the wicked. The punishment is stern, but it is just.

d. The devouring nation (5:15-18). Jeremiah again speaks of the **nation** that is to be the rod in the hand of God for punishing Judah. He no doubt refers to the enemy from the north. His description is one that would strike terror to the bravest heart: **I will bring a nation . . . from far . . . a mighty nation . . . ancient . . . whose language thou knowest not** (15). **Their quiver is as an open sepulchre** (16), i.e., their arrows are deadly and their soldiers are **mighty** warriors. When these people come they will **eat up** (devour and destroy) **the harvest . . . bread . . . sons . . . daughters . . . flocks . . . herds . . . vines . . . fig trees** (17). The walled **cities** that the people thought were impregnable will collapse before their astonished gaze, and **the sword** will do its fearful work. The ferocity of the attack could well fit the barbarous Scythians, but refers more probably to the Chaldeans, who were fully cruel enough to carry the meaning here.

There follow words of hope, **Nevertheless . . . I will not make a full end** (18). These words have now become almost like a refrain. But is this not like the God of the Bible, who into the darkest night brings a ray of hope? God must punish, but He weeps while He punishes.

e. The reasons for divine judgment (5:19-31). **Wherefore doeth the Lord . . . all these things unto us?** (19), the people ask. God is not slow to set forth His reasons. (*a*) *A backsliding heart* is the first: **ye have forsaken me.** This estrangement from

347

God is to end in the wretchedness of exile, **in a land . . . not
yours.** Every backslidden heart knows the wretchedness of a
strange land. The next reason (b) is *spiritual stupidity;* **O foolish
people, and without understanding . . . eyes, and see not . . .
ears, and hear not (21).** (c) *Lack of reverence for God* is the
point of 22-25. **Fear ye not me? . . . will ye not tremble at my
presence?** (22) God's creative power in the world should cause
men to stand in awe, but to this they are blind. In 22 we are
reminded that the physical universe obeys God's will for it, but
often this is not true of men. "The fear of the Lord is the beginning of wisdom" was a well-known maxim in Judah. However,
these people gave no reverence to God at all, but had **a revolting
and a rebellious heart (23).** Further, (d) they were *guilty of
social injustice;* **wicked men . . . lay [in] wait . . . set a trap**
(26). There were no bounds to their wickedness; they grew **fat**
(wealthy) by trampling on the rights of **the fatherless** and **the
needy (28).** Then (e) *religious perversity* is **the wonderful** (lit.,
astounding) **and horrible thing (30)** that is prevalent in the
land. **The prophets prophesy falsely (31).** This perversity had
taken hold of **prophets, priests,** and **people.** Every stratum of
society was infected with moral rottenness, and God said sadly,
My people love to have it so. The expression **The priests bear
rule by their means (31)** is translated, "The priests rule at their
[the false prophets] beck and call" (Moffatt).

The blistering indictment of this section is brought to a
close with a burning question, **What will ye do in the end?** (31)
The question rings through the mountains and valleys of Judah,
and reverberates in the streets of Jerusalem, but to no avail.
Spiritual stupidity and moral perversity had done their deadly
work; the nation is "past feeling" (Eph. 4:19).

3. *The Advancing Foe* (6:1-30)

In this section the prophet continues to alternate between a
description of coming judgment, the guilt of Judah and Jerusalem,
and giving vent to the searing pain in his own heart.

We must recognize that Jeremiah viewed things from a
different perspective than the people. Standing, as he did, in the
councils of God, he saw things that the people did not see.
Throughout his career he was constantly penetrating the divine
mysteries, perceiving things from God's perspective. However,
since he was finite, he saw only in part. What he saw was
authentic, but he never had the whole of truth, or the whole of

reality before him at any one time. This is the case with all the prophets; they could relate only that portion of truth that they themselves were able to comprehend. (Cf. Paul's position, I Cor. 13:12.)

a. Preparation for siege (6:1-8). With the advance of the foe from the north, Jeremiah perceives that Jerusalem will not be taken immediately, but that the city will be placed under siege. In his deep concern for human life, he calls for an evacuation of the city, **O . . . children of Benjamin . . . flee** (1). The reference to **Benjamin** is not too strange when it is remembered that Jerusalem, or at least part of it, was sometimes thought of as lying within the tribe of Benjamin.[25] The **sign . . . in** (on) **Beth-haccerem** (lit., house of the vineyard) apparently refers to a high point several miles outside Jerusalem used for signaling. **Tekoa** refers to a small city[26] lying twelve miles south of Jerusalem (see map 2) where the mountainous terrain and many caves offered protection for the evacuees. There is a great sense of urgency in the prophet's words.

Jeremiah describes the preparations that will be made to put the city under siege. **The shepherds** (chiefs or generals) **pitch their tents against her round about** (3). Plans for taking the city by surprise are discussed: first **at noon** (4), during the "siesta," but somehow this misfires; then they plan to **go by night** and **destroy her palaces** (5). This too seems to fail, so they **hew . . . down trees, and cast a mount against Jerusalem** (6). The description of siege preparations is characteristic of the Assyrians and Chaldeans during this period of history.

What Jeremiah saw in prophetic vision he now uses to warn **Jerusalem** of her fate, and to exhort her concerning the desperate state of her moral and spiritual life. **This is the city to be visited** (besieged, 6), for "as a well [**fountain**] keeps its waters fresh, so she keeps fresh her wickedness" (7, RSV). It is characteristic of Judah's sinful nature to spew forth fresh wickedness constantly. Jeremiah will eventually push this thought further and say that, for both nations and individuals, spiritual cleansing and transformation are necessary to change the outflow of one's life. **She is wholly oppression** (6) means, "There is nothing but oppression within her" (RSV). The city, morally corrupt at heart, cannot but have it said that **violence and spoil**

---

[25]See IB, V (exeg.), 856.

[26]The prophet Amos was a native of Tekoa (Amos 1:1).

is heard in her; she is filled with **grief and wounds** (7), for like
produces like.

In v. 8 Jeremiah turns from portraying the calamity that is
coming, to exhorting Judah to do something constructive about
her moral and spiritual life: **Be thou instructed, O Jerusalem ...
lest I make thee desolate** (8).

b. Punishment will be thorough (6:9-15). Verse 9 has been
variously interpreted.[27] One thing about the passage is certain,
Judah is likened to a vineyard. **They shall throughly glean** (9)
seems to refer to the enemy as the **grapegatherer.** His gleaning
of Judah appears to refer to the thorough punishment coming on
her. So desperate is Judah's sin that Jeremiah, who often pleads
with God in behalf of his people, is found crying, **I am full of the
fury of the Lord; I am weary with holding in** (11). The depths
of depravity are so great, and the moral rottenness so vile, that
Judah's sins literally cry for punishment. No one will be spared!
All ages and sexes, and every stratum of society, **from the least**
(poorest) **even unto the greatest** (richest; 13) are guilty and
ripe for punishment.

What then are the sins of which Judah is so flagrantly guilty?
The prophet does not mince words. Judah is spiritually deaf:
their ear is uncircumcised (10). Also, **the word of the Lord** is an
object of **reproach** and scorn. The prophet's message is a frustrating irritant that interferes with their desires, so they close
their ears and refuse to hear. **I will stretch out my hand** (12)
means, "I will exert my power." The people are **given to covetous-
ness** (13), greedy for material gain, and it does not matter how
they obtain the gratification of their desires.

The prophet and **the priest** are no better than the people,
every one dealeth falsely. In fact, these "religious sinners" are
the worst of all. They have proclaimed that which is not true,
saying, **Peace, peace; when there is no peace** (14). Instead of
healing **the hurt** of the nation, they have lulled the people to sleep
with a false sense of security. Were these prophets and priests
ashamed **when they ... committed abomination? Not at all** (15).
They had become so shameless in their sin that they cannot **blush**
(cf. Eph. 4:19). For them as well as for others the punishment
will be thorough; **they shall fall** and there will be none to help
them.

[27]For alternate interpretations see IB, V, 859.

c. *Prescription for deliverance* (6:16-21). In true prophetic fashion, the yearning heart of Jeremiah feels compelled to prescribe a remedy for Judah's ills. He points the way out of the dark! **Ask for the old paths, where is the good way, and walk therein, and ye shall find rest for your souls** (16). The prophet is referring to the original way in which Israel had followed the Lord under the hand of Moses (2:1 ff.). It was a covenantal relationship—God and Israel living together in holy fellowship and mutual love. The people of Jeremiah's time understood what he was talking about. They knew about the ancient paths and **the good way.** It was a good way, not because it was old, but because it was the right way—God's way. Walking in **the old paths** had always brought rest of soul to the nation. But the stiff-necked and stubborn men of Judah refused the way out of their predicament by saying, **We will not walk therein.**

Again Jeremiah tries to stir the people by reminding them of the many times God had sent **watchmen** (prophets) who had sounded the **trumpet** (17) of warning and instruction. He implied that if they would listen to him there was help and hope for the nation even yet. But they continued to rebel saying, **We will not hearken.**

The prophet now turns and makes a threefold appeal. He calls for the **nations,** the **congregation**[28] of Israel (18), and **the earth** (19), to take note that Judah had rejected God's **law** and scornfully refused to give heed to His **words. The fruit of their thoughts** means their devices.

Despite these grievous sins the nation was formally religious. They multiplied offerings and ritual with abandon. Not content with the **old paths,** they had devised some new religious ideas on their own! But God asks them about these unauthorized practices, **To what purpose . . . incense from Sheba, and the sweet cane from a far country?** (20)[29] God says, Your new-fangled ways of worship **are not acceptable, nor your sacrifices sweet unto me.** Sacrifices and religious ceremony are repugnant to God unless they are accompanied with righteous living. **This people,** saith the Lord, shall stumble and **perish** (21).

---

[28]The use of the word **congregation** is rather strange; the Hebrew is obscure but it seems to refer to Israel as a whole. See Peake, *op. cit.,* p. 142.

[29]**Sheba** is a tribe of noted traders in southwest Arabia, and **sweet cane** is probably not sugarcane, but calamus, an herb used in making incense.

Against the dark backdrop of Israel's sin and disobedience we see in 16 "God's Good Counsel" to men who are missing the way of life. (1) Look for **the old paths**—God's eternal truths; (2) Ask for **the good way**—the way of righteousness; (3) **Walk therein** —act on the best you know; (4) **And ye shall find rest for your souls** (A. F. Harper).

d. *Painful lamentations* (6:22-26). Jeremiah returns again to the enemy **from the north country** (22) and describes this **people as a great nation . . . raised from the sides** ("farthest parts," RSV) **of the earth.** They are being stirred up and brought forth by God to punish Judah for her sin. They have a fearful mein: ruthlessly expert with **bow and spear; they are cruel, and have no mercy (23).** The sound of their coming is like the roaring of **the sea.** Even now they are marching toward Judah arrayed for battle.

Jeremiah sees the result of their coming. **The fame** of this dread people is such that the men of Judah will be paralyzed with fear; **our hands wax (grow) feeble, and pain** takes **hold** of them **as of a woman in travail (24).** There is lamentation in the city. Furthermore, the danger is so great that no one dares go outside the city **into the field** or **by the way,** for **fear of the sword (25).** Consternation and terror are **on every side.** Jeremiah cries to the people to put on their **mourning** robes, for the day that is coming is one of great **lamentation. Wallow thyself in ashes** and **make bitter lamentation: for the spoiler shall suddenly come upon us (26).** One can feel the throb of pain in the heart of the man of God as he conveys to his people what he sees in the offing.

e. *Put to the test* (6:27-30). The Hebrew text of these verses is difficult, and the metaphors are mixed, but the general meaning is reasonably clear. God says to Jeremiah, **I have set thee for a tower and fortress** ("assayer and examiner," Berk.) . . . **among my people, that thou mayest know and try their way** (27). Judah is put to the test by a severe refining process. But alas, human beings are not like ore from the earth; they have wills of their own. Although **the bellows are burned** (29, blow fiercely) and although **the lead,** the oxidizing agent, which carries off the dross, melts properly, yet the work is done **in vain.** The people **are all grievous revolters** (28); they reject the refining process, and **the wicked** (29) remain in control of the nation. God has put the people to the test and the refining process has failed. The men of Judah are but slag for the refuse heap. **Reprobate silver shall men call them** (30). Because they would not respond positively to the transforming process, therefore **the Lord hath rejected them.**

Three truths of judgment stand out clearly: (1) The people's refusal of God, 27-29; (2) God's consequent refusal of the people, 30*b*; (3) What God has refused, all men count reprobate, 30*a* (G. C. Morgan).

D. The Temple Sermon, 7:1—8:3

There is a break between chapter 7 and the foregoing chapters. The theme is still the same, but new information is given to us about the prophet. In the background of the sermon is the attitude of the people toward the sacrificial system and the Temple. Jeremiah revealed that there was something tragically amiss with the then current Hebrew religion. It is clear that what is lacking is at the core of Judah's present trouble. Thus the Temple sermon marks an important point in the career of Jeremiah, for here he lays his finger on the most sensitive religious nerve of the nation.

Scholars have long debated the relation of c. 7 to c. 26. Some are confident that 26 gives the results of the sermon in 7 and proves without doubt that the sermon here was given in the first year of Jehoiakim (608 B.C.). Others are just as certain that the sermon was given in the last years of Josiah, and that Jeremiah repeated the sentiments at a later date, in c. 26. There are good arguments for both views, but the first seems preferable.

1. The Delusions of a Hardened Conscience (7:1-15)

God commissions Jeremiah to deliver a message to the people of Judah at the Temple gate. **Hear the word of the Lord, all ye of Judah** (2) suggests that the occasion was a national religious festival, one which the entire kingdom attended.

The prophet first pleads with the people to **amend** their **ways** (3), i.e., to be genuine and wholehearted in their repentance. He then outlines what this would involve in a practical way: **Trust ye not in lying words** (4), deal justly with one another, **oppress not the stranger, the fatherless . . . the widow . . . shed not innocent blood,** forsake other gods (6). His tone is conciliatory and encouraging. The result: they would remain in **the land** and **dwell in peace** (7). Jeremiah assures the people that God's thoughts toward them are good.

However, as the prophet moves on into his sermon his tone changes as he reminds the nation of its sins. **Behold, ye trust in lying words** (8) . . . **ye steal, murder** . . . **commit adultery** . . . **walk after other gods** (9). Then after having broken the law of God they had the audacity to come into the Temple—**this house, which is called by my name** (11)—and say, " 'We are delivered!'—only to go on doing all these abominations" (10, RSV). They were actually making God's house **a den of robbers** (11; see Matt. 21:13, *et al.*) Also they were laboring under the delusion that, since the Temple was the dwelling place of God, He would never let it be violated, thus the nation was safe. They thought they could say, **The temple of the Lord, the temple of the Lord** (4), and by this magic formula ward off any kind of disaster. **Ye trust in lying words** (8) suggests that the false prophets had put these ideas in the minds of the people. Such notions, however, are the delusions of a hardened conscience, and the lowest kind of religious superstition.

Reaching back into Israel's history, Jeremiah reminded them of **Shiloh, where I set my name at the first** (12). Shiloh had been a place of worship during the period of the judges, but when the people made a fetish out of the ark (I Sam. 4:3 ff.) the village had been destroyed. God says, **See what I did to it** (Shiloh) **for the wickedness of my people . . . Therefore will I do unto this house** (the Temple) . . . **as I have done to Shiloh** (12, 14).

With this prediction Jeremiah touched the most sensitive nerve in the religious life of the people. They reacted (see c. 26) with resentment and anger, for it exposed their self-deception and their moral poverty. To satisfy their own depraved desires, the people were attempting to make God over into their own image, and had reduced His moral precepts to superstitious delusions. Here is an inherent tendency in man's fallen nature (Rom. 1:22 ff.).

God declared, **You are not safe as you suppose, but I will cast you out of my sight, as I have cast out all . . . of Ephraim** (15). The reference here is to the exile of the Northern Kingdom, which had already taken place (721 B.C.), and is also a clear prediction of the exile of Judah. Self-deception always ends in tragedy and desolation (cf. Matthew 23).

2. *Forbidden to Intercede* (7:16-20)

It must have taken unusual courage for a sensitive person like Jeremiah to proclaim such a horrifying message. He involuntarily starts to cry out in prayer for his beloved nation, but God forbids him to intercede: **Pray not thou for this people . . . neither make intercession to me** (16).

God was not through indicting the people, nor was the revelation ended. **Seest thou not what they do in . . . Judah and in the streets of Jerusalem?** (17) **Children . . . fathers . . . women . . . make cakes to the queen of heaven** (18). The people had become so utterly brazen in their sin that they were offering sacrifices to **other gods** openly in the streets. **The queen of heaven** apparently refers to Ishtar, the goddess of a Babylonian fertility cult that had been imported to Judah. She is mentioned to indicate the depths to which the people had fallen in their sin. The point they had reached marks the beginning of the end for the nation. God declared, **My fury shall be poured out on this place** (20); such perverseness cannot go unpunished.

3. *Obedience Is Better than Sacrifice*[30] (7:21-28)

Jeremiah next strikes a blow at the wrong use of religious ritual. He affirms with no uncertain sound that religious ceremony without ethical content is meaningless. If sacrifices did not enforce and strengthen morality in the nation, they were worse than nothing. This is true with all ritualism in religion. Unless formal religious ceremony (or informal religious ceremony) strengthens morality and holy living, it is effort expended in vain.

There is sarcasm in Jeremiah's words, **Put your burnt offerings unto your sacrifices, and eat flesh** (21). He is saying, You may just as well put your **burnt offerings** (which were completely devoted to God, and which none might eat) with your peace offering (which was eaten by the worshipers) and eat them together. Under such circumstances your sacrifices have no religious validity; they are just so much flesh.

Verse 22 has been variously interpreted.[31] On the surface it seems difficult to reconcile with Hebrew history and religious practice. However, when it is read in context, it simply means

---

[30]Cf. I Sam. 15:22.
[31]See Calvin, *op. cit.*, p. 391; IB, V, 875; Peake, *op. cit.*, p. 152; Clarke, *op. cit.*, p. 274.

that God's primary commandment did not deal with **burnt offerings** or **sacrifices** when He **brought them out of the land of Egypt** (21-22). The primary emphasis at that time was, "Obey My voice; then I will be your God; then you will be My people" (lit.). The moral demands of God are always important. The sacrificial system was instituted for the purpose of promoting moral obedience and making God a real factor in the lives of the people.

Instead of obeying God's moral requirements, the people began to walk **in the imagination** (stubbornness) **of their evil heart** (24) and became even more wicked and sinful. When they failed to learn from the sacrificial system, God instituted the office of prophecy. The prophets were commissioned to assist the people in fulfilling the demands of the law that had been given at Sinai. The people now had twofold help: the object lessons in holy living set forth by the sacrificial system, and the preaching of the prophets. Moffatt interprets **daily rising up early and sending them** (25) to indicate God's deep concern: "I have been sending you all of my servants the prophets eagerly and earnestly." Instead of listening to either of these "agencies of help," **they hearkened not unto me, nor inclined their ear, but . . . did worse than their fathers** (26). **They . . . hardened their neck,** i.e., grew more stubborn. Now God sees that **they will not hearken** and **will not answer** (27) when Jeremiah speaks to them. Therefore the prophet is told to pass the verdict: **This is a nation that obeyeth not the voice of the Lord . . . nor receiveth correction** (28). Only judgment and destruction await them.

4. *The Irony of Sin's Rewards* (7:29—8:3)

Cut off thine hair (29) seems to be addressed to the daughter of Zion, i.e., **Jerusalem,** since the verb is feminine. The rest of the verse indicates that cutting the hair is an act of mourning. It may refer to the hair of the Nazarite, which was a symbol of his consecration to God. **Jerusalem,** as a city, had been "a Nazarite to God, but must now cut off her hair, must be profaned, degraded, and separated from God."[32] **The Lord hath rejected and forsaken the generation of his wrath**—"the race

[32]C. W. Eduard Naegelsbach, "The Book of the Prophet Jeremiah," *A Commentary on the Holy Scriptures,* ed. John Peter Lange; trans. Philip Schaff (New York: Charles Scribner's Sons, 1915), p. 97.

that has roused him to wrath" (Smith-Goodspeed); there was therefore ample reason for mourning.

Jeremiah gives several reasons why lamentation would be in order in Jerusalem. (*a*) Judah had become so shameless and irreverent that she had set up **abominations** (i.e., idols) **in the house** (30) of the Lord, and had profaned that holy place. (*b*) They had also built a shrine to the god Moloch (II Kings 21:5) **in the valley of the son of Hinnom** (31), and there had made human sacrifices—a thing so hateful in the eyes of God that He declared, It "never entered my mind" (Moffatt). Although the place had been named **Tophet,** it would now be called **the valley of slaughter** (32), since so many would die there in the coming destruction of Jerusalem. The place where they had practiced such gross wickedness would become their grave. Such is the irony of sin. (*c*) Another reason for mourning was the prediction that on the day of judgment the slaughter would be so great that many bodies would not be buried, but should be meat for the birds and **the beasts . . . and none shall fray** (frighten) **them away** (33). No greater indignity could be suffered by a Hebrew than to have his dead body remain exposed to the elements. (*d*) Still further, the time was soon coming when **the voice of mirth . . . of gladness, the voice of the bridegroom, and . . . the bride** (34) would no longer be heard. The land would be utterly desolate; there would be nothing but the stillness of death. (*e*) The desecration of the graves of the honored dead was to climax Judah's sorrows. **The bones of the kings . . . princes . . . priests, and . . .** false **prophets shall be spread** out before the heavenly bodies **whom they had worshipped, and they shall be for dung upon the face of the earth** (8:1-2). (*f*) As for those who escape destruction in the capture of the city, their fate in exile will be so horrible that they would gladly have **chosen** death **rather than life** (3).

E. Miscellaneous Oracles, 8:4—10:25

The following undated oracles are of varying lengths, and seem to have no sequence with those that precede or follow them. However they carry the same general theme—the arraignment of the house of Jacob for judgment. Their location here supports the assumption that Jeremiah's prophecy was compiled topically rather than chronologically. Almost the entire section is in poetic form (cf. Moffatt and RSV).

1. *The Unnaturalness of Judah's Sin*[33] (8:4-7)

The Lord laments the unbelievable conduct of Judah. "When men fall down, do they not get up? If one turns away, will he not return?" (8, lit.) Yet **this people** turns away in **a perpetual backsliding** (5), and no one repents **of his wickedness** (6). They are so willful and stubborn that they rush headlong into sin like a horse into battle. Nothing can turn them from their course. They have become set in their way of habitually sinning. **The stork in the heaven . . . and the swallow** (7) unerringly obey their natural instincts, fulfilling their destiny. On the other hand, the people of God do "not obey the law of their being,"[34] but are constantly thwarting the divine purpose. They have done the wrong thing so long that it seems right. They seem oblivious to the divine ordinances, although God's law is written in every sinew of their being.

2. *The Fate of the Self-deceived* (8:8-13)

God now accuses the people of being deceived into thinking that they **are wise** (8). He places the blame for this upon their religious leaders. The false **pen of the scribes** has made **the law** into a lie. **The prophet** and **the priest . . . dealeth falsely** (10), saying, **Peace, peace; when there is no peace** (11). Although the people claim to be wise, it cannot really be so, for both the people and their leaders **have rejected the word of the Lord** (9). Therefore, **what wisdom** could be **in them?** These so-called **wise men,** says God, will be **dismayed and taken,** and I will **give their wives (and their fields) unto others** (10). They had become so hardened in their self-deception that when their abominations were brought to light **they were not at all ashamed** (12; see comment on 6:13-15). Furthermore, God continues, Judah is like a worthless grape **vine** or **fig tree** (13) that will bear no fruit; even its leaves will wither and **fade.** The once fine fruit and luxuriant foliage that were the Southern Kingdom, **I will surely consume.** They rejected **the law of the Lord** (8), when they should have meditated in it day and night (Psalms 1), and now the people and their religious leaders shall **fall** (12) and there will be none to help.

---

[33]See also 2:10-11; 5:22-23; 18:13-17.
[34]Kuist, *op. cit.,* p. 39.

3. *There Is No Escape* (8:14-17)

In this paragraph the people of the countryside are speaking. They recognized their peril more keenly than those in the cities. Yet they seemed to sense that even though they fled to **the defenced cities** (14) they would eventually **be silent there.** The word for **silence** actually means the silence of death. **Water of gall** would be bitter or poisoned water. Although they wait for **peace,** nothing **good** arrives; although they hope for healing, there will be nothing but **trouble** (15). Already the enemy is near. **The snorting of . . . horses** is **heard from Dan,** the north border of Judah. **They are come, and have devoured the land** (16). The coming calamity is so certain that the prophet speaks as though it were already accomplished. The enemy is likened to **serpents** and **cockatrices** (adders; 17) that cannot be **charmed** but will **bite** and devour the land.

4. *The Wail of Despair* (8:18—9:1)

What the prophet sees is so terrifying and so inevitable that, when he tries to comfort himself concerning the fate of his beloved land, his heart faints. He seems to hear the people as though they were already in exile, crying in consternation, **Is not the Lord in Zion? is not her king in her?** (19) God answers their questions immediately, **Why have they provoked me to anger?**

Knowing the true state of things, the prophet cries with great lamentation, **The harvest is past, the summer is ended, and we are not saved** (20). We find three things in this text: (1) The acknowledgment of opportunity; (2) A confession of neglect; (3) The anticipation of doom (Lange, p. 108).

But Jeremiah is not finished with his lament, **For the hurt . . . of my people am I hurt . . . astonishment** ("confusion," Berk.) **hath taken hold on me** (21). **I am black,** i.e., I mourn. One can feel the searing pain in the heart of the prophet as he breaks forth anew, **Is there no balm in Gilead?** (22) The expected answer is, Yes. Gilead had long been known for the **balm** made from the resin of the mastic tree. **Is there no physician?** Again the expected answer is, Yes. Since there is a **physician** near, and a remedy at hand, **why then** is there no healing? There can be but one answer. The people have not applied to the Physician. They have sought no remedy. They have neglected the one sure source of help. Heedless, blind, and stubborn, they are rushing headlong toward the precipice of doom. The shepherd heart of the prophet breaks under his load of grief, and the compassionate cry bursts from his lips, **Oh that my head were waters, and mine eyes a fountain of tears** (9:1). It is this lamentation that gained for Jeremiah the title of "the weeping prophet."

5. *The Grief of a Loving Heart* (9:2-22)

There is a close connection between the end of c. 8 and the beginning of c. 9. The prophet's breaking heart has vented itself in deep, irreconcilable sorrow over the fate of his people. He is also distressed at his growing isolation. No one understands him; he is shunned by some, and abused by others (11:21 ff.). He is so overcome with grief that he longs to fly away to **a lodging place** in **the wilderness** (2). (In this he has expressed the sentiments of many weary prophets of a later day!) Since it is impossible for him to get away, he spends his grief in a series of laments. These at times seem vindictive, but they only appear so, for underneath they express the sorrow of a loving heart.

a. The treacherous people (9:2-8). Jeremiah is now given an insight into the inner lives of the people. What he beholds fills him with great sadness. The whole nation has gone in one way—**they be all adulterers, an assembly of treacherous men** (2). Their treachery takes several forms. They are spiritual **adulterers,** yes, but they are guilty of physical adultery as well (cf. 5:7-8). They are also guilty of falsehood; **they bend their tongues like their bow for lies** (3). One dare not trust his neighbor, **for every brother will utterly supplant** (4). The Hebrew word for **supplant** is the same as the word "Jacob," and the reference is to the treachery of Jacob with his brother, Esau (Gen. 27:5 ff.). "The descendants are like their ancestor, each 'Jacobs' his brother."[35]

They have taught their tongue to speak lies, and actually **weary themselves** (go to unusual lengths) **to commit iniquity** (5). They live in the midst of **deceit,** and **refuse to know the** Lord (6). Their wickedness is willful and deliberate. They are especially deceptive with their tongues (cf. Jas. 3:5 ff.), expressing goodwill to their neighbor outwardly, while inwardly they are planning his ruin.

---

[35]Peake, *op. cit.,* p. 165.

b. The coming desolation (9:9-11). Another reason for Jeremiah's grief stems from the desolation that he knows is coming on the land, and especially Jerusalem. Everything will be swept away. I will **take up a weeping and wailing,** cries the prophet, because the land is **burned up . . . none can pass through . . . the fowl . . . and the beast . . . are gone** (10). He then describes Jerusalem as lying in **heaps,** i.e., ruins, **and a den of dragons** (jackals), and **the cities of Judah desolate, without an inhabitant** (11). This prophecy was fulfilled in 586 B.C. when the city was reduced to rubble.

c. The lack of understanding (9:12-16). The prophet laments because of the spiritual stupidity of the people. A **wise man** would have asked some questions: **Why does the land perish** (lit.), **and is burned up so that none passeth through?** (12) A discerning person would have readily seen the reason: **They have forsaken my law and walked after the imagination** (stubbornness) **of their own heart** (13-14). A wise person would have looked ahead and known that sorrow and tragedy would be the outcome of such conduct: **I will feed them . . . with wormwood, and give them . . . gall to drink. I will scatter them also among the heathen** (15-16). Since the time of Jeremiah the expression "wormwood and gall" has been used to characterize extreme affliction and sorrow. The reference to scattering them among the heathen is a prediction of exile. Judah should have learned from the fall of Israel, but apparently she had learned nothing. Jeremiah weeps because no one discerns the fate of the nation. He insists that, had they known the character of God, they could have read "the signs of the times."

d. Death's relentless harvest (9:17-22). God speaks again to the prophet, and His words are the reason for a fresh outburst of grief. The message is of such solemn import that Jeremiah is urged to call in professional mourning women. The **cunning** (skillful) **women** are the same as the **mourning women.** This is an instance of parallel structure in Hebrew poetry. The women are to **take up a wailing** in order to stimulate the people of Jerusalem to weep over the city, that **our eyelids** may **gush out with waters** (17-18). The cry goes up, **How are we spoiled!** (19) Possessions have been swept away and exile has come; "they [the enemy] have thrown down our dwellings" (lit.).

But there is a still greater reason for grief than the loss of possessions. For this, hired lamentation is not sufficient. Every

woman of Judah should not only take up a lament, but the
women should **teach** (20) a dirge to their **daughters** and their
neighbors as well. **Death is come up into our windows and into
our palaces,** and our **children** and our **young men** (21) are
gone. **Death** has appeared in a sudden and unexpected way, and
there is no security against him. Here is cause for real weeping.
The bodies of the **men shall fall** (22) in the **field** like sheaves
after the harvestman (reaper). **None shall gather them,** i.e.,
they will not be given a proper burial, but their **carcases** will be
treated as refuse. Death is personified here as one who cuts
down the inhabitants of the land as a reaper cuts grain. The
idea of death as a "grim Reaper" apparently arises from this
passage.[36]

6. *Wisdom—the False and the True* (9:23-24)

On the surface these verses seem to have little relation to
what precedes and yet they are appropriate. They could very
well set forth the only way of escape from the coming destruction. They certainly draw a contrast between false security and
genuine safety. They also contrast the wisdom of men with the
wisdom of God. The men of Jeremiah's day, like men of every
age, boasted in "human wisdom (culture), military might (technical skill), material wealth (economic plenty)."[37] Actually,
this is the height of foolishness, for these things are transient and
offer no solid basis for security. Therefore **let not the wise man
glory in his wisdom** (23).

On the contrary, the only real basis of wisdom and happiness lies in knowing God. The character of God is best understood by what He loves, and how He deals with men. He takes
delight in **lovingkindness** (gracious favor, steadfast love),
judgment (equity, fairness, impartiality), and **righteousness**
(straightness, uprightness) (24). These things are the ground of
true wisdom. **Righteousness** (*tzedek*), **judgment** (*mishpat*), and
lovingkindness (*hesed*) are the great triumvirate of the Old
Testament. On these an individual or nation can build securely.
Without them the greatest and strongest are hopelessly weak.

[36]IB, V (expos.), 892.
[37]Kuist, *op. cit.,* p. 40.

7. The Punishment of the Uncircumcised (9:25-26)

The Hebrew of this little oracle is difficult, and scholars have translated it variously,[38] but the meaning is reasonably clear. Jeremiah is stressing the primacy of inward religion as over against outward conformity to religious practices. Jeremiah anticipates St. Paul here by quoting God as saying, **The days come** when **I will punish the circumcised with the uncircumcised** (25); i.e., "circumcision is nothing, and uncircumcision is nothing, but the keeping of the commandments of God" (I Cor. 7:19). Whether **Egypt** or **Edom,**[39] or even **Judah,** practiced circumcision, it does not matter, for the fate of the **uncircumcised in the heart** will be the same as the **uncircumcised** in flesh. Therefore the circumcision (in the flesh) of the Jew will be treated as uncircumcision unless an "inner circumcision" is effected with the outward act (cf. 4:3-4). Outward conformity to religion without inward grace is totally insufficient. Since **Judah** had missed the deeper meaning of the outward acts of her religion, she will be punished with the heathen, for she is no better than they. In this emphasis on inward religion Jeremiah is definitely pointing toward the gospel age.

8. The Emptiness of Idols (10:1-16)

There is a break in the thought of the prophet at the beginning of c. 10 that is rather puzzling;[40] however, the contents of the passage are quite appropriate to the general theme. The passage is addressed to the **house of Israel** (1). Does this mean the Northern Kingdom, which is already in exile, or is he addressing Judah under the generic name of Israel? Whomever he addresses, he speaks as though they are in exile. This writer holds that it is altogether possible that Jeremiah is speaking to the exiles of the Northern Kingdom in faraway Assyria. In doing so he could have had a twofold aim: (1) to sincerely urge the exiles to be faithful to the Hebrew religion in a strange land;

---

[38]See ASV, RSV, and C. F. Keil and F. Delitzsch, "Jeremiah," *Commentaries on the Old Testament* (Grand Rapids, Mich.: Wm. B. Eerdmans Publishing Co., 1956, reprint), p. 192; IB, V, 896; NBC, p. 616; and J. F. Graybill, "Jeremiah," *The Wycliffe Bible Commentary* (Chicago: Moody Press, 1962), p. 666.

[39]*Ibid.*

[40]Kuist, *op. cit.*, p. 41.

and (2) that his words to the exiles of Israel should be an indirect lesson to sinful Judah.

Kuist points out two perils that surrounded every exiled Hebrew in his heathen environment. One had to do with pagan interpretations of happenings among the heavenly bodies which were calculated to produce great terror; the other had to do with the manufacture of idols which sought to give tangible form to intangible spiritual realities.[41] Concerning both of these, the prophet issues stern warnings to the exiles. **Learn not the way of the heathen** (2), i.e., their religious practices. He enforces his warning with reasons: **The customs** (practices) **of the people are vain** (empty and stupid; 3). He elaborates by drawing a contrast between the living God and idols. He describes how an idol is made: the **workman cutteth a tree . . . deck it with silver,** etc. (3-4). He pours scorn upon these manufactured objects by comparing them to "scarecrows in a cucumber field" (5, RSV). They **speak not . . . cannot go** (walk) **. . . cannot do evil** (harm), **neither also is it in them to do good** (5). **They are . . . brutish** (stupid) and **foolish** (8). "The instruction of idols is but wood!" (RSV), i.e., their wisdom is wooden like themselves. You may dress them up with **silver . . . from Tarshish, and gold from Uphaz**[42] (9), but they are still empty and worthless, **a work of errors** (15) that **shall** soon **perish from the earth** (11).

In contrast to the idols that he has just described, the prophet speaks of the majesty, wisdom, and creative activity of God (6-7, 12-16). Jeremiah asks, **Who would not fear thee, O king of the nations?** (7) "For this is thy due" (RSV). God's wisdom and might far surpass the petty foibles of men, for **every man is stupid and without knowledge,** and every maker of a **graven image** is at last put to shame by his own foolish inventions. But **the portion of Jacob** (16) is the One who **made the earth by his power,** and **established the world by his wisdom** (12), **for he is the former** (Fashioner) **of all things . . . Israel is the rod** (tribe) **of his inheritance: The Lord of hosts is his name** (16).

Verse 11 is the only verse in Jeremiah in the Aramaic language. Why it appears thus is not known. Some scholars think

---

[41] *Ibid.*

[42] **Tarshish** in Spain or Sicily was the westernmost extremity of the known world, noted for its silver; **Uphaz** is unknown, but thought by some to be the land of Ophir, noted for its gold.

that it was originally a marginal gloss that finally was incorporated into the text. Whatever the answer, its sentiments are true to Jeremiah's teaching and its meaning is not hard to discern.

9. *Exile Is Near* (10:17-22)

These verses seem to be in the form of an imaginary dialogue between the prophet and the mother city—Jerusalem. The prophet commands the inhabitants **of the fortress** (17; the city), "Pick up your bundle from the ground" (lit.), apparently to begin the long journey into exile. **Thus saith the Lord, Behold, I will sling out the inhabitants of the land** (18). This is violent language, but indicates the manner in which the city will be taken. The mother city is now heard to say, "Woe is me for my hurt! my wound . . . this is an affliction, and I will bear it" (19, lit.). She continues the lament, **My tabernacle** (tent) . . . **my children . . . my curtains** (20). The figure is of the Eastern desert dwelling with its tent, supporting ropes, and side curtains. In prophetic vision Jerusalem has fallen. The mother city reflects on her hopeless condition, and mourns to think that **the pastors** (21; leaders) had been too **brutish** (stupid) "to gather in the scattered flock."[43] **The noise of the bruit** (22) is a redundancy. **Bruit** is a French word meaning "noise."[44] The literal translation is "the sound of a report" (rumor or message), **a great commotion** has come **out of the north country** (22). All this can only mean that "the desolation of the cities of Judah is about to begin"[45]—exile is at hand!

10. *A Plea for Correction and Retribution* (10:23-25)

The terror that he sees drives the prophet to prayer. This is the first of Jeremiah's prayers that we shall consider. Others will follow. He seems to perceive the frailty and impotence of the human race. He acknowledges for himself, and for all men, that man is a finite, dependent creature; **it is not in man . . . to direct his steps** (23). He implies that he himself is badly in need of God's help. Since man, left to himself, will wander off into error, Jeremiah prays, **O Lord, correct me;** i.e., discipline and

[43]Kuist, *ibid.*, p. 42.
[44]Clarke, *op. cit.*, p. 284.
[45]Kuist, *op. cit.*, p. 42.

guide me. But seeing his own human frailty in light of the majesty and holiness of God, he hastens to cry, **Oh, blend mercy with judgment** (justice) **. . . lest thou bring me to nothing** (24). Justice alone would destroy him; mercy is his only hope. Thus it is with all men.

Jeremiah next prays that God will **pour out** His **fury** on the nations that **have eaten up Jacob** (25). This seems like an unbecoming prayer for a prophet of God. But one must not read twentieth-century morals into Jeremiah's day. Also we must remember that he conceived of the enemies of Israel as the enemies of God and thus felt justified in praying for their destruction.

Section IV Confessions and Predictions

Jeremiah 11:1—20:18

This section contains a miscellaneous collection of narratives and predictions, along with several dialogues between the prophet and God. The narratives and predictions shed light upon the career of Jeremiah, but the dialogues have special value in that they reveal to us the inner life of the prophet. There is no chronological arrangement of the material, but most of it seems to come from the time of Josiah (640-609 B.C.) and the earlier years of Jehoiakim (608-597 B.C.). The prophet's dialogues with God are his prayers that came to the surface in times of great crisis. They have long been called the "confessions of Jeremiah."

A. JEREMIAH AND THE COVENANT, 11:1—12:17

1. Judah's Violation of the Covenant (11:1-17)

Jeremiah is commanded to speak to the men of Judah (2), cities of Judah (6), and to the inhabitants of Jerusalem (2), concerning the covenant. The use of "Amen" (5, margin, KJV) and reference to the curses pronounced upon those who violate the covenant indicate that Jeremiah is talking about the Sinai covenant (Deuteronomy 27—30) with its emphasis on the moral law. It is also possible that the recent renewal of that covenant under Josiah (II Kings 23:3) was in the background.

God reminds the people that, on His part, the covenant has been sealed by His redemptive acts in their behalf, I brought them forth out of the land of Egypt (4). This is evidence of His grace (unmerited favor) and concern for them. The iron furnace is a furnace in which iron is smelted and thus a figure of severe suffering. Rising early (7) indicates God's special attention to Israel. In turn, He demanded good faith on the part of His people: Hear ye the words of this covenant, and do them (6). But, God declares, Israel has not kept the vows made at Sinai. Your fathers (7) obeyed not, nor inclined their ear (listened), but walked . . . in the imagination (stubbornness) of their evil heart (8).

God said to Jeremiah, There is a conspiracy . . . among the men of Judah (9). They are turned back to the iniquities of

their forefathers (10). The words **turned back** may refer to the fresh violation of the covenant so recently renewed under Josiah. Because of this flagrant disloyalty, judgment is pronounced upon Judah, **I will bring evil upon them** (11). It is foreseen that when this **evil** comes, the people will **cry** to all the false **gods** that they worship, but **they shall not save them . . . in the time of their trouble** (12). For v. 13 see comments on 2:28; 7:17-18. Because of these things, Jeremiah is again forbidden to intercede for Judah, **Pray not thou for this people** (14).

The condemnation of God is further enforced in 15-16 by the lines of what seems to be a mutilated poem. The Hebrew is difficult to translate. RSV has gone to the Septuagint rendering, which at least fits the context, and is perhaps the best solution. "What right has my beloved in my house, when she has done vile deeds? Can vows and sacrificial flesh avert your doom?" (15) The prophet seems to be saying, "No [sacrificial] offering, however costly, could ever be a substitute for wholehearted dedication."[1]

The poem continues as Judah is likened to an **olive tree,** which in the beginning was beautiful and productive but has become diseased and unfruitful. Her branches will be consumed by fire—**with the noise of a great tumult** (16). Since God had **planted** it, He could also destroy it. However, it is Judah's violation of the covenant that has brought her to this place of ruin (17).

2. Confessions of Jeremiah (11:18—12:17)

While carrying on his prophetic duties, Jeremiah suddenly discovered that his relatives and neighbors in Anathoth had conspired to kill him. The discovery left him greatly tortured in mind. The rest of the passage is taken up with a dialogue between God and the prophet about the value and meaning of his task.

a. The plot at Anathoth (11:18-23). Jeremiah's knowledge of the plot against his life seems to have been revealed to him by God, **Thou shewedst me their doings** (18). He is amazed at how naive and unsuspecting he had been, **I was like a lamb . . . brought to the slaughter** (19). In this passage the prophet shows his acquaintance with Isaiah 53.[2] **Let us destroy the tree . . .** (19)

---

[1]Kuist, *op. cit.,* 47.

[2]This is a point in favor of the unity of Isaiah, since if the last half of Isaiah were written by a "second Isaiah" in the period of the return from Exile, Jeremiah could not have known about it.

seems to have been some kind of proverb. In great distress of mind, Jeremiah appeals his case to the bar of God's justice. He asks vindication for himself and **vengeance (20)** for his enemies. **The reins** would be the thoughts.

God immediately asserts himself in behalf of His servant with a word of assurance, **I will punish them (22) . . . there shall be no remnant of them (23). The year of their visitation** means "the year fixed for their punishment" (Moffatt). The words of God bring a measure of relief to the prophet's heart. But Jeremiah has, for the first time, looked death fully in the face, and it has left his mind greatly troubled.

b. Jeremiah questions God (12:1-4). Deeply shaken by the treachery of his relatives and neighbors, Jeremiah complains to God. He confesses his faith in the integrity of God, **Righteous art thou, O Lord (1),** but admits that he is painfully distressed and puzzled by what is happening. **Wherefore doth . . . the wicked prosper?** It would seem that God is on the side of the wicked, **Thou hast planted . . . they grow (2).** They succeed in their schemes, but their hypocrisy is shockingly evident. The name of God is on their lips, but **far from their reins** (hearts)! How can God permit these things to go on? This was Job's problem (Job 12:6) and the problem of many a good man who suffers.

Jeremiah reminds the God who knows all things of the purity of his own intentions (3). He requests that God evidence His concern for moral values by vindicating him in the wrongs that he has suffered. In his discouragement and despondency he cries, **How long shall the land mourn** because of **the wickedness of them that dwell therein? (4)** The Septuagint renders the latter part of 4 as, "God will not see our ways," which seems to catch the meaning of the Hebrew if not the words.

c. God questions Jeremiah (12:5-6). God does not give Jeremiah a direct answer to the above questions, but counters with some questions of His own. It is up to Jeremiah to interpret the signals and obtain his answer from the questions that God asks. God queries, **If . . . footmen . . . wearied thee, . . . how canst thou contend with horses? (5)** If in a **land of peace** (your hometown) you stumble, what will you **do in the swelling** (lion-infested jungle) **of Jordan,** i.e., when real trouble comes? Both questions are cast in the form of proverbs. The import of God's word startled the prophet; the worst is still to come!

After letting this truth penetrate the consciousness of Jeremiah, God attempts to prepare him for future events. He warns him not to trust his own family or his neighbors at Anathoth. Although they may **speak fair words** (6), they cannot be trusted. **They have called a multitude after thee** is better, "They have raised a hue and cry after you" (Moffatt). This revealed to the prophet how utterly alone he was. Jeremiah against the whole land!

d. *The divine lament* (12:7-13). Just as Jeremiah must forsake his family and friends because of treachery, God is compelled to forsake His people for the same reason. Thus God's lament over Israel is parallel to Jeremiah's sorrow over his home and family. Several different figures are used to describe Israel: she is God's **heritage** but forsaken by Him (7), **a lion** turned against her Maker (8), **a speckled bird** about to be attacked by others (9), **a vineyard** trampled and ruined (10). As ruthless **pastors** (lit., shepherds) tear and trample a **vineyard,** so Israel will be crushed and dismantled by foreign rulers. The land will become utterly **desolate** from one end to the other **because no man layeth it to heart** (is concerned, 11). **Although** Israel has **sown wheat,** she has reaped **thorns** (13). **They shall be ashamed of your revenues** (harvests). She has exhausted herself in her endeavors, but to no **profit.**

e. *The divine plan* (12:14-17). This oracle seems to say that God is interested in all men—even the enemies of Judah. Therefore Jeremiah has a message for the Gentile nations of his day. Such a ministry was in keeping with Jeremiah's commission (1:10). These nations will certainly be punished for what they do to **Judah** (14), but if they repent and **learn the ways of my people** (16; i.e., the ways of the Lord), then they shall **be built** up **in the midst of my people.** But the **nation** (17) that does not learn will be destroyed. This passage teaches the universal sovereignty of God. All nations are under the power of His control. He blesses those who are righteous, and punishes those who are wicked.

B. Parables and Pronouncements, 13:1-27

1. *The Parable of the Waistcloth* (13:1-11)

Scholars have held various views concerning the historicity of this incident. It seems improbable (though not impossible) that Jeremiah would have made two 400-mile trips (see map 1) to the **Euphrates** River just to bury a dirty loincloth and dig it up again. With the change of one Hebrew letter in the text it could refer to a place five or six miles northeast of Jerusalem (Wadi el-Farah), which would fit the description in the story very well. It is perhaps best to take the incident as a parable and not try to press the historical aspect too far.

The parable teaches that any object is of value only when used for its intended purpose. A loincloth designed to be worn on the loins of a man is not useful when buried in the damp earth (4) and never washed (1). It would certainly become **marred** (7)—soiled and rotted. Likewise **Judah** (9) is useless as a nation unless she is fulfilling God's purpose for her. **The imagination of their heart** (10) would be the way of their own proud choosing. The parable implies that **Judah** is as corrupt morally as Jeremiah's waistcloth was physically—the fabric is rotten and broken. Sin decays the moral sensibilities of man and reduces him to a useless object, fit only for the scrap heap of the universe.

God had bound Israel to himself in covenant relations as closely and intimately as a man would bind a waistcloth around his loins. It is a moving thought to remember that God clothes himself with those who profess to follow Him. Despite the special privileges the covenant brought, Judah failed God. Consequently, as a man casts away a useless waistcloth, so God will mar the pride of **Judah** (9) by casting her out of her land.

2. *The Parable of the Wine Jar* (13:12-14)

God commands Jeremiah to speak a commonplace proverb concerning a wine jar (12) to the men of Judah, with the express purpose of getting a peevish reply. Apparently the occasion was a festival where wine jars were in clear view of prophet and people. God tells him what their reply will be, and how he is to answer them. Thus a bit of wry humor becomes the occasion for a rapier-like thrust of divine truth: **I will fill all . . . this land . . . with drunkenness** (13) **. . . I will dash them one against another . . . I will not pity** (14).

Drunkenness is often taken in the Bible as symbolic of the "wine of God's wrath," i.e., His judgments (Jer. 25:15; 51:7; Ps. 75:8; Isa. 19:14; Rev. 16:19). This idea, without doubt, is present here. But there is something more. The contents of the wine jar seem to represent the people of Judah. As the particles in a wine jar jostle against each other in the process of fermentation, just so the inhabitants of Judah will dash against each other in civil strife and moral confusion. As the turmoil and confusion of the fermentation process is transferred to the man who drinks the wine, so Judah will be as confused and bewildered as a drunken man in the day of judgment. From the king on the throne to the peasant in the field the land will be in a state of bewilderment and confusion. This state of bewilderment in Judah is symbolic of the confusion there is in the life of an individual who has not found (or has lost) the organizing power of the Spirit of God.

3. *Sinners, Be Not Proud* (13:15-19)

In this oracle Jeremiah pleads with his sinful countrymen to turn from their pride and **give glory to the Lord** (acknowledge His sovereignty; 16), lest **darkness** come upon them and they **stumble** as in the night (John 12:35). Pride blinds one to proper values and brings darkness. The alternatives are clear for Judah. **Give ear** (heed, 15) to the voice of God, else the **light** shall be turned **into the shadow of death** (16). **But if ye will not hear . . . my soul shall weep in secret places . . . because the Lord's flock** will be **carried away captive** (17). If there is no turning, exile is inevitable.

Verses 18 and 19 are addressed to **the king** (probably Jehoiachin, cf. II Kings 24:8-12) and **the queen** (mother). **Humble yourselves** (18) . . . else **your principalities** (crowns; "head tires," KJV, margin) **shall come down,** i.e., you will no longer rule. There will be no help from **the south** (19; i.e., from Egypt). Exile threatens Judah and her ruling family. This prediction probably came true in 597 B.C. when Jehoiachin, his mother, and thousands of the people were carried to Babylon (II Kings 24:14-16).

4. *The Deep-seated Nature of Sin* (13:20-27)

Jerusalem (or Judah) is addressed as a shepherdess who has lost her **flock** (20; probably the best of her inhabitants). "What will you say when he [the Babylonian conqueror] shall set as head over you those whom you have taught to be friends to you?" (See 21; II Kings 20:12-13.) Great will be the shame and humiliation of Jerusalem when her former allies become tyrannical rulers over her. And if the city wants to know the reason for all this, she shall be told it is because of **the greatness of thine iniquity** (22). Moffatt translates, "It is for a host of sins that you are exposed and stripped."

The prophet elaborates by describing the deep-seated nature of Judah's sin. **Can the Ethiopian change . . . or the leopard?** (23) We may as well expect the Ethiopian to change the color of his skin and the leopard the spots in his coat as to expect the men of Judah to alter their evil habits by their own power. Sinning had become a second nature[3] with them. There is no denial of man's freedom here, but there is an acknowledgment that man's moral perversity is so deep-seated that he cannot change himself unaided. Man therefore needs God to do something for him that he cannot do for himself. This is the rationale behind all the redemptive acts of God. An inner transformation of man's moral nature is needed. Only God can do that (4:3-4).

Verse 24 describes what the lot of those will be who refuse to turn to God for help; **I will scatter them as the stubble** blown **by the wind.** The figure is that of the chaff blown away from the winnowing floor. Their shame will be so evident that all will know and see the humiliation of Judah. The sin of the nation is described in the baldest terms, **adulteries, neighings** ("lustful cries," Moffatt), **lewdness** (27). This deplorable condition, says God, has come about **because thou hast forgotten me, and trusted in falsehood** (lies, 25). In disconsolate tones the prophet cries, "O Jerusalem! How long will it be before you are made clean?" (27, RSV)

C. The Drouth and Its Moral Implications, 14:1—15:9

1. *The Ravages of the Drouth* (14:1-6)

A fearful drouth gave the prophet an occasion to teach some moral lessons to the people. The date of the drouth cannot be fixed, but the horrors of it are depicted in graphic terms. The whole land **mourneth . . . the cry of Jerusalem is gone up** (2). **They are black unto the ground** means, "Her people are mourning on the ground" (Berk.). The rich and the poor, men and animals, suffer because they can find no water; **little ones** (servants) **return with their vessels empty** (3). **The ground is chapt** ("cracked," ASV), **for there was no rain** (4). **The hind** (doe) **forsook** her newborn calf **because there was no grass** (5). The glazed eyes and the gasping breath of the wild animals reveal the terrible plight of the land. Jeremiah apparently believes that this natural calamity has come upon the people as a direct result of their sin.

---

[3]Clarke, *op. cit.,* p. 291; Lange, *op. cit.,* p. 143; see also E. Stanley Jones, *Christian Maturity* (New York: Abingdon Press, 1947), p. 173.

2. *Frantic Prayers Are Evil* (14: 7-9)

There now follows an example of what it means to pray when frantic. The people in great distress cry to the Lord, but not in genuine repentance. They rush through their confession with more self-pity than deep acknowledgment of sin. **O the hope of Israel . . . why shouldest thou be as a stranger in the land?** (8) **Why shouldest thou be as a man astonished** (astounded, confused) **. . . that cannot save? We are called by thy name; leave us not** (9). Underneath there is a tendency to blame God for their suffering. They practically demand that He get them out of their dilemma. In doing so they reduce God to a being who is as fickle and shallow as themselves. It is evident that their problem lies in a wrong conception of God.

3. *The Verdict of God* (14: 10-12)

God seems to see through the veneer of Judah's pretended religiosity. There is no deep-seated sorrow for sin. Their prayers are but lip service; **they loved to wander, they have not refrained their feet** (10) from going to false gods. Therefore, says the Lord, I will **remember their iniquity, and visit** (punish) **their sins.**

God says to Jeremiah, "Do not pray for the welfare of this people" (11, RSV). He saw that their prayer was shallow, and that they sorrowed only because they suffered. He would be less than God if He acceded to their frantic praying when it had in it no element of genuine faith. **When they fast . . . I will not accept them . . . I will consume them by the sword** (12).

4. *The Root of the Trouble* (14: 13-16)

Jeremiah attempted to excuse the people by pointing out that the false **prophets** had misled them by prophesying lies and saying, **Ye shall not see the sword** (13). The Lord seems to agree that **the prophets** are at fault; **I sent them not . . .** (they) **prophesy lies** (14). **A false vision and divination** would be "a lying vision, a hollow superstition" (Moffatt). But the inference is that **the people** (16) were willing to be deceived, for the lies flattered their sinful passions. They had heard the true prophets preach repentance, but to this truth they had closed their ears. The root of the trouble was that **the people** preferred a lie to the truth. Therefore, **people** and **prophets** must share the same punishment; they will **be cast out in the streets of Jerusalem . . . they have none to bury them** (16).

5. *Lamentation and Confession* (14:17-22)

Jeremiah here gave vent to his grief over the plight of the nation. But somehow the prophet's grief is also an expression of God's own deep sorrow. **Let mine eyes run down with tears night and day . . . the virgin daughter of my people is broken . . . with a very grievous blow** (17). He then describes the results of the drouth as being civil strife, plunder, and death. If **one ventures into the field** he sees those killed by **the sword;** inside the city people **are sick with famine** and disease. All the while the false prophets and priests traffic in "pseudo-holiness" throughout the land (see 18, RSV).[4] Everywhere there are wickedness, frustration, and death.

Perhaps encouraged by God's own grief to intercede for the nation, the prophet breaks out in new lamentations. He asks whether mercy and **healing** could yet be obtained: **Hast thou utterly rejected Judah?** (19) With a bitter cry he confesses **the iniquity** of the **fathers** (20), and then reminds God of the jeopardy to His own name and begs Him to **remember** His **covenant** with the nation. Jeremiah gladly acknowledges that the Lord is the only God: **Are there any among the vanities (gods) of the Gentiles that can cause rain?** (22) The prophet is convinced that there is no hope but in the living God. He declares his intention to **wait upon** the Lord until his petition is granted.

6. *The Verdict Reaffirmed* (15:1-4)

Despite Jeremiah's strong avowal of faith, God refuses his intercession "with a decisiveness that allows for no repetition."[5] The people are rejected once for all: **Though Moses and Samuel stood before me, yet my mind could not be toward this people: cast them out of my sight** (1). The people had not repented as Israel had done in the days of Moses and Samuel; consequently there was no hope. **If they say . . . whither shall we go?** (2) the prophet is instructed to reply, **Such as are for death, to death,** etc. Four kinds of punishment will be inflicted on them. Also four instruments will be used in their destruction, **the sword to slay . . . dogs to tear . . . fowls . . . and the beasts . . . to devour and destroy** (3). Furthermore, Judah will **be removed** ("tossed to and fro," ASV). She will thus become "a horror to all the kingdoms of the earth" (RSV, 4). The reason for all this is that the nation has never recovered from the wicked reign of **Manasseh** (II Kings 21:1-26; 24:3-4). The idolatrous practices that he

[4]Keil and Delitzsch, *op. cit.*, p. 253.   [5]Lange, *op. cit.*, p. 150.

introduced were still loved by the people of Jeremiah's day (cf. 44:1-30).

7. *A Lamentation over Jerusalem* (15:5-9)

These five verses form a poetic dirge (cf. Smith-Goodspeed). Seeing that the sinful people are to be ill-used by all the kingdoms of the earth, Jeremiah begins another lamentation. He bewails the fact that there will be no one to look with **pity** (5) on the city. No one will so much as inquire about her welfare. To make matters worse, he hears God saying, **Thou hast forsaken me . . . thou art gone backward . . . I am weary of repenting** (relenting, and giving them another chance, 6). "I have winnowed them with a winnowing fork" (RSV) but "they have not turned from their [wicked] ways" (7, lit.).

The description of the plight of the city is continued by saying that her **widows** have **increased as the sand of the seas** (8). The **mother** city, and its widowed mothers, are **suddenly** spoiled at **noonday** because the death of her sons leave her defenseless. She who is still in full bodily vigor (having **borne seven** sons) **hath given up the ghost** (lit., "breathed out her life"); **her sun is gone down while it was yet day** (9). Thus is described the unnecessary and premature death of the city and the nation. The epitaph over her ruins might well have been, "If love could have saved thee, thou needst not have died." This is also the case of every man who rejects God.

D. CONFESSIONS OF JEREMIAH, 15:10-21

1. *The Conflict of a Soul* (15:10-19)

Jeremiah's dialogue with God here is one of the most poignant passages in Sacred Writ. It lifts the curtain for a moment on the inner life of the prophet—the wrestling of his soul with God.

This is the first of what scholars have long called "the confessions of Jeremiah." (Others will be found in 17:12-18 and 20:7-18. Some scholars would also put 1:4-19; 4:19; 6:11; 8:21—9:1; 11:18-23; 12:1-3 in the same category.) They have been given this title because in them the prophet lays bare the innermost secrets of his heart and confesses to the spiritual pain and mental anguish that he passes through at times. He reveals that uncertainties and perplexities haunt him. He acknowledges that on occasion the hopelessness of his predicament and God's inscrutable methods of operation all but drive him to despair. These passages par-

take of the nature of prayer, meditation, and of intimate conversation with God.

a. Life tumbles in (15:10). Jeremiah is overwhelmed by
the events that have been taking place. There was the opposition
of his king and people, and the plot against his life by his own
family and former friends. The horrible drouth that came upon
the land, what he saw as a prophet concerning his nation and
its fate, and the terrible isolation that had come to him were
almost more than human flesh could bear. As the years passed
and there seemed to be no hope of a change for the better, the
human spirit rebelled. The prophet is plunged into a period of
great despondency. He wrestles with the awful temptation to
doubt God. In this he is not alone, for the holiest men of all ages
have suffered similar moments of dark temptation: Abraham,
Job, Elijah, and Paul. In bitter anguish of soul he cries, **Woe is
me . . . a man of contention to the whole earth!** (10) He feels
himself pitted against the entire world. He sees himself as
despised as a money lender who is cursed by **every one** he meets.
Life has tumbled in on the prophet, and he carries his complaint
before the Lord.

b. God speaks to his need (15:11-14). The Hebrew is obscure here, and many things have been conjectured about this
passage. The ASV has the most literal translation and is to be
preferred to the KJV at this point. God replies in 11 to the
prophet's complaint and gives words of encouragement. **It shall
be well with thy remnant,** i.e., "I will leave you some who shall
prosper again" (Berk.). Verse 12 has been variously interpreted,
but appears to be Jeremiah's answer to God's statement in 11.
The ASV margin has the literal rendering, "Can iron break
iron from the north?" i.e., Can my strength break the strength
of Babylon? From the depths of self-pity he makes a rather
facetious response, "Do you expect me to stem the Babylonian
tide?" (paraphrase). Jeremiah is so despondent that God's
promise seems to mock him.

Verses 13 and 14 are much like 17:3-4 (see ASV). In both
places they appear to refer to Judah, and are interpreted as a
prediction of exile. However, it should be noted that in some
respects 14 fits Jeremiah's case. He did pass with his enemies
into a land that was strange to him (cf. 43:4-7).

c. The "valley of the shadow" (15:15-18). Thus far Jeremiah's dialogue with God had not lifted his spirits. Indeed, it
seems to have deepened the gloom that had fallen across his

soul. His pleading cry of pain is renewed with greater vehemence, **O Lord, thou knowest . . . revenge me . . . take me not away in thy longsuffering** with my enemies . . . **for thy sake I have suffered** (15). A fleeting glimpse of previous joys passes before his mind, **Thy words were found, and I did eat them . . . the joy and rejoicing of mine heart** (16).[6] However, the remembrance of the past only plunges him deeper into gloom, **I sat alone because of thy hand . . .** "sharing all thine indignation" (17, Moffatt). He sinks in despair. In 18, Jeremiah reaches bottom emotionally. In the bitterness of his soul he cries, **Why is my pain perpetual . . . my wound incurable?** All the frustration of thirty years of opposition and ridicule are gathered up in this outburst of grief. Has he suffered all these things for nought? In desperation he cries, "Wilt thou indeed be unto me as a deceitful brook, as waters that fail?" (18, ASV) He cries out in his agony of soul, searching for some shred of meaning to his predicament. He reminds us of Job at this point (Job 3; 6—7).

d. The voice of iron (15:19). God does not seem to show much sympathy with Jeremiah's outburst. "Instead of praise for the past or tender comfort for the present, we have an implied rebuke."[7] There is a touch of iron in the voice of God: **If thou return,** i.e., repent of your lack of faith, **then will I bring thee again** (restore you, 19). **If thou take forth** (bring out) **the precious** (highly valued words) **from the vile** (base or insignificant), then **thou shalt be as my mouth.** God is saying, If, instead of this doleful wail which is unbecoming to a man of God, you speak forth truth and faith, then you shall be My spokesman. God requires utter commitment, if one is to fill His high calling. The touch of iron in the voice of God seems to shock the prophet back to himself again.

2. The Comfort of God (15:20-21)

Now that the emotional storm has passed and the chastened prophet has become a sadder but wiser man, he finds the comfort of God surrounding him. For His broken ones, God's severity is always followed by His consolation. The promises that God had given to Jeremiah when he was inducted into the prophetic office are now renewed: **I will make thee . . . a fenced brasen wall** (20) . . . **I will deliver thee out of the hand of the wicked, and I will redeem thee out of the hand of the terrible** (21). Jeremiah had battled against "principalities and powers" and had won a

[6]Cf. Ezek. 2:8—3:3; Rev. 10:9-10.   [7]Peake, *op. cit.,* p. 213.

signal victory. However his days of deprivation and suffering were by no means over.

E. MISCELLANEOUS MATERIALS, 16:1—17:18

This cluster of material is a good example of the composite form of the Book of Jeremiah. In these two chapters there is a mixture of personal vignettes, prophetic indictments and predictions, hope for the future, and two prayers. Some of these have only a casual relation to the others, but all of them fit appropriately under the theme "Confessions and Predictions."

1. *The Prophet's Personal Loss* (16:1-9)

Jeremiah, whose sensitive and affectionate nature craved companionship and social intercourse, is now forbidden these things. He stands isolated from his fellows, a lonely figure against a darkening sky. God forbids him the comforts of home and family: **Thou shalt not take thee a wife, neither shalt thou have sons or daughters in this place** (2). Jeremiah is the only one of the prophets who was forbidden to marry. But there are tragedies greater than loneliness. The prophet was instructed to use his **Concerning the sons and . . . daughters . . . born in this place . . . their mothers . . . and . . . fathers . . .** all **shall die of grievous deaths** (3-4).

Jeremiah was next forbidden to go to **the house of mourning** (5). This was strictly contrary to custom, and could be used as an object lesson for the people. It was a sign that the coming destruction would be so great that the rites for the dead would not be performed. Carcasses would **not be buried**, no lamentation made, no making **themselves bald** (6), no **cup of consolation** (7) offered. The meaning of 6-7 is clarified by Moffatt thus:

> *Throughout the land both high and low shall die*
> *   and all unburied lie,*
> *with none to lament or gash themselves*
> *   or cut their hair for them,*
> *with none to press the mourner to take food*
> *   on their account,*
> *and none to hand a cup of comfort*
> *   for a father or a mother's death.*[8]

For a Jew this was the darkest picture that could be painted.

---

[8]For further explanation of the various rites for the dead, see Keil and Delitzsch, *op. cit.*, pp. 267 ff., or Lange, *op. cit.*, pp. 158 ff.

The final prohibition had to do with **the house of feasting** (8). This was to be a sign that all pleasurable things would soon be cut off. No longer would there be the happy sounds of the wedding festival—**the voice of mirth, and the voice of gladness (9)** would cease. Only the silence of death would prevail over a once joyous city.

2. *The Meaning of Judah's Fate* (16:10-21)

The prophet is warned that the people will inquire of him as to why God's punishment would be so severe. The meaning of Judah's fate is found in the answer he is instructed to give.

a. The stubbornness of an evil heart (16:10-13, 16-18). In his answer to their inquiry, Jeremiah traces the doom of the nation to a disposition of mind in the people themselves; **Ye walk every one after the imagination** (stubbornness) **of his evil heart (12)**. The expression "imagination of their evil heart" is mentioned eight times[9] in the Book of Jeremiah. These words apparently refer to a state of mind which had become characteristic of the people. This disposition manifested itself in a resentment toward authority—a settled determination to gratify one's own desires regardless of the cost. This temper of mind had been characteristic of the **fathers**, but had become even more firmly set in the hearts of the men of Jeremiah's day. Although Judah and Jerusalem knew that their **fathers** had suffered grievous punishment because of their sins, people still had the temerity to defy God to His face. In fact, they had now become shameless in their sinning and deliberate in their perverseness.

This lawless spirit was opposed to all the gracious overtures of God. Social mores, cultural patterns, and natural desires had crystallized in the direction of the evil and the vile. Nothing short of utter catastrophe could ever change this pattern or break the mold. This is why exile was inevitable: **Therefore will I cast (hurl) you out of this land . . . I will not shew you favour (13)**.

The intention of God to shatter the structure of an evil civilization is further confirmed in 16-18. Here He indicates that the shattering process will be performed with deliberate thoroughness: **I will send for many fishers . . . will . . . send for many hunters, and they shall hunt them (16)**. No stone will be left unturned to ferret them out for punishment. Besides, **their ways**

---

[9]Cf. 3:17; 7:24; 9:14; 11:8; 13:10; 18:12; 23:17.

. . . **are not hid from my face** (17) . . . and **I will recompense
their iniquity and their sin double** (18).

b. *The prediction of a new exodus* (16:14-15). These verses
have no apparent connection with those that precede or follow.
They are hopeful, while the material on either side is very
dark. Some scholars feel that they are misplaced, for they appear
again in 23:7-8, where they fit the context better. They break
in here like a shaft of light in the midst of deepest gloom. It
may be that they are placed here to soften the blow that verses
10-13, 16-18 deliver to the nation. However, as they are seen
here, they contain the prediction of a "new exodus." It shall no
more be said, **The Lord . . . brought up the children of Israel
out of the land of Egypt: but . . . from the land of the north**
(14-15). This time it will be an exodus from the north country,
i.e., from exile. These verses stress the fact that beyond judgment
there will be a return—a new beginning. A new vessel is to be
formed out of the marred clay (cf. 18:1-10).

c. *A vindication of God's wrath* (16:19-21). This passage is
a magnificent affirmation of faith in the living God. The prophet
firmly believes that the divine severity in dealing with Judah
will be vindicated in the future.[10] He envisions a day when the
Gentiles will be converted and will say to God's people, **Surely
our fathers have inherited lies** (idolatry, 19). They will acknowledge the vanity of idols, and will turn and worship the true God.
What a moment of shame this will be for Judah, who has clung
so stupidly to these same false idols! God further affirms concerning the Gentiles, **They shall know that my name is The
LORD** (21), i.e., that I AM THAT I AM, the Eternal, the living
One! In that day Judah will see that God has dealt justly with
her in every situation.

3. *The Nature of Judah's Sin* (17:1-4)

A pen of iron and **the point of a diamond** (1) are used
here to emphasize the ingrained quality of Judah's sin. The iron
stylus and the diamond were used for engraving on the hardest
substances known to the ancient world. The prophet declares
that the **sin of Judah** had become so deeply engraved on her
heart (inner being) that ordinary means are insufficient to
remove it. Sinning had become her nature—her settled disposi-

---

[10]Kuist, *op. cit.*, p. 55.

tion. Her affection, her habit of mind, her will had crystallized in one direction, so that evil had become the dominant tone of life—a state of being. Forgiveness could never change this situation. God has no way of dealing with a sinful disposition except to break it to pieces, as a potter breaks an earthen vessel. Out of the fragments He forms a new creation.

The latter part of 1 and all of 2 are difficult to translate. The Hebrew apparently means that Judah's sin is as indelibly written on her religious rites **(the horns of your altars)** as on her **heart.** Pagan ideas and practices had so corrupted Temple worship that the **children** can **remember** (2) only heathen ways of doing things. Revealed religion had fallen upon such difficult days, and Temple worship had become so distorted and twisted, that there was no possibility of reform. God had decreed that both nation and Temple were to be broken in pieces in order that a completely new start could be made.

The outlook for the present is only punishment and loss. **I will give thy substance . . . thy treasures to the spoil (3) . . . I will cause thee to serve thine enemies in the land which thou knowest not (4).** God's hatred of Judah's sin is revealed in the assertion, **Ye have kindled a fire . . . which shall burn for ever.** He has sworn eternal vengeance on the disposition in man that is opposite to the nature of God. "A fallacy of his [Jeremiah's] day was that the people thought God could easily and would readily forgive sin, that the standard ritual [would] at once atone for it and comfortable preaching bring assurance of its removal."[11] But the facts are to the contrary. Nor does God pamper sin today, as some would believe. He has but one plan for sin and that is to destroy it (Rom. 6:6; I John 3:8). The **groves, green trees, high hills,** and **mountain** refer to typical places of idol worship.

4. *A Psalm of Contrasts* (17:5-8)

In a manner reminiscent of Psalms 1, Jeremiah contrasts the fate of him who trusts in man with the fate of one who trusts in God. "Dependence upon the flesh, the antithesis of the spirit, sets forth the vanity and perishableness of man and all earthly things."[12] The man[13] who trusts in **flesh** (5; all temporal things)

---

[11]G. A. Smith, *op. cit.*, p. 346.   [12]Keil and Delitzsch, *op. cit.*, p. 281.

[13]Some scholars think Jeremiah is referring to Zedekiah when he put his trust in Egypt. See IB, V (exeg.), 950.

shall be like the heath (dwarfed juniper) **in the desert** (6). The picture of **parched places, salt land,** and **wilderness** is drawn to discourage sinners.

On the other hand, the man who puts his trust in the Lord flourishes even in time of drought. **Shall not be careful** (8) means "is not anxious" (Berk.). Since he has found the secret springs of God, he can safely endure all the misfortunes of life. The evil man is in distress even in times of plenty, for he can be cut off at any moment.

In 7-8 we see "Characteristics of the Blessed Man." (1) He flourishes in adverse circumstances; (2) Hidden resources are the secret of his strength; (3) He lives without anxiety; (4) He produces fruit.

5. *Sin Is a Disease of the Heart* (17:9-11)

These verses could well have followed 1-4 with their discussion of Judah's sin. Although cast in a different literary form (that of two proverbs), they seem to carry on that discussion.

In order to understand 9 and 10, one needs to recall the Hebrew custom of using the physical organs to symbolize the activities of man's inner life. The term **heart** as used here signifies the "inner man," or "the essential self" from which all action, will, and reasoning spring. Likewise, **reins,** or the kidneys, were thought of as the seat of the emotions.

Jeremiah is saying: **The heart** (man in his essential being) is ʻaqob[14]—**deceitful** and treacherous (9). Furthermore, it is "desperately sick" (or diseased—ʼanush is more accurately rendered "sick" or "incurable" than **wicked**). Jeremiah's penetrating eye has perceived that Judah's trouble can be traced to the heart or inner disposition of her people. "Treacherous is the heart [of the man of Judah] above all things, and incurably sick—who can understand its true nature?" (paraphrase) Since the pagan nations were considered even more vile than Judah, this treacherous heart must be characteristic of all men.

The passage clearly teaches that "something indeed is desperately wrong about man, and Jeremiah with all the skill of a physician was pointing precisely to the source of man's illness as well as to the One who can bring healing."[15] **I the Lord**

---

[14]The same Hebrew form from which we get the word "Jacob."
[15]Kuist, *op. cit.,* p. 57.

search (am constantly searching) **the heart, I try** (am constantly testing, examining) **the reins** (man's deepest longings and greatest loves). Jeremiah sees that man in his "existential predicament" is a bundle of contradictions. He does not even understand himself. God alone is capable of dealing with him.

The second proverb (11) "emphasizes the insecurity of ill-gotten gain."[16] It was believed by the Hebrews that **the partridge** (species uncertain) took over the nest and hatched out the eggs of other birds. For a little while she struts in great pomp with her illegitimate brood, but the fledglings soon desert their foster mother at the very time she needs them most to bolster her ego. She is left looking like the **fool** she is. So it is with ill-gotten gain; it is apt to fly away just when a man needs it most.

6. Faith and Petition (17:12-18)

a. A prayer of hope and praise (17:12-13). The Hebrew text is difficult, and the passage has been variously interpreted. But these two verses seem to be a confession of faith on the part of Jeremiah. "A throne of glory, lofty from the beginning is the place of our refuge. The Hope of Israel is the Lord. All who forsake Thee shall be ashamed. They who turn aside from Me[17] [i.e., spurn My message] shall be written in the dust, **because they have forsaken the Lord, the fountain of living waters**" (lit.). These are words of hope and praise. **Sanctuary** here means a place of refuge or security for the nation. Those who do not trust in the Lord will pass away like writing **in the earth** (dust).

b. A prayer of petition (17:14-18). While keenly aware of the might and power of God, Jeremiah suddenly remembers his own miserable predicament and the taunts of his enemies. He cries, **Heal me . . . save me . . . Behold, they say unto me, Where is the word of the Lord?** (14-15) Moffatt translates the last part of 15, "Where is the Eternal's word? Come on with it!" The prophet defends himself before God, insisting that he has not desired the task of delivering a message of doom, nor has he sought to bring in the day of calamity. He calls God to remembrance that the persecutors are not only his enemies, but

---

[16]*Ibid.*

[17]This phrase can also be read, "they who chastise [mistreat] me [Jeremiah]."

384

God's enemies. He asks for protection and vindication: "Let the double crushing crush them" (18, lit.).

F. SYMBOLIC ACTIONS: MEANING AND RESULTS (17:19—20:18)

Jeremiah now performs certain symbolic acts which bring various reactions from the people. Each of these incidents has a message for the **inhabitants of Jerusalem** (20). Both **kings** and **people** (19) come in for a portion of the prophet's invective. As a result, Jeremiah suffers at their hands. A storm of protest is gathering around the head of the unfortunate prophet. His message of doom is not acceptable to the pleasure-loving people, and they react with characteristic viciousness.

1. *The Sacredness of the Sabbath* (17:19-27)

Jeremiah is given a message to deliver at the Gate of the People[18] in the city of Jerusalem. He is instructed to address both **kings** and **people** concerning the keeping of the **sabbath day** (22). Apparently the people of Jerusalem had been profaning the Sabbath by carrying on their secular activities. They brought their produce from the field to the city and marketed their wares in utter disregard of the law. Jeremiah set about to rectify the situation, not because he was a legalist, but because of the deeper implications of their actions. The secularization of the **sabbath** was a straw in the wind; it symbolized the moral decay of the nation. It spoke of greed for material gain, of wickedness in high places, and of forgetting God.

Moses himself would agree that the **sabbath** was not instituted merely to bind men to a law, or make it the negative, joyless day that was observed by the Pharisees of the New Testament. On the other hand, both in the Old Testament and the New it was meant to be a day of joyful honor to God, and spiritual and physical refreshment for the people. The nation which dishonors the Sabbath soon forgets the God who made the Sabbath. The promise to the people was that, if they kept the Sabbath, the **city shall remain for ever** (25). If they did not, there would be

---

[18]Only here do we hear of **the gate of the children of the people.** Despite many conjectures, any sure identification of this gate remains uncertain. A decision is not important since Jeremiah was further instructed to go to all the gates of Jerusalem.

kindled **a fire** . . . that would **devour the palaces of Jerusalem** (27).

2. *The Potter and the Clay* (18:1-17)

Jeremiah was informed that a message from God awaited him **at the potter's house** (2),[19] to which he now journeyed. As he watched the work he became keenly aware of **the potter** (4), **the wheels** (3), and the **clay** (4). As he watched the practiced hand of the potter knead the clay, he perceived that a message from God was beginning to form. Before the eyes of the prophet an exquisite vessel began to take shape. Then suddenly, to Jeremiah's surprise, the vessel **was marred in the hand of the potter.** Did a wave of deep sadness pass across the face of the potter? If so, it did not stop his skillful hands. He broke the marred vessel into a shapeless mass and began anew to knead and pummel. After sufficient working and refining, he returned (note KJV margin, "returned and made") and **made it again another vessel.**

a. The symbolism of the incident (18:1-6). God spoke to Jeremiah and the message came clear and plain to his mind. God is **the potter, Israel** is the **clay,** and apparently **the wheels** represent the circumstances of life. All along God has had a purpose for Israel. On the **wheels** of life God has been working out His purpose for the nation. But something has happened to spoil God's plan. Something in Israel—"a stone of stumbling" or "a rock of offence"—has marred the work of the Master Craftsman. God is grieved over the impurity in the nation's life. Things cannot continue as they are. In this situation, forgiveness alone will not suffice. Judgment is inevitable. There is no other way except for the existing form of national life to be broken and refined, and then reshaped into **another vessel** (4).

The process of life is seen in the **wheels.** Every man and every nation is present and involved because God has a purpose for men and nations. The object lesson teaches the sovereignty of God: **Cannot I do with you as this potter?** (6) But it also teaches the freedom of man[20]—the response of the clay had

[19]The potter's workshop was probably located in the valley of Ben Hinnom, south of Jerusalem. It would include, beside the shop, a "field for storing and treading the clay, a kiln for vessels, and a dump for discards" (IB, V [exeg.], 961).

[20]See G. A. Smith, *op. cit.,* pp. 186 ff.; John Skinner, *Prophecy and Religion* (Cambridge: University Press, 1957), pp. 162 ff.

thwarted the potter's purpose. Men are free to respond to the dealings of God. If they respond positively to the touch of the Master Potter, His purpose is achieved in the formation of a vessel such as He has planned. If men respond negatively, God's work is **marred**. If on the wheel of life men and nations resist God's will, the breaking process ensues. This is never a pleasant moment for either the potter or the clay. Although there is an element of hope in the fact that another vessel will be formed, it does not relieve the rigors of a judgment now! After refinement there comes the moment of reshaping into another vessel as it **seemed good to the potter to make it** (4). How long this breaking and re-forming process goes on is here hidden in the purposes of God, but it is clear from subsequent verses in Jeremiah, and from the Gospels, that men come to a point beyond which there is no hope.[21]

G. Campbell Morgan sees in this passage: (1) *The principles* —the sovereignty of God, and man as free to surrender to Him; (2) *The purpose*—God has a plan for men, the universe is bathed in purpose; (3) *The person*—at the heart of the universe is a Person, and we see Him in Jesus.[22]

b. God's method with men (18:7-12). These verses teach that God deals with men on a moral basis[23] rather than a strictly legal one: **If that nation ... turn ... I will repent of the evil that I thought to do ...** (8). Since God operates on a moral basis, He can deal with men as they respond to Him. This presupposes that man is not an inanimate piece of clay, but a free person like God himself. This makes it possible for God to repent (change His mind) concerning proposed judgment, and instead of destroying men or nations, forgive them. The reverse of course is also true. **At what instant** (7, 9) means "If at any time" (RSV).

If law alone had been God's method of operation, the race would have been destroyed long ago. There would have been no divine revelation, no sacrifice for sin, no mediating priest, no prophets preaching repentance, no Temple, and no prayers. If men were judged strictly by the law, none would survive.

[21]Smith, *op. cit.*, p. 189; cf. Matt. 25:46; Luke 19:41-44.
[22]*Studies in the Prophecy of Jeremiah* (New York: Fleming H. Revell Company, 1931), pp. 107 ff.
[23]Smith, *op. cit.*, pp. 186 ff.

Since this is true, "God's threats, like God's promises, are conditional (and contingent)."[24] "The people are told that it is only by reason of their stiff-necked persistency in wickedness that they render threatened judgment certain, whereas by returning to their God they might prevent ruin of the kingdom."[25] When there is no longer any hope, the shattering process begins.

Despite the offer of God to spare the nation on the grounds of moral obedience (repentance), the people disdainfully reply to God's threat of judgment; **There is no hope: but we will walk after our own devices** (desires, plans, 12). This leaves God with no alternative but to punish.

c. *The moral stupidity of Judah* (18:13-17). God now chides the people because of the unnaturalness of their evil practices: **Ask ye now among the heathen, who hath heard such things** (13). The reference to **Israel** as a **virgin** only magnifies the enormity of her sin. Verse 14 is difficult to translate, but it appears to mean that **the waters** of **Lebanon** (perhaps Mount Hermon, see map 2) are constant and dependable year after year, "but Judah's conduct is fickle and unnatural"[26] (cf. 2:13; 8:7). Because of her faithlessness to the living God, and because of her devotion **to vanity** (false gods that have no existence), Judah has wandered far **from the ancient paths**, and finds herself on "a dead-end street," **a way not cast up** (15). Because of her moral stupidity, Judah's once proud land will be an object of derision and **hissing** (16). She will not be able to stand before her enemies in battle, and will be scattered in utter confusion. God's **back** will be turned to the people **in the day of their calamity** (17) because they have forsaken "the fountain of living waters."

3. *A Plot and an Unworthy Prayer* (18:18-23)

Jeremiah discovered that the religious leaders of the nation had plotted against him. The priests, prophets, and even the wisdom teachers, felt that his denunciation of corrupt worship and his prediction of the destruction of the Temple was leveled

---

[24]L. Elliot Binns, "The Book of the Prophet Jeremiah," *Westminster Commentaries* (London: Methuen and Co., Ltd., 1919), p. 147.

[25]Keil and Delitzsch, *op. cit.*, p. 296.

[26]Binns, *op. cit.*, p. 149.

at them. If allowed to go on, they knew that Jeremiah's mesage would undercut their position with the people—**the law** would **perish from the priest** (18). His blistering words of doom apparently drew forth a malignant conspiracy. They fiercely rejected Jeremiah's prophecy that they and their offices would soon **perish. Let us smite him with the tongue** means that, by premeditated libel, they would undermine any influence that he might have had with the people.

The old wounds suffered from the plot at Anathoth (11:21-23) were reopened and their hurt was now multiplied tenfold. With the religious leaders of the nation against him, Jeremiah's future—and the future of the nation—was indeed dark. It was these very people he had sought most to help. Jeremiah's whole soul revolted within him at their treachery and at what their attitude foreshadowed for the nation. These religious leaders were the prophet's last hope for national reform. With this hope gone, he turned in great bitterness of spirit to God in prayer. He complains about his unhappy state, **Shall evil be recompensed for good? for they have digged a pit for my soul** (20). He reminds God of how he had interceded for these very people and had begged God **to turn away** His **wrath from them.** Now with this deeper insight into the magnitude of their wickedness he breaks out in earnest demand that they, and their households, receive their just reward: **Forgive not their iniquity,** etc. (23).

Some scholars think that this vindictive prayer is unbecoming to Jeremiah, and view it as an editorial addition. The words are filled with wrath, at least in part, because the prophet conceived his enemies to be even more the enemies of God, as indeed they were. To this extent his indignation is not an unholy thing, but partakes of the quality of God's own wrath. But even when reasonable allowance is made for these moods and words, we must admit that they are sub-Christian in the light of New Testament teaching and experience (cf. Matt. 5:38-48; Luke 23:34; Acts 7:58-60).

4. The Earthern Flask (19:1-13)

In another symbolic action Jeremiah is instructed to take an earthen flask (a *baqbuq*—the most delicate and expensive of ancient ceramic objects) and go to the Potsherd Gate (a reading better than **east gate**), which opened out on **the valley of the**

son of Hinnom (2).[27] On his excursion Jeremiah was instructed to take some of the elders of the people and some of the older members of the priesthood. Older people are usually serious-minded and would more likely take his message to heart. The story is best followed by reading 10 after 2. At the Potsherd Gate, **in the sight of** (10) all the elders, Jeremiah shattered the **bottle** and proceeded to interpret his actions.

He declares that in a similar fashion, because of their grievous and persistent wickedness, Judah and Jerusalem will be shattered by their enemies. And just as the broken vessel **cannot be made whole again** (11), so the old Judah cannot be mended. The past is gone forever. If there is to be a future for the nation, it will be vastly different from what it could, and would, have been. Here we see the "once-for-all-ness" of opportunity.

The prophet went on to describe what was going to take place in the city and why. In the coming destruction, the city of **Jerusalem** would become like **Tophet** (cf. 7:32), a rubbish heap. This will be her fate because of the idolatrous practices carried on in the homes of Jerusalem, **upon whose roofs they have burned incense unto all the host of heaven, and have poured out drink offerings unto other gods** (13). **The kings of Judah** had been just as guilty as the people. In that day the slaughter will be so great that every available place about the city will be used to bury the slain. All of Jerusalem will become unclean like the **valley of the son of Hinnom** (6).

Verses 3-9 seem to be the message given by Jeremiah in the Temple court (14-15) to the **kings of Judah, and inhabitants of Jerusalem** (3). The message is essentially the same as in 11-13, but in greater detail. Here are found such expressions as **his ears shall tingle**, indicating the magnitude of the coming destruction. **I will make void** (*baqqothi*, empty out) **the counsel of Judah** (7). The evil plans of Judah and Jerusalem will be emptied like water from the flask (*baqbuq*). Before **the siege is** over and the city is taken, the hunger will become so great that men will **eat the flesh of their sons and . . . daughters** (9). The last half of 9 has been translated, "through the stress of the

---

[27]This valley, to the south of Jerusalem, had been made into a place of worship to false gods by the wicked Mannaseh (II Chron. 33:6). Children were sacrificed there to these false gods. When Josiah instituted his reform, this place was made into a rubbish heap for the city (II Kings 23:10) and its name changed to Tophet. In other scriptures this place is likened to hell, the rubbish heap of the universe.

siege which their enemies—even those who seek their lives—
shall press upon them" (Smith-Goodspeed). In the end the
city will be so thoroughly destroyed that people who later pass
by will **hiss** (8; lit., whistle) in astonishment.

5. Jeremiah in the Stocks (19:14—20:6)

From the Potsherd Gate, Jeremiah returned to the Temple
court (14-15), where he apparently repeated his message (as
contained in 3-9) to all the people. Such caustic words must have
created a riot among the people, for **Pashur, the chief governor
(chief of the Temple police) in the house of the Lord** (20:1),
hearing these things, arrested Jeremiah. After beating the
prophet, **Pashur** (whose name seems to be of Egyptian origin)
put him in the stocks . . . in the high gate of Benjamin,[28] where
he was exposed to the ridicule and jeers of his enemies. In this
torturous position Jeremiah remained all night. This is the first
time that hands had been laid on the prophet. There had been
threatenings before, but now the rising tide of hatred among
the religious leaders made this type of affliction inevitable.

The next day, when **Pashur brought forth Jeremiah out of
the stocks** (3), the prophet seized the opportunity to supplement
the message he had delivered the day before. He told **Pashur**
(no doubt the crowd was listening) that God had changed his
name, **The Lord hath not called thy name Pashur, but Magor-
missabib,** which means "terror on every side." The incident
centers in the fact that **Pashur** had **prophesied lies** (6) to the
people. The passage implies that he had been refuting Jeremiah's
preaching by telling the people that Egypt would come to the
help of Judah if Babylon attacked. He had deceived them by
saying, "Peace, peace; when there is no peace" (8:11). Jeremiah
now tells Pashur that henceforth in accordance with his change
of name he will be a **terror** ("a cause of fear," *Basic Bible*) to
himself and to all his **friends.** The prophet then reminds the
people that **the king of Babylon** (4) would surely come and
take **all the precious things** (5) of the city, and **the treasures
of the kings of Judah** for a spoil. **Strength** and **labours** are
interpreted to mean "riches" and "gains" (ASV), and are thus
parallels to **precious things** and **treasures.** Pashur will see all
these things, and will himself be taken captive to **Babylon** (6).

---

[28]To be distinguished from the city gate of that name—this was
probably the north gate of the Temple's inner court.

There he will **die** in disgrace among the very people he had deceived.

6. *Jeremiah's Anguish* (20:7-18)

This is one of the most powerful and impressive passages in the book. It is certainly Jeremiah's saddest and bitterest complaint. For a moment the curtain is pulled aside and the reader is given a glimpse of the inner feelings of the prophet. "It is significant that Jeremiah's inner struggles and persecutions never led him to doubt the reality of his divine commission, and his sense of being overpowered by God never made him lose his own personality."[29]

a. Jeremiah's complaint (20:7-10). This time of dark reflection may have come directly out of the anguish and pain of Jeremiah's day and night in the stocks as he reflected on that experience. Or it may be that these moments came periodically to a man of the poetic emotional temperament of the prophet. In either case, life for the moment had come to the point of despair—he felt boxed in from every side. All that was human and finite cried out against the odds that faced him. The days, months, and years of his prophetic career seem to have flashed before him. He remembers again the details of his call, and how he sought to be released. He recalls the insistence of the divine voice (1:7-10). What has God done to him? His emotions rise to the breaking point! Broken, suffering, finite man cries out in the bitterness of his grief: **Thou hast deceived** (enticed, seduced; cf. same Hebrew word in Exod. 22:16) **me, and I was deceived: thou art stronger than I, and hast prevailed** (7). He continues by reminding God that he is daily a laughingstock; all who meet him mock him. When he opens his mouth to prophesy, nothing but predictions of **violence and spoil** (8) come out. It is this kind of preaching that has made him **a reproach** and **a derision.** A bearer of evil tidings is never popular, and the prophet's very humanness rebels against the painfulness of his situation.

However, when he had resolved: **I will not . . . speak any more in his name,** he discovered that the will of God was still the great driving force in his life—**His word was in mine heart as a burning fire shut up in my bones . . . I could not stay** (9).

---

[29]IB, V (exeg.), 973.

Still, frustrated at every turn, he felt that there was no way out, no place to hide, no alternative. He constantly heard his enemies whispering behind his back, calling him "Old Mr. Terror-on-every-side." The name he had given to Pashur was being thrown back in his face, probably at the instigation of that gentleman himself. But it was heartbreakingly true that terror, **violence and spoil** (8) was the theme of every message that he delivered. To make matters worse, those who had been his friends had turned against him with bitter hatred, and were watching for the slightest slip in his words or actions. **Peradventure he will be enticed** (deceived, seduced) . . . **and we shall take our revenge on him** (10).

b. An outburst of praise (20:11-13). Just at the breaking point the tide changes (cf. I Cor. 10:13). Jeremiah's thoughts shift to the greatness of God. Immediately there is a difference. As he ponders the character of God, his spirits begin to rise. He cries to himself, **The Lord is with me as a mighty terrible one** (terrifying warrior); **therefore my persecutors shall stumble** (11). His faith takes firm hold of God. **They shall not prevail: they shall be greatly ashamed.** When he remembers that it is God **who triest the righteous, and seest . . . the heart,** he launches into an appeal for the vindication of his **cause** (12). At the remembrance of these things his faith begins to soar. He bursts into a song of confidence. In characteristic Hebrew fashion, he proclaims that what he believes God for is already done!

> *Sing to the Lord;*
> *praise the Lord!*
> *For he has delivered the life of the needy*
> *from the hand of evildoers* (13, RSV).

c. Jeremiah curses the day of his birth (20:14-18). From the heights of religious ecstasy Jeremiah lapses into even greater despair. The fact that these verses come immediately after a song of confidence is puzzling. Many scholars think they do not logically follow here, but come from some other occasion in Jeremiah's life. Binns quotes Buttenwieser: "It would be psychologically impossible . . . for such faith, such surrender, such exultation . . . to be followed immediately by such utter dejection and bitterness of spirit."[30]

---

[30]*Op. cit.,* p. 155. Other scholars want to solve the problem by inserting vv. 14-18 after 10. This would make vv. 11-13 follow 18.

On the other hand, these verses may be given to reveal the inner workings of Jeremiah's mind: "the ebb and flow, the rise and fall, of the inner thoughts" of an extremely human individual.[31] Although a true prophet of God, he was subject to all the limitations of the human. The direction in which he looked, the thing that caught his attention, made all the difference. Certainly when seen from the human side alone, the prophet's despair is understandable. Jeremiah was just earthling enough that his emotions followed the direction of his gaze.

Apparently then, at v. 14, Jeremiah's attention is caught again by the hopelessness of his human situation. A pall of intense gloom falls upon his spirit. In great bitterness he cries, **Cursed be the day wherein I was born.** All outward conditions are against him. He feels the merciless hatred that swirls around him. His deeper instincts tell him that matters will never be any better, and his utter helplessness causes him to continue his lament: **Cursed be the man who brought tidings to my father** (15). It was customary to reward the man who brought tidings of the birth of a son; but Jeremiah cried, **Let that man be as** (16) Sodom and Gomorrah **because he slew me not from the womb** (17).

The passage must be taken rhetorically rather than literally. No particular man is meant. It is worth noting that the curse of despair does not fall upon God, nor upon "those who bore him, nor even [upon] the fact of his being born, but rather it points once more to the curse of Israel's betrayal of her heritage."[32] Momentarily crying out of deep human frustration, Jeremiah is saying that, with the kind of life he was compelled to live, it would have been better for him to have been slain at birth, or for his mother to have been killed while he was yet in her **womb** (17). If the latter could have happened, then neither of them would have lived to see this wretched day.

The ultimate question is, Why? **Wherefore came I forth ... to see labour and sorrow, that my days should be consumed**

---

[31]The Bible nowhere teaches that the life with God is a placid journey. On the contrary, it teaches that men of God in all ages have had at times the fiercest kind of temptations, frustrations, inner struggles, periods of deep questionings, and battles of faith. They have had to stand, as it were, at the doors of their souls with a drawn sword and fight off the demonic forces that sought to destroy them. Even the Master had His moments of fierce struggle (Matt. 26:37-44; Mark 15:34; Luke 4:1-13).

[32]IB, V (exeg.), 976.

with shame? (18) Jeremiah would certainly have been less than human had he not felt the torture of the question. His conduct is no worse than Job, who is called a perfect (blameless) man by the inspired writer (Job 1:1; 2:3), or the Man on the middle cross, who in His agony cried out, **My God, my God, why . . . ?** (Mark 15:34) The Scriptures record for the encouragement of all subsequent generations the fluctuations of Jeremiah's emotions and the range of his thoughts and feelings under extreme pressure. Although he may not be admired for having these thoughts, he is to be respected, and imitated in not succumbing to the temptation to doubt God. That he maintained his integrity in the face of stupendous odds, the rest of the book gives ample evidence.

Section **V** *A Forecast of the End*

Jeremiah 21:1—29:32

It is obvious that a new section of the book begins here. The transition of thought is abrupt and without explanation. The material is not in chronological order and covers a wide range of subject matter. Included in these chapters are historical incidents, pronouncements, matters dealing with the political and religious affairs of Judah, and events from the international scene, all interwoven.

The one dominant note is the end of Judah and the Davidic dynasty. The kings of Judah are dealt with first. After this the religious leaders come in for a goodly share of the prophet's invective. Then the Gentile nations are brought to the bar of justice; "The Lord hath a controversy with the nations" (25: 31). Jeremiah sees all nations being brought into servitude to the king of Babylon, but only according to divine decree. The captives who are already in Babylon are instructed to prepare themselves for the fall of Judah and for an extended exile. The whole section serves as a forecast of the end of Hebrew national life.

A. BEGINNING OF THE FINAL SIEGE, 21:1-10

Without announcement, the reader is suddenly carried to the beginning of the final siege of Jerusalem (probably 588 B.C., cf. 37:3—38:28). The Babylonians have appeared outside the walls of the city. The situation is becoming grave. In distress, Zedekiah (see Chart A) sends his trusted servants[1] to Jeremiah to obtain some word from God, **Enquire . . . of the Lord for us** (2). Zedekiah's reference to **all** of God's **wondrous works** indicates that the fearful king was hoping for a miracle similar to that Hezekiah had experienced through the intercession of Isaiah a hundred years before (II Kings 19:1-7; Isa. 37:1-7). But, alas, the outcome is to be far different! Jeremiah's reply is immediate and unequivocal: **Thus saith the Lord . . . Behold, I will turn back the weapons . . . in your hands, wherewith ye fight . . .**

---

[1]The **Pashur** listed here is not the same Pashur mentioned in c. 20. This one is **the son of Melchiah,** the other "the son of Immer."

396

I myself will fight against you (4-5). This is the beginning of the end. There is to be no reprieve for the nation this time; **I will deliver Zedekiah . . . his servants, and the people . . . into the hand of Nebuchadnezzar king of Babylon** (7).

To go up from us (2) would be to withdraw from the siege. The **great pestilence** (6) may refer to the siege of the city with all of its horrors or more narrowly to actual pestilence that would follow famine and water shortage. **His life . . . for a prey** (9) means "as a prize of war" (RSV).

Jeremiah knew that the end of the nation was already determined and there was nothing he could do about it. He does, however, have a word for the people. He offers them "two courses of action: the way of life and the way of death. To desert to the enemy meant life; to resist meant death because the doom of the city was certain."[2] This does not mean that the prophet was a traitor to his country, but it does mean that he saw the way God was moving, and moved along with Him.

The passage shows that Jeremiah's status had changed considerably from c. 20. He was now the highly revered elder statesman whose advice was earnestly sought in a time of crisis.[3] The passage also teaches that Jeremiah's "two ways" are symbolic of the choices men are constantly required to make. There are always two courses of action open to every individual. One way is an expression of faith and dependence on an eternal God and it leads to life. The other is an expression of trust in man's wisdom and ability to direct his own life, and leads to death. The way of life demands faith to believe that God's word is true even when it is contrary to human reason and desire—you "bet your life" on God. The way of death stakes everything on what is humanly reasonable and appropriate—you "bet your life" on man.

B. The Fortunes of the House of David, 21:11—23:8

This section does not logically follow 1-10, and must therefore come from another period in the life of Jeremiah. The messages are addressed to the house of David in general, and

---

[2]Kuist, *op. cit.*, p. 67.
[3]*Ibid.*

especially to the several kings who reigned during Jeremiah's lifetime.

1. *A Message to the Royal House* (21:11—22:9)

Jeremiah addresses the whole **house of David** (12) concerning the task and duties of all good kings. He insists that **judgment** is to be executed **in the morning,** i.e., daily, and not spasmodically or at the whim of an official. The king is also held responsible for the acts of his officers. The weak and the helpless are to be delivered from **the hand of the oppressor** by the king. God warns the royal house that His **fury** will be visited upon them if they fail to rule with equity and with justice.

Verses 13-14 are obscure. The word **inhabitant** is feminine, and may therefore refer to Jerusalem. However the language is figurative, and since it is found here in the middle of a passage that deals with the kings of Judah, it is probably meant to refer to the royal family. Moffatt has Jeremiah address Jerusalem:

> O *dweller in the glen*
> *on the rocks of the tableland.*

Whether Jerusalem or the kings of Judah are referred to, someone is guilty of saying boastfully, **Who shall come down against us?** (13) It is the language of self-sufficiency and pride. God counters this immediately by saying that all such arrogance will be punished. **Kindle a fire in the forest** (14) may very well mean to burn the palaces of the kings, which were constructed of "choice cedars" **(22:7).**

Again, Jeremiah is commanded to **go down to the house of the king of Judah** (22:1) and speak to the royal court. He reiterates what was said in 12 above, but is more detailed in this sermon. He speaks at length concerning the rewards that come to the royal family that rules justly! **If ye do this . . . then shall** (4). The prophet then changes his tone and cries, **But if ye will not hear these words, I swear by myself . . . that this house** (palace) **shall become a desolation** (5). Although the royal family and the city of Jerusalem are as fair as the balsam heights of **Gilead,** or the wooded crest of **Lebanon,** yet the Lord declares, **I will make thee a wilderness, and cities . . . not inhabited** (6). Later when foreign people **pass by** (8) and ask why the Lord permitted such destruction to come to His own city, the answer will be, **They have forsaken the covenant of the Lord their God, and worshipped other gods** (9).

398

2. The Fate of Shallum (22:10-12)

This is the first of a series of oracles against specific kings. It is directed against **Shallum** or Jehoahaz (see Chart *A*), **the son of Josiah** (11). When Josiah was slain in the battle of Megiddo by Pharaoh-necho, the people of Jerusalem took Shallum, his third oldest son, and made him king. After about three months Pharaoh-necho took Shallum off the throne and put his brother Eliakim (Jehoiakim; see Chart *A*) in his place. Shallum (Jehoahaz) was carried away to Egypt and died there (II Kings 23:30-34). Apparently the people of Judah wept long for Josiah, but Jeremiah rebuked them. He cried, **Weep ye not for the dead** (10), i.e., Josiah, **but weep sore for him that goeth away** (Shallum): **for he shall return no more.** Jeremiah was saying that Shallum's going away into captivity, and his death there, foreshadowed the end of Judah itself. Thus in the fate of **Shallum** was a portent of the end of the royal house.

3. The Oracle Against Jehoiakim (22:13-23)

Jeremiah's bitterest denunciations are reserved for **Jehoiakim** (18). He was the most ruthless and wicked of all the kings who reigned during the prophet's lifetime. The king was callously indifferent to the misery of his subjects. In a time of great need, he squandered money on a palace of cedar, which he built merely to gratify his own pride. To gain his objective he forced his own people to work **without wages** (13), "and caused the innocent to be condemned in judgment that he might grasp their goods to himself . . . he also put to death the prophets who rebuked his unrighteousness, 26:23, and used every kind of lawless violence."[4]

Jeremiah demands of him, "Do you think you are a king because you compete in cedar?" (15, RSV) The prophet then compares him to his father, Josiah. He was certainly no ascetic, **but did eat and drink** (15). At the same time he gave earnest attention to his duties as king: **he judged the cause of the poor and needy** (16). Jehoiakim, on the other hand, neglected his kingly duties and attended only to his own pleasure. He did not hesitate to stoop to **oppression** and to **shed innocent blood** (17) to gain his ends.

---

[4]Keil and Delitzsch, *op. cit.*, p. 340.

The Lord now assesses condemnation. Jehoiakim's life shall end in shame and disgrace. **They shall not lament for him, saying, Ah my brother!** (18) **He shall be buried with the burial of an ass, drawn** (dragged) **and cast forth beyond the gates of Jerusalem** (19). Although the Old Testament does not give us the details of Jehoiakim's death, there is no reason to doubt that dishonor and shame attended his end.[5]

In 20-23 it seems that Judah and/or Jerusalem was urged to lament because of the wickedness and lack of integrity on the part of such **pastors** (22; rulers) as Jehoiakim. **Go up to Lebanon and cry . . . in Bashan . . . all thy lovers are destroyed** (20).[6] The passages has been translated "Abarim." It is literally "the parts across," and refers to a range of mountains east of the Dead Sea. The meaning is, Go north, east, and south to the allies you have depended on. The human agencies in which the king and the nation had placed their trust were gone. Jeremiah reminded Judah and her king that God **spake unto thee in thy prosperity** (in a day of peace when no calamity threatened); **but thou saidst, I will not hear** (21). Now the game is up! Shame, consternation, and captivity are to be the portion of Judah and the peoples who consorted with her.

In the Old Testament, Lebanon is sometimes used to refer to Jerusalem. In 23, **O inhabitant of Lebanon** seems to refer to that city and to Jehoiakim, her king. **Thy nest in the cedars** refers to the palaces of the king, since they were constructed of cedar from Lebanon. These buildings were the pride and joy of the people of Jerusalem. But Jeremiah shatters their sense of ease and complacency with a dire prediction, "How you will groan" (lit.) **when pangs come upon thee!** Again, a forecast of the end.

[5]Scholars have sought to discover just what happened at the death of Jehoiakim. Some think he died in a palace revolt, and his body was desecrated. Others think that, dying during the siege, he was hastily buried, and the Chaldeans, learning of this (8:1 ff.), disinterred and dishonored his body. Still others think he was captured by the Chaldeans in a foray outside the walls of the city (597 B.C.) and was bound in chains but died of disease and exposure in the camp of the enemy—and in the events that followed the capture of the city, his body was dishonored and never given a decent burial. Cf. Lange, *op. cit.*, p. 202; Keil and Delitzsch, *op. cit.*, p. 341.

[6]"It is not clear to whom the words of 22:20-23 are addressed, but they affirm the same principle for which Jeremiah has been pleading" (Kuist, *op. cit.*, p. 70).

4. Oracles Against Jehoiachin (22:24-30)

There are two short oracles here concerning Jehoiachin (called **Coniah**; 24, 28). The first was given before he was carried away into captivity; the other, after that sad event had taken place.

At the age of eighteen years **Coniah** (Jehoiachin, see Chart *A*) had succeeded his father, Jehoiakim, to the throne of Judah. Apparently he was as wicked as his father, for in the first oracle God is highly displeased with him: **Though Coniah** (probably a personal name; he was also known as Jeconiah, 28:4) **. . . were the signet upon my right hand, yet would I pluck thee thence** (24). Jeremiah then predicts the king's captivity and death in a foreign land (25-27). Jehoiachin reigned three months in 597 B.C. and then surrendered to Nebuchadnezzar, who was beseiging the city. He and his mother, Nehushta, his wives, and 10,000 of his people were carried to Babylon as captives.

In the second oracle the people of Jerusalem seem to question why Jehoiachin received such a fate, **Wherefore are they cast . . . into a land which they know not?** (28) It would appear that many "Judeans continued to consider him the legitimate king, even in exile, rather than Zedekiah, his uncle (28:1-4; Ezek. 17:22)."[7] This also appears true of the Jewish exiles (29:1-14). Weary and exasperated with the people because they do not seem to grasp the meaning for the nation of Jehoiachin's fate, Jeremiah cries out in bitterness of soul, "O land, land, land, hear the word of the Lord!" (29, RSV) He then eliminates the captive king from ever being a factor in the ongoing purposes of God for the nation: **Write ye this man childless** (30), i.e., without a descendant on the throne of Judah. Jehoiachin had failed to be a useful instrument for the divine purpose. His demise from national life foreshadowed the demise of the nation itself.

5. The Messianic King (23:1-8)

This section (21:11—23:8) on the fortunes of the house of David began with a general statement; it now closes with another. In this passage Jeremiah gathers up all that he had said of the kings of Judah in a concluding statement that exposes them as evil **pastors** ("shepherds," ASV, RSV) who have scattered **the sheep** (1). He apparently includes Zedekiah along with the

[7]IB, V (exeg.), 985.

others, though that king is not mentioned specifically by name. The term "shepherd" in the Old Testament often refers to the king, but sometimes it is expanded to mean the king's court, or "ruling officials in general."[8] It may be thought of in that fashion here.

Jeremiah's denunciation of the evil shepherds is also a forecast of the end of the nation, for the rulers are the ones who have led Judah to this place of ruin. But in his pronouncements concerning the end of the nation the prophet also gives us a glimpse "beyond judgment." He seems to take for granted that God's redemptive purpose in judgment will be accomplished and that a better day is coming.

The accomplishment of God's purpose will comprise at least three things, none of which are new to Old Testament prophecy. The first deals with the return of the remnant (3). Isaiah had made much of this idea, and the other prophets had caught something of it also. **I will gather the remnant of my flock out of all countries . . . and will bring them again to their folds.** With Jeremiah's emphasis here, and that found elsewhere in the OT, the idea of the remnant's return became a firm expectation on the part of the covenant people. The third thing is so closely allied with the first that it should be treated with it. This is the idea that when the return takes place it will be thought of as a "New Exodus." So glorious will be this deliverance that people will no longer say, **The Lord liveth, which brought up the children of Israel out of the land of Egypt; but, The Lord liveth, which brought . . . the seed . . . of Israel out of the north country** (7-8; cf. 16:14-15).

Another important point (the second of the above series) is the coming of an ideal King: **I will raise unto David a righteous Branch** (*tsemach tsaddiq*) (5) **. . . he shall be called, THE LORD OUR RIGHTEOUSNESS** (*Yahweh tsidhqenu*); "our salvation, or deliverance" (6). Judah's kings had been her undoing. Now a King is to come who will **execute judgment and justice in the earth,** and under His rule **Judah shall be saved, and Israel shall dwell safely.** The term **Branch** (*tsemach*) is better translated "shoot" or "sprout." "The figure suggested is that of the stump of a tree . . . suddenly showing fresh life . . ."[9] The tree of David, cut to the ground by the fall of the monarchy, will sprout again

[8]*Ibid.*, p. 987.
[9]Binns, *op. cit.*, p. 173.

and send forth a "Shoot." This new King of David's line represents all the unfulfilled longings of men for an ideal ruler. The Church has always seen in this passage the figure of Christ, the Messianic King (cf. also 30:9; Isa. 11:1; 53:2; Ezek. 34:23-24; 37:24; Zech. 3:8; 6:12).

C. Oracles Against False Prophets, 23:9-40

Having dealt with the political leaders in the previous section, Jeremiah now turns his attention to the religious leaders of his nation. No group had been so troublesome to Jeremiah as the professional prophets and certain of the priests. The time is the same as that of the previous section, probably in the reign of Zedekiah.

1. *The Pain of Jeremiah* (23:9-10)

Jeremiah felt crushed over what he perceived going on among the religious leaders of his day: **Mine heart . . . is broken . . . my bones shake; I am like a drunken man** (9). Despite the curse[10] of a drouth with its attendant calamities, the people were flagrantly immoral. **The land is full of adulterers** (10), **their course** of living is incorrigibly evil, "and their might is not right" (RSV). When the prophet saw these conditions in the light of the character of God and His holy word, he was overcome with grief.

2. *The Profaneness of the Prophets* (23:11-15)

Jeremiah wastes no time getting to the real cause of this situation: **both prophet and priest are profane** (11). These men who were supposed to reverence God and all holy things were guilty of sacrilege; **in my house have I found their wickedness.** They handled sacred things irreverently. **The year of their visitation** (12) would be their time of judgment. The Northern Kingdom had been openly apostate. In Samaria the prophets had blatantly **prophesied by Baal** (13), and had thus been the basic cause of Israel going into exile. But Judah had far outstripped Israel in wickedness. The prophets in Jerusalem were guilty of the vilest kind of sins—**they commit adultery, and walk in lies** (14)—yet proclaim the word of the Lord with great

---

[10]The word **swearing** (Heb., *'alah*) may be translated "cursing," or "oath," but it fits the context much better to render it "the curse" (see RSV).

bravado. **An horrible thing** ("filthiness," KJV, marg.) may very well refer to the sin of sodomy, since Jerusalem is compared to **Sodom** and **Gomorrah.** The capital city of Judah was a "sinkhole" of moral perversity. Worst of all, these religious leaders seemed permanently settled in their evil ways, for **none doth return from his wickedness.**

Profaneness, however, has within itself the seeds of decay and death: "their way shall be to them like slippery paths in the darkness" (12, RSV). Furthermore, **saith the Lord . . . I will feed them with wormwood, and make them drink . . . gall** (15). This is the biblical way of saying that their end will be filled with calamity and sorrow.

3. *The Proclamation of Error* (23:16-22)

Jeremiah now upbraids these false prophets for prophesying error. His reasons for denunciation are not hard to find: (*a*) They gain their ideas from the wrong source, from **their own heart** (16). (*b*) They proclaim what they know the people want to hear, **Ye shall have peace . . . No evil shall come upon you** (17). (*c*) They have not **stood in the counsel** (*sodh*) **of the Lord** (18), else they would have known what the word of God was for this hour: **A whirlwind of the Lord is gone forth in fury . . . The anger of the Lord shall not return, until he have executed . . . the thoughts of his heart** (19-20). (*d*) They have gone forth and spoken without a commission or without a message: **I have not sent . . . I have not spoken to them, yet they prophesied** (21). (*e*) If they had been willing to listen to the **counsel** (22) of the Lord, they could have known the true word, and saved both themselves and the nation.

4. *The Provocation of God* (23:23-32)

God is provoked at the stupidity of these false prophets. The meaning of 23 is, Do they think I am a limited God? **Am I a God at hand . . . Can any hide himself in secret? . . . Do not I fill heaven and earth?** (23-24) They act as though their sins are hidden from God, but He was aware all along of the "lying pretensions of these men."[11] They also used dreams to propagate their **lies** (25). **Dreams** had been a legitimate medium of revelation for centuries, but these false prophets had used **dreams** to their own ends, and thus distorted the character of God (27).

---

[11]Kuist, *op. cit.*, p. 73.

Jeremiah insists that "the dream and the word of God must be sharply distinguished, for straw has nothing to do with wheat, the worthless stubble with the Bread of life; they must not be blended together."[12] A genuine word from God is known by the divine energy that accompanies its proclamation. **Is not my word like as a fire? ... and like a hammer that breaketh the rock in pieces?** (29) No one need be in doubt about God's word; it authenticates itself. It is evident that these false prophets did not know how to obtain the divine word. God accuses them of stealing His word ... **every one from his neighbour** (30), and then going out with glib **tongues** and saying, **He saith** (31). God repeats that He is against people who "give second hand messages and tell lying dreams as though they were God's truth."[13]

5. *The Perversion of a Divine Word* (23:33-40)

The false prophets are sternly reprimanded for their perversion of a term **the burden of the Lord** (33), that, up to then, had had a sacred meaning. **Burden** (*massa*) is derived from a verb root (*nasa*) that means "to lift up." A message from God was something the prophet took up and cried forth to (or was laid upon) the people. Also it was often thought of as something that lay heavily on the heart of God and the consciences of men. Thus *massa* came to mean **the burden of the Lord,** or an "utterance" or "oracle." Jeremiah's messages from God were particularly heavy with doom for the nation. In time they became hard for the people to bear. His messages were especially burdensome to the false prophets, for in their gay way they saw him as out of step with the times. So deeply did they resent him that they ruined a perfectly good prophetic term by asking him mockingly, **What is the burden of the Lord?** (33) They apparently taunted him so constantly with this question that the word was no longer usable. Any message given this title appeared ridiculous. Instead of helping God's cause, it hindered it. God therefore commanded that the term be eliminated. **The burden of the Lord shall ye mention no more** (36); in its place you shall say, **What hath the Lord ... spoken?** (35)

On the surface the matter seems trivial. However the problem reveals in a glaring way the moral perversity of the false prophets, indeed of the whole nation, for all the people were

[12]Peake, *op. cit.,* p. 269.
[13]Kuist, *op. cit., ad loc.*

caught up in this downgrading of a divine message. The Septuagint and the Vulgate answer the question, **What is the burden of the Lord?** by saying, "You are the burden, and I will cast you off, says the Lord." God turns the jest on their own heads.

D. The Parable of the Figs, 24:1-10

Sometime after Jehoiachin and 10,000 of the choice families of Judah had been deported to Babylon in the debacle of 597 B.C. (cf. II Kings 24:8-16), the Lord spoke to the prophet. Jeremiah was aware of the situation faced by the exiles in Babylon, and he was also keenly conscious of the situation in Jerusalem. He saw that there was a message of deep spiritual significance in this incident for both groups. (Jeremiah's letter to the exiles in c. 29 should be read in conjunction with this chapter in order to get the full picture.)

The Lord called Jeremiah's attention to **two baskets of figs** sitting **before the temple** (1). **One basket** contained very excellent **figs** . . . **the other basket** contained the poorest kind of **figs**, totally unfit to eat (2). After gaining Jeremiah's attention, the Lord made this commonplace incident a moment of deep spiritual insight for the prophet, and a forecast of the end of Judah.

The Lord explained that the **good figs** (3) represented the exiles in Babylon; the **naughty** (very evil) **figs** represented the people then living in Jerusalem. God further explained that the difference between the two groups lay in the response they were making to Him and His actions in history. The response of the group in Babylon is summed up in the words: **They shall return unto me with their whole heart** (7). The group in Jerusalem responded, "We will walk after our own devices" (18:12).

The exiles in **Babylon,** although deprived of the Temple and the customary aids to religious living, were going to discover through the discipline of suffering and hardship that God is not bound to institutions and forms. He can be found anywhere when men search for Him with all their hearts (29:10, 13). On the other hand the people of Jerusalem, despite the presence of the book of the law, the Temple, and the faithful prophets, had no time for anything but their own carnal desires. For explanation of **Zedekiah** and **them that dwell in the land of Egypt** (8), cf. II Kings 25:1-26 and Chart *A*.

There are several truths that we may learn from the parable of the figs. (1) God's ways are not our ways. "It was natural that the Jews who were left behind in Palestine should attribute their escape from captivity to their superior excellence. This complacent estimate is contradicted in this chapter."[14] What appears often as something good can really be very bad. The Exile of itself was not necessarily a bad thing. God was working out His purpose. These people were cured forever of idolatry. At the same time the people of Jerusalem were living under a doomed system and were too blind to see it. (2) The devastating power of a closed mind: The men of Jerusalem were unwilling to learn. They refused to listen to anything that ran counter to their own desires. They were unable to hear the newer word from God. For them anything new could not be true. (3) God's view of the good: For God the highest good was not in civil and political well-being, as the men of Jerusalem thought (though it is not to be despised), but in constant spiritual renewal gained by listening to the voice of God. (4) God's view of what is bad: God counts men as evil (a) when they are blind to eternal verities, (b) when they see only the present as important and are intensely concerned with creature comforts, and (c) when they rely on human wisdom rather than the word of God.

E. A PREVIEW OF THE END, 25:1-38

In this chapter the reader is suddenly shifted backward from the reign of Zedekiah to the fourth year of Jehoiakim (from *cir.* 588 B.C. back to 605-604 B.C.; see Chart *A*). In this year the whole of the Near East was in a process of great change. The battle of Carchemish had been fought shortly before (606 B.C.), and this engagement was one of the most decisive events in the history of the ancient world. The last remnant of the Assyrian army had joined forces with the Egyptian hosts under Pharaoh-necho to fight Nebuchadnezzar, the crown prince and general of the armies of Babylon. When the battle was over, Nebuchadnezzar was victorious; Assyria was no more, and Egypt had lost its bid to dominate the politics of the Fertile Crescent. Babylon stood supreme. Among the smaller nations there was a mad scramble for realignment.

After the battle of Carchemish, Nebuchadnezzar apparently

[14]Peake, *op. cit.*, 271.

pursued the armies of Pharaoh-necho to the gates of Egypt. While in that area he seems to have taken the city of Jerusalem,[15] or at least took hostages, and compelled Jehoiakim to change his allegiance from Egypt to Babylon (II Kings 24:1; Dan. 1:1). Judah was now to be a vassal of Babylon (cf. Isa. 39:5-7) until the end of Babylonian domination of the Near East (539 B.C.).

Jeremiah had keen insight into international events. He had been commissioned a prophet to the nations (1:10) and he was fully aware of what was going on around the Fertile Crescent. Nor was it difficult to know the current news, for the international highway from Egypt to Babylon ran along the coastline of Palestine. Hopper quotes A. B. Davidson as saying, "Like a lightning flash, Carchemish lighted up to (Jeremiah) the whole line of God's purposes with his people right on to the end."[16] The battle of Carchemish with its results brought many things into focus for Jeremiah. The identity of the foe from the north was now clear. God's plan to use the Chaldeans as the instrument of His wrath had become apparent. The fate of Judah was discernible in the light of these happenings. These events were to influence Jeremiah's prophetic activities for the rest of his life.

After a brief summary of his prophetic career, Jeremiah gives a preview of the end of Judah, the breakup of the Babylonian Empire, and the final judgment of all nations.

1. *Recollection* (25:1-7)

No preview of the future is really adequate without a glance at the past. Standing at this crucial point in history, Jeremiah addressed **all the people of Judah** (1). He reminded the people that he himself had served as God's spokesman for twenty-three years, **from the thirteenth year of Josiah** (see Chart *A*) . . . **I have spoken unto you** (3). Also that for centuries God had, **rising early** ("persistently," RSV), **sent to them his servants the**

---

[15]It is only fair to say that there are chronological difficulties concerning Nebuchadnezzar's appearance at Jerusalem in 606-605 B.C. Various arguments are given. For a cross-section of the different views see the following: E. J. Young, *Introduction to the Old Testament* (Grand Rapids: Eerdmans Publishing Co., 1949); G. L. Archer, *A Survey of Old Testament Introduction* (Chicago: Moody Press, 1964), pp. 369 ff.; J. E. H. Thompson, "The Book of Daniel," *Pulpit Commentary* (Grand Rapids: Eerdmans Publishing Co., 1950), XIII, i ff.; R. H. Pfeiffer, *Introduction to the Old Testament* (New York: Harper and Brothers, 1948), p. 756.

[16]IB, V (expos.), 999.

prophets (4). Jeremiah then repeats the central message of all the prophets, including the theme of his own ministry: **Turn ye again now every one from his evil way** (5) . . . **go not after other gods** (6). He also reminds the people what their response had been, "You have not given ear to me . . . so that you have made me angry" (*Basic Bible*).

Standing here at the middle point of his career, Jeremiah emphasizes (*a*) hearing, (*b*) turning, and (*c*) dwelling. Although they had heard, they had not heard well, for they did not turn from the **worship** of false **gods** (6). Consequently they will no longer be permitted to **dwell** in their own **land** (5). The sin of idol worship had been their ruin. They had not been content to live by faith; they insisted on living by sight—by what was humanly reasonable. So, says the prophet, instead of the living God, you have worshiped **the works of your** own **hands** (7). Their sin and disobedience has found them out.

2. *Resolution* (25: 8-14)

From his recollection of the past, Jeremiah now turns to a preview of the future. The key to that future lies in what has happened in the past, **Because ye have not heard my words** (8). God's plans for the future were conditioned upon their response in the past. He now communicated to Jeremiah what He had resolved to do in regard to Judah and Babylon.

(1) In His eternal wisdom God had decreed that the nation of Judah must come to an end. He indicated how this was to come about, **I will . . . take all the families of the north . . . and Nebuchadnezzar the king of Babylon . . . and . . . bring them against this land** (9). **My servant** means only that God was using Nebuchadnezzar as an instrument to punish Judah. There were to be eighteen more years of national life, but God's decision was final: **I will take from them the voice of mirth . . . of gladness . . . of the bridegroom . . . of the bride . . . this whole land shall be a desolation, and an astonishment** (a ruin and a waste; 10-11). **The sound of the millstones, and the light of the candle** were familiar signs of village life.

(2) God had also determined the length of Judah's period of exile: **This whole land . . . and these nations shall serve the king of Babylon seventy years** (11). This is understood to be a round figure. but Judah's period of servitude to Babylon came

very close to this figure. The battle of Carchemish was fought in 606 B.C. and it gave Babylon control of all the area of the Near East from Egypt to the mouth of the Euphrates River (II Kings 24:7). This would include Judah, and there is some indication that Jewish captives were taken to Babylon in 606-605 (see fn. 16). Babylon herself fell to the Medes and Persians in 539 B.C., and the first group of Jews returned to Jerusalem in 536 B.C. From the first deportation of captives to Babylon in 606-605 to the first return of Jews to Jerusalem in 536, there is an approximate period of **seventy years.** Some scholars prefer to count from the fall of Jerusalem in 586 B.C. to the dedication of the second Temple in 516 B.C. This also gives a period of **seventy years.**

(3) God further resolved that Babylon would not go unpunished, **I will punish the king of Babylon . . . And I will bring upon that land all . . . which I have pronounced against it** (12-13). Although Babylon will be the instrument in the hand of God for punishing the Jews, yet that great nation will have to answer to God for her own sins. **Many nations and great kings will** "make them slaves" (14; Berk.). Jeremiah sees that God not only controls the destinies of the Jews, but the great empire of Babylon as well.

3. *Retribution* (25:15-29)

Jeremiah here sees still further into the events of the future. He moves beyond the punishment of Judah and envisions the day when **all the nations** (15) will be brought to judgment. God commands Jeremiah **to take the wine cup** of His **fury . . . and cause all the nations . . . to drink it.** He then describes what takes place: Beginning at **Jerusalem** (18), nation after nation is compelled to drink of the wine of God's wrath, and last of all **Sheshach** (26; Babylon). All of them shall become "a desolation, a horror, a derision, and a curse" (18; Moffatt). The **mingled people** (20, 24) are mixed foreign populations.

All the nations to whom the oracles are addressed in cc. 46—51 are mentioned here (see maps 1, 2, and 3) except Damascus. Several nations, however, have been added that do not appear in 46—51. **Arabia** (24) mentioned here is the same as Kedar in 49:28-33. **Elam** (25) and Media are here mentioned together, where only Elam is named in 49:34-39. "In addition [there are] Uz (closely connected with Edom); Tyre and Sidon; Dedan and Tema (north Arabian tribes); Buz and all who cut the corners of their hair; Zimri [is] (unknown)."[17] **All the kingdoms of the world, which are upon the face of the earth** (26) shall drink, and in drinking they shall become "drunk and vomit, fall and rise no more" (27, RSV). The retributive justice of God shall begin its mighty work. If any **refuse . . . to drink** (28), the prophet is instructed to say, "You must drink!" (RSV) **For, lo, I begin to bring evil on the city which is called by my name, and should ye be utterly unpunished? The** answer is, **Ye shall not be unpunished** (29).

4. Retribution Reenforced (25:30-38)

The prophet changes from prose to poetry in this section (cf. Smith-Goodspeed or RSV). The figures change. The judgment scenes pictured above are drawn out and deepened to provide a preview of the end of the age and of the final judgment. The Lord is pictured as a **lion,** coming forth from his **covert** (38), roaring with great ferocity. He shall also **shout, like they that tread the grapes** (30; cf. Isa. 63:1-3). The whole passage is a judgment scene. **The Lord hath a controversy with the nations, he will plead with all flesh** (31, a universal judgment), and the wicked will be punished with great destruction. There will be **a great whirlwind** (32, tempest) in which **nation** after **nation** will be involved. On that day **the slain of the Lord shall be . . . from one end of the earth even unto the other,** and the number of the dead will be so vast that they will **not be lamented . . . gathered, nor buried** (33).

The final verses of this section are addressed to the **shepherds** (rulers) and the **principal** ("lords," RSV) **of the flock** (34). **Howl, ye shepherds, and cry . . . wallow yourselves in the ashes. There shall be no way to flee** or to **escape . . . the Lord hath spoiled their pasture** (35-36)—i.e., their source of help is cut off. **Ye shall fall like a pleasant vessel** (34) means to be slaughtered like choice, fattened lambs. They are left with no place to hide. The final day has come, and who will be able to stand? God holds the whole world in His hand; all nations, tribes, and people must be judged by Him.

The theme of this entire chapter is "God's Judgment of Men." (1) Judgment begins at the house of God, 29; (2) Judgment is necessary because of the wickedness of men, 5-7, 10, 12, 14; (3) There will be no place to hide from the wrath of God, 33, 35;

[17]Kuist, *op. cit.,* p. 79.

(4) All nations and peoples will be involved in the judgment of this great day, 32-33.

F. OPPOSITION TO PREDICTIONS OF DOOM, 26:1—29:32

These chapters form a collection of incidents and oracles that come from different periods of Jeremiah's life. They are brought together here under one theme because they reveal the reactions of various individuals and groups to the prophet's preaching. He insisted that Judah and the neighboring nations must submit, at least for a period of time, to the rulership of the king of Babylon. The king and the people of Judah naturally resented this kind of prophesying, but Jeremiah's bitterest foes were the religious leaders of the nation. The professional prophets and the priests opposed him with great vehemence. He likewise saved his most blistering invective for these men who were most responsible for leading the nation astray. From the human standpoint the odds were against Jeremiah, for the false prophets were cunning and capable men. But this section proves again that one man and God are a majority.

1. *The Sermon in the Temple Court* (26:1-6)

As this chapter opens the reader finds himself in the first year **of the reign of Jehoiakim** (1; see Chart *A*); the events of c. 25 took place in the fourth year. At this time (608 B.C.) the whole of the Near East was agog with excitement. The empire of Assyria was breaking to pieces; Egypt was seeking a voice in the politics of Asia; Babylon, determined to deal a deathblow to Assyria, was moving in for the kill. The armies of all these nations were maneuvering for the showdown which was soon to come at Carchemish in 606 B.C.[18] At the moment everything was in a state of flux, and no one knew what the outcome would be.

Judah herself was going through a painful period of adjustment, still mourning the death of Josiah. Jehoahaz (Shallum), his successor, had been removed by the victorious Egyptians. Jehoiakim, ruling at the pleasure of Pharaoh-necho, was inexperienced, unscrupulous, and filled with grandiose ideas. The religious situation had worsened since the passing of Josiah. Jeremiah saw the nation standing at the crossroads, and knew that the only hope was in a return to God. He was also aware that

---

[18]Paterson, *op. cit.*, pp. 538, 545.

if a blow were to be struck for true religion it must be done soon. Under the compulsion of God, and disregarding the danger to himself, Jeremiah makes a last desperate appeal to the nation and its young king to throw themselves on the mercy of God. The prophet steps into the "public light as a statesman of intrepid courage and political insight."[19]

God commands Jeremiah to take his **stand** in the Temple **court** and to speak **all the words that I command thee ... diminish** (omit) **not a word** (2). The occasion seems to have been a national festival to which people from **all the cities of Judah** came. An important message could be delivered here that would affect the whole land. He is to tell the people of God's offer to pardon and to make it plain. "It may be they will listen, and every one turn" (RSV), **that I may repent me of the evil, which I purpose to do unto them** (3). But he is also instructed to say, **If ye will not hearken** (4), **then will I make this house like Shiloh** (6; destroyed by the Philistines and never rebuilt, cf. I Samuel 4). The expression **rising up early** (5) means "whom I have been sending to you early and late" (Smith-Goodspeed).

Many scholars think that this is the same sermon and the same occasion as is found in c. 7 (cf. comments on 7:1-14). There the sermon is given in greater detail, but here is seen the reaction of the people to the sermon. The present writer would concur with this point of view. The unwelcome point in the sermon is Jeremiah's prediction of the destruction of the Temple and the city of Jerusalem. The inviolability of the Temple and the city of Jerusalem was the most popular religious dogma of the day.[20] The professional prophets and the priests had made much of this idea by telling the people that they were secure, since God would never let His dwelling place be destroyed. With one stroke Jeremiah undercut their most cherished dogma. Thus the priests and the prophets could not let Jeremiah's sermon go by unchallenged.

2. Jeremiah's Arrest and Acquittal (26:7-19)

Jeremiah's sermon brought an immediate reaction from the religious leaders of the nation. They flew into a rage. Claiming that Jeremiah was guilty of prophesying falsely in the name of the Lord, they condemned him on the spot: **Thou shalt surely die**

[19]Kuist, *op. cit.*, p. 80.
[20]Paterson, *op. cit.*, p. 545.

(8). The people in town for the feast were swept along by their religious leaders, and Jeremiah was in danger of being stoned to death. His "guilt" lay in the fact that his sermon had contradicted what the professional prophets had been telling the people.

The news of the mob action in the Temple court spread rapidly. **The princes,** i.e., the officials of the king's court who were charged with keeping the peace, hurried to the judgment seat, which was set at the entrance of **the new gate** (east gate) **of the Lord's house** (10). Apparently this was the place where religious problems affecting the populace were discussed.

The religious leaders lost no time in accusing Jeremiah before **the princes** and **the people,** claiming, **This man is worthy to die** (11). However, the princes seemed to be fair-minded men, and would not be hurried. Despite the pressure of the religious leaders, they gave the prophet an opportunity to speak for himself.

Jeremiah defended his position in admirable fashion. He was forthright, resolute, and he spoke with power: **The Lord sent me to prophesy** (12). **Therefore now amend your ways . . . and the Lord will repent him** (13). **As for me . . . I am in your hand** (14). The prophet was prepared for any eventuality.

Then said the princes and all the people (16)—note where the people stand now—**This man is not worthy to die.** Immediately some of **the elders of the land** (17; probably from the smaller towns of Judah, present for the festival) stepped forth and reminded the princes and the people of the words of the prophet **Micah.** A hundred years before **Micah** had **prophesied** that **Zion shall be plowed like a field, and Jerusalem shall become heaps** (18; cf. Mic. 3:12). **Did Hezekiah . . . put him at all to death?** (19) The answer was, No. By this time the tide had turned; the prophets and the priests had lost their bid to destroy Jeremiah; he was acquitted. In the prophet's favor had been his confident manner, the ring of authenticity in his words, and the help of influential friends. **Ahikam the son of Shaphan,** from one of the best families in the land (II Kings 22:12; 25:22; Jer. 39:14), became a political friend of great value (24).

3. *The Arrest and Execution of Urijah* (26:20-24)

This incident of itself has no connection with Jeremiah's trial and acquittal. It is introduced at this point to show what grave danger Jeremiah faced, and how easily his life could have been snuffed out. It shows the deep-seated hostility of the religious leaders of the nation and the king to the true prophets of God. **Urijah** had **prophesied** against Judah and Jerusalem **according to all the words of Jeremiah** (20). He was ruthlessly murdered and his body cast into a public burial place (23). This account also reveals that influential friends in strategic places can be of great value to the cause of God. Most of all it reveals that God was keeping His word to Jeremiah acording to 1:17-19, and that his acquittal was no mere happenstance.

4. *The Yoke of Babylon Remains* (27:1—28:17)

Jeremiah's predictions that Babylon would rule the nations of the Near East for seventy years aroused the anger of the political and religious rulers of Judah. All would concede that Babylon ruled then (593 B.C.), but there was strong expectation this this would shortly be changed. The religious leaders were angry with Jeremiah because their own predictions were being contradicted; the political leaders, because their nationalistic aspirations were in danger of being thwarted by such preaching. The professional prophets were the most openly antagonistic at this time. Despite their malicious hostility, Jeremiah held firmly to the position that his pronouncements were of God, and that Babylon would continue to be the overlord of Judah and the nations.

a. Foreign kings (27:1-11). It is conceded by practically all scholars that **Jehoiakim** in 27:1 is a copyist's error, and is probably taken from 26:1. Verses 3, 12, and 20 make it clear that Zedekiah is meant (see Chart *A*).

In the beginning of the reign (1) should be understood as "in the beginning years of the reign of Zedekiah"; for 28:1 indicates that the events there happened in the same year, and states that it was in the fourth year of Zedekiah.

Verse 3 tells of the appearance in Jerusalem of envoys from five of Judah's neighbor nations, seeking a conference with Zedekiah. It can be ascertained from Jeremiah's message to the kings of **Edom, Moab, the Ammonites, Tyrus** (Tyre), and **Zidon** (Sidon; see map 2) that they were seeking to enlist Zedekiah's help in a revolt against Nebuchadnezzar, king of Babylon. While the messengers were conferring with **Zedekiah** and his princes, the Lord gave Jeremiah a message for the kings of these nations.

The prophet was instructed to dramatize his message by the use of **bonds and yokes** (2; yoke-bars). Apparently Jeremiah made seven pairs of yoke-bars, one for each of the kings, including Zedekiah, and one for his own use. He seems to have appeared in the streets of Jerusalem for several days with a yoke-bar around his neck, proclaiming the message God had given him. The envoys of the five kings were commanded to give God's message to **their masters** (4).

The substance of Jeremiah's message to the kings is found in seven points. (*a*) **The Lord of hosts, the God of Israel** (4) is the Creator of **the earth, man,** and the beasts (5). He controls the destinies of all nations, and gives the sovereignty of them to whomever He sees fit. (*b*) For the time being, He has given control of these lands **into the hand of Nebuchadnezzar the king of Babylon** (6) and there is no appeal from this decision. On **my servant,** see comment on 25:9. (*c*) Anyone who prophesies differently, whether by dreams, divination, enchantments, or sorcery, is lying and does not have the best interests of his own people at heart (9-10). (*d*) Those who refuse to accept **the yoke of the king of Babylon** (8) will be severely punished and will be removed from their own **land, to perish** in captivity (10). (*e*) Those who accept **the yoke** will be able to **remain still in their own land** (11); their lives and homes will be saved. (*f*) On God's timetable Babylon herself is scheduled to answer to God for her own sins. In that day **many nations and great kings shall serve themselves of him** (Nebuchadnezzar; 7, cf. comment on 25:12-14). (*g*) The great lesson to be learned is, despite the conniving of kings and nations, God's word through Jeremiah stands firm. The yoke of Babylon remains!

b. Zedekiah the king of Judah (27:12-15). **I spake also to Zedekiah** (12) indicates that Jeremiah made a personal effort to make clear to his king that God's message applied to him also. The prophet was aware that **Zedekiah** was "a weak, vacillating king who was willing to listen to counsels of revolt."[21] He also knew that the king was under pressure from the professional prophets to join the rebellion; they were loudly proclaiming, **Ye shall not serve the king of Babylon** (14).

Something was needed to bring the king to his senses, and Jeremiah posed the startling question, **Why will ye die?** (13) Zedekiah was in a dilemma. The kings and the false prophets represented the natural reactions of human nature apart from God. Jeremiah presented the spiritual side of life—the wisdom

---

[21]IB, V (exeg.), 1012.

of God. The king must choose between them. In this case submission to Nebuchadnezzar was, in reality, submitting to God, for He had decreed that the yoke of Babylon should remain upon Judah. It was a matter of seeing behind events, and recognizing the hand of God shaping the affairs of men. It was a choice between faith and sight.

    c. Priests and people (27:16-22). Jeremiah next turned his personal attention **to the priests and to all this people** (16). The professional **prophets** had been prophesying that **the vessels** which had been taken from the Temple (597 B.C.) and carried to **Babylon** would **shortly** be returned. But Jeremiah warned the priests, **They prophesy a lie unto you.** He urged them to readjust their thinking, for the yoke of Babylon was not to be lifted for many years. Therefore they should **submit to the king of Babylon, and live** (17).

    To enforce his message, Jeremiah challenged the false prophets to a test. **If they be prophets . . . if the word of the Lord be with them, let them** pray to the Lord that **the vessels which yet remain in the house of the Lord, and in the house of the king . . . go not to Babylon** (18). There is no uncertainty here on the part of Jeremiah. His challenge rings loud and clear as he flings down the gauntlet, **Thus saith the Lord . . . They shall be carried to Babylon** (19, 22). He does not deny that the vessels from the house of the Lord will eventually be returned to Jerusalem, but he affirms that it will be at the time when God decrees it (22). History has proved that Jeremiah was right and the priests were wrong. For a description of the items in 19 see comments on I Kings 7:15-50. On the events of 20, see II Kings 24:8-16.

    The underlying note in all these episodes was that Jerusalem was doomed, and the end of the nation was near.

    d. False prophets (28:1-17). In this chapter Hananiah represents the entire guild of professional prophets. The incident has been included here to bring out in bold relief the error of these men, and to show that what they were doing was in the worst interest of the nation. They may have been sincere, but they were grievously wrong.

    In the same year (1), i.e., in the year in which the events of c. 27 occurred. **In the beginning of the reign of Zedekiah** means "in the beginning years of his reign," for he says that it was **in the fourth year.** The events in cc. 27 and 28 apparently took place close to the same time; in fact, 28 may have preceded 27:16-22.

Jeremiah seems to have been prophesying in the streets of Jerusalem for several days, dramatizing his message by wearing yoke-bars. He was suddenly confronted in the house of the Lord by one of the professional prophets. Hananiah . . . of Gibeon (see Gibeah, map 2), with a great show of religious fervor, contradicted Jeremiah's preaching before a large gathering of the priests and the people. He cried, Thus speaketh the Lord of hosts . . . I have broken the yoke of the king of Babylon. Within two full years will I bring again . . . all the vessels . . . that Nebuchadnezzar . . . carried . . . to Babylon . . . and . . . Jeconiah [Jehoiachin; see Chart A] . . . with all the captives of Judah (2-4).

Jeremiah's reply was a fervent Amen (6). He devoutly wished that what Hananiah was saying could be true, for he loved his nation and his people. Nevertheless (7) said Jeremiah, these words are not in accordance with the prophets who prophesied before me and before thee (8). In the past the true prophet of God had not prophesied smooth things without emphasizing the responsibility of the people. This Hananiah and his friends were failing to do. The true prophet spoke of ethical conduct and eternal verities. He knew that God dealt with people on a moral basis, not on what appeared merely desirable in human eyes. And because men's hearts were "desperately wicked" (17:9), the old prophets spoke of war, and of evil, and of pestilence (8). The word of the true prophet must carry a mixture of the negative and the positive, for only then is the word of the Lord given forth in proper balance. Consequently, a man who spoke only smooth things was suspect until his words came true.

Without warning, Hananiah tore the yoke from . . . Jeremiah's neck, and brake it (10). He repeated even more firmly his previous prophecy, declaring that the yoke of . . . Babylon will be broken from the neck of all nations within the space of two full years (11). With this, Jeremiah turned and walked away. His silence was more eloquent than anything he could have said. He could have argued, but with the mood of the mob, and the excited state of Hananiah, further words were useless.

The last word, however, had not been spoken. Sometime later God gave Jeremiah a message for this false prophet, "You have broken wooden bars, but you have made in their place bars of iron" (13, lit.). Verse 14 explains what is meant, Thus

saith the Lord . . . I have put a yoke of iron upon the neck of all
these nations, that they may serve Nebuchadnezzar . . . and they
shall serve him. The last phrase emphasizes just how wrong
Hananiah had been, and how final is the decision of God.

The Lord also had a personal word for Hananiah, **Thou mak-
est this people to trust in a lie . . . The Lord hath not sent thee**
(15). **This year thou shalt die** (16). **So Hananiah . . . died . . .
in the seventh month** (17). Kuist has observed, " 'Two years . . .
two months . . .' Grim end!"[22]

Hananiah's crime was that he "with a light heart made
promises in Jehovah's name inconsistent with the moral condition of the people, and [which] therefore could not be realized."[23]
He was a fanatic—he expected results without laying the proper
foundation for bringing about those results. "With great assurance he puts a two year limit on his prophecy: fanatics are
always in a hurry."[24]

5. Letters to People in Exile (29:1-32)

Two letters are mentioned in this chapter. The first has to
do with the general welfare of the people in exile, and contains
a warning against false prophets. The second is addressed to
the entire community, but deals with one false prophet in particular.

Jeremiah was not only troubled by false prophets in Judah,
but the same type of men were creating difficulty among the
exiles in Babylon. These exiles were, no doubt, a homesick,
unhappy lot. They were thus an easy prey for the pseudo-
prophets who were predicting a speedy end to the Captivity and
an early return to their native land. News of their activity
reached Jerusalem, and Jeremiah felt constrained to oppose them
just as he had opposed Hananiah, and others of his stripe, in
Judah. This chapter has a very definite connection with cc. 24—
28, and c. 24 especially should be read along with c. 29.

a. A general letter (29:1-23). (1) *Background* (29:1-3).
Taking advantage of emissaries going to Babylon for Zedekiah,
Jeremiah sent a letter to the exiles by the hand of two trustworthy officials. One was **Elasah the son of Shaphan** (3) and
brother of Ahikam who had already proved a great friend to

---

[22]*Op. cit.*, p. 70.
[23]Binns quoting Cheyne, *op. cit.*, p. 210.
[24]Paterson, *op. cit.*, p. 554.

Jeremiah (26:24). The second was **Gemariah, son of Hilkiah** (3; probably the Hilkiah who was high priest when the law book was found in the Temple—II Kings 22:4, 8, 14). The historical record of the events of v. 2 are to be found in II Kings 24:8-16.

(2) *Basic instruction* (29:4-19). The contents of this letter can be summarized under six headings. (*a*) The exiles were instructed to prepare themselves for a long sojourn in captivity. They were to **build . . . plant . . . eat . . . take ye wives . . . bear sons and daughters; that ye may be increased there, and not diminished** (5-6). (*b*) They were to **seek the peace** and pray for the welfare of their adopted city (first admonition to pray for one's enemies in the OT), for they would prosper as the land prospered (7). (*c*) They were not to be deceived by **prophets** and **diviners** ("Do not listen to their dreams," 8, Berk.)—**I have not sent them, saith the Lord** (8-9). (*d*) They must understand that God will **visit** them in **Babylon . . . after seventy years,** and that He will not fail to keep His **word** to them (10-14). (*e*) They must realize that God has a plan and purpose for them, but that He is more concerned with their moral advancement than with their political aspirations. For **an expected end** (11) read "a future and a hope" (Berk.). God has their welfare at heart, and His worship is not bound to any particular time or building (the Temple)—**Ye shall seek me, and find me, when ye search for me with all your heart** (13). (*f*) They were more fortunate than their brothers in Jerusalem whom they envied. In God's sight, the people at Jerusalem had become **like vile figs,** unfit to be eaten (17; cf. 24:1-10). Consequently the Davidic monarchy, the city of Jerusalem, the Temple, and the people will be swept away. They will become a **curse . . . an hissing** (18), **because they have not hearkened to my words** (19). For **rising up early,** read "early and late" (Smith-Goodspeed).

In 4-11 we see "God's Word to His People in a Wicked World." (1) Take adequate care for your physical needs, 5; (2) Plan for a next generation of God-fearing people, 6; (3) Be as good citizens as possible where you live, 7; (4) Don't be easily swayed by rumors and rebellions, 8-9; (5) You are still under God's providence and He has plans for your lives, 4, 10-11 (A. F. Harper).

(3) *Warning against lying prophets* (29:20-23). Jeremiah lays bare the falseness and the fate of the two most popular

prophets among the captives in Babylon, **Ahab** and **Zedekiah** **(20)**. In blunt language he indicts them for prophesying **a lie** in the Lord's **name (21)**, and for having committed **adultery with their neighbours' wives (23)**. Their fate will be so terrible that it will henceforth be used in pronouncing a curse, **The Lord make thee like Zedekiah and like Ahab, whom the king of Babylon roasted in the fire (22)**.

b. Letter concerning Shemaiah (29:24-32). This letter seems to have been a result of a previous one. Jeremiah's words about an extended exile aroused the antagonism of a prophet in Babylon, **Shemaiah the Nehelamite (24)**.[25] In his anger **Shemaiah** wrote a fiery letter to **Zephaniah** (and to others also), a priestly officer in Jerusalem whose duty it was to keep order in the house of the Lord **(26)**. He demanded that **Zephaniah** imprison and punish a **mad . . . prophet** by the name of **Jeremiah of Anathoth (27)** for writing a letter to the exiles, saying that the **captivity** would be of **long** duration **(28)**.

Zephaniah was evidently a believer in the integrity of **Jeremiah,** for he read Shemaiah's **letter to the prophet (29)**. Jeremiah replied sternly, addressing another letter to all the captives in Babylon concerning this false prophet. **Thus saith the Lord . . . Because . . . I sent him not, and he caused you to trust in a lie: therefore . . . he shall not have a man to dwell among this people (31-32)** i.e., "He shall have no descendant among you who lives to see the happiness I am about to bring to my people" (Moffatt).

It is clear from cc. 21—29 that Jeremiah's forecast of the end of Judah brought him into open conflict with the national authorities, and especially with the religious leaders. A bearer of evil tidings is never popular, and this was one of Jeremiah's greatest crosses. However, because of the opposition and intense suffering through which he was called to pass, he developed into a mighty warrior for God whose exploits will never die.

---

[25]**Nehelemite** means "dweller of Nehelam," but no such place name is found in the OT. Its etymology suggests "to dream" and this has given rise to the marginal rendering, "dreamer" (ISBE).

Section **VI** *The Book of Consolation*

Jeremiah 30:1—33:26

These four chapters are the only consistently hopeful part of the entire book. Chapters 32 and 33 are precisely dated in the tenth year of Zedekiah, while the prophet was imprisoned in "the court of the guard." Chapters 30 and 31 cannot be so easily dated. Scholars have assigned them to periods all the way from the time of Josiah to the governorship of Gedaliah. While the time of composition cannot be settled with perfect certainty, it is reasonable to assume that they were written at the same time as the other two, in the tenth year of Zedekiah.[1] The tone, the mood, the viewpoint, and the subject matter have much in common.

The period when Jeremiah was imprisoned in "the court of the guard" was a dark period in the life of the prophet and the nation. Jerusalem had been under siege for a year. Famine, pestilence, and misery were everywhere in the city. But this sorrowful hour gave birth to one of the most beautiful passages in the entire Bible. Chapters 30—31 can be likened to "a Song in the Night." Also, these chapters seem to fulfill Jeremiah's commission—"to build, and to plant" (1:10).

Morgan reminds us that:

> Nearly seven years had passed since the conflict with the false prophets. Events had quietly moved on, every hour contributing fresh evidence of the divine authority of Jeremiah's teaching. Hananiah had predicted that within two years the power of Babylon would be broken; the vessels of Jehovah's house would be restored to the Temple; and Jeconiah, together with the captives of Judah, returned to the city. The prediction had been demonstrated false. Things had gone from bad to worse in the life of the nation, and now the foe was at the gates.[2]

Jeremiah's predictions concerning the national and international situation had proved to be correct over a period of forty years. Therefore there was no reason to question what he now

[1]Keil and Delitzsch, *op. cit.*, II, 2; IB, V (expos.), 1043; G. C. Morgan, *op. cit.*, p. 160.

[2]*Op. cit.*, p. 160.

gave as his insights for the future of the nation. This is not to
say that Jeremiah saw the future clearly. He did not. He saw
things as did the other prophets, "through a glass, darkly" (I Cor.
13:12). Much of the time the near and the far are blended in
that strange way so characteristic of Hebrew prophecy. During
the years Jeremiah had been given glimpses of events that were
to take place "beyond judgment," so this passage is not unique.
Subsequent history in some cases, and subsequent biblical writers
in others, have confirmed the authenticity of his insights.

A. THE PREFACE, 30:1-3

Jeremiah is commanded to **write** down **in a book** (2) of
consolation **the words** God has spoken to him concerning the
future of His covenant people. These first three verses serve to
identify and introduce to the reader the remarkable words that
are to follow.[3]

For, lo, the days come (3) points to a certain, but indefinite,
time in the future. This gives the whole section an eschatological
perspective. There is also found here the clear prediction of a
return from **captivity.** Both **Israel and Judah** are expected to
possess again **the land** God had given **to their fathers;** the kingdom visualized is a united kingdom.

B. FROM TRAGEDY TO TRIUMPH, 30:4—31:1

The actual content of "the book of consolation" begins
with v. 4. What follows speaks of pain and trouble, "but the
ultimate [theme] is always that of joy."[4] It is through the valley
of tragedy and unbelievable sorrow "that the people of God are
to be brought to triumph."[5]

1. *The Time of Jacob's Trouble* (30:4-7)

The salvation of the people of God is plainly set forth but
it is to be preceded by a time of great trouble. **Alas! for that day
is great, so that none is like it** (7) . . . **a voice** (sound) **of trem-**

---

[3]Some scholars think that the **book** referred to here comprises only
cc. 30—31, while others include 32—33. The present writer holds to the
latter view. The Hebrew word for book (*sepher*) may be used for either a
short letter or a large volume such as the Book of Genesis, or Isaiah.

[4]Morgan, *op. cit.,* p. 162.

[5]*Ibid.*

bling, of fear, and not of peace (5). What kind of day will it be when men will be in such convulsive pain as to clutch their **loins** like a **woman** in childbirth, with **faces pale**[6] and lacerated with horror (6)? The words seem to be pointing beyond the present destruction of Jerusalem to a day in the distant future. They are similar to the words spoken by other preexilic prophets concerning "the day of the Lord" (Isa. 2:12-21; Joel 2:11; Amos 5:18-20), and seem, indeed, to refer to that day. If this be true, all nations will be involved. The passage ends by calling this moment of history **the time of Jacob's trouble** (7), but proclaiming that **he shall be saved out of it.**

2. *The Yoke Is Broken from Jacob* (30:8-11)

A shaft of light breaks through the darkness of this awful day—**I will break his yoke from off thy neck** (8). Jacob's day of slavery to foreign nations will be ended, and Israel **will serve the Lord . . . and David their king, whom I will raise up unto them** (9). This does not mean that David will be raised from the dead, but that the Righteous Branch from the house of David— the Messiah—will sit on the throne, and the Golden Age will be ushered in.

The overthrow of Babylon will mark the beginning of God's defense of His people,[7] and will serve as a foretaste of what He will do for them right on down to the time of the End. **I will save thee from afar, and thy seed from the land of their captivity** (10), is but a further guarantee that God will never forget His people. Therefore the true Israel of God, **my servant Jacob,** has nothing to **fear,** for Israel shall surely **return** to dwell **in rest** and quietness in her own land. She must remember, however, that the divine punishment that has come to her in just **measure** was "designed to correct Israel, and so to bring God's people to their appointed end."[8] There is much for Israel to rejoice about, for while it is God who has punished, it is that same God who will save (11). Verses 10-11 appear again in 46:27-28.

3. *Zion's Wounds Are Healed* (30:12-22)

For the moment, however, Jeremiah returns to Judah's present plight. Zion's wound is **incurable** (12), and no human

---

[6]T. K. Cheyne, "The Book of Jeremiah" (Expos.), *The Pulpit Commentary,* XI (Grand Rapids, Wm. B. Eerdmans, [reprint] 1950), 600.

[7]Keil and Delitzsch, *op. cit* II, 6.

[8]Kuist, *op. cit.,* p. 89.

help is available. The nation is destitute of anyone to **plead** her **cause**; all her **lovers have forgotten** her (13-14). God was the One who had afflicted Zion, but she richly deserved her suffering because of **the multitude of thine iniquity.**

The thought takes a sharp turn at 16. A marginal reading, "Nevertheless," makes clearer meaning than **therefore.** God has punished Israel, but He will now defend her by punishing her enemies: **They that devour thee shall be devoured.** He is impartial in His dealings with all nations, including His own. Since God has afflicted her, He is the only One who can help her now. Healing will be performed when punishment has accomplished its purpose.

Despite the ridicule of her enemies—"It is Zion, for whom no one cares!" (17, RSV)—the day will surely come when Zion's health will be restored. Jerusalem will be "rebuilt upon its mound, and the palace shall stand where it used to be" (18, RSV). All "the things that accompany salvation" (Heb. 6:9; i.e., spiritual health) will be evident among the restored people: songs, laughter, **thanksgiving,** increase of number, honor, and settledness (19-20). No foreign ruler will impose his will upon them. On the contrary, **their nobles ... and their governor** (21, ruler), who will be on intimate terms with the Lord, will be of their own race. To climax it all, the old covenantal relationship will be restored: **Ye shall be my people, and I will be your God** (22).

4. God's Purposes Relentlessly Executed (30:23—31:1)

In this passage the power (energy, perhaps Spirit) of God is likened to a **whirlwind** (23; a relentless tempest), which goes forth to execute **the intents of his heart** (24). He will not slacken His pace until (1) evil has been thoroughly punished, and (2) **all the families of Israel** (31:1) acknowledge His lordship. The term **in the latter days** (30:24) sounds as though the time is far off, but nevertheless certain. **Ye shall consider it** means "you shall understand."

C. RESTORATION ASSURED, 31:2-40

In this chapter Israel's song of triumph rises to even loftier heights. Verses 2-22 deal for the most part with the Northern Kingdom, 23-26 mainly with the Southern Kingdom, and 27-40 with both kingdoms. The Lord seeks to assure His people that their restoration is certain. This restoration is assured by (1) God's everlasting love, (2) A joyful homecoming, (3) Comfort for Rachel, (4) The restoration of Judah, (5) The reestablishment of a united kingdom, and (6) The institution of the new covenant.

1. *God's Everlasting Love* (31:2-6)

God's love, manifesting itself in **grace** (divine favor), had aided the Israelites as they came out of Egypt, and had given them **rest** in Canaan. This same **grace** is still operating now in behalf of those living **in the wilderness** (2) of exile. Thus God's love has remained steadfast toward His people through the centuries; **I have loved thee with an everlasting love** (3).

God's **lovingkindness** ("faithfulness," RSV) has worked in Israel's behalf in a thousand different ways. He has drawn them with travail and with kindness, by scattering and by gathering. This teaches that God's everlasting love "leads through tragedy as well as triumph, and . . . all pain and suffering are somehow or other within the compass of that love."[9]

The fact that God still loves Israel can be taken as an indication that there is hope for a restoration beyond judgment, **Again I will build thee** (4). This restoration will include planting and reaping, rest and security, laughter and feasting (4-5). Pure worship (6) will also be an ingredient of this idyllic scene. **Arise ye, and let us go up to Zion unto the Lord our God.**

These verses reveal that Jeremiah was no gloomy or morose individual, but one who could have enjoyed the sunnier side of life had circumstances been different.

2. *A Joyful Homecoming* (31:7-14)

Jeremiah calls upon the people to **shout** for joy and to **publish** (7; proclaim) the news of a glorious homecoming for the captives of Israel: **I will bring them from the north country, and . . . the coasts** (8), i.e., "the farthest parts of the earth" (RSV). Time may intervene, but on the word of the Lord the thing is as good as done. What are the ingredients of this joyful proclamation? (*a*) The tenderness of God is revealed by the way He guides them home. He gathers **the blind and the lame, the woman with child** (8); He gently leads them by **rivers of waters**

[9]Morgan, *op. cit.*, p. 170.

(9) and on a level path where they will **not stumble.** (*b*) That God has the heart of a father is seen in His attitude toward **Ephraim, His firstborn.**[10] (*c*) The thoughtfulness of God is disclosed by the proclamation to the **nations, and . . . isles** (Israel's enemies) that, although God has **scattered Israel** (10), He has not forgotten to **gather** them again. (*d*) The restoring strength of God is revealed by His redemption of **Jacob** (11) from hands too strong for him. (*e*) The goodness of God is seen in all the wonderful things that He does for them; they will **sing** again on the heights **of Zion** (12); the two nations will **flow together** (Isa. 60:5) and flourish like a **watered garden.** (*f*) The resources of God are manifest in His supplying them with an abundance of **wheat, wine, and oil.** (*g*) The comfort of God is revealed in the happiness that will be theirs. **Their mourning** will be turned **into joy** (13). **They shall not sorrow any more at all** (12); rejoicing will be the order of the new day.

3. *Comfort for Rachel* (31:15-22)

These words are directed to **Rahel** (15, Rachel), the grandmother of Ephraim and Manasseh. Ephraim was the leading tribe of the Northern Kingdom; thus Israel is sometimes referred to as Ephraim, and Rachel is sometimes thought of as the maternal ancestor of the northern tribes. She is pictured here in uncontrollable grief at the departure of her children to exile. **Ramah** (height) was a high point on the boundary between the Northern and Southern kingdoms. **A voice** crying here could be heard for a great distance. It has also been said that **Ramah** was the gathering place of the exiles for deportation to Babylon in the days of Jeremiah (see comments on 40:1-6). There is a tradition that Rachel died near Ramah (I Sam. 10:2), although the traditional site of Rachel's tomb is near Bethlehem.

God speaks to Rachel and bids her **refrain . . . from weeping** (16). Her children will surely return to their own land, and **there is hope in thine end** (17; future). Verses 18-19 contain an account of Ephraim's repentance, which seems to be honest and sincere. Although **Ephraim** (20) has been a wayward son, and punishment has been administered to him, yet God's loving

---

[10]In the Near East to this day, the firstborn son has a special place in the father's heart. I Chron. 5:1 says that, because Reuben defiled his father's couch, the birthright was given to the sons of Joseph. This explains the reference to Ephraim, Joseph's son, in v. 9 above.

heart has yearned for his return. Now since he is repenting, God will surely have mercy on him. To smite the **thigh** (19) was a gesture of grief. **My bowels are troubled** (20) means, My emotions are stirred.

Verses 21 and 22 are difficult to interpret. Jeremiah passes from talking about **Ephraim my dear son** (20) to the **virgin of Israel** (21). Although both terms have been previously used, this is an abrupt change. In 21 the certainty of return from captivity is emphasized. The **virgin of Israel** is urged to send out an advance party to set . . . **up waymarks** and signposts to direct the returning exiles on their way home. In the latter part of 22 we are told that God has **created a new thing in the earth, A woman shall compass a man,** perhaps in the sense of cleaving to her loved one, as Israel will cling to the Lord in that day (Berk., marg.). Most scholars conclude that there is a proverb here, the meaning of which has been lost.

4. *The Restoration of Judah* (31:23-26)

God's people are further assured of deliverance and salvation by the restoration. **The land of Judah** (23) and her **cities** are pointedly mentioned, as being re-inhabited. The weight of the statement, however, is on pure religion being once again practiced in the land: **The Lord bless thee, O habitation of justice, and mountain of holiness.** This is understandable since corrupt religion was the main cause of her captivity. Idyllic conditions will prevail when **Judah** (24) returns to her homeland. Peace and harmony are pictured, with the "farmers and those who wander with their flocks" (RSV) happily dwelling together. **The weary soul** (25) will find rest, and **sorrowful** hearts will find abundant comfort. Completely new conditions will prevail, reminding us of Isaiah's Golden Age.

Verse 26 constitutes a sudden break in the thought. It is not quite clear as to who the speaker is. It cannot refer to God or the exiles, so the most likely figure is the prophet. The verse would imply that the prophecies just enunciated had come to him in a dream. Since they were hopeful and pleasant (contrary to Jeremiah's usual proclamations), it is understandable how they might seem **sweet** to him.

5. *Reestablishment of a United Kingdom* (31:27-30)

Three things seem to stand out in these verses. (1) God will bless a returned Israel and Judah with prosperity (in both **man** and **beast, 27)**, and they shall be one again. The divided kingdom had been a great grief to the prophets; now that breach will be healed. (2) There will be a reversal of God's policy concerning the welfare of the land. Because of Israel's sin, His policy had been one of punishment—to **pluck up, and to break down (28)**; but since punishment has done its healing work in their hearts (cured them of idolatry), God's policy now is **to build, and to plant.** (3) There will be a new type of morality demanded. Individual responsibility will be the mark of the new age. Heretofore the basic unit of responsibility had been the nation. Apparently the people of Jerusalem and the exiles already in Babylon had complained that it was unfair for them to have to suffer for the sins of their fathers. Thus the proverb, **The fathers have eaten a sour grape, and the children's teeth are set on edge (29)**, will no longer be true. **Every one shall die for his own iniquity (30).** This new emphasis in morality will constitute a marked advance in the faith of Israel. It can be conceived as paving the way for Jeremiah's idea of the new covenant, and also as preparing the way for the gospel age.

6. *Institution of a New Covenant* (31:31-34)

Jeremiah's conception of a new covenant was born out of his many years of experience in the prophetic office. In the reforms of Josiah he had seen his people pour all their hope into outward forms of religion, but with no corresponding improvement in ethical living. Nationalized religion did not furnish adequate grounds for the individual to feel personally responsible. Thus "the old religion broke down at the point of individual responsibility."[11]

It was apparently during Josiah's reforms that Jeremiah became convinced that the only hope for the nation was an internal, individual revolution: "Break up your fallow ground . . . take away the foreskin of your heart" (4:3-4). As the years went by, the prophet seems to have become more and more convinced that religion must be individualized.[12] His own experience bore out the fact that individual religion was possible. He himself knew God and had fellowship with Him; this relationship was

[11]Fred M. Wood, *Fire in My Bones* (Nashville: Broadman Press, 1959), p. 152.

[12]Paterson, *op. cit.*, p. 556.

immediate and internal. What was possible for him should be possible for every individual in the nation.[13]

It would be foolish to say that Jeremiah saw everything with perfect clarity. However he was able to see the outline of things to come, and this is what he passed on to the Hebrew people. What then are the distinctive features of the new covenant as set forth by Jeremiah?

(1) The new covenant will be eschatological in character, for it lies at the heart of the redemptive purposes of God. It is not a divine afterthought. Just as Mosaic religion was a part of the redemptive scheme, so the new covenant will appear in the fullness of times.

(2) The next feature will be the introduction of a new methodology. Heretofore God had worked through the nation as a unit, but the nation was soon to disappear. In order to accomplish the purposes of God, a new method must be found. He will now work through the individual. God's new methodology will involve three things: (*a*) A different kind of motivation, **I will put my law . . . in their hearts** (33); (*b*) Immediate knowledge of God, **They shall all know me** (34); (*c*) Individual pardon for sin, **I will forgive their iniquity.** God could deal now with the mainsprings of human action. Then, in working through the individual, religion could become universal.

(3) There will be a new spiritual dimension. Religion will no longer be merely external; inwardness will be the dominant note in the future. Heretofore the laws of God had been written on tables of stone; now they are to be written in the heart. Instead of treating outward symptoms, God will be dealing with inner principles. Under the new covenant men will respond from inward motivation, rather than from outward forms of compulsion.

(4) There will be a new relationship. Under the new covenant, man's relationship with God will be intimate and personal, **They shall all know me** (34). Under the old covenant, man's relationship with God was formal; under the new, it would be spiritual. When the law is written in the heart, religion has a dynamic quality that carries infinite possibilities.

(5) There will be a new level of morality. Judah had suffered from a "deceitful" and "desperately wicked" heart (17:9).

---

[13]Keil and Delitzsch, *op. cit.,* II, 39.

There was great need for a moral transformation—a changed heart. Under the new covenant this will be a glorious possibility. True religion will, henceforth, have aspirations based on a personal knowledge of God, and will operate from spiritual laws written in the heart. The result will be that new moral principles will govern society.

The restoration of Israel reaches its climax with the institution of the new covenant. These are perhaps the four most important verses in the Book of Jeremiah, because they forecast so much of what has happened in the field of religion since his day. Paul took up Jeremiah's idea, making a clear distinction between the old covenant and the new (II Cor. 3:6, 14-16). The author of the Epistle to the Hebrews begins and ends his exposition of the ministry of Jesus by quoting Jer. 31:31-34.[14] Jesus himself instituted the Lord's Supper by saying, "This is my blood of the new testament [covenant], which is shed for many" (Matt. 26:28; Mark 14:24). Individual religion can trace one of its beginnings to Jeremiah. He was the chief link between the old order in Israel and the new.[15]

7. *Perpetuity of the Nation* (31:35-37)

God here makes the people a promise regarding the future of the nation. Israel is guaranteed an existence as long as the **sun** and **moon** (35) shall last. The **ordinances** mean "the fixed order" of nature (RSV). Thus far God has kept His word to His people. The survival of Israel as a distinct entity is one of the miracles of history.[16] "It is hardly explainable on any but supernaturalistic grounds."[17]

8. *The Rebuilding of Jerusalem* (31:38-40)

God further confirms His word to the nation by saying that Jerusalem will be rebuilt. The statement, "The days are coming" (38, RSV), throws the passage into an eschatological perspective, and one may expect to find here a blending of the near and the far. The mention of a **measuring line** . . . **Gareb** . . . **Goath** . . . **brook of Kidron** (39-40) could refer to the time of the return

---

[14]Kuist, *op. cit.*, p. 97.

[15]James Fleming, *Personalities of the Old Testament* (New York: Chas. Scribner's Sons, 1946), p. 329.

[16]Binns, *op. cit.*, p. 240; also James, *op. cit.*, p. 1.

[17]J. F. Graybill, *op. cit.*, p. 679.

under Ezra and Nehemiah. On the other hand, the disappearance
of all unclean places and the sanctification of places that had
once been used for burying the dead and casting rubbish may
have reference to the spiritual Jerusalem of the Messianic age.[18]
Although the earthly city has been captured and recaptured many
times since Jeremiah's day, it has never been **thrown down . . .
for ever.** It still exists. This cannot be said concerning Nineveh
and Babylon.

D. Restoration Dramatized, 32:1-44

In this chapter the dominant note is still optimistic. God led
Jeremiah to portray in dramatic action a prophecy of the reestablishment of the nation. In order to better understand what
takes place here, one should read also cc. 37—38.

1. *The Prelude* (32:1-8)

The time is the **tenth year of Zedekiah** (1), about 597 B.C.
The place is "the court of the guard" (2, RSV), which was a part
of the palace complex in the city of Jerusalem.[19] Jeremiah was in
prison because of his prediction that Jerusalem would be taken
by Nebuchadnezzar: **Zedekiah . . . shut him up, saying, Wherefore dost thou prophesy?** (3) The king and his princes were
highly displeased with the prophet, for he seemed to be a traitor
to his own nation. He had prophesied that Judah's king would
become a captive and thus "speak to [the king of Babylon]
personally and see him face to face" (4; Moffatt; cf. 21:9; 38:2).
But Jeremiah's predictions were in the process of coming to pass
at that very moment. The Babylonians were just outside the
walls, and the city was in danger of being taken at any time.

One day Jeremiah heard **the word of the Lord** (6) to the
effect that **Hanameel** was coming to see him about the **field in
Anathoth,** for it was his by **the right of redemption** (7). Sometime later when Hanameel came to the prison and asked Jeremiah
to buy his field, the prophet records, **Then I knew that this was
the word of the Lord** (8).

---

[18]Keil and Delitzsch, *op. cit.,* II, 46.

[19]**The court of the prison** (2) was a part of the king's palace. It seems
to have been an open court around which were situated the barracks of
the king's bodyguard. It was "used for political prisoners who did not
require strict confinement" (IB, V [exeg.], 1043). Apparently outside people
could view what went on in the court (10, 12). See Binns, *op. cit.,* p. 245.

2. *Act I: Faith in Action* (32:9-15)

And I bought the field of Hanameel . . . and weighed him the money (9). Every legal step was taken with precision. Since the Hebrews did not use coined money, the **silver was weighed.** The matter was properly written up, and duly witnessed (10, 12). Two copies were made **according to the law and custom;** one was **sealed,** and the other left **open** (11). **Baruch** (13) was instructed to **put them in an earthen vessel,** in order that they might be preserved **many days** (14). This transaction gives us the details of a real-estate transaction in preexilic Judah, the only instance in the OT where this is done.[20]

The whole transaction was an act of faith on the part of Jeremiah. The prophet was painfully aware that the field he purchased in Anathoth, a few miles north of Jerusalem, was even then in the hands of the Babylonians. Although he knew this, he paid "the full fair price"[21] for the land, and was careful to see that all legal requirements had been met. Before a large group of witnesses he dramatized his faith in God's word that **houses and fields and vineyards shall be possessed again in this land** (15). Apart from a hope of restoration, this act would have been meaningless. It is evident from the following passage that Jeremiah himself did not know how this could be, but faith faces the impossible and cries, "It shall be done!"

3. *Act II: Faith Put to the Test* (32:16-25)

After the transfer of the property had been completed, Jeremiah took himself to prayer. What he had acted out seemed so humanly incredible that he felt the need of talking to God about it. In this prayer of communion he dwells first on the greatness of God as Creator (17), then on His **lovingkindness,** wisdom, and might (18-19), and finally reviews His redemptive acts in behalf of His covenant people (20-22). **Made thee a name** (20) would be "didst win for thyself . . . renown" (Smith-Goodspeed). He deplores the unfaithfulness of Israel, and recognizes the reason for the present plight of the nation, **therefore thou hast caused all this evil to come upon them** (23). **Mounts** (24) were siege mounds. Jeremiah's mind apparently turns back across the history of Israel, the preaching of the other prophets, and his own long years of experience, and cries, **What thou hast spoken**

[20]IB, V (exeg.), 1045; John Bright, *op. cit.,* p. 239.
[21]Paterson, *op. cit.,* p. 556.

is come to pass (24), He seems to be saying, "I know all this, yet my finite mind cannot grasp how Israel is to be restored. It seems such an impossible thing," but **thou hast said unto me . . . Buy thee the field,** though (KJV, marg.) **the city is given** to **the Chaldeans** (25).

G. Campbell Morgan has well said, "Obedience by faith does not mean that there will be no inquiry, no question, no sense of difficulty . . . if there be no risk, then there is no faith."[22] The Bible nowhere indicates that faith is easy to come by, or that genuine faith has no questions to ask. The contrary is more nearly the truth. God has never been displeased with honest, sincere doubt, nor does God fail to help His perplexed children.

4. Act III: The Faithfulness of God (32:26-44)

God's answer to Jeremiah's perplexity is fourfold. (1) By changing Jeremiah's statement in v. 17 into a very probing question, **Is there any thing too hard for me?** (27) He declares that He, "not the Chaldean (Nebuchadnezzar), is the Lord of history."[23] (2) He reiterates the certainty of judgment; therefore the immediate outlook for the city is, indeed, grim (28-36). (3) The way of redemption lies through tragedy, but redemption is certain. God will not fail to **gather them out of all countries** (37) to repossess their own land. "Moreover, there will be a regeneration of heart and soul, and the people will not depart from their God."[24] (4) Jeremiah's act of faith is confirmed as authentic: **Fields shall be bought in this land** (43). **Men shall . . . subscribe evidences, and seal them, and take witnesses . . .** (44).

E. FURTHER ASSURANCES OF RESTORATION, 33:1-26

The oracles of c. 33 continue the theme of judgment and restoration. The appearance of the Messianic King and the picture of ideal conditions in a united kingdom bring the Book of Consolation (cc. 31—33) to a glorious climax.

1. The Divine Invitation (33:1-3)

God speaks to Jeremiah a second time in the court of the guard, and shares with him His secret plans. Verse 2 is difficult as there seems to be something missing. The RSV follows the

---

[22]*Op. cit.,* pp. 193 ff.   [23]Paterson, *op. cit.,* p. 628.

[24]F. Cawley, "Jeremiah," *The New Bible Commentary,* ed. Francis Davidson, *et al.* (Grand Rapids, Michigan: Wm. B. Eerdmans Publishing Co., 1956), p. 628.

Septuagint: "Thus says the Lord who made the earth." This makes the verse intelligible, and is perhaps the best solution. God is now conceived to be stressing His role as the Creator, and with it His sovereignty over men and nations.

The background of His gracious invitation in 3 is the desperate condition of Jerusalem: famine, pestilence, the prophet's own brush with death (38:7-13), and the imminent fall of the city.[25] **Call unto me, and I will . . . shew thee great and mighty (hidden) things** (3). The invitation here is to Jeremiah, but he represents all of God's servants. The verse highlights prayer as one of the great agencies through which God reveals spiritual truth to men. It also shows "the need for human cooperation if the Divine revelation, which God is willing and anxious to unfold, is to become possible."[26]

2. *Afflicted Jerusalem Is Healed* (33:4-13)

Verses 4-5 bring the reader to the very eve of the fall of Jerusalem. One can feel the sense of desperation that prevails among the people as the city makes its final stand. **Mounts** (4) would be siege mounds. **Houses** built next to the walls are torn down and the space and material are used in the defense of the city. The prophet's heart is breaking because the end is in sight. God's word is still the same: **I have hid my face from this city** (5). There will be no reprieve.

Even though God's decision to destroy the city cannot be repealed, He does not leave the prophet hopeless. Afflicted Jerusalem will be healed. Verse 6 contains God's goal of restoration: moral health and material well-being, "I will heal them and reveal to them abundance of prosperity" (6, RSV). **As at the first** (7); i.e., as in an earlier, happier day. Verse 13 indicates that all sections of Judah shall share in the restoration. The rest of the passage indicates that God's method of restoration involves three things:[27] (1) In Jerusalem's particular situation, destruction is the gateway to restoration. Death is the gateway to life. There is to be no slight healing of the situation; all evil must be swept away. In the redemptive processes of God "old Israel" must die in order for "new Israel" (the Church) to arise.

(2) Moral cleansing is the gateway to spiritual wholeness (health); **I will cleanse them from all their iniquity** (8). If

---

[25]Kuist, *op. cit.*, p. 102.   [26]Binns, *op. cit.*, p. 253.
[27]Cf. G. C. Morgan's exegesis of this passage, *op. cit.*, pp. 200 ff.

spiritual wholeness is ever to exist again in Israel, a radical moral cleansing is necessary. The Hebrew for *cleansing* (*taher*) is a strong word and means "to purify" or "make clean." Spiritual health is God's goal for man. Where there is spiritual wholeness, there will be **the voice of joy, and the voice of gladness . . . the voice of them that shall say, Praise the Lord** (11). But the moral cleansing comes first. There must be a "purification of the springs of life, in order that life may become full of joy and full of gladness."[28]

(3) Spiritual health is the gateway to material well-being. This too is always God's order. However, men often try to reverse it. They put the primary emphasis on material prosperity and vow that this will bring spiritual blessedness. But sinful men have always gotten matters turned around. First let there be spiritual wholeness; then there will be heard **the voice of them that . . . shall bring the sacrifice of praise into the house of the Lord—the voice of the bridegroom . . . bride** (11). **In this place, which is desolate . . . again . . . shall be . . . shepherds** (12). Afflicted Jerusalem will be healed, but on God's terms, and through eternal principles.

3. *Davidic Kings and Levitical Priests* (33:14-26)

The lofty language of this final section is designed to bring the Book of Consolation (cc. 30—33) to a splendid climax.

(1) The opening words, **Behold, the days come** (14), immediately throw the whole passage into an eschatological perspective, and point to the coming of a new order which is to find its fulfillment in a certain but indefinite future. (2) The material is addressed both to **the house of Israel and to the house of Judah** and points to the expectation of a united kingdom when the new order arrives. (3) At the proper time, God will raise up a true offspring of David, **the Branch** ("Shoot" or "Sprout") **of righteousness** (15). These words are almost identical with 23:5-6. There is a difference, however, for here the Messianic name, **The Lord our righteousness** (16), is applied to the city of **Jerusalem.** At first glance this seems rather strange, but on second thought, it is to be expected. *The holy city has taken on the character of its King.*[29] (4) In the new order the Davidic house will never lack for a man to rule the kingdom (17), and the Levitical priest-

---

[28]*Ibid.*, p. 204.

[29]Keil and Delitzsch, *op. cit.*, II, 72; Morgan, *op. cit.*, p. 201.

hood will never lack for a man to perform the proper religious duties (18). The two pillars of God's administration[30] in the world have always been the kingship and priesthood, the state and the Church. (5) In order that His people may have a sure hope, God binds himself by a pledge that, as long as His **covenant of the day, and . . . night** (20) lasts, His word to Israel will not fail. **Ordinances** (25) are the orderly processes of nature. (6) To those who were doubtful about the future of the nation, God had an answer. He assured them that the promise made to the Davidic and Levitical houses (20-21) stood good for all **the seed of Jacob** (26). Thus **mercy** to both Israel and Judah is doubly sure.

These prophecies have never been fulfilled in a narrow nationalistic sense. Perhaps they were never meant to be, for the new order could never be like the old, any more than the butterfly is like the cocoon from which it comes. But in a spiritual and wider sense the prophecy has been fulfilled: "Jesus Christ is 'the root and offspring of David.' "[31]

[30]Keil and Delitzsch, *op. cit.*, II, 73; Paterson, *op. cit.*, p. 557.
[31]Cawley, NBC, p. 628.

Section **VII** *Counsel for Kings*

Jeremiah 34:1—36:32

In this section is found a group of incidents from the life of Jeremiah, and sayings of his, that relate for the most part to kings of Judah, and secondarily to the people. In an instance or two the people are addressed, but even here it is hoped that the ear of the king will be reached. The material comes from different periods in the life of the prophet and is not arranged in chronological order.

A. COUNSEL CONCERNING BABYLON, 34:1-7

The date of this passage can be ascertained from 7. Lachish and Azekah[1] were still holding out against the armies of the Babylonians. This would suggest that the siege of Jerusalem was only in its early stages, and as yet things were not critical. The rest of the chapter would indicate that Zedekiah and his princes were hoping for help from the Egyptians. It may be that it was his conniving with the Egyptians that prompted Jeremiah to give serious counsel to Zedekiah.

Ever since the fourth year of Jehoiakim (c. 25) Jeremiah had not wavered in his position concerning the future of the Near East. He had been consistent in his advice to Jehoiakim, Jehoiachin, and now Zedekiah, in that Nebuchadnezzar had been decreed by God to be the overlord of the area for many years to come. Jeremiah insisted that any attempts at rebellion against the king of Babylon would be futile; therefore, why not "serve him . . . and live" (27:12)? In counseling obedience to the king of Babylon, Jeremiah did not consider himself disloyal to his

---

[1]Lachish (see map 2) was a fortress city twenty-three miles southwest of Jerusalem, which commanded the highway that ran from the coastal plain (the Shephelah) to Jerusalem. Before the capital city could be forced to capitulate, this stronghold would have to be taken. Excavations at this site have uncovered the *Lachish Letters* written during the very period under consideration. See Introduction for a discussion of the importance of the *Lachish Letters* to an understanding of the life and times of Jeremiah. Azekah was between Lachish and Jerusalem.

nation or his king. He was convinced that, since God had decided the matter, Judah's best interests lay within His decree.

Jeremiah's warning to Zedekiah here is similar to warnings given by him in 21:1-10; 32:3-5; 37:8-10, 17; 38:17-23. **All the kingdoms of the earth** (1) would be the countries subject to Babylon. **The cities thereof** would be the cities of Judah. In this passage Jeremiah goes into detail concerning Zedekiah's fate— he shall **not die by the sword** (4), but **in peace** (5). Jeremiah adds that they shall **burn odours for thee . . . with the burnings of thy fathers** they shall **lament** (6). Hebrews did not cremate their dead, but they burned spices and hired professional mourners. According to 52:8-11, Zedekiah was carried to Babylon and died there as a royal prisoner (cf. 39:7; II Kings 25:5-6; Ezek. 12:13). If, at his death, the king of Babylon permitted Zedekiah to be buried in that land according to the customs of the Jews, with the burning of spices and lamentations, then the prophecy may be considered to have been fulfilled.[2] But many scholars think the passage must be interpreted "as a conditional promise that was unfulfilled because the king did not follow its condition,"[3] i.e., submit to the king of Babylon.

B. COUNSEL CONCERNING SLAVES, 34:8-22

At a very dark point during the siege of the city of Jerusalem, Zedekiah made a covenant with the people to let their Hebrew slaves go free. Apparently one reason was to gain the favor of God. **To serve himself of them** (9; cf. 10) was to enslave them. According to the law of Moses (Exod. 21:2; Deut. 15:2) a Hebrew slave was to go free at the beginning of the seventh year of service, but in Judah the matter apparently had not been given attention for many years.[4] Verses 15 and 19 indicate that a solemn covenant had been made in the Temple between the people and their slaves. One can almost feel a wave of piety sweep over the city. **All the people,** including **princes** and

---

[2]Cf. Keil and Delitzsch, *op. cit.,* p. 81.

[3]IB, V (exeg.), 1054; see also Peake, *op. cit.,* II, 137; Graybill, *op. cit.,* p. 680.

[4]Binns observes, "The number of slaves must have been very great as the frequent invasions had ruined the small landowners, who were oppressed by the greed of the great proprietor and in their poverty reduced to servitude" (*op. cit.,* p. 260).

priests ... passed between the parts of the calf[5] (10, 19), i.e., took the vow to let their slaves go free. This was an excellent step toward God, and Jeremiah heartily approved.

Shortly after this was done, the Babylonian armies suddenly lifted the siege against Jerusalem and went away. When 21-22 are read with 37:1-10 it is clear that an Egyptian army had appeared from the south. Nebuchadnezzar immediately shifted his troops to meet the newcomers. Jerusalem for the moment was relieved and there was great jubilation in the city. Since the fields outside the walls could be worked again, the leaders in Jerusalem quickly repudiated their vows. The freed slaves were re-enslaved and put to work.

In no uncertain terms, Jeremiah denounced both king and people. He said, "You recently repented ... but then you turned around and profaned my name" (15-16, RSV). He quoted God as saying that, since they had not hearkened unto Him **in proclaiming liberty, every one to his brother ... behold, I proclaim a liberty for you ... to the sword, to the pestilence, and to the famine** (17). Furthermore, God said, **I will command ... them** (the Babylonians) **to return to this city; and ... fight ... take ... and burn it** (22).

A study of the actions of Zedekiah and his people reveals the moral poverty of Judah in this sad hour. (1) The leaders of the nation had broken a covenant voluntarily made and duly ratified in God's house. (2) They had thus profaned the character of God, in whose name the vows had been taken. (3) They were irresolute and double-minded in their devotion to God. (4) They quickly bowed to the law of expediency. (5) Their repentance was superficial,[6] for (a) it was motivated only by a fear of consequences, (b) it was a change of conduct with no real change of heart, (c) its results were shallow and temporary.

C. THE EXAMPLE OF THE RECHABITES, 35: 1-19

Jeremiah did not hesitate to use various methods to present God's truth to men. In this instance he used a whole tribe of

---

[5]In ancient times a covenant between two parties was confirmed by killing an animal, preferably a calf, and cutting it into halves. Between these pieces the two parties passed, intimating "that if either of them broke the covenant it would fare with him as the slain and divided animal" (Unger's *Bible Dictionary*, p. 224).

[6]On "superficial repentance" see Jer. 34:8-11 *Pulpit Commentary*, XI, 87.

people whose singular devotion to family ideals permitted him to drive home the truth to the people of Judah.

The incident is undated except that it occurred during the reign of Jehoiakim (see Chart *A*). A date shortly after the battle of Carchemish would fit quite well, since Nebuchadnezzar was in the area at the time, and **the Syrians** (11) could easily have been active then. However, a date toward the end of Jehoiakim's reign (*cir.* 598 B.C.) should not be ruled out, for the king of Babylon captured the city of Jerusalem in 597 B.C.

The Rechabites were a nomadic family apparently of Kenite descent (I Chron. 2:55). As a desert tribe they worshiped the Lord, and threw in their lot with the Israelites during the Exodus (Judg. 1:16). **Jonadab the son of Rechab** (6) is thought of as the spiritual father of the tribe, since his ideas made them distinctive. It was he who welded them into a close-knit group of desert-dwellers who shunned the settled, agricultural life of Canaan. Jonadab is mentioned in II Kings 10:15-28 as a partisan of Jehu, the king of Israel.

1. *Jeremiah Offers Wine to the Rechabites* (35:1-5)

God instructed Jeremiah to go to **the house** (the camp) **of the Rechabites . . . and bring them into the house of the Lord** and offer them **wine to drink** (2). The prophet sought out the leader of the tribe and eventually persuaded the whole group to accompany him to the Temple. The men named in 3-4 are not mentioned elsewhere except **Maasiah**, identified as a priest in 29:25. Jeremiah describes the location of the chamber to which he **brought them** (4), so that the reader may know that the incident took place openly, before the officials of the Temple, and before the eyes of the people of Jerusalem. These chambers were "arranged around the courts of the temple, serving partly as storehouses and partly as residences for priests" (Berk., fn.). Cf. I Chron. 9:27; Ezek. 40:17; Neh. 10:37-39. Inside the room Jeremiah set pitchers **full of wine**, with **cups**, before **the Rechabites**, and bid them, **Drink ye wine** (5).

2. *The Rechabites Refuse to Drink* (35:6-11)

The Rechabites not only refused to drink, but unhesitatingly presented their reasons for total abstinence. They reminded Jeremiah that **Jonadab**, two centuries before, had commanded them that they should not **drink . . . wine** (6), **build houses** (9), **sow seed** (7), or **plant** vineyards, but instead should dwell in

441

tents and live the life of nomads all their days. They completed their answer by saying, **We have . . . done according to all that Jonadab our father commanded us** (10). They told Jeremiah that they were in Jerusalem only temporarily **for fear of the army of the Chaldeans, and . . . the Syrians** (11). When the emergency was past they would be away to the desert again.

3. *An Object Lesson for Judah* (35:12-17)

The presence of a group like this in the Temple area could not help but create a sensation in Jerusalem, and Jeremiah seized the opportunity to deliver God's message to the people. In telling fashion he focused attention on the faithfulness of this family to the command of a dead ancestor. In contrast, Jeremiah sought to arouse the conscience of Judah to her pathetic spiritual condition, pointing out her unfaithfulness to the requirements of God. The Rechabites had remembered to keep their father's command although he had been dead for two centuries, but despite the fact that God had constantly sent **prophets** (15) to remind His people, Judah had forgotten Him. In clarion tones Jeremiah calls the people to repentance: **Return ye** (15). **Rising early** (14; cf. 15) is a figure of speech meaning earnestly or repeatedly.

God's message, however, seemed to fall on deaf ears: **This people hath not hearkened unto me: therefore . . . I will bring upon Judah . . . all the evil that I have pronounced against them** (16-17).

4. *The Promise to the Rechabites* (35:18-19)

The outlook for Judah was grim, but for the Rechabites the prospects were bright: **Jonadab the son of Rechab shall not want a man to stand before me for ever** (19). God promised to reward this desert tribe, not because of their peculiar ways or ascetic practices, but because their faithfulness to the precepts of their father is a rebuke to infidelity and double-dealing wherever it is found. Their faithfulness will stand in biblical literature forever as a living example of the utter devotion that God seeks from men. Even to this day among the Bedouin peoples of the Near East there are said to be tribes who live by the rules of **Jonadab.**[7]

---

[7]Merrill F. Unger, *Unger's Bible Dictionary* (Chicago: Moody Press, 1957), p. 913; IB, V (exeg.), 1062; Paterson, *op. cit.*, p. 557.

D. COUNSEL PRESERVED IN A BOOK, 36:1-19

This is one of the most valuable sections of the Book of Jeremiah. (1) The passage throws light on the origin of the book. The process of writing and compiling his various prophecies began here. Eventually many different oracles, incidents from his life, and historical information were arranged to comprise the book as it stands today. (2) It provides important details concerning how one biblical book came to be written. Involved in the process were a roll book, pen, ink, the selection of a scribe, and the actual dictation. No other OT book gives us such detailed description of its production. (3) The events related here mark a turning point in the career of Jeremiah. Up to this time he was well-known only in one of the smallest countries of the Near East, but with the writing of his messages he was destined to influence the world. From this point on he belongs to the ages.

1. *God's Words Written Down* (36:1-8)

The incident occurred **in the fourth year** (1) of King **Jehoiakim** (605 B.C.). God instructed the prophet to **write** down in **a book** all the prophecies that He had given him **from the days of Josiah** (i.e., from the day he was called), **even unto this day** (2). God's purpose for doing this is found in 3. **It may be . . . Judah will hear all the evil which I purpose to do and may return . . . that I may forgive their iniquity.** It is amazing how many different methods God has used as recorded in the Book of Jeremiah to get His people to turn from their wickedness to serve Him. One has to say with Isaiah, "What could have been done more?" (Isa. 5:4) Only an eternal love could be so ingenious and so persistent.

Jeremiah complied with God's request by securing the services of **Baruch the son of Neriah** (4) to be his scribe. **Baruch** (appearing for the first time in 32:12) seems to have belonged to one of the noble families of Judah. His brother Seraiah was in the service of Zedekiah (51:59). Josephus tells us that Baruch "was exceptionally well instructed in his native tongue."[8] **And Baruch wrote from the mouth of Jeremiah all the words of the Lord** (4). The period of time used for dictating and writing must have been several days and even weeks. The **roll of a**

---

[8] *Antiquities of the Jews* X. 9.1.

book would be a scroll, rolled up for convenience in storing and reading.

There came a day when Jeremiah said to Baruch, **I am shut up** (detained); **I cannot go into the house of the Lord** (5): **therefore go thou, and read** (6). Just why Jeremiah could not go to the Temple is not told. Scholars have conjectured sickness, being ceremonially unclean at the moment, or forbidden by Temple authorities because of previous incidents such as the Temple Sermon. All agree that he was not in prison at this time. **Baruch did as Jeremiah . . . commanded him** (8).

2. *Baruch Reads God's Word in the Temple* (36:9-10)

God's word through Jeremiah was written "in the fourth year of Jehoiakim" (1; 605 B.C.), but an appropriate time for reading it did not come for several months. Finally in the **ninth month** (our December) of Jehoiakim's **fifth year . . . a fast** was **proclaimed** (9) for the entire kingdom of Judah, perhaps in mourning for the attack on Jerusalem by Nebuchadnezzar the year before. People from all the cities of Judah were in Jerusalem for this solemn fast. Jeremiah apparently hoped that, by probing their consciences with a pungent message from God himself, this religious ceremony could be turned into a revival of genuine religion (7). Baruch read the message to the multitudes from a strategic place in the Temple area, **the chamber of Gemariah . . . at the entry of the new gate** (10). The reading brought an immediate reaction.

3. *Baruch Reads to the Princes* (36:11-19)

Michaiah the son of Gemariah (11) heard the reading in the Temple court. Deeply disturbed, he hastened to **the scribe's chamber** (12) of the king's palace to report what he had heard. His father and the other **princes** were there in session. Upon hearing Michaiah's report, **the princes sent for Baruch** (14) and the scroll, and requested that it be read to them. **So Baruch read it in their ears** (15). It was the princes' turn to be upset; "they turned one to another in fear" (16, ASV), and told Baruch that the matter would have to be reported to **the king**. To clarify the matter further, they questioned Baruch about his part in the affair (17). He replied, **He pronounced all these words unto me with his mouth, and I wrote them with ink in the book** (18). Convinced that the matter required the king's attention, but fearful about what his reaction would be, **the princes** said to **Baruch, Go, hide thee, thou and Jeremiah** (19).

E. THE BOOK DESTROYED, 36: 20-26

Leaving the scroll in the room of **Elishama the scribe** (20),
the princes went directly to **the king**. Jehoiakim was in his
winterhouse (22), probably a part of the palace that caught the
rays of the winter sun. It was the **ninth month** (our December),
and a **fire** was **burning** in a brazier. Upon hearing the report of
the princes, he demanded to see the scroll (21). It was brought
and read to him with his officials standing **beside** him. Sullen
anger gripped the king as he heard the counsel given to him in
the scroll. As **Jehudi** (23) read **three or four leaves** (columns),
Jehoiakim in bitter contempt **cut** them off with his **penknife** and
threw them **into the fire**. He continued this until the entire
roll was consumed.

The king did this despite the protestations of several of the
princes (25). Arrogant and high-handed, Jehoiakim was completely unconcerned and unafraid at what he had done, and so
were a number of his courtiers (24). His attitude and actions
were a far cry from those of his father, Josiah, when he heard the
book of the law read in a similar situation (II Kings 22:10-14).
Disregarding the counsel of God and the princes, Jehoiakim immediately ordered **Baruch** and **Jeremiah** (26) to be arrested. But
God was protecting His servants. The prophet and his scribe
could not be found, for **the Lord hid them** (26). There is no doubt
that Jehoiakim would have killed Jeremiah as he had done Urijah
(26:20-24) had he been able to lay hands on him.

Scholars have long speculated on just what words the scroll
contained. It could not have contained all of Jeremiah's words,
since it was read three times in one day. It is quite certain that
the scroll was made of papyrus, since "any writing material
made of animal skins would have been difficult to cut with a
penknife, and would have made an intolerable stench when
burned."[9]

F. THE BOOK REWRITTEN, 36: 27-32

Sometime later, in his place of hiding, Jeremiah was instructed by the Lord to prepare another scroll, **and write in it
all the former words that were in the first** scroll (27-28). The
prophet did as he was bidden and dictated again the **words of the
book which Jehoiakim . . . had burned in the fire: and there**

---

[9]IB, V (exeg.), 1064.

were added besides unto them many like words (32). This
second writing would contain material from approximately the
first half of Jeremiah's ministry. Since there were still seventeen
to twenty years of activity left to the prophet, much more
material would be added to this.[10]

The rewritten scroll contained stern words for **Jehoiakim**
(29). God took him to task for burning the first scroll, which
had contained wise counsel for the king. **Thou hast burned this
roll, saying, Why hast thou written therein?** (29) God then
declared that Jehoiakim would never have a son **to sit** (30) on
David's throne (Jehoiachin, his son, did reign for three months,
but the Heb. term rendered **sit** implies some degree of permanence).[11] Jeremiah predicted a violent and dishonorable death
for the king (see comments on 22:18).

[10]Kuist, *op. cit.*, p. 110.
[11]Unger's *Bible Dictionary*, p. 561.

These chapters deal with those last sad events that took place just before the fall of Jerusalem. Throughout this time Jeremiah's life was constantly in danger, and he suffered many indignities. In addition, there was the spiritual anguish of seeing his beloved city go down to destruction. Zedekiah was an indecisive monarch who suffered from the pressures of a troubled conscience on the one hand and a group of angry and ill-advised young princes on the other. The final scenes show the Babylonians pressing in for the kill, with the city tottering and falling beneath their onslaught. All the time, one is conscious of the fact that if love could have saved a city, this one need not have died.

A. THE FATAL FLAW IN THE CITY'S DEFENSES, 37:1-2

These verses[1] introduce **Zedekiah** as though the reader had not met him before. This is a little strange, since he appears many times in our story prior to this. Although the arrangement of the Hebrew is a bit odd, the major emphasis in v. 1 is on the fact that **Zedekiah** was **made king** of Judah by Nebuchadnezzar. This means that he was subject to the king of Babylon. According to Jeremiah, the nation's security rested on Zedekiah's faithfulness to these vows (27:11-15). The following pages reveal the tragic consequences of his failure to keep his word. Verse 2 indicts the king still further, **Neither he . . . nor the people . . . did hearken unto the words of the Lord.** This weak and vacillating king had neither kept his vows to men nor had he taken to heart the word of the Lord.

B. HOPES WITH NO FOUNDATION, 37:3-10

The siege had been lifted. Pharaoh-hophra's **army** (5; cf. 44:30) had crossed over into Palestine and was marching toward

---

[1]Some scholars see 1-2 as a transition device of the editor (perhaps Baruch) to notify the reader that he is moving from the reign of Jehoiakim (c. 3) to the reign of Zedekiah. The change is so abrupt that the editor thought the reader should be notified.

Jerusalem. The Babylonians had shifted their forces to meet this new threat. With the enemy gone, people came and went once more through the gates of the city. Hope ran high in Jerusalem. With the help of the Egyptians the Chaldeans might yet be defeated!

The apprehensive king sought confirmation of his hopes. He sent a deputation to Jeremiah, saying, **Pray now unto the Lord our God for us** (3). Jeremiah sensed that Zedekiah's request for prayer was really an inquiry; he wanted to know what the outcome would be. Jeremiah predicted **Pharaoh's army . . . shall return to Egypt** (7). **And the Chaldeans shall come again** (8), **and burn this city with fire** (10). Furthermore, said Jeremiah, if **the Chaldeans** were all **wounded men,** they would still **rise up** and **burn this city.** The prophet here used hyperbole to emphasize his point.

The king and the people had based their hopes on human agencies and not on the living God. The prophet cries, **Deceive not yourselves** (9). The only true foundation for hope is a knowledge of the character of God, and a willingness to bring one's life into line with that knowledge. The men of Judah did not possess this knowledge. "They know not me, saith the Lord" (9:3); "My people know not the judgment [requirements] of the Lord" (8:7).

C. JEREMIAH ARRESTED AND IMPRISONED, 37:11-15

While the siege was lifted, Jeremiah decided to visit his home in Anathoth, a few miles north of Jerusalem, apparently to take care of personal business. Moffatt renders the last part of 12, "to take over some property among his own people." Many scholars conjecture that his proposed trip had to do with the purchase of the field (32:6-12). Jeremiah, however, did not reach Anathoth; he was arrested at **the gate of Benjamin** (north gate) by the sentry and charged with deserting **to the Chaldeans** (13). The accusation had some plausibility, since Jeremiah had openly recommended desertion as a way to save one's life (21:8-10). The prophet vigorously denied that he was deserting. Nonetheless, the incident gave some of **the princes** (14) the chance they had been waiting for (38:1-6). The older officials under Jehoiakim had been friendly to Jeremiah (36:11-19), but these counsellors had been deported in 597 B.C. The young men who had replaced them hated Jeremiah, and had often influenced Zedekiah to disregard the counsel of the prophet. Now in a violent rage they beat Jeremiah **and put him in prison in the house of Jonathan the scribe (15).** This building had been **made** into a **prison** —and a very foul one.

D. A Secret Conference, 37:16-21

Jeremiah **remained** in **the dungeon** (lit. "house of the pit") for **many days (16),** where, according to v. 20, his health was greatly endangered. **The dungeon, and . . . the cabins** is often translated "the dungeon cells." During his stay in prison, the Egyptian army had returned to its own land, and the Babylonians renewed the siege of Jerusalem with greater ferocity than ever. Jeremiah's predictions had come true.

With the siege renewed, **Zedekiah** was in great distress. Jeremiah was **secretly** brought **(17)** to the king's apartments, and **Zedekiah** eagerly inquired of him, **Is there any word from the Lord?** The prophet replied, **There is . . . thou shalt be delivered into the hand of the king of Babylon.**

Taking advantage of his opportunity, the prophet reasoned with the king about the treatment that he had received from the hands of the princes. He reminded the king that his own predictions had come true, while the king's prophets had prophesied nothing but lies. His words imply the question, Who really deserves to be in prison? Jeremiah ended his argument with an earnest plea not to be sent back to the **house of Jonathan the scribe, lest I die there (20).**

Disappointed by Jeremiah's message, but condemned by his own conscience, Zedekiah commanded that the prophet be kept in the **court of the prison (21).** He further specified that he was to receive a daily ration of bread while it lasted. Although he was still a prisoner, the prophet's living conditions were greatly improved.

E. A Cistern Episode, 38:1-13

The princes were apparently highly displeased at Jeremiah's being transferred to the court of the guard, but they could do nothing at the moment, so they bided their time. Everything indicates that they planned the death of the prophet. The final stage of the siege had come. Only days remained. In a situation like this tempers flare easily, and a scapegoat is needed. Jeremiah could very well serve that purpose.

As a prisoner in the court of the guard, the prophet was apparently able to converse with the soldiers, and even the populace of the city (32:9, 12). He was overheard by some of the princes giving forth the word of the Lord to the people, **He that remaineth in this city shall die . . . he that goeth forth to the Chaldeans shall live** (2) **. . . This city . . . the king of Babylon's army . . . shall take it** (3). The expression **his life for a prey** (2) means his life shall be his only share of the spoils. In anger the princes accused Jeremiah of high treason. They demanded of the king, **Let this man be put to death . . . he weakeneth the hands of the men of war** (4).

It is true that Jeremiah had uttered such words on numerous occasions (21:9; 34:2, 22; 37:8). Now pressed beyond measure by his officials, the king cried in exasperated weakness, **He is in your hand: for the king is not he that can do any thing against you** (5). No record reveals so clearly the helplessness and instability of Zedekiah.

From a military point of view the princes were right in their accusation. "The mistake the princes made was due to the fact that they could not see that Jeremiah spoke with an authority above his own person and mind."[2]

The princes seized **Jeremiah** and **cast** (6) him into a nearby **dungeon** (perhaps a cistern, for there were many of these in Palestine) by letting him down with ropes. There was **no water** in the cistern, but plenty of mud, and **Jeremiah sunk in the mire.** The princes plainly hoped that they had seen the last of this troublesome prophet.

But the princes had not reckoned with one of the king's **eunuchs, Ebed-melech,** an **Ethiopian** (7). This man seems to have been a firm believer in the integrity of Jeremiah. Upon learning how the princes had disposed of the prophet, he hastened to **the king** and begged permission to rescue him, lest he **die** of **hunger** (9) and exposure. For once Zedekiah acted decisively. He ordered Ebed-melech to take **thirty men**[3] and remove Jeremiah from the cistern, **before he die** (10).

Ebed-melech proved to be an efficient leader of the rescue operation. He came to the king, **sitting in the gate of Benjamin**

---

[2]Cawley, NBC, p. 630.

[3]Most modern translators have changed this to read "three men." However it seems best to follow the Masoretic text, for perhaps the anger of the princes, and the opposition that might have been encountered, required the thirty men.

(7) in the north wall of the city, holding court there. Taking his men, he stopped only long enough to get some "old rags and worn-out clothes" (11, RSV). At the mouth of the cistern, he let these rags down to Jeremiah by ropes. He instructed the prophet to put the rags under his armpits and to arrange the ropes over them. There would be great strain under the armpits because of the suction of the mud and the depth to which Jeremiah had sunk in the mire. A few minutes later the prophet stood safe and free in **the court of the prison** (13). He remained a prisoner there until the fall of the city (28).

F. A FINAL INTERVIEW, 38:14-28

Shortly after Jeremiah's rescue from the cistern, **Zedekiah** sought another interview with him. The prophet was taken to the **third** entrance of the Temple (precise location unknown) to meet the king. It turned out to be his final interview with that unfortunate monarch. The king was almost frantic and seemed to be desperately hoping for some good word from the Lord as he begged Jeremiah, **Hide nothing from me** (14). At the same time he was unwilling to do the very thing that would have saved himself and his people.

Jeremiah probed the king severely, "If I tell you, will you not be sure to put me to death? And if I give you counsel, you will not listen to me" (15, RSV). Zedekiah then took a vow not to harm Jeremiah himself, and that he would not let the princes harm him. **This soul** (16) means "this life of ours" (Smith-Goodspeed). Convinced by the king's vow that he was sincere, Jeremiah advised him to surrender **to the king of Babylon's princes** (17). He assured Zedekiah that, if he did, it would not only save his own life and that of his family, but it would save Jerusalem as well: **This city shall not be burned with fire.** Jeremiah declared, on the other hand, that if Zedekiah did not surrender, the **city** would be burned and he himself would fall into the hands of the **Chaldeans** (18).

The mental anguish of **the king** was painfully evident as he confided to Jeremiah, **I am afraid of the Jews that are fallen to the Chaldeans, lest they deliver me into their hand, and they mock me** (19). Zedekiah's fear at this point was not altogether unfounded, for this often happened in that ancient day. But Jeremiah assured him that it would not take place in his case (20).

From this incident it is clear that God's terms for our salvation are always hard on flesh and blood. (1) They attack our pride; (2) They crush our self-will; (3) They require real faith.[4]

Jeremiah continued to warn Zedekiah about the price of refusing to surrender. He seems to have seen in a vision or a dream **the women** of the king's household marching out as captives to the Babylonians chanting a lament:

> *Your trusted friends have deceived you*
> *and prevailed against you;*
> *now that your feet are sunk in the mire,*
> *they turn away from you* (22, RSV).

Why this reference to **the mire?** Does mud from the pit still cling to Jeremiah's clothing? Perhaps. The prophet ends his warning by saying to the king, **And thou shalt cause this city to be burned with fire** (23); i.e., the blame for the city's destruction will rest on Zedekiah. Still the king cannot find the strength to follow the prophet's advice.

Zedekiah exacted a promise from Jeremiah, **Let no man know of these words** (24). He instructed Jeremiah what to say if **the princes** should ask about his interview (25-26). His precautions in this case were well-justified, for **all the princes** (27) pounced on Jeremiah when he returned from the king, plying him with questions. He calmly and carefully answered them as he had promised the king, which was the truth as far as it went. Was he attempting to protect himself or the king? How much truth was he obligated to reveal? It is difficult to say. It was certainly not to save his own life that he parried the questions of these wicked men, and gave them only what was appropriate for the moment, for he was not afraid to die. His answer seemed to satisfy the princes, and they bothered him no more, "for the conversation had not been overheard" (27, RSV). Without further harassment he was permitted to remain in the court of the guard **until the day Jerusalem was taken** (28).

G. The City Falls, 39:1-10

Similar accounts of the fall of Jerusalem are found in c. 52; II Kings 25; and II Chron. 36:11-12, and should be read along with this (cf. comments there). Recent archaeological discoveries

[4]*Pulpit Commentary,* XI (II), 138.

indicate quite certainly that the words **Rab-saris** and **Rab-mag** (3), heretofore taken as names of individuals, are Babylonian titles of high-ranking officers, and that **Samgar** may be the corrupt form of another title.[5]

The city of Jerusalem had fallen! The hour that Jeremiah had long predicted had at last come. After eighteen months of siege **the city was broken up** (2), i.e., a breach was made in the walls. **All the princes of the king of Babylon came in, and sat in the middle gate** (3), i.e., took over the administration of the city. The location of the **middle gate** is unknown, but was perhaps a gate in the wall that separated the upper and lower parts of the city.

Seeing that the situation was hopeless, **Zedekiah** slipped **out of the city by night** through **the gate betwixt the two walls** (4; i.e., where the inner and outer walls came together). This gate apparently gave access to the Kidron valley, and looked toward the Jordan River. However, the desperate attempt for freedom was a failure. The Babylonians **overtook** him **in the plains of Jericho** (see map 2) and transported him to the headquarters of **Nebuchadnezzar** at **Riblah**[6] in Syria. Harsh **judgment** (5) was measured out to the rebellious king by Nebuchadnezzar. His **sons** (6) were slain **before his eyes,** and his **nobles** whom he had so cravenly feared were put to death. Last of all, his own eyes were **put out** and he was **bound** (7) with fetters of bronze. Sometime later he was carried **to Babylon,** where he languished in prison until his death.

Apparently **the princes** of Babylon named in 3 were busy with mopping-up operations for several weeks. According to 52:12, **Nebuzar-adan** (9), the chief executioner or field marshal of the king of Babylon, did not come to Jerusalem for a month after the city fell. When he arrived he put the city to the torch.

---

[5]**Rab-saris** has usually been translated as "chief eunuch," and **Rab-mag** as "chief Magi, or soothsayer." These translations are not satisfactory, but a high military or diplomatic official is most certainly meant. (See J. B. Pritchard, *Ancient Near Eastern Texts* (Princeton: Princeton University Press, 1950), pp. 307-8; also, IB, V (exeg.), 1078 ff.; Bright, *op. cit.,* p. 243.

[6]**Riblah in the land of Hamath** (see map 1) was a very strategic military point in the ancient world. It lay at the crossroads of western Asia. From there the highway moved south toward Damascus, Jerusalem, and the gates of Egypt; to the east, the Euphrates and Babylon; to the southwest, Tyre and Sidon; to the north, the central plains of Asia Minor. Pharaohnecoh had quartered here before the battle of Carchemish.

The king's house (8) was burned, and "the house of the people" (lit.) —which may mean the Temple—and the **walls of Jerusalem** were broken down. The people who had already deserted to the Babylonians, and those who were taken in the fall of the city, were prepared for deportation to **Babylon. The poor of the people** (10), who **had nothing,** Nebuzar-adan left in **Judah,** and **gave them** the devastated countryside.

H. Jeremiah Gains His Freedom, 39:11-14

This is one of two accounts which records how Jeremiah gained his freedom. The other is 40:1-6, and seems in some details to contradict the account here. However, amid the destruction of a city and the confusion of deporting hundreds of captives, there may have been two episodes in Jeremiah's release. See comments on 40:1-6.

In this passage, **Nebuzar-adan** is instructed by **Nebuchadnezzar** to **look well** to the needs of Jeremiah, and to do whatever the prophet might **say** to him. It would appear that **Nebuzar-adan** and the princes mentioned in 3 joined in freeing Jeremiah from the court of the guard. How Nebuchadnezzar knew about Jeremiah and his activities is not clear. Kuist has conjectured[7] that, on the advice of Jeremiah, Gedaliah and his family had gone over to the Babylonians early in the siege (it was Gedaliah's father, Ahikam, who had protected Jeremiah after he had preached the Temple Sermon, 26:24), and that it was Gedaliah who informed Nebuchadnezzar of Jeremiah's attitude toward Babylon. Whatever the answer, Jeremiah was taken from the court of the guard and **committed** (14) to the care of **Gedaliah,** who apparently took him to his **home** in Jerusalem, where he remained for the time being.

I. The Rewards of Faith, 39:15-18

This passage concerning the Ethiopian eunuch would fit much better chronologically after 38:13. In its position here, however, it does give a bright ending to a dark chapter.

While still in the **court of the prison** (15) Jeremiah was given a message for **Ebed-melech** (16). When, in the course of his work, the eunuch should appear, Jeremiah was instructed to **go** to him with the following message of hope from **the Lord.**

[7]*Op. cit.,* p. 116.

(a) God had not at all relented in His purpose to punish Jerusalem. (b) The city's punishment would take place before the very eyes of the eunuch. (c) Ebed-melech's life would be endangered, but **I will deliver thee . . . saith the Lord** (17). **Thy life . . . a prey unto thee** (18) means that his life would be given to him as a prize of war. (d) Deliverance is promised from **the men of whom thou art afraid** (17). These would perhaps be the princes who hated him for rescuing Jeremiah, or maybe the Babylonian invaders.

The passage emphasizes the rewards of faith, and stands in strong contrast to the story of Zedekiah. Ebed-melech believed in something, and at great risk acted decisively; Zedekiah also believed that a certain course was right, but did not have the courage or faith to act decisively. One man gained his life, and eternal honor; the other received death, and eternal disgrace.

J. JEREMIAH MAKES HIS CHOICE, 40: 1-6

This further account of how Jeremiah gained his freedom differs in some details from the account in 39:11-14. The main difficulty can be reduced to a single question, Why should Jeremiah be found **in chains** in **Ramah** (1) when he was (seemingly) freed from the court of the guard some time before?

In c. 39, Jeremiah was freed from prison and committed to the care of Gedaliah. That individual took him to his own home in Jerusalem, where he apparently remained for some time. But a final disposition of Jeremiah's case by Babylonian authorities had not yet been made. Gedaliah's administrative duties for the king of Babylon (he may have already been secretly nominated as governor of Judah) would have demanded that he go to Mizpah to attend to matters there. Jeremiah remained at Gedaliah's house in Jerusalem, for "he dwelt among the people" (39:14). Finally when the walls of Jerusalem had been broken down, and all that was valuable had been removed from the homes and buildings, and the city was ready for the torch, the captives of Jerusalem were removed to **Ramah** (the processing point for deportation to Babylon). Since no final decision had been made concerning Jeremiah, the officer in charge of the people in Jerusalem could only send him along with the rest to Ramah.

When **Nebuzar-adan** found him among the captives in **Ramah,** he quickly and apologetically stripped him of his **chains.**

The great captain, having heard of Jeremiah's predictions concerning Jerusalem, used the prophet's words (2-3) to excuse what he had done to Jeremiah's beloved city. Nebuzar-adan then said to Jeremiah, **Behold, I loose thee this day from the chains . . . If it seem good unto thee to come with me into Babylon, come . . . but if it seem ill unto thee . . . all the land is before thee (4). Now while he was not yet gone back (5),** i.e., while he was still in the process of making up his mind about going to Babylon, Nebuzar-adan suggested that, since **Gedaliah** was now **governor of Judah,** perhaps he would like to go there. When Jeremiah made the choice to remain with **Gedaliah (6),** he was given a supply of food and a present and sent on his way. So Jeremiah dwelt **among the people** at **Mizpah** with **Gedaliah** the governor. **Mizpah** was about four and one-half miles northwest of Jerusalem.

Section **IX** *In the Wake of Ruin*

Jeremiah 40:7—44:30

This section traces the fortunes of Jeremiah and the Jews who remained in Judah, from the departure of the captives for Babylon until Jeremiah gave his final prophecy in the land of Egypt. It should have been said of Jeremiah that he lived his remaining years in peace at Mizpah, and died of a ripe old age. But alas! No such good fortune was to come his way. His life was to be filled with turbulence and sorrow to the end.

In Judah, the period that followed the fall of Jerusalem was filled with turmoil and anarchy. The small guerilla bands of Jews, who had fled to the mountain fastnesses during the Babylonian invasion, now gave vent to their own particular brand of venom. Gedaliah was the only man who could have brought some semblance of order out of the chaos and he was cruelly murdered early in the period. From then on, matters became increasingly worse, until the disillusioned and frustrated remnant of Judah[1] sought refuge in the land of Egypt. This happened over the protests of Jeremiah. Even in Egypt conditions continued to grow worse for the fugitive Jews. Through it all Jeremiah did not once step out of character. He was a prophet to the end.

A. THE GOVERNORSHIP OF GEDALIAH, 40:7—41:3

After the fall of Jerusalem, Palestine became a province of the Babylonian empire. Nebuchadnezzar appointed Gedaliah, member of a prominent Jewish family, as governor of Judah. Gedaliah's father, Ahikam, had been an important figure at the court of Josiah and Jehoiakim, and a good friend of Jeremiah (26:24; II Kings 22:12, 14); his grandfather, Shaphan, appears to have been the secretary of Josiah (II Kings 22:3, 10). Gedaliah seems to have been a devoted follower of the Lord, and to have shared Jeremiah's faith and perspective on the national and international situation. It is possible that he was convinced

---

[1]This phrase appears seven times in this section: 40:11; 42:15, 19; 43:5; 44:12, 14, 28; "remnant in Judah," 40:15.

by Jeremiah that Jerusalem was going to be destroyed, and that he went over to the Babylonians with the hope that in the debacle that was to come he might render a service to his people. Whatever the situation, he was a great help in gaining Jeremiah's freedom, and he rendered effective service to the remnant of Judah after the city's fall. It is not certain how long Gedaliah ruled. Some scholars think it was a period of about five years because 52:30 speaks of a final deportation of Jews to Babylon taking place in 582-581 B.C., and that this was punishment for the assassination of Gedaliah.[2] In 41:1 and II Kings 25:25, Gedaliah appears to have ruled for only a few months.

1. *Gedaliah's Attempt at Reorganization* (40:7-12)

The appearance of **the captains of the forces** (7; guerilla chieftains) in **Mizpah** (8; cf. 40:6, comment) was their recognition of Gedaliah's jurisdiction over Judah under Babylonian authority. There was not, as will be seen, a unanimous acceptance of that jurisdiction. The list of names includes **Ishmael, Johanan, Seraiah,** and **Jezaniah.** These men represented widely different sections of Palestine, and constituted a force that Gedaliah would have to reckon with in any attempt to reorganize the broken nation. In this interview Gedaliah sought to quiet their fears and secure their assistance in rebuilding the land. He counselled them, **Dwell in the land, and serve the king of Babylon, and it shall be well with you** (9). He promised faithfully that he would take their interests to heart and would represent them fairly before the Babylonians. He encouraged them to **dwell in your cities** (10), and to gather food for the coming winter from the trees and vineyards.

In addition to the guerilla chieftains and their bands, many fugitives who had fled across the Jordan at the approach of the Babylonians sought to return when they heard that **Gedaliah** was governor of Judah. Many of these had taken refuge in **Edom** and **Moab** and among the children of Ammon (11). They now returned to Judah and likewise **gathered wine and summer fruits very much** (12). All seemed happy to be under the leadership of the new governor.

Jeremiah is not mentioned in these verses, but no doubt he was dwelling quietly among the people at Mizpah, recovering from the effects of his imprisonment.

---

[2] IB, V (exeg.), 1084.

2. *Gedaliah's Life Is Threatened* (40:13-16)

Among the guerilla chieftains appearing before Gedaliah at Mizpah was **Ishmael son of Nethaniah** (14). According to 41:1, Ishmael was of the royal family. He appears here as a vengeful individual who resented Gedaliah serving as governor. It may be that he felt that he himself, being of the royal seed, should have been governor, or he may have felt that Gedaliah was a traitor to Judah in collaborating with the Babylonians. He clearly seems to have been a man of small caliber under the influence of **Baalis the king of the Ammonites.** Apparently **Baalis** was using the ill-tempered **Ishmael** as a tool to gain his own ends. He may have desired to take over either all or part of Judah for himself. At any rate, the two laid plans to murder Gedaliah.

Johanan the son of Kareah (15), another of the chieftains, was aware of the conspiracy of **Ishmael** and Baalis, and informed **Gedaliah** of the plot against his life. Gedaliah refused to believe that Ishmael was planning to harm him. Johanan, however, pressed the matter further by going to Gedaliah **secretly** and asking for permission to slay the wretched **Ishmael** without anyone knowing about it. He insisted, **Wherefore should he slay thee, that all the Jews . . . should be scattered, and the remnant in Judah perish?** (15) These words reveal Johanan's assessment of Gedaliah's importance to the Judean community, and what would happen if he were removed. Gedaliah, a man of noble character, refused to permit Johanan to carry out his proposal, and also refused to believe his life was in danger.

3. *Gedaliah's Assassination* (41:1-3)

Gedaliah apparently felt that his effectiveness as governor of Judah depended upon his being accessible, at all times, to the guerilla chieftains, whose help and influence were so important in unifying the country. But it was while **Ishmael** and **ten of his men** (1) were enjoying the kindness of **Gedaliah** that they suddenly turned on their host and **slew him** with the **sword** (2). **The seventh month** would be our October. Ishmael also killed **all the Jews** (3) who were with Gedaliah, as well as the Chaldean soldiers who were present.

The deed was so dastardly that it was almost impossible to believe that it had happened. No one in the Near East would be suspected of murder who had accepted the invitation to eat at another man's table. The "hospitality code" required that "the

host was bound to protect his guests, and the guests were honor
bound to reciprocate in good faith. Gedaliah was thus unsuspecting and, in effect, defenseless."[3] In postexilic times the Jews
observed the third day of the seventh month as a fast-day in
remembrance of Gedaliah's death.[4]

B. Ishmael's Atrocities, 41:4-18

1. *Massacre of Seventy Pilgrims* (41:4-9)

The murder of **Gedaliah** had been so stealthily executed that
no one outside of Mizpah knew that a crime had been committed.
On the **second day** (4), Ishmael struck again. This time his
victims were eighty pilgrims, bearing **offerings** (5), who were
passing Mizpah on the highway that led to Jerusalem. The
shaved **beards,** torn **clothes,** and **cut** bodies were typical signs of
mourning. The pilgrims were evidently lamenting over the recent destruction of the Temple. **Ishmael . . . went forth . . . to
meet them** (6), simulating their mourning by **weeping** aloud. In
the name of Gedaliah he persuaded them to turn off the highway
into Mizpah. Once inside Mizpah, he murdered seventy of them
in cold blood. **Ten** of the **men** escaped with their lives by offering
to show him where stores of **wheat, barley, oil,** and **honey** (8)
were hidden. The **bodies** (9) of the seventy dead pilgrims were
cast into a large cistern that King Asa had dug three hundred
years before as a part of a defense system for Mizpah against
Baasha king of Israel (I Kings 15:22).

No intelligible motive can be discerned for this crime. On
the surface it appears that Ishmael was cunningly insane.

2. *The Capture of Mizpah* (41:10)

Ishmael further compounded his evil deeds by taking **captive
. . . the people** at Mizpah (10). They were apparently herded
together like cattle, including **the king's daughters**[5] (not necessarily the daughters of Zedekiah, but princesses of the royal
house), and hurried away toward the land of Ammon. Certainly
Ishmael's mentor, the king of the **Ammonites,** should have been
satisfied with the results of this raid. As an effect of this crime,

[3]Bright, *op. cit.,* p. 254.

[4]Keil and Delitzsch, *op. cit.,* p. 132.

[5]The Chaldeans apparently left some members of the royal house in
Palestine; Peake, *op. cit.,* p. 189.

the political and economic life of Judah was to be in a state of disruption for many years to come.

3. *Ishmael's Defeat* (41:11-18)

When Ishmael's dastardly deeds became known, **Johanan the son of Kareah** (11) and the other chieftains took their warriors and set out to avenge Gedaliah's death and to recover the people of Mizpah. They found Ishmael **by the great waters of Gibeon** (12).[6] When the captives **from Mizpah** saw the rescue party, they broke rank and joined **Johanan** and his army (14). However, in the skirmish that took place, **Ishmael** and **eight** of his **men** made their escape to the land of **the Ammonites** (15).

Even though they had been successful in rescuing the people of Mizpah, Johanan and the chieftains were at a loss to know what to do next. The Babylonians could be expected to avenge the death of Gedaliah, and they would not be careful as to whom they punished. Therefore, fearful of the Chaldeans, the group moved quickly southward. They finally camped at the **habitation** (inn or sheepfold) **of Chimham** (17), near **Bethlehem**, intending to go to **Egypt**.

C. The Flight to Egypt, 42:1—43:7

It is while the people are camped near Bethlehem that Jeremiah returns to the narrative. The prophet has not been mentioned since he went to Mizpah to dwell among the people there (40:6). Apparently he and Baruch were living in Mizpah during the incidents related in 40:7—41:18. Also, the two must have been among the captives carried away by Ishmael. Rescued with the other captives by Johanan and his army, they continued with the group on their journey. The only other alternative is that they were away from Mizpah during Ishmael's raid and joined the group later by their own choice.

1. *Jeremiah's Counsel Sought* (42:1-6)

Both the leaders and the people were uncertain as to what course they should pursue. They would have preferred to remain in Judah, but they greatly feared Babylonian reprisals for the death of Gedaliah, and they were sick of killings and blood-

---

[6]Archeologists have uncovered the remnant of an excellent water system here. It is the modern Ej Jib.

shed (cf. 14). It appeared that the safest thing to do was to flee to Egypt. It was not likely Nebuchadnezzar would pursue them there. To human reason this seemed to be the right course, yet underneath there seems to have been an inner prompting that they should remain in Judah.

The leaders of the group, **Johanan, Jezaniah,**[7] and the other chieftains, accompanied by **all the people** (1), approached Jeremiah and begged him to pray to the **Lord** (2) for them. They promised him with an exaggerated humility that they would do whatever the Lord said. (Were they remembering how the inhabitants of Jerusalem had rejected God's message through Jeremiah, yet how his predictions had come true?) Jeremiah replied, **I have heard you . . . I will pray unto the Lord . . . according to your words** (4), i.e., on the basis of their promise. Again they pledged to follow the Lord, going so far as to call upon Him to **witness** (5) their vow: **Whether it be good, or whether it be evil, we will obey the voice of the Lord** (6).

2. *Jeremiah's Response* (42:7-22)

Ten days went by before God made His will known. Jeremiah refused to speak until he was certain that the message was from God. It is likely that both leaders and people became impatient before the ten days were up, and were greatly disgusted with the prophet. It is characteristic of unbelief always to be in a hurry.

When the message was clear to the prophet's mind, Jeremiah called for the entire encampment to hear God's word. It is interesting to note that God took just as much pains to make His will clear to this small group as He did with the nation of Judah and the city of Jerusalem. His answer to the inquiry of the company can best be summarized under the following points.

(1) It was God's will that the people remain in Judah, **If ye will still abide in this land, then will I build you, and not pull you down** (10). This, of course, would require faith in Him. To remain would be contrary to human reason, for the only sensible thing would be to put themselves under the protection of Pharaoh.

---

[7]"Jezaniah is here called the son of Hoshaiah; in 40:8 he is called the son of the Maachathite; in 43:2 Azariah is named as the son of Hoshaiah. There must have either been two Jezaniahs and two Hoshaiahs, or there is an error in the text" (*Lange's Commentary*, p. 342).

(2) God's attitude toward them was one of goodwill, **I repent me of the evil that I have done unto you.** "To the modern
reader this suggests that Yahweh regrets what He has done,
and if He were again placed in the same situation would act
differently . . . (but not so) . . . It is no confession of mistake or
remorse for the evil He has inflicted. But now His righteous
judgment has been executed, His attitude toward His people
is changed, and for the future He is prepared to build up those
whom His justice has forced Him to pull down."[8] God deals
with men on a moral basis, not on a legalistic one; thus He is
able to change His attitude when certain conditions are met
(cf. comments on 18:7-12). Bright renders this part of the verse
aptly, "For I regard the hurt that I have inflicted upon you as
sufficient."[9]

(3) Their fears concerning the king of Babylon were ground-
less, **Be not afraid of the king of Babylon . . . I am with you to
save you . . . to deliver you** (11). Many troubles that seem
overwhelming never come.

(4) The thing to avoid was an evil heart of unbelief, **But if
ye say, We will not dwell in this land . . . we will go into . . .
Egypt** (13-14). Jeremiah anticipates what their reply will be,
and undercuts all their objections. He continues, **If ye say** (13),
**In Egypt we shall see no war, nor hear the sound of the
trumpet, nor have hunger of bread** (14), then **the sword, which
ye feared, shall overtake you there in the land of Egypt** (16).
If ye wholly set your faces (15), i.e., if you are determined. This
little group of Jews was confronted with the age-old dilemma of
faith versus unbelief. It still faces Jews and Christians every day.

(5) It is the mistake of the centuries to suppose that God
has changed His character, or that the moral law has been abro-
gated. **Mine anger . . . shall . . . be poured forth upon you, when
ye . . . enter into Egypt** (18). "You shall become an object of
execration and horror; accursed and derided" (18; Moffatt).

(6) They were in danger of making God a liar. They sent
Jeremiah to the Lord, solemnly vowing to do all that the Lord
would say. Yet when that word came with great clarity, they
refused to accept it as God's word (20-21).

(7) Their choice determined the outcome. If they chose to
remain in Judah, there would be help and hope for the future;

---

[8]Peake, *op. cit.,* p. 193.   [9]*Op. cit.,* p. 251.

if they insisted on going to Egypt, they would **die by the sword, by the famine, and by the pestilence** (22). Jeremiah already knew by some intuition of the mind what their decision would be.

3. *Jeremiah Defied by the People* (43:1-3)

The people heard the prophet through his address without interruption, but by the time he had finished, "the light had gone out of the meeting." It was evident that both the leaders and the people were determined not to obey God. It was the leaders who confronted Jeremiah: **Then spake . . . all the proud** (insolent) **men** (2)—and their words seemed to come out through clenched teeth—"You are telling a lie. The Lord . . . did not send you to say, 'Do not go to Egypt' " (RSV). Their decision was made; unbelief had hardened into apostasy.

Their search for a scapegoat was ludicrous, but nevertheless they try: **Baruch the son of Neriah setteth thee on against us . . . to deliver us into the hand of the Chaldeans** (3). When small men make up their minds, all the pearls of wisdom cannot change them. There is no indication that Jeremiah tried.

Baruch was still with Jeremiah. All the trouble that both had endured had not severed their relationship. Apparently Baruch survived the destruction of Jerusalem as well as the nefarious schemes of Ishmael. It may be that this section of the book is graphic and clear because the reader is studying the account of an eyewitness.[10]

4. *On to Egypt* (43:4-7)

Once their minds were made up not to obey the voice of God, Johanan and the people made preparations for moving into Egypt. All the **men, and women, and children, and the king's daughters** (6) were organized for the trek southward. **Jeremiah** and **Baruch** are both listed in the number that went to Egypt. It is inconceivable that Jeremiah went willingly, since it was contrary to his conception of the will of God. No doubt the angry leaders forced him and Baruch to go, in order that they might share the fate of the group, if what Jeremiah had predicted came to pass.

They ended their flight at **Tahpanhes** (7), a fortress city inside the Egyptian border. This city, now known as Daphne, is

---

[10]Kuist, *op. cit.*, p. 120.

located in the northeastern part of the Nile delta, on the highway
that leads from Egypt to Palestine (see map 3).

D. JEREMIAH IN EGYPT, 43:8—44:30

Jeremiah's prophetic powers did not desert him in Egypt.
In his two final discourses recorded in this section there is the
same intensity, the same directness, that had characterized his
preaching all through the forty years of his ministry.

1. *Nebuchadnezzar's Coming Predicted* (43:8-13)

Jeremiah's first recorded discourse in Egypt was delivered
shortly after the arrival of the Jews in **Tahpanhes** (8). Here, as
on so many occasions, Jeremiah dramatized his message. He took
some large **stones** (9) and buried them "in mortar in the brickwork" (ASV) in front of **Pharaoh's house in Tahpanhes.** This
was not his royal palace, for that was in another city, but
Pharaoh's official residence when visiting Tahpanhes. Just how
and when this was done is not known. Some scholars think it was
done at night, but at least the leaders of the Jewish colony were
present to get the message. After burying the stones in the
brickwork, Jeremiah predicted that Nebuchadnezzar would come
to Egypt and **set his throne upon these stones** (10). For **my
servant** see comment on 25:9. Furthermore, Jeremiah continued, the king of Babylon would **smite the land of Egypt** (11),
and **burn** (12) the temples, and carry the images of **the gods**
away.[11] In that day, pestilence, captivity, and the sword would
be visited upon those individuals for whom they were appointed.
All this, Nebuchadnezzar would perform with no more trouble
than it takes for **a shepherd** to put on his mantle.

The message for the Jewish colony at Tahpanhes was obvious. (1) The very thing that they feared would overtake them.
They had fled to Egypt to escape Nebuchadnezzar's reprisals,
but he would come and punish them there. (2) In fleeing to
Egypt they had sought the help of man, rather than the help of
God. (3) Dependence on any earthly power is utterly in vain.
(4) Real security is found alone in obeying and serving God.

A fragmentary inscription recovered from Nebuchadnezzar's archives speaks of his punishing Egypt in the thirty-seventh

---

[11]**Images of Beth-shemesh** (13) would be "the obelisks of Beth-shemesh"—House of the Sun—a famous temple dedicated to the sun, with a row
of obelisks in front of it (Berk., fn.).

year of his reign, about 568 B.C.[12] Although he did not conquer the whole land, he overran most of it, and thus prevented Egypt from meddling in the affairs of Asia for many years. Josephus, however, tells of an invasion of Egypt by Nebuchadnezzar five years after the fall of Jerusalem in which he killed the king of Egypt, and carried away the Jews of Egypt to Babylonia.[13] It is possible that Nebuchadnezzar invaded Egypt twice.

2. A Prophet to the End (44:1-30)

This is Jeremiah's final discourse. The last glimpse the reader has of the old prophet, he is proclaiming the word of God. He was a prophet to the end.

a. The Egyptian Jews denounced (44:1-14). Jeremiah's last recorded sermon was directed toward **all the Jews** in **Egypt.** The record mentions the various communities (see map 3) where Jews were dwelling—**Migdol** (site unknown, but apparently in northeastern Egypt, not far from **Tahpanhes**), **Noph** (Memphis), **and in the country of Pathros** (Upper Egypt). It is impossible to ascertain the date when this incident took place, but it was apparently several years later than the previous discourse. The occasion seems to have been a religious festival in which "a great multitude" **(15)** of Jews had burned incense to the Queen of Heaven (the goddess of the fertility cult known as the "Great Mother"; see comments on 7:16-20). Verse 15 sounds as though the festival took place in "Pathros" (Upper Egypt), but again, certainty is impossible. It appears that Jeremiah's righteous soul was desperately tried by what his eyes beheld of the utter corruption of his people.

As usual, Jeremiah made his first appeal to history. He reminded the Jews of the recent destruction of **Jerusalem** and **the cities of Judah (2).** He insisted that the reason these cities stood empty and desolate was that the people served **other gods (3),** the very thing the Jews were doing in Egypt even then. **Rising early (4),** i.e., "persistently," God had sent His **prophets,** saying, **Oh, do not this abominable thing that I hate.** But the people did not give heed, they did not **turn (5).** This was why their cities were **wasted and desolate, as at this day (6).**

Jeremiah makes his application, **Wherefore commit ye this**

---

[12]Pritchard, *op. cit.*, p. 308; IB, V (exeg.), 1095; Kuist, *op. cit.*, p. 121.
[13]*Antiquities* X. 9.7.

great evil against your souls? (7) **Have ye forgotten** so quickly the sins of **your fathers . . . the kings of Judah, and . . . their wives . . . your own wickedness, and . . . of your wives . . . in the streets of Jerusalem?** (9) The prophet's mention of the **wives** of **the kings** and the **wives** of the men present was like striking the audience with a whiplash. Resentment flared among the women of Judah because they had been aggressors in the worship of the Queen of Heaven.

Ignoring the reaction of the audience, Jeremiah pronounced God's sentence against the Jews in Egypt: **Behold, I will set my face against you for evil** (11). **The remnant of Judah** living in Egypt **shall die,** but their memory will live on in the minds of men as **an astonishment, and a curse, and a reproach** (12). Just as **Jerusalem** had been **punished . . . by the sword, by the famine, and by the pestilence** (13), so God will punish the Jews who worship other gods in Egypt. No one will escape, and none shall ever **return to Judah** "except some fugitives" (14, RSV).

b. The reply of the Jews (44:15-19). Jeremiah's words touched a sensitive nerve. The women were aroused, and the men were angered by having to defend their wives as well as themselves. In a defiant manner they replied to the aged prophet, **As for the word that thou hast spoken unto us in the name of the Lord, we will not hearken unto thee** (16). With stinging words they defended their idolatrous practices. They admitted that they had made vows to **the queen of heaven** (17), but so had their **fathers,** their **kings,** and their **princes** before them. Furthermore, in those former days things had gone **well** with the nation. But since they had **left off** burning **incense** (18) to the goddess, they had lacked everything, and one disaster after another had struck them. The women added a word in their own defense by saying: "Yes . . . and had we not the consent of our husbands when we sacrificed to the Queen of heaven and poured libations in her honour and made cakes in the shape of her?" (19, Moffatt)

The Jews of Egypt were harking back to the reign of Manasseh and the early years of Josiah. Much idolatry had been practiced then and nothing upsetting had occurred. But the reform under Josiah had no sooner commenced than one calamity after another had struck the nation. These difficulties did not end until Jerusalem was destroyed. They claimed that it was only when they had started trying to serve the Lord *exclusively,* and had neglected the other gods, that distress and trouble came upon them. Jeremiah was reading history one way and they were reading it another.

c. *Jeremiah's final word* (44:20-30). Jeremiah takes extra pains to include the women (20, 24-25) in his final reply to the people. Although broken in health and in heart, the old prophet's last address is very much like his first. His final trumpet blast gives forth no uncertain sound. He insists that the people have misread the character of God; they have things precisely in reverse. Because God did not punish them immediately in the days of Manasseh for their idolatrous practices, it did not mean that He had not taken note nor remembered (21). It merely meant that in His long-suffering He had borne with them until He **could no longer bear . . . the evil** of their **doings** (22). The truth is as simple as this: **Ye have sinned against the Lord . . . therefore this evil is happened unto you** (23).

A touch of irony now creeps into the prophet's voice; since they have made these very important vows, most assuredly they must perform them! **Spoken with your mouths, and fulfilled with your hand** (25); i.e., "You . . . have pledged your word and have fulfilled it in actual deed" (Smith-Goodspeed; cf. I Kings 8:15, 24). Then the prophet becomes deadly serious. They must also know that in carrying out those vows they are making their choice of gods! And since they have chosen the Queen of Heaven, the living God will see to it that they will perform no more religious observance in His **name** (26). They are now guilty of total apostasy. Henceforth He will be "wakeful" over them **for evil, and not for good,** to make an **end of them** (27). All the Jews who had fled to Egypt will be destroyed. However, a **remnant** will escape; but all will **know whose word shall stand, mine, or theirs** (28).

So that there can be no mistake, God will further confirm His word in a singular circumstance. The man to whom **the remnant of Judah** had fled for help—the one whom they sought instead of God—**Pharaoh-hophra** (30), will **fall into the hand of his enemies** just as **Zedekiah** of Jerusalem fell into the hands of the **king of Babylon.** Hophra was delivered into the hands of the people of Egypt by Amasis and was strangled to death.[14]

[14]See Clarke, *op. cit.,* IV, 367; Peake, *op. cit.,* p. 208; Binns, *op. cit.,* p. 314.

Some have found a problem with v. 26 because a great Jewish colony was existing in Egypt some two hundred years later. But the passage here was addressed to the **remnant of Judah,** and has nothing to do with Jews who may have migrated to Egypt years later.[15]

[15]See Keil and Delitzsch, *op. cit.,* pp. 168 ff.

Section X   God's Message to Baruch

Jeremiah 45:1-5

From a chronological standpoint this excerpt from the life of Baruch, Jeremiah's scribe, would have fitted much better after 36:8. If it had been placed there, however, it would have interrupted the carefully arranged order of that passage as it stands today. Its present position is to be preferred. Some scholars insist that it was not written until long after the event had taken place. While this is possible, "the precise language" of v. 1 militates against this view.[1]

As the chapter opens the reader is suddenly shifted back to **the fourth year of Jehoiakim,** and the writing of Jeremiah's prophecies by **Baruch the son of Neriah** (1). By the time Baruch had finished writing Jeremiah's words, he was in great distress of mind. The inference is that there was some relationship between his own troubles and what he had written. His affliction of mind became very great and very real. In the midst of his pain, the Lord gave Jeremiah a message for him. God reminded Baruch of his words of anguish, **Woe is me now! for the Lord hath added grief to my sorrow; I fainted in my sighing, and I find no rest** (3).

The reasons for Baruch's intense sorrow are not given. It may be that through Jeremiah's prophecies he had gotten an insight into the corrupt spiritual condition of the nation, and the horrifying sight brought sorrow to his soul. Then when he realized that his own future, so hopefully planned, was to be swept away, along with the city, the Temple, and all the familiar things that he had known, his grief became almost unbearable.

In the midst of his sorrow, God pointed out to Baruch His own great sadness. **That which I have built will I break down, and that which I have planted I will pluck up** (4). "It was a time of suffering for God himself for he must destroy His own creation."[2] The Lord seems to chide Baruch by saying, **And seekest thou great things for thyself? seek them not** (5). In

[1]Kuist, op. cit., p. 123.
[2]Pulpit Commentary, XI, 201.

other words, God was saying, And you are upset over your own small affairs! **Behold, I will bring evil upon all flesh.** Thus God informed the scribe that His purpose must be carried out regardless of whom it affects. However, the Lord consoles Baruch by promising him that his **life** will be given to him as **a prey,** i.e., as a prize of war.

All indications point toward the fact that out of this experience Baruch came to "a moment of truth" concerning himself and God. Something of deep spiritual significance happened. After this Baruch will continue to have human frailties, but the trend of his life will be forever in a new direction.

As these verses are analyzed, several things are worth noting. (1) The passage recapitulates the central theme of Jeremiah's own message—purgation, followed by new life on a higher level— *root out, pull down, destroy, build, plant* (1:10). The old pattern of life must go, the old mold must be broken; then life can be formed anew on a different basis. (2) Baruch is a truly human individual with troubles like everyone else. (3) God's ways of executing His plans and purposes distressed his finite mind. (4) He experienced a "shattering process" that led him through the valley of personal despair to a surrender of self. (5) Self-renunciation led to a reorganization of life around a new center, with new perspectives. (6) The passage speaks of a continuing obedience to God's spoken word. (7) Other references to Baruch in the book indicate that he accepted the challenge of God. "Whatever his feelings, and regardless of his personal interests, he stayed with Jeremiah to the end."[3]

---

[3]Bright, *op. cit.,* p. 186.

According to 1:5, Jeremiah was ordained a prophet to the nations. His first duty was to "the covenant people," but the prophet's sense of obligation to the other nations is evident in the book. This was quite characteristic of a Hebrew prophet and especially those which influenced the destinies of the house of Jacob (cf. Amos 1:3—2:3; Isaiah 13—23; Ezekiel 25—32; etc.).

In the Septuagint the nine oracles of this section are inserted after 25:13, where, in some respects, they fit better than they do here. However, when inserted there, they disrupt the sequence of thought. Consequently their present position is to be preferred (cf. comments on c. 25). The fact that these oracles have been moved about as a self-contained block of material lends some weight to the view that, at one time, they were a separate collection of Jeremiah's writings.

Jeremiah believed that it was the Lord who had created the world and man. It was the Lord who controlled the destinies of nations and guided the affairs of earth. Therefore Jehovah was the Lord of all nations.

A. Preface, 46:1

Verse 1 serves as a heading for all the oracles in this section. It also identifies the material as **the word of the Lord** to the Gentile nations of that day, and Jeremiah is identified as God's agent in its delivery. The claim of divine authority rests on this material in the same fashion as on the other portions of the book.[1]

B. Oracle Against Egypt, 46:2-28

1. Egypt and God at Carchemish (46:2-12)

Verse 2 informs the reader that this oracle is about Pharaoh-necho's defeat at the battle of Carchemish, at the hands of Nebuchadnezzar, and dates it in **the fourth year of Jehoiakim . . . king of Judah,** or about 605 B.C. Keenly aware of interna-

---

[1]Kuist, *op. cit.,* p. 125.

tional politics, Jeremiah evidently sensed the importance of this battle in the history of the Near East. It proved to be one of the most decisive conflicts of ancient times. Jeremiah, of course, was concerned with its import for the purpose and plans of God, and saw it as a **day of the Lord** (10). Here two of the world's great powers battled for the mastery, but it was God who made the difference in the outcome.

The oracle is in poetic form and is made up of two strophes comprising vv. 3-6 and 7-12. In the first strophe one views the scene on the eve of the battle and feels the thrill of excitement and expectancy that vibrates through the Egyptian camp. **Order ye buckler and shield, and draw near to battle** (3). **Harness the horses . . . put on the brigandines** (4; breastplates or armor). One can almost feel the rush of men and horses as the two armies collide. Then the scene changes to horror and dismay as the panic-stricken Egyptians give way. **Their mighty ones are beaten down** (5) and there is none to help. There is terror on every side. They do not even look back, so great is their desire to flee. But they are not swift enough; they **stumble, and fall** (6) in the **north** country **by the . . . Euphrates.**

In the second strophe the same event is pictured but from a different angle. The Egyptian army under Pharaoh-necho is likened to the surging Nile in **flood** stage (8), roaring, moving, leaping, covering the whole earth as it presses on toward Carchemish. At last the foe is sighted. There is the shout of battle, **Come up, ye horses; and rage, ye chariots** (9). Egypt's mercenary soldiers are seen advancing to the fray, **Ethiopians, Libyans,** and **Lydians,**[2] wielding their weapons of war. But again consternation reigns in the ranks of the Egyptians. This time, however, it is God who directs affairs. It is His **day,** and He avenges himself on **his adversaries** (10). **The Lord . . . of hosts hath a sacrifice . . . by the river Euphrates** and the Egyptians are the sacrificial victims. It is a sad day for Pharaoh-necho. The retreating **cry** of this proud nation **filled the land** (12), and her **shame** is evident to all **nations.** Even though she should **go up** to **Gilead** (11) for healing "balm" (8:22), her wound is incurable. Mighty Egypt has fallen. She has lost her bid to dominate the nations of the

---

[2]**Libyans** and **Lydians** were people from ancient Put and Lud. Put is probably "Punt," a people along the east coast of Africa near Egypt. Lud was probably a Libyan people west of Egypt (Ludim or Lubim). See Peake, *op. cit.,* II, 217; Bright, *op. cit.,* p. 306.

world. But God, not Nebuchadnezzar, is the effective cause of
her downfall.

2. The Aftermath of Carchemish (46:13-26)

This poem has a heading of its own (13), and was written
sometime after the preceding one. In this oracle Jeremiah evalu-
ates the military position of Egypt after the battle of Carchemish.
The utter rout of the Egyptian armies "has left Egypt open to
later invasion."[3] Jeremiah's opening cry is to alert the border
towns (see map 3), **Migdol . . . Noph . . . Tahpanhes** (14), to
their danger. At the same time Jeremiah indicates that the men
of these cities stand hopeless before the foe. It is possible that
Nebuchadnezzar had already appeared (605-604 B.C.) on the
Philistine plain, threatening "the gates of Egypt."

Verse 15 is better read as in ASV, "Why are thy strong
ones[4] swept away [lit., prostrated]? they stood not, because
Jehovah did drive them" [lit., thrust them down]. If the singular, "strong one," is used, the reference could be to Pharaoh-
necho; and v. 17 can be read to support this view. God has
thrust Pharaoh down, and Egypt's chance for conquest is a thing
of the past. Even Pharaoh's own people call him "Big noise—who
missed his chance,"[5] i.e., the one who let his hour of opportunity
go by. Verse 16 is obscure, but probably contains the words of
the mercenary soldiers of Pharaoh, who, beaten by the foe, say
to each other, **Let us go again to our own people.**

Jeremiah now predicts the sure coming of a conqueror, who
will loom as high above the king of Egypt as **Tabor** and **Carmel**
(18) tower above the hills of Palestine. It is evident from v. 26
that he is referring to Nebuchadnezzar. His coming is so certain
that the inhabitants of Egypt are instructed to prepare for exile,
for their capital city, **Noph** (Memphis), will be laid waste (19).

The plight of Egypt is further emphasized by the use of
several figures. She is compared to a beautiful **heifer** (20),

---

[3]Cawley, NBC, p. 634.

[4]In Hebrew all the words are singular except "strong ones" (ASV,
text; valiant men, KJV). The LXX and the Vulgate plus sixty-five other
MSS. read it in singular.

[5]This is John Bright's paraphrase (*op. cit.*, p. 303). ASV renders it,
"They cried there, Pharaoh king of Egypt is but a noise; he hath let the
appointed time pass by."

feeding in luxuriant grass, who suddenly finds herself pained and fleeing from the sting of a tiny gadfly (the meaning of the Heb. term translated **destruction**) from the **north**. Another figure likens her **hired men** (mercenary soldiers) to fat young bulls, untrained and clumsy, who have no taste for real war, so they melt away before the enemy (21). Verses 22 and 23 are obscure, but they seem to say that Egypt's fleeing armies are like hissing serpents that slither away before the woodsmen. They can only emit a hiss of defiance as they wriggle back to their holes.

On the other hand, the hosts of Babylon will demolish the cities of Egypt like an army of woodcutters clearing a **forest** (23). In fact, the foe from the **north** (24) will come like an army of **grasshoppers** (23), too numerous to count. Even Upper Egypt with her famous capital of **No** (25; Thebes) will fall into the hands of Nebuchadnezzar (26) along with Pharaoh, and everyone who depended on the wisdom of that unfortunate monarch.

3. *The Salvation of Israel* (46:27-28)

These verses must be seen in relation to the above oracles against Egypt. The prophet could not think of the defeat of Egypt without reflecting on the salvation of **Israel** (27). Although he speaks of punishment, it will be in a **measure** (28) just and fair. Israel's salvation is so certain of accomplishment that the prophet speaks of it as though it had already happened. These verses are also found in 30:10-11, where they fit the context better than they do here. See comments there.

C. ORACLES AGAINST THE PHILISTINES, 47:1-7

God warned the Philistines through Jeremiah that a terrible scourge from the **north** (2) was bearing down upon them. According to v. 1 the oracle was given to Jeremiah **before . . . Pharaoh smote Gaza**. Just which **Pharaoh** is meant is uncertain, and the particular occasion when **Gaza** was captured is not clear. Scholars have speculated[6] but have found no definite solution. The scourge from the north probably referred to the coming of Nebuchadnezzar and the armies of Babylon after the battle of Carchemish. The Babylonian Chronicle[7] indicates that Neb-

---

[6]For fuller treatment see Keil and Delitzsch, *op. cit.*, pp. 197 ff.

[7]D. J. Wiseman, *Chronicles of Chaldean Kings* (London: British Museum, 1956).

uchadnezzar moved southward in pursuit of the fleeing Egyptians in 605-604 B.C. taking Philistine cities along the route (see map 2). **Ashkelon** (5) is specifically mentioned as having been taken and ravaged.

Jeremiah's vision includes several figures of speech. (*a*) **Waters** (2) are seen rising **out of the north,** ever increasing until they become an **overflowing** torrent, covering the whole **land. Men . . . cry** aloud and **all the inhabitants** wail because of the distress that has come upon them. (*b*) This **overflowing flood** can be discerned as a military host. There will be the sound of stamping **hoofs, rushing . . . chariots,** and **rumbling . . . wheels** (3). (*c*) Worn-out from fighting against such overwhelming odds, **the fathers** will not have strength to give thought to saving **their** own **children.** (*d*) The destruction will be so great that even **Tyre and Sidon** (4) will be affected. This seems rather strange, since Tyre and Sidon are Phoenician cities (see map 2), but apparently the two people were allies at this period of history. (*e*) The magnitude of the distress is revealed by the mention of **baldness** in **Gaza** (5) and "the cutting of flesh" in **Ashkelon.** Both were signs of deep mourning. (*f*) A cry for mercy is addressed to the **sword of the Lord** (6) by the people of Philistia. **How long will it be ere thou be quiet? put up thyself into thy scabbard.** Men often seek for God to sheath His sword so they can go on unchecked in their evil ways. (*g*) The prophet answers their question with a query of his own, **How can it be quiet, seeing the Lord hath given it a charge?** (7) The answer is that it cannot be sheathed until its work is done, for the **sword of the Lord** is the righteousness of God. Sin cannot go unpunished. Justice must be done. Right must be established. All nations, not only Israel, must learn to obey the moral law of God. Not only must the Egyptians drink of the wine cup of God's wrath, but the Philistines find the cup pressed to their lips also (25:15-20). **Caphtor** (4) is referred to in Amos 9:7 as the homeland of the Philistines. It probably means the island of Crete (Ezek. 25:15-16).

D. Oracle Against Moab, 48:1-47

Among the oracles found in cc. 46—49, this prophecy is unique because of its length, its large number of place names, and its similarities to other portions of scripture.[8] Because of its

---

[8]IB, V (exeg.), 1112.

similarities to portions of Isaiah,[9] some scholars have insisted that it does not belong to Jeremiah.[10] That it has parallels to other scriptures cannot be denied. However, it would appear that, in this instance, Jeremiah gathered up into a new whole the utterances concerning Moab made by earlier prophets as far back as Balaam. He reaffirms these predictions in his own fashion, adding to them ideas of his own. This should not be thought strange, since he was well acquainted with Hebrew history, and was familiar with the utterances of his predecessors in the prophetic office. It is probable that Isaiah's prophecies concerning Moab were especially strong in his mind at the moment and that they fitted his mood and cast of thought. He used them because they reflected his own understanding of what was to take place in the Moabite nation.

1. The Consequences of Misplaced Trust (48:1-10)

The prophecy starts out with a description of the destruction that is coming upon Moab (see map 2) from the God of Israel. The land will be invaded by an unnamed foe whom the Lord will send. The cities will be broken down, **Nebo** (not the mountain), **Kiriathaim, Misgab** (1), and their inhabitants will flee in con‐ sternation, **weeping** (5) as they go along. **The going up of Luhith** and **the going down of Horonaim** would be the roads ascending to and descending from these cities. Verse 6 has been translated as a warning: "Flee! Save yourselves! Be like a wild ass in the desert!" (RSV) Even the god **Chemosh** (7) will be carried **into captivity** along with the **priests** who served him. **No city shall escape: the valley also shall perish, and the plain shall be destroyed** (8). The destruction will be so complete that if Moab were to escape she would need the **wings** of a bird (9). All of this will happen **because thou hast trusted in thy works**[11] **and in thy treasures** (7) instead of trusting in the Lord. Further‐ more, the wickedness of Moab is so great that a curse is pro‐

---

[9]Vv. 29-34 are parallel to parts of Isaiah 15—16; vv. 43-44 are parallel to Isa. 24:17-18; 45-46 are parallel to Num. 21:28-29; 24:17. Cf. BBC comments on these passages.

[10]For more detailed opinions, see Keil and Delitzsch, *op. cit.*, p. 129; IB, V (exeg.), 1112; Cawley, NBC, p. 635.

[11]While RSV translators and John Bright in the Anchor Bible go to "strongholds" for the word **works** in v. 7, it does not change the meaning. The Moabites still were guilty of putting their trust in the wrong place.

nounced upon any invader who is negligent in doing the Lord's work of destruction, or who keeps **back his sword from blood** (10).

2. The Calamity of Undisciplined Living (48:11-17)

Moab was famous for its vineyards, and the prophet seems to have had wine and the wine jar in mind as he prophesied. The lot of the people of Moab had been an easy one; **he hath not been emptied from vessel to vessel** (11). The country, at times, had been invaded and put under tribute, but their cities had not been demolished, nor had the people **gone into captivity.** So Moab had settled down to a life of undisciplined ease. The prophet compared her to wine **settled on his lees.** Inferior wine when it sits too long undisturbed tends to take on the **taste** and **scent** of **the lees** (dregs) and thus develops a bitter taste. This was the case with Moab. Indolence and lack of hardship had brought a great deterioration in the moral fabric of the nation.

The prophet sees that this easy life is going to be disturbed. Moab's day of judgment is coming, "I shall send to him tilters who will tilt him, and empty his vessels, and break his jars in pieces" (12, RSV). Moab will collapse when a real emergency arises. When this hour arrives, Moab will **be ashamed of Chemosh,** his god, just **as the house of Israel was ashamed of Beth-el** (13; i.e., the golden calf at Bethel). Both were mere idols made by the hands of men, and could not help their people. Israel had already gone into captivity, and Moab was soon to experience the same fate. The Moabites had said of themselves, **We are mighty and strong men for the war** (14), but alas, undisciplined living had taken its toll, and **Moab is spoiled** (15); his choice **young men** have **gone down** in terrible defeat. His friends are encouraged to lament for him, for the mighty scepter —the **staff** of his sovereignty is broken (17).

3. Disaster Strikes (48:18-28)

The spoiler of Moab (18) has done his deadly work. The nation's inhabitants are toppled from their place of **glory** and **sit in** ignominy and shame. Moab's mightiest fortresses are destroyed, and when the fleeing inhabitants are asked by the people **of Aroer** (19) what has happened, they cry, **Moab is confounded; for it is broken down** (20). The people are called upon to lament, **howl and cry,** for city after city has been taken until not one remains.[12] Consequently his **horn** (the symbol of power) is cut off and his **arm** (symbol of authority) is **broken** (25).[13] All this has happened because Moab has **magnified himself against the Lord** (26). Moab's arrogant attitude toward Israel has come home to him. He who skipped **for joy** (27) at Israel's fate has himself become a **derision.** His inhabitants are urged to flee like a mourning **dove** to the rocks and holes in the mountains (28), for utter catastrophe has struck the nation!

4. *A Lament for a Proud Moab That Has Fallen* (48:29-39)

Moab's pride had been the most hateful thing about him. Using Isaiah's prophecy (Isa. 16:6-14) as the basis of his remarks, Jeremiah piles word upon word to describe the arrogance and haughty **pride** (29) of this nation. A hypersensitive spirit, with outbursts of **wrath** (30) and the telling of **lies,** are always characteristic of a proud heart. RSV interprets 30:

> I know his insolence, says the Lord;
>   his boasts are false,
>   his deeds are false.

In v. 31, the prophet takes up what seems to be a personal lament for this nation. It seems rather strange that Jeremiah would wail over the downfall of an enemy of Israel, yet it is as Raschi says, "The prophets of Israel differ from the heathen prophets like Balaam in this, they lay to heart the distress which they announce to the nations."[14] So it is not unreasonable to suppose that the I in vv. 31-32 is that of Jeremiah. Somehow the tender heart of the man from Anathoth weeps over the men of Moab. He continues to describe the lamentable conditions that will exist there: the vineyards that had been famous for their choice quality are hopelessly ruined; the orchards are stripped bare; weeping and crying are heard throughout the land; **joy and gladness** (33) have ceased. The desolation is so

---

[12]In 1868 archeologists found the Moabite Stone of Dibon. This has added greatly to our understanding of this period of OT history. Mesha, king of Moab, recorded his victories over Israel on this stone. The names of the following cities mentioned in this chapter are found on the Moabite Stone: Nebo, Dibon, Horonaim, Aroer, Kiriathaim, Jahzah, Kerioth, Bozrah, Beth-meon, and Beth-diblathaim.

[13]Kuist, *op. cit.*, p. 130.

[14]See Keil and Delitzsch, *op. cit.*, p. 226.

great that sacrifice will no longer be offered at the shrines, nor will **incense** be burned to the **gods** (35). In fact, the gods have been taken captive and there are no priests to offer sacrifice (7). The whole land is in a state of mourning; baldness appears everywhere; beards are **clipped** (37), and people have gashed themselves, to show the intensity of their grief. Wails come from **the house tops** (38), as well as from **the streets**. They lament over Moab crying, "How it is broken! How they wail! How Moab has turned his back in shame!" (39, RSV)

5. *There Is No Escape from Judgment* (48:40-47)

In the prophet's vision the conqueror of **Moab** is likened to **an eagle** (40) for swiftness and wingspread. The figure of an **eagle** is a favorite description of a victorious leader. It apparently refers to Nebuchadnezzar here, who, according to Josephus, destroyed Moab, Ammon, and the neighboring peoples in 582-581.[15] His strength is deadly, **Kerioth is taken, and the strong holds are surprised** (41). The hearts of Moab's mightiest warriors will be terror-stricken as a **woman in her** birth **pangs**. The entire land will **be destroyed** (42), and eventually the nation of Moab will be no more. This will happen because Moab was too arrogant and proud to serve the God of Israel, and **magnified himself against the Lord**.

There will be no escape from the dread conqueror. He who flees because of terror will **fall into the pit** (44), and he who gets **out of the pit** will fall into a **snare**. There will be no place to hide. The first part of 45 may be read

> *In the shadow of Heshbon*
> *fugitives stop without strength* (RSV).

Heshbon, although a strong city, can offer no protection for the weary fugitives, for a **fire** will go **forth out of Heshbon** (45) as in the days of **Sihon**, king of the Amorites (Num. 21:28-30), and will **devour** those who seek refuge there. **The corner of Moab** is better "the brow of Moab" (Smith-Goodspeed). The prophet seems to be saying that all the ancient predictions concerning Moab, even Balaam's prophecy, will find fulfillment in the coming destruction.[16] The **sons** and the **daughters of the**

[15]*Antiquities* X. 9.7.
[16]Keil and Delitzsch, *op. cit.*, p. 233.

people who worshipped the idol **Chemosh** (46) instead of the living God will go into exile. However, after the fires of discipline have done their work, there is some hope of a day of restoration for **Moab** (47).

E. ORACLE AGAINST AMMON, 49:1-6

This denunciatory oracle against **the Ammonites** (see map 2) can be viewed from three standpoints: (1) the things of which the Ammonites are guilty, (2) the punishment that will be meted out to them by God, (3) explanations concerning the text.

The Ammonites were guilty because (*a*) they had been crooked and treacherous in their dealings, and (*b*) they trusted in material things instead of the Lord. Concerning their treachery, they had occupied Hebrew territory by might and not by right. God questions them, **Hath Israel no sons ... no heir?** (1) Then why did Ammon take over the land of Gad when that tribe had to go into exile (734 B.C. to Assyria)? This had been Ammon's disposition all along. Other incidents bear this out.[17] Then on the matter of misplaced trust, the Ammonites boasted in their fertile valleys and flowing streams, their fortified cities, and their treasures of fruit and grain, saying, "Who can attack me?"[18] The Ammonites have deceived themselves into thinking that they are safe, but there is no security outside the God of Israel.

The punishment that Jeremiah predicted will fall upon Ammon involves: (*a*) the loss of the territory taken from Israel, which will be restored to the tribes of Jacob (2); (*b*) an unnamed foe will invade the land, and **Rabbah,** the capital, and all **her daughters** (cities) **shall be burned with fire;** (*c*) utter confusion will reign in the land, as the people, girded with **sackcloth ... run to and fro** among the **hedges** (3), lamenting with uncontrollable grief; (*d*) Milcom (see next paragraph), the god of the Ammonites, will be taken into exile, along with **his priests** and **princes** (3)—the poor idol is really more helpless than the people; (*e*) there will be no help for the Ammonite fugitives,

---

[17]The double-dealing nature of the Ammonites is revealed by the following: "In the times of Jeremiah they appear (*a*) as allies of Babylon (II Kings. 24:2); (*b*) leagued against Babylon (Jer. 27:3); (*c*) offering refuge to fugitive Jews (Jer. 40:14); (*d*) plotting to murder Gedaliah (Jer. 40:14)," Binns, *op. cit.,* p. 343.

[18]Bright, *op. cit.,* p. 325.

for the terror-stricken people will be driven away to captivity in such haste that there will be no one to care for the stragglers (5). Still, at some future time the fortunes of **Ammon** will be restored (6).

Several things may be observed concerning the text. The city of **Heshbon** is addressed (3), although it belongs to Moab rather than to Ammon. However, it was on the border between the nations, and invasion may have struck Ammon first. Besides the two peoples were kinsmen, being descendants of Lot (Gen. 19:37-38). The mention of **Ai** is difficult, for no city of that name is known east of the Jordan River. RSV has followed the Septuagint, the Syriac, and the Vulgate in translating the word **king** (1, 3) as "Milcom," the chief god of the Ammonites. Although there are difficulties, this seems to be the better course.[19] **Rabbah** (3) is today the modern city of Amman, capital of Jordan.

F. ORACLE AGAINST EDOM, 49:7-22

In this oracle against Edom (see map 2), Jeremiah follows the same pattern as that found in his oracle against Moab (48: 1-47). Using his own ideas and insights as a framework, he gathers up into a new whole some thoughts from earlier prophets. Jeremiah especially draws upon Obadiah[20] at certain points in his prophecy (vv. 9-10 are parallel to Obad. 5-6). Jeremiah was certainly familiar with the writings of his predecessors, so it would not be unusual if something of the flavor of their thinking crept into his own writings.

Edom was the traditional enemy of Israel. Although closely tied by blood, yet since the days of Esau and Jacob a feud had raged between these two peoples. Some of the bitterest language in the Old Testament involves the feelings between the descendants of the two men.

1. *The Announcement of Edom's Coming Doom* (49:7-13)

In a bold but subtle manner God announced the doom of Edom by chiding her concerning the vaunted **wisdom** (7) of

---

[19]See Peake, *op. cit.*, pp. 239 ff.; Keil and Delitzsch, *op. cit.*, pp. 237 ff.

[20]This, of course, raises the question of the date of Obadiah. Some scholars think Obadiah was not written until 585 B.C. If this is true, then both Jeremiah and Obadiah quote from an oracle that is older than either of them.

Teman, a district in the north of Edom (cf. Job 2:11; Amos 1:12). He implies that the mightiest wisdom of man is useless in the face of the judgment of God. He then reveals the approaching doom of Edom by appealing to her neighbors, the Dedanites,[21] to **flee** (8) to "some impenetrable retreat, lest they be overwhelmed by the blast of judgment that is to sweep over Edom."[22] God further makes known His intentions by the thoroughness of His judgments. He will strip **Esau** (10, Edom) **bare;** and since Edom will be unable **to hide himself,** he will be plundered of his treasures. The men of the nation will perish in battle, and the Lord, whom the Edomites have hated so intensely, will be the only One left to look after their **fatherless children** and **widows** (11).[23] In this manner, Edom must **drink of the cup** (12) of the wine of God's wrath (25:15-26). If God's own children, whom He would ordinarily spare, must **drink,** certainly Edom cannot **go unpunished.** This will include the destruction of **Bozrah** (see map 2), the capital of Edom, and the other **cities** of Edom which are destined to **be perpetual wastes** (13).

2. *The Occasion of Edom's Doom* (49:14-16)

Jeremiah now confirms Obadiah's vision concerning Edom, by using the language of the other prophet almost verbatim (Obad. 1-4). However, Jeremiah introduces some changes that are consistent with his own immediate situation. The doom of Edom is occasioned by the action of God. God takes the initiative, and sends messengers among **the heathen** (14) to summon them to **battle** against Edom. They are invited to the spoil because God has decreed that **Edom** shall be the least among the nations (15). The reason for God's decision is Edom herself, **Thy terribleness,** i.e., the terror you inspire, **hath deceived thee** (16). Edom had been misled by the reputation she had gained as being invincible. Already proud, her vanity now knew no bounds. Since her city was built high **in the clefts** of the mountain gorge, and was easily defended, Edom was confident that no invasion could be successful against her. God now pierced her arrogant and haughty spirit, by declaring, **Though thou shouldest**

---

[21]Dedan was an Arabian city just outside the borders of Edom. Traders from Dedan were often found dealing with the merchants of Teman and Bozrah.

[22]Peake, *op. cit.,* p. 244.

[23]Keil and Delitzsch, *op. cit.,* II, 244.

make thy nest as high as the eagle, I will bring thee down from thence. Thus Edom's pride and overconfidence became the occasion for her downfall.

3. *The Fall of Edom* (49:17-22)

There is no promise of restoration for Edom such as is found in the oracles against Moab and Ammon. The execution of God's judgment against Edom will be so thorough that the people who pass by will **hiss** (whistle) in astonishment at the **desolation** (17). Edom's destruction will remind men of **Sodom and Gomorrah** because it will become a waste, where **no man** can **dwell** (18).

The invader whom God will send against Edom is compared to **a lion** (19) that comes from **the swelling** (jungle) of the **Jordan** to pounce upon a flock of sheep (50:44). He will attack the Edomites and put them to flight. No **shepherd** (ruler) can stand before him, for God has formulated plans to bring Edom down from his high place with a terrible crash. The sound of his **fall** (21) will shake **the earth,** and the wail that will arise from Edom will be **heard** at **the Red Sea.** Edom's conqueror is also compared to an **eagle,** against whose strength of wing and swiftness of flight Edom's inaccessible heights offer no barrier. When he spreads **his wings** against **Bozrah,** the warriors of Edom turn pale and faint away like **a woman in her pangs** (22).

The last part of 20 may be read: "Even the youngest of the flock shall be dragged away, and their fold shall be shocked at their fate" (Smith-Goodspeed).

G. ORACLE AGAINST DAMASCUS, 49:23-27

The reference to **Damascus** (23) more likely means the kingdom of Aram (Syria), of which **Damascus** was the capital, and **Hamath** and **Arpad** were two chief cities (see maps 1 and 2). Although **Damascus** (Syria) is not mentioned in c. 25, it is unthinkable that, in a judgment in which all nations are compelled to drink of the cup of God's wrath, Syria would be exempt. Syria before its fall in 732 B.C. had been a thorn in the side of the Northern Kingdom at numerous times (I Kings 15:18-21; 20:1-21; 22:3; II Kings 5:2; etc.), and gave Judah much difficulty at least on one occasion (II Kings 16:5-6; Isa. 7:1-16).

The oracle describes the consternation that takes place in **Hamath** (110 miles north of Damascus) **and Arpad** (95 miles

north of Hamath) when the **tidings** of the fall of Damascus comes
to them: "They melt in fear, they are troubled like the sea
which cannot be quiet" (23, RSV).[24] **Damascus,** the famous city,
beautiful for location, wealthy and richly supplied with the good
things of life, has become **feeble** (24). Paralyzed by fear, and
bowed in sorrow, she stands helpless before the foe. Verse 25 is
an exclamation of sadness: "How the renowned city is forsaken,
the city of My joy!" (Berk). Her warriors have fallen and **her
young men** (26) have died in the **streets** of the city (50:30).
The ruthless invader goes unnamed, but that does not matter, for
it is God who has brought about her destruction. Thus Damascus
drinks of the cup. **Ben-hadad** (27) was the name of several kings
of Damascus (I Kings 15:18-20; II Kings 13:24).

H. ORACLE AGAINST KEDAR AND HAZOR, 49:28-33.

Apparently these two peoples represent the Arabian tribes
residing in the desert to the east of Palestine. **Kedar** and **Hazor**
are not mentioned in c. 25, but they are probably represented
there under the names of "Dedan, Tema, Buz, and all who cut
the corners of their hair" (25:23, RSV). In this oracle God summons Nebuchadnezzar (28) to smite the "people of the east"
(RSV).

Kedar (Gen. 25:13) seems to have been a nomadic tribe
of the family of Ishmael, noted for its skill with the bow (Isa. 21:
16-17). The tribe is mentioned by Jeremiah (2:10) and also by
Ezekiel (27:21). Nebuchadnezzar is urged to plunder their
tents, and to seize their **flocks, curtains** (tent hangings), and
camels as spoil (29).

There are several Hazors mentioned in the OT, but the
Hazor here seems to represent a seminomadic people residing in
the desert, and very much like the people of **Kedar.** The people
are **wealthy** (31), they possess a **multitude** of **cattle** (32), and
their villages have no **gates** or **bars.** They dwell at ease, and the
men cut the corners of their hair (see comments on 9:26). Nebuchadnezzar is assured of much **booty** if he attacks them. The
inhabitants (30) are urged by the prophet to **flee** swiftly and
hide themselves securely from the Babylonian scourge. As for

---

[24]This verse has given translators trouble. The literal "Anxious care
is on the sea" does not make sense. The RSV has the apparent meaning.

Hazor, it will become uninhabited—a **dwelling for dragons (jackals), and a desolation for ever (33).**

I. ORACLE AGAINST ELAM, 49:34-39

Elam was located in the hill country east of Babylon and north of the Persian Gulf. Its capital was Susa (or Shushan; see map 1), and the country had had a long history reaching back to the earliest times.[25] In frequent conflict with Assyria, it had been conquered by Ashurbanipal *cir.* 640 B.C.,[26] but had apparently regained its independence after the fall of the Assyrian empire. There are indications that **Elam** gave the Babylonian empire serious trouble, and that Nebuchadnezzar had to subdue the nation *cir.* 596-595 B.C.[27] The details of Elamite history are obscure but there is ample evidence that she lived on as a political entity for many years.[28]

What provoked Jeremiah to deliver this oracle against Elam? There is no knowledge of a Jewish-Elamite contact of any sort at this time. It must be that the Jewish exiles, as they arrived in Babylon, learned that **Elam** was giving Nebuchadnezzar considerable trouble, and seized upon the hope that Babylon might be overthrown by the Elamites. When this information reached Jeremiah in the **beginning** years of **the reign of Zedekiah (34),** he wrote the oracle to dispel this false hope.

The main ideas of the oracle are: (*a*) The **Lord will bring evil (37)** upon the Elamites; **I will set my throne in Elam (38),** i.e., God will judge them. (*b*) Destruction will come upon this people **from the four quarters of heaven (36),** but the details are not known. (*c*) The Elamites will be no match for the foe, and will flee in terror before the enemy. (*d*) Their great skill as archers, for which they were famous (Isa. 22:6), will not deliver them now: **I will break the bow of Elam (35), saith the Lord.** (*e*) As they flee before the enemy, **the sword** shall consume them (37). (*f*) They will be scattered to the four **winds** of heaven among all nations. (*g*) But **in the latter days (39)** the nation will be restored.

[25]J. W. Swain, *The Ancient World* (New York: Harper and Brothers, 1950), I, 187 ff.

[26]*Ibid.,* p. 178.

[27]Bright, *op. cit.,* p. 338; see also Ezek. 32:24.

[28]Elamites evidently were forcibly settled in Samaria, according to Ezra 4:9, and Jews from Elam were present at Pentecost (Acts 2:9).

J. ORACLE AGAINST BABYLON, 50:1—51:64

In the light of 25:12, 26, it is fitting that Jeremiah's prophecies against foreign nations should conclude with an oracle against Babylon. Also, it is not surprising to find that it is the longest of the oracles, and one that is filled with a great deal of emotion. Since Babylon exerted such an influence on the life and destiny of Judah, this oracle would naturally require more than ordinary attention.

The material in these chapters is put together in a rather unusual fashion. The oracle is made up of a series of poems. Between some of the poems there are prose sections. This makes it difficult to arrange the material in logical order.[29] The dominant theme is the imminent overthrow of Babylon and the early restoration of Israel. There is no progression in the theme, but a recurrence of the same note again and again.

Jeremiah's authorship of this oracle has been contested. That there is a decided difference from earlier sections of Jeremiah in time, viewpoint, and attitude cannot be denied. There seems no compelling reason, however, why these words could not have come from the pen of the prophet. Edward J. Young proposes to solve the problem by suggesting that Jeremiah wrote a first draft (or the original nucleus) of the oracle in the fourth year of Zedekiah. He then sent a copy to Babylon by Seraiah precisely as recorded in 51:59-61. Later on, however, in Egypt, after the Temple had been destroyed and the nation had gone into exile, Jeremiah expanded that original nucleus to its present state.[30]

1. *Babylon's Doom and Israel's Restoration* (50:1—51:58)

As noted above, the material in these two chapters is not organized in a logical fashion. The most noticeable feature is an alternation between Babylon and Israel, indicated below by the letters *B* and *I*. Following almost every message of doom for Babylon there is an encouraging word for the exiles of Israel.

Verse 1 serves as a title for the two chapters. It declares that what follows is **the word** of **the Lord** concerning **Babylon,** as given through **Jeremiah the prophet.**

B— (50:2-3). **Babylon is taken** (2). This news is to be published to **the nations.** To **set up a standard** would be to post an

---

[29]Bright, *op. cit.,* p. 359.
[30]E. J. Young, *op. cit.,* p. 228; also NBC, pp. 636-37.

announcement or fly a victor's emblem. In the prophet's vision
the deed is as good as done. An enemy **out of the north** (3) has
captured the city. The gods of Chaldea (**Bel** [lord] came to be
identified with **Merodach** [Marduk], the chief god of Babylon)
are destroyed. Babylonian religion is thrown into confusion.

I— (50:4-10). **In that time . . . Israel . . . and . . . Judah . . .
shall go, and seek the Lord** (4). God's people will repent, and
will, therefore, have a chance to escape from exile. They shall
turn **their faces** toward **Zion,** and in humbleness of heart desire
a renewal of the **covenant** (5). **My people hath been lost sheep**
(6). **Their shepherds** (leaders) had led them **astray.** The nations
devoured them greedily, saying, "We are not guilty, for they
have sinned against the Lord" (7, RSV). Israel must flee from
the midst of Babylon (8), for the Lord is bringing a company of
nations (9) against Babylon, and she shall be plundered, and all
of **Chaldea** (10) will be spoiled. To **be as the he goats before
the flocks** (8) would be to lead the way, to get out first. *The
Berkeley Version* clarifies 9 thus: "Their arrows are like an
expert warrior who returns not empty-handed."

B— (50:11-16). **Her foundations are fallen, her walls are
thrown down** (15). Although Babylon has been the first among
the nations, she will now be **hindermost** (12). She **rejoiced** (11)
with glee at the fall of Judah, but men will be **astonished** (13)
at her own destruction. God calls for the nations to array themselves against her, for she has **sinned against the Lord** (14).
When Babylon is laid waste, the exiles from all nations will **flee
every one to his own land** (16).

I— (50:17-20). "I will restore Israel to his pasture" (19,
RSV). Though they have been **scattered** like **sheep** (17), **devoured** by the **king of Assyria,** and gnawed like a bone by the
king of Babylon, nevertheless the **iniquity** of Israel and **Judah**
(20) will be pardoned and they will be restored to their native
land. The kings will **be** punished, but God's people will be **satisfied** (19) abundantly.

B— (50:21-27). **I have laid a snare for thee . . . O Babylon**
(24). **Merathaim** (21, double rebellion) and **Pekod** (punishment)
are synonyms[31] for Babylon. The words suggest the crime of
which she is guilty, and the judgment that is coming upon her.

---

[31]"There is a play on the Hebrew roots *Mrh* and *Pqd*. *Mar marrati* was
a district of southern Babylonia; the *Puqudu* was a people of eastern
Babylonia. *Mrh* means "to rebel" and *Pqd* means to "punish."

The hammer of the whole earth is broken (23), for Babylon the great is caught (24) in the snare of the Lord. God's armoury (25) is open and the weapons of his indignation are brought forth, for the time of Babylon's punishment has come!

I— (50:28). There is a voice . . . in Zion. Those who have escaped from a burning, falling Babylon declare in Jerusalem that the desecration of the temple has been avenged. God has not forgotten His people.

B— (50:29-32). Recompense her according to her work (29). Because Babylon has been proud against the Lord, the warriors of the nations are called to surround the city so that none may escape. The . . . proud shall stumble and fall (32), and there will be none to raise him up. Babylon's day of recompense has come (31).

I— (50:33-34). Their Redeemer is strong (34). Although enemies of Israel and Judah have oppressed (33) them greatly, and refused to let them go, yet the Lord of hosts will deliver them with a strong arm. He will give them rest, but disquiet to their enemies.

B— (50:35-38). A sword is upon the Chaldeans (35). The sword of the Lord is upon the people of Babylon: princes . . . wise men . . . liars (36; diviners); and they shall dote (be fools). The sword is upon their horses, and . . . chariots (37). Mingled people would be foreign troops. Their mighty warriors shall become like women. Babylon's treasures will be taken, and a drought (38) shall plague her land, because the people "are mad over idols" (RSV). Babylon shall become the home of "wild beasts of the desert" (39, ASV). No man shall abide there (40). Babylon will become as desolate as Sodom and Gomorrah. From the north (41) shall come a fierce people and many kings "from the remote corners of the earth" (Berk.). The sound of their coming is like the roar of the sea (42). At the sound, anguish shall take hold of the king of Babylon (43). Her conqueror will burst upon the land like a lion leaping in the midst of a flock— a lion from the swelling (jungle) of Jordan (44) comes. The earth will be moved at the noise of the taking of Babylon (46). A shepherd (44) would be a leader of a nation. On the last part of 45 see comments on 49:20.

B— (51:1-14). Babylon's destroyer (51:1-5) will be like a wind (1) that winnows the chaff from the grain and like archers whose arrows pierce the strongest brigandine (3, armor). Chaldea will be winnowed (sifted) because of her **sin against the Holy One of Israel,** but **Israel** and **Judah (5)** are assured that God has not **forsaken** them. **The golden cup is fallen (7-8). Babylon** is taken. **Flee . . . deliver every man his soul: be not cut off in her iniquity (6). Babylon** is beyond healing—**balm (8)** will not help her. Israel's **righteousness (10,** vindication) is reflected in Babylon's destruction. **O thou that dwellest upon many waters** (Babylon in the midst of her rivers), **thine end is come (13).** The Lord has stirred up **the kings of the Medes (11),** for He has plans **against Babylon.**

I—(51:15-24). The **Lord is the former** (Creator) **of all things (19).** Men are stupid, and graven images are in error, for it is Israel's God who created the **earth . . . established the world . . .** and **stretched out the heaven (15).** He is a living God who guides the destinies of nations. God encourages His people by saying, "I will requite Babylon . . . before your very eyes" **(24,** RSV). Although God had used Babylon as His agent, **my battle ax and weapons of war (20-23),** yet God will requite him for the **evil** he has **done to Zion (24).**

B—(51:25-33). For God to address Babylon as a **destroying mountain (25)** seems strange. Babylon was built on a plain. The reference may be to Nebuchadnezzar's artificial mountains, waterfalls, and hanging gardens which he had built in Babylon. On the other hand, it may refer to Babylon's exalted position over the nations. In either case God said, **I . . . will make thee a burnt mountain (25).** God's command is, **Prepare the nations against her (27).** The figure at the end of 27 is, "Bring up horses like bristling locusts" (RSV). In the pupa stage the locust's wings are enveloped in hornlike projections on its back (Berk., fn.). Various people are called to organize themselves against Babylon: **Ararat, Minni** (ancient peoples living in Armenia), and **Ashchenaz** (unknown, but probably a neighboring people), and **the kings of the Medes (28). The Medes** are especially singled out, and seem to be the leaders of the attacking armies. As the assault is launched, messengers are sent to **the king of Babylon (31)** to tell him that his warriors have ceased fighting, the city is on **fire (32),** and **the passages** (the fords of the river as means of escape) **are stopped.** The day of God's vengeance has come!

I—(51:34-37). Here the cries of God's people are heard bewailing the distress and sorrow they have suffered at the hands of the king of Babylon. **The violence** (35) and bloodshed require satisfaction. God says, I **will plead thy cause, and take vengeance for thee** (36) by making **Babylon** (37) a heap of ruins.

B—(51:38-44). **How is Sheshach (Babylon) taken! and how is the praise of the whole earth surprised!** (41) God will prepare a feast for the Babylonians where they will **roar . . . like lions** (38) and go "beside themselves" in their orgy. They will fall into a drunken stupor from which they will never awake (Belshazzar's feast?). The first part of 39 may be read, "While they are inflamed I will prepare them a feast" (RSV). The stupefied soldiers will be slaughtered like animals, and the nation's sovereignty will be destroyed (39-40). Thus will Babylon's **cities** (43) be made desolate and **Bel** (44), her god, will be punished.

I—(51:45-51). **My people, go ye out of the midst of her** (45). **Every man** is urged to save **his** own **soul.** The day of Babylon's **judgment** (47) has come. When **the slain of Israel** (49) are avenged, even **the heaven and the earth** will sing (48). In this hour of destruction, **let Jerusalem come into your mind** (50). Those who escape from Babylon must never forget the **shame** that Zion has suffered because of the desecration **of the Lord's house** (51).

B—(51:52-58). **The Lord hath spoiled Babylon** (55). God's decrees have gone forth. The spoilers have come. **Though Babylon should mount up to heaven** (53), nothing can save the doomed city. Moffatt has rendered 55:

> *'Tis the Eternal battering down Babylon,*
> *still the din of her city-life!*
> *The enemy surge in like the roaring tides,*
> *shouting aloud.*

God has made her rulers and leaders **drunk** (57) so that they may not be able to defend the city. Instead, they will be slain in their drunkenness and will thus **sleep a perpetual sleep** (the sleep of death). Babylon's great walls will be thrown down, and all her glory will come to nought.

> *So ends the toil of nations, ends in smoke,*
> *and pagans waste their pains* (58, Moffatt).

2. *Jeremiah's Words to Seraiah* (51:59-64)

According to this passage **Zedekiah the king of Judah** (59) made an official visit to Babylon **in the fourth year of his reign,** about 594 B.C. There is no mention made of this visit elsewhere in the Scriptures. No reason is given for the trip, but many scholars have conjectured that Zedekiah went to Babylon to clear himself of the suspicion of revolt (27:2-11). The king's **quiet prince** (quartermaster; lit., prince of the resting place) was **Seraiah the son of Neriah,** apparently the brother of Baruch, Jeremiah's secretary.

Learning of the trip, Jeremiah seized the opportunity to enlist the help of Seraiah in carrying out a special mission. Jeremiah had written on a scroll a prophetic oracle announcing **all the evil that should come upon Babylon** (60). On arriving in **Babylon** (61), Seraiah was to **read all these words** of the prophecy. The message was probably for the Jewish exiles or their leaders and not read publicly. After a prayer (62), Seraiah was to **bind a stone to the scroll and cast it into the midst of Euphrates** (63). This was to symbolize the fate that awaited Babylon. As the scroll sank in the waters of the river, Seraiah was to say, **Thus shall Babylon sink, and shall not rise from the evil that I will bring upon her** (64).

This was an act of faith on the part of Jeremiah. It proclaimed to the leaders of the Jewish exiles that their hated oppressor would not go unpunished. Thus by this symbolic action God's judgment against Babylon was "set in motion."[32] In God's own time His moral purposes in relation to both Babylon and the exiles would be achieved.

[32]Bright, *op. cit.,* p. 212.

Section XII *Historical Appendix*

Jeremiah 52:1-34

This chapter is mainly reproduced from II Kings 24:18—25:30, though with some significant variations. Since only differences from the account in the Book of Kings will be noted in the following paragraphs, the reader should consult BBC comments on II Kings for a general exposition of the material.

A. ZEDEKIAH'S ACCESSION AND REVOLT, 52:1-3 (II Kings 24:18-20)

B. THE SIEGE OF JERUSALEM, 52:4-5 (II Kings 25:1-2)

C. THE FAMINE DURING THE SIEGE, 52:6 (II Kings 25:3)

D. THE FALL OF JERUSALEM, 52:7 (II Kings 25:4-5)

E. ZEDEKIAH'S CAPTURE AND FATE, 52:8-11 (II Kings 25:6-7)

Verses 10-11 are slightly expanded from the account in II Kings, and additional information is given here concerning the fate of **Zedekiah.**

F. DEMOLITION OF JERUSALEM, 52:12-16 (II Kings 25:8-12)

Verse 12 reads **tenth day** while II Kings 25:8 reads "seventh day." Verse 15 reads **the poor of the people** but should probably be omitted as a copyist's error, since it contradicts v. 16.

G. TEMPLE VESSELS TAKEN, 52:17-23 (II Kings 25:13-17)

Verses 17-23 are slightly shortened in Kings.

H. FATE OF THE PRINCES, 52:24-27 (II Kings 25:18-21)

Verse 25 reads **seven men** while II Kings 25:19 reads "five men." The chapter here completely omits II Kings 25:22-26 because it is superfluous, the material having already been given in Jer. 39:11—43:7.

493

I. THREE DEPORTATIONS OF CAPTIVES, 52:28-30

These verses which treat of the deportation of Jewish captives to Babylon are totally lacking in II Kings. The statistics given here are found nowhere else in Scripture, and add something to the several accounts of the capture of Jerusalem. The writer apparently had access to a separate statistical source. He speaks of a deportation in the **seventh year** of Nebuchadnezzar's reign, another in the **eighteenth year,** and still another in his twenty-third year. These do not altogether correspond with other accounts of deportations, and raise the question as to just how many deportations there may have been.[1]

The first deportation mentioned here is said to have taken place in Nebuchadnezzar's **seventh year,** and 3,023 persons were carried to Babylon. This deportation is described in II Kings 24:12-14 as taking place in Nebuchadnezzar's eighth year and including 10,000 deportees. The discrepancy is usually reconciled by saying that the smaller figure represents only males of fighting age. The difference in years is explained by two different methods of counting the reign of kings. One method uses the "non-accession year system," which starts counting with the very year the king ascends the throne; the other is the "accession year system" which counts an "accession year" before the "first year" of the king begins. This would apparently solve the above problem.

The second deportation occurred in the **eighteenth year** of Nebuchadnezzar ("nineteenth year" in v. 12) and corresponds to the time of the destruction of Jerusalem in 587 B.C. However, 832 (29) seems a rather pitifully small figure for the garrison in Jerusalem in 587 B.C., even if it represents only males of fighting age.

The third deportation is not mentioned elsewhere in the Scriptures. It is interesting to note, however, that Josephus states that Nebuchadnezzar in the twenty-third year of his reign deported Jews from Egypt, and the suggestion is that in so doing he avenged the murder of Gedaliah.

---

[1]The present writer thinks that there may have been several more deportations than scholars have previously supposed. He believes that those listed in 28-30 are included here because they had not been recorded elsewhere.

J. Favor Shown Jehoiachin, 52:31-34 (II Kings 25:27-30)

The final section of this chapter corresponds almost identically with the II Kings passage. It contains a hopeful note in that it tells how Jehoiachin, prisoner-king of Judah, gained the favor of the Babylonian court. In the thirty-seventh year of his captivity (he had been taken to Babylon when eighteen) Evil-merodach (561-559 B.C.), the son and successor of Nebuchadnezzar, lifted up his head (31), i.e., restored him to royal favor. He was taken from prison, given proper food and clothing, and assigned "a seat above the seats" (32, RSV) of the other captive kings in Babylon. He was treated kindly, and given a pension for the rest of his life (34). In order to achieve this success, he evidently learned to adjust himself to a hostile environment in such a way as to win the respect of his enemies. As Hopper suggests, "He emerges at last with sudden character."[2]

Why this historical appendix should have been attached to the prophecies of Jeremiah has been debated at length by scholars. It does seem a bit strange, since the prophet's name is not mentioned even once, and most of the material can be found in the Book of Kings. On the other hand, it cannot be said to be inappropriate. It is generally conceded that it was placed here to show that Jeremiah's prophecies concerning Jerusalem were most certainly fulfilled. In this manner, history itself could vindicate the long years of suffering endured by the most maligned and least understood of the Old Testament prophets. Also, Jehoiachin's good fortune raised expectations of a brighter day "beyond judgment," an expectation that Jeremiah voiced again and again in the more hopeful moments of his life.

[2]IB, V (expos.), 1142.

Bibliography

I. COMMENTARIES

BALL, C. J. "The Prophecies of Jeremiah." *The Expositor's Bible.* Edited by W. ROBERTSON NICOLL. New York: George H. Doran, n.d.

BINNS, L. ELLIOT. "The Book of the Prophet Jeremiah." *Westminster Commentaries.* London: Methuen and Co., Ltd., 1919.

BRIGHT, JOHN. "Jeremiah." *The Anchor Bible.* Edited by W. F. ALBRIGHT and D. N. FREEDMAN. New York: Doubleday and Company, Inc., 1965.

CALVIN, JOHN. "The Book of the Prophet Jeremiah." *Calvin's Commentaries.* Translated by JOHN OWEN. Grand Rapids, Michigan: Wm. B. Eerdmans Publishing Co., 1950 (reprint).

CAWLEY, F. "Jeremiah." *The New Bible Commentary.* Edited by FRANCIS DAVIDSON, *et al.* Grand Rapids, Michigan: Wm. B. Eerdmans Publishing Co., 1956.

CHEYNE, T. K. "The Book of Jeremiah" (Exposition). *The Pulpit Commentary.* Edited by H. D. M. SPENCE and JOSEPH EXELL. New Edition. Chicago: Wilcox and Follett, n.d.

CLARKE, ADAM. *The Holy Bible with a Commentary and Critical Notes,* Vol. IV. New York: The Methodist Book Concern, n.d.

GRAYBILL, J. F. "Jeremiah." *The Wycliffe Bible Commentary.* Edited by CHARLES PFEIFFER and E. F. HARRISON. Chicago: Moody Press, 1962.

HOPPER, STANLEY R. "The Book of Jeremiah" (Exposition). *The Interpreter's Bible.* Edited by GEORGE A. BUTTRICK, *et al.,* Vol. V. New York: Abingdon-Cokesbury Press, 1951.

HYATT, J. P. "The Book of Jeremiah" (Exegesis). *The Interpreter's Bible.* Edited by GEORGE A. BUTTRICK, *et al.,* Vol. V. New York: Abingdon-Cokesbury Press, 1951.

KEIL, C. F., and DELITZSCH, F. "Jeremiah." *Biblical Commentaries on the Old Testament.* Translated by D. PATRICK. Grand Rapids, Michigan: Wm. B. Eerdmans Publishing Co., 1956 (reprint).

KUIST, H. T. "Jeremiah." *Layman's Bible Commentaries.* London: SCM Press, Ltd., 1961.

MORGAN, G. CAMPBELL. *Studies in the Prophecy of Jeremiah.* New York: Fleming H. Revell Co., 1931.

NAEGELSBACH, C. W. EDUARD. "The Book of the Prophet Jeremiah." *A Commentary on the Holy Scriptures.* Edited by JOHN PETER LANGE. Translated by PHILIP SCHAFF. New York: Charles Scribner's Sons, 1915.

PATERSON, JOHN. "Jeremiah." *Peake's Commentary on the Bible.* H. H. ROWLEY, Old Testament editor. New York: Thomas Nelson and Sons, 1962.

PEAKE, A. S. "Jeremiah." *The New Century Bible.* Edinburgh: T. C. and E. C. Jack, 1910.

SMITH, GEORGE ADAM. *Jeremiah.* New York: George H. Doran and Company, 1922.

II. OTHER BOOKS

ARCHER, GLEASON L. *A Survey of Old Testament Introduction.* Chicago: Moody Press, 1964.

BROWN, F., DRIVER, S. R., BRIGGS, C. A. (eds.). *A Hebrew and English Lexicon of the Old Testament.* Oxford: Clarendon Press, 1907; reprinted, 1953, 1957.

HYATT, J. P. *Prophetic Religion.* New York: Abingdon Press, 1947.

JAMES, FLEMING. *Personalities of the Old Testament.* New York: Charles Scribner's Sons, 1946.

JEFFERSON, CHARLES EDWARD. *Cardinal Ideas of Jeremiah.* New York: The Macmillan Company, 1928.

JONES, E. STANLEY. *Christian Maturity.* New York: Abingdon Press, 1947.

JOSEPHUS, FLAVIUS. *Antiquities of the Jews.* "The Works of Flavius Josephus." 2 volumes. Philadelphia: J. B. Lippincott Co., 1895.

PATERSON, JOHN. *Goodly Fellowship of the Prophets.* New York: Charles Scribner and Sons, 1948.

PFEIFFER, R. H. *Introduction to the Old Testament.* New York: Harper and Brothers, 1948.

PRITCHARD, J. B. *Ancient Near Eastern Texts Relating to the Old Testament.* Princeton: Princeton University Press, 1950.

ROBINSON, C. A. *Ancient History.* New York: The Macmillan Company, 1951.

SKINNER, JOHN. *Prophecy and Religion.* Cambridge: University Press, 1951.

SWAIN, J. W. *The Ancient World.* New York: Harper and Brothers, 1950.

THOMPSON, J. H. "The Book of Daniel." *The Pulpit Commentary.* Edited by H. D. M. SPENCE and JOSEPH S. EXELL, Vol. 13. Grand Rapids, Michigan: Wm. B. Eerdmans Publishing Co., 1950 (reprint).

TORCZYNER, HARRY (ed.). *Lachish Letters.* London: Oxford University Press, 1938.

UNGER, MERRILL F. *Unger's Bible Dictionary.* Chicago: Moody Press, 1957.

WESLEY, JOHN. *Wesley's Works.* Kansas City, Missouri: Beacon Hill Press, 1958 (reprint).

WISEMAN, D. J. *Chronicles of the Chaldean Kings.* London: British Museum, 1956.

WOOD, FRED M. *Fire in My Bones.* Nashville: Broadman Press, 1959.

YATES, KYLE M. *Preaching from the Prophets.* Nashville: Broadman Press, 1942.

YOUNG, E. J. *Introduction to the Old Testament.* Grand Rapids, Michigan: Wm. B. Eerdmans Publishing Co., 1949.

III. ARTICLES

ALBRIGHT, W. F. "A Supplement to Jeremiah: The Lachish Ostraca." *Bulletin of the American Schools of Oriental Research,* No. 61 (February, 1936), pp. 15-16.

———. "A Re-examination of the Lachish Letters." *Bulletin of the American Schools of Oriental Research,* No. 73 (February, 1939), p. 16.

THE LAMENTATIONS
OF JEREMIAH

C. Paul Gray

Introduction

A. Historical Background

The terrifying calamity that befell the land of Judah and the city of Jerusalem in 587-586 B.C. forms the backdrop for this little book. The Babylonian army under Nebuchadnezzar had laid siege to Jerusalem for eighteen long months. When the famine-stricken and disease-ridden city was finally taken, it was totally demolished and put to the torch. It was a tragic and heartbreaking occasion for the Jewish people. The security of Jerusalem had been held as a precious doctrine by the inhabitants of the city ever since the time of Isaiah (701 B.C.). Now those who lived to see the city lying in ruins and the Temple leveled to the ground could scarcely believe their eyes. Their grief knew no bounds. In the months and years that followed, their minds were plagued with many unanswered questions about their past history and their future destiny.

These five poems came out of the excruciating pain of those trouble-filled days that followed the destruction of the city, the capture of King Zedekiah, and the deportation of the people to Babylon. "The torrent of emotion" that flows through the book reveals the depths of despondency to which the people had fallen. These poems are an outpouring of all the grief and suffering that was pent up in their hearts. It is now poured out in a description of their evil plight mingled with a confession of their sin and accompanied with anguished cries of penitence. Their grief was really too deep for words, but an inner compulsion drove them to express their sorrow in some form. As with people in all ages, poetry and song were the most natural way to give vent to their emotions.

B. Title and Place in the Canon

In the Hebrew text the book has no title, but like the books of the Pentateuch, it was long known by its first word, "How!" 'ekah (also first word of cc. 2 and 4). However, somewhere through the centuries the Rabbis began to refer to it as "lamentations" or "dirges" (Qinoth), and it is listed under that name in the Babylonian Talmud. The translators of the Septuagint, Greek version of the Old Testament, followed the Rabbis by using the Greek term for lamentations, Threnoi. They went a step further and ascribed the book to Jeremiah. Consequently the later Greek versions, the Syraic, the old Latin, Jerome's Vulgate, and the English versions have given it the longer title, "The Lamentations of Jeremiah."

In the Hebrew Bible today Lamentations is not found among The Prophets, but is listed in The Writings (*Hagiographa*). It is one of the Five Rolls (*Megilloth*) in that section (the third) of the Hebrew Scriptures. That it was not always listed there is especially evident from the Septuagint and the writings of Josephus. The Septuagint consistently placed Lamentations with the prophecy of Jeremiah. In a comment on the number and nature of the Holy Scriptures,[1] Josephus does the same. Speaking of the books of the Old Testament, Josephus states that their number is twenty-two, and divides them into three groups, giving the number that belonged to each group. While he does not mention Lamentations by name, to arrive at the number twenty-two he had to count Lamentations with Jeremiah and Ruth with the Book of Judges. He apparently followed the Septuagint in putting Lamentations among The Prophets and not in The Writings.

Melito, bishop of Sardis (A.D. 180) likewise reckoned the number of books at twenty-two, and he was followed in this by Origen (A.D. 250), Augustine (A.D. 420), and Jerome (A.D. 405). This would mean that all these men thought of Lamentations as belonging with The Prophets and not in the *Hagiographa*. Jerome, however, mentions that "some would include Ruth and Lamentations in the *Hagiographa* and by adding these compute the number of books as twenty-four, etc."[2] He may have been referring to II Esdras and the Talmud, which follow the twenty-four numbering and place Lamentations in The Writings. It is apparent from the foregoing that during the intertestamental period and first centuries of the Christian Church no official order of the books of Scripture had been established. The Book of Lamentations in one catalogue was found in The Writings and in another among The Prophets. Our English Bibles follow the arrangement found in the Septuagint and list Lamentations with Jeremiah.

C. Authorship and Date

No one is named as the author of Lamentations in the Hebrew text. But a long line of tradition affirms that Jeremiah

---

[1] *Apion*. I.8.

[2] C. W. E. Naegelsbach, "Lamentations," *Lange's Commentary on Holy Scripture*. (Grand Rapids: Zondervan Publishing House, [reprint], n.d.), p. 1.

composed the book. That the book is written in the spirit of Jeremiah, and has many similarities to his prophecy, cannot be denied. The Septuagint, however, is the earliest written source that ascribes the poems to Jeremiah. Although II Chron. 35:25 has often been quoted as a biblical reference to the authorship of Jeremiah for Lamentations, this passage merely states that Jeremiah wrote a lament on the death of king Josiah that was known to the Temple singers of a later day. It does connect Jeremiah with the lamentation type of literature, but this only corroborates what we already know from the prophet's own book. There is no certainty that this passage refers to the Book of Lamentations, for the Temple choir must have had many songs of lamentation in its repertoire.

The Septuagint is quite explicit in its view of the authorship. This Greek version of the book carries an introductory note (apparently based on a Hebrew original) that clearly attributes the book to Jeremiah. It reads: "And it came to pass after Israel was carried away captive and Jerusalem was made desolate that Jeremiah sat weeping, and he lamented with this lamentation over Jerusalem, and he said"—then follows the first verse of the Hebrew text. The Vulgate carries this introductory note with a slight variation; the Arabic reproduces it exactly; and the Targum (paraphrase of) Jonathan replaces it with this line: "Jeremiah the prophet and chief priest said." These authorities are followed by the Talmud and the Church Fathers in assuming that Jeremiah was the author. For centuries Jeremiah's authorship was never questioned.

Today, however, many outstanding scholars reject the Jeremianic authorship. They do so on the basis of structure, diction, and the attitude toward the destruction of Jerusalem assumed by the writer. They claim that the acrostic form with its preciseness, the presence of many new terms and phrases not found in Jeremiah's prophecy, the bewildered attitude of the writer over the destruction of Jerusalem, is alien to Jeremiah. These scholars can tabulate an impressive array of *differences* from the prophecy, and are quite confident that the poems do not come from the pen of Jeremiah.

On the other hand, scholars just as well qualified to render an opinion strongly favor the traditional view. They base their findings on the *similarities* that exist between the two books. The view that punishment had come to Israel because of the nation's persistent sinning and its reliance on weak and treacherous allies is common to both books. The same attitude toward false prophets and priests characterizes the two volumes. Similar words and phrases point to a common author. The anguish and tears of the writer of Lamentations reflect vividly the personality of Jeremiah. The detailed description of the city's ruin argues well for Jeremiah's authorship. We know that he was present when the city fell and remained behind to look upon its desolate wastes. Thus the affinity in content, spirit, tone, and language, all speak strongly for Jeremiah.

The date of the two books, generally speaking, is the same. The closing events recorded in the Book of Jeremiah would fall close to 580 B.C. and there is nothing in the Book of Lamentations that would require a later date.

D. Structure

Of the five poems that make up the book, the first four are dirges, while the fifth is more in the form of a prayer. In the Hebrew, the first four poems are alphabetic acrostics. Poems one, two, and four each have twenty-two verses, corresponding in number and order to the Hebrew alphabet. Verses in poems one and two have three lines each with only the first line following the acrostic form. Poem four is the same except it has only two lines to the verse. Poem three is still more unusual in that all the letters of the alphabet are repeated three times in succession. Because of this the Masoretes thought of each line as a verse and divided the poem into sixty-six verses. The fifth poem has twenty-two verses of one line, but no acrostic arrangement is evident.

It is not known just why the author chose to use the acrostic form. Although it is artistic and well-suited to express the grief of a sorrowing nation, it does restrain and hamper the free movement of thought. Kuist has suggested that it may have been used as a mnemonic device to aid the memory, or to keep the explosive emotional element under careful control, or to give "a sense of continuity and completeness to the communal expressions of grief and guilt and striving for hope which these elegies encouraged."[3]

It should be noted, however, that the acrostic was a familiar literary device[4] in biblical times and that the author took his freedom at certain points. In poems two, three, and four the letters *ayin* and *pe* of the Hebrew alphabet are transposed, and

[3]H. T. Kuist, "Lamentations," *Layman's Bible Commentaries* (London: SCM Press, Ltd., 1961), p. 141.
[4]See Psalms 25; 34; 35; 111; 112; 119; 145; and Prov. 31:10-31.

verse 7 of poem one and verse 19 of poem two have four lines instead of three.

The metrical structure used here is known as the *Qina* rhythm. It is the metre most commonly used for chanting dirges over the dead or over national calamities in ancient times. Its use of parallelism, repetition, apostrophe, and its play on words were admirably suited to communicate the unfathomable depths of suffering and sorrow that the human soul is capable of experiencing.

E. Purpose and Usage

These poems are dirges composed with the expectation that they would be recited by the congregation of Israel to express their great sorrow over the loss of their national identity. They contemplate all the great subjects of public grief. Their purpose is to express therapeutically the deepest and most profound emotions of a broken and ruined people. The poems enabled the people to confess that God had dealt with them justly, and in so doing to find strength to bear an unutterable burden of woe without despair. They were intended to help the people learn a lesson from the past and at the same time to retain faith in God even when confronted with overwhelming disaster. Opening the doors of prayer, they pointed the way to repentance and faith, and thus aroused hope in the mercy of God.

That the Jewish people have recognized the value of these poems is seen in their usage. Lamentations is included in the Five Rolls which are read on important anniversary days every year in Judaism. Our little book is read on the ninth of Ab (near the end of July), a fast day that is observed in the commemoration of the destruction of the first and second Temples. The Roman church uses passages from Lamentations for the last three days of Holy Week. Passages from the book are also included in certain Protestant liturgies. Its use in the synagogue and in the church through the centuries is an abiding testimony to its influence on the religious life of the world, and may well show why the canonicity of Lamentations has never been questioned.

Outline

Section **I** *The Song of a Mourning City*

Lamentations 1:1-22

A. THE CITY'S PLIGHT, 1:1-7

This song of deep sorrow begins with a description of the captive city of Jerusalem personified as a woman bereft of her husband and children. The unhappy state of her widowhood is mourned. **How!** was the only appropriate way to begin a dirge. It opened the way for any expression of grief that was suitable for the occasion. Here it prepares the way for a disclosure of the city's tragic predicament. The loneliness of widowhood is emphasized, **How doth the city sit solitary!** (1) Once it **was full of people,** and had a name **among the nations;** but it is now empty, and her children are in captivity. **Her lovers** (2; political allies), after humbling her, have tossed her aside as a soiled plaything. Betrayed and afflicted, she weeps **in the night,** finding **no rest** (3), and there is **none to comfort her.** The expression **between the straits** means "in the midst of her troubles" (Smith-Goodspeed).

In addition to all this she lives in a widowed state spiritually. The religious life of the city has stopped. The Temple has been destroyed. **The ways** (roads) to **Zion** are empty; no worshippers appear for her **solemn feasts; her gates are desolate;** and the **priests** groan (4). There is the **bitterness** of remorse, for her day of grace is past. To make matters worse, her judgment comes from a divine hand. **The Lord hath afflicted her** (5). But in this the prophet recognizes divine justice; Jerusalem's troubles are due to **the multitude of her transgressions. Her beauty is departed** (6); her adversaries have the upper hand; her families are in exile. So destitute of **strength** are **her princes** that they are like stags without **pasture;** weakened by famine and winded before their pursuers, **they are gone**—they fall to rise no more.

In this weakened and widowed condition, haunting memories come to increase the city's sorrow. Jerusalem remembers the **pleasant things** that were hers **in the days of old** (7). This is the reason for loud outcries and weeping. But there is no alleviation of her suffering, for her **adversaries** take delight in her misery. **Her sabbaths** is better "her downfall" (RSV).

B. THE CITY'S PERVERSITY, 1:8-11

The secret of Jerusalem's trouble lay in the fact that she had **grievously sinned** (8). Her sinning had not been a surface thing. The word **removed** is rendered "filthy" in RSV and "unclean" in ASV. **Her filthiness is in her skirts** (9) indicates that her sin was an inward perversity, i.e., an inner disposition. Jerusalem was as unclean morally as a menstrous woman was unclean ceremonially. Therefore Jerusalem's basic problem was an evil heart (Jer. 17:9).

They have seen her nakedness (8) means that her true nature has been revealed; polluted and impure, she turns away in shame. **She came down wonderfully** (9), i.e., "she degenerated astoundingly" because she followed the inclinations of a perverse heart. She failed to consider the ultimates of life. **She remembereth not her last end**; she lived only for the present. Verse 10 refers primarily to the desecration of the Temple. **Her pleasant things** were the "utensils for the sacrificial offerings" (Berk., fn.). But there is a deeper spiritual implication. The enemy had **entered . . . her sanctuary** (10), and had taken **her pleasant things,** i.e., robbed her of her virtue; and now **her people** (11) groan under the magnitude of their sin. She acknowledges that she is **vile.** The sorrows of widowhood are only increased by the knowledge of her uncleanness. The literal meaning of 11 is made clear by Smith-Goodspeed: "They give of their treasures for food to keep themselves alive."

C. THE CITY'S PLEA, 1:12-19

The accumulated weight of her tragic condition has become too great to bear. Judah cries aloud in her anguish, **Is it nothing to you, all ye that pass by?** (12) Although the Hebrew is difficult, KJV has caught the sense. Addressing any who may hear her cry, she begs for compassion, insisting that there is no **sorrow like unto my sorrow.** She confesses that her punishment is from **the Lord,** and beginning with this, she enumerates all the things which she has suffered at His hand. God has kindled a **fire** (13) in her **bones. It prevaileth against them** probably means, "It has subdued them" (Berk.). **A net** has been **spread** for her feet; her **transgressions** have been **wreathed** into an intolerable **yoke** about her **neck** (14). Her **mighty men** (15), as well as the flower of her youth, have been cast into the **winepress** of God's wrath. The contemplation of her many woes brings a new outburst of tears, **For these things I weep; mine eye . . . runneth down with water** (16). But there is no **comforter** to assuage her grief, and the **enemy** has **prevailed** over her.

While she is so choked with tears that she cannot speak, a voice seems to be heard saying that, although **Zion** (17) holds out **her hands** in pitiful supplication, God has **commanded** that she must be thus afflicted. The reference to **a menstrous woman** (her enemies) is a figure of speech meaning, "Jerusalem has become among them as one who is unclean" (Berk.). After regaining a measure of composure, Zion acknowledges that God has dealt justly with her. She confesses that she has **rebelled against his commandment** (18). There is no resentment in her words, and no disposition to defend herself. She further acknowledges, **My lovers** (alien nations and gods to whom Judah had turned) **deceived me**. Because of this her children are in **captivity**; her **priests** and . . . **elders** have expired. The sadness of her condition overwhelms her as she makes a final plea, **Hear . . . all people, and behold my sorrow** (18-19).

D. The City's Prayer, 1:20-22

Betrayed, broken, and punished, Zion now lifts up her voice in prayer, **O Lord, . . . I am in distress . . . I have grievously rebelled** (20); **there is none to comfort me** (21). In 20, **My bowels are troubled** is better, "My soul is wretched" (Moffatt). In this rehearsal of her predicament there are all the elements of a repentant heart: deep sorrow, confession, self-abasement, self-despair, and faith. Judah turns to the Lord because she is now convinced that He alone can help her. There is no effort to excuse any of her sins, and she accepts her punishment as just. She does, however, express the faith that somewhere God will vindicate her before her enemies: **Thou wilt bring the day that thou hast called, and they**, i.e., her enemies, **shall be like unto me** (21). Here is the faith that in a morally ordered universe no transgressor will get off scot-free. **Let all their wickedness come before thee** (22) is a recognition that all evil will be punished. Her enemies will also know the penalty for sin. A sovereign God will make all things come right.

Section **II** *The Song of a Broken People*

Lamentations 2:1-22

This poem continues the general theme of c. 1, a lamentation over the city of Jerusalem. However, it seems to broaden its scope to include the people of Israel in general and Judah in particular. As an acrostic poem it is almost identical in form with c. 1, with the exception that the sixteenth and seventeenth letters of the Hebrew alphabet are transposed. Despite this, there is no interruption of the thought. This phenomenon occurs again in cc. 3 and 4. Chapter 2 continues the theological assumption that the people's punishment is a direct result of their disobedience to God, and that their punishment is wholly deserved.

A. The People's Antagonist, 2:1-10

The awful reality of Zion's affliction is now revealed. The detailed account indicates that the writer was an eyewitness to the catastrophe that he describes. The astonishing thing about the poem is that the Lord is seen as Judah's real Antagonist. The writer portrays what it means for one to have God as his Enemy. It illustrates the New Testament statement that "it is a fearful thing to fall into the hands of the living God" (Heb. 10:31). This is all the more amazing when it is set over against God's continuing love for His people. But the admission that one's punishment comes from the hand of God can be very salutary in its effect. It may mark the beginning of repentance.

The anger of the Lord is a very real and awesome thing. **The day of his anger** (1) saw a number of unusual incidents taking place among His people. **A cloud** indicates a calamity of gigantic proportions. God has **cast down . . . the beauty of Israel** (the Temple), and **remembered not his footstool** (mercy seat). He has **thrown down . . . the strong holds . . . of Judah** and dishonored **the kingdom** and her **princes** (2). **He hath cut off . . . the horn** (power) **of Israel** (3) by withdrawing **his right hand** from her defense. At the same time He has **poured out his fury like fire** (4). He has destroyed the delight of their eyes (the Temple) and **swallowed up all her palaces** (5). He has multiplied the mournings and the lamentations of **the daughter of Judah.**

510

God's actions are seen as a vindication of His righteousness. He does not look with approval upon sin anywhere; **he hath violently taken away his tabernacle** (booth), and stopped the mockery of Judah's appointed **feasts** and **sabbaths (6)**. The expression **as if it were of a garden** seems to be a figure of God's power and man's insecurity; God destroyed the stone Temple as though it were a gardener's temporary booth made of branches and leaves. Even **the king and the priest** have felt the rod of divine wrath. He has **scorned his altar (7)** and **abhorred his own sanctuary,** indicating that something more than outward ritual is needed to prevent the judgment of a holy God. The shout of the enemy has been heard in the holy place as though gathering for a **feast** day. God's face was so set against Zion that He made deliberate plans for her destruction and marked off His purposes with **a line (8)**. **Rampart** and **wall** stand for the whole defense of the city. As a result the city's **gates are sunk into the ground (9)**, her **bars** (defenses) are **broken, her king and her princes** are in exile, **her prophets** are without **vision,** and **the law** is suspended. **The elders (10)** wrap themselves in **sackcloth,** and pour **dust upon their heads,** while **the virgins** hang **their heads** in shame.

B. THE PEOPLE'S ANGUISH, 2:11-16

While the prophet has been setting forth the physical destruction of the city and nation, the tide of emotion has been rising in his soul. When he turns to contemplate the condition of the individuals involved, he cannot restrain his grief. He breaks out in a personal lament over what he has so recently seen with his own **eyes (11)**. These words reflect the compassionate spirit of the prophet (Jer. 9:1; 14:17). He cries aloud in his great suffering, **Mine eyes . . . my bowels . . . my liver.** All of these are Oriental expressions of extreme anguish. He then relates what his eyes have beheld of the suffering of his people. With the city falling in shambles all about him, the tenderhearted prophet sees young **children** and babes swooning from hunger and disease. Their piteous cries are heard as with gasping breath they beg **their mothers (12)** for food; and only moments later pour out **their soul,** i.e., expire, upon their mothers' breasts.

In the midst of his distress the poet tries to think of some like catastrophe with which to compare the people's present situation. He hoped to bring **comfort** to the suffering nation **(13)**, but alas, he knows of nothing with which to compare this great sorrow. It is as measureless as **the sea.**

Jeremiah then lays his finger on the real cause of the trouble; the catastrophe has a moral basis. This overwhelming debacle can be traced directly to the deceptive visions and misleading oracles of the false **prophets** (14). They were not faithful in exposing the **iniquity** of the people: "Your prophets saw for you vanity and whitewash" (14, lit.). Their lack of faithfulness to proclaim God's truth had now brought **banishment** and exile. Jeremiah has laid the ax to the root of the tree; a nation or a church always dies first in its leaders. **The prophets** (cf. Jer. 14:14-16; 23:9-40) are held accountable for the whole tragic situation, although the people are not excused for their willingness to be led astray.

The poet now portrays the unrestrained derision that the people of Judah and Jerusalem endure from all who **pass by** (15). Even the travellers who do not necessarily bear any hate for Jerusalem express amazement and contempt for the once proud city. They **wag their head** and **clap their hands,** saying, **Is this the city** called **The perfection of beauty?** The **enemies** of the Jews, on the other hand, show no sense of restraint. They **hiss** and **gnash** their **teeth** in fiendish glee, crying, **Certainly this is the day we have looked for** (16).

C. THE PEOPLE'S ANSWER, 2:17-22

In search of a solution, the prophet begins an exhortation to the people. He reminds them that there is a moral government operating in the universe. **In the days of old** (17) the Lord had made a covenant with His people at Sinai. At that time He gave commandments for the welfare of the nation. These commandments contained both blessings and curses. All through the centuries God had **fulfilled his word** in every detail. Their punishment now was due to their failure to keep His commands. He had not spared or pitied, in order that Israel might know that the laws of God operate inexorably in the lives of men. **The horn of thine adversaries** (17) would be the strength of their enemies.

But since God is holy, He not only punishes sin with great severity; He forgives all those who repent with broken and contrite hearts. The God who afflicts will also heal. The prophet insists that the answer to their situation is to be found in sincere,

earnest prayer. In 18-19 he proceeds to put the kind of prayer
they ought to pray in their hearts and in their mouths. In KJV
it is not clear who is addressing whom. It seems clearest to
understand it as Jeremiah exhorting the people of Jerusalem. In
an Oriental fashion that seems strange to Western minds, the
broken **wall** of Jerusalem is addressed as representing the city
and its inhabitants. They are bidden to cry **day and night (18)**
in supplication to God, to **let tears run down like a river . . . give
thyself no rest.** His exhortation is reinforced in 19, where he
urges them to pray all through **the night . . . lift up thy hands
toward him.** The Jews divide the night into three **watches.** The
implication is that the God who heard the cries of the children
of Israel in Egypt (Exod. 3:7) and through all their later history
will hear them now.

In 20 the people begin to entreat the Lord. They pray,
Behold, O Lord, and consider to whom thou hast done this.
There follows a prayer of lamentation in which they rehearse all
the tragic things that have taken place, **Shall the women eat . . .
children? shall the priest . . . be slain in the sanctuary? The
young and the old lie . . . in the streets (21).**

It is a sorry tale of woe. There is, however, in this rehearsal
an implied request (readily understood by the ancient mind) for
mercy and deliverance. They believed that God could not be
indifferent to an enumeration of all these outrages against natural
instincts (20b), religious sanctities (20c), and human life (21-22).
And their faith in God was right. He is never indifferent to
those who are truly penitent. Thus the chapter ends with a veiled
expression of hope.

Section III The Song of a Suffering Prophet

Lamentations 3:1-66

This poem would have been appropriate as a part of c. 20 of Jeremiah's prophecy, or better still following the cistern episode of c. 38. This chapter is actually the same length as cc. 1 and 2, but the construction is different, so that the verses are only one-third as long and there are three times as many of them. Instead of only the first line of each stanza beginning with a consecutive letter of the Hebrew alphabet, as in cc. 1 and 2, all three lines of each stanza begin with the same letter. Thus lines 1, 2, and 3 all begin with *Aleph,* and 4, 5, and 6 begin with the letter *Beth,* etc. Unlike the two previous chapters, each line is considered a verse in itself, thus bringing the total verses to sixty-six instead of the usual twenty-two.

The poem is written from the standpoint of an individual, and all the verses carry "I," "me," or "my," except vv. 40-47. This use of the first person does not preclude the poem from being used as a communal lament, since the writer identifies himself with the community in its affliction. Their trouble is his trouble, and their grief is his grief. "He is organically related to them and seeks to lead them into the same religious apprehension of their affliction as he has, in order that they may share his faith."[1]

A. A CRY OF DESPERATION, 3:1-18

The poet identifies himself as an individual who has experienced in his own life all the suffering that the nation has undergone: **I am the man that hath seen affliction** (1). Apparently he conceives of himself as typical of the nation. As their representative before God, he has borne their griefs and carried their sorrows. He has repeatedly felt the **rod** of divine **wrath.** In his pain he cries aloud that God has changed his **light** into **darkness** (2), and it seems like the darkness of **they that be dead** (6; in Sheol). God has **turned** against him and

---

[1]A. S. Herbert, "Lamentations," *Peake's Commentary on the Bible* (London: Thomas Nelson and Sons, Ltd., 1962), p. 566.

punishes him **all the day** (3). Disease has wracked his body until he is prematurely **old** (4). **Gall and travail** (5; bitterness and hardship) have been his portion. There is no pleasantness to life and it is a struggle to survive.

He hath hedged me about (7), i.e., God has fenced him in and he has lost his freedom. He complains that he carries the **heavy chain** of a prisoner. Although he cries out in his anguish, there is no answer to his **cry—he shutteth out my prayer** (8). **Hewn** (firmly fixed) **stone** blocks his way and drives him into wrong **paths** (9). Everywhere he turns there is trouble; his frustrations are almost unbearable. As if these things were not enough, God actively takes the field against him. Like **a bear** or **a lion** (10), God lies **in wait** to ambush him. He pursues him relentlessly with **bow and arrow** (12), so that his **reins** ("heart," RSV) are filled with the shafts of God's vengeance (13).

I was a derision (14), i.e., his own **people** made him their **taunt-song all the day.** He has no rest for mind or body; his heart is **filled** with bitter sorrow, and he is drunk **with wormwood** (15; cf. Jer. 23:15).[2] God has **broken** his **teeth with gravel** (16), i.e., given him **stones** for bread. **He hath covered me with ashes** means that he has not suffered merely light embarrassment, but has rather plumbed the depths of disgrace and humiliation. **Peace** (17) has long since fled, and the prophet has "forgotten what happiness is" (RSV).

Jeremiah is in the depths of despair; he cries out, **My strength and my hope is perished** (18). Blocked at every turn, broken in body and mind, torn with a thousand sorrows, and suffering the pangs of the damned, strength is gone and hope has fled. But man's extremity is God's opportunity. It is precisely at this point that his faith finds solid footing.

B. A Confession of Faith, 3:19-39

The prophet has poured out his complaint before the Lord. His strength is gone, his heart is broken, he lies spent and helpless. All the tenseness and all the struggle have gone out of him. He turns loose of himself. Humble and quiet, he waits before God. In the stillness there comes a change. He begins to pray softly, "Oh, remember my **affliction . . . My soul** is **humbled**

---

[2]**Wormwood** was a bitter substance, usually associated with gall. Smith-Goodspeed interpret it, "He hath sated me with anguish."

(bowed down) within me" (19-20, lit.). Insight and understanding begin to dawn: **This I recall to my mind** (21)—he begins to remember many things that he had forgotten while in frantic grief. God does not despise the broken and humble in heart (Ps. 51:17)!

Surely here is "A Message of Faith and Hope." (1) The **mercies** of God never cease; **his compassions fail not** (22). Even if we fail, He remains faithful! Furthermore, His mercies **are new every morning** (23). The ceaselessness of God's mercy is a proof of His truthworthiness,[3] and so the prophet cries aloud, **Great is thy faithfulness!**[4] These thoughts bring a hearty response and the prophet continues, **The Lord is my portion** (i.e., the sum total of my desires); **therefore will I hope in him** (24). As the prophet confesses his faith in God, other things impress themselves upon his mind.

(2) God's way is the best way. (*a*) He is favorable **to the soul** (25) that seeks guidance from Him. (*b*) Patience and **hope** (26) open the channels of **salvation**. (*c*) Discipline in **youth** (27) makes for dependability and success in adulthood.

(3) Blessed is the man that endures temptation. (*a*) That man has completely yielded himself to God. (*b*) He has "bit the **dust**" in self-abasement (29). (*c*) He has given up his rights and, like Jesus, **he giveth his cheek** (30) to the smiters (Isa. 50:6; Matt. 5:39); and though **filled . . . with reproach,** he reviles not again (I Cor. 4:12; I Pet. 2:23).

(4) Suffering has a moral purpose. (*a*) God tests His people but His rejection is not permanent—He **will not cast off for ever** (31). (*b*) Although He permits suffering to come, He loves men too well to forsake them or give them one trial too much (32). (*c*) He takes no delight in men's afflictions (33), but He does allow afflictions to overtake men in order that a higher good may come to the sufferer.

(5) We may rest assured that God sees and disapproves of all evil. (*a*) He is against all mistreatment and injustice done to the helpless (34). (*b*) Any perversion of justice, whether for religious reasons or on political grounds, must suffer His displeasure and punishment (35-36).

---

[3]W. F. Adeney, "Lamentations of Jeremiah," *Pulpit Commentary* (Grand Rapids: Wm. B. Eerdmans Publishing Company, 1950 [reprint]), p. 39.

[4]Vv. 22-23 were the inspiration for, and furnish key phrases in, the language of Thomas Chisholm's hymn "Great Is Thy Faithfulness."

(6) Mourning unduly over one's afflictions is wrong. Nothing is done without God's permission. He allows both **good** and **evil** (38) to exist in the world. As a free agent, man does not have to choose **evil** with its resultant **punishment** (39). Therefore he should not **complain** over his sufferings when he has sinned, but he should rather lament over his **sins,** which cause his sufferings.

C. A PLEA FOR REPENTANCE, 3: 40-47

Since transgression and rebellion on the part of the people have brought suffering and punishment, the prophet makes a plea for the people to **search** (examine) and **try** (test) their **ways** (40; conduct). He insists that the least they could do would be to analyze their situation honestly. Instead of blaming God for their sufferings, they should ascertain the meaning and purpose of the trouble that has come upon them by taking thought to themselves. The object of all this should be to adjust matters between themselves and God, i.e., **turn again to the Lord.** In the Hebrew, **turn** or "return" (*shub*) means "to repent."

Since prayer is the proper way to approach God, Jeremiah admonishes them to begin their examination with earnest, sincere petition. They should, therefore, **lift up** their **heart with** their **hands unto God** (41). The emphasis on the heart indicates that inward submission must accompany outward acts of supplication, if prayer is to be genuine. Heretofore they had prayed, but their hearts had not accompanied their **hands** in the exercise.

In 42-47 the prophet speaks the words that the people ought to say. Here is a lamentation for what rebellion against God has done to the people.

There must be confession of sin, **We have transgressed and . . . rebelled** (42), and their confession must be accompanied by lamentation (mourning, godly sorrow).

In these verses we see "The Results of Rejecting God." (1) Rebellion cuts off the mercies of God; **Thou hast not pardoned,** 42. To be true to His own nature, God could not pardon until repentance was genuine. (2) Rebellion produces swift and relentless punishment, **Thou hast slain and hast not pitied,** 43. Sin is a terrible boomerang. (3) Rebellion separates from God; **a cloud** of transgression lies between man and God, so **that** no **prayer** can get **through,** 44. It is only when people turn from rebellion that God can hear prayer (Ps. 66:18). (4) Rebellion brings humiliation and grief; **Thou hast made us as the off-scouring and refuse,** 45. (5) Rebellion brings terror and confusion; **Fear and a snare is come upon us,** 46-47. "The way of transgressors is hard," and the prophet pleads with the people to bring forth "fruits meet for repentance" (Matt. 3:8).

Verses 40-47 deal with the theme "What to Do When Conviction Comes." (1) Admit that we are under God's condemnation, 42-47; (2) Honestly examine our lives, 40*a*; (3) Turn to the Lord, 40*b*; (4) Be utterly sincere in our prayer, 41 (A. F. Harper).

D. THE PAIN OF INTERCESSION, 3:48-54

As the prophet contemplates what sin and rebellion have done to his people, he breaks into a prayer of intercession, **Mine eye runneth down . . . for** (in behalf of) **. . . my people** (48). Time passes, but he does not cease to pray. He is determined to continue his intercession **till the Lord look down . . . from heaven** (50). Although his intercession takes a terrible toll of his physical powers, he continues to pray, "**Mine eye** (his weeping stands for travail of soul) deals severely with my life" (51, lit.). In agony of soul Jeremiah actually faces physical death. At this moment his mind seems to turn to his cistern experience before the fall of Jerusalem (Jer. 38:6-13). Verse 52 seems to be saying that he faced death in similar fashion then. Without excuse, his **enemies** had hunted him down. They planned to **cut off** (53) his **life** by casting him **in the dungeon** and covering the mouth of the pit with a **stone.** He sank in the mire and the **waters** of death (figuratively speaking) **flowed over** his **head.** In despair he had cried, **I am cut off** (54), i.e., "Death has come." These words are certainly written in the spirit of Jeremiah, whose life was one long martyrdom. They are placed here so that the prayer of the prophet might become a prayer of intercession on the lips of the people.

The passage shows "The True Prayer of Intercession." (1) Intercession involves taking on oneself as it were the sin and guilt of the ones prayed for; (2) Intercession involves a sense of desperation (48-51) similar to that of Queen Esther, "If I perish, I perish" (Esther 4:16); (3) There can be no intercession without suffering and humiliation; (4) Intercession may actually mean the death of the intercessor—at least one must be willing to give his life (Exod. 32:32).

E. A Song of Confidence, 3:55-66

As the prophet looks back upon his cistern experience and compares it to the present moment, his faith begins to rise. He soon breaks forth into a song of confidence and trust, **I called upon thy name, O Lord . . . Thou** didst hear **my voice** (55-56, lit.). He continues to sing, **Thou** didst draw **near . . . thou** didst say, **Fear not** (57, lit.). He now brings all of his troubles, both past and present, before the Lord and cries, **Thou hast pleaded . . . thou hast redeemed** (58). **. . . thou hast seen . . .** (59-60). **Thou hast heard . . .** (61). Thou wilt **recompence** (64, lit.). The Hebrew of the last part of 56 is not clear. It may mean, "Close not Thy ear to my sighs and my cries" (Berk.). **I am their musick** (63) means, "I am the theme of their taunt-song" (Berk.).

The passage expresses the confidence of the poet that God will vindicate His people, and will eventually make all things come right. Thus he rejoices over the presence of a moral Governor in the universe who will judge the cause of the poor and needy. He looks forward to the day when God's people shall be avenged of their enemies: **Persecute and destroy them . . . from under the heavens of the Lord** (66). In that day right shall prevail over the whole world, and "the earth shall be full of the knowledge of the Lord, as the waters cover the sea" (Isa. 11:9).

The mood reflected in 64-66 has been called the "imprecatory" element in the Old Testament. It is sometimes difficult to understand. The curses which are invoked upon enemies appear sub-Christian and far below the standard given by Jesus in Matt. 5:43-48. However, it should be kept in mind that it is difficult to distinguish between the Hebrew forms, "Let this happen" and "This will happen." We can be sure that at least some of the maledictions are simple predictions of what will happen as a result of rebellion against God (cf. BBC, Vol. III, "The Book of Psalms," Intro.).

Section IV *The Song of a Ruined Kingdom*

Lamentations 4:1-22

This poem is a song of contrasts. It compares the former glory of the kingdom of Judah, as represented by Jerusalem, to its present wretched condition. Jeremiah was an eyewitness to the terrible disaster of 587-586 B.C., when Jerusalem fell to the Babylonians. One can feel the throb of sorrow that prevailed during the siege, and that followed the demolition of the city. The poem is an alphabetic acrostic like cc. 1 and 2 with the exception that the stanzas here have two lines instead of three. The sin of Judah is the most prominent theme in the chapter. This idea is not entirely lacking in the preceding chapters but it is now set forth as the primary reason for the collapse of the kingdom. The magnitude of Judah's sin is dealt with in 1-12, and the consequences of her sin is the theme of 13-22. Thus the moral reasons for Judah's fate are uppermost in the poet's mind.

A. THE DEGRADING POWER OF SIN, 4:1-12

The depths to which Judah and Jerusalem had fallen can be traced to rebellious hearts. The descriptions here reveal the degradation into which a nation can fall when its moral foundations are removed. The wail of the prophet as he laments over the glory of the Judah that once was, and the devastated condition in which he sees her now, is enough to break the heart. "How are the mighty fallen!"

The poet sings a dirge over the unbelievable change that has come to this once proud nation and its capital, **How is the gold become dim!** (1) Blackened and tarnished, the golden city lies in a desolate ash heap. He bewails the utter ruin of the Temple— **The stones of the sanctuary are poured out in the top of every street**; i.e., scattered all over the city. The youth of the nation, the hope of its ongoing life, lie dead in the streets. In life they were **comparable to fine gold**, (2); now they are mere lumps of clay, like broken **pitchers** on the refuse heap **of the potter!**

The mothers of Judah, deranged from suffering, treat their babies worse than the wild animals treat their young. Despite

520

the fact that **sea monsters** (3; better "jackals") are violent beasts of prey, yet they do not forget their offspring. Although **ostriches** are notorious for being neglectful and cruel to their young (Job 39:13-17), the mothers of Judah are even worse; they have **become cruel** (inhuman). With their motherly instincts dead, they let their nursing infants die for lack of nourishment. The younger **children** cry for **bread** (4), but no one takes note of their need. Women who were once clothed **in scarlet** (purple) and feasted on dainty food now wander aimlessly about **the streets.** They are reduced to circumstances in which they **embrace dunghills** (5) in their search for food.

Jerusalem has had a sadder fate than **Sodom.** That city **was overthrown . . . in a moment** (6) by the hand of God, but Jerusalem's punishment has been drawn out almost beyond endurance. The reference to Sodom emphasizes the magnitude of Jerusalem's guilt. She was the city that had had the Temple, the law, and the prophets. Since so much light and privilege had been hers, she deserved a severer punishment than Sodom. It must have been difficult for a Jewish poet to write v. 6, and it portrays in an unforgettable fashion Jeremiah's understanding of the degrading power of sin.

"Her princes"—rather than **Nazarites** (7)—once beautiful in appearance, well-fed, and popular with the people, are now in a lamentable condition. Their faces are "darker than blackness" (8, lit.); their names are forgotten; people do not recognize them, for they are but walking skeletons, shriveled and withered **like a stick.**

The condition of Judah and Jerusalem is so deplorable that those **slain with sword** (9) **are better** off than the living. The siege had deprived the living of even the bare necessities of life. Some **pitiful women** (10), driven by hunger, boiled **their own children** for food. No one would have thought that Jerusalem could have come to this! Even **the kings of the earth** (12) are astonished at the fate of this nation and city. Sin when it has run its course brings forth death (Jas. 1:15).

In 1-12 we see "Sin's Degrading Effects." (1) Life's beauty goes, 1; (2) The resources of youth are lost, 2; (3) Womanhood sinks lower than the beasts of the field, 4-5, 10; (4) Sin's effects are greatest where light has been brightest, 6; (5) Even leaders become confused and broken men, 7; (6) Final punishment is frighteningly thorough, 11-12.

B. The Demoralizing Power of Sin, 4:13-16

The responsibility for the ruin of Judah is laid squarely on the religious leaders of the nation.

> *This was for the sins of her prophets*
> *and the iniquities of her priests* (13, RSV).

It is in the lives of these men that we see the demoralizing power of sin. They could have saved the land from ruin. Instead, (1) Their teachings and their example crippled the moral life of the nation. (a) They could not discern between the voice of God and the voice of their own hearts. (b) They prophesied that which was false, saying, "Peace, peace; when there is no peace" (Jer. 6:14). (c) They succumbed to the pressure of the times and preached what the people wanted to hear; they did not expose the sins of the people, so that they could be healed (2:14). (d) They were afraid to stand up for the right; they placed popularity above righteousness. (e) They came to believe a lie to be the truth, and a truth a lie. Jeremiah had earlier thundered against these false leaders of the people (Jer. 5:31; 6:13; 23:11-16), but they thwarted his every effort to influence the people toward genuine repentance.

(2) They were guilty of murder, perhaps not directly, but indirectly. Under the guise of religion, they **shed the blood of the just in the midst of** the nation (13). Their counsel and influence had brought about the death of the righteous (see Jer. 26:20-24). (3) There came a day when their world tumbled in on them. When the city of Jerusalem was destroyed, they became bewildered; **They . . . wandered** (staggered) **as blind men in the streets** (14). Their confusion was a result of the blindness of their hearts. They were not adequate for the emergencies of life. (4) Their sin found them out. Their masks came off when their predictions were proved false. Men then recognized them for what they were, vile and wretched impostors. It was their punishment to be treated as moral lepers. Men cried after them, **Depart ye . . . unclean . . . depart . . . touch not** (15). (5) They were driven from their own land by their own people. The curse of Cain rested on them. **They wandered . . . among the heathen** (15), but even here they were not wanted. (6) They suffered divine retribution; **The anger of the Lord** has scattered them (16). Despite the fact that they were **priests and elders,**

no favor was granted them by either God or man. As the moral Governor of the universe, God took the responsibility to see that they were punished.

C. The Deceiving Power of Sin, 4:17-20

This section is an acknowledgment that the nation had put its confidence in the wrong place. The poet confesses for the people. Jeremiah is looking back to the time of the siege (17-18), the fall of the city (18), the flight of the king and his nobles (19), and the capture of Zedekiah (20).

The prophet declares that (1) the nation was deceived into placing its trust in foreign allies. **We have watched for a nation that could not save us (17).** Jeremiah, and other prophets, had warned Judah against putting her confidence in men, but the nation had rejected the word of the Lord and continued to rely on Egypt. Pharaoh had made an attempt on one occasion to come to the rescue of Jerusalem (Jeremiah 37), but the whole episode had been a sorry failure. The Psalmist had likewise cried, **Vain is the help of man** (Ps. 60:11), but it is amazing what people "fall for" when they are out of step with God.

(2) The nation had been deceived into thinking that it could successfully resist Babylon. Although Jeremiah had repeatedly proclaimed that God had delivered the Near East into the hand of Nebuchadnezzar (Jeremiah 25), the people of Judah would not believe. They continued to rebel until the city fell. **Our days are fulfilled; for our end is come** (18). (3) They were deceived into thinking that they could escape by fleeing. **They pursued us upon the mountains** (19). This apparently refers to the flight of Zedekiah and his princes (Jer. 39:4-7). When people begin to disobey God, they keep thinking that the next move will be the right one. It never is. (4) The nation was deceived into thinking that God's promises to the Davidic house were unconditional. They had completely misunderstood the character of God, and His methods of operation. Now they wail, **The breath of our nostrils, the anointed of the Lord, was taken in their pits** (20). The reference here is to the capture of Zedekiah by the Baby-lonians in the "jungle" of the Jordan, and the end of the Davidic monarchy. The verse reveals the loyalty of the people of Judah to their royal house, but it also reveals that reliance upon man as the ultimate source of wisdom and strength is grievously misplaced.

D. THE DESTRUCTIVE POWER OF SIN, 4:21-22

Here is an example of how the sin of pride can destroy a nation. Edom (see map 1), although a descendant of Abraham and a kinsman of Judah, was always arrogant and haughty where Israel was concerned. Her pride reached classic proportions in her reaction to the fall of Jerusalem in 587-586 B.C. She herself had "played things smart." She had collaborated with the enemy, betrayed her neighbors, and withheld her help from the needy. Taking advantage of the misfortune of her kinsman, she went so far as to annex some of Judah's territory (Ezek. 35:10-12). Now she rejoices with fiendish glee at the punishment of Judah, and her own escape from the horrors of war. But at the height of her exultation a voice is heard pronouncing her doom.

The beginning of 21 is sheer irony, **Rejoice and be glad, O daughter of Edom**—i.e., have your fun now—**the cup shall pass through unto thee.** The reference is to the cup of God's fury as prophesied by Jeremiah (25:15-28). **Thou shalt be drunken,** and all the things that accompany drunkenness will be hers: shame, confusion, sorrow, and destruction.

In 22 the poet frankly confesses that Judah and Jerusalem have been severely punished at the hand of the Lord. But Judah has taken her punishment and it is over; **The punishment of thine iniquity is accomplished.** For her a better day is coming; **He will no more carry thee away into captivity.** The implication is that Judah has a future but Edom has none. When Edom's day of punishment arrives, **He will discover** (uncover) **thy sins.** Edom will fall to rise no more (Obad. 18).

Section V The Prayer of a Penitent Nation

Lamentations 5:1-22

In this closing poem there is no alphabetic acrostic. However there are twenty-two verses, which indicates that these five poems belong together. This chapter is more of a prayer than a song of lamentation. Although a large part of the material is a recital of the miseries that the people have suffered, they are enumerated so as to appeal to the compassion of God and to gain His help. They are used confessionally here (recited by the congregation) in order to lead the people to a place of humility and penitence where they may cast themselves on the mercies of God. The poet calls upon the Lord to look with mercy upon their miserable condition. He acknowledges that their afflictions are a result of sin (7). There is much grief on account of these things, and over the desolate condition of Zion. Their only hope arises from the fact that, unlike the thrones of earth, God's throne is eternal, and He is utterly trustworthy in His dealings with men.

A. THE FINAL APPEAL, 5:1-6

Remember, O Lord (1). There is more in this **remember** than appears on the surface. It is the language of prayer. There is in it a sense of great urgency. It breathes of hope and faith. It implies that, if God's attention can be gained and His consideration given, help will soon be forthcoming.

In this fervent appeal Jeremiah calls the attention of God to the suffering and the **reproach** that His chosen people have undergone. **Strangers** and **aliens** (2) have occupied **the inheritance** (land) and the **houses** that God had given them. God's people were as helpless as **orphans** and **widows** (3) who had no fathers or husbands to defend them. The most necessary things of life have to be purchased from their captors; **our water for money; our wood is sold unto us** (4). Did they have to pay the enemy for water from their own cisterns? If this is a picture of Judah following the fall of Jerusalem, it may be so. The yoke of servitude was especially galling; **Our necks are under perse-**

cution (5). They were forced to **labour** constantly for the enemy, and were given no time for decent **rest**. The humiliation of having to give **the hand** (submit) **to the Egyptians and to the Assyrians** in order to keep from starving was almost more than one could bear. The mention of Egyptians and Assyrians is symbolic of enemies east and west; i.e., they were surrounded by foes on every side.

Judah makes her final appeal with strong crying and tears. There seems to be no resentment against God for the punishment she suffers, only penitence and shame. The appeal is made with the faith that, although God has punished, He will also forgive. Since they have gained His attention and He has seen their afflictions, their sufferings will not last forever, nor will He let their oppressors escape judgment.

B. THE COMPLETE CONFESSION, 5: 7-18

The poet confesses that there is a moral reason for the nation's plight: **Our fathers have sinned . . . we have borne their iniquities** (7). He recognized that there was a solidarity in the Jewish nation that no generation could escape. The children suffered for the sins of the parents. They were enslaved by their former **servants** (8). They obtained their **bread with the peril of their lives** (9), because of the desert robbers, the fierce Bedouin, who are likened to **the sword of the wilderness**. Their **skin was black like an oven** (10); i.e., hot because of the fever brought on by hunger. Their **women** had been **ravished** (11), their **princes** and **elders** (12) dishonored. The young men **grind at the mill** (13), i.e., do women's work, and even "boys stagger under loads of wood" (RSV). All the **joy** (15) of living has disappeared; only **mourning** remains. Prosperity and honor disappear. **The crown is fallen from our head** (16); i.e., national sovereignty and statehood is gone for the Jews. The nation is no more.

The climax of this passage is reached when the poet himself confesses for his generation, **Woe unto us, that** (for) **we have sinned!** (16) The whole truth is confessed at last! Jeremiah will no longer allow Judah to put all the blame on the past generation, **our fathers** (7), although they were guilty. It is always a good sign when men quit confessing the sins of others and begin to acknowledge their own guilt. Now that the confession has started, he makes it complete. Because of sin, "the whole head is sick," and the whole **heart is faint** (17; Isa. 1:5). Because of sin the **eyes are dim** through weeping. Because of sin **Zion** lies **desolate** and in ruins.

C. The Only Hope, 5:19-22

With their confession complete, hope begins to rise in the hearts of the people. Loosed from a preoccupation with themselves, thoughts of the greatness of God begin to fill their minds. They cry in exultation, **Thou, O Lord, remainest for ever** (19). Unlike the gods of the heathen, the Lord is the Eternal One— the Ever Living One. All other powers and kingdoms may crumble and fall, but **thy throne** (His moral governorship over men) continues throughout all generations. All else may disappear, but God remains! Here is an anchoring place for the soul! Here one's heart may safely rest! Here is ample ground for hoping! "Since His throne endures eternally in heaven, He cannot let His kingdom perish on earth."[1] Therefore it does not seem illogical, when one understands Hebrew psychology, for the people to make a request in the form of a question, "Why dost Thou forsake us so long a time?" (20, lit.) Underneath the surface, the question is packed with hope, for it is based on a Hebrew conception of the character of God.

Verses 21-22 must be taken as a unit. It is stated awkwardly for the modern mind, but in the Hebrew the meaning can be discerned when read in the light of 19. Since God is forever the moral Governor of the universe, His people may have hope. This is what happens in the last two verses of the book—*the people cast themselves without reservation on the mercies of God.* They have become fully aware that submission and surrender is the only way out of their predicament, "Turn us back to thyself, O Lord, that we may be turned . . . unless Thou hast **utterly rejected us,** unless Thou art exceedingly angry with us" (21-22, lit.). Verse 22 is difficult, and it is almost certainly an admission that Judah deserves to be **utterly rejected.** Nevertheless it throbs with ill-concealed hope and unutterable longing.

Thus the book closes on a note of reckless faith—a faith that throws everything in one vast sweep of utter abandonment on the mercies of an eternal God.

[1]Carl F. Keil and Franz Delitzsch, "Lamentations of Jeremiah," *Commentaries on the Old Testament,* II (Grand Rapids: Wm. B. Eerdmans Publishing Co., 1956, [reprint]), 455.

Bibliography

ADENEY, W. F. "Lamentations of Jeremiah." *Pulpit Commentary*, Vol. XI. Grand Rapids: Wm. B. Eerdmans Publishing Co., 1950 (reprint).

ANDERSON, G. W. *A Critical Introduction to the Old Testament.* London: Gerald Duckworth & Co., 1960.

CLARKE, ADAM. "The Lamentations of Jeremiah." *Commentary and Critical Notes,* Vol. IV. New York: Abingdon-Cokesbury, n.d.

HERBERT, A. S. "Lamentations." *Peake's Commentary on the Bible.* Edited by MATTHEW BLACK and H. H. ROWLEY. London: Thomas Nelson and Sons, Ltd., 1962.

KEIL, CARL F., and DELITZSCH, FRANZ. "Lamentations of Jeremiah," Vol. II. *Commentaries on the Old Testament.* Grand Rapids: Wm. B. Eerdmans Publishing Co., 1956 (reprint).

KUIST, H. T. "Lamentations." *The Layman's Bible Commentaries.* London: SCM Press, Ltd., 1960.

MEEK, T. J. "Lamentations." *The Interpreter's Bible.* Edited by GEORGE A. BUTTRICK, *et al.,* Vol. VI. New York: Abingdon Press, 1956.

NAEGELSBACH, C. W. E. "Jeremiah and Lamentations." *Lange's Commentary on the Holy Scriptures.* Grand Rapids: Zondervan Publishing House (reprint).

PEAKE, A. S. "Jeremiah and Lamentations," Vol. II. *The Century Bible.* Edinburgh: T. C. and E. C. Jack, Ltd., 1911.

PRICE, ROSS E. "Lamentations." *Wycliffe Bible Commentary.* Edited by CHARLES PFEIFFER and E. F. HARRISON. Chicago: Moody Press, 1962.

STEPHENS-HODGE, L. E. H. "Lamentations," *New Bible Commentary.* Grand Rapids: Wm. B. Eerdmans Publishing Co., 1963.

THOMPSON, J. G. S. S. "Lamentations." *The Biblical Expositor.* Edited by CARL F. H. HENRY. Philadelphia: A. J. Holman Co., 1960.

The Book of the Prophet

EZEKIEL

J. Kenneth Grider

Introduction

A. Ezekiel Himself

Ezekiel's name means "one whom God sustains." He was taken captive into Babylon by Nebuchadnezzar[1] in 597 B.C. (II Kings 24:14). In Jerusalem he had been a priest (1:3). Perhaps he had ministered in the Temple itself, since his writings show that he was minutely acquainted with that sanctuary. During the fifth year (1:2) of his captivity, in 592 B.C., he was called of the Lord to be a prophet, and exercised that office for at least twenty-two years (29:17).

Along with Ezekiel, in the first major deportation, Nebuchadnezzar had taken 10,000 of the most prominent men of the country—including the skilled workers, the nobility, and King Jehoiachin himself. Nebuchadnezzar thought that, with the leaders in his own land, he could better subject the populace of Jerusalem and Judah to his will. (See Chart B.)

In exile, although King Jehoiachin was imprisoned, the Israelites in general had considerable freedom. Ezekiel had his own house (3:24; 20:1) and was married (24:18). He lived rather comfortably at Tel-abib, near the river Chebar. While Daniel lived out the seventy years of captivity, Ezekiel must have died before it was over.

Ezekiel was a watchman to warn the faithless, and a man with balm for the faithful. Unlike the false prophets, who had been given nothing to say but nevertheless spoke (Jer. 29:31), Ezekiel received his oracles from the Lord. Perhaps more than any other prophet, what he had to say he felt compelled to say.[2]

B. The Times of the Prophet

For the Israelites, being subjected to another power and taken into exile was a disgrace indeed. Canaan had been prom-

---

[1]This king's name appears in the Book of Ezekiel and frequently in these comments. The Babylonians pronounced the name with an r, Nebuchadrezzar; hence most recent commentaries use the r. It is found according to both spellings in the Hebrew of Ezekiel but usually with the n. Therefore Babylon's king is more widely known according to this spelling.

[2]R. B. Y. Scott of Princeton Seminary would certainly have included Ezekiel when he said, "The prophets were driven by an overpowering will to say what they shrank from saying" (1960 presidential address to the Society of Biblical Literature and Exegesis at Union Seminary in N.Y.C.).

ised to them, and finally delivered into their hands by the power of their God. But from Moses onwards they had been told by the prophets that if they rebelled against the Lord they would be punished, driven from the land, and dispersed among the nations (Lev. 26:14-45; Deut. 28:15-68). Already, in 721 B.C., the northern kingdom of Israel, composed of ten of the twelve tribes, had fallen to Assyria. Just before Ezekiel's time, Jeremiah prophesied that a similar fate would come upon Judah, including Jerusalem. Jeremiah had specifically foretold that exile would be their lot and that it would last seventy years (Jer. 29:10).

Ezekiel rose to prominence as a priest just in time to be taken in the Captivity. Nebuchadnezzar of Babylon had first invaded Judah in 606 B.C. He captured Jerusalem and carried away several outstanding young men, including Daniel. This began the seventy years of captivity. Eight years later, in 597, after Jerusalem had revolted, Nebuchadnezzar invaded the Holy City a second time, now taking into exile 10,000 leading men, including Ezekiel.

Zedekiah was made king in Jerusalem. But after eleven years, hoping for help from Egypt, he revolted against Nebuchadnezzar. The king of Babylon then turned his fury against Jerusalem a third time. After a siege of some three years he destroyed the city, the Temple, and the kingdom, killing or deporting the people in large numbers.

It was in such times as these that Ezekiel lived. To such times as these he spoke his warnings and gave his comforts as a prophet of the Lord.

C. The Prophecy Itself

The prophecy of Ezekiel is one of the major prophetic books of the Old Testament. It was divided into forty-eight chapters probably in the thirteenth century A.D. The first twenty-four chapters have to do with Ezekiel's call to be a prophet and with his prophecies concerning the fall of Jerusalem—the final Babylonian destruction, which occurred in the eleventh year of Zedekiah's reign. Chapters 25—33 contain prophecies of judgment against seven heathen nations—Ammon (25:1-7), Moab (25:8-11), Edom (25:12-14), Philistia (25:15-17), Tyre (26:1—28:19), Sidon (28:20-23), and Egypt (29—32). The last section, chapters 33—48, contains prophecies about the restoration of Jerusalem and hope for the future of Israel.

Ezekiel makes it clear that he was an exile in Babylon when he was called to be prophet. He prophesied from Babylon both against his fellow exiles and against those still living in Jerusalem before its final fall during Zedekiah's revolt (1:3; 3:11, 15, 23; 10:15, 20, 22; 11:24-25).

Some have suggested that Ezekiel did not write chapters 40—48. Others would include also chapters 38—39 as from another author. There are scholars who suggest that a redactor added other materials, such as the verses which place the prophet in Babylon as he writes. But there is no serious evidence against the traditional view that the prophecy as a whole is from that dauntless watcher and warner known to the centuries as Ezekiel.

The style of the prophecy is difficult because of the poetic symbolism with which it is adorned. This style caused the ancient Jerome to despair of ever plumbing the book's truth. It may be the reason why John Calvin wrote a commentary on only the first twelve chapters, and why Martin Luther did not give it any special attention. Howie says, "The Prophecy of Ezekiel, written in apocalyptic style and replete with obscurities in text and meaning, has baffled more scholars and given rise to more strange ideas than perhaps any other book of the Bible."[3]

Yet with all the book's symbolic mystery, it yields truths of spiritual worth to those who slacken their rapid pace long enough to dig out what is at the book's depth.

[3]Carl Gordon Howie, *The Date and Composition of Ezekiel* (Philadelphia: Society of Bib. Lit., 1950), p. 1.

Outline

I. The Call to Be a Prophet, 1:1—3:27
   A. Preface to the Call, 1:1-28
   B. The Call Itself, 2:1—3:27

II. Prophecies Against Jerusalem, 4:1—24:27
   A. Four Symbolic Acts, 4:1—5:17
   B. Two Discourses on Israel's Doom, 6:1—7:27
   C. Abominations and Judgments, 8:1—11:25
   D. Prophecies Against Jerusalem, 12:1—19:14
   E. Prophecies Dated 590 B.C., 20:1—23:49
   F. Last Prophecy Before Jerusalem's Fall, 24:1-27

III. Prophecies Against Heathen Peoples, 25:1—32:32
   A. Ammon, Moab, Edom, and Philistia, 25:1-17
   B. Tyre and Sidon, 26:1—28:26
   C. Egypt, 29:1—32:32

IV. Restoration and Hope, 33:1—48:35
   A. Restoration of Israel, 33:1—39:29
   B. Hope, Temporal and Eternal, 40:1—48:35

Section I The Call to Be a Prophet

Ezekiel 1:1—3:27

A. PREFACE TO THE CALL, 1:1-28

Ezekiel . . . the son of Buzi (3) had been a priest in Jerusalem. Now, a captive of Nebuchadnezzar in **the land of the Chaldeans,** the Lord called him to be a prophet.[1] As a priest, he had brought men to God; as a prophet, he will continue this ministry but will need to be nearer to God than before. As a priest he was near to men in their sorrows in order to bring them to God. As a prophet he must be near enough to God to receive His messages for men.

1. What Precipitated His Call (1:1)

The opening words of Ezekiel's prophecy are, **Now it came to pass . . . I saw visions of God** (1). What had occurred that precipitated Ezekiel's call? False prophets had arisen among the exiles who told them what they wanted to hear, that there would be a speedy return to the homeland. Jeremiah, prophesying at the time in Jerusalem, had sent a letter to the exile community telling them that their captivity would endure for seventy years and that meanwhile they should submit themselves to God's will and ways (Jeremiah 29). Not everyone liked what Jeremiah had said, and there was unrest along the Chebar. This message had been sent during the fourth year of Zedekiah's reign (Jer. 51:59), which was also the fourth year of the Captivity. Soon after, in the fifth year of the Captivity, God raised up Ezekiel from among the exiles. He, like Jeremiah, would authentically declare God's truth to the people.

2. The Time of His Call (1:1-2)

a. *"The thirtieth year"* (1:1). No one knows to what event or point in time **the thirtieth year** refers. It had been thirty years

---

[1]The word *prophet* means "one who speaks for another." Cf. Exod. 7:1, "Aaron thy brother shall be thy prophet." Aaron was to be Moses' spokesman. We also read, "He [Aaron] shall be thy [Moses'] spokesman" (Exod. 4:16). The prefix *pro* in the word *prophet* does not mean "beforehand," as in "procession," but "instead of," as in "pronoun." The prophet is God's spokesman who speaks to men in God's stead. See A. C. Knudson, *The Beacon Lights of Prophecy* (New York: Eaton and Mains, 1914), p. 30.

since the book of the law had been located in Temple debris, which precipitated a change in Judah's worship. But there is no general dating of events from that time. Indeed, it was not customary to date from the time of a significant happening within a king's reign.

Some scholars have suggested that this was the thirtieth year since the last year of jubilee. But again, such a method of dating was not customary.

Perhaps those are correct who suggest that this is the thirtieth year in Ezekiel's own life. The thirtieth year of a Jewish man's life was peculiarly significant in his attaining maturity. **The fourth month** would correspond to our late June or early July.

b. "The fifth year" (1:2). **Jehoiachin's captivity** began in 597 B.C., after he had been king only three months. Ezekiel's call came during **the fifth year** of the king's imprisonment,[2] which was also the fifth year of Ezekiel's exile in Chaldea.

3. The Place of the Call (1:1-3)

Ezekiel was **among the captives by the river of Chebar** (1) (meaning "great river") in Chaldea—of which Babylon was the capital city. This river is perhaps the same as the Chaboras River of Mesopotamia, which finally empties into the Euphrates near Kirkesion (see map 1).[3]

Because Ezekiel is so familiar with the Temple and seems often to speak to the people of Jerusalem, some scholars say that he actually wrote from there and not from Babylon. However Babylon is specifically indicated as the place of his call; it is also repeatedly mentioned as the place of his labors (1:3; 3:11, 15, 23; 10:15, 20, 22; 11:24-25).

4. The Manner of His Call (1:1-3)

The heavens were opened (1). This means that Ezekiel began to see things which were not revealed to other men. Since he was to be God's spokesman, God revealed to him the high and holy things of heaven. It is a good day for any man when the heavens are opened above him. Until this happens, a man is

[2]**Jehoiachin's captivity** was an actual imprisonment, and it was not relaxed until 561 B.C.
[3]**The Chebar** may have been a canal, and the captives employed in digging it.

earthbound indeed. When it happens, he can see higher things than men can see to whom the heavens above are closed.

He saw **visions of God**. Reasoning, the art of making thought fit into rational moulds, characterized the ancient Greek philosophers. Vision, in which a man sees to the center of things and into the future, is what most characterized the Hebrew prophets. Of none of them was this more true than of Ezekiel. He was a seer of the Most High God, a mystical man of refined faith whom God could entrust with visions of himself and of other high verities.

Daniel was also in Babylon at this same time, holding high political office and foretelling the things which were to come. Ezekiel did not move among the Chaldeans as Daniel did, but rather among the exiles along the banks of the Chebar. Both were apocalyptic seers of things to come. Ezekiel saw visions predominantly of the near future. They required men to line up with the Lord, then and there. In contrast, Daniel's visions were primarily of things a great way off.

5. *The Purpose of His Call* (1:3)

Ezekiel was called, not to dispense his own opinions, nor to tell the people what they wanted to hear. He was called, as all prophets are called, to declare the truth of God. This is why we read, **The word of the Lord came ... unto Ezekiel** (3). He would deliver messages to the forlorn and forgetful exiles, but they would not be his own messages. They would not be his own ideas—truths of his own choosing. Instead, they would be the Lord's word. This word came to him **expressly**. The word "verily" or "authentically" would give the sense of what is meant.

6. *Assurance in the Call* (1:3)

The account goes on to add, **And the hand of the Lord was ... upon him**. It had not been easy for a patriot such as Ezekiel to spend five years in exile. And it is never easy for a man to declare for the Lord what he must declare when the message is precisely what willful men do not want to hear. Besides, Ezekiel was a young man, probably only thirty, and the Israelites did not listen to young men. At least from Moses onwards the Israelites had special respect for the words of old men—elders in the land. But in spite of all this—perhaps because of it—Ezekiel was peculiarly aware that **the hand of the Lord was ... upon him** to guide him, to strengthen him, to free him from his fears.

God's hand was upon Ezekiel not only during this preface to his call. Six other times it is stated that God's hand was upon the dutiful man from the side of the Chebar (3:14, 22; 8:1; 33:22; 37:1; 40:1). Any man who will hear and obey God's word will receive the needed strength from God's hand to implement that word in the lives of men and nations.

"God Cares for a Captive" is the theme of 1-3, with 1 as the key verse. In the context of Ezekiel's circumstances as a captive along the Chebar, two special points are made: (1) God gives him an uplook, opening the heavens and giving him visions, 1; (2) God gives him an outlook, enabling him to help others with messages from the Lord, 3. This passage speaks to all who are captives in times that try the soul. God cares and offers both an uplook and an outlook.

7. *Summary in a Vision* (1:4-28)

The preface to Ezekiel's call is concluded with an account of his first vision. This vision suggests something of the compelling reality and at the same time the baffling mystery of God's revelations of himself to the human spirit.

a. A whirlwind (1:4). Ezekiel looks and first sees a **whirlwind** ("stormy wind," ASV), significant of a judgment with destruction in it. The wind **came out of the north**—the direction from which judgment came at various times in Israel's checkered history (e.g., Assyria, 721 B.C.; see map 1). At the time Ezekiel wrote, 10,000 leading citizens were already in exile, as judgment from Babylon. After six more years Jerusalem would be utterly destroyed by this "stormy wind" from **the north.** Chapters 4—24 recount predictions of that destruction.

A great cloud and **fire** were in the midst of the "stormy wind." Both of these symbols signify God's presence—in this instance, His presence in judgment upon Judah.

b. The four living creatures (1:5-14). In his vision Ezekiel saw **four living creatures** who **had the likeness of a man (5).** These probably represent the forces of Nebuchadnezzar which were to be loosed in their full fury upon Jerusalem. They had **wings (6),** suggesting peculiar abilities which ordinary armies, not led of Jehovah, do not have. The living creatures, although they represent heathen forces, were being sent by the Lord, so there would be no stopping them.

Their **wings** joined **one to another** (9; cf. 11), implying unity of purpose; and **they went . . . straight forward** (cf. 12), suggesting the resoluteness of their intention.

Each of these living creatures had four faces (10): that **of a man,** showing their basic identity as human avengers; that **of a lion,** indicating their power and terror;[4] that **of an ox,** suggesting their steady strength in God's service; and that **of an eagle,** showing that they will be swift to rise above even the strongest opposition that Jerusalem will offer (see Rev. 4:7).

These living creatures were being guided by the Lord, for Ezekiel says, **Whither the spirit was to go, they went** (12).

c. *The wheels* (1:15-25). Ezekiel also saw some wheels (15 ff.). He saw them on **the earth** (15), and **lifted up from the earth** (19). Each living creature had a wheel within a wheel; and around the rims there were eyes. These wheels, with their perfection in roundness, signify God's presence even as do the cloud and the fire. When Ezekiel says that **the spirit of the living creature was in the wheels** (21), he means that the Lord was in them (cf. "the Spirit impelled them," Moffatt). The **eyes** on the **rings** (18; "rims" ASV) of the wheels signify God's ability to observe in all directions. His omniscience is basic to His being an all-wise Judge. The general **appearance of the wheels and their work** (construction) **was like a beryl** (16), or perhaps a "chrysolite" stone (RSV). The gem intended is a matter of uncertainty. If beryl, it would be perhaps deep green or blue-green. If chrysolite, perhaps a yellow-green (see Exod. 28:20; 39:13; Ezek. 28:13; Rev. 21:20).

Over **the heads** (22) of these living creatures, winged and accompanied by wheels, was a **firmament,** an expanse, the visible arch of the sky. The KJV says **the firmament** was **upon** their **heads,** but ASV and RSV makes the meaning clearer with "over." Above this firmament **was the likeness of a throne** (26), again signifying judgment.

d. *The mention of mercy* (1:26-28). Exciting indeed is what follows in this vision. Up to this point the Lord's judgment has been portrayed; but now is pictured the mercy of the Mighty One. Ezekiel is to prophesy about God's judgment on Jerusalem (cc. 4—24) and of seven heathen nations (cc. 25—32); but at

---

[4]The lion was the national emblem of Babylon. In the Louvre Museum in Paris one can view clay lions from ancient Babylon, in varying degrees of ferocity.

last the prophet is to speak comfortably to the people about restoration and hope (cc. 33—48). The last part of this early vision sums up the final message which Ezekiel is to deliver and there is hope in it.

The prophet seems to get a glimpse of the Christ, who will one day come forth transmuting judgment into mercy. The RSV makes this clear: "And seated above the likeness of a throne was a likeness as it were of a human form" (26). The fire that enveloped this figure is characteristic of Bible accounts of the revelation of God (cf. Exod. 3:2; 19:16-18; II Kings 18:36-39). Supporting the interpretation that this was a vision of Christ, the promised Redeemer, is the fact that the brightness of this "human form" gives **the appearance of the bow that is in the cloud in the day of rain** (28). The rainbow had been given to Noah as just such an everlasting promise (Gen. 9:13-17). Evidently this inclusion of a rainbow in the vision means that mercy is in the offing. When Ezekiel saw the glory of the Lord, he took the only appropriate posture for a man in these circumstances—**I fell upon my face.**

B. The Call Itself, 2:1—3:27

Chapter 1 is a sort of preface to the prophet's call. Chapters 2 and 3 describe the call itself.

1. *The Prophet's Designation* (2:1a)

In v. 1 and in eighty-six other instances, the Lord addresses Ezekiel as **Son of man** (cf. Num. 23:19; Job 25:6). Only Ezekiel, of all the prophets, is so addressed. This designation is a reminder to the man called to a prophetic ministry that he is still a creature, frail and finite. He is of no use as a prophet except the Lord fill his mouth with the things he is to speak.[5] In Ps. 8:4 and Dan. 7:13 this term, "Son of man," has a Messianic significance. There may be a degree of such significance in its use in the case of Ezekiel. As spokesman for God along the Chebar, he anticipates the One who will later come in human flesh to speak

[5]For a full discussion of the phrase see "Son of Man" in HDB. In this article we read, "Ezekiel has a profound sense of the majesty of Jehovah; and the expression is no doubt intended to mark the distance which separated the prophet, as one of mankind, from Him" (James Hastings, ed., *Dictionary of the Bible* ([N.Y.: Scribner's Sons, 1923]), IV, 579.

for the Father once and for all. It is significant that according to all four Gospels the title "Son of man" became Christ's favorite designation of himself—but He added the definite article to make it "*the* Son of man."

The fact that the designation "Son of man" appears throughout the prophecy of Ezekiel testifies to the book's unity, as does the recurrence of other phrases (e.g., "Lord God," 217 times; and "the hand of the Lord was upon" him, 3:14, 22; 8:1; 33:22; 37:1; 40:1).

2. The Prophet's Summons (2:1b-3a)

Ezekiel was told, **Stand upon thy feet** (1); and as he recounts the experience, he says, **The spirit** ("the Spirit," RSV) **entered into me . . . and set me upon my feet** (2). He was to stand up and stand out for the Lord, but the Holy Spirit helped him to obey the command. He was weak, admittedly, if only his own resources were taken into account. But it was just such a man whom God could place before the exiles to warn them of the necessity for personal righteousness.

To this man, drafted for divine service, the Lord says, **I send thee to the children of Israel** (3).[6] There does not seem to be any churchly ordaining act here, as in the New Testament (Acts 14:23). There is, however, a divine ordination. Ezekiel was sent by the Lord to declare stern, yet hopeful messages to all the children of Israel, both those in exile and those still in Judah.

3. The People to Whom He Is Sent (2:3b-8a)

Israel is **a rebellious nation** (3; "a nation of rebels," RSV). Its people are **impudent** (4; lit., hard of face, i.e., hardheaded, brazen). They therefore would not weep in repentance over sin, nor in any other way break up in contrition. Also, they are **stiffhearted**, i.e., stubborn. Their hard faces meant that their hearts were also hardened. It is not far from a hard face to a hardened heart. **Their fathers** had rebelled against the Lord, and so do they. God describes them as **briers and thorns** (6), even **scorpions**. Notice the progression here in hurtfulness: from small needlings as briers, to piercing as thorns, to poisonous stinging as scorpions.

---

[6]It should be kept in mind that after Israel, the northern ten tribes, fell to Assyria in 721, Judah itself was frequently called Israel, as here.

As briers, thorns, and scorpions lie in wait to damage men, so the **rebellious house** would strike back at Ezekiel with **their words** and their hard **looks**.

It was a difficult work to which **the Lord God** (4) called the young priest. But God's man was being sent by One who knows all about the emotionless faces and the stubborn hearts of the people. It was God himself who would give him the messages which he was to bear. A man can be strong when his message is backed up by **Thus saith the Lord God** (4).

4. *The Prophet's Preparation* (2:8b—3:3)

God's true spokesmen never bear a message which is impersonal to them, with which they have not wrestled firsthand, over which they have not wept or exulted. The word they deliver to the souls of men has first gone through their own souls—gladdening them or saddening them.

So it was with Ezekiel. He is to speak for God, but that word must first be internalized. Therefore, as the Lord held forth **a roll of a book** (9),[7] He said, **Open thy mouth, and eat that I give thee** (8; cf. Rev. 10:8-11). The **book** was filled with messages to be delivered, lettered not only on one side, as was usual in those days, but **written within and without** (10; "on the front and on the back," RSV).

What the Lord gave Ezekiel may have been a figurative representation of the words which he was to deliver. Or as some think, it might have contained the Book of Jeremiah. Whatever it was (*a*) it was from the Lord, and (*b*) it was not very pleasant, containing as it did **lamentations, and mournings, and woe** (10). Heartbreaking though it was, Ezekiel must get the message internalized. No superficial mouthing of the truth would do, no telling of it without first being heart deep in it, no pronouncement of such woes without his first feeling those woes and weeping over them. Insistence in our time upon a divine-human encounter, or upon an I-Thou kind of relationship, has been thought to have "a new look" about it; but it is not new at all. Ezekiel had living, authentic encounter with the Thou who was

---

[7]This book would have been made from either animal skins sewn together or long strips of papyrus, in scroll form. The fact that papyrus was often used is in part the reason so few ancient manuscripts have survived. When papyrus could not be obtained, skin was used. What was a difficulty to men in ancient times has become a blessing to us in the better survival of the skins which were used.

his God, and every dimension of his being was touched by the things he was to teach. His prophecies would be his own, and God's, even at points where another man of God (such as Jeremiah) may have been the first to declare these truths and may have influenced Ezekiel.

Still receiving "visions of God" (1:1), the prophet was told to **eat this roll, and go speak** (3:1). First there would be the intake, and then the issuing forth. In receiving the message, Ezekiel had to open his own **mouth** (2), but God **caused him to eat.** The man's preparation was not made apart from his own effort, but neither was it made apart from God's decisive help. Since the preparation had about it this two-way-ness, the word he received was in his **mouth as honey for sweetness** (3; cf. Ps. 19:10; 119:103).

5. *The Prophet's Commission* (3:4-15)

As was so with the later Son of Man, Ezekiel's great Antitype, the prophet was commissioned to go to **the house of Israel** (4). Broadly, he was to prophesy to all Israel, but more specifically **to them of the captivity** (11).

He is reminded that they are not **many people** (6), not small and divergent tribes; and that they are not **of a strange speech and of an hard language, whose words** he would not be able to understand. Instead, he is sent to his own people, the people of God. Heathen **would have hearkened,** but not these light-and-mercy-rejecters "of a hard forehead and of a stubborn heart" (RSV; cf. Isa. 48:4).

Ezekiel is to find the people stubborn indeed, but God will make him more stubborn for the divine message than the people are against it. They are as hard as flint, but Ezekiel will be **an adamant harder than flint** (9). The word for **adamant** is sometimes translated "diamond" (Jer. 17:1). He is not to **fear them** nor their flintlike **looks,** rebels though they be. Greater is He who will be for Ezekiel than those who will be pitted against him. Ezekiel is the most poetic of all the prophets, an idealist who was inclined to teach by symbolic act in which the message was dramatized. He was not a man for whom controversy came naturally, and would tend to shrink from "crossing swords" with those hard after what they wanted. But even as a weeping Jeremiah was given strength for a task not natural to him (Jer. 1:18; 20:7-18), so was Ezekiel.

Whether the people **will hear, or whether they will forbear** (11), Ezekiel is commissioned and strengthened to pronounce their doom (cc. 3—24), that of their pagan neighbors (cc. 25—32), and also the dawning of a new day (cc. 33—48).

Again **the spirit** (12) takes him up. **The wings of the living creatures . . . touched** (lit., kissed) **one another** (13); there was **a noise of a great rushing** (earthquake); and **the hand of the Lord** (14) **was strong upon** the prophet.

Ezekiel **sat for seven days** (15; the time set for mourning, Job 2:13) in the midst of the captives **at Tel-abib**—the word means "hill of young ears [of barley]." As he sat he was **astonished**, i.e., overwhelmed, amazed, and silent. This was perhaps also a part of Ezekiel's preparation for his task. A time of silence, in a place apart, has been given to many at the outset of their service (e.g., Jesus after His baptism and Paul in Gal. 1:17).

6. *The Prophet's Responsibility* (3:16-27)

When the seven days of sitting and silence had passed, the Lord revealed to Ezekiel what a responsible office had been given to him. He is to be a sentry, **a watchman** over the interests of many, **warning** them against folly (17). Habakkuk had also been a watchman (Hab. 2:1), as had Isaiah (Isa. 56:10) and Jeremiah (Jer. 6:17). But they had been principally watchers over the destiny of Israel as a whole. Ezekiel is likewise a watchman for the nation; but his charge here was particularly to warn individuals.

Take a given **wicked** man. If Ezekiel were not to warn him, and he should die, the man would suffer the consequences of evil—and Ezekiel would be guilty of **his blood** (18), i.e., of manslaughter or murder. But if Ezekiel were to warn the man, Ezekiel would not be responsible, even if the man continued headlong and headstrong in his sin (19). **Delivered thy soul** means "saved your life" (RSV) or "saved yourself" (Smith-Goodspeed).

Also, Ezekiel was to warn the **righteous man** (20) not to **turn from his righteousness, and commit iniquity. When . . . I lay a stumbling block before him** is translated by Moffatt, "when I put temptation before him." Not until a thousand years later was unconditional election and eternal security taught, when Augustine, steeped in Stoic and Gnostic ways, became a Christian in middle life and soon a theologian. Calvin and Calvinism

544

would not appear for some two thousand years. Ezekiel could hardly have conceived that their teaching would one day be advocated by a broad segment of the people of God. But as if to prohibit the birth of such teaching he says simply that a man, ever so righteous, might fall away and **die in his sin,** and that **his righteousness which he hath done shall not be remembered.** Surely it would take a twisting of texts to teach that believers can never be lost, in the face of teachings such as this (see also Rom. 11:22).

Ezekiel, then, is called to be a watchman to warn individuals that they must turn from iniquity to righteousness and that they must continue in righteousness as long as life lasts.

The prophet who is to speak words of warning to Israel is first to shut himself up in his own house (24), refraining from prophetic utterance, and practice God's presence. Then, at such times as God will **open** his **mouth** (27), he will announce God's word for the **rebellious house.** It is not known what **plain** is indicated in 22-23.

"The Call of the Chebar Captive" reflects truths relevant to Christian workers. The text could be, "Son of man, I send thee" (2:3); and the scripture reading all of c. 2. (1) The messenger's audience (2:3b-8a; (2) The worker's preparation, 2:8b—3:3; (3) The commission, 3:4-15; (4) The responsibility, 3:16-27.

Ezekiel 4:1—24:27

Chapters 4—24 contain prophecies directed to the people of Jerusalem, made prior to the city's destruction by Nebuchadnezzar in 586 B.C. In these prophecies there are symbolical actions, as well as spoken oracles that are delivered in the name of the Lord. Riddles, allegories, and symbols are used as vehicles for the message which the Lord gave Ezekiel for Israel. There are times of hope when it is made clear to Israel that she can receive forgiveness and a new-made heart. But the general tenor of these chapters is one of denunciation.

A. FOUR SYMBOLIC ACTS, 4:1—5:17

Immediately after Ezekiel's call to be God's spokesman, the Lord shut him up to his own house (3:24), prohibiting him from opening his mouth to speak (3:26). Instead of a spoken ministry God directed him to act out four special messages to the rebellious house of Israel. The prophet's audience included those still living in Judah, for there was considerable communication between the exiles and the homeland.

To us of the West, the symbolical actions of Ezekiel seem strange. But in that area of the world, acting out a message was not unusual. Theology in our time, after having passed through many centuries of Platonic dominance emphasizing abstract ideas, is getting back to the biblical emphasis on the importance of concrete action such as one sees here in Ezekiel. We call the emphasis "existential," and it sounds like something new. But at its best it is the Hebrew emphasis and the emphasis also of the New Testament Scriptures. God comes concretely among us in Christ and dies on a real Roman cross and rises bodily and ascends literally and announces that He will return visibly.

1. *A Clay Model of the Siege* (4:1-3)

Ezekiel was to take a **tile** (1), portray Jerusalem upon it, and act out the siege of the city which he had prophesied in c. 1. The siege began about four years after that prophecy. The tile he used would have been a clay brick about fifteen inches square and five inches thick. That is the sort found in the walls of Babylon, and many of them can be viewed in the British Museum today. It was customary in those times to write upon such tiles.

With soft clay, Ezekiel was to mold a fort, a camp, and battering rams. He used an iron pan, or a flat plate, to depict the strong wall between the besiegers and the city.

Battering rams (2) were arranged within movable towers. From these towers a city being besieged could be observed and its defenders fired upon with arrows. The principle of the ram was the same as that still used to break up the walls of buildings being razed. A large beam was swung from the tower. Men would pull this beam up, and let it swing downward against a city's walls.

2. Bearing Their Iniquity (4:4-8)

Ezekiel was to lie on his **left side** (4) for 390 days to bear **the iniquity of the house of Israel,** and 40 days on his right side to bear that **of Judah** (6). **Thine arm shall be uncovered** (7), or "with your arm bared" (Berk.). There will be **bands** (8) upon him, and he will not change his position until the siege is ended. Probably through the main part of the day, each day, the prophet would take this position, and so would instruct by symbolic act all who came into the home of this strange and silent man. The actual siege of Jerusalem which ended in 586 B.C. lasted much longer than 430 days, according to Jer. 39:1 and 52:4-7 (see also II Kings 25:1-2).[1] However, during this period Nebuchadnezzar had to leave Jerusalem alone for a time and fight the Egyptians, so the actual siege may not have lasted any longer than the 430 days.

There is also, in the passage, a suggestion that each of the 390 days represents a year that Israel had been sinful, and that the 40 days are for a like number of years during which Judah had been untrue to God. We read here that the days are "equal to the number of the years of their punishment" (5, RSV). The 390 days, now thought of as years of iniquity for which Israel deserves the punishment of the siege by Nebuchadnezzar, may refer to the years from their first king, Saul (10:8), to the fall of Israel in 721; but as we reckon those dates, the years would be 350 instead of 390. As regards the 40 years of Judah's punishment,

[1]It seems to have lasted from Jan. 15, 588, to July 19, 586 B.C.

there is no obvious period of Judah's history to which this can be referred with certainty.

The Septuagint reads 190 days in verses 5 and 9 instead of 390, and the 190 includes the 40. In this case, the first 150 days might refer roughly to the 148 years from the deportation under Tiglath-pileser in 734 B.C. to the fall of Jerusalem in 586 B.C. On this basis the forty days could refer roughly to the period from 586 to Judah's return to her homeland in 536 B.C.

The significant truth here, however, is that, by the siege and fall of Jerusalem, both Israel and Judah will be punished for the years of their iniquity. Ezekiel, lying upon his side, is to bear that iniquity symbolically, anticipating the time when the divine Son of Man will bear the iniquity of many upon a Roman cross. Here there is a foregleam of the vicarious, substitutionary suffering of Christ.

3. *Rationing of His Food and Water* (4:9-17)

Ezekiel was to **make . . . bread** (9), and eat only a small portion of it each day. The word **meat** (10) here should be translated "food." He was to have **twenty shekels a day.** This would be about eight ounces, taking an amount midway between twenty Hebrew shekels and a like number of Babylonian shekels (the writer does not say which measurement he is using). **Water** allowed to Ezekiel each day with this bread would be **the sixth part of an hin** (11), or about a pint and a half. In vv. 16-17, God made clear to Ezekiel the meaning of these symbols in the life of Judah. We know from Jer. 37:21 that bread was actually rationed during the siege.

The bread was to be baked with **dung that cometh out of man** (12). This defilement of the bread was to signify the way that Israel's religion was to be **defiled . . . among the Gentiles** (13), among whom they were to be dispersed by the hand of God. After Ezekiel complained, somewhat in the way that Peter did later (Acts 10:14), that he had not before eaten anything ceremonially unclean, the Lord permitted **cow's dung** to be used instead (14-15).

4. *Cutting Off His Hair and Beard* (5:1-17)

Ezekiel was next instructed to **take . . . a sharp knife** (1), probably a short sword, sharp as a razor, examples of which can be seen in the British Museum. He was to cut off his hair and

beard, dividing the hair into three lots. From v. 12 it is clear what each lot represented as happening to the inhabitants of Jerusalem when the siege of Nebuchadnezzar was successful.

This is Jerusalem (5) means, This hair represents Jerusalem. The Chinese called themselves the Middle Kingdom because they thought they had been placed in the middle of the world; and the Latins later said that their capital city was central because "all roads lead to Rome." So Jerusalem was thought of as being at the center of things. God had given her a special place and importance. The Lord said of Jerusalem, **I have set it in the midst of the nations and countries that are round about her.**

But the city had fallen into sin, more so even than had the heathen nations. So God changed His attitude toward its people, and would **execute judgments in the midst of thee in the sight of the nations** (heathen; 8).

The one-third portions of Ezekiel's hair (1-4) represented what would befall the inhabitants of Jerusalem. One-third would die from disease and **famine** (12); one-third would **fall by the sword;** and one-third would be scattered **into all the winds** by their exile. Only a few would be left in the land, under Gedaliah, these being represented by the few hairs taken from the last of the three portions and bound in the prophet's **skirts** (robe; 3). Even these would suffer greatly, as is signified by the prophet's burning, later, the few hairs which represented those left in the land. Punishment would come to **all the house of Israel** (4).

Thus cc. 4 and 5 describe the four symbolic acts by which the prophet revealed what was soon to happen to Jerusalem. Nebuchadnezzar, a heathen king, would execute the punishment, but he would do so on behalf of the God of Israel himself.

Chapters 6—24 spell out in detail the judgments that will irrevocably befall the nation which has had everything and, because of its sin, will soon have nothing.

B. Two Discourses on Israel's Doom, 6: 1—7: 27

Evidently the silence of the seer is broken, and he can now utter prophecies on the doom that is soon to befall the land of Israel. Chapter 6 contains a discourse about the judgment awaiting Israel for its idolatry, with mention of a remnant who will be saved. Chapter 7 is a separate discourse but deals with the imminence and inevitability of the coming disaster. Both discourses follow from the symbolical action of c. 5, in which the prophet's shorn hair and beard, divided into three parts, represents the doom that awaits Jerusalem. But while c. 5 deals only with Jerusalem, these discourses include the whole land of Israel in the denunciations.

1. *The First Discourse* (6:1-14)

The trouble with Israel, its sin of sins, was idolatry. Just as people today who covenant only halfway with God have a dividedness that gives them a desire to be like the world about them, so it was with Israel. All about her there was idolatrous worship, especially of Baal, the sun-god; and Israel perennially fell into the ways of the world that surrounded her.

Especially upon **the hills** was Baal worshipped. Thus Ezekiel personifies **the mountains** (3) and directs his prophecies against them. He cries out against the pagan shrines called **high places** (3, 6).

The Ten Commandments had been given nearly a thousand years previously, and only a few years before Ezekiel's time under King Josiah there had been a revival of emphasis upon keeping God's laws. The Israelites could not therefore have been unaware that idolatry was a great sin. But they yielded repeatedly to that sin.

Often in the Old Testament idolatry is portrayed as the worst of all sins. That is why Jeroboam sinned more than all the kings previous to him. Saul had sinned, as had Solomon, and David. But Jeroboam[2] was an idolater and led the people into heathen worship; he was therefore declared to be worse than any king up to his time (I Kings 14:9).

The reason idolatry is the worst of all sins is that it is an affront not only to what God commands, but also to the person of God himself. Idolatry is unfaithfulness to God and is therefore often described as spiritual adultery in the Old Testament (cf. Hos. 1:2).

In this chapter God declares that the idols and idolaters will both be **broken** (4). And the idol shrines will be polluted with the **bones** of the dead (5). **I am broken with their whorish heart** (9) is reversed in the modern translations, e.g., "I have broken their adulterous hearts" (Berk.). Only **a remnant** (8) of the

[2]This was the first of the two Jeroboams who ruled the northern kingdom of Israel.

people will escape **the sword, and the famine, and the pestilence** (11). Always when the populace had been headstrong in its sin, there had been a remnant who had not bowed the knee to Baal. Upon all those who worship the living and loving God, He will have mercy. Ezekiel himself was one of them, as were Jeremiah and Daniel at the same time.

More desolate than the wilderness toward Diblath (14) takes on added significance in *The Berkeley Version,* "a desolation and a waste from the [south] desert to Riblah." This would represent the maximum extent of Israel's territory, from the wilderness of Judah to northern Syria (I Kings 8: 65).

2. *The Second Discourse* (7: 1-27)

Another similar discourse on doom immediately follows the one given in c. 6.

a. Scope of the doom. **The four corners** (2), i.e., the land in all directions, north, south, east, and west, will suffer the judgment of God. In this chapter there is not even any mention of the remnant.

b. Imminence of the doom. **Now** (3) is the time when **the end** of Israel's **abominations** ("detestable doings," Moffatt) is to come about. In the New Testament, judgment on sin is usually deferred until the willful soul suffers eternally in hell—although there are a few exceptions, such as the immediate judgment which came upon Ananias and Sapphira (Acts 5: 1-11). In the Old Testament, whereas eternal punishment is occasionally taught, (e.g., Dan. 12: 2), the usual method of the Lord was to begin to punish men for their sins in this life. Thus it is in this chapter. God will not permit the sinners to flourish as the green bay tree; instead, He will cut them down in the midst of their sin, as an object lesson to all that the Lord is Lord indeed. **Mine eye shall not spare thee** (4) means, "I will have neither mercy nor pity" (Moffatt).

c. Distinctiveness of the inevitable doom. The coming doom will be **an evil, an only** (a final) **evil** (5). It will be an evil such as had never been seen. The phrase, **The morning is come unto thee** (7) perhaps should read, "The circuit of thy sins is finished." The word here is not the usual one for **morning** and it might mean "circuit."[3] Shroder may be more nearly correct

[3]See F. Gardiner, "Ezekiel," *An Old Testament Commentary,* ed. Chas. Ellicott (N.Y.: Cassell & Co., 1844), V, 220.

in suggesting that it could be translated, "The turn comes to thee."[4] The sense is that the doom is sure to come, the day of destiny is about to dawn. **Not the sounding again of the mountains** has been rendered, "no joyful shouting upon the mountains," and it is interpreted as "neither joyous cries of harvest nor pagan shouts of idolatrous worshippers" (Berk., fn.). In 9, Ezekiel recognizes the justice of God, who declares, **I will recompense thee according to thy ways . . . and ye shall know that I am the Lord.**

d. Description of the doom. As soon as Judah's turn at suffering comes, the destruction will be complete. The last part of 10 and the first clause of 11 have been translated, "Pride has blossomed, insolence has budded, violence has grown into a shoot of wickedness" (Smith-Goodspeed). In the expression **neither shall there be any wailing** (11), the word translated **wailing** may refer to what is glorious or beautiful. The RSV renders it "preeminence," while admitting in a footnote that the Hebrew is unclear. The passage probably means that there will not be left anything outstanding or distinctive in all the land.

A **buyer** (12) of land will not **rejoice** in his possession, for it will be of no use to him. A **seller** need not **mourn** over having had to sell by reason of his want; it would have been of no use to him had he been able to keep it. **All the multitude** indicates that everyone in the city will be under the judgment of God's punishment.

A land **seller shall not return** (13) refers to property law among the Jews. In Jewish law there was private ownership, but curbs were placed on the accumulation of land by wealthy individuals and families. Sales of land were valid only until the year of jubilee, which occurred every fifty years; at that time all land reverted to its original possessors. Here it is implied that, even if a seller should live, the Exile would last too long for him to come back for this land. The Hebrew of the last part of 13 is obscure. Moffatt interprets it to mean, "Wrath falls upon the entire city . . . and none shall prosper by iniquitous dealing."

Verse 14 declares that normal human preparations for protection are useless in the face of God's wrath. Verse 15 indicates that those who escape one part of the destruction will be caught in another phase of it. A few persons will **escape** (16) to the

---

[4]W. J. Shroder, "Ezekiel," *A Commentary on the Holy Scriptures,* ed. John P. Lange (Edinburgh: T. & T. Clark, 1876), *loc. cit.*

mountains; but they will not have escaped from their consciences. **All of them** will be **mourning, every one for his iniquity.** In 17 we see the source of a common figure of speech, **weak as water.**

Even if they take money with them, **their silver and their gold shall not be able to deliver them in the day of the wrath of the Lord (19).** Ezekiel declares that not only will money fail to satisfy their souls, but under the punishment of God it will not even fill their stomachs **(bowels).** Verse 18 indicates two common symbols of mourning among the Jews—**sackcloth** and **baldness** (shaved heads). **Shame** and **horror** will be reflected in their faces. If the Israelites needed to hear this from Ezekiel, how much more do men need to hear it in our materialistic age, when the chief purpose of life for so many is to amass for themselves an abundance of this world's goods!

The Berkeley Version translates 20, "They made of it [silver and gold] beautiful ornaments with which to adorn their idols, and out of it they made detestable and loathsome images; therefore, I will make it for them an unclean thing." Because Israel has thus polluted her wealth, God will **give it into the hands of strangers . . . for a spoil (21).** Even **my secret place (22;** the Temple) shall be plundered and defiled. RSV interprets **Make a chain (23)** as "make a desolation." In this day of calamity none of Israel's leaders will be able to help—neither **prophet (26),** nor **priest,** nor **ancients** (the elders), nor **king (27),** nor **prince.**

C. ABOMINATIONS AND JUDGMENTS, 8:1—11:25

Chapters 8—11 form a unit within the prophecies of Jerusalem's fall. They spring from visions given to Ezekiel, and have to do with the abominations going on in the homeland of Judah— as well as with the judgments which are to fall.

1. *The Date* (8:1)

No other prophet is as careful about dates as Ezekiel is. As he begins to present this series of prophecies, he tells us to the day when they were delivered. The **sixth year (1)** is 591 B.C., the sixth year from the time of King Jehoiachin's imprisonment. It is the **sixth month** and the **fifth day** of the month—early September, 591.[5] The time of these prophecies, then, is fourteen

⁵Nobody knows whether the Hebrews at this time were starting their year in the spring or in the fall. Dates are given according to the theory that they were using the older calendar, beginning the year in late March or early April. This seems evident from 45:21, which places the Passover in the "first month."

months after the previous oracles (1:2; 3:16) which relate
Ezekiel's first vision and his call. The prophet does not give
another date until 20:1, and the date there given is August,
590 B.C., so we may assume that what is in chapters 8 to 19 was
delivered between September, 591, and August, 590, B.C.

2. *Forms of False Worship* (8:1-18)

On that September day in 591 B.C., Ezekiel sat in his own
house with **the elders of Judah** (1; the leaders of the exiles in
Babylon) in front of him. God's power fell upon him there.
The description of God's **appearance** (2) parallels what Ezekiel
saw in 1:26-27 (see comments there). **The form of an hand** (3)
seemed to take the prophet by the hair of the head and trans-
port him **to Jerusalem.** That he was taken there spiritually, not
bodily, is suggested by the statement that he was brought **in the
visions of God to Jerusalem.** Instead of **the door of the inner
gate** the RSV has "the gateway of the inner court," which agrees
with the Temple description in I Kings 7:12 and II Kings 20:4
(see Chart C).

a. *"The image of jealousy."* This image was an idol so
named because its presence in the Temple at Jerusalem provoked
the Lord **to jealousy** (3). It might have been the image which
had stood there during the reign of Manasseh, just before King
Josiah's reform. That image had been taken away, but it may
have been returned by Ezekiel's time (see II Chron. 33:7, 15).

b. *Animal idols.* The figure of the **hole in the wall** (7) is to
suggest a means of discovering what was going on in secret behind the wall. The animal idols **pourtrayed upon the wall round
about** (10), on the inner part of the Temple, were worshipped
in the dark (12). The men engaging in this idol worship ought
to have known and done better; they were the **seventy men of
the ancients of the house of Israel** (11) who were depended upon
for their wisdom. **Jaazaniah the son of Shaphan** is otherwise
unknown. They were mistaken when they said, **The Lord seeth
us not** (12). What was done in the dark in those days was seen
by the Lord, even as it is today. Thick walls and thick darkness
do not hinder in the least the X-ray sight of Him who views all
things.

c. *Tammuz.* This god was worshipped openly at the north
door of the gate of the Lord's house (14; see Chart C) by
idolatrous **women.** Not only were the men far from God. Even

the women, who often seem to fare better in the faith than men do, were equally unfaithful to God. **Tammuz,** to whom they bowed, was a god that the Babylonians had inherited from the Sumerians, who had previously flourished in that area. He was the god of vegetation and fertility.[6]

The sun was also being worshipped by twenty-five men inside the Temple. **Between the porch and the altar** would be in the holy place of the Temple itself. They turned **their backs toward the temple** (16) and faced the sun. Sun worship had been practiced by the Canaanites, and had been recently introduced through the powerful Assyrians to the north. There seems to be a progression in these abominations, making sun worship the worst of all (15). This might be because the sun, not made with man's hands, but instead a mysterious source of light and life, was more readily accepted than the equally mysterious God.

Lo, they put the branch to their nose (17) is a literal rendering but leaves the reader wondering what is meant. Moffatt puts interpretation into his translation, "They are filling my nostrils with their stench!" This makes sense; as does, "See! they are thrusting their obscenity against my very nostrils" (Smith-Goodspeed). For all these abominable worship practices the Lord will **deal in fury** (18) with Judah.

3. *The Slaughter of the Sinful* (9:1-11)

In c. 9, Ezekiel passes from a charting of Judah's abominations to a prophecy of God's sure judgment. **Six men from the north** (2), who are evidently angels, are to execute the slaughter of all the people who choose idols instead of God. Their coming from the north is typical, since their mission is judgment (see 1:4). It is possible that Ezekiel here sees the slaughter which Nebuchadnezzar is soon to work, and that these six angels, with the seventh one (who places a mark on those to be left), represent the host of the Babylonian king.

In his vision Ezekiel saw **the glory of the God of Israel** (3) in His dwelling place in the Temple. His presence gives assurance that in all this slaughter there is an accompanying mercy; those who are righteous are to be spared. Before the six destroying angels go in, a seventh angel is to go through the city and

---

[6]See W. L. Wardle, "Ezekiel," *The Abingdon Bible Commentary*, ed. F. C. Eiselen, Edwin Lewis, and D. G. Downey (N.Y.: Abingdon, 1929), p. 719.

mark the people who are to be spared. This angel was **clothed with linen** (3), the cloth of cleanness in those times—as opposed to wool, which would cause more perspiration from the wearer. He was to **set a mark upon the foreheads of the men that sigh and that cry for all the abominations** (4). Those who were so marked, and only those, were to be spared. This is similar to what John the Revelator saw in Rev. 7:3-4; 22:4.

There are times when moral judgment becomes more important than ceremonial righteousness. In the Old Testament, men became ceremonially unclean when they touched a dead body. Conversely, a guilty man might be safe if he took refuge in a holy place (cf. I Kings 1:51-52). However, in the time of God's judgment, His servants are instructed even to **defile the house** (7) in order that righteousness may prevail. According to this prophecy God is willing to show mercy wherever it is possible. There are times, such as that here portrayed, when God's people have exemption from suffering as well as enjoying redemption. There are other times when His people have only redemption, the hurt of suffering being upon them as well as upon the unjust. It is for God to decide whether they will be exempted from suffering or suffer in a finite way for the good of others. It is for the righteous person to be thankful for redemption, whether or not he has exemption from the times that try the soul. The Christian who has made a whole response to God's will, and who has the far view, does not require that he get his so-called just deserts while in this life. He suffers with Christ if so be that he may be glorified in a day of brightness yet to come. In 9 it is clear that lack of faith was the great sin of Israel: **They say, The Lord hath forsaken the earth, and the Lord seeth not.**

4. *The Fire and the Glory* (10:1-22)

In this vision Ezekiel sees again much of what he saw in c. 1 (see comments there). But some new details are introduced here. **The cherubims,** the **coals of fire** (2), and **the cloud** (3) remind one of Isa. 6:1-6. While they refer to soon-coming judgment, the judgment is a cleansing of the sin of the land. It is the same angel who in c. 9 is asked to mark the righteous so that they will be spared. He is here directed to set fire to **the city** (2).

Three times in this chapter (vv. 15, 20, 22) the prophet tells us that **the living creature** which he sees in this vision, and which he identifies with **the cherubims** (15), is what he saw in his earlier vision when he was near the river Chebar. The new vision of what is to happen, therefore, simply corroborates the earlier one, although there are in it new details. The meaning of the symbols seen by Ezekiel is not always as clear to us as we wish it were. Perhaps, however, this very fact suggests the essential element of mystery in the revelation that God gives to us. Who can adequately describe the wonder of those times when God's presence is most clearly felt?

5. Redemption for the Remnant (11:1-23)

Chapter 11 talks about judgment, as do most chapters in this section of Ezekiel. In his vision the prophet saw twenty-five of Jerusalem's leaders at the Temple. They had been advising the people to rebel against Nebuchadnezzar and to side with the less powerful country of Egypt. They did not want the people to settle down with their lot. Instead, they agitated against the Babylonian rule. In v. 3 these leaders were obviously attempting to refute Ezekiel's prophecies that the time of destruction was near. They thought of Jerusalem as a protecting **caldron** (11) in which her people would be preserved. Through Ezekiel, God refuted them, saying, "This city shall be no caldron for you, and you will not be the flesh inside of it; as far as the borders of Israel I will punish you" (11, Berk.). Among these twenty-five men were two **princes of the people, Jaazaniah** and **Pelatiah** (1). In his vision, Ezekiel saw **Pelatiah** fall dead even while he himself was speaking his prophecy against these idolaters (13).

Such immediacy of judgment unnerved the prophet and he asked the Lord whether everybody was to receive that kind of fate, or if the Lord would look favorably upon the **remnant of Israel** who were righteous. The answer which Ezekiel received is one of the highest and most hopeful messages to be found in the forty-eight chapters of this prophecy.

The RSV clarifies the meaning of 15 thus: "Son of man, your brethren, even your brethren, your fellow exiles, the whole house of Israel, all of them, are those of whom the inhabitants of Jerusalem have said, 'They have gone far from the Lord; to us this land is given for a possession.'" But these reports circulating in Jerusalem were false.

Yes, Ezekiel may take heart. Not all the Israelites are like the twenty-five false leaders who told the people simply what they wanted to hear. Not all the Israelites sided with these leading figures. There were at least a few, a remnant of the exiles, who would escape the doom. These were mostly in captivity now, Ezekiel's "fellow exiles," who had not bowed the knee to such false and flattering hopes. These were the people who were listening to the true prophets such as Jeremiah and Ezekiel. The faithful prophets wanted the people to accept God's judgment and to bear the oppression of Nebuchadnezzar. They advised Judah not to revolt with the hope that an already weakened Egypt would join them and be able to crush Babylon. Jeremiah had said that the oppression would last seventy years (Jer. 25: 11-12). There was no use trying to escape the yoke after only a few years—as Israel soon tried to do under Zedekiah.

Jerusalem would be **the caldron** for many, and her people generally would be **the flesh** cooked in the pot (7). But those who had been scattered abroad and who served the Lord would receive God's mercy. God would be "a sanctuary to them for a while in the countries where they have gone" (16, RSV). The word for **little** is an adverbial form, and should therefore be translated as "a while" rather than a **little sanctuary.**

Several things will happen for good to this remnant. The prophecy of 18 was exactly fulfilled after the return from Babylon. Israel was never troubled with idolatry after her exile. There was also a striking parallel between what is to happen to them and what will happen to God's people in the coming dispensation of the Holy Spirit (cf. 36:25-29).

"Redemption for the Remnant" is a theme illustrated in this chapter. The central thought is found in the question, **Ah Lord God! wilt thou make a full end of the remnant of Israel?** 13; and the answer, **I will be to them as a little sanctuary,** 16. (1) **One heart,** 19*a*; (2) **A new spirit,** 19*b*; (3) **An heart of flesh,** 19*d*.

a. One heart (11:19). No longer would they be torn between whether or not they would serve the Lord. No longer would they be double-minded, their hearts divided, and hence unstable in living for the Lord. They would have pure hearts; that is, they would be motivated by just one thing—God's will. They would be able to say, as Paul did in New Testament times, "This one thing I do, forgetting those things which are behind . . . I press toward the mark for the prize of the high calling of God in Christ Jesus" (Phil. 3:13-14). What the remnant of Israel would be given was what the Early Church was later granted. Of them it was said, "And the multitude of them that believed were of one heart and of one soul" (Acts 4:32).

b. *A new spirit.* The remnant would exchange the spirit of murmuring for the spirit of praise. Again we have a prediction of what was most fully realized in the dispensation yet to come. After they returned to Jerusalem, the Jews rebuilt the Temple and soon returned to the external trappings of ceremonialism. It took Christ, who leveled His hardest statements against the externalistic Pharisees, to establish the **new spirit** within men.

c. *A heart of flesh.* The Israelites had often enough been stony-hearted, resisting the prophets and turning "every one to his own way" (Isa. 53:6). But through Ezekiel, God here promises to take out of them **the stony heart,** hardened by self-will, and put in its place **an heart of flesh.** This new heart is one that can be moved to regret over failures and to compassion for others; it is a heart that readily performs God's will. Much earlier, a similar promise had been made to God's people: "And the Lord thy God will circumcise thine heart, and the heart of thy seed, to love the Lord thy God with all thine heart" (Deut. 30:6).

Such promises were fulfilled in a measure at various times during Israel's history but not in fullest measure until the fullness of the times had come. This fullness of times would come when the Sun of Righteousness arose with healing in His wings—the Desire of all nations, a Light to lighten the Gentiles, and a Glory indeed to Israel itself. Ezekiel here, and in 36:26-27, means to say that real, inward faith of the heart is to appear in the remnant who are restored to Jerusalem. But Jeremiah, who proclaims a similar prophecy at about the same time, makes it quite clear that its highest fulfillment awaits a redemptive age yet to come. "Behold, the days come, saith the Lord, that I will make a new covenant with the house of Israel . . . I will put my law in their inward parts, and write it in their hearts" (Jer. 31:31-33). This is most truly fulfilled in the Pentecostal baptism of believers with the Holy Spirit, "purifying their hearts by faith" (Acts 15:9; cf. Acts 2:4). Ezekiel and Jeremiah both say what is coming, although theirs were the "not yet" times when men still looked for deliverance after a new fashion.

In spite of the glowing promise for the remnant, God was bringing judgment on Jerusalem. **The glory of the God of Israel** (22) which had been in the Temple at the beginning of the vision

559

(9:3) now withdrew from Jerusalem to the mountain which is on the east side of the city (23; "the Mount of Olives," Berk., fn.).

6. *Back to Chaldea* (11:24-25)

With the message for Jerusalem ended, Ezekiel is returned in his vision to **Chaldea** (24). This is a common biblical name for the land of Judah's exile. The Chaldeans were at first a tribe which flourished to the southeast of Babylonia. They later became the main tribe of Babylonia, after which the whole country was sometimes referred to as **Chaldea**. It was the land to which Ezekiel and many others had been taken as captives. It was to his fellow captives in the land that the man of visions now told the things that he had seen (25).

D. PROPHECIES AGAINST JERUSALEM, 12:1—19:14

Ezekiel was a man of many visions (1:1-28; 8:1 ff.; 11:24; 12:27; 37:1-14; 40:1-4; 47:1-12). The previous four chapters (8—11) contain a record of a special kind of vision—a vision in which the man of God was transported in spirit to a different locale and was enabled to see to the center of things in that environment.

There are also visions connected with what Ezekiel sees in cc. 12—19. But here the vision consists of what the prophet sees in Babylon. Its subject is the same as the theme of cc. 8—11. What he sees as soon to happen is a day of doom for the rebellious and restless city of Jerusalem. The people will not accept the Babylonian yoke, as Ezekiel and Jeremiah counsel them to do. This is because they do not see the enormity of their sin. They will not accept the nearness of such a colossal judgment as the total destruction of the city. Rebel against Nebuchadnezzar they will, and rebel they do—in 588 B.C., the ninth year of Zedekiah's reign (II Kings 17:15-18; 24:20). Nebuchadnezzar marches against them immediately and begins to lay siege against the city. For two and a half years the siege lasts. It would have ended sooner had not Egypt finally thrown its armies against Nebuchadnezzar. He withdrew his forces from Jerusalem for a time in order to attack and defeat the new enemy. Jerusalem thus had cause for a short-lived hope; but soon Nebuchadnezzar was back at her gates and she fell in 586 B.C. All this Ezekiel sees as soon to happen; and in cc. 12—19, he prophesies against the

rebellious house—a phrase found in 12:2-3, and elsewhere in Ezekiel's prophecy (cf. Isa. 6:9-10; Matt. 13:13-15).

1. *More Symbolic Acts* (12:1-28)

Ezekiel is not like any other prophet. Others can be content with speaking the message but Ezekiel must frequently act out his prophecy. He figures that people would disregard what he says, but that it would be more difficult for them to forget his dramatized prophecies. As it happened, they disregarded what he acted out as well as what he did. But at least his soul had been delivered. He had used good pedagogy in employing the eye-gate, and he had used good psychology in acting out what was to happen, allowing the onlookers to reach their own conclusions. In cc. 4—5 he had resorted to symbolic acts, and now turns to them again in c. 12.

a. Ezekiel acts out the Exile (12:1-16). The people **have eyes to see, and see not** (2)—having disregarded his acted-out prophecies of cc. 4—5. **They have ears to hear, and hear not** —having disregarded his spoken prophecies of c. 6 onwards. So the Lord again directs Ezekiel to portray exile for Jerusalem. **Prepare thee stuff for removing** (3) is literally, "Make thee vessels of exile." The RSV has, "Prepare for yourself an exile's baggage." Ezekiel is to **remove by day in their sight**; i.e., simulate going into exile as they look on. Perhaps this will cause them to **consider.** He is to pack his baggage in the daytime. **At even** (4), he is to dig through the sun-dried, clay-brick wall of his house and carry the things out through the hole. Always it is to be **in their sight**; this phrase appears seven times in vv. 3-7. **Thou shalt cover thy face** (6) was to symbolize the coming blindness of king Zedekiah.

The curious folk did just what God knew they would do; they asked Ezekiel, **What doest thou?** (9) The **burden** ("this bearing of a burden"; Moffatt) applied to **all the house of Israel** (10), but mainly to **the prince in Jerusalem.** This phrase refers to the king, whom Ezekiel always calls a prince. Perhaps the reason was that Zedekiah was Nebuchadnezzar's choice, whereas Ezekiel knew that the real king was the imprisoned Jehoiachin. The prince would escape but he would be caught, and would **not see** (13) Babylon because he would be blinded (cf. 17:20; II Kings 25:4-7; Jer. 52:7-11). Verse 14 has been translated, "And all his attendants, his retinue, and his guard, I will scatter to the winds; and them, too, I will pursue with my unsheathed sword"

(Berk.). In 15 and 16 there is given the reason for God's action. It runs like a refrain through the message of the prophet: **And they shall know that I am the Lord.**

b. *Life under the siege* (12:17-20). Ezekiel next acted out what life during the siege and the period of exile was going to be like. He ate his **bread with quaking** (18) and drank **water with trembling** to show that both food and water would soon be scarce. The middle part of 19 has been translated, "They shall eat their bread with anxiety, and shall drink their water with dismay" (Smith-Goodspeed).

c. *Ezekiel opposes a proverb* (12:21-28). It had become customary in Israel to say that God's day of judgment was a long way off (27), and that **every vision** (22) of the prophets fails to materialize. To the careless and cynical, God declares that the people will **no more use** (23) this **proverb,** because judgment will soon be levied (28). **Divination** (24) is foretelling the future by reading omens or drawing lots. The seeming success of this false kind of prophecy will soon come to an end.

The rebellious house of Israel, in putting off the day of God's wrath, were not a peculiar people. Sinful men of all generations have been prone to this error. It is a flimsy hope to which the sinful heart tends to cling.

2. *False Prophets Are Denounced* (13:1-23)

Chapter 13 consists of denunciations against false prophets (1-16) and false prophetesses (17-23). They have prophesied **out of their own hearts** (2; "minds," RSV; cf. Jer. 23:9-40). They have followed "what they feel" (3, Moffatt), and have not seen any vision at all. They were as worthless as **foxes in the deserts** (4). They say that they have seen **peace** (10) coming, and that "all is well" (Moffatt). That is what the people wanted to hear, but it is not what God intended to tell them. The fate of the false prophets was to be cut off from God's people: "They shall not . . . be enrolled in the register of the house of Israel" (9, RSV).

The false prophets constructed a flimsy wall of hope for the people, and **daubed it** with "whitewash" (10, RSV). It looked nice for a time, but soon everybody would know how wrong these dishonest builders were.

There were likewise prophetesses who said nice things that the people wanted to hear (17-23). They divined for **handfuls of barley and for pieces of bread** (19). The falsehood here was in mixing up the truth. They said that the souls who were to live would die and that those who were to die would live. Instead of **pillows** (18), we should think of their putting "magic charms" (Berk.) upon the people. Also they put **kerchiefs upon the head of every stature,** or "veils around the heads of persons great and small" (Berk.). These were to remind the people of the nice things the prophetesses had said. The evil of their actions was in making the **righteous sad** (22) and in giving the unrighteous a false sense of security that no judgment was forthcoming—**promising him life.**

It is a sad day when those who purport to speak for the Lord say simply what the sinful multitudes want to hear. It is a sad day when such persons twist the truth, so that the wicked are put in a good light and the righteous in a bad light. It happened in Ezekiel's day, however, and it has happened in other days—e.g., in the days of Hitler, when a strong segment of the Christian Church in Germany supported his racial and national superiority theories and went along with his program of mass murder. But Germany had its Martin Niemoellers and its Dietrich Bonhoeffers. And Israel in exilic times had its Ezekiel and its Jeremiah.

3. *Idolatrous Elders* (14:1-11)

Certain **elders of Israel** (1), leaders in the exiled community, **came** and **sat before** Ezekiel as if to hear some oracle from him. Perhaps they were simply curious or more probably they wished to appear to listen to God's message. In reality they were idolaters. God told Ezekiel, **These men have set up their idols in their heart** (3). The word of the Lord to them was, **Repent, and turn yourselves from your idols; and . . . from all your abominations** (6). In 4-5, God declares that He himself will give these men an answer, "so that I may grip the house of Israel in their own thoughts" (5, Berk.), i.e., convict them of their sin. These men and the false prophets who deceive them (9) will be punished (10). Of such a man God says, "I will make an example of him, I will make him a byword" (8, Moffatt). This will be done to keep Israel from going yet further astray and **that they may be my people, and I may be their God** (11).

4. *Personal Righteousness Rewarded* (14:12-23)

Ezekiel knows little of the kind of social righteousness stressed at our century's turn by Walter Rauschenbusch and others. With Ezekiel, the really important matter is whether or not the individual person serves God. In vv. 12-23 he says that the Lord is to judge Israel by a **famine**, wild **beasts**, the **sword**, and **a pestilence**, and that nobody is to be spared unless he himself is righteous. **Break the staff of the bread** (13) has been interpreted as "the support of its bread is broken, and I make it short of food" (*Basic Bible*). Even if a person is as righteous as **Noah, Daniel,**[7] **and Job** (14, 20), his righteousness would be sufficient only for his own deliverance, not for that of even his **sons** and **daughters** (16).

Ezekiel was an "Arminian" many centuries before there were any Arminians as such. Individual persons needed to "repent, and turn" themselves (6) to God, and remain in moral obedience to Him, else they would be the objects of the Lord God's wrath. It was not enough to be an Israelite, or the son of the best of the Israelites. There is no thought in Ezekiel about a person's being acceptable with God because of some decree of election on the part of God. An individual is righteous only if indeed he himself is righteous. Covenant or no covenant, the Lord looks for individuals who from their hearts truly yield themselves to God and obey Him.

Even so, some Israelites are to survive the **four sore judgments** (21) of the Lord. The KJV calls them a **remnant** (22), but they might better be called simply "survivors" as in RSV, since they are not righteous, as "a remnant" in the biblical meaning usually is. They do not suffer death because the Lord wants to let these survivors of Jerusalem's sinfulness reveal to other people by their corrupt lives how just He was in punishing the majority (22-23).

5. Israel Is like a Wild Vine (15:1-8)

The people of God are often compared to a vine (Gen. 49:11; Isa. 5:1-7; Jer. 2:21; Hos. 10:1). Probably some were saying that Jerusalem was the vine of God's own planting, and therefore He would not destroy it. But the comparison is usually between God's people and the cultivated vine with its luscious fruit. Here it is between Israel and the wild **vine tree** of the **forest** (2). Such vines are worthless from the standpoint of fruit, and one

---

[7]This is probably the Daniel who, like Ezekiel, was a captive of Babylon. Contra, see G. R. Beasley-Murray, "Ezekiel," *The New Bible Commentary,* ed. F. Davidson (Grand Rapids: Wm. B. Eerdmans Publishing Co., 1953), p. 653.

cannot even make anything useful from their wood. Verse 3 asks, "Is even a peg cut from it, to hang a vessel on?" (Moffatt) Apart from its function of bearing fruit, the vine is useless. **Meet for (4-5)** means "fit for." Israel is now like a wild, unfruitful vine, and it is soon to be burned. But as always, God's action is designed to be redemptive: **Ye shall know that I am the Lord, when I set my face against them (7)**.

6. *The Unfaithful Wife* (16:1-63)

This chapter consists of a detailed allegory of Jerusalem as a cast-off child (1-7) whom the Lord cared for in childhood and married in her youth, but who becomes an unfaithful wife. Parts of the chapter would be out of present-day taste to read in public. Yet it can be drawn upon as illustrative of the sin of ingratitude and of God's continuing love even for those who forsake Him and seek other loves. The figure of God as Husband was not frequently used in those times, but it did appear; e.g., in Hosea and the Song of Songs, if the latter be interpreted allegorically.

The prophet traces Israel's history and explains thereby why she must be judged. She was born of mixed parentage (3) and therefore considered as low-caste. As was common outside of Israel, especially in the case of girl babies, she was taken out and left to die. **To supple thee (4)** should be read "to cleanse you" (RSV). **Thou wast not salted** refers to a custom, still practiced in the East, of rubbing a newborn child with salt to signify dedication to God. But the Lord saw her and had compassion on her. When she became a beautiful maiden, He married her. **Come to excellent ornaments (7)** means "came to womanhood" (Moffatt). **Shod thee with badgers' skin (10)** probably means "put leather shoes on your feet" (*Basic Bible*). After her marriage she became even more glorious in her beauty and strength—a possible reference to Israel's glory during the reigns of David and Solomon.

But alas! after all this love was lavished upon her, and after her increase in beauty and status, she forsook the One who had rescued her as a foundling child. The essential nature of sin, as self-instead-of-God, is seen in 14-15: **Thy renown . . . was perfect through my comeliness . . . But thou didst trust in thine own beauty.** She played **the harlot (15)**, i.e., turned to idolatry, and made **images of the jewels and gold and silver (17)** which had been given her. She became even worse than the professional harlot who sells herself to earn a living (31). Israel had no reason for her idol worship after all the revelation of himself that God had given to her. The nature of Israel's false worship was child sacrifice (20-21) and erecting pagan altars in prominent places (24-25, 31). She had adopted from neighboring nations any pagan worship that appealed to her: from **the Egyptians** (26), **the Assyrians** (28), and the Canaanites (29). Even the pagan **Philistines** would be **ashamed of** her **lewd way** (27). All this sinfulness had spilled over into **Chaldea** (29), not being confined simply to the city of Jerusalem, that was soon to fall.

Because of all this poured-out **filthiness** (36), God will pour out upon her the fury of His holy wrath (37-41). The figure for Judah's punishment is the punishment meted out to a faithless wife in Israel. Since her sins were greater than those of **Sodom, her sister** (48), her punishment would be still greater than Sodom's. Her sins were greater than Sodom's partly because of their being done in the wake of greater love expended upon her. The geographical note in 46 envisions the reader standing in Jerusalem facing Babylon to the east. In this position **Samaria** lay north to the **left hand** and **Sodom** lay south **at thy right hand.** Sodom was probably in the vicinity of the Dead Sea. It is assumed that the site is now covered by water (see map 1).

But God is a God of mercy. He is holy. He is righteous and requires righteousness of His people. Yet He will show mercy when Israel becomes **ashamed** (61) of her great sin. At that time He will reestablish His **covenant . . . and thou shalt know that I am the Lord** (62). So thorough will be His forgiveness that, after Israel has received her pardon, she will never need to **open** her **mouth** again to say anything about the **shame** into which she had sunk (63). This probably means that today, after a person has been forgiven, he should not recount in his testimonies any lewd or otherwise unsavory details of the sins for which he has been forgiven.

7. Zedekiah's Breach of Treaty (17:1-21)

Ezekiel was a poet, a man who worked best with symbols. He sometimes acted out what he wanted to say, or as here, he put it into an allegory—a riddle or parable. He sometimes presented his parable and let his hearers draw conclusions for themselves. Or, as in this case, he might intrigue them at first by a parable (1-10) and then explain its meaning (11-21). Ezekiel here describes and interprets events occurring in Palestine, although he remained in Babylonia.

In this allegory the **great eagle** (3) is **the king of Babylon** (12), who has **divers** (different) **colours** (3), signifying the various countries under his dominance. He comes to **Lebanon,** i.e., Jerusalem, and takes the **highest branch of the cedar** (King Jehoiachin). The **land of traffick** and **city of merchants** (4) was Babylon, where Jehoiachin was held in official custody. In Jehoiachin's place, Nebuchadnezzar plants **the seed of the land** (5, Zedekiah) **in a fruitful field,** hoping that it would flourish as a **willow tree,** i.e., prosper in peace with the overlord nation. This seed becomes a **spreading vine of low stature,** not very strong by comparison with Babylon, and it **turned toward** (6) that country obediently.

Now there was **another great eagle** (7; Egypt), and the vine **did bend . . . toward him**—it "sent out its tendrils for him to water" (Berk.). This vine will not **prosper** because the Lord does not want Judah to turn toward Egypt but to accept His punishment as it will be meted out through Babylon. Indeed, the Lord will **pluck it up by the roots** (9) and it shall **utterly wither** (10). **Make for him in the war** (17) means "shall do nothing for him on the day of battle" (Smith-Goodspeed). In **breaking** his signed pledge (18) with Nebuchadnezzar, Zedekiah was opposing the Lord. This is the way Ezekiel saw it, and it is the way Jeremiah saw it (cf. Jer. 21:1-10).

8. *Message on the Messiah* (17:22-24)

After this allegory about Zedekiah, Ezekiel was inspired to speak also (22) of a greater than Zedekiah—a **tender** twig which will be planted upon **an high mountain and eminent,** i.e., Mount Zion. **It shall bring forth boughs, and bear fruit, and be a goodly cedar** (23). This is no doubt another of the times when men of old speak of the Messiah (cf. Ps. 2:6; Isa. 53:2; Jer. 23:5; Mic. 4:1-3).

9. *Individual Responsibility* (18:1-20)

Here Ezekiel becomes a theologian. He is usually a pastor, burdened with the care and the cure of souls; or he is a prophet, declaring God's counsels with forthrightness. But here he deals with doctrine.

He picks up a false **proverb** and shatters it. This common saying, also referred to in Jer. 31:29-30, was, **The fathers have eaten sour grapes, and the children's teeth are set on edge** (2). The meaning of the proverb is that, because of the sins of the fathers, their children will suffer. Something similar to this is taught in Lam. 5: 7, "Our fathers have sinned, and are not; and we have borne their iniquities." Also in Exod. 20: 5, we read, "I the Lord thy God am a jealous God, visiting the iniquity of the fathers upon the children unto the third and fourth generation of them that hate me." Experience, too, surely shows that the righteousness or unrighteousness of parents affects their children.

What Ezekiel says is that, while children might suffer from the sins of their fathers in the natural order of cause and effect, God will not himself punish a son for the sins of his father and will not consider an unrighteous son to be righteous because his father happens to be righteous. Twice in this chapter Ezekiel says, **The soul that sinneth, it shall die** (4, 20). The word **soul** (*nephesh*) is used as a synonym for the whole personality. In Ezekiel's day the Israelites were using the proverb to justify themselves and to blame their national misfortune on their fathers. But there is universal truth in this clear declaration of God's attitude toward right and wrong. There are in it clear overtones of spiritual and eternal death.

Ezekiel follows mainly Deuteronomy and Leviticus in listing what a person should refrain from doing and what he should do. The sins he lists were common sins in Israel. The expressions **hath restored to the debtor his pledge** and **hath spoiled none by violence** (7) are clarified in the *Basic Bible* thus: "has given back to the debtor what is his, and has taken no one's goods by force." Eating **upon the mountains** (6, 11, 15; cf. Isa. 65: 7) means joining in idolatrous feasts there. Taking **any increase** (8, 13, 17) probably refers to usury, i.e., excessive interest (cf. 22: 25); Lev. 25: 36; Deut. 23: 19; Ps. 15: 5). **Hath taken off his hand from the poor** (17) is interpreted as "withholds his hand from crime" (Smith-Goodspeed).

The theme of this passage is "The Requirement of Individual Righteousness." The key thought is in v. 20, **The soul that sinneth, it shall die.** (1) You cannot honestly blame your forebears, 2; (2) You cannot truthfully blame your surroundings, 6-8; (3) You must not blame God, for He is fair and merciful, 20, 23.

10. *The Righteous Can Fall from Grace* (18: 21-32)

Ezekiel explains that **if the wicked will turn from all his sins . . . he shall surely live** (21). God is glad to give him life

(23). On the other hand, the prophet asks, **When the righteous turneth away from his righteousness . . . shall he live?** (24) The answer is, "No." **All** ("none of," ASV) **his righteousness that he hath done shall . . . be mentioned** ("remembered," ASV) **. . . and in his sin that he hath sinned . . . shall he die** (24). The prophet explains further, **When a righteous man turneth away from his righteousness, and committeth iniquity, and dieth in them; for his iniquity that he hath done shall he die** (26). Such a person really has been righteous, and has really fallen from grace. If he does not come back to God, but dies in his fallen state, he will suffer God's holy wrath.

It is ever so mistaken an idea, but ever so widely accepted in Protestantism, that once one is a Christian he cannot fall from grace and be lost. This was taught by John Calvin (1509-64), by the Calvinists in the time of James Arminius, and is still taught by many Calvinist authorities who have nonetheless accepted Arminianism at other important points—e.g., that anyone may be saved. It is difficult to understand how one can reconcile a theology of "once in grace, always in grace" with the clear biblical teaching of this passage.

The use of the term **equal** in 25 and 29 is strange to twentieth-century readers. It means "just" or "fair." Moffatt translates v. 29, "Israel complains, 'The Lord is not acting fairly!' My methods not fair, O Israel! Is it not rather your methods that are not fair and right?" Ezekiel concludes the chapter with a call to sinners to turn from their **transgressions, to receive a new heart and a new spirit: for why will ye die, O house of Israel?** (31)

11. *A Lamentation for Israel's Princes* (19:1-14)

Ezekiel here presents a **lamentation for the princes** (kings) **of Israel** (1). Their **mother** (2) is the nation, and her two **whelps** (3) are evidently Jehoahaz and Jehoiachin. Jehoahaz (1-4), after a reign of but three months, was taken captive to Egypt by Pharaoh-necho (see II Kings 23:21; Lam. 4:20). Jehoiachin (5-9) was taken to Babylon and imprisoned in 597 B.C. (cf. II Kings 24:8-16). The use of the figure of a lion to represent the royal family is apt, for the lion was used of the Davidic line (Gen. 49:9; Num. 23:24; Mic. 5:8; Rev. 5:5). Also, the throne of Judah's kings was decorated with lions (I Kings 10:18-20). **Taken in their pit** (4, 8) means caught in their trap. **He knew their deso-**

late palaces (7) probably means, "He ravaged their strongholds" (RSV).

The figure of the vine, another familiar symbol to the Old Testament mind, is used here (10-14) of Judah. The meaning of 11 is clarified by the RSV:

> *Its strongest stem became a ruler's scepter;*
> *it towered aloft among the thick boughs.*

This form reminds us that Ezekiel was a poet. The entire chapter should be read as a narrative poem (cf. its form in other modern translations, e.g., Moffatt and Smith-Goodspeed). The soon-coming destruction of the Holy City and the capture of Zedekiah are described (cf. II Kings 25).

The dirge closes with the statement that it is **a lamentation** (14) and that its purpose is to cause the reader to lament what had happened to Judah's kings and what would soon happen to Judah. Because of the evil deeds of her ruler, Judah's strong branch, Ezekiel writes:

> *A fire has gone out from her branch,*
> *has devoured her boughs.*
> *And she has no strong branch*
> *As a royal scepter.*

> (14, Smith-Goodspeed)

E. PROPHECIES DATED 590 B.C., 20:1—23:49

The prophecies of this section are dated as of about September 1, 590 B.C. This would be the **seventh year** (20:1) after Ezekiel's deportation to Babylon in 597 B.C. It was approximately a year after the last previous date which Ezekiel gives (8:1). These chapters contain further indictments and denunciations against the rebellious house of Israel—both those in exile and those in the homeland.

1. *Israel's Apostasies and God's Mercy* (20:1-44)

a. The occasion (20:1-4). The **elders of Israel** (1) came to Ezekiel **to enquire of the Lord.** Moffatt calls them "sheikhs of Israel." These were the mature and supposedly wise men living in exile with Ezekiel. What they inquired of is not told us. According to an ancient interpretation, they asked about setting up a temple in Babylon where idols would be worshipped. This interpretation is based on Ezekiel's answer where he seems to say that what is in their minds, an intention "to serve wood and stone" (32), must never happen. Another and more plausible interpretation is that they asked about setting up in Babylon a temple for true worship. Even this, Ezekiel opposed.

b. *The apostasies* (20:5-30). Ezekiel answered their question by recounting Israel's sins of the past and of the present. He tells them that a temple in Babylon is out of the question because their loss of a homeland and the Temple is a punishment from the Lord. To build a new temple would be a human attempt to avert a just punishment. He reminds them of their departures from the Lord in **Egypt** (5-9), in **the wilderness** (10-26), and in Canaan (27-30).

God repeatedly says in this passage that He had been merciful to Israel even though she had sinned. His **eye spared them** (17); He **withdrew** His **hand** of judgment (22). They had defiled His **sabbaths** (24), but He was merciful. And they had **caused to pass through the fire all that openeth the womb** (26, cf. 31)—a reference to sacrificing children to the god Moloch (16:20-21; II Kings 16:3).

It is grammatically possible to translate vv. 25-26 so as to say that God caused them to do this sacrificing. Moffatt probably comes closer to the truth when he interprets it: "I let them have laws that were evil and customs that could not bring them life, and I made their very sacrifices befoul them, as they burned their first-born children alive." If God ever makes men sin, surely it is only indirectly—in making them free and in permitting them to go on for a time unpunished in their sins. Repeatedly, the Lord says that He was merciful, and did not punish Israel immediately, so that men **might know that I am the Lord** (26; cf. 9, 14, 22).

In this section, **lifted up my hand** (15, 23, 28) refers to the act of taking an oath. RSV translates it, "I swore to them." Ezekiel here "places great emphasis on keeping the Sabbath [vss. 12, 13, 16, 20, 21, 24]. Its importance as a religious institution would be increased in the exile. To profane the Lord's Sabbaths meant oblivion of the covenant promise [cf. Exod. 24:3; Amos 8:5]" (Berk., fn.). **Bamah** (29) means "High Place."

c. *God's mercy* (20:31-44). In 9, 14, 22, and 26, the Lord's mercy is declared as for His name's sake. When Israel sinned, she was not punished in ways that she might have been punished.

This was to put on display the name of the Lord as a God of mercy. In the present passage Ezekiel answers the question of the elders who came to inquire. He says that the Lord will not be inquired of by people so vile as to **make your sons to pass through the fire** (31) and who are guilty of other polluting sins. What they have in **mind** (32), perhaps the building of a temple in Babylon, is not to be.

But God has a plan in mind, and it will come to pass. What He has in mind is to restore Israel, in acts of mercy, in spite of her past sins. He will **gather** the people **out of the countries wherein** they **are scattered, with a mighty hand, and with a stretched out arm** (34). He will bring them out of the heathen nations to the land of promise and, as He says, I will **plead with you face to face** (35). Imagine! Israel sins on and on; but God purposes to plead on and on, if perchance she will see the folly of her sin and turn to Him with all her heart. He says, **Ye shall loathe yourselves in your own sight for all your evils** (43). And **ye shall know that I am the Lord, when I have wrought with you for my name's sake, not according to your wicked ways** (44).

To pass under the rod (37) is the figure of a shepherd who brings his sheep to the fold at night, making each one pass under his staff so that he may be sure that all are in. The **bond of the covenant** is "the yoke of God's mercy and of man's duty" (Berk., fn.).

2. *The Fire and the Sword* (20: 45—21: 32)

Between 44 and 45 there is a break, for with 45 a new subject is begun. The Hebrew Bible begins c. 21 at 20:45 of the English versions.

a. The fire (20:45-49). These verses contain a parable about Judah's destruction with **fire** (47). The opening verses of c. 21 contain a sort of interpretation of this parable, but with the sword as the principal symbol of the destruction.

The prophet is to **drop** (46) his **word**. It may be translated "inveigh". (Smith-Goodspeed), or even "preach" (RSV). He is to send his word **toward the south** (46). In Hebrew there are three words denoting three areas of Judah, but all three are simply gathered up and translated as **south**. They all denote Judah. It was due west of Babylon (see map 1), where Ezekiel was writing; but it was south from the standpoint of the direction from which Nebuchadnezzar would invade the area. This is a parable (49), or, as the Hebrew word may be translated, an allegory. It has to do with the soon-coming destruction of Jerusalem and of Judah as a whole.

b. *The sword* (21:1-32). The sword of destruction will be that of Nebuchadnezzar, the heathen king, but the Lord calls it **my sword** (3-4). The **righteous and the wicked** (3), **all flesh** (4), will suffer and thereby **the Lord** (5) will bring a judgment upon them. This, of course, refers to temporal tragedy and not to personal destiny. Good men often suffer with evil men in this life but God's final reckoning draws a clear line between them. The sword **shall not return any more** to the sheath until the destruction is total. Men are now to **sigh** (6) at the description of the horror, for **all hands shall be feeble, and every spirit shall faint, and all knees shall be weak as water** (7). These verses interpret what the prophet means by his parable in 20:45-49.

The breaking of thy loins (6) means "with breaking heart" (RSV). God's sword will be **sharpened, and also furbished** (9) —sharpened so that it will cut, and polished so that it will "flash like lightning" (10, Moffatt). **It contemneth the rod of my son, as every tree** may be understood as in *The Berkeley Version*, "You have despised the rod, my son, with everything of wood." Having refused to profit by the lesser judgments, they would be destroyed by the greater. **Smite therefore upon thy thigh** (12) is "an Oriental gesture of despair, often used upon receiving heart-rending news [cf. Jer. 31:19]" (Berk., fn.). Verse 13 is clarified thus by Smith-Goodspeed:

> *For there is a trial in store;*
> *And who can despise the rod of my wrath?*

Smite thine hands together (14; cf. 17) was a signal that the action should begin.

The heathen Ammonites also are to suffer from the Lord's sword (vv. 20, 28-32; 25:1-7; Jer. 49:1-6). **The king of Babylon** (19) is pictured as poised to move both against Jerusalem and against the Ammonites. **Rabbath** (20), capital of Ammon, is the Amman of today. Nebuchadnezzar uses the pagan arts of **divination** (21) in order to determine where to strike first. Still presuming that their city is safe, the Israelites look upon the Babylonian decision as **a false divination** (23). But their doom is sealed, and Zedekiah, **the profane wicked prince of Israel** (25), is warned that there is no escape. The Ammonites also will be destroyed (28-32).

3. *A Listing of Jerusalem's Sins* (22:1-31)

Since the Lord sees all the sins that men do in the dark, He inspires Ezekiel to catalog them in this chapter (cf. 18:5-18; Rom. 1:18—2:1). Three times **the word of the Lord** came to the prophet (1, 17, 23), thus indicating three separate oracles (1-16, 17-22, 23-31). In the first, the sins of Jerusalem are named one by one. In the second, Jerusalem is melted down and found to be dross. In the third, the **prophets** (25) and the **priests** (26) and the **princes** (27) are accused of conspiring against the Lord. These three groups are analogous in our time to the preachers, the religious leaders, and the political officials. With these three influential groups agreeing to oppose God, it is no wonder that all Jerusalem had followed them into the ways of sin. The common people—**people of the land** (29)—aped their elders in doing evil.

Verse 6 is clarified thus in the RSV: "Behold, the princes of Israel in you, every one according to his power, have been bent on shedding blood." **Men that carry tales to shed blood** (9) are those "who murder their fellows by false evidence" (Moffatt). Those who **eat upon the mountains** are they who engage in idolatrous feasts there. **Humbled her that was set apart for pollution** (10) means, "They lie with menstruous women" (Moffatt). **Gifts to shed blood** (12) refers to taking bribes to commit murder. The first half of 16 is obscure. RSV translates it, "And I shall be profaned through you in the sight of the nations." Verse 24 indicates the tragedy of Judah's plight—not cleansed from sin and therefore punished by drouth.

So total had that sinfulness become that God sought for a person of prayer who would intercede for the sinful city, but **found none** (30). Because He found nobody to pray, He must go on with His plan to punish the people. Nowhere in all the Bible is the importance of intercessory prayer stated more clearly than in 30-31. Even one person, **a man** (30), can by prayer bring a reprieve from God's holy judgment against sin. And God even searches for such a man to appear upon the horizon of human history. In this case He looked in vain.

In 23-31 we see "The Princely Privilege of Intercessory

Prayer." (1) The need for such prayers, 23-29; (2) The difference such prayers make, 30b-31; (3) God searches for intercessors, 30.

4. *The Sins of Two Sisters* (23:1-49)

These prophecies, dated in 590 B.C. (cf. 20:1), are concluded by a description of the sins of **Samaria** (the Northern Kingdom) and **Jerusalem** (representing all of Judah). The two areas are spoken of as two sisters, **Aholah** and **Aholibah** (4).[8] This chapter recounts their inclinations towards and alliances with such heathen nations as Egypt, Assyria, and Babylon. A significant part of the evil of the alliances was Israel's tendency to accept the heathen worship of her allies.

This prophecy describes the alliances in terms of fleshly whoredoms which would not be appropriate for public reading today. There would seem to be an effort on Ezekiel's part to describe Israel's sin in as loathsome language as possible. He perhaps thus tried to create a revulsion against those sins.

Verses 9-10 clearly refer to the fall of Samaria in 722 B.C. Verses 11-21 refer to the alliance of Judah with Babylon (II Kings 20:12-21; 24:1). Judah **(Aholibah)** is warned that **the Babylonians** and their Aramaic mercenaries **(all the Chaldeans, Pekod, and Shoa, and Koa)** together with their Assyrian associates (23) will execute God's judgment against her (24-26).

Verse 27 was literally fulfilled. It is a fact of history that, after the exile in Babylon, Israel never again lapsed into the sin of idolatry. The **cup of astonishment** (33) is "a cup of horror" (RSV). Of this cup v. 34 says:

> *You shall drink it, and drain it—*
> *You shall drain it to the dregs;*
> *And your breasts you shall tear,*
> *For I have spoken* (Smith-Goodspeed).

There are here several important lessons. For one thing, sin tends to snowball in its enormity. The whoredoms **increased** (14) and **multiplied** (19).

Another lesson about sin contained here is that the parties in sin became alienated from each other. God says to Aholibah,

---

[8]**Aholah** means "her tent"; **Aholibah,** "my tent is in her." "The Arabs today frequently give names of similar rhythm to their children" (Berk., fn.).

I will raise up thy lovers against thee, from whom thy mind
(or soul) is alienated (22). God also speaks of her lovers as
them whom thou hatest (28).

Still another fact is that sin simply does not pay. Even
those with whom Judah sinned will deal with her hatefully
(29), and leave her naked and bare, and will disclose to others
the sins she has done. Both sisters will be laughed to scorn (32)
and spoken of in derision. In 38-39, God reveals the depths to
which one may sink when religion is divorced from righteousness. These men violated almost every commandment of God
and then came the same day into my sanctuary (39) to worship.

Sooner or later it will be clear that the holy God is displeased
and will visit the unrepentant ones with judgment (46-49).
God is saying through Ezekiel that He is going to employ Judah's
partner in sin, Babylon, to storm her city and her citadels with
fire and fury the likes of which the world had not seen.

F. LAST PROPHECY BEFORE JERUSALEM'S FALL, 24:1-27

About January 15, 588 B.C., two years and five months after
the previous recorded date (20:1), Ezekiel gave a parable. *The
Berkeley Version* gives a clear rendering of v. 2: "Son of man,
write down the date of this day, for on this day the king of Babylon has besieged Jerusalem." (Cf. II Kings 25:1; Jer. 52:4). The
parable of the caldron (3-5) is interpreted in 6-14. The caldron
is the city and the flesh boiled in the kettle is the rebellious house
of Israel. Even the best of the people would suffer—every good
piece (4) and the choice of the flock (5). Let no lot fall upon it
(6) means that no one would have a chance to escape the judgment coming on Israel. Moffatt renders 7-8: "For the blood of
her murderers is in her; she poured it out on the bare rock, not
on the ground for the dust to hide it." Blood violently shed, if
left uncovered, was said to cry out from the ground. The meaning
of spice it well (10) is not clear. The thought of the verse seems
to be a completely consumed people. RSV has it, "Heap on the
logs, kindle the fire, boil well the flesh, and empty out the broth,
and let the bones be burned up." Verse 11 continues the picture.
"Then set it empty upon the coals, that it may become hot, and
its copper may burn, that its filthiness may be melted in it, its
rust consumed" (RSV). Here is the symbol of sin cleansed by
fire. The judgment, issuing from a heathen king, is nonetheless
the Lord's own judgment (14).

On the evening of this day Ezekiel's **wife died** (18). But he goes on prophesying the next morning without any of the usual Oriental demonstrations of mourning. His wife had been the **desire of** his **eyes** (16), but he will put a **tire** (turban; 17) on his **head,** so as not to show the uncombed hair of a mourner; he will wear **shoes** whereas mourners went barefoot; he will not **cover** his **lips,** which mourners did; and he would not eat **the bread of men,** which it was customary to prepare for people who mourned (see Jer. 16: 5-7).

Ezekiel is to bear his own personal sorrow without mourning as a way of showing the exiles how they are to bear the news they will soon receive of their homeland's destruction. He was to keep silent, except perhaps for prophesying against the heathen nations (cc. 25—32), until news of Jerusalem's fall reached the Chebar community—**until he that escapeth . . . shall come unto thee** (26). This occurred some two years later (see 33:21). The fulfillment of Ezekiel's prophecy would be **a sign unto them; and they shall know that I am the Lord** (27).

Over the centuries, men of God have been called upon to bear difficult loads; and over the centuries, men of God have borne them. That is why the gospel was proclaimed in spite of martyrdom during the first glorious century of Christian history. It is why Luther and his like stood for something revolutionary and revitalizing in the sixteenth century. It is the reason the learned and holy Mr. Wesley took his stonings with nonchalance in the eighteenth century. It is why five missionaries died at the hands of the Auca Indians in the twentieth century.

Section III   Prophecies Against Heathen Peoples

Ezekiel 25:1—32:32

The siege against Jerusalem has now ended. The time was about two years after the events and prophecies just described (cf. 24:1-2; 26:1). But before Ezekiel's prophecy gives us word of the city's fall, he records how God will judge the heathen nations and cities round about Judah. The immediate neighbor nations, Ammon, Moab, Edom, and Philistia, first come up for denunciation (25:1-17). Then Tyre and Sidon, two proud, commercialized cities, are condemned in detailed statements (26:1—28:26). Most specific of all is the statement of how God intends to judge Egypt (29:1—32:32). There are in all seven such nations; the number suggests completeness of judgment.

It is the Lord himself who will judge these nations, and He will do so particularly because they have taken advantage of Israel in her distress. Babylon, interestingly, is not mentioned in Ezekiel's list. Her judgment and fall, which did indeed occur after her years of glory, are not mentioned. To have included Babylon would have encouraged the Israelites who were quite sure that Babylon was no tool in God's hands.

A. Ammon, Moab, Edom, and Philistia, 25:1-17

It can be seen from maps 1 and 2 that these nations were on Judah's doorstep. All four, for centuries, had been as thorns in the side of Judah and Israel.

1. Ammon (25:1-7)

Ammon, to the northeast of Jerusalem, had chuckled an **Aha** (3) when Nebuchadnezzar had finally stormed into Jerusalem, **profaned** the **sanctuary,** and laid the land **desolate.** She had even **clapped** her **hands, and stamped with the feet, and rejoiced in heart** (6) over Jerusalem's calamity. No doubt her earlier opposition to the Hebrews (Judg. 10:9—11:49) also figured in Ammon's **fate.** After the Northern Kingdom had been defeated by Assyria in 721 B.C., Ammon had taken Gad for herself (Jer. 49:1; see map 2). She attacked Judah in 600 B.C. All this, with her rejoicing at Judah's fall to Nebuchadnezzar, brought God's judg- ment—in order that **ye shall know that I am the Lord** (5). **The men of the east** (4) who would conquer Ammon were the Babylonians who had just destroyed Judah. **Rabbah** (5; see map 2) was the chief city of Ammon. **A couching place** means "a fold for flocks" (RSV). **Stretched out mine hand** (7) is a figure to describe an exertion of God's power. Here the stretching out of God's hand may be a literary parallel to the clapping of Ammon's **hands** (6).

2. *Moab* (25:8-11)

To the southeast lay Moab (see map 1), another longtime enemy of Judah. She gloated in the apparent fact that **Judah is like unto all the heathen** (8), not having the special protection from God she had so often enjoyed. **Upon Moab,** also, God will **execute judgments** (11). **Seir** (8) belonged to Edom, not Moab. It is not included in the Greek text of Ezekiel in the Septuagint.[1] This fact suggests that it might have been added to the Hebrew manuscript after the translation of the Hebrew into Greek. **I will open the side of Moab from the cities** (9) has been translated, "I am laying open Moab's flank, the cities of its frontier" (Berk.). The cities mentioned have survived to our time. **Beth-jeshimoth** is now Tel el-'Azelmeh, two and one-half miles northeast of the Dead Sea; **Baal-meon** is now Ma'in, nine miles east of the Dead Sea; and **Kiriathaim** is now called el-Qereiyat, ten miles south of Ma'in. **The Ammonites** (10) lived to the north of Moab.

3. *Edom* (25:12-14)

Real and lasting had been the animosity between Edom (see map 1) and the Jews. Edom had not permitted the Israelites to pass through her area to get to Canaan in Moses' time, and the Israelites therefore had to go the long way around. The brief prophecy of Obadiah, sometimes called "a hymn of hate,"[2] re-

---

[1]This variance from the Hebrew, and many others, can be checked by the Bible student who does not understand the Greek, in an English translation of the Septuagint by Charles Thompson and edited by C. A. Muses (*The Septuagint Bible,* Indian Hills, Colo.: The Falcon's Wing Press, 1960).

[2]John Paterson, *The Goodly Fellowship of the Prophets* (New York: Charles Scribner's Sons, 1948), p. 178.

flects the deep animosity between the two peoples. This feeling was perhaps enhanced since Edom had descended from Esau, the twin of Jacob, the ancestor of the Israelites (Gen. 35:22—36:43). Edom even took an active part in the destruction of Jerusalem, murdering the escaping Jews as they fled southward (see Obadiah). For her sins of the centuries Edom will suffer. **Teman** and **Dedan,** two of her cities, would be made **desolate** (13). This prophecy was so completely fulfilled that no one now knows where they were located (cf. 35:1—36:15, extended comments).

4. *Philistia* (25:15-17)

The Philistines had entered the land of promise many centuries earlier, and it was from them that the name of Palestine become attached to the area. The prophets often denounced the Philistines (Isa. 14:29-32; Jer. 25:20; Amos 1:6-8). Their conflicts with the Jews had a long history (cf. Judg. 3:31; 14:1-16; I Sam. 4:1-6; II Chron. 26:6-7). They wanted Judah destroyed due to **the old hatred** (15). God says He will **cut off the Cherethims** (16)—another name for them, perhaps because they seem to have come from Crete, or Caphtor, as it was known in the Old Testament (Deut. 2:23; Jer. 47:4; Amos 9:7).

B. Tyre and Sidon, 26:1—28:26

Tyre and Sidon are not nations as such, but seacoast cities (see map 2) bent upon commercial interests. Tyre, called **Tyrus,** comes in for a lengthy, passionate denunciation (26:1—28:19); and Sidon, spelled **Zidon,** is denounced swiftly in only four verses (28:20-23).

1. *Tyre* (26:1—28:19)

Tyre had had a long history as a trading center of note. Even at the time of Ezekiel's prophecy she was a center of mercantile power, although, like Jerusalem, she was nominally subject to Babylonia. Tyre was a **renowned city** (26:17), **strong in the sea.** She was jealous that Jerusalem had been a center for trade between Babylonia and Egypt, and thus **the gates of the people** (26:2). Jerusalem's fall would mean that the trade would be **turned unto me,** so that now she would be **replenished.** Selfish she was, big in material interests but small in soul.

Tyre had about her certain small towns, **daughters in the**

field (26:8), which came under her influence. And she traded with numerous nations and cities listed with care in c. 27.

The king of Tyrus (28:12), Ithobaal II, was the really proud one. His heart was **lifted up** (28:2) to such extent that he said, **I am a God, I sit in the seat of God.** Tyre, rich and selfish, producer of Jezebel (I Kings 16:31) and many others of her kind, would be brought low—her proud king included.

At about the time of Jerusalem's fall, Nebuchadnezzar (spelled here with the *r*—**Nebuchadrezzar,** 26:7) laid siege against Tyre for thirteen years, according to Josephus.[3] Tyre's sails were brought so low that they were never really raised again. Today she is an insignificant town of some 6,000 people.[4]

Scrape her dust from her (26:4) and **make thee like the top of a rock** (26:14) may be allusions to Tyre's traditional lack of farming land. Some four hundred years earlier Solomon had exchanged grain and oil for timber to build the Temple (I Kings 5:11). A comparable allusion occurs in 12, "They will plunder your wealth . . . casting . . . your garden soil into the sea" (Berk.). **The princes of the sea** (26:16) would be the rulers of maritime nations with whom Tyre traded. Verse 17 begins a brief poem. It has been rendered:

> *How you have perished, have vanished from the sea,*
>   *O city renowned*
> *That was strong upon the sea,*
>   *herself and her people,*
> *That struck the terror of her might*
>   *upon all who dwelt there!* (Smith-Goodspeed)

Also in poetic form are 27:3-9, 25-36 and 28:2-19 (cf. RSV). The extent of Tyre's commerce is graphically shown by the list of places mentioned in 27:5-25, ranging from Spain on the west (**Tarshish**, 12) to Mesopotamia on the east (**Haran,** 23).

Thy merchant (27:12 ff.) means a nation with whom Tyre engaged in trade. **Suburbs** (27:28) has been rendered "countryside" (RSV). **Utterly bald** and **sackcloth** (27:31) refers to shaving the head and wearing sackcloth as signs of mourning. Moffatt translates **shall be astonished** (27:35; 28:19), "All seafaring folk shall be appalled at the sight of you." **Shall hiss at thee** (27:36)

---

[3] *Against Apion,* I, 21.

[4] To read further about Tyre, and other Bible places, see the *International Standard Bible Encyclopedia,* edited by James Orr.

means to whistle, or "make sounds of surprise" (*Basic Bible*).
Daniel (28:3)—cf. 14:14, comment and footnote. The meaning of
anointed cherub (28:14) and **covering cherub** (16) is uncertain.
Ezekiel apparently is thinking of God's sovereign dealings with
people other than Israel. It was God who prospered them and
God who punished them on moral grounds. RSV translates:
"With an anointed guardian cherub I placed you; you were on
the holy mountain of God . . . till iniquity was found in you . . .
so I cast you as a profane thing from the mountain of God, and
the guardian cherub drove you out."

The decline of Tyre is an example of what happens to a
nation that loves gold more than God. Here is the destiny of all
who can gloat over the suffering of others if only that suffering
fills their own coffers with the goods of this present world. His-
torian Arnold Toynbee sees materialism as one of the major
factors in the fall of past civilizations. The example of Tyre is
still followed by the twentieth century, with its quantitative
thinking, that brought in the jet age and the "get age." Two
centuries ago Goethe observed that "the spirit tends to take to
itself a body." He was talking about us, for whom material things
are too often what matter most.

"The Error of Our Era" could be the title of a message
based on 28:1-8. (1) The error itself: matter is what matters
most, 28:1-5; (2) Results of the error—the effects upon Tyre,
and us, of an overstress on material prosperity, 28:6-8; (3) Right-
ing the error by (*a*) the vertical view maintained by Ezekiel;
(*b*) raising the sights of our affections, Col. 3:1-2; and (*c*) putting
first things first, Matt. 6:33.

2. *Sidon* (28:20-23)

In early times Sidon may have been a larger city than Tyre.
This is suggested by its being mentioned without any reference
to Tyre in Gen. 10:19. It was no mean city (Josh. 19:28), and
had its kings (Jer. 25:22; 27:3). Often, in Scripture, it is mentioned with Tyre (Isa. 23:1-2; Mark 7:24-26; Acts 12:20). In
Ezekiel's day the two were seaside partners in sin.

God is **against** (22) Sidon and will **send into her pestilence,
and blood** (23)—both disease and **the sword.** In both 22 and 23
it is clear once more that God's power poured out in judgment is
intended to be a revelation of himself to men: **they shall know
that I am the Lord.**

582

3. *Restoration of Israel* (28:24-26)

In a brief three-verse anticipation of what the prophet will enlarge upon in his later chapters (33—48), Ezekiel says that the time will come when no nearby nation will be to Israel a **pricking brier** (24). At that time God **shall have gathered the house of Israel from the people among whom they are scattered, and shall be sanctified in them in the sight of the heathen** (25). God's being sanctified, as here, is an indication that the word "sanctification" not only refers to moral purity, as it does frequently in the NT (e.g., Eph. 5:25-27; I Thess. 4:3; 5:23), but also (particularly in the OT) to being set apart from all else. In this case, after judging Tyre and Sidon for their sin, and after restoring Israel to her own land, **the Lord God** will be seen to be the God of real power and care. Thus He will be **sanctified.**

C. EGYPT, 29:1—32:32

In even more detail than in the case of Tyre, Ezekiel makes complaint against **Egypt** and announces the doom that she soon will endure. Only Egypt, of the seven heathen nations on Ezekiel's list, was a real empire at this time. Next to Babylon, she was a power to be reckoned with. Archaeological findings in recent years confirm the political strength of this nation that stretched itself out along the Nile and bowed down to none. The unfaithful Israelites hoped that Egypt would come to their aid and defeat Babylon. But Ezekiel and Jeremiah saw that this was not to be.

In order to make it crystal-clear what God was to do to the land of the Nile, Ezekiel devotes seven oracles to the fate and the fall of this fabled land. Each of the seven oracles begins with the phrase, **The word of the Lord came unto me, saying** (29:1, 17; 30:1, 20; 31:1; 32:1, 17). The first oracle is dated in the **tenth year** of the exile (29:1); and the latest, which comes second in the series, is the latest date for a prophecy given in Ezekiel's writings: **the seven and twentieth year, in the first month, in the first day of the month** (29:17). This is the twenty-seventh year of Jehoiachin's captivity—probably April, 571 B.C.

1. *First Oracle* (29:1-16)

This oracle, delivered during the siege of Jerusalem (see 24:1), is directed mainly against **Pharaoh** (2). In his pride and prosperity he thought he had things going his own way. Unlike

583

other kings who sometimes said that they were descended from the gods, Pharaoh claimed to be himself a god.

And how proud he was of his Nile River! Of it he said, **My river is mine own, and I have made it for myself** (3). Today, along with the Mississippi and the Amazon, the Nile is still one of the great rivers of the world. As this is being written its course has been changed so that a dam can be finished which will make it more useful than ever before. Even in Ezekiel's time, the Nile was a boon to the land. It was so wide that it was sometimes called a sea, so long that a vast length of land was made fertile by its silt and productive by its water. Camels could sense the difference it made in the air a half-day's journey from it.

Pharaoh did not see that God is the Creator of all things and that in the use of nature's blessings men are to be thankful for His provisions. Instead Egypt's king, **the great dragon** (3; sea monster), wallows in the wealth of his river, proclaiming that he himself made it and that he made it for none other than himself.

Ezekiel tells how God will set himself **against Pharaoh . . . and against all Egypt** (2). The king will be brought up out of the protection of his river; **the fish** (4), i.e., the people of Egypt, who are small but similar, will stick to the **scales** (4) of the big fish Pharaoh. All will be **thrown into the wilderness** (5), and die without burial—which was considered calamitous by the Egyptians and other ancient peoples. Several MSS. have "buried" in v. 5 instead of **gathered.** The RSV therefore translates, "You shall . . . not be gathered and buried." The fact that **beasts** and **fowls** will eat their bodies further suggests that there will be no burial.

Egypt has been a **staff of reed to the house of Israel** (6). The Israelites had leaned on Egypt as one leans on a staff, but Egypt has given poor support, a flimsy reed instead of solid wood. Verse 7 has been translated: "When they took a grip of you in their hands, you were crushed so that their arms were broken; and when they put their weight on you for support, you were broken and all their muscles gave way" (*Basic Bible*).

Egypt will be laid waste from the north to the south. Instead of **from the tower of Syene** (10; cf. 30:6) we should read "from Migdol to Syene" (RSV). Migdol, which means "tower," is a town (see Exod. 14:2; Num. 33:7) in the north, and Syene, the modern Aswan, where the massive dam is now being built, is in the extreme south near Ethiopia (see map 3). To say "from

Migdol to Syene" in Egypt was comparable to saying "from Dan to Beer-sheba" in reference to the Holy Land.

Egypt will be punished for **forty years** (12), interestingly the same as the time of Israel's wandering in the wilderness after she had escaped from Egypt's yoke (Num. 14:33; Ps. 95:10). This is a rounded figure standing for the Persian occupation of Egypt from 525-487 B.C.

Restoration will then come to **the land of Pathros** (14), i.e., Upper Egypt (see Isa. 11:11; Jer. 44:1). But the south will be neglected, and in general Egypt will be a **base** (insignificant) **kingdom** (14). Because Egypt will no longer be a great power, **the house of Israel** (16) will not again be tempted to place **confidence** in the strength of her southern neighbor. The oracle closes with God's eternal purpose for man and Ezekiel's prophetic refrain, **They shall know that I am the Lord God.**

2. Second Oracle (29:17-21)

This oracle has to do with Egypt's spoils being wages (18-19) for Nebuchadnezzar's **great service** (18)—a thirteen-year effort against Tyre. The campaign against Tyre had resulted in little booty, since the city seems to have removed its treasures before it fell to the Babylonian king.

The oracle is closed with reference to restoration through **the horn of the house of Israel** (21). Since the phrase is coupled with **the opening of the mouth** (or lips), **the horn** may refer to a contemporaneous situation. The one whose lips are to be opened might well be Ezekiel himself, since his had been sealed by the Lord so that for a time he could speak only to the foreign nations and not to Israel. However, "the word 'horn' implies power and prosperity. . . . The vision of a Coming One may be back of it, a Messianic hope" (Berk., fn.).

3. Third Oracle (30:1-19)

This undated message is a poetic[5] listing of the woes that will befall Egypt on her **cloudy day** (3), **the day of the Lord** when God will visit her in judgment. These woes will spill over to her sister gentile nations. **The time of the heathen** means "a time of doom for the nations" (RSV). **Chub** (5) appears only here in the Bible, and we do not know what area the word

---

[5]See the poetic form in one of the modern-language translations, e.g., Moffatt, Smith-Goodspeed, or RSV.

designates. The Septuagint reads Lud or Libya. The exclamation, **Howl ye, Woe worth the day!** (2) is rendered vividly as "Wail aloud, woe for the day" (Moffatt). For **the tower of Syene** (6) see comment on 29:10. In v. 9, **the careless Ethiopians** are listed specifically as a neighboring nation which would come under judgment along with Egypt.

The statement, **I will make the rivers dry** (12), is rendered less literally, "I will dry up the Nile," in Moffatt and RSV. The passage probably means that the Nile would not rise high, and that its waters would therefore not go out into the canals for watering the land. **The day shall be darkened** (18) is another example of figurative language used to describe the evils which were to come on Egypt.

The cities mentioned in verses 13-18 were the leading cities of ancient Egypt. **Noph** (13) was Memphis, the capital of Lower Egypt. **Pathros** (14) was Upper Egypt (see 29:14). **Zoan** was Tanis in the northeast delta region. **No** was another name for Thebes in Upper Egypt, once the country's most magnificent capital, the present-day Karnak. **Sin** (15) later became known by its Greek name Pelusium, and is the present Tell Farama on the seashore about twenty miles southeast of Port Said. **Aven** (17) or On is the later Heliopolis, a city dedicated to the worship of the sun. **Pi-beseth** is Bubastis, an ancient city on the Nile in Upper Egypt, thirty miles southwest of Zoan. It had a famous temple dedicated to a cat-goddess. **Tehaphnehes** (18), or Tahpanhes, was in the east delta region near Migdol (see map 3).

4. *Fourth Oracle* (30:20-26)

This is a brief prose prophecy against Pharaoh, and is dated in April, 586 B.C. **the eleventh year** of the Exile (20). Ezekiel foresees that Pharaoh's power will be broken and given to another king, Nebuchadnezzar—the purpose being to declare that Jehovah is **the Lord** (26). **The arm of Pharaoh** (21) would be his power. **A roller to bind it** means a bandage to support and strengthen it.

5. *Fifth Oracle* (31:1-18)

This word against Pharaoh, dated less than two months after the previous oracle (cf. 30:20), likens Egypt's king to a **cedar** tree, the typical tree of Assyria, which has flourished but which will now flourish no more.

The KJV rendering makes it sound as if there is a switch from Pharaoh to an **Assyrian king** (3). The long description of the **cedar** appears therefore not to apply to Pharaoh, but to another. But the oracle is addressed to **Pharaoh** in 2, and concluded by reference to him by name in 18. It is possible that there is a very slight copyist's error between what is now the text and what seems to have been in the autograph. With the addition of one letter, plus a change from another letter to one that is almost identical, the text would read, "I will liken you to a cedar." The reference to **the waters** (4) as the source of the cedar's prosperity probably had a direct implication for Pharaoh's situation in Egypt, since the waters of the Nile formed the basis of the nation's agriculture (cf. 29:3, 9-10).

The garden of God (8-9) appears to refer to the Garden of Eden. The word **hell** (16-17; *sheol,* place of the dead) refers to a place of destruction or oblivion. It is not here the place of eternal punishment, because the reference is to the fate of the nation rather than of persons. The difficult last part of 16 is interpreted to mean that other nations which had feared Egypt and had gone down to destruction, perhaps before Egyptian armies, would rejoice in Egypt's downfall. Moffatt translates it, "In the regions . . . the best trees of Lebanon, nourished by water, were all consoled by his fate." To **lie in the midst of the uncircumcised** (18) would be a great indignity to the Egyptians. They practiced circumcision and considered peoples who did not "as outside the pale of civilization" (Berk., fn.).

6. *Sixth Oracle* (32:1-16)

Again we have a dated oracle (1), having been delivered in March, 585 B.C., about a year and nine months later than the prophecy of 31:1. In it the Lord laments Pharaoh and describes what will happen to him. The king is likened to **a young lion** (2), fiercest of beasts on the land; and to **a whale** or perhaps crocodile, fiercest of animals in the water.[6] Moffatt translates it, "You are like a monster in the streams, snorting water from your nostrils, splashing the river with your feet, fouling the streams."

Verses 3-5 are almost a duplication of 29:3-5. See comments there. In 5, **height** does not make the meaning clear. Most recent translations interpret the word as "carcass" (RSV) or "worms" (ASV, fn.). In 7-8 the desolation of the land is likened to the lights going out and the **bright lights of heaven** (8) being dark-

---

[6]For this contrast see Adam Clarke, *A Commentary and Critical Notes* (N.Y.: Abingdon, n.d.), *loc. cit.*

ened. Verses 13-14 show Egypt's judgment in terms of cattle being destroyed, and the turbulent, silt-filled Nile River running placidly **like oil,** or "clear" (Berk.), without its fertilizing silt.

7. *Seventh Oracle* (32:17-32)

The last of the seven oracles against the seventh of the heathen nations, Egypt, is dated as of **the twelfth year, in the fifteenth day of the month** (17). No month is given but the month and the year are probably the same as that of the previous oracle, 585 B.C. No prophet was as careful as Ezekiel about recording dates.

This oracle has to do with Egypt's place among the various uncircumcised[7] nations (19, 21, 24-30, 32), i.e., the Gentiles, going down to Sheol, or **the pit** (18). It opens (cf. 17) and closes by asserting that Pharaoh **shall be laid in the midst of the uncircumcised** (32) along with **all his multitude,** i.e., the people of Egypt. Pharaoh and his people will have no better places in the **nether parts of the earth** (18) than other Gentiles. This will be true even if some of them have been embalmed and put into great tombs as mummies. That might be why they are asked, **Whom dost thou pass** (surpass, RSV) **in beauty?** (19)

In 21 this nether world is called **hell.** The word in the Hebrew is *sheol,* which means simply the place of the dead, for all persons (see comments on 31:17). *Sheol* here is not to be identified with the place of eternal punishment spoken of so often and so vividly in the New Testament (e.g., Matt. 18:9; Rev. 20:10-15).[8] While the Book of Daniel (12:2) teaches eternal rewards and punishments, the Old Testament as a whole does not say what existence beyond this life is to be like. It took Christ's teachings about the resurrection (John 11:25-26), and His own resurrection from the dead (cf. I Corinthians 15), to send Christians forth with a strong confidence about the next life—and with warnings to the willful about the fate awaiting them (Rev. 20:8).

Asshur (22) is, in the newer versions, translated as "Assyria" (see map 1). Assyria had been conquered by Babylon in 612 B.C. "After Assyria, Elam [24] was the next most formidable warrior state. . . . They inhabited the region east of the Tigris and joined the Assyrian army against Jerusalem in Isaiah's time" (Berk.,

[7]See comments on 31:18.
[8]In the NT *hades,* the underworld, is a comparable expression (Luke 10:15; Acts 2:27).

fn.; cf. Isa. 22:6). **Meshech** and **Tubal** (26) "were remnants of
the old Hittite population, sons of Japheth" (Berk. fn.; cf. Gen.
10:2). All of 26 and 27 seems to refer to Meshech and Tubal
with 28 pointing out Egypt's similar fate. Moffatt's translation is
helpful: "Meshek and Tubal are there, with all their folk in the
graves around them, all lying in a shameful death, victims of the
sword, because they were a terror in the land of the living; they
shall not lie beside the mighty warriors of old, who went down to
the underworld with their weapons, their swords lying under
their heads, and their shields upon their skeletons, because they
were a terror in the land of the living. (And, Pharaoh, you shall
lie among the defeated in disgrace, the victims of the sword.)"

Section **IV** *Restoration and Hope*

Ezekiel 33:1—48:35

Not only does the scene change at this point in Ezekiel's prophecy, but also the subject changes and the tenor, the atmosphere, and the spirit. No longer is there any exclusive engagement with prophecies directed to foreign nations, although they receive some attention in 36:7; 38—39. For the most part, the man of God now focuses upon the people of God, Israel. No longer is doom the order of things to come. We have here restoration and hope, insight and foresight.

A. RESTORATION OF ISRAEL, 33:1—39:29

In this section there are passing references to the doom awaiting certain Israelites (e.g., 33:23-29), and the nearby heathen nations (36:7). But summed up, these seven chapters tell of good days ahead for the people of the Lord in the land of the Lord.

1. Ezekiel's Office of Watchman Restated (33:1-9)

Always **the word of the Lord** (1) comes to Ezekiel. Never is the word one of his own, conjured up and thought out on his own part. He is never like the sun, emitting light from within himself. Instead, he is more like the moon. As the moon would have no illumination were it not for the sun, Ezekiel would have no light to give were it not for **the word of the Lord** that came to him.

Again, as so frequently, he is addressed as **son of man** (2; see comments on 2:1). As the word of the Lord for his **people,** Israel (2), comes to Ezekiel, he first declares simply that any prophet is a **watchman** to warn the wayward. This has been stated earlier in 3:16-21. Outside of Ezekiel, the figure of the prophet as watchman appears in Isa. 21:6; Jer. 6:17; Hab. 2:1. What is said in this section is clear enough: The watchman's responsibility is to **warn the wicked** (8), and **the wicked** person's responsibility is to **turn from his way** (9).

A man of their coasts (2) means "a man from among their number" (*Basic Bible*). His blood shall be upon his own head (4); i.e., "That man is responsible for his own death" (Moffatt). Hear the word at my mouth (7) is better as "Hear the word from My mouth" (Berk.). Delivered thy soul (9) means, "You will have saved your life" (RSV) from the condemnation of God.

2. Individual Responsibility (33:10-20)

Ezekiel was a believer in man's moral freedom, emphasizing individual responsibility. He would have been shocked by even the suggestion of anything like the unconditional predestination of individuals as taught by John Calvin and his followers.

Earlier, Ezekiel had spoken of the individual's own personal responsibility before God, stating that if a person who had been righteous turned from God and sinned, he would surely die. Of the righteous person's turning from God, and his resulting punishment, Ezekiel says that "in his sin that he hath sinned . . . shall he die" (18:24; see comments on 18:21-32).[1]

Here Ezekiel returns to the same emphasis. It is as if, under the Holy Spirit's guidance, he can see a time to come when Augustinianism and Calvinism would damage the nerve of spiritual endeavor by advocating that what men do (such as repenting and believing) or refrain from doing has no bearing on their eternal destiny—that they are elected or reprobated before they are born. The prophet, an Arminian two thousand years before Arminius, says: The righteousness of the righteous shall not deliver him in the day of his transgression (12; "when he transgresses," RSV). The fact that a person is righteous, or justified before God, will not help him any whatever if he willfully transgresses God's law. Ezekiel further explains that if the righteous trust to his own righteousness, and commit iniquity, all his righteousnesses shall not be remembered; but for his iniquity that he hath committed, he shall die for it (13). This seems to be in pointed opposition to the doctrine of "once in grace, always in grace," often also called the doctrine of "eternal security."

Against the second prong of that doctrine is Ezekiel's repeated explanation of the case of the wicked person who turns

---

[1]A highly quotable statement is made in this connection by Walter R. Roehrs: ". . . there is no group insurance against God's judgment" ("Ezekiel," *The Biblical Expositor* [Phila.: Holman Co., 1960], II, 251).

from his wickedness. Such a person's individual destiny was not decided in eternal decrees made before he was born. It is decided by whether or not he turns from sin to God. God declares, **When I say unto the wicked, Thou shalt surely die; if he turn from his sin . . . without committing iniquity; he shall surely live, he shall not die** (14-15).

People were saying that **the way of the Lord is not equal** (just, fair; 17). Ezekiel explains that God's ways are most fair, each individual being treated according to whether or not he is righteous. They are told, **O ye house of Israel, I will judge you every one after his ways** (20).

If it be suggested that this is Old Testament teaching and that New Testament truth might have been different, let two things be said. First, the New Testament follows Ezekiel's teaching (Matt. 10:22; Col. 1:23; Heb. 3:6; II Pet. 1:10). Second, proponents of unconditional election and perseverance do not give any reason for a change from need for individual responsibility in Old Testament times to no requirement of it in New Testament times.

3. *News Arrives of Jerusalem's Fall* (33:21-22)

Jerusalem had fallen to Nebuchadnezzar; and a detailed description of the fall was given to Ezekiel **in the twelfth year of our captivity, in the tenth month, in the fifth day of the month** (21; see 24:26). News did not travel with telegraphic rapidity in those days, and yet general news of the fall must have reached the Chebar community in a rather short time. Now, however, an eyewitness comes and tells Ezekiel the happenings firsthand.

The fugitive may have been detained by his captors, for according to most MSS. his coming seems to be a year and a half after the event. However, on the theory that the year began in the autumn, there would have been a lapse of less than six months between the event and this news of it.[2] According to Ezra 7:9 it took 108 days for a company of people to make the same journey.

Ezekiel had been told that, when "he that escapeth in that day" (24:26) would bring word of the city's fall, the prophet's mouth would be "opened to him which is escaped" (24:27). Ezekiel's mouth was to be closed from speaking to the Israelites, although he spoke during this time to the heathen nations (cc.

---

[2]See Herbert G. May, *op. cit.*, VI, 247-48.

25—32). Regarding the fugitive's coming, we read, **Now the hand of the Lord was upon me in the evening, afore he that was escaped came; and had opened my mouth, until he came to me in the morning . . . and I was no more dumb** (22).

4. The First Prophecies After Jerusalem's Fall (33:23-33)

One of Ezekiel's first prophecies has to do with the punishment of those who had fled to the **wastes of the land of Israel** (24) as the city fell to Nebuchadnezzar (23-29). These people reasoned that the land was theirs by promise. They said that God had given it to Abraham; and that if God had given it to **one** (24) person, surely the **many** descendants of Abraham should have the land as their own. But they did not think of their sin, and of the fact that God's promises always have conditions attached to them.

Ezekiel here catalogs their sins. For one thing, **Ye eat with the blood** (25). This no doubt means that they ate meat with the blood still in it, due to failure to kill the animal in the proper way. To abstain from blood was a rule still maintained in New Testament times (Acts 15:20). They are also told, **Ye stand upon your sword** (26). The RSV has, "You resort to the sword." Adam Clarke comments, "Ye live by plunder . . . and murder."[3] Other sins are also listed, including **abomination** (26), which has to do with idolatry. These rebellious fugitives will **fall by the sword, and . . . the pestilence** (27), and **the land** will be made **most desolate** (28).

Another prophecy made soon after the news of Jerusalem's fall had to do with the attitude of the people toward Ezekiel. They liked him, which is clear if **against** (30) is translated "about" or "concerning," as it is in the Septuagint.[4] They tell one another that the prophet is a man from whom they may **hear . . . the word that cometh forth from the Lord** (30). Ezekiel is to them **a very lovely song** (32), especially as he prophesies of restoration and hope, as he now does. He even **hath a pleasant voice, and can play well on an instrument.** A really popular preacher, this! But, lo! they **hear** his **words, but they do not do them.** Nonetheless, **when this cometh to pass** (33), which Ezekiel has prophesied, **then shall they know that a prophet hath been among them** (33).

[3]*Op. cit.*, IV, 512.
[4]See Alfred Rahlfs, ed., *Septuaginta* (N.Y.: Societate Biblica Americana, 1949), II, 831.

5. *Restoration Promises* (34:1—39:29)

a. *Restoration under a good shepherd* (34:1-31). As the prophet was called a watchman, the rulers of Israel are here called **shepherds** (2). They include such persons as the kings, the princes, and the magistrates. Clarke includes also the priests and Levites.[5] These have been unfaithful shepherds to God's people. They have not fed the Lord's **flocks** (2), Israel. Instead they have seen to it that they themselves were well fed and well clothed (3). They have had no mercy toward the **diseased** and the wounded. They have not **sought that which was lost** (4), as Christ, the Good Shepherd, was to do in a later day (John 10:11, 14).

Beautiful and gracious indeed are the things which God promises to do for His flock, He himself becoming a Good Shepherd to them (11-31). He will search for the lost **sheep that are scattered** (12). This evidently refers to the Israelites who were dispersed to many lands. Being a timeless promise of the Eternal One, it no doubt refers to God's grace which still seeks out the sinner and urges him to return to the fold. **The cloudy and dark day** is a figure for a time of uncertainty and fear.

The word for **fat** (14) has a variety of meanings. In 14 it refers to "rich" pastures (Berk.). In 16 and 20 there are clear overtones of a self-centered prosperity, gained at the expense of others. The Lord says of these selfish leaders, **I judge between cattle and cattle** (17). "The he-goats are the strong, leading men of the community, who ignore the rights of common people" (Berk., fn.). Of them, God says, **I . . . will judge between the fat cattle and between the lean cattle** (20). Responsibility for Israel's exile is charged to these leaders: "You plump creatures, you have pushed the lean sheep away, with your sides and shoulders, butting at these feeble creatures with your horns till you have scattered them abroad" (21, Moffatt).

God will show no mercy to such evildoers but He has glorious plans for His people. Over them He **will set up one shepherd** (23), **and he shall feed them, even my servant David.** This Messianic prophecy has to do with the coming of Christ in David's lineage; He will shepherd all the sheep who follow Him (John 10:4).

The clear Messianic message of 23-25 blends with the nearer

[5]*Op. cit.,* IV, 513.

promise of Israel's restoration to Jerusalem. **My hill** (26) probably refers to Mount Zion, on which the Temple had stood. Along with spiritual redemption through **one shepherd** from David's lineage (23), God promises to look after their life necessities (25b-29). Instead of **I will raise up for them a plant of renown** (29), which might seem Messianic, the Hebrew reads: "I will raise up unto them a plantation for renown" (ASV).[6] No longer would they be **consumed with hunger** (famine). Nor would they any longer **bear the shame of the heathen,** who were sure that Israel's God had let His own people down every time Israel was in dire need. **Those that served themselves of them** (27) means "those who enslaved them" (Berk.). The assertion, **Thus shall they know that I the Lord their God am with them** (30), clearly refers to the material blessings promised in 25b-29. But does it not also refer to the revelation of God in the Messiah (23-25), and to every manifestation of himself to those who serve Him? There is from time to time a strong inner assurance of the Divine Presence to all who sincerely walk with God.

b. Restoration of Israel (35:1—36:15). The next chapter and a half refer to one matter. When chapter divisions were made in the thirteenth century A.D. it would have been more accurate to begin the new chapter at 36:16 instead of at 36:1. The subject of this section is the restoration which God promises to Israel, and the message is directed principally to Ezekiel's fellow exiles in Babylon. Mostly, it is said that restoration will come to Israel's **mountains** (36:1, 4, 8), which are used to personify the nation. But included also are **the rivers** and **the valleys** (36:4), the waste places and the **cities** (see 36:6)—i.e., all the land. This is the promise which the prophet makes for the God who lives and who therefore can fulfill the promises (35:6).[7]

But as a contrast to what God proposes to do for the mountains of Israel, the judgment which He is to bring to **mount Seir**

---

[6]See discussion in F. Gardiner, *op. cit.,* p. 301.

[7]It is the living God, as opposed to the lifeless idols made by men, who is behind all these promises of restoration—and who is therefore able to follow through and fulfill the promises. This is why the phrase as **I live** appears so often in this section (33:11, 27; 34:8; 35:6). For a superb discussion of God as the living God see Otto Baab, *The Theology of the Old Testament* (N.Y.: Abingdon, 1949), pp. 24-28. Baab says, "Perhaps the most typical word for identifying the God of the Old Testament is the word 'living'" (p. 24). See Josh. 3:10; Ps. 42:2; 84:1-2. For the oath, "As the Lord liveth," see Judg. 8:19; Ruth 3:13; I Sam. 19:6; 20:21.

(2; the poetic name for Edom) is delineated (35:1-15). **I will stretch out mine hand** (3) means, I will exert My power.

Edom has already come up for the Lord's rebuke (25:12-14). Descended from Esau,[8] this neighbor of Israel (see map 1) had been a thorn in her side for a long time. She had had a **perpetual hatred** (35:5) for Israel.

When Moses and the children of Israel were making their way toward the Promised Land, they asked permission to pass through Edom and go directly into Canaan. The permission was refused (Num. 20:18), and Israel had to go the long way around. That action was long remembered by Israel. Centuries after Ezekiel's time, Edom produced the Herods who were so cruel to the Saviour.

But just before Ezekiel gave this "prophecy in contrasts" between Edom and Israel, Edom opposed Israel and aided Babylonia. In Jerusalem's most difficult day, when she fell to Nebuchadnezzar, Edom stood "on the other side . . . as one of them" (Obad. 11). When there was no use holding out longer, some of the Israelites fled into neighboring Edom. But she was only neighboring, not neighborly. In a fiendish hatred she "stood in the crossway, to cut off those of his [of Judah] that did escape" (Obad. 14). Her warriors stood at the main crossroads just inside Edom, and murdered the scattering escapees. After Obadiah had reminded them that they had cut down the escapees he says, "Neither shouldest thou have delivered up those of his that did remain in the day of distress" (Obad. 14). When they had had enough of blood, they elected to capture the escapees and watch them writhe when turned over to the enemy. Ezekiel says that Edom **shed the blood of the children of Israel by the force of the sword in the time of their calamity** (35:5). **In the time that their iniquity had an end** is more simply and accurately translated, "the time of their final doom" (Berk.).

Edom looked the situation over and "rejoiced over the children of Judah in the day of their destruction" (Obad. 12). Besides, she boasted that no such humiliation had come to her. Obadiah says, "Neither shouldest thou have spoken proudly in the day of distress."[9] Moreover, the Edomites "entered into the

---

[8]This is why Judah (Israel) is called Edom's "brother" (Obad. 10, 12).

[9]For further graphic description of this and other phrases in this passage see "Obadiah," *Biblical Commentary on the Old Testament*, by C. F. Keil and F. Delitzsch, *Minor Prophets*, II, 364.

gate" of the destroyed city, "looked on their affliction," and looted "their substance" (Obad. 13). God said to Edom, "Because you are guilty of blood, therefore blood shall pursue you" (35:6, RSV). In 35:11 we see something of divine justice. God declares, **I will even do according to thine anger, and according to thine envy.** Paul writes, "Vengeance is mine; I will repay, saith the Lord" (Rom. 12:19).

Before Rebekah had given birth to the twins, Jacob and Esau, the Lord told her, "Two nations are in thy womb, and two manner of people" (Gen. 25:23). **These two nations** (35:10) refer to Mount Seir and Canaan. Israel had her wanderings and her sins, but her history had been under the hand of God. Edom, on the contrary, was "heathen" (Obad. 2). Esau himself had been a "profane person" (Heb. 12:16), and he had begotten a profane people. The Old Testament makes no mention of their worshipping any gods whatever, although archaeologists have found remains of their idol deities. Profane they were—materialists, smart traders with many nations, wise in the wisdom of men, forgetting God. John Paterson says, "Edom was interested solely in buying and selling things: beasts and [other] livestock were its main concern. It was a commercial civilization and prided itself on its business acumen and commercial astuteness."[10]

Edom's smallness might have contributed to her attitude. She was only about a hundred miles in length, and nowhere more than twenty miles in width—a mere speck on the map. But mainly her arrogance arose because of her allegedly impregnable geographic situation. Her capital city, Sela (Heb., "rock"), was well-located for fortification. Its name was later changed to Petra, a Greek word of similar meaning. It was situated on both sides of a deep ravine which winds like a river for a mile and a half. On either side of the gorge were cliffs, in which there were both natural and hewn caves, where people lived. The earlier inhabitants of the area, then named **mount Seir** (35:2-3, etc.), were called cave dwellers (or "Horim," see Gen. 14:6; Deut. 2:12, 22). In those days of foot soldiers and chariots it was exceedingly difficult for any enemy to defeat the people of Petra; also the country generally was easily fortified.

The proud and pompous Edom, also called **Idumea** (35:15), will become **perpetual desolations** (35:9). Moffatt translates it

[10]*Op. cit.*, 178.

vividly: "I will lay you desolate for all time." On the contrary, the humbled and scattered Israelites will be restored to their land and blessed. In 36:8, God promised fruitfulness to the mountains of Israel and explained the reason: It was for **my people of Israel; for they are at hand to come.**

c. Restoration of the sinful hearts of men (36:16-38). If the prophecy of Ezekiel reaches a peak which is higher than all other peaks, it is in the last part of this chapter. In this passage Ezekiel tells what God proposes to do for the hearts of the Israelites; but he prefaces that word by explaining the deep-down reason why He proposes to redeem men in this way. He is to make men holy because He himself is holy.

First, the prophet points out the sins of the people. They have **defiled** the land **by their doings** (17).

Then the Lord says that **their way was before me as the uncleanness of a removed** (ceremonially unclean) **woman.** Sinful people were to be held off from fellowship with God. The people had **their idols** (18); and when God had **scattered them** (19) due to their idols they **profaned** His **holy name** (20). They dragged God's name in the dust among the heathen. In the Old Testament God's **name** is often synonymous with His nature. Thus God is deeply concerned that His name be not profaned, i.e., that His nature be not misunderstood; for if men do not rightly understand God, they cannot rightly worship and love Him. It is significant that Israel's profanity was not in cursing God—it was in their failure to obey Him.

Note that it is His **holy name** (20) which they have profaned. When God is said to be holy, it means that He exists in a category by himself, both metaphysically and morally. The word for "holiness" (Heb., *kodesh*) originally had to do with separation or cutting off.[11] When applied to things, it means that they are set apart from ordinary uses, for God's use. Thus sacrifices and tithes were holy (Exod. 29:33 ff.; Lev. 21:22; 22:10; Num. 18:25-32; Deut. 12:26). When applied to persons, Old Testament holiness usually signified that they were set apart for God's special work, e.g., the priesthood. But even in His employ, they defiled His holy name if they were not morally pure of heart (18-24). When applied to angels, holiness means that they share the Cre-

---

[11]For a more thorough discussion of this subject see A. C. Knudson, *The Religious Teachings of the Old Testament* (N.Y.: Abingdon, 1918), pp. 137-53.

ator's nature and are dedicated to His service (Dan. 8:13; Matt. 25:31).

When applied to God himself in the Scriptures generally, holiness means that He is set apart from all other so-called gods of men. He is the absolutely holy One. So we read: "There is none holy as the Lord" (I Sam. 2:2). Isaiah often uses "Holy One" as a synonym for God (e.g., Isa. 40:25). All the attributes of God, metaphysical and moral, are subsumed under His holiness.[12] That is what He is—Holiness. Thus Amos can speak of God at one time as swearing "by his holiness" (Amos 4:2), and at another time as swearing "by himself" (Amos 6:8). God's great name (23) is here used as a synonym of His holy name (22).

In our present passage, however, it is God's moral holiness that demands holy lives in men (cf. 17-23). See also comments on Ezek. 43:7, where God as a holy God requires holy lives.

Holiness, then, is what God is, His very nature. His holiness is absolute, of course, and underived, so it will be on a far higher level than when it is given to men. But God as a holy God has expected men to be holy in both the Old Testament and the New Testament. In Lev. 11:44 we read, "Ye shall be holy; for I am holy" (cf. Leviticus 11—18).[13] And the Apostle Peter says, "But as he which hath called you is holy, so be ye holy in all manner of conversation [living]; because it is written, Be ye holy; for I am holy" (I Pet. 1:15-16). This holiness in men includes their being set apart as the Lord's own possession. It also includes purity of heart—a singleness of spirit in which a man loves the Lord's will and work without the inner opposition which has its roots in the carnal nature or original sin. This purity of heart is essentially what the believing disciples received on the Day of Pentecost (Acts 2:4; 15:8-9).

[12]The Scriptures of course connect God's holiness with His moral nature (e.g., in the passage being treated and very explicitly in Ezek. 43:7). But they also connect His holiness with His metaphysical attributes. It is connected with His power and majesty, e.g., in many places. In Isa. 6:3 we read, "Holy, holy, holy, is the Lord of hosts"—the angelic hosts, here. Such is shown in Ps. 47:8: "God reigneth over the heathen: God sitteth upon the throne of his holiness." God is "the high and lofty One that inhabiteth eternity, whose name is Holy" (Isa. 57:15).

[13]Although there is much of ceremonial holiness in those chapters, the so-called ceremonial matters often have moral connotations—e.g., the prohibitions against improper relationships with various relatives (Lev. 18:6-24).

Ezekiel sees perhaps more clearly than any other Old Testament figure the heart purity made available at and after Pentecost.[14] The prophet naturally does not cast his foregleams of heart holiness in the language of systematic theology. But what he sees is what is fulfilled in the new covenant dispensation—and particularly in those who are sanctified wholly (I Thess. 5: 23).[15]

Speaking for the Lord, the prophet says, **Then** (some time after Israel's restoration to the land) **will I sprinkle clean water upon you, and ye shall be clean** (25). Adam Clarke comments, "The *truly cleansing water;* the influences of the Holy Spirit typified by *water,* whose property is to *cleanse, whiten, purify, refresh,* render *healthy* and *fruitful.*"[16]

The Lord further promises, **A new heart also will I give you** (26). This has to do with new appetites and a new will to serve God—for "heart," in the Hebrew, has volitional overtones and not simply emotional ones as it does in the English. **A new spirit** will also be put **within** the people—a new yearning to perform God's will even at personal cost. And note that all this will be **within.** Religion had been quite external as Israel was brought along God's ways. In the new thing which God will do, the faith is to be internalized. So internal will it be that imparted righteousness as taught in Wesleyan-Arminianism is implied, instead of mere imputed righteousness (reckoning a person as righteous because he is Christ's, when he himself is not actually righteous).[17]

[14]Jer. 31:31-34 is a similar passage. This passage in Jeremiah is quoted in Hebrews 8 and 10. See comments in H. Orton Wiley, *The Epistle to the Hebrews* (Kansas City, Mo.: Beacon Hill Press, 1959), pp. 382 ff.

[15]For one of the most thorough of biblical and historical studies of the doctrine and experience of entire sanctification, as emphasized by John Wesley, see George Allen Turner, *The Vision Which Transforms* (Kansas City, Mo.: Beacon Hill Press, 1965), 352 pp.

[16]*Op. cit.,* IV, 521.

[17]This prophecy is a peculiarly fertile source of what has come to be known as Arminianism. For a resumé of this theological stance, see Gerald O. McCulloh, *Man's Faith and Freedom* (N.Y.: Abingdon, 1962), 128 pp. See Rom. 8:4 as an outstanding "imparted righteousness" passage. Calvinists have often taught that God's requirements are fulfilled only in Christ, and not in the individual Christian. But Paul there says, "That the ordinance of the law might be fulfilled in us, who walk not after the flesh, but after the Spirit" (Rom. 8:4, ASV). See Daniel Steele's comments on this passage in his *Half Hours with St. Paul* (Chicago: The Christian Witness Co., 1909), p. 71.

This high peak of Old Testament prophecy continues with the promise that the **stony heart** will be taken away, and the **heart of flesh** put into its place. Israel had had its bouts with **the stony heart.** The people had often wanted to go their own way, and they often did. And the more one goes his own way, the more flintlike does his heart become. More and more he hardens himself against God's call. Ezekiel sees the time when by a divine surgery God will remove the stony heart as a surgeon might cut out a cancer. Then God will put in its place a heart that is responsive to His wishes.

For all this there will need to be an enablement. This is supplied by the Lord's Spirit, the Holy Spirit, indwelling the trusting soul. God therefore says, **And I will put my spirit within you, and cause you to walk in my statutes** (27). This seems to be what Joel also had seen (Joel 2:28-29). It was fulfilled at Pentecost (Acts 2), and has seen a thousand thousand reverberations in the modern holiness movement which God used John Wesley to fan into a flame in the eighteenth century. On verse 27, Adam Clarke says: "Here is the salvation that is the birthright of every *Christian believer: the complete destruction of all sin in the soul, and the complete renewal of the heart;* no *sin* having any place *within,* and no *unrighteousness* having any place *without.*"[18]

In 36:25-38 we see "Pentecost in Ezekiel's Prophecy." **Then will I sprinkle clean water upon you, and ye shall be clean, 25.** (1) **A new heart, 26;** (2) **A new spirit, 26;** (3) These will be possible because of the dynamic indwelling of the Holy Spirit, **And I will put my spirit within you, 27.**

The remainder of this chapter (28-38) has to do mainly with the ways in which God's people, restored in their hearts, will be blessed temporally in the land of promise and plenty. In 37-38, God promises that the sparsely peopled land of Israel shall **increase . . . with men like a flock.** But the promise is not for mere numbers alone. God promises to increase them with men **as the holy flock.** The comparison is to the special flock consecrated to God. Like begets like. When His people are consecrated— dedicated to a holy purpose—God promises that they shall increase like **the flock of Jerusalem.**

---

[18]*Op cit.,* IV, 521. It is also worthy of note that this is the only Old Testament text included in John Wesley's famous "Thirty Texts" upon which he placed major emphasis in teaching Christian perfection.

d. Restoration of the dry bones (37:1-14). These verses are probably the best known of any in the entire prophecy, thanks to the lively and popular spiritual about the dry bones.

Here we rejoice with the man of God who sees another vision. This time it is about **dry** bones (2). He sees them in a **valley** (1), but the sight he sees has put many a Christian upon a mountaintop spiritually. The dry bones are the scattered Israelites. The expression **We are cut off for our parts** (11) is dramatically translated, "We are completely done for!" (Berk.) Their getting connected to each other, and being clothed with **flesh** (6) and enlivened with **breath** is a poetic way of saying that they will be returned to the land of their love (12, 14).

The picture of opening Israel's tombs and of bringing the people **up out of your graves** (13) is to be taken symbolically. However, the symbolism would probably not have been used if there had not been, even at this time, some kind of faith in the resurrection of the body—which faith bursts out in full glory in the New Testament (e.g., I Corinthians 15).

Applying the symbolism of this passage spiritually, an evangelistic message could be given on "Ezekiel's Vision in the Valley." (1) The pity of the sinful state, the dry bones of those dead in trespasses and sins, 1-2; (2) The place of preaching, **O ye dry bones, hear the word of the Lord,** 4; (3) The power of God, to make dry bones live, 5-14.

e. Restoration of Israel's earlier unity (37:15-28). Ezekiel would always rather give an example than a definition. This prophet who was a doer as well as a thinker takes two sticks and with them gives an object lesson. With it he captures the attention, and when its meaning is made clear, truth is fixed in the memory. He wrote, **For Judah** (16), on one of the sticks and, **For Joseph,** on the other. Then he joined the two sticks together **into one stick** (17), and told the disheartened captives that thus God would join together in the restoration the Southern Kingdom of Judah and the Northern Kingdom known as **Israel, Joseph,** or **Ephraim.** At Solomon's death in 931 B.C., the kingdom had been divided. In 721 the Northern Kingdom had fallen, and in 586 the Southern Kingdom had gone down. Now the two will be restored and united. God says, **I will make them one nation in . . . the mountains of Israel; and one king shall be king to them all** (22). This one king is to be **David** (24), and he is to be **their prince for ever** (25). This is a reference to Christ, the

Prince of David's lineage who is to reign eternally over the redeemed hearts of men.

f. *Restoration in spite of evil powers* (38:1—39:29). In
these two chapters there is a prophecy against "Gog, of the land
of Magog" (28:2, ASV). **Gog** is **the chief prince** (38:2), or king,
of **Magog**, an area far to the north, which includes the lesser
areas of **Meshech and Tubal.** Gog and his hordes will, **in the
latter years** (38:8), war against the restored land of Israel, and
are to be defeated utterly. Allied with Gog there will be **Persia,
Ethiopia, and Libya** (5)—"Persians, Ethiopians, and East Afri-
cans." **Gomer** (38:6) refers to the "Cimmerians, who originally
dwelt north of the Black Sea" (Berk., fn.). **Sheba, and Dedan**
(38:13) were great trading centers in Arabia. Gog seems to be
symbolic of all the evil powers which will be arrayed against
God's people in the future. And yet **Magog** seems to be also a
real country or group of countries; it is included in a list of
nations in Gen. 10:2 and I Chron. 1:5 along with Meshech and
Tubal.

Many leading enemies of Israel have been suggested by
different Bible scholars as the Gog of these chapters. For some,
Alexander the Great—the Greek general who overran Palestine
in the late fourth century B.C.—has seemed to fit the descriptions given here. Others have said that Gog is Antiochus Epiphanes, king of Syria, who polluted Israel's worship in the early
second century B.C. Likewise Magog has been suggested to be
various countries: Persia, Syria, Scythia, Russia.

After studying these chapters as carefully as possible, and
with what help there is from recent archaeology, the identity of
both Gog and Magog remains unclear. Some suggest that even
to the inspired writer himself their identity might not have been
altogether clear. Adam Clarke speaks of "the ocean of conjecture"[19] that surrounds them, and says, "This is allowed to be the
most difficult prophecy in the Old Testament."[20]

But whether Gog is a specific future opposer and Magog
is a given country or coalition of countries are not the important
matters here. The significant fact is that God is on the side of
His people and promises to thwart the attempts of their enemies
to do them hurt. Whoever may play the part of Gog, God will
protect His own people, and thereby His own **holy name** (39:7).

[19]*Op. cit.*, IV, 526.
[20]*Ibid.*

In 38:16, God declares, **I shall be sanctified in thee, O Gog.**
Moffatt renders the meaning graphically: "I will indeed bring
you against my land, to let the nations learn what I am, when I
show them my dread divinity in handling you, O Gog."

Hamon-gog (39:11) means "the multitude of Gog" (RSV,
fn.). Smith-Goodspeed clarifies 39:14 thus: "And they shall set
apart a standing commission of men who shall pass through the
land, searching for those who remain unburied. . . . At the end
of seven months they shall begin the search."

John the Revelator must have alluded to Ezekiel's prophecy
about enemy forces when he spoke of "Gog and Magog" (Rev.
20:8). The apostle seems to think of Gog as a nation instead of a
king. But he might well have interpreted both Gog and Magog
symbolically—as representing the nations which Satan will deceive at end-time and which will then war against God and
God's people (see Rev. 20:7-9).

B. Hope, Temporal and Eternal, 40:1—48:35

Chapters 40—48 are high paeans of hope. They tell of hope
through a rebuilt temple (40:1—42:20), the divine glory in the
temple (43:1-12), restored sanctuary ordinances (43:13—46:24),
a ministry to others (47:1-12), and an inheritance for this life and
the next (47:13—48:35).

1. *Background of the Hope* (40:1-4)

These prophecies, so full of hope, are dated as in **the five and
twentieth year of our captivity** (1), or 572 B.C. They came to the
prophet **in the tenth day of the month,** and in **the beginning of
the year.**[21] This last phrase might mean "in the first month,"
which is the way the Septuagint reads.[22] This was **the fourteenth
year** after Jerusalem's fall.

The prophecies consist of what Ezekiel saw in another of
his visions. In spirit he was **brought . . . into the land of Israel**
(2), **set . . . upon a very high mountain,**[23] and allowed to see

[21]This might mean New Year's Day. According to Lev. 25:9 the tenth
day of the seventh month was New Year's Day, although that special
occasion was moved to the first day of the seventh month (Lev. 23:24;
Num. 29:1). Cf. G. A. Cooke, "The Book of Ezekiel," *The International
Critical Commentary* (N.Y.: Charles Scribner's Sons, 1937), II, 429.

[22]See Alfred Rahlfs, ed., *op. cit.,* p. 843.

[23]This is probably Mt. Zion (see Ps. 48:2; Isa. 2:2).

sights which even the less privileged people of God will also see sooner or later. **By which was as the frame of a city on the south** is rendered, "upon which was a building like a city in front of me" (Moffatt).

A man (3), i.e., an angel, is near him, with a **measuring reed** in his hand (cf. Rev. 21:15-27), who tells him to look and listen and to **declare . . . to the house of Israel** (4) all that he sees.

2. *Hope Through a Rebuilt Temple* (40:5—42:20)

Ezekiel saw a **house** (40:5), the temple, similar to Solomon's Temple, which had been destroyed. The various measurements of it are given in cubits. The "long cubit"—**the cubit and an hand breadth** (5)—which Ezekiel used was about twenty-one inches; the shorter, more common cubit was just under eighteen inches. The angelic guide used **a line of flax** (3), a kind of tape measure for long measurements; and **a measuring reed,** used as a "yardstick" (about ten and one-half feet long) for the shorter measurements.

For a clearer picture of 41:6-7 and 42:5-6, see *The Berkeley Version.* **The separate place** (41:12-15; 42:1, 10, 13) was "the yard" (RSV).

In these chapters there are, however, far more important matters than measurements. Basic among them is the very fact that in his vision Ezekiel sees a restored temple. The one which had been built some four centuries earlier was in ruins, but another one figured in Israel's destiny. Israel still needs a temple, and a temple she will have.

With one central place for sacrifice and worship, Israel will have it dramatized that there is but one God. With the once-for-all sacrifice of Christ still half a millennium away, Israel will need the temporary ministries of the repeated sacrifices of animals. The time will come when men will worship the Father in spirit (spiritually) and in truth (living out the faith) anywhere and everywhere, temple or no temple (John 4:23-24). And since Titus destroyed the Temple in A.D. 70, even the Jews have had none. But that time had not yet come. Meantime, another Temple will be built soon after Israel returns to Palestine. And a third one, called Herod's Temple, will be built before the "not yet" times are turned into the times of New Testament fulfillment.

The temple which Ezekiel envisioned was somewhat different from Solomon's Temple, as can be seen by a comparison of details in Ezekiel with those in I Kings 6—7. Ezekiel's envisioned temple was also somewhat different from both of the temples which were yet to be built. For example, the wall around **the inner house** is **five hundred reeds** (42:15-19) in each direction, about five hundred feet, or nearly a mile, each way. Such distances were greater than the dimensions of the actual temples, and greater than could literally fit on Mount Zion. It may be that much of what Ezekiel saw was to be fulfilled literally, yet some of it is to be understood symbolically. It seems to refer to a temple "not made with hands, eternal in the heavens." This is borne out by the fact that God promises to dwell **for ever** (43:9) in this temple.

Most editions of the KJV read **utter court** (40:17, 31, 37; 42:1-10), but it should be "outer court," as in ASV.

3. Hope Through Divine Glory (43:1-12)

The appearance of the divine glory is an exciting Old Testament phenomenon. It may be defined as the outward manifestation of God's holiness. The thrice holy Lord of the angelic hosts fills all the earth with His glory (Isa. 6:3). Sometimes this outward manifestation of His holiness reveals itself in His might that is manifest in nature and history, as in Isa. 2:10. At other times it is at least a quasi physical appearance indicative of the Divine Presence. As such, it is seen in prophetic vision in Ezek. 1:26-28; 8:1-2; 9:1-3; 10:4; 11:23; 44:4. On this occasion Ezekiel says the appearance was similar to **the vision which I saw** (3) on two previous occasions (8:1-2; 9:1-3; and 1:26-27). The visible presence of God was also observed at times by persons who were not prophets (e.g., Exod. 16:10; 24:16-18; 29:43; 40:34).

In 43:1-12 this glory of God, this outward manifestation of God's holiness, comes to dwell in the temple which Ezekiel sees. Here it is something that a person can **behold** (2). The prophet says that the glory came by **way of the east.** This manifestation of God's presence **came into the house** (temple) **by the way of the gate** (4), the one "facing east" (RSV).

God's glory, so observable, will not mix with defilement of any sort, because the glory is bound up with God's holiness.

Harlotry and idolatry are both moral sins. **Whoredom** (7) would defile God's **holy name,** as would **the carcases of their kings in their high places.** This expression may mean the idols of the kings, since kings were not buried within the Temple as far as is known.[24]

There is such an aloofness about God as the Holy One that the glory will not mix with ordinary people in their ordinary lives, even apart from their sinning. God says that Israel has defiled His holy name by building houses too close to the Temple. The charge is, **In their setting of their threshold by my thresholds, and their post by my posts, and the wall between me and them, they have even defiled my holy name** (8). This becomes clearer when one supplies the word "only," as in RSV; there is "only a wall between me and them." Even in our dispensation, we should maintain a real reverence for God, who is high and holy; and we ought never desecrate holy places by occupations which in other locations would be legitimate.

4. Hope Through Restored Ordinances (43:13—46:24)

Some things about the temple which Ezekiel sees make it a heavenly one, e.g., as noted earlier, that God will dwell in it forever. But most of what he saw was to be fulfilled in the next two earthly temples. Summed up, he sees a restoration of Temple procedures connected with sacrifices, and an apportioning of the land.

a. Requirements of the priests (43:13—44:31). Instructions for building the altar are given with its various measurements mentioned. Here, too, the long cubit is used as the standard of measurement (see comment on 40:5). The **settle** (43:14) is the ledge about the base of the altar, on which the priests walked. **Four horns** (43:15, 20) point upward from the altar's four corners. In connection with the offerings offered on the altar the priests were to **cast salt upon them** (43:24). "Salt signified covenant keeping. 'There is salt between us,' says the Arab, after eating with another" (Berk., fn.).

The priests are to be **the Levites that be of the seed of Zadok** (43:19; cf. 44:15; also I Kings 1:7-8 for Zadok himself

---

[24]Keil concludes, "The corpses of the kings are therefore the dead idols, for which the kings (for example Manasseh) had built altars or high places in the sanctuary, i.e., in the courts of the temple (II Kings 21:4, 5-7)" (*Prophecies of Ezekiel,* II, 281).

with II Sam. 8:17; 15:24 ff.). The other Levites **shall not come near unto me, to do the office of a priest** (44:13). Instead, they will be attendants: **keepers of the charge of the house, for all the service thereof** (44:14). This was a punishment for **their abominations** (44:13). The selection of the sons of Zadok was because they had **kept the . . . sanctuary when the children of Israel went astray** (44:15). God has ways of remembering faithfulness!

The priests were to wear **linen garments; and no wool** (44: 17) during their **inner court** ministrations. There is here an implication that they did not wear the priestly garments all the time. Wool would cause **sweat** (44:18): also, it was an animal product, and touching it would make a priest ceremonially unclean. Linen is of course a vegetable product. **Utter court** (44:19) is the "outer court."

The priests **shall only poll their heads** (44:20)—that is, not **shave** them, but cut the hair short. They could drink wine moderately, but not when ministering (44:21). Only the Nazarites took the vow of total abstinence.

The priests married, within Israel, of course, a maiden, or the **widow** of a **priest** (44:22). Prophets and priests married, as did the apostles in New Testament times. The celibacy of the priesthood stems from neither the Hebrew nor the Christian tradition, but from Greek influences, in which nature in general and the human body in particular were considered as inherently evil.

Priests were not to eat **any thing that is dead of itself** (44:31), since the blood would not have been drained properly. The opposition to eating blood extends into New Testament times (Acts 15:28-29).

b. *Allotment of the land* (45:1-7). In this passage we have still more of the symbolism in this book which bursts historical and logical bounds and talks in heavenly terms. In the restoration, land is to be allotted to **the sanctuary, the priests, the prince** (king), and the city itself. The people were to **divide by lot** (1), which in this case probably means allotment; the very order of the division shows that **lot** in the sense of chance is not intended. But this division of the land was not used at any previous time, nor at any time subsequent to Ezekiel's day. Like much of the rest of what the man of many visions sees, it has a spiritual fulfillment in God's eternal kingdom.

Several lessons can be learned from the passage. One is that, even as the portion of land for God's **sanctuary** (2) comes first in this allotment, so God's portion always comes first in the matter of possessions. And this is not only a duty. What we set aside for God is an **oblation** (1, 6-7; an offering).

Another lesson is that God's sanctuaries are holy. We are to give them a respect and reverence not accorded to ordinary human places. There was to be an area about the temple, **the suburbs** (45:2; open places), in which even the priests were not to build their houses. This area was to be **fifty cubits** or about eighty-five feet in width.

Another insight is that, even as God looked after **the priests** in those days by allotting land for them (45:4), so He has made a provision for His ministers in our day. The obscure last part of v. 5 has been rendered, "It shall be their possession for their houses in which to live" (Berk.).

c. Fairness and consistent measures (45:8-12). A further lesson is that God cares for the poor, of whom the world has so many in every age. God says, **My princes shall no more oppress my people** (8; cf. 34:1-31). God was not asleep when Hitler and his cohorts were having their brief day upon the stage of human history. He is not slumbering at present while His own are taunted in Russia and China. God is never content when the princes of nations oppress any people. He has a way of looking after His own—if not in this life, then in the next—and of subjecting world leaders to His ultimate will.

God's interest in the poor is further shown when He says to the princes, **Remove violence and spoil** ("oppression," RSV), **and execute judgment and justice, take away your exactions from my people, saith the Lord God. Ye shall have just balances** (9-10). The poor are not mentioned outright, but one is quite sure that they are in the Lord's mind. Various measurements are mentioned in what follows, the modern equivalents of some of them being unknown to us.[25]

d. An order of worship (45:13—46:24). This section deals

---

[25]See Herbert G. May, *op. cit.*, p. 317, for a study of the measurements. The approximations in *The Berkeley Version* are helpful: **ephah** equals about one bushel; **bath**, about ten gallons; the **homer** or cor was equal to ten ephahs or baths. The **shekel** was a little more than half an ounce, and the **gerah** at one-twentieth of a shekel would be worth about four cents. The **maneh** was about one and one-half pounds.

with the order of sacrifice and worship to be observed in the ideal temple and community. There will be no divorcement between religion as such and the state. The prince is given land, and is **to give burnt offerings, and meat offerings, and . . . prepare the sin offering . . . to make reconciliation for the house of Israel** (45:17; see also 46:1-12). The separation of church and state in the American tradition does not mean that the state is to be divorced from religion as such. We refer to God on our coins and in the salute to our flag; we favor the faith by waiving taxes on religious buildings, and by providing chaplains to the armed forces. But the nation does not make any one religious group the official, established one. Not freedom *from* religion, which is the guarantee of Russia's constitution, but freedom of religion, is the guarantee of Article One of America's constitution.

Regular provisions were established for ritual purification of **the sanctuary** (18). This was to be done twice a year, at the beginning of the **first** (18) and **seventh** (25) months, corresponding roughly to the beginning of April and the first of October of our year. As always throughout both the Old Testament and the New, **blood** (19) was the cleansing agent.

The gate of the inner court that looketh toward the east (46:1) was to be **shut** during **the six working days,** but opened **on the sabbath** and on **the day of the new moon,** i.e., the first day of each month. **Prince** (2) and **people** (3) alike are to worship (2-8). An interesting provision was made whereby those who entered through one gate were to leave by another (9). May this not suggest that worship is to be a life-changing activity? We should not leave as we came, but lifted and better. Offerings and sacrifices were to be a stated part of worship (10-15).

Special care was to be taken to preserve the property of **the prince** (16-18), probably both to safeguard the lands of the ruler and to prevent his taking property from the people. Ezekiel was shown the places provided for the preparation of the sacrifices (19-24).

5. *Hope Through Living Waters* (47:1-12)

The allotting of the land begun in 45:1-8 is continued in 47:13—48:35. But there is a high, poetic interlude here about refreshing **waters** for the nations. They came **from under the threshold of the house** (Temple) **eastward** (1); originating along **the south side of the altar**—relating the water to redemption.

610

In his vision Ezekiel was led around the stream as it flowed through the Temple. Because the water was flowing out of the south side, the prophet was **brought . . . out** (2) of the north gate, thence to the **utter** (outer) **gate,** and then eastward paralleling the flow of the stream.

The river gets larger and larger as it goes along, but without any tributaries flowing into it—evidently miraculous and symbolical. The angelic guide has the prophet test the river's depth at thousand-cubit intervals as it leaves the Temple and the top of Mount Zion. At first the waters are **to the ancles** (3), then **to the knees** (4), then **to the loins;** and finally **waters to swim in, a river that could not be passed over** (5). Already the vision is reminding us of redemption. There were **very many trees on the one side and on the other** (7), suggesting the tree of life seen in Adam's garden; and **every thing that liveth, which moveth, whithersoever the rivers shall come shall live** (9).

The **east country** and the **desert** (8) refer to the deep Jordan valley, especially the section between the Sea of Galilee and the Dead Sea. **The waters** of **the sea** refer to the salt waters of the Dead Sea. **En-gedi** and **En-eglaim** (10) refer to fishing points on the north and northwest shores of the Dead Sea (Berk., fn.). **The great sea** would be the Mediterranean. Verse 11 is translated, "But its swamps and marshes will not become fresh; they are to be left for salt" (RSV).

Other prophets also saw symbolical rivers. Joel had earlier said, "All the rivers of Judah shall flow with waters, and a fountain shall come forth of the house of the Lord, and shall water the valley of Shittim" (Joel 3:18). Shortly after Ezekiel's time, Zechariah, the prophet of peace who dreamed dreams during the days of the rebuilding of the Temple, says, "Living waters shall go out from Jerusalem; half of them toward the former sea, and half of them toward the hinder sea" (Zech. 14:8). Much later John the Revelator, evidently referring to Ezekiel's river, sees a "pure river of water of life" (Rev. 22:1). No doubt what Ezekiel sees, and what other prophets saw, is the increasing reign of God in the hearts of men, the increasing redemption which flows from Christ and refreshes all who will be refreshed.

The prophets did not always know the full meanings of the things they saw. But from our vantage point we can see that many of them were talking about Christ. In Acts we read, "To him give all the prophets witness, that through his name whosoever believeth in him shall receive remission of sins" (Acts 10: 43). He was "the Master light of all their seeing."[26] Kirkpatrick says, "It was the function of the prophecy to prepare for Him. It was the function of prophecy to bear witness to Him."[27] On this subject Andrew Blackwood says, "The prophets rose to their loftiest heights when they pointed men's weary eyes to the Redeemer."[28] And he adds, "The great reason, after all, why we should study the prophets is because they prepared the way for the coming of Christ."[29] Of God's prophets even the liberal A. C. Knudson can say, "These men were not merely preachers of repentance. They were heralds of the coming kingdom of God."[30] Most of the Jews missed the Messiah when He came, but their Talmud states, "All the prophets have only prophesied the days of the Messiah."[31]

It never dies, that dream. It never even fades. Malachi, last of the Old Testament prophets, the Hebrew Socrates who asks and answers questions, is as sure as are any of the others that "the Sun of righteousness [will] arise with healing in his wings" (Mal. 4:2). He is "the desire of all nations" in Hag. 2:7; "a light to lighten the Gentiles," and surely "the glory of . . . [all] Israel" (Luke 2:32). This is what the burning in the bones of the prophets (Jer. 20:9) was about supremely. This is in the main the cherished legacy that they left. Christ himself knew that Ezekiel and all the others had spoken of Him, for "beginning at Moses and all the prophets, he expounded unto them in all the scriptures the things concerning himself" (Luke 24:27).

"God's River of Redemption" is the subject of 47:1-12. This symbolical river is similar to other rivers of redemption in scripture (Joel 2:18; Zech. 14:18; Rev. 22:1). (1) It flows from the Temple—and now from the Church, 1-2. (2) It is ever-enlarging, 3-5, including more and more persons as the generations pass. (3) It is all-refreshing, including **every thing . . . whithersoever the rivers shall come;** and it has by-products—**all trees** on both

---

[26]Quoted without reference by Edwin Lewis, *The Drew Gateway* (Madison, N.J., University), spring issue, 1958.

[27]*The Doctrine of the Prophets* (N.Y.: Macmillan, 1907), p. 521.

[28]*The Prophets: Elijah to Christ* (Chicago: Fleming H. Revell, 1917), p. 35.

[29]*Ibid.*, p. 46.

[30]*The Beacon Lights of Prophecy*, p. vii.

[31]Sanhedrin XXXIV, col. 2.

its banks become refreshed, and the **fish** thrive within its waters, 9-12.

6. Lessons from the Temporal Arrangements (47:13—48:35)

Ezekiel was indeed a man of many visions (1:1-28; 3:1-3; 8:1; 11:25; 12:27; 37:1-14; 40:1-4; 47:1-12). And a vision might come upon him at almost any time. The vision about the ever-increasing stream of redemption seems to have caught him in the middle of his rather prosaic outline of the allotments of the land at the time of the restoration. Out he comes with that vision, and in it he takes us to one of the highest peaks of the Old Testament. Once the vision is recorded, however, he climbs down from the high pinnacles of ecstasy and engages himself again with the same ordinary matter.

We might have wanted him to cut off the prophecy while it was at a Mount Everest of glory. But life is not all visions. And just as it often does not cut off when a person is at the pinnacle of his powers, so the prophecy of Ezekiel comes down to what is quite ordinary as it is rounded off at its conclusion. What is in this closing passage is plain enough, not requiring particular exegetical explanations to make it clear.

Ezekiel in Babylon looked forward to restoration in the land of Israel and here set forth a possible relocation of the twelve tribes. In 47:13 he says, **Joseph shall have two portions.** This refers to the tribes named for the two sons of Joseph, Ephraim and Manasseh. In 14-20, Ezekiel recounts the general boundaries of the Promised Land. The border would be near **Damascus** (17) in the north. On the east, the line runs down through **Gilead** along **Jordan** and the east side of the Dead Sea (18). The south border turned westward through **Kadesh** (19) and thence **to the great sea** (the Mediterranean). The Mediterranean coast was the western boundary. Ezekiel saw that God's material blessings were not to be confined to Israel, and that they were not to be a selfish people—**the strangers that sojourn among you** shall also **have inheritance with you** (22-23).

In 48:1-7 and 23-27 the tribal allotments are given. The listing is from north to south. A comparison of this arrangement with that which prevailed in the time of the judges shows a general parallelism. Ezekiel sees **Dan** in the far north; also **Issachar, Zebulun,** and **Gad** are located in the far south.

Verses 8-22 expand upon Ezekiel's description in 45:1-8 of

the areas to be allocated to the Temple, priests, Levites, and the king.

In 30-35, Ezekiel saw a picture of the Holy City which is a foreglimpse of John's vision of the city that "lieth foursquare" (Rev. 21:9-16), with its three gates on each of its four sides.

Certain meanings ought not to be missed in these concluding passages. One is that, although God may be a long time in fulfilling His promises, they will be fulfilled in His own time if men will bend their ways to His ways. Also these promises will be fulfilled in such a way that nobody is neglected; God's concern for the stranger and the individual tribes will bear this out.

Another lesson to be learned is that, while God is a God of redemption in the eternal sense, He is also a God who cares about temporal matters. The Judeo-Christian faith is not a world-denying faith that looks at the common needs of men and laughs them off as unimportant. Biblical religion is down-to-earth. It affirms that the person who turns to God in this world, and serves God faithfully here, is the man who will make it with his Maker in the next.

Bibliography

I. COMMENTARIES

BEASLEY-MURRAY, G. R. "Ezekiel." *The New Bible Commentary.* Edited by FRANCIS DAVIDSON, *et al.* Grand Rapids: Wm. B. Eerdmans Publishing Co., 1956.

CALVIN, JOHN. "Ezekiel," *Calvin's Commentaries.* Edinburgh: T. Constable, 1846.

CLARKE, ADAM. *A Commentary and Critical Notes.* New York: Abingdon Press, n.d.

COOKE, G. A. "A Critical and Exegetical Commentary on the Book of Ezekiel," *The International Critical Commentary.* New York: Charles Scribner's Sons, 1937.

GARDINER, F. "Ezekiel," *Commentary on the Whole Bible.* Edited by J. EL-LICOTT, Vol. V. New York: Cassell and Co., n.d.

HARTFORD, JOHN B. *Studies in the Book of Ezekiel.* Cambridge: University Press, 1935.

KEIL, CARL FRIEDRICH. "Biblical Commentary on the Prophecies of Ezekiel," *Biblical Commentary on the Old Testament.* Edited by C. F. KEIL and F. DELITZSCH. Grand Rapids: Wm. B. Eerdmans Publishing Co., 1950.

MAY, HERBERT G. "The Book of Ezekiel" (Exegesis). *The Interpreter's Bible.* Edited by GEORGE A. BUTTRICK, *et al.,* Vol. VI. New York: Abingdon Press, 1951.

REDPATH, HENRY A. "The Book of the Prophet Ezekiel," *Westminster Commentaries.* Edited by WALTER LOCK. London: Methuen and Co., 1907.

ROEHRS, WALTER R. "Ezekiel," *The Biblical Expositor,* Vol. II. Edited by CARL F. H. HENRY. Philadelphia: Holman Co., 1960.

SHRODER, W. J. "Ezekiel," *Commentary on the Holy Scriptures.* Edited by JOHN PETER LANGE. Grand Rapids: Zondervan Publishing House, n.d.

SMITH, JAMES. *The Book of Ezekiel: A New Interpretation.* New York: Macmillan Co., 1931.

WARDLE, W. L. "Ezekiel," *The Abingdon Bible Commentary.* Edited by F. C. EISELEN, *et al.* New York: Abingdon-Cokesbury, 1929.

II. OTHER BOOKS

AALDERS, JAN GERRIT. *Gog and Magog in Ezekiel.* Amsterdam: J. H. Kok, N. V. Kampen, 1951.

BAAB, OTTO J. *The Theology of the Old Testament.* New York: Abingdon Press, 1949.

BLACKWOOD, ANDREW. *The Prophets: Elijah to Christ.* Chicago: Fleming H. Revell, 1917.

BROWNE, LAWRENCE E. *Ezekiel and Alexander.* London: S.P.C.K., 1952.

BURROWS, MILLAR. *The Literary Relations of Ezekiel.* Philadelphia: Jewish Publication Society Press, 1925.

CARNELL, E. J. *Christian Commitment.* New York: The Macmillan Company, 1957.

———. *The Kingdom of Love and the Pride of Life.* Grand Rapids: Wm. B. Eerdmans Publishing Co., 1960.

HOWIE, CARL GORDON. *The Date and Composition of Ezekiel.* Philadelphia: Society of Biblical Literature, Monograph Series, Vol. IV, 1950.

KIRKPATRICK, A. F. *The Doctrine of the Prophets.* New York: The Macmillan Co., 1907.

KNUDSON, A. C. *The Beacon Lights of Prophecy.* New York: Eaton and Mains, 1914.

———. *The Religious Teaching of the Old Testament.* New York: Abingdon Press, 1918.

PATERSON, JOHN. *The Goodly Fellowship of the Prophets.* New York: Charles Scribner's Sons, 1948.

RAHLFS, ALFRED, Editor. *Septuaginta,* 2 vols. New York: Societate Biblica Americana, 1949.

ROBINSON, H. WHEELER. *Two Hebrew Prophets.* London: Lutterworth Press, 1948.

THOMPSON, CHARLES, Translator. *The Septuagint Bible.* Edited by C. A. MUSES. Indian Hills, Colo.: The Falcon's Wing Press, 1960.

III. ARTICLES

DRIVER, S. R. "The Son of Man," *Hastings Dictionary of the Bible.* Edited by JAMES HASTINGS. N.Y.: Charles Scribner's Sons, 1923.

LAURIN, ROBERT B. "Sheol," *Baker's Dictionary of Theology.* Edited by E. F. HARRISON. Grand Rapids: Baker Book House, 1960.

The Book of

DANIEL

Roy E. Swim

Introduction

The Book of Daniel stands to the fore as "the Apocalypse of the Old Testament." The word *apocalypse* means an unveiling, a disclosure of things hidden, a revelation of divine mysteries.[1]

The Book of Daniel and the Book of Revelation have much in common, although in certain important respects they are different. The dramatic crises, the clash of forces on a cosmic scale, and the focus on the time of the end appear in both books. Many of the symbolic images of Daniel are reflected in Revelation. The horned beasts of Daniel, representing earthly powers, find their counterpart in the beasts of Revelation. In both books we see a vision of the Glorious One whose presence overwhelms the onlooker. In both we see thrones, and the throne where sits the Ancient of Days. Both depict the culmination of history, when the kingdoms of men yield to the triumphant and eternal kingdom of God.

Daniel and Revelation do not stand alone in the apocalyptic tradition. A number of other books both in the Old Testament and in the New Testament contain sections characterized as apocalyptic. Isaiah 24—27 has been called "The Isaiah Apocalypse." Zechariah contains distinctive apocalyptic elements such as the visions of mystic symbols of horses and chariots, of candlesticks and flying scroll. The prefiguring of the Messiah, both Priest and King, is suggested in the two "anointed ones," Joshua and Zerubbabel. And the climactic judgment of the nations depicted in Zechariah 14 is most clearly apocalyptic.

In the New Testament, each of the three Synoptic Gospels contains apocalyptic sections. These are found in Matt. 24:1—25:46; Mark 13:1-37; and Luke 21:5-36. The section in Mark has been called "The Little Apocalypse." A Pauline apocalypse is found in II Thess. 1:7—2:12. Each of these New Testament sections clearly reflects elements found in the Book of Daniel.

Apocalyptic literature is distinctive in a number of characteristics, all of which the Book of Daniel well illustrates. There is first of all the element of mystery contained in visions and unusual symbols. There is also the element of disclosure. Apocalypticism is related primarily to the future and to the ultimate

[1]Henry George Liddell and Robert Scott, *A Greek-English Lexicon.* Revised 1940 (London: Oxford University Press, 1951), p. 201.

consummation of God's plan. As distinctive from the function of prophecy, which proclaims God's more immediate word within history, apocalypse reaches beyond history. It pictures events of the end time in cataclysm and judgment. It reveals God's ultimate purposes fulfilled through a divine manifestation that breaks up the historic order. Most important, the Messianic element looms large in apocalypse.

The Book of Daniel became during the intertestamental period and for more than a century within the Christian era the model and stimulus for an amazing number of apocalyptic writings. None of these was ever admitted into the canon of scripture, for they lack the essential marks of inspiration that Daniel possesses. But they do reveal the longings and hopes of God's people in times of intense trial.[2]

A. Place in the Canon

Daniel's place in the canon of the Old Testament scriptures has never been seriously challenged. Among the Jews as well as among Christians through all the centuries this book has been highly regarded. It bears within itself the marks of divine inspiration and the superior qualities demanded of those writings acknowledged as scripture. It carries the message of God and clearly brings to bear the revelation of God upon life and upon history. It has the quality of timelessness as well as timeliness engrained within it.

In the Hebrew Bible, Daniel is placed, not among the Prophets (*Nebhiim*), but among the Writings (*Kethubhiim*). Some have complained that this was done to lessen the authority of Daniel because of the prominent witness which the book gives to the Messiah. But such a reason seems not quite plausible in view of the place of authority which the book received in the sacred canon. If there had been a serious intent to lessen Daniel's authority, it would have been kept out of the canon altogether. Pusey explains that Daniel himself indeed was not technically nor professionally a prophet, but a statesman. He did not hold the prophetic office. So he was not listed in the Hebrew scriptures among the prophets.[3] But Daniel did fulfill

[2]Among these apocalypses, often called *pseudepigrapha,* are I and II Enoch, Book of Noah, Testaments of the Twelve Patriarchs, Assumption of Moses, Apocalypse of Baruch, Apocalypse of Abraham, Apocalypse of Elijah, Testament of Job, Syballine Oracles, Apocalypse of Peter, Apocalypse of Paul, Revelation of Bartholomew, and many others.

[3]*Daniel the Prophet* (New York: Funk and Wagnalls, 1885), pp. 308-10.

the prophetic function. So his book is in the canon of Holy Scriptures and his message is recognized in the Scriptures themselves as prophecy. Young follows much the same line of reasoning respecting the placement of Daniel in the Hebrew scriptures.[4]

B. AUTHORSHIP

Through the centuries both among the Jews and among Christians, the book has been traditionally credited to Daniel as its author. The writing identifies itself in important sections as being directly from Daniel. The first person singular, "I Daniel," is used repeatedly. Chapter 7 begins with the statement, "Daniel had a dream and visions of his head upon his bed: then he wrote the dream, and told the sum of the matters" (Dan. 7:1).

But for the past century and a half authorship of the Book of Daniel has been a major battleground. It has become the habit to credit the book to an unknown writer living in the times of Antiochus Epiphanes, 175-169 B.C. Consistent with this view it is assumed that the Book of Daniel is an allegory written somewhat in code to undergird and inspire the Jews who were suffering under the tyrannies and persecutions of Antiochus. The stories of the book therefore were not to be taken literally but symbolically. The book would be placed in the category of pseudepigrapha (later writings presented in the names of great men of an earlier day), which had certain resemblances to it.

To those who view divine inspiration from the supernaturalistic standpoint there is no valid reason to deny the traditional Christian belief in the integrity of the Book of Daniel. To search for reasons why Daniel could not have written this book ascribed to his name would itself be unreasonable. To take the book at face value, after all the questions have been raised against it, is far more than credulity. It is faith. This faith would be still and listen to what God has to say to us in our day about the firm purpose which He has established within time and for the ages to come.

Daniel does not stand alone and undefended within the Bible itself. Without question the most striking and authoritative reference is to Dan. 9:27 in Jesus' own apocalyptic message: "When ye therefore shall see the abomination of desolation, spoken of by Daniel the prophet . . ." (Matt. 24:15; cf. also Mark 13:14). Jesus seems clearly here to give His endorsement both

[4]*The Prophecy of Daniel* (Grand Rapids: Wm. B. Eerdmans Publishing Co., 1949), *ad loc.*

to the validity of Daniel as a prophet and to the genuineness of his message.

Inferential references to Daniel's prophecy are also quite numerous in other teachings of Jesus, particularly in His use of the phrase "Son of man." In Matt. 24:30, we read: "They shall see the Son of man coming in the clouds of heaven with power and great glory." These words seem a clear echo of Dan. 7:13-14, "I saw in the night visions, and, behold, one like the Son of man came with the clouds of heaven . . . And there was given him dominion, and glory, and a kingdom" (cf. Matt. 16:27-28).

When Paul writes of "that man of sin . . . the son of perdition; who opposeth and exalteth himself above all that is called God, or that is worshipped" (II Thess. 2:3-4), he is clearly referring to Dan. 11:36, "He shall exalt himself, and magnify himself above every god, and shall speak marvellous things against the God of gods."

References from Daniel reflected in the Book of Revelation are sufficiently numerous to justify the inference that the authority of this New Testament book supports the integrity of its Old Testament counterpart.

It is of some interest to note that the Covenanters of the Qumran community, who produced the oldest existing biblical manuscripts now known, had a special interest in the Book of Daniel. From the fragments recovered from their caves it is evident that they possessed numbers · of copies of this book. Living as they did in the turbulent times following Antiochus and until the destruction of Jerusalem in 71 A.D., they had a deep interest in the apocalyptic hope.[5]

C. HISTORICAL SETTING

The Book of Daniel itself quite definitely describes the historical setting and times ir. which it originated. The siege or raid which made Daniel and his princely companions captives occurred in the third year of Jehoiakim. This was in the early days of the rise of the Neo-Babylonian empire. Nabopolassar had thrown off the yoke of Assyria and with his son, Nebuchadnezzar, was bringing into subjection all the lands of the Near East as well as Egypt. Judah was likewise falling under the power of Babylon. From 606 B.C., the year of Daniel's exile, to

---

[5]Harold H. Rowley, *Jewish Apocalyptic and the Dead Sea Scrolls* (London: Athlone Press, University of London, 1957), pp. 17, 23; Miller Burrows, *The Dead Sea Scrolls* (New Haven: American Schools of Oriental Research, 1950), pp. 28, 63.

536 b.c., the year of Babylon's fall to Cyrus the Persian, the Neo-Babylonian kingdom rose and declined. Most of this time was occupied with the reign of the mighty Nebuchadnezzar, 606 to 561 b.c. Within this period and extending into the early years of the Persian period, Daniel lived and served. It would seem probable that he attained an age past ninety.

The period covered by the time of Daniel's life and service coincided with an age of tremendous international upheaval. Assyria, which had raged for centuries across the lands of the Middle East, had been banished forever by the combined forces of her onetime subjects, the Babylonians, the Medes, and the Scythians. Egypt, which had for a thousand years sought to control not only Africa but the lands of the eastern Mediterranean, had been reduced to subjection. Babylon climbed meteorically into the ascendancy. Under the genius of Nebuchadnezzar, military leader, political organizer, and civic builder, the land of the Chaldeans came into a position of power, wealth, and world leadership beyond anything it had ever known.

But while ancient empires were vanishing and a new empire was writing its brilliant but brief history, Daniel's own people, the people of the promise, were passing through a dark night of trial. Exiled from their homeland of promise, servants in a pagan land, they hanged their harps on the willows and hoped for the dawning of the day.

Although the Book of Daniel contains an outlook that is worldwide in its implications and that reaches to the end of time, its chief focus is in the lands of the Middle East and of the Mediterranean. It leaves entirely out of account the kingdoms and civilizations that preceded Daniel's day. It has nothing to say about the civilizations and the rise and fall of dynasties of the Far East, of China or of India. Its center is the land where the drama of redemption was to be enacted with its goal-event, the coming of Messiah and the consummation of His kingdom.

D. Message of the Book

The Book of Daniel is an unveiling of a mystery. And while it unfolds the mystery, at the same time it enfolds it in wonder, leaving much of the mystery of revelation remaining.

Daniel was a man of extraordinary wisdom and insight. Living in the midst of sudden and world-shaking changes, he was able to keep his poise and sanity, viewing what was happening with a steady gaze. He was servant to kings. He was a valued counsellor to governments. But most important, he was an intimate with the God of heaven. He stood with his feet firmly planted on earth among mundane affairs. But his head was in a clearer atmosphere; he lived among the realities of eternal things.

Some truths become clear in Daniel's message revealing God's plan for earth and its inhabitants. *First*, earthly power and circumstance are exceedingly temporary. The mightiest tyrannies endure but for a little while. *Second*, God makes the wrath of man to praise Him, and the remainder of it He restrains. Both Nebuchadnezzar, the raging despot, and Cyrus, wise and genial sovereign, attest this truth. *Third*, God keeps His promise to His people; He will not forget. *Fourth*, God has His own time to do His work. He will be neither hurried nor delayed. *Fifth*, the kingdoms of this world are destined to give way to the kingdom of our Lord and of His Christ. *Sixth*, while God has an eternal and a cosmic view, He has a loving interest in the minute affairs of a single individual.

The Book of Daniel was a book for Daniel and for the struggling remnant of God's people in the days of long ago. This too is a book for the ages, designed to keep history in perspective. It is as truly a book for us and for our day. Certainly we are nearer the time of consummation of the kingdom of God than any people who have lived before us. Let us, in days of deepest darkness or of most crucial conflict, draw hope and courage from the message given to Daniel.

Outline

625

Section I The Story of Daniel's Exile

(A Hebrew Section)

Daniel 1:1-21

A. HISTORICAL PRELUDE, 1:1-2

A clearly focused historical setting introduces the Book of Daniel. Interestingly, this brief section is in Hebrew, while the part of the book following, 2:4—7:28, is in the Aramaic or Chaldean language. Then the concluding section of the book returns to the Hebrew. Interpreters have differed as to the reason for this unusual feature. The most plausible explanation seems to be that this section and the closing part of the book are marked by their language as pertaining especially to the people of God in exile. The Chaldean portion by its language is marked as pertaining to the pagan nations, of which Babylonia was first and most immediate. Both languages were current in Daniel's time and both were understood by the people of the Exile and of the centuries following. The use of these two related tongues helped to keep in graphic relation the historical setting of the book and its pertinence to the people for whom it was written.

The Book of Daniel records, **In the third year of the reign of Jehoiakim king of Judah came Nebuchadnezzar king of Babylon unto Jerusalem, and besieged it** (1; see Chart A). This would be less than three years after Necho had appointed Jehoiakim king, so quickly did political fortunes change.

While Nabopolassar was indeed the reigning monarch of the new kingdom of Babylon, his vigorous son Nebuchadnezzar was his recognized heir apparent and already co-regent with him. He had scarcely gathered his booty of treasure and hostages when an emergency call came from Babylon. His father had died and he must hasten back to take the throne.

Thus Daniel and his three companions with other royal and princely youth from the court of Judah found themselves in a strange land fifteen hundred miles from home. And with them had come sacred treasure from **the house of God** (2) in Jerusalem to adorn the Temple of Bel in Babylon. **Shinar** was the central plain of Babylonia.

B. YOUTH ON TRIAL, 1:3-16

1. *The King's Policy* (1:3-5)

Flushed with victory and his new power, the young king of the new Babylonian kingdom moved with cunning to consolidate his realm. How better could he strengthen his authority than to choose the most gifted princes of his newly won territories and train them for political leadership? We know nothing of the outcome for the other princes from Judah. All were selected for their native gifts and for their excellent appearance. They were given the best training that the Babylonian court could contrive. These were youths **of the king's seed, and of the princes (3) . . . in whom was no blemish, but well favoured, and skilful in all wisdom, and cunning in knowledge, and understanding science, and such as had ability in them to stand in the king's palace (4).**

The program of education included **the learning and the tongue of the Chaldeans,** a three-year course of intensive training. Their physical welfare was provided for by the best that the realm could supply, viands from the imperial table.

2. *Young Men of Character* (1:6-16)

Standing out among all the winners of the competitive examinations were the four heroes of the Book of Daniel. These, **of the children of Judah,** were reputed to be of the line of David. They were **Daniel, Hananiah, Mishael, and Azariah (6).**

These four youths from Judah carried with them in their names a testimony to the one true God. Whatever the limitations of their religious environment in Judah had been, their parents had given them names which spoke with clear witness. **Daniel** meant, "God is my judge"; **Hananiah** signified, "The Lord has been gracious"; **Mishael** proclaimed, "He is one who comes from God"; and **Azariah** declared, "The Lord is my Helper." The sequel of the story would seem clearly to indicate that, however others in Judah may have failed their children, the parents of these boys had given them a grounding in convictions and responsibility that went far deeper than their names. Their godly training had nurtured deep roots of character.

In deference to the king and to his pagan gods the prince of the eunuchs attached new names to the four youths. **Belteshazzar (7)** meant "the treasure (or secrets) of Bel." **Shadrach** signified "the inspiration of the sun." **Meshach** suggested "he who belongs to the goddess Sheshach." And **Abed-nego** meant "servant of Nego (the morning star)." How lightly these names rested on the youths who bore them the following narratives of the book reveal.

With unshakable conviction, holy daring, and delicate finesse of courtesy Daniel and his companions early revealed their extraordinary gifts of wisdom and character. Whether they should partake of the king's viands was much more than a question of expediency or of health. It related to the integrity of their vows of consecration as Hebrews to the God of Israel. The ceremonial significance of food, clean or unclean, meant everything to deeply committed descendants of Abraham. To partake of food dedicated to the pagan gods of Babylon would constitute a breach of faith with Jehovah. They must risk the peril of refusal. But they must make their refusal in a manner that was courteous to their superior and considerate of those charged with their keeping.

When **the prince of the eunuchs** (8, 10) declined the request, a sensible suggestion to the lieutenant, **Melzar** (11), in immediate charge of the boys, took the pressure off the superior officer and opened a way to a solution. The **ten days** (12) period of trial was fair and sufficient to provide adequate demonstration of the good hygienic sense of the request and to give God opportunity to vindicate His youthful servants. **Pulse** means, literally, "seeds," but included in general a vegetable fare.

C. Integrity Vindicated, 1:17-21

Whether the final examination on their studies came at the full end of three years or whether the time was shortened is not altogether clear. The outcome of the test was a complete vindication in the presence of the king of the course of self-discipline and diligent effort followed by the **four children** (17; youths). **The king communed** (19) is better "the king spoke with them" (RSV). How much the king knew of their religious commitment we are not informed. But Daniel and his companions knew full well that God had sustained them in all their decisions and endeavors. We can be sure that this undergirding fact of God's faithfulness served to confirm their convictions and courage to live by them. Their appointment to places of prominence and responsibility was an obvious recognition of their superior gifts and attainments. **Therefore stood they before the king** (19). **For magicians and astrologers** (20), see comments on 2:2.

The statement that **Daniel continued even unto the first year of king Cyrus** (21; 539 B.C) is clearly not intended to limit the span covered by his life, but rather to show its general extent. In 10:1 we are informed that Daniel was still living in the third year of Cyrus.

Section **II** The Chaldean Apocalypse

(A Message to the Nations in Aramaic)

Daniel 2:1—7:28

A. NEBUCHADNEZZAR'S DREAM, 2:1-49

1. *Haunting Dreams Beyond Recall* (2:1-3)

The first three verses of this section continue the narrative in Hebrew. Following the words, **Then spake the Chaldeans to the king in Syriack** (4), the Aramaic section begins and continues until the close of c. 7.

Most evangelical expositors identify this chapter and its counterpart, c. 7, as the key passages in the book. Here we see the God of heaven revealing to a pagan king the divine intent through the ages and stages of history until the consummation in the kingdom of God.

Nebuchadnezzar (1) was in the prime of his young manhood and had but recently fallen heir to the throne. The power that was accumulating under his hand was increasing at an astonishing rate. Furthermore, by an imaginative and daring program of building in the cities through his own land he was winning both the religious leaders and the civilian population to enthusiastic support of his leadership.

At this juncture in his career the king showed a remarkable quality of greatness. Instead of driving on in an increasing frenzy of achievement he brought himself to a halt in order that he might think about the meaning of his own life and of the power that had come to him. What would be his destiny? And what would be the outcome of the empire which he had helped so recently to found? As he pondered he dreamed and his dreams, though confused, served to stimulate even more profound thoughts and questions about destiny and ultimate meaning. **His spirit was troubled, and his sleep brake from him** (1). God was behind these questions and dreams.

So urgent did these questions become to Nebuchadnezzar that he took extreme measures to solve his problems. His own intellectual efforts were not sufficient to answer his questions. He called the experts and specialists in science, philosophy, and

630

religion into consultation. The special function of each of the four groups mentioned is not altogether clear. But it seems **the magicians** (2) were experts in the occult arts, **the astrologers** were supposed to have access to supernatural knowledge through the study of the heavens, **sorcerers** were manipulators of supernatural powers through incantations, and **the Chaldeans** were the leaders of a priestly caste in Babylonian society.

The question naturally arises, Why did not Nebuchadnezzar include Daniel and his friends in his summons at the first? It is quite probable that these newcomers had not yet won a recognized place among the professional wise men and advisors. Furthermore, these Hebrews, gifted though they were, had not been accepted into the priestly caste.

2. A Despot's Impossible Demands (2:4-13)

The king presented to his wise men the problem of his deep concern about the dream which had awakened him and started his thoughts flowing in a troubled stream. The priestly representatives, **the Chaldeans** (4), became spokesmen for the rest and requested a more exact statement of the problem. They asked for the specific details of the dream before they would undertake an interpretation. This demand nettled the king. He accused them of talking **till the time be changed** (9), i.e., simply stalling for time. If their profession of supernatural ability was genuine, they must guarantee their interpretation by telling him what the dream was. This of course pulled the cover off their hypocrisy, for they had no way of knowing what the dream was.

Because the king had made this a matter of life and death for all the wise men, they began desperately to maneuver for their survival. When they found that even the king could not help them, for he had forgotten the dream, they saw how hopeless their case was. Driven to the wall, they were driven to the truth. **It is a rare thing that the king requireth, and there is none other that can shew it before the king, except the gods, whose dwelling is not with flesh** (11).

Keil[1] insists that the king had not really forgotten the dream, but was determined to test the genuineness of the ability of these professed wise men. If they could accurately produce the details

[1] "The Book of the Prophet Daniel," *Biblical Commentary on the Old Testament,* C. F. Keil and F. Delitzsch, trans. by M. G. Easton (Edinburgh: T. and T. Clark, 1862), pp. 89-90.

of his dream, he would be sure that their interpretation would have validity. But if they could not even produce the dream, their profession of supernatural ability was a fraud and the dire punishment the king had threatened would be their just desert. But whether or not the dream had been forgotten, the plight of the wise men had become desperate.

The punishment decreed by Nebuchadnezzar was quite usual among the Babylonians (see 3:29). Dismemberment of captives of war had even been practiced by the Hebrews (I Sam. 15:33) as a manifestation of extreme judgment. Nebuchadnezzar added to this horror the confiscation of property and the desecration of the victims' homes by turning them into **a dunghill** (5), i.e., public latrines.

3. God Gives Daniel the Key (2:14-23)

Though Daniel and his companions had escaped the summons to the king, they did not escape involvement in the edict to **slay the wise men** (14). They too were marked for execution. When Daniel learned the nature of the edict and the reason for its severity, he went at once to the king. The fact that he had such access gives witness to the high standing he had earned in the examinations which he had so recently passed (1:19-20). In the presence of Nebuchadnezzar, Daniel daringly placed himself on record by promising that he would **shew the king the interpretation** (16), if given **time**. The king, so recently furious with the desperate manipulations of the wise men, was evidently impressed with the sincerity and firm confidence of Daniel.

Daniel's own action was consistent with the man of God he was. He called his three companions with him into a time of desperate intercessory prayer. The answer to that prayer was not long in coming. When Daniel himself beheld the dream in a night vision, he broke out in a hymn of exultant praise to God.

> *Blessed be the name of God for ever and ever,*
>   *to whom belong wisdom and might.*
> *He changes times and seasons;*
>   *he removes kings and sets up kings;*
> *he gives wisdom to the wise*
>   *and knowledge to those who have understanding;*
> *he reveals deep and mysterious things;*
>   *he knows what is in the darkness,*
>   *and the light dwells with him* (20-22, RSV)

4. *Daniel's Presentation to the King* (2:24-30)

Daniel's confidence in God and in the answer he had received was complete, **I will shew unto the king the interpretation** (24). The vision God had given him was identical with what the king had seen, for God had given both. So he need not even inquire of the king to test it.

Arioch's excitement in learning that Daniel was so soon ready was evident in his actions; he **brought in Daniel before the king in haste** (25). When the dubious king asked whether Daniel could fulfill his difficult demand, he faced a man who stood on firmer ground than the soil of Babylon. Daniel humbly declared that his source of knowledge was a revelation from the **God in heaven that revealeth secrets** (28). He disclaimed any particular wisdom of his own. Furthermore, this particular revelation was directed from God to the king himself, that he might know the thoughts of his own heart and **what shall be in the latter days.**

5. *Daniel's Interpretation* (2:31-45)

Thou, O King, sawest, and behold a great image. This great image, whose brightness was excellent, stood before thee; and the form thereof was terrible (31; "its appearance was frightening," RSV). This immense and dazzling sight had overwhelmed and confused the king. Although the image was one, it was a composite. It started with shining **gold** at the **head** (32) and rapidly deteriorated in quality through chest and **arms of silver, belly and . . . thighs of brass** or bronze, **legs of iron** (33), and **feet** a mixture **of iron** and brittle **clay.** Then out of a mountain **a stone** (34) was cut with no **hands** in evidence. When the stone **smote the image** at its base it crushed the whole structure and ground it to bits that were scattered like **chaff** (35) and **carried** off by the wind. **The stone** itself grew into a **great mountain.**

Daniel instantly identified the king with the image he had seen. **Thou, O King, art a king of kings: for the God of heaven hath given thee a kingdom, power, and strength, and glory** (37). Furthermore, and more specifically, **Thou art this head of gold** (38).

It is not difficult to imagine the amazement and the exultation which the king must have felt at this remarkable disclosure. Here in clear focus were the very details of the dream he could scarcely remember. And with it was a sure guarantee of the truth of its supernatural message to him. But as he listened he learned that he was but the first in a succession of empires. They all had one goal in history—dissolution under the triumph and dominance of the kingdom of the God of heaven, which shall never be destroyed. **It shall break in pieces all these kingdoms, and it shall stand for ever** (44).

Then Daniel clinched the purpose of the dream which, he reminded the king, had come from God. **The great God hath made known to the king what shall come to pass hereafter** (45). The king's most profound questionings were answered. The meaning of destiny for him and for all earthly rulers was that the hand of God is upon the course of history and the ultimate goal is not man's rule in increasing splendor but the rule of God over the ruins of man's folly.

Although interpreters have differed in identifying the five kingdoms of Nebuchadnezzar's dream, the mainstream of tradition and of evangelical interpretation has agreed almost unanimously. The first (38), is clearly stated; the **head of gold** is the Neo-Babylonian empire. The fifth (44) is just as clear; it is the kingdom of God. The second (39*a*) is quite generally conceded to be the Medo-Persian empire. The third (39*b*) and the fourth (40) have had a wider range of difference, especially among those who would make the fourth kingdom the Grecian rule or the rule of those who succeeded Alexander. These would focus the last messages of the Book of Daniel on the reign of Antiochus Epiphanes. But for the most part, since the days of Jerome, the third kingdom has been identified as that of Greece founded by Alexander, and the fourth as Rome. Verse 43 has been interpreted as reflecting either the weakness of mixed marriages or the rapid decline of society in the collapse of the fourth kingdom (Berk., fn.). Since the image of Nebuchadnezzar's dream and Daniel's vision of c. 7 are obviously parallel, the interpretation of the dream must be controlled by the content of the vision.

6. *Daniel's Exaltation* (2:46-49)

The response of Nebuchadnezzar to the remarkable revelation was total and overwhelming. Pagan that he was, he reacted in the only way he knew. He fell in worship before this manifestation of the supernatural embodied, as he thought, in Daniel. He ordered the pouring of **an oblation** (46) and the burning of incense. Then he gave praise to Daniel's God, **a God of gods, and a Lord of kings, and a revealer of secrets** (47). To show his gratitude in a practical way he poured out gifts on Daniel and advanced him to **chief of the governors over all the wise men of Babylon** (48). At Daniel's request, his three companions were given important political appointments. **But Daniel sat in the gate of the king** (49) means that he remained at the king's court.

B. NEBUCHADNEZZAR'S COLOSSUS, 3:1-30

1. *An Emperor's Self-deification* (3:1-7)

A vigorous defense of Nebuchadnezzar and his intention is made by J. A. Seiss. He argues that the daring concept of the great image was a direct result of the dream the king had seen. Had he not himself fallen in worship before the man who bore the message from the God of heaven?

> Now all his realm would bow before this wonderful idea revealed to him. In his mixed up pagan mind this was a wonderful tribute to the God of Daniel and his Hebrew friends. This would make their refusal all the more unreasonable and infuriating.
>
> Under the clear and full light of revelation and the divine institutes which Nebuchadnezzar did not have, it is very plain that he made a great mistake which can by no means be justified or excused on Biblical grounds. But the mistake was in the method and not in the motives. It was the mistake of defective education, not of intent. He meant it honestly, to acknowledge and glorify that very God of heaven who had so remarkably communicated with him. He intended that his empire, through all its assembled representatives, should thus acknowledge that God in a tangible copy of the image given in the dream. All the depths of his religious nature, experiences and convictions would thus rise up to insist upon the duty and propriety of compliance with what he had so devoutly and honestly arranged and commanded."[2]

But it is likely that this effort at a defense of Babylon's pagan king does not cover all the ground. It does not seem likely that Nebuchadnezzar would be erecting the image to one of the ancient gods of Babylon, since the land was filled with competing deities and their temples. It is, however, possible that his dream had had a profound effect upon him as to his own place in the world and in history. Was not he the head of gold? Did he not stand first and highest of all the earthly kings to be? It is not difficult to conceive of the growing vanity of this Oriental despot

[2]*Voices from Babylon* (Philadelphia: The Castle Press, 1879), pp. 96-105.

whose heathen mind failed to fathom the real meaning of the insights God had tried to share with him. This statue eighteen feet wide and standing ninety feet tall, towering over **the plain of Dura** (1) so as to be visible for miles, would proclaim to all the brilliance of the man who designed it and the glory of the king whom it symbolized. **The plain of Dura** was apparently near Babylon, but its exact location is otherwise unknown.

Whatever may have been Nebuchadnezzar's motive, the edict which summoned all the political leaders of the realm, great and small (3), left no doubt as to what the king required. Instantly, at the prearranged signal, the sound of the imperial orchestra (5), every man was to fall in worship before the image.

2. *Plot Against the Hebrews* (3:8-18)

It is hardly surprising that the three Hebrews, so recently advanced to political leadership, should have aroused some jealousy among the officials. That Daniel seems to have been ignored in the summons can be explained only by some absence on business, or the fact that some special assignment by the king engaged him. **Certain Chaldeans** (8), not the priestly caste but Babylonian citizens, saw to it that the three Hebrews did not escape. When they were reported to the king, he flew into a **rage** (13) and summoned them immediately. Without giving them a chance to defend themselves he presented them another chance to do obeisance at a special sounding of the music. A refusal would mean the immediate execution of the irreversible decree—they would be cast into the **burning fiery furnace; and who is that God that shall deliver you out of my hands?** (15) raged the king.

The poise and calm of the three servants of the most high God was in clear contrast to the unrestrained turbulence of the king. The daring of their faith was matched by their self-possession. **O Nebuchadnezzar, we are not careful** (cautious, or calculating results) **to answer thee in this matter. If it be so, our God whom we serve is able to deliver us from the burning fiery furnace, and he will deliver us out of thine hand, O king. But if not, be it known unto thee, O king, that we will not serve thy gods, nor worship the golden image which thou hast set up** (16-18).

⚫ True faith is not linked to circumstances nor to consequences. It is founded upon the immutable faithfulness of God. And faith is strong in relation to the element of faithfulness in the

believer. It might have seemed a small thing to rationalize ever
so little. Did they not owe the king some small courtesy of consideration? Could they not bow with their knees and stand up in
their hearts? A small concession to the king's limited understanding of divine things would be a small matter.

But no! The very reputation of the character of the true
and living God depended on this moment. Multitudes of heathen
from many lands were watching. Whether God chose to deliver
them from the flame or not, they must be faithful to the honor
of His name.

3. *Trial by Fire* (3:19-25)

The threatened punishment was put into almost immediate
execution. In the king's mounting fury "the expression of his
face was changed" (19, RSV), and the fires were stoked to a
sevenfold heat. A picked group of the king's mightiest soldiers
were ordered to bind (20) the three unresisting prisoners, dressed
as they were "in their mantles, their tunics, their hats, and their
other garments" (21, RSV), and cast them in. As Shadrach,
Meshach, and Abed-nego fell into the flames, their executioners
died before them, overcome by the intense heat.

Nebuchadnezzar was hardened to seeing men die, even by
the most horrible means. But what happened galvanized him
into amazed action. Springing to his feet, he called to his counsellors. **Did not we cast three men bound into the midst of the
fire? . . . Lo, I see four men loose, walking in the midst of the
fire, and they have no hurt; and the form of the fourth is like
the Son of God (24-25).**

Seiss,[3] following Keil and many others, renders the last
phrase of 25, "like to a son of the gods." Keil[4] explains:

> The fourth whom Nebuchadnezzar saw in the furnace was like
> in his appearance . . . to a son of the gods, i.e., to one of the race of
> the gods. In verse 28 the same personage is called an angel of God,
> Nebuchadnezzar there following the conception of the Jews, in con-
> sequence of the conversation which no doubt he had with the
> three who were saved. Here, on the other hand, he speaks in the
> spirit and meaning of the Babylonian doctrine of the gods. . . .
> Nebuchadnezzar approached to the door of the furnace and
> cried to the three men to come out addressing them as the servants

[3]*Ibid.*, p. 342.
[4]*Op. cit.*, pp. 131-32.

of the most high God. This address does not go beyond the circle of heathen ideas. He does not call the God of Shadrach, Meshach, and Abed-nego the only true God, but only the most high God, the chief of the gods.

Whether or not we limit the depth of Nebuchadnezzar's insight into the identity of **the fourth** who walked in the flames, it is clear that here was a manifestation of the supernatural, and the king was not too blind to see that. God was there in the furnace of affliction with His servants. And the presence of the God who created the very principle of light and heat was sufficient to control the effect of these natural forces upon the persons of these men who had dared to put their trust in Him.

4. *Nebuchadnezzar's Tribute to the True God* (3:26-30)

Nebuchadnezzar's summons to his three Hebrew servants as they stepped forth unharmed from the maw of the inferno contained a spontaneous tribute to the mighty God whom they trusted. And in that tribute he recognized that they served a higher Master than himself. **Ye servants of the most high God, come forth, and come hither** (26). The amazement of the king and of his assembled officialdom was instant and evident. How could it be that three defenseless men thrown to the flames could escape not only unharmed but without even the smell of smoke upon their clothing? But there before their eyes was the evidence! The supernatural was at work.

This was a vivid moment of revelation. The king cried out in praise to this living God whose mighty work he had just seen. **Blessed be the God of Shadrach, Meshach, and Abed-nego, who hath sent his angel, and delivered his servants that trusted in him** (28).

Nebuchadnezzar further uttered a remarkable testimony to the fidelity and courage of these three servants of God. They had trusted in God, regardless of consequences. They had dared to change **the king's word** as they **yielded their bodies, that they might not serve nor worship any god, except their own God** (28).

The Lord, our God, is most clearly made known as He reveals His glory through fleshly vessels of His humble servants. To the king this was **the God,** not of the cosmos nor of eternity, but **of Shadrach, Meshach, and Abed-nego** (29). And in their helplessness, in their trial by fire in the furnace of affliction, the power and glory of God were disclosed.

Furthermore, it was in the furnace that **the form of the**

fourth was revealed. Here half a millennium before the miracle of the Incarnation, God's eternally preexistent Son came and walked with those who were His own in the midst of the affliction. Here shone the glory of the Word which was to become flesh and dwell among us (John 1:14). Later that same glory shone brilliant and dazzling from the midst of the candlesticks (Rev. 1:13).

The king was deeply moved by this experience. Throughout his realm he ordered a reverent respect for this **God of Shadrach, Meshach, and Abed-nego.** The dire threat of dismemberment and destruction of property which accompanied the edict characterized the pagan cruelty of this king to whom religion by coercion and fear was a natural way of thinking. There is little evidence that King Nebuchadnezzar was converted, even though he was forced to admit that **there is no other God that can deliver after this sort** (29). The gods of Babylon were not renounced, but for the time the most high God was exalted as the greatest among them.

As a practical response of appreciation for the three faithful witnesses the king forthwith **promoted Shadrach, Meshach, and Abed-nego in the province of Babylon** (30). The Aramaic expresses it, "He made them to prosper."

C. NEBUCHADNEZZAR'S PERSONAL JUDGMENT, 4:1-37

1. *Ascription of Praise to the Most High God* (4:1-3)

The fourth chapter of Daniel has been described as the most remarkable state paper that has come down to us from ancient times. Bearing within it the inscription of **Nebuchadnezzar the king** (1), it spoke with imperial authority to **all people, nations, and languages** recognizing his authority. Without shame or apology this proclamation exalted **the high God** (2). Few world leaders of any age have excelled Nebuchadnezzar in giving glory to God or in rightfully setting forth His exalted character. This could well be called the "Emperor's Theodicy"—an exalted vindication of God's judgments and His justice.

> *How great are his signs,*
> *how mighty his wonders!*
> *His kingdom is an everlasting kingdom,*
> *and his dominion is from generation*
> *to generation* (3, RSV).

2. A Troubled Dream (4:4-18)

There is no clear indication as to what time in Nebuchadnezzar's reign this humbling and enlightening experience came to him. Keil suggests that it occurred "in the later period of his reign, after he had not only carried on wars for the founding and establishment of his world-kingdom, but also, for the most part at least, finished his splendid buildings."[5]

There was nothing in his environment but what would give the king deep satisfaction. He had swept the world in his conquests. He had been eminently successful as a designer and builder, both in Babylon and throughout his realm. Now at home in his palace he **was at rest . . . and flourishing** (4). But his peace and satisfaction were broken by a dream that deeply disturbed him. As he had done before on a similar occasion, he called in **all the wise men of Babylon** (6). But for all their vaunted wisdom **they did not make known** (7) the king's mystery. Whether Daniel had been contacted in the first summons is not altogether clear. Perhaps he had been purposely excluded by the king until the majority of the wise men had been given opportunity to prove what they could do. **But at the last Daniel came in before me** (8). Of him the king testified, **I know that the spirit of the holy gods is in thee** (9).

The king had seen in his dream **a tree** (10) growing ever taller and broader until it **reached unto heaven** (11) and seemed to cover **the earth.** The foliage was so verdant and the fruit so copious that it furnished food and shade **for all** (12), man, bird, and beast. Then a heavenly being called a **watcher . . . an holy one** (13) appeared and rent the silence with a mighty command, **Hew down the tree, and cut off his branches, shake off his leaves, and scatter his fruit** (14).

The heavenly messenger went on with specific details of the frightening dream that sounded ominously like a portent of judgment. And judgment it was, but judgment tempered with mercy. For Nebuchadnezzar was set on a collision course, and God would be faithful to him.

Keil[6] suggests it is possible that in the king's identification

[5]*Op. cit.*, p. 138.
[6]*Ibid.*, pp. 149-51.

of **the decree of the watchers** (17) there is a hint of the ancient Babylonian theology. In the hierarchy of deities there were thirty counselling gods serving the five great planetary gods. Fifteen of those were in charge of the upper world, and fifteen of the nether world. Each ten days a messenger from each council would visit the other world and bring some word. But whatever theological limitation Nebuchadnezzar may have had, he came clearly to know that a greater God, **the most High ruleth in the kingdom of men.**

3. Daniel's Interpretation (4:19-27)

When the pagan philosophers and scientists of the court had given up in confusion, Daniel was ushered in and greeted by the king with a deference that revealed his high opinion of this servant of God. **Thou art able; for the spirit of the holy gods is in thee** (18), spoke the king. But Daniel, when he had heard the dream, was overwhelmed with a great astonishment and stood speechless for an hour. Then, encouraged by the king, he gave the reason for his dismay. **My Lord, the dream be to them that hate thee, and the interpretation thereof to thine enemies** (19).

The towering tree was indeed the king himself. Its amazing growth and strength were an accurate picture of his great power. **Thy greatness is grown, and reacheth unto heaven, and thy dominion to the end of the earth** (22). But the tragic sequel was that this greatness was decreed soon to end. The king, renowned throughout the earth for his genius, would lose his reason and turn to grovel on the ground like a beast. Indeed he who was honored as the greatest of living human beings would forfeit his humanity and consider himself to be an ox feeding on grass. **Till seven times pass over him** (23) indicated seven years of insanity for the king.

But in the midst of this shocking foretoken of doom, that to the king must have seemed more terrible than death, came assurances of God's infinite faithfulness and mercy. Though the tree was cut down, **the stump** (23) was left to revive and grow again. Furthermore it was encircled with a **band of iron and brass,** a symbol of the firmness of God's promise of survival and restoration. At the end of his interpretation, Daniel stood before the king and pled that he would repent of his **sins** of injustice and oppression, that God might prolong his **tranquillity** (27).

4. Fulfillment and Dethronement (4:28-33)

Nebuchadnezzar's failure to heed the warnings and turn to God in genuine repentance is a graphic reflection on human weakness and wickedness. **Twelve months (29)** went by and the terrifying vision faded. Perhaps it would not happen after all.

One day in a high mood of self-gratification the king began to exult in the glory of his achievements. As he walked "on the roof of his royal palace" (RSV), beneath his feet was the most splendid edifice Babylon had ever seen, adorned in gold and brilliant colors of glazed tile. Nearby were the artificial mountain and the magic hanging gardens built for his queen from the mountains of Media. There was **this great Babylon (30)**. From a small town on one side of the Euphrates he had doubled its area to both sides of the river. He had filled it with new buildings and temples of a distinctive architecture. He had surrounded it with walls renowned for their height and thickness. Chariot teams could race abreast upon their top. One hundred and thirty miles of these walls encompassed the city. One hundred gateways, with brass gates, controlled access to the city. And outside was a reservoir 138 miles in circumference, conserving and controlling the waters of the Euphrates. Canals for navigation and irrigation laced the area. Dikes lined the Euphrates to the sea, and breakwaters made the Persian Gulf safe for shipping.

With such a vision filling his mind we can well conceive the king's elation. He who already had everything took glory to himself: **Is not this great Babylon, that I have built . . . for the honour of my majesty? (30)** Inflated to the bursting point with his self-esteem, he collapsed into the abyss of spiritual and mental darkness.

Nebuchadnezzar's interlude of insanity here reported is not known otherwise, as we can well understand. Any reference to it in the Babylonian sources would be carefully obliterated after the king regained his sanity and his position. The monarch's extreme pride was punished by striking and humiliating judgment. The particular form of Nebuchadnezzar's delusion is known as lycanthropy.

5. Restoration (4:34-37)

The king's recital of his recovery and his ascription of praise to God, **the most High,** properly climax this chapter. As God had promised, his kingdom had been preserved to him. His cabinet of counsellors, among whom Daniel could very well have been one, administered the kingdom throughout the "seven times" (32) of the king's incapacity. If this was seven years, as most commentators interpret it, it shows something of the esteem in which the king's subjects held him, as well as God's faithful providence which so inclined their hearts.

We may well ask, Why did God permit the restoration? Even more, why did God guarantee it, to such an ego-centered autocrat as Nebuchadnezzar? Was it not that God might through this man reveal His glory?

God had designed this experience as a special discipline of learning to Nebuchadnezzar. Its special purpose was, in Daniel's words, "till thou know that the most High ruleth in the kingdom of men, and giveth it to whomsoever he will" (25). And we note that his recovery came when **I Nebuchadnezzar lifted up mine eyes unto heaven** (34).

The king had learned his lesson well. Whatever he had known of God before, much or little, he now broke forth in praise that was profound in the depth and breadth of its meaning. The nature of the Most High God stands out in clear relief against the paganism and superstitution of that day. Here we see disclosed: (1) *God's eternity*—**Him that liveth forever** (34); (2) *His sovereignty*—**Whose dominion is an everlasting dominion, and his kingdom is from generation to generation;** (3) *His omnipresence*—**He doeth according to his will in the army of heaven, and among the inhabitants of the earth** (35); (4) *His omnipotence*—**None can stay his hand, or say unto him, What doest thou?** (5) *His justice*—**"All his works are right and his ways are just"** (37, RSV).

D. FALL OF THE CHALDEAN EMPIRE, 5:1-31

The first half of the Book of Daniel is the record of a series of crucial encounters between the vaunted pride and power of puny men and the great and good God, who in the ultimate sense governs the affairs of men whether or not they acknowledge it. The incident of this fifth chapter comes as a climax to the story of the meteoric journey through history of the Neo-Babylonian kingdom.

At the death of Nebuchadnezzar, his son, Evil-merodach,

succeeded to the throne. This is the king who gave special honor to King Jehoiachin after his thirty-seven years of exile by releasing him from prison and assigning him a pension (Jer. 52: 31-34; II Kings 25:27-30).

After two years Evil-merodach's brother-in-law, Neriglissar, led a revolt and assassinated him. Neriglissar had married a daughter of Nebuchadnezzar and claimed some royal right, especially through his young son, Labashi Marduk. But the lad won no support and soon was dispatched by his trusted friends. The generals and political leaders selected Nabonidus, another son-in-law of Nebuchadnezzar, and a tried and trusted aid throughout much of his reign. Nitocris, daughter of Nebuchadnezzar, bore Nabonidus a son, Belshazzar. Because of his royal blood, Belshazzar, three years after Nabonidus' accession to the throne, was made co-regent with his father. He was given the special assignment to govern the city and province of Babylon. This was the Belshazzar of Daniel, as the cuneiform tablets have disclosed after decades of confusion even by conservative scholars as to the historical identity of this king.[7]

1. *Belshazzar's Profane Orgy* (5:1-4)

For all his royal heritage from the great Nebuchadnezzar, his grandfather, Belshazzar became renowned for his profligacy and cruelty. Xenophon is credited with the story of a hunting incident in which one of Belshazzar's nobles outshot the king and brought down the game. Thereupon Belshazzar slew the noble on the spot. Later at a feast one of the guests was complimented by one of the women. The king ordered the guest mutilated to eliminate any further occasion for such compliments.[8] Brought up in luxury, with power and adulation thrust early upon him, he could scarcely escape growing up to be an insensate egotist and a heartless autocrat.

But now fourteen years as second in command in the kingdom, Belshazzar was faced with serious responsibility. Nabonidus, his father, was in the field with the Chaldean army trying to fend off the blows of the combined forces of the Medes and Persians. One after another of the lands about Babylon had

[7] R. P. Dougherty, *Nabonidus and Belshazzar* (New Haven: Yale University Press, 1929), pp. 42-47, 59-66, 134, 192-200.

[8] Seiss, *op. cit.*, p. 141.

fallen. Now the armies of Cyrus surrounded the capital itself as their final prize.

But was not this great Babylon impregnable? Its walls could withstand any assault. Its wealth of provisions and its inexhaustible water supply could outlast any siege. To demonstrate his reckless disdain of the Persian threat, Belshazzar proclaimed a festival for the whole city. By special invitation to **a thousand of his lords** (1) he called a feast in the royal palace. He invited the women of the royal harem to add gaiety to the party. Then the king himself led the festivities by demonstrating his prowess with drink. At length, "inflamed by the taste of wine" (2, Berk.), Belshazzar followed a reckless impulse. He ordered brought in the sacred **vessels** which his grandfather had carried to Babylon from **Jerusalem** (3) fifty years before. They would drink from these as none had ever before dared to drink and praise all **the gods** (4) of Babylon. So noisy did the din become that Xenophon reported Cyrus' general, Gobryas, to have declared, "I should not be surprised if the doors of the palace are now open, for the whole city seems tonight to be given up to revelry."[9]

2. *The Apparition of Doom* (5: 5-9)

Suddenly without warning the revelries were frozen into stunned silence. Against the plastered wall appeared **a man's hand** (5) slowly writing a message. But not a word could the king make out, nor any of his courtiers. "Then the king's color changed, and his thoughts alarmed him; his limbs gave way, and his knees knocked together" (6, RSV). When Belshazzar found his voice, he began to shout loudly for the experts in wisdom, **the astrologers, the Chaldeans, and the soothsayers** (7), to come and explain this mystery. The king promised every inducement of reward and advancement to anyone who could read the writing and show the interpretation of its message. He would be **clothed** in **scarlet** (royal purple), be decked about the neck with a golden **chain,** and promoted to the third place in kingdom rulership. This was the highest spot available, for Nabonidus held first place and Belshazzar second.

When the wise men could find no answer at all, the king and all the company were smitten with fresh consternation. The

[9]*Ibid.,* pp. 141 ff.

Aramaic term used here, *mishettabbeshiyn,* implies much more than astonishment; rather there was "confusion and great commotion in the assembly."[10]

3. *Daniel Called* (5:10-12)

As men cried out and women screamed, **the queen** (10; queen mother, Nitocris), who had absented herself from the feast, came in from her quarters in the palace to the assembly hall. Taking command of the hysterical situation with poise and dignity, she gently chided the king, her son, and instructed him what intelligent action to take. She reminded him of **a man . . . in whom is the spirit of the holy gods** (11). This man had proved his remarkable ability again and again to unlock supernatural secrets in the days of his grandfather Nebuchadnezzar. This was none other than **Daniel . . . named Belteshazzar** (12), onetime chief of the wise men of Babylon.

4. *Daniel's Interpretation* (5:13-29)

Then was Daniel brought in before the king (13). Long neglected and all but forgotten, now God's man was the man of the hour. Offered the same extravagant reward that the king had previously promised (16), Daniel brushed aside the baubles (17) and went straight to the crisis facing the drunken king and his city. Daniel courteously but forthrightly faced him with a message from God. The lessons that Belshazzar should have learned from history, especially from the life of his grandfather and God's dealings with him, were recalled. Nebuchadnezzar's pride and his tragic humiliation were pointed out (18-22). Then came a thrust to Belshazzar's own conscience: **And thou his son, O Belshazzar, hast not humbled thine heart, though thou knewest all this; but hast lifted up thyself against the Lord of heaven** (22-23).

The writing on the wall was finished. Four cryptic words glowed on the plaster. They were in Chaldean, plainly written, but what did they mean? **Mene, Mene, Tekel, Upharsin** (25). Daniel explained each word with a twofold meaning. **Mene, Mene** meant "numbered, numbered"; **God hath numbered thy kingdom, and finished it** (26); **Tekel**—"weighed"; **thou art weighed in the balances, and art found wanting** (27). *Pharsin*—"broken fragments" (the *U* means "and"). Using the singular participial

[10]Keil, *op. cit.,* p. 185.

form, **Peres**—fragmented, Daniel prounonced the final doom, **Thy kingdom is divided,** or broken to pieces, **and given to the Medes and Persians (28).**

5. *Collapse of the Empire* (5:30-31)

Scarcely had the honored decorations been placed on Daniel when the shouting soldiers of Gobryas and Cyrus broke into the palace. Tradition has had it that the engineers of Cyrus diverted the river and walked inside the defenses along the dry channel. But more solid evidence seems to indicte that insurrectionists within the city had opened the gates and invited the Persian armies inside. The city fell with little loss of life beyond that of Belshazzar. When King Nabonidus' army had been soundly beaten, Cyrus assigned him a permanent residence in Carmania, a not far distant province, where he lived out his days.

But for Belshazzar, Nabonidus' son, how pathetically futile was the father's prayer recorded on a large cuneiform cylinder found in the Ziggurat at Ur! Addressed to Sin, the Moon-God, it reads: "As for me Nabonidus, the king of Babylon, the venerator of thy great divinity, may I be satisfied with the fulness of life, and as for Belshazzar, the first son of my loins, lengthen his day; let him not turn to sinning."[11]

In c. 5 against the background judgment of v. 27 we see the theme "When God Pronounces Doom." (1) When men will not learn from the experience of others, 17-22; (2) When men ignore and defy God, 22-23; (3) When men live in sensuality, 1-3; (4) When men worship other gods, 23. Cf. also Seiss.[12]

E. THE REIGN OF DARIUS, THE MEDE, 6:1-28

The final verse of c. 5 with the first verse of c. 6 introduces us to a new government. Though Cyrus was the conqueror, Darius the Mede is introduced as the ruling monarch in Babylon. It seems to have been the policy of Cyrus to leave the administration of government in the hands of others while he pressed on to new conquests.

For many years one of the crucial problems of the Book of Daniel has been the identity of Darius the Mede, the son of Ahasuerus (5:31; 9:1). Secular history throws no light on the prob-

[11]R. P. Dougherty, *op. cit.,* p. 94.
[12]*Op. cit.,* pp. 139 ff.

lem. The same could have been said of Belshazzar until the cuneiform inscriptions began to disclose their secrets. Josephus thought that Darius was the son of Astyages, known to the Greeks by another name.[13] This would mean that he was grandson to Cyaxeres, the great Median ally of Nebuchadnezzar.

Some have sought to identify Darius with Gobryas, the general of Cyrus' army which took Babylon. He is credited with governing for a brief time. But his death within two months after the capture of Babylon would scarcely support this theory.

John C. Whitcomb in his book, *Darius the Mede,* suggests strong reasons for identifying the Median Darius with a Gubaru whose name was discovered in the cuneiform records. This Gubaru is called "Governor of Babylon and the District Beyond the River." Under the authority of Cyrus, Gubaru appointed governors to rule with him in the absence of Cyrus, who resided for extended periods in his capital at Ecbatana. Gubaru was given practically unlimited power over the huge satrapy of Babylonia. Even into the reign of Cambyses, Cyrus' son, Gubaru continued his authority.[14]

1. *Daniel's Political Advancement* (6:1-3)

In the reorganization of the government, Darius followed the liberal policy of Cyrus and moved immediately to distribute responsibility of administration. The appointment of 120 **princes (1)**, over whom **three presidents (2)** were placed, may have been a more or less temporary arrangement to assure the orderly levying of taxes and maintaining a system of collection and accounting. The brief explanation in 2 seems to indicate this: **that the princes might give accounts unto them, and the king should have no damage.**

Of the three presidents, **Daniel was first.** And Darius found in him such **an excellent spirit (3)** that he moved to extend his authority over the whole realm.

Daniel was now in his middle or late eighties. He had been through the testings of one political crisis after another. Now his reputation for integrity and honesty had carried through to the new rulers. Perhaps informants had advised the new rulers of Daniel's stand on the fateful night of Belshazzar's fall. What-

[13]*Antiquities of the Jews,* Book X. 11. 4.

[14]*Darius the Mede* (Grand Rapids: Wm. B. Eerdmans Publishing Co., 1959), pp. 66 ff.

ever the circumstances, God's man was ready to serve where he was needed.

2. Plot of the Princes (6:4-9)

A man of fidelity and honesty is disconcerting to disreputable schemers. To see Daniel about to receive a further promotion beyond them was more than the **presidents and princes (4)** could endure. They must destroy Daniel at any cost. Their failure to find flaws in Daniel's administration of his office made them know they must attack him on his strongest point—his religion and **the law of his God (5)**.

The king was gullible for the suggestion. It was fairly common for a Median or Persian ruler to stand in the place of one of their gods and call for the worship of the people. Darius was flattered with being the center of religious devotion for a month, so **signed the writing and the decree (9)**.

3. Daniel's Courageous Devotion (6:10-24)

Daniel's response was unequivocal. To alter his habits of devotion or to become secretive about his relation to his God would be base denial. **He kneeled upon his knees three times a day, and prayed, and gave thanks before his God, as he did aforetime (10)**. This was a law that had no right to be on the statute books. To make a matter of deep conscience an illegality is high treason against the God of heaven. The issue of the authority of the state and the right of individual conscience has become crucial again and again in our enlightened century. And like Daniel, men have been betrayed for a conscientious stand. The plotting princes reported to Darius, "That fellow, Daniel, one of the Jewish captives, is paying no attention to you or your law. He is asking favors of his God three times a day" (13; LP).

The king was dismayed when he was faced with the implications of his action. He **set his heart on Daniel to deliver him (14)** out of the legal trap in which together they had been caught by this nefarious plot. The schemers pressed their advantage heartlessly and shamelessly (15). They drove the king to do what he revolted from doing, to **cast Daniel into the den of lions (16)**.

The den was **sealed** with the royal **signet (17)**, so that there was no chance for escape. The king returned to the palace, but not to eat or to sleep. Darius **passed the night fasting (18)** and no doubt in praying to what gods he knew. The dawn had scarcely come when the king hurried to the den. The RSV renders it, "When he came near to the den where Daniel was, he cried out in a tone of anguish and said to Daniel, 'O Daniel, servant of the living God, has your God, whom you serve continually, been able to deliver you from the lions?'" (20)

With a forlorn hope the evening before he had said to Daniel, "May your God, whom you worship so faithfully, deliver you" (16, Berk.)

Daniel's reply from the depths of the cave was the most wonderful sound the king could hope to hear. **O king, live for ever. My God hath sent his angel, and hath shut the lions' mouths** (21-22).

The king's joy reveals the esteem in which he held Daniel. And his sense of outraged justice is seen in his effort to right the wrong he had done by the immediate reversal of the edict and the peremptory punishment of the evil schemers.

4. The Decree of Darius (6:25-28)

While the immediate reaction of Darius was to correct the injustice that had been done to Daniel and to punish the real offenders, he went much further than this. He recognized that the real wrong had been done against Daniel's God. In truth, the edict which had put Daniel in the lions' den had for a time outlawed **the living God** (26) in the realm of the Medes and Persians. That edict must be counteracted by one as sweeping in its outreach and as specific in its implications. So where the first edict had forbidden prayer to any but to the king, the second commanded reverence for Daniel's God throughout the realm. Whether true worship can ever be insured by royal edict, it most surely can be encouraged. The king's command and ascription of praise set forth the glory of God in terms almost as comprehensive and clear as those proclaimed by the great Nebuchadnezzar, the Chaldean. **The God of Daniel . . . he is the living God, and stedfast for ever, and his kingdom that which shall not be destroyed, and his dominion shall be even unto the end. He delivereth and rescueth, and he worketh signs and wonders in heaven and in earth** (26-27).

Darius' recognition of the supernatural character of Daniel's deliverance is disclosed in the two Aramaic terms used in 27 to describe God's work—*'athiyn* and *thiymhiyn*, **signs and wonders.** The singular noun *'ath* implies "a signal or beacon" and so "a portent, a miracle or sign." The second word, *temah,* implies "amazement, astonishment, marvel," and so also, "miracle, wonder." That hungry beasts should be held in such control as to leave God's man unharmed is indeed a miracle, especially so since when in a short time those same animals, released from the power that restrained them, broke in pieces the bones of those who had defied God. Such a miracle is utterly unacceptable to those who insist on a natural explanation for every event. But to those who accept the revelation of a God who has disclosed himself to be free to act within His own created universe, this miracle is no more impossible than any other act of God by which He has chosen to fulfill His purposes. Both the Old Testament and the New Testament are filled with such incidents. By this means is unfolded the kind of God we serve, **the living God . . . stedfast for ever** (26).

In c. 6 we see "Courage and Its Consequences." (1) Courage to be faithful, 1-10; (2) Courage tested, 11-17; (3) Courage vindicated, 18-23; (4) God's kingdom advanced, 25-27 (A. F. Harper).

Verse 28 relates the reigns of **Darius** the Mede and **Cyrus the Persian** to Daniel, who served under both. History makes clear that these monarchs were co-regents, Darius the Median serving at Babylon under Cyrus, who had consolidated the kingdoms of the Medes and Persians and was their recognized head. It seems that Darius could not have reigned more than two years at the most. Other dated references mention only the first year of Darius (9:1; 11:1).

F. Empires Rise and Wane Until the Consummation, 7:1-28

Daniel 7 concludes the Aramaic section of the book (see comments on 1:1-2) and closes the messages relating to the heathen world-powers. In a sense this chapter forms a bridge between the Gentile section and the Jewish section following. The first, couched in the language of the lands into which Israel and Judah had been exiled, brought God's word to the emperors and empires of the Gentiles. The second, in the language of promise to the people of the promise, brought God's sure word to the remnant of Israel. The perspective of the first is the Gentile world order. The perspective of the last brings God's kingdom into the foreground, albeit in conflict with the world forces. Thus this seventh chapter converges both perspectives, **the earthly and the heavenly. Together with c. 2 it has been characterized as the heart of the message of Daniel.**

1. The Four Beasts (7:1-8)

a. *The beasts and Nebuchadnezzar's image* (7:1-3). **The first year of Belshazzar** (1) would be fourteen years prior to the fall of the Neo-Babylonian kingdom. Daniel's **dream** of the shape of things to come swept the vistas of time from where the prophet stood, more than five centuries before Christ's birth, down through our times, to the end of the ages. From his vantage point, surrounded by the quiet darkness of the **night** (2), there emerged a picture of sound and fury—raging **winds of the heaven** wrestling together over **the great sea,** roaring **beasts** (3) ascending from the waters, stalking across the earth, each in turn pursued by another.

The winds of heaven striving upon the sea is a graphic picture of the two dimensions of reality in history. There is the earthly existence of peoples and nations represented by the tumultuous sea and the solid earth. There is the heavenly, supernatural order. Both realms are involved in the course of human affairs, and between them and within them there is a dynamic conflict of forces.

There is a striking parallel between Daniel's vision depicted here and Nebuchadnezzar's vision of the great image. Indeed they quite clearly depict the same historical realities, though from different viewpoints. Chapter 2 pictures history as God permitted a pagan monarch to glimpse it. The image had in it elements of Nebuchadnezzar's own situation. In Daniel's vision here we share the view of a man of God who catches a glimpse of God's outlook.

Nebuchadnezzar saw the world order towering in magnificent grandeur, a gleaming golden colossus, but Daniel saw the same substance as frightful and ravening beasts.

Stevens notes the pertinence of the symbol of beastliness as applied to the tyrants of history. "We must bow in respect to this expression of the divine estimate of the character of the world's imperial rule. What are the attributes of beasts? To keep their own at any cost within their might; to quarrel over what they do not have, but what they want; to fly easily into blood-thirsty rage at any affront . . . under passion to take utmost satisfaction in the blood, the agonies, the loss, the death of the objects of their rage. . . . God foresaw this spirit prevalent in the world empires down to the end. Indeed it is the very spirit of world-empire. And militarism is its indispensable implement."[15] Truly "the Lord seeth not as man seeth" (I Sam. 16:7).

b. *The winged lion* (7:4). The identification of the first three beasts seems quite clearly to parallel the interpretation by Daniel of the image of c. 2. The **lion** with **eagle's wings . . . lifted up . . . and made** to **stand** on its feet as a **man** and receiving a **man's heart** suggests Nebuchadnezzar as the great personification of the Babylonian empire. His degradation is suggested in the denuded wings, and his restoration in the gift of **a man's heart** and a man's erect stance. The king of beasts for strength and ferocity and the king of birds for grace, swiftness, and rapacity combined to picture the regal power and grandeur of this king and his kingdom.

c. *The lumbering bear* (7:5). The **second** beast, **like to a bear,** "having its paw raised, ready to strike" (Berk.), came next to the lion in ferocity. The **three ribs** in its **mouth** and the command, **Arise, devour much flesh,** depict its predatory character. The kingdoms of Babylonia, Lydia, and Egypt are suggested by the ribs held in the bear's teeth.[16]

Pusey graphically describes the lumbering stolidity of the bearish Persian empire—massive and ponderous in its military strategy, wasteful of human life and resources. Xerxes' expedition against Greece, which met its initial defeat at the Battle of Marathon, more nearly resembled the migration of vast hordes than the movement of an army. It was estimated to have consisted of more than two and a half million fighting men.[17]

d. *The fleet-winged leopard* (7:6). The **leopard** with **four wings of a fowl** is an apt symbol of the Greek, Alexander, whose amazing speed and striking power quickly laid Persia and the world at his feet. The fourfold division of his realm soon after his death is suggested in the **four heads.**

e. *The indescribable monster* (7:7-8). The fourth beast becomes the special subject of the angel's interpretation in 15-28. This dreadful, but nondescript creature strongly recalls the heter-

[15]*The Book of Daniel* (Los Angeles: Bible House of Los Angeles, 1943), pp. 97-98.
[16]Keil supports this view and cites Hofmann, Ebrard, and Kliefoth in agreement; *op. cit.,* p. 226.
[17]E. B. Pusey, *op. cit.,* pp. 123-25.

653

ogeneous character of the lower part of Nebuchadnezzar's image with legs of iron and feet and toes a mixture of iron and miry clay (2:40-43).

(1) *Power, pillage, and terror* (7). The distinctive character of the fourth beast is the terror it is calculated to arouse in the beholder; it was **dreadful and terrible, and strong exceedingly; and it had great iron teeth.** "It devoured and tore its victims in pieces, and stamped the remaining portions of it with its feet" (Berk.). Its marked difference from the other beasts before it is especially noted.

(2) *Ten horns* (7). Growing out of the head of this beast were **ten horns.** Symbols of military might these horns represent ten kings or kingdoms (cf. 24). Springing from the one head they presented a unity in diversity, as parts of the one beast. They also belonged to the same period in history in contrast to the successive appearance of the beasts.

(3) *The frightful little horn* (8). Springing out of the same head and displacing **three of the first horns** was a **little horn.** More devastating than any of its predecessors, this horn becomes a chief subject of the remainder of the chapter. A human being, gifted with extraordinary intelligence and sagacity, with towering pride, is suggested by **the eyes of a man, and a mouth speaking great things.**

2. *The Ancient of Days Sits in Judgment* (7:9-14)

a. *The thrones of judgment* (7:9-10). As the fury of the fourth beast reached a climax, Daniel saw thrones being placed,[18] and the Ancient of Days takes His seat of judgment. Clothed in ineffable light, surrounded with multiplied millions who serve Him, the Judge summons to **judgment . . . and the books were opened.** This picture is clearly reflected in Rev. 20:4.

b. *The judgment of the beast and of the beasts* (7:11-12). The fourth beast meets his end in the judgment of God. **The beast was slain, and his body destroyed, and given to the burning flame.** With him went the little **horn. The rest of the beasts** were granted some surcease, though their authority was taken from them and brought under the divine dominion.

---

[18]RSV and Berk. translate "thrones were placed" rather than **thrones were cast down.**

c. A new king and a new kingdom (7:13-14). There follows a beatific vision of **one like the Son of man** (13), who comes with the **clouds of heaven** and receives **an everlasting . . . kingdom** (14) of which **all people, nations, and languages** become subjects. Jesus' own choice of the title "Son of man" inevitably identifies the new King. And Jesus' proclamation of the Kingdom identifies the new dominion.

The relation of this vision to that of 2:44 is evident. There the stone cut from the mountain displaces the kingdoms (cf. Matt. 24:30 and Rev. 1:7).

3. The Angel's Interpretation (7:15-28).

a. Explanation of the beasts (7:15-18). Little wonder that Daniel was overwhelmed and **troubled** (15) at the vision he had just seen. Wise as he was in the ways of God, he had insight enough to comprehend something of the significance of the panorama that had swept before him. But the breadth of it, and the dark implications for earth's peoples, and for his own people, were more than Daniel could calmly take in.

God is good to provide His children help when they sorely need it. God's angel was there to assist Daniel toward clearer understanding. The four **beasts,** he explained, were **four kings** (17), or kingdoms. But the final outcome of history is a fifth Kingdom, the rule of **the saints of the most High** (18).

b. The fourth beast (7:19-26) was Daniel's chief anxiety, as it has been the concern of students of Daniel's book ever since. So the angel concentrated on this aspect and gave it major attention.

This **beast** with great **teeth . . . of iron** and claws **of brass** (19) was indescribably dreadful. It was more wanton in its destructiveness and heartless in its cruelty than any of its predecessors. Though at first it had **ten horns** (20), another little horn sprang up to displace three others and distinguished itself in its vigor and growth. In ferocity and boastfulness it **was more stout than his fellows.** At last it attacked God himself, the Most High, and **made war with the saints, and prevailed against them** (21).

This **fourth beast,** the angel explained, **shall be the fourth kingdom upon earth . . . diverse from all kingdoms, and shall devour the whole earth, and shall tread it down, and break it in pieces** (23).

(1) *What empire is this?* What kingdom in history can be identified with the dread picture of this fourth beast? Following the interpretation adopted in c. 2 it would be the Roman Empire, though most modern interpreters disagree with this view. The popular view is that the dragon-like beast represents the Greeks, whose ten horns represents the ten rulers who succeeded Alexander. The little horn is Antiochus Ephiphanes.[19]

(2) *Rome identified.* Young in support of the Roman view says, "It is probably correct to say that the traditional view is that this fourth empire is Rome. This was expressed as early as the time of Josephus, and it has been held very widely. We may mention Chrysostom, Jerome, Augustine, Luther, Calvin as expounders, or at least adherents, of this position. In later times such great believing scholars as E. W. Hengstenberg, H. Ch. Hävernick, Carl Paul Caspari, Karl Friedrich Keil, Edward Pusey and Robert Dick Wilson [supported this view]."[20]

Young gives two reasons why the Roman view came to ascendancy in New Testament times and has held its ground with conservative interpreters since.

a) "Our Lord identified himself as the Son of Man, the heavenly figure of Daniel 7, and connected the 'abomination of desolation' with the future destruction of the Temple (Matt. 24)."

b) "Paul used the language of Daniel to describe the antichrist, and the Book of Revelation employed the symbolism of Daniel 7 to refer to powers that were then existent and future.

"The reason why the Roman view became so prevalent in the early church is because this view is found in the New Testament, not because men thought they had found a simple way out of the difficulty."[21]

(3) *What is the "little horn"* (8, 11, 20-22, 24-26)? Conservative interpreters quite universally agree that the little horn of Daniel 7 is the Antichrist, who is to come in the end of time. Against Porphyry, Jerome insisted on this.[22] Few who accept

[19]*The Oxford Annotated Bible,* ed. Herbert G. May and Bruce M. Metzger (New York: Oxford University Press, 1962), p. 1078.
[20]E. J. Young, *The Messianic Prophecies of Daniel* (Grand Rapids: Wm. B. Eerdmans Publishing Co., 1954), p. 17.
[21]E. J. Young, *The Prophecy of Daniel* (Grand Rapids: Wm. B. Eerdmans Publishing Co., 1949), pp. 293-94.
[22]*Commentary on Daniel,* trans. by Gleason L. Archer (Grand Rapids: Baker Book House, 1938), p. 129.

for Daniel a supernatural inspiration have questioned Jerome's contention. However a number insist that the little horn of this chapter is not to be identified with the smaller horn of c. 8. As for the little horn, the blasphemous audacity, the towering egotism, of this human being who comes forth from the political soil of human history marks him as the culmination of iniquity and godlessness. His characterization as having **the eyes of man** (8) suggests that he is a man of extraordinary genius, possessing intelligence, sagacity, and insight far beyond his contemporaries. He will win the world by reasonableness and logic as much as by armed might. His **mouth speaking great things** (8) indicates gifts of eloquence, and persuasion, a power of communication that serves as weapons of war against God and man.

This is Paul's "man of sin . . . the son of perdition; who opposeth and exalteth himself above all that is called God, or that is worshipped; so that he as God sitteth in the temple of God, shewing himself that he is God" (II Thess. 2:3-4). This is the "mystery of iniquity" (II Thess. 2:7), the "lawless one" (II Thess. 2:8, RSV). That this evil one should be identified as Antiochus Epiphanes is impossible. That tyrant had been dead for some two hundred years by Paul's time. He might well symbolize the "lawless one," but Paul placed Antichrist at the end of the age, at the culmination of the conflict between God and Anti-God.

The clause, **He shall speak great words against the most High** (25), is controlled by the preposition **against.** The Aramaic word *letsadh* signifies "at the side of, against." "It denotes that he would use language by which he would set God aside, and give regard to another. He would give himself out as God, making himself like God and destroy the saints of God."[23]

c. *The kingdoms of men and the kingdom of God* (7:13-14, 18, 22, 27-28)

(1) *Divergent theories.* What is this **kingdom** (18) which the Most High shall deliver to **the Son of man** (13) and through Him to **the saints of the most High** (22)? Where is it located? Who are its citizens? When does it come? Numerous theories have clustered around this most important theme. Perhaps there is no more important aspect of revelation, aside from redemption itself, than the kingdom of God. Nor is there any subject more

[23]C. F. Keil, *op. cit.*, p. 241.

essential to understanding the full implications of redemption and the meaning of the gospel in its universal setting.

(a) *Israel is God's "anointed,"* and provides the core of the Kingdom. This is the liberal view and relates closely to the theory that the fourth kingdom is Greece, and the little horn is Antiochus Epiphanes. There is no recognition of a personal, superhuman Messiah. It is sometimes allowed that Onias, the high priest who resisted Antiochus and was slain by him, could be "the anointed." But it is argued that the writer of Daniel could not have known anything of a personal Messiah to come, and certainly nothing of one who would become the King of God's kingdom.

(b) *A spiritualizing view.* This view is credited first to Origen and has been followed by many interpreters down through the centuries. From this point of view there does not need to be any time of final, crucial judgment. Christ is Judge now and has been ever since His first advent. The Kingdom is already here, and wherever the realm of God extends its sway over men's hearts. Most Catholic writers, following Augustine, hold this view in some modified respects, identifying the Kingdom with the Church. Augustine's *The City of God* is a classic example of its presentation. Neoorthodoxy in its eschatology leans to the spiritualizing interpretation of the continuous encounter of men and nations with the righteous Judge and His judgment.

(c) *Israel in Palestine.* This theory is held by most dispensationalists and fundamentalist interpreters of prophecy. Gabelin, Ironside, Blackstone, Larkin, and many others have ably promoted this "parenthesis view."[24] It is so called because of the long parenthesis or hiatus required by the theory between the First Advent and the Second Coming. The Church age or dispensation is viewed as a blank in prophecy, a time of waiting until God can work out His purposes in bringing Israel back from banishment to the land of promise, Palestine. The Old Testament covenant is made with the literal Israel and can be fulfilled only in her.

The Kingdom is viewed as a political Kingdom of which Christ is King and Israel the government. The locale is earth, and a small spot on earth, Palestine. The time of this golden age is a thousand years at the end of time, the millennium.

[24]Arno C. Gaebelein, *The Harmony of the Prophetic Word* (New York: Fleming H. Revell Co., 1907), p. 70.

(d) The Kingdom in continuity to the consummation. This theory combines two of the preceding theories in a sort of larger synthesis. It holds that the kingdom of God is that same rule of God which Jesus instituted in His ministry, death, and resurrection. It was this which He proclaimed when He said, "The kingdom of God is come." It was this He intended His disciples to pray for whenever they prayed: "Thy kingdom come. Thy will be done in earth, as it is in heaven" (Matt. 6:10).

But the kingdom of God is more than this. Jesus proclaimed the growth and increase of the Kingdom in such parables as that of the sower. He made clear also in parables of judgment that there was to be a culmination of the Kingdom in the end of time. That culmination would be in tribulation and judgment, but more importantly it would ensue in the total victory of God and His people in a reign of righteousness and peace on earth.

Jesus had nothing to say of a millennium, nor does Daniel. The Kingdom is to be an everlasting Kingdom and its rule to cover all nations. Young points out that in the second (and so, in the seventh) chapter of Daniel, "The Messianic kingdom is represented as being of eternal duration. For that reason we are not warranted in identifying it with a millennium of only one thousand years' length."[25]

The representation of the Scripture that the Kingdom is to be eternal is a strong argument against the assumption that it is to last for only one thousand years.[26]

Yet further, the kingdom of God is more than a narrow political regime with one small race, downtrodden as it has been, exercising autocratic control over all other people. The kingdom of God to come will not contravene the principles of grace which Jesus established. The essential character of salvation, of personal relationship in holy living, will not be set aside in the time of consummation. Rather, this will be a time of fulfilment when the angel's message announcing Messiah's birth will come to pass—"On earth peace among men with whom he is pleased!" (Luke 2:14, RSV)

Then will He whom Isaiah named "Prince of Peace" (Isa. 9:6) reign in righteousness and "the earth shall be full of the knowledge of the Lord, as the waters cover the sea" (Isa. 11:9; Hab. 2:14).

[25]E. J. Young, *The Messianic Prophecies of Daniel*, p. 30.
[26]*Ibid.*, pp. 31 ff.

(2) *The Kingdom and the kingdoms.* One of the most disputed problems of this chapter is the relation of the kingdom of God in its consummation to the kingdoms of men in the end time. The parenthesis theory requires the hypothesis of a revived Roman Empire, headed by ten kings and finally by the Antichrist himself, who displaces three kings. The dealings of this evil one will be specifically with a reconstituted Israel who will regard him as Messiah and pledge themselves to him in a covenant. This covenant the king breaks unconscionably and turns his fury on Israel itself. These are **the saints** with whom the little **horn made war . . . and prevailed against** (21); indeed he **shall wear out the saints of the most High** (25) and would destroy them except for divine intervention.

Both Keil and Young resist this interpretation.[27] In interpreting both the second chapter and this chapter Young points out that the God of heaven sets up His kingdom, not after, but "in the days of these kings." Indeed c. 2 requires, and c. 7 allows, that these kingdoms in some sense endure until the final consummation. The image of c. 2 remains whole until in the last stage it is smitten in the feet. In 7:12 we read, **As concerning the rest of the beasts, they had their dominion taken away: yet their lives were prolonged for a season and time.** And in Rev. 11:15, "The kingdoms of this world are become the kingdoms of our Lord, and of his Christ." Further we read, "And the kings of the earth do bring their glory and honour into it" (the New Jerusalem, Rev. 21:24). It would seem that human existence on the earth has not ceased in the time of the consummation, nor have the social structures of law and order vanished. We could well reason that in the coming of earth's proper King what is good in human living would rather be enhanced than displaced or destroyed.

But we must go further. The Messianic kingdom not only has a beginning; it has a consummation! That we should fail to see in Daniel's symbols of empire the essential unity of the successive kingdoms would seem to be an important oversight.

There is an essential cultural link through all succeeding ages. Just the fact that an emperor has been dethroned does not imply that his people have disappeard from the face of the earth. Nor have they forgotten what they have learned from their

---

[27]Keil, *op. cit.,* pp. 269-70; E. J. Young, *The Messianic Prophecies of Daniel,* pp. 27-28.

fathers, if it has seemed good or useful. The pomp and magnificence of Babylon merged into the giantism of Persia, and Persia's sensuous and materialistic civilization flowed into Greece, as did the brilliance of Grecian literature and art and philosophy make Romans more Greek than the Greeks. And to this day the iron of Rome's laws and political structures is a part of the warp and woof of Western civilization.

As to the ten kings, depicted as ten horns of the fourth beast, Keil and Young both show that the number ten is not to be taken mathematically but symbolically. The ten signifies a round number of completeness and sufficiency.[28]

An interesting sidelight on this discussion is furnished by the picture of the beast of end time disclosed in the Apocalypse. "I stood upon the sand of the sea, and saw a beast rise up out of the sea, having seven heads and ten horns, and upon his horns ten crowns, and upon his heads the name of blasphemy. And the beast which I saw was like a leopard, and his feet were as the feet of a bear, and his mouth as the mouth of a lion: and the dragon gave him his power, and his seat, and great authority" (Rev. 13:1-2).

Obviously this beast is a composite of the four beasts of Daniel 7. All the elements of power and culture and wickedness are blended into one. It would seem clear that the political manifestation in the end time will grow directly out of world civilizations and will become a supremely evil manifestation of all that is godless.

But the saints of the most High shall take the kingdom, and possess the kingdom for ever, even for ever and ever (18). The end of history is not to be an atomic explosion, nor the destruction of what is good. The goal of God's design is the kingdom of God and the consummation and preservation of all that is good and beautiful and true and holy.

---

[28]Young, *ibid.*, pp. 40-41.

Section **III** *The Hebrew Apocalypse*

(A Message to the Chosen People, in Hebrew)

Daniel 8:1—12:13

Keil regards the eighth chapter as the beginning of the second part of the Book of Daniel. He gives it the title "The Development of the Kingdom of God."[1] This is in line with earlier analyses of the book (see comments on 1:1-2 and the introductory paragraph on 7:1-28).

A. DANIEL'S VISION OF WARRING EMPIRES, 8:1-27

The vision of c. 8 pictures God's people under the rise and fall of the second and third world empires foreseen in c. 7.

1. *The War of the Ram and the Goat* (8:1-12)

a. Occasion and place of the vision (8:1-2). In this **third year of the reign of king Belshazzar** two years had elapsed (cf. 7:1) since Daniel's vision of the four world-kingdoms. If Daniel's exile to Babylon occurred when he was between fifteen and twenty years of age, he would now be nearing seventy-five. He had served his age illustriously under the great Nebuchadnezzar. Under succeeding kings, Daniel seems to have gone somewhat into the shadows as far as public notice was concerned. But he was still God's man and the years had ripened him in wisdom. Now God was about to unveil to him the most treasured secrets of His plan for Israel and for humanity. The setting was **at Shushan** (2), the summer **palace** of the Persian kings, some two hundred miles east of Babylon (see map 1). **The river of Ulai** was a canal connecting the Kerkha and Karun rivers.

b. The Medo-Persian ram (8:3-4). In Daniel's first vision in c. 7, the beasts which symbolized world power were wild beasts. Now the temper of the vision changes and two of these same world powers appear as domesticated animals—a ram and a goat. Could it be that the Spirit of God is here depicting another important phase of human life and history, the cultural aspect? Whereas in c. 7 the emphasis was upon the political

---

[1]*Op. cit.*, p. 283.

662

power of the nations, in c. 8 it is upon the cultural influences. If this be accepted it would be possible to conceive of the two aspects, coming through two different kingdoms, converging at one time in one culminating manifestation of evil, the Antichrist.

Whatever may be the meaning in the change of the character of the beasts, the ram and the goat were soon furiously at war. The **ram** first appears, **pushing westward, and northward, and southward** (4). Keil suggests that the direction of the pushing seems to indicate that the eastward-looking exploits were not so strategically important as the other directions. Both Cyrus and Darius led successful campaigns eastward to India. But it is their Occidental impact that most seriously affected history.[2]

The two-horned beast, with the second growing higher, clearly suggests Medo-Persian history. Cyaxeres the Mede was a powerful leader allied with the Chaldean Nabopolassar and his son, Nebuchadnezzar, in overturning the Assyrian empire in 612 B.C. Next to Babylonia, Media stood ascendant in its day. But with the rise of the gifted Cyrus (whom tradition says was a grandson of Astyages, king of the Medes) his prowess became so evident that he quickly climbed to the top in the Medo-Persian alliance.

The word **beasts** (*chayywoth*) signifies living creatures in general and carries no connotation of either wildness or domestication. "No living creature could stand before him, and there was no one who could rescue from his power; he did as he pleased and made himself great" (4, lit.) **Became great** (*higddil*) does not here mean "became haughty" but rather "did great things." So in 8; cf. Ps. 126:2-3, "The Lord hath done great things for us."[3]

c. *The Grecian goat* (8:5-12). A new factor enters history with this scene. Hitherto the center of gravity in world power was Oriental. Now for the first time the West comes into view. **Behold, an he goat came from the west on the face of the whole earth** (5). The attack of the goat on the ram was swift and shattering. **Moved with choler against him** (7); i.e., "in brutal rage he butted him" (Berk.). **There was none that could deliver the ram out of his hand.**

(1) *The broken horn and its four successors.* At the zenith of the ram's power **the great horn was broken** (8) and in its

---

[2]*Ibid.*, p. 291.
[3]*Ibid.*

place **four** other horns sprang up. The significance here clearly relates to four kings and their kingdoms which succeed them.
(2) *The little horn that waxed great.* As Daniel watched, an astonishing thing began to happen. One of the four horns sprouted **a little horn, which waxed exceeding great** (9). **The pleasant land** was "the land of Israel" (LP). The same word "became great" (*gaddal*) is used here as in 4 and 8. But the context describes another kind of growth, a growth in evil. The towering pride of the despicable little horn magnifies itself even against **the prince of the host** (11). He attempts to attack God by destroying **some of the host and** his **stars** (10; His saints).

Much diversity surrounds the identification of **the prince of the host.** Some have supposed it referred to the high priest, Onias, at the time of Antiochus Epiphanes. Some have said it was Israel's God. Could it be that here again we see the eternal, preincarnate Christ, who appeared to Joshua saying, "As captain ['prince,' margin] of the host of the Lord am I now come" (Josh. 5:14)? Clearly **the prince** refers to the divine authority which rules over the saints of God. As the foreordained Anointed Prince of God's people, who could better fill this role than the Second Person of the divine Trinity?

To carry out his blasphemous purposes the little horn stops **the daily sacrifice** and desecrates the **sanctuary** (11). This was a time when the usual restraints against evil and evildoers were removed. "As a result, truth and righteousness perished, and evil triumphed and prospered" (12, LP).

2. The Meaning of the Vision (8:13-27)

a. *"How long?"* (8:13-14) To Daniel, God revealed through the conversation of nearby holy beings that the time of evil would not be prolonged. The question was, **How long shall be the vision concerning the daily sacrifice, and the transgression of desolation, to give both the sanctuary and the host to be trodden under foot?** (13) The answer came, **Unto two thousand and three hundred days; then shall the sanctuary be cleansed** (14). How are we to consider this symbol of numbers? Jerome gives a very simple and commonsense interpretation:

> If we read the books of the Maccabees and the history of Josephus, we shall find there recorded that . . . Antiochus entered Jerusalem, and after wreaking a general devastation he returned again in the third year and set up the statue of Jupiter in the Temple. Up until the time of Judas Maccabaeus . . . Jerusalem lay

waste over a period of six years, and for three of those years the Temple lay defiled; making a total of two thousand three hundred days plus three months.[4]

b. *God's messenger Gabriel* (8:15-19). The deep wonderment of Daniel at the vision he had seen quickly found an answer in **the appearance of a man** (15)—a special messenger sent from God. It was **Gabriel** (16) who appeared, announced by **a man's voice.** For **the banks of Ulai** cf. comment on v. 2.

Gabriel (Heb., "God has shown himself mighty") is well-known in Scripture. He was God's messenger to Daniel (8:16; 9:21); and the messenger of the annunciation of John the Baptist's birth, as of the conception of Jesus himself (Luke 1:19, 26). To the aged Zacharias, Gabriel explains his office: "I am Gabriel, that stand in the presence of God; and am sent to speak unto thee, and to shew thee these glad tidings" (Luke 1:19).[5]

In his awe at the presence of the angel, Daniel writes, "I fell on my face . . . while he was speaking to me I swooned face down to the ground; then he touched me and . . . said, 'I am here to acquaint you with the final events . . . for the end comes at the appointed time'" (17-19, Berk.).

c. *The interpretation* (8:20-27). (1) *The ram—Medo-Persia* (8:20). The identification of this rampaging creature is direct and unequivocal. It is **Media and Persia** (20) in their two-sectioned rise to power. Cyaxeres, the great Median leader of Nebuchadnezzar's day, had led his land to power and prestige. With Lydia to the northwest, Media had been one of the victorious allies with the Babylonians in the vanquishment of Assyria. At the time of Nineveh's fall in 612 B.C., Persia was a small and little noticed land to the south and eastward of Media and Elam. But when the young genius, Cyrus the Persian, arose he moved rapidly to absorb the whole land. His allies, and relatives, were Medes.

Jerome shares what knowledge he has gleaned on the relation of the Persians and the Medes by going back to Josephus:

> Now Darius who destroyed the empire of the Babylonians in cooperation with his relative Cyrus—for they both carried on the

[4]*Commentary on Daniel,* trans. by Gleason L. Archer, *op. cit.,* p. 86.
[5]For an interesting discussion of the place of angels in the divine scheme, cf. Arno C. Gabelein, *Gabriel and Michael the Archangel* (New York: Our Hope Publications, 1945).

war as allies—was sixty-two years of age at the time he captured Babylon. . . . When Babylon was overthrown, Darius returned to his own kingdom in Media, and brought Daniel along with him in the same honorable capacity to which he had been promoted by Belshazzar. There is no doubt but what Darius had heard [of] the sign and portent which had come to Belshazzar, and also of the interpretation which Daniel had set forth, and how he had fore-told the rule of the Medes and the Persians. And so no one should be troubled by the fact that Daniel is said in one place to have lived in Darius' reign, and in another place in the reign of Cyrus. The Septuagint rendered Darius by the name of Artaxeres. . . . And so it was under this Darius who put Belshazzar to death that the events took place of which we speak.[6]

(2) *The rough goat of Greece* (8: 21-22). **The rough goat is the king of Grecia: and the great horn that is between his eyes is the first king** (21). This seems to describe Alexander the Great of Macedon. His brilliant strategy swiftly laid everything before him. At Thebes he conquered Egypt. At Jerusalem the high priest and his retinue opened wide the gates in welcome and received favored treatment for their foresight. Twice on the way northward and eastward he met the hosts of Persia. At last on the plains of Arbela in Syria he laid low Darius III and scattered his armies. Everywhere Alexander went he was wel-comed either by acclaim or by easy victories, until at last he stood on the borders of India on the banks of the Indus River. At this first aggressive encounter of West against East the West had gloriously won and changed the face of history and the cur-rents of culture for two and a half millenniums.

Alexander's empire was the most fragile and least enduring of any. Like a meteor it flashed across the sky of history and exploded into fragments. These fragments were **four** (22), ham-mered into visible **kingdoms** by four of his hardiest generals. Macedonia and Greece were taken by Alexander's half brother, Phillip Aridaeus. Asia Minor fell to Antigonus. Egypt went to Ptolemy, son of Lagos. The great mass of Syria, Babylonia, and all the kingdoms eastward to India became the dominion of Seleucus Nicanor.

(3) *The fierce and despicable "little horn"* (8: 9-12, 23-25). Most interpreters have joined in noting the distinct difference between the **little horn** of this chapter and that of c. 7. This horn sprouts out of one of the four other horns. The little horn

[6]Jerome, *op. cit.*, p. 63.

of c. 7 springs up among the ten and displaces three. This horn is a product of the third kingdom. That of c. 7 is from the fourth kingdom.

Almost without dissent interpreters agree that whoever the little horn of c. 7 is, Antichrist or other, the little horn of c. 8 is Antiochus Epiphanes.

But as clear as is the picture of Antiochus here, there lurks in the background, like a dim double exposure on a photographic film, another, the dread Antichrist. Jerome points out this fact and suggests that Antiochus is a type of Antichrist as Solomon was of Christ, the Anointed.

The interpretation which Gabriel gives lends support to this view. We read: **At the time of the end shall be the vision** (17); **At the time appointed the end shall be** (19); **In the latter time of their kingdom, when the transgressors are come to the full** (23). This latter passage reminds us of Paul's reference and his application of it to "that man of sin . . . the son of perdition" (II Thess. 2:3), who shall identify the end-time.

(4) *Daniel's Massive Secret* (8:26-27). The reaction of the prophet is revealing of the deep spiritual and emotional impact this revelation had upon him. **I Daniel fainted, and was sick certain days** (27). In his heart there burned the secret which he must needs shut up for future times. But the call of the present day was upon this servant of God. He did not fade away into idle dreaming. **I rose up, and did the king's business; and I was astonished at the vision, but none understood it** (27).

B. DANIEL'S INTERCESSION FOR ISRAEL, 9:1-27

Toward the close of his earthly journey we see Daniel engaged in one of the crucial battles of his life. We are reminded of Paul's declaration about the nature of prayer: "We wrestle not against flesh and blood, but against principalities, against powers, against the rulers of the darkness of this world, against spiritual wickedness in high places" (Eph. 6:12).

1. *The Occasion for Daniel's Prayer* (9:1-3)

A change in government brought sharply to Daniel's mind the conviction that some great providential change must be imminent for the remnant of his people in exile. The kingdom of the Chaldeans had come to an end with the fall of Babylon (5:30-31).

The rule of the Persians and their Median allies had displaced it. If **Darius, who was made king over the realm of the Chaldeans** (1), was indeed the aging relative of the Persian Cyrus, the political situation was nonetheless unstable. The balance of power was shifting from Media to Persia. Cyrus would within two years assume civil as well as military leadership.

But Daniel was seeing beyond the secular scene. He **understood by books . . . the word of the Lord** (2). Daniel was well aware of how minutely faithful had been the fulfillment of the warnings God had given His people. He had lived through the harrowing days of calamity graphically depicted in Lev. 26: 14-35. Even the recompense requited for neglected sabbatical years was becoming intelligible. God's promise of mercy and restoration based on the covenant with the fathers (Lev. 26: 40-45) with the requisite condition of repentance closely followed. God was waiting on the response of His people. Then Daniel came upon Jeremiah's startling prophetic reference to a series of sabbatical cycles that climaxed in those very days: "Thus saith the Lord, That after seventy years be accomplished at Babylon I will visit you, and perform my good word toward you, in causing you to return to this place" (Jer. 29:10; cf. 29:11-13; II Chron. 36:21). He knew that the time was at hand and he saw clearly what he must do. In Jeremiah's prophecy he discovered God's design for the times in which he lived.

The earnestness of Daniel's prayer struggle is suggested in the phrases which recount it: **I set my face . . . to seek by prayer and supplications, with fasting, and sackcloth, and ashes** (3).

Here was a man engaging in an extraordinary period of soul searching and seeking divine aid. Calvin remarks that "when God promises anything remarkable and valuable, we ought then to be the more stirred up and to feel this expectation as a sharper stimulus." He goes on to point out that Daniel's use of sackcloth, ashes, and fasting were used, not as meritorious works to win God's favor, but as helps to increased ardor in praying. "Thus, we observe Daniel to have made use of fasting correctly, not wishing to appease God by this discipline, but to render him more earnest in his prayers."[7]

In 9:1-3 we see "Factors in Effective Prayer": (1) An opened heart to **the word of the Lord,** 2*a;* (2) An overpowering convic-

---

[7]*Commentaries on the Book of Daniel,* Vol. II, trans. by Thomas Myers (Grand Rapids: Wm. B. Eerdmans Publishing Co., 1948 [reprint]), pp. 137-38.

tion that God's time is now, 2b; (3) Observing the disciplines of importunate prayer, 3.

2. *Daniel's Prayer of Confession* (9:4-14)

As Daniel entered this crucial ministry of intercession he did what every true intercessor must do. He identified himself with those for whom he was interceding. The sins of his people were his sins. Their woe was his woe. Their punishment was his punishment, fully deserved. He did not stand above his people on a superior plane, judging them from an exalted position. It is true that Daniel personally was no idolatrous rebel against God. But he went down into the valley of humiliation among his erring people and took their guilt and shame upon himself. How vividly this reflects our Saviour's estate as He took upon himself the sins of a lost world! How pointedly it suggests to all who would enter into the fellowship of His suffering that we must in some real sense become identified with the erring whom we would bear before the throne of grace!

In Daniel's approach to God, he had a clear view of the nature of the character of God, whose face he sought. God was personal and available, for Daniel addressed Him as **my God** (4). He was also sovereign and holy, **the great and dreadful God.** God was faithful, **keeping the covenant and mercy to them that love him.**

Daniel's confession was more than generalizations and platitudes. He became specific in opening up the dark horrors which were his people's sins. There is searching meaning in the four Hebrew terms with which Daniel described the evil of Israel. **We have sinned** (5; *chata*) means to make a misstep, to err from the right. We **have committed iniquity** (*'awah*) goes more deeply into motives; **iniquity** implies to be perverse. **We have done wickedly** (*rasha'*) means to do wrong in rebellion against God. The following phrase, **have rebelled** (*marad*) **even by departing from thy precepts,** serves to reinforce this third term. **Confusion of faces** (7 and 8) means shame or shamefaced.

Israel's sin was far more serious than some superficial error. It was a deeply ingrained wickedness that controlled actions in perverse ways. It had stopped the ears and blinded the eyes and hardened the hearts of king and commoner so that God's efforts to influence them through His servants the prophets had been of no avail. God is righteous and holy. Men are evil and corrupt. God is merciful and gracious. The people are rebellious and stubborn. God's judgments are just. Israel's calamity is deserved; it is simply the exact fulfilment of **the oath that is written in the law of Moses the servant of God** (11). The evil of man serves but to accentuate the righteousness of God.

3. *Daniel's Prayer of Supplication* (9:15-19)

In the light of the undimmed holiness of God, and in the face of the unabated wickedness of his people, Daniel could only throw himself upon the divine mercy. Any hope that Israel might have for restoration or salvation could have no basis at all in merit. It must be of grace or not at all. So even before the age of grace we see the manifestations of grace breaking through. **O Lord, according to all thy righteousness ... let thine anger and thy fury be turned away . . . because for our sins, and for the iniquities of our fathers, Jerusalem and thy people are become a reproach to all that are about us** (16).

Then Daniel's importunity breaks over all boundaries and overflows the channels of speech. **O my God, incline thine ear, and hear; open thine eyes, and behold . . . O Lord, hear; O Lord, forgive; O Lord, hearken and do; defer not, for thine own sake, O my God** (18-19).

Surely here was an instance where "the effectual fervent prayer of a righteous man" (Jas. 5:16) did avail much.

In 15-19 we see "Appropriate Approaches in Prayers of Petition." (1) Recall God's earlier blessings, 15a; (2) Confess our own unworthiness, 15b, 16b; (3) Pray persistently, 19a; (4) Ask in the name of God's goodness and in the interests of His kingdom, 16a, 17-18, 19b (A. F. Harper).

4. *God's Answer* (9:20-27)

a. *The angel messenger Gabriel* (9:20-23). Like the bright light which illuminates the dark background of an overcharged storm cloud, God's answer broke upon Daniel in the midst of his desperate prayer. One of God's angel messengers, whose ministrations Daniel had once before experienced (8-16), came swiftly to him. This was **Gabriel** (21), the messenger of God's special revelations (Luke 1:19, 26).

What comfort must have overwhelmed Daniel's heart when he heard God's assurance: **O Daniel, I am now come forth to give thee skill and understanding** (22). Then Gabriel informed him that from the beginning of his prayer God had been listening and answering. Already the wheels were in motion to bring to fulfilment what Daniel had been praying for—and more. Then to climax the message of personal comfort he gave Daniel a witness of personal assurance from God, **Thou art greatly beloved** (23). In this we are reminded of Luke's account of a greater Intercessor in a garden called Gethsemane to whom in His agony "there appeared an angel unto him from heaven, strengthening him" (Luke 22:43).

b. *The revelation of the seventy weeks* (9:24-27). Strangely, the message of understanding which Gabriel brought to Daniel seems to bear not at all upon the immediate subject of Daniel's prayer. He had been thinking of Jeremiah's prophecy of the seventy years and of the fact that the completion of this time was near at hand. This fulfillment did indeed soon come in the edict of Cyrus and the release of the Jews to return to Jerusalem. But in the message which Gabriel brought, another door of prophetic insight opens into a larger dimension of God's purpose, not only for Israel, but for the world. This larger dimension of revelation concerns the work and reign of the Messiah. This subject had been introduced in previous visions and dreams, as to Nebuchadnezzar in the great image (2:44-45) and as in Daniel's vision of the four beasts (7:13-14). But here the message comes from another angle and in greater detail.

(1) *The ministry and times of the Messiah* (9:24-25). Some interpreters would limit the scope of the **seventy weeks** and the work therein included to the people of Israel, the land of Palestine, and the city of Jerusalem. It does seem that to this land and to this people there is a special pertinence in this message, for the first clause states, **Seventy weeks are determined upon thy people and upon thy holy city** (24). But as the message develops, it becomes clear that the clause has an inclusive rather than an exclusive connotation. God's plan in the Messiah is indeed for Israel, and the main redemption-events transpire in Palestine and at Jerusalem. But in salvation for Israel is salvation for all (Rom. 11:1, 11-12, 25-26). For salvation is through Christ and Him alone, whether for Jew or for Gentile.

(a) *The sixfold work of Messiah* (24). Within the wholeness of the symbolic **seventy weeks** a complete work of redemption is to be done. It would seem that in extent of time this would reach even beyond the desolations, "until the consummation"

671

(27), that is, to the end of this world. Furthermore, since the key to this passage is the Messiah, it is evident that this work is Messiah's work.

Six aspects of the Messiah's work of redemption are given in 24:

1. **To finish the transgression**
2. **To make an end of sins**
3. **To make reconciliation for iniquity**
4. **To bring in everlasting righteousness**
5. **To seal up the vision and prophecy**
6. **To anoint the most Holy**

The first three have to do with the conquest of sin. The second three have to do with the positive aspects of the completion of redemption; to bring all things for all time under the righteous rule of God; **to seal up the vision and prophecy** by bringing these to fulfillment; and **to anoint the most Holy,** the heavenly sanctuary which is the eternal antitype of the earthly holy of holies.

Keil holds that:

> we must refer this sixth statement (to anoint the most Holy) also to that time of the consummation, and understand it of the establishment of the new holy of holies which was shown to the holy seer on Patmos as "the tabernacle of God with men," in which God will dwell with them, and they shall become His people, and He shall be their God with them (Rev. 21:1-3). In this holy city there will be no temple, for the Lord, the Almighty God, and the Lamb is its temple, and the glory of God will lighten it (vv. 22-23). Into it nothing shall enter that defileth or worketh abomination (v. 27), for sin shall then be closed and sealed up; there shall righteousness dwell (2 Pet. 3:13), and prophecy shall cease (1 Cor. 13:8) by its fulfillment.[8]

(b) *Messiah's advent and prophetic expectation* (25). However variously the words have been understood, **from the going forth of the commandment . . . unto the Messiah the Prince shall be seven weeks, and threescore and two weeks,** this much is well-established: At the time of Christ's first advent there was an unprecedented surge of expectancy of the Messiah. The documents of the Qumran community from the Dead Sea caves with their heightened tone of apocalyptic excitement confirm

[8]*Op. cit.,* p. 349.

this. John the Baptist was not the first in his day to cry out for preparation. And whence, can we suppose, did the wise men from the East gather the hint that a King in Judah was to be born at that particular time? The star alone would hardly have been sufficient without some tradition or teaching that would give a basis for an approximate time of expectancy. These men came from Daniel's country, where these weeks of years were known and discussed.

So we may be sure that Gabriel's mystic message, couched in terms of times and numbers, caused eager hearts to yearn with hope and expectation long after Daniel had departed. For the Messiah-Prince, the Anointed Priest and Leader, was the Hope of Israel and of the world.

(2) *The symbolic weeks* (9:25-27). The **seventy weeks** of Daniel have been the rock on which an unending succession of systems of interpretation have broken themselves. Perhaps there is no subject of Scripture that has occasioned a greater variety of opinions.

Young outlines four principal classes of interpretation which show the divergences of views:

(a) The Traditional Messianic Interpretation. This view holds that the seventy weeks prophesies the first advent of Christ, especially His death, and culminates in the destruction of Jerusalem. Following Augustine, who first described this interpretation, its proponents have included Pusey, Wright, and Wilson. Young also supports this view.

(b) The Liberal Interpretation. This view regards the seventy weeks not so much as prophecy as description of the days of Antiochus Epiphanes and his overthrow under the Maccabees. The Messiah who was cut off is identified as the high priest Onias, who was slain for his defiance of Antiochus.

(c) The Christian Church Interpretation. In this the sevens are understood, not as exact weeks of years, but rather as symbolical numbers covering the period between the edict of Cyrus to repatriate the Jews through Messiah's first advent and death to the time of Antichrist and his destruction in the time of consummation.

(d) The Parenthesis Interpretation. Here the seventy sevens of years are divided into periods of seven sevens, sixty-two sevens, and a final seven detached from the rest by an indefinite parenthesis or hiatus. The sixty-nine sevens cover the period to

Messiah's first coming and death and the destruction of Jerusalem. The final seven is the period of Antichrist in the end of the age.[9]

Most interpreters since the days of Jerome, except those of the liberal school, have understood the 70 sevens as weeks of years, totaling 490. Jerome wrote, "Now the angel himself specified seventy weeks of years, that is to say, four hundred and ninety years from the issuing of the word that the petition be granted that Jerusalem be rebuilt. The specified interval began in the twentieth year of Artaxerxes, king of the Persians, for it was his cupbearer Nehemiah who . . . petitioned the king and obtained his permission that Jerusalem be rebuilt."[10]

If we accept the year 454 B.C. as the twentieth year of Artaxerxes' reign and calculate the 7 plus 62 sevens, 69 sevens or 483 years, we come to the year A.D. 29. This is the climactic year of the ministry of Jesus. In the spring of that year He appeared in Jerusalem as both Messiah and Prince, riding in triumph attended by a rejoicing multitude (Zech. 9:9; Matt. 21:5).

But Calvin insists that the reckoning must begin with the edict of Cyrus for the return of the exiles to Jerusalem, thus directly connecting Jeremiah's prophecy of 70 years to Daniel's 70 weeks.[11] By this means Calvin identifies Christ's baptism as the time of His manifestation. This would mean that the total of the years would not coincide, for more than 530 years intervene between the edict of Cyrus in 536 and the birth of Jesus in 4 B.C., plus 30 additional years to His baptism. To the death of Jesus in A.D. 29 the time would be extended to 565 years. This Calvin does not think important.

Young agrees with Calvin and holds that the exact number of years is not significant since they are symbolical rather than chronological. He says:

"Seventy heptads"—7x7x10—is the period in which the divine work of greatest moment is brought to perfection. Consequently since these numbers represent periods of time, the length of which is not stated, and since they are symbolical, it is not warrantable to seek to discover the precise length of the sevens. This cannot be done, nor for that matter, can the length of any of the individual sevens be discovered or determined. . . .

[9]E. J. Young, The Prophecy of Daniel, pp. 192-94.
[10]Op. cit., pp. 95-96.
[11]Op. cit., pp. 212-13.

674

> One thing, however, should be clear. It is that, according to Daniel, the important matters are not the beginning and ending of this period but the remarkable events which took place within it. . . . We believe . . . that when the seventy sevens were completed, so also the six purposes of verse twenty-four were accomplished. And that is the important matter. When Jesus Christ ascended to heaven, the mighty salvation which He came to accomplish, was actually accomplished.[12]

Keil also supports the symbolical view of this measure of time. "By the definition of these periods according to a symbolical measure of time, the reckoning of the actual duration of the periods named is withdrawn beyond the reach of our human research, and the definition of the days and hours of the development of the kingdom of God down to its consummation is reserved for God, the Governor of the world and the Ruler of human destiny."[13]

But where Keil holds that the seventy weeks cover the history of the kingdom of God to the consummation in the end of time, Young believes that the cutting off of Messiah (26) culminates not only the sixty-nine weeks but the seventieth as well. **The covenant** that is confirmed **with many** (27) is the gospel which Christ proclaimed, and His crucifixion **in the midst of the week** put an end to the validity of all other sacrifice and oblation. Moreover, it rendered the Temple which was dedicated to such sacrifice an abomination. The desolation which came upon the Temple and the city of Jerusalem under the hand of Titus was but an outward enactment of the inner desolation that had already overtaken them.

But others insist that the years of the seventy weeks be taken much more literally. Pusey settles on the year 457 B.C. as the base from which he begins his calculations and interpretation of the 7 and 62 weeks, 483 years. This date he takes to be the time of the first authorization of Artaxerxes Longimanus given to Ezra to return to Jerusalem.[14] This would bring us to the beginning of the year of A.D. 27, the time of Jesus' baptism at Jordan and the occasion of His anointing by the Holy Spirit. The first half of the seventieth week of years is occupied with the public ministry of Jesus. His "cutting off" comes in the middle

[12]E. J. Young, *The Messianic Prophecies of Daniel*, pp. 56, 82.
[13]*Op. cit.*, p. 400.
[14]*Op. cit.*, pp. 184 ff.

of this crucial week after 3½ years. For 3½ years more the gospel is preached exclusively to the Jews until at the house of Cornelius the door of opportunity is opened to Gentiles and Israel's special privilege ends. In due course the destruction of the Temple and the devastation of Jerusalem follow.

Seiss, Gabelein, and others of the dispensational school also take an exact view of the seventy weeks. The particular characteristic of this interpretation is the hiatus or parenthesis between the close of the sixty-ninth week, when Messiah is cut off, and the opening of the seventieth week, which is reserved for the end of the age and the reign of Antichrist. The **prince that shall come** (26) is not **Messiah the Prince** (25), but the "little horn" of c. 7. **The covenant** which he confirms (27) is a perfidious treaty by which he wins the Jewish people to his side. After three and a half years, **in the midst of the week,** he renounces the covenant, outlaws religion, and opens the floodgates to the torrent of unrestrained evil which constitutes the "time of trouble" (12:1).

C. A HEAVENLY VISION OF EARTHLY CONFLICTS, 10:1—12:13

Most interpreters agree that the final three chapters of the Book of Daniel constitute one unit. Keil describes the contents of this section as "The Revelation Regarding the Affliction of the People of God on the Part of the Rulers of the World till the Consummation of the Kingdom of God."[15] This section is not in the nature of a dream or a vision. It is a revelation, given directly to Daniel by a glorious One who acts as the Mediator of truth. **A thing was revealed unto Daniel** (10:1) contains the word *niglah,* the passive form for the verb which means "to unveil, disclose, reveal." This climaxing disclosure experienced by Daniel came to him on the highest level of revelation, through direct confrontation with Deity. Keil describes this experience as a theophany, a manifestation or appearance of God.

The unveiling which Daniel beheld brought a glorious realization of divine power. At the same time it opened up a scene of tragic conflict through the ages. Moffatt renders 10:1, "A revelation was made to Daniel . . . the true revelation of a great conflict." The KJV gives this clause, **The thing was true, but the time appointed was long.**

---

[15]*Op. cit.,* pp. 402-3.

This revelation in a special sense pertains to the people of Israel even to the end of time. In 10:14 we read, **Now I am come to make thee understand what shall befall thy people in the latter days.**

1. *Daniel's Vision of the Glorious One* (10:1—11:1)

   a. *Daniel's vigil* (10:1-3). Four years or more had passed since Daniel's experience of revelation through Gabriel. At that time Darius the Median (see comments on 6:1-28) was serving as interim king in Babylon. Now **Cyrus king of Persia** (1; see Chart B) was in his third year. Daniel, who must by this time have been in his nineties, was launched in an extended prayer enterprise. Again he was giving himself not only to prayer, but to fasting. **I Daniel was mourning three full weeks** (2). "I ate no delicacies, I never tasted flesh or wine, and I never anointed myself" (3, Moffatt). Such importunity could not fail to open the portals to heavenly places.

   b. *Appearance of the Glorious One* (10:4-11). What follows is an unveiling of a glorious Being to Daniel's view that reminds us of what John the Revelator saw on Patmos (Rev. 1:10-20). Here beside the river **Hiddekel** (4; Tigris) Daniel saw a **man clothed in linen** (5). There, on Patmos, John saw one like unto the Son of Man clothed with a garment down to the foot. Both were **girded with . . . gold.** Both glowed from head to foot with supernal light. Both looked with **eyes** like flame for brilliance and spoke like **the voice of a multitude** (6). The Person John saw identified himself: "I am he that liveth, and was dead; and, behold, I am alive for evermore" (Rev. 1:18). Who could doubt that Daniel saw in a different setting the same Being, the Eternal Word?[16] **Daniel alone saw the vision** (7), although his companions were awe-struck apparently by an accompanying light and sounds.

   The effect on Daniel and on John was identical. **There remained no strength in me** (8), Daniel confessed. "I fell at his feet as dead" (Rev. 1:17), John recorded. The limits of human capacity to absorb heavenly wonder were surpassed in both cases. "On hearing the sound of his words I fell unconscious with my face to the ground" (9, Berk.). Though the prophet fainted at **the voice** of the messenger, he was aroused to full conscious-

---

[16]C. F. Keil identifies the Being who appeared to Daniel as The Angel of Jehovah, the divine Logos, and refers to Rev. 1:13 (*op. cit.*, p. 410).

ness as God's message was given to him. **Behold, an hand touched me** (10), Daniel testified. Added to the strengthening touch was a comforting word, **O Daniel, a man greatly beloved** (11). What more assuring word could there be from the lips of Deity?

c. *The Prince of Peace and earth's princes* (10:12—11:1). Another comforting word comes from Daniel's experience. The Lord who cares takes notice of our prayers. Three weeks Daniel had been praying in holy desperation. Had God heard? The effulgent One speaks, **Fear not, Daniel: for from the first day ... thy words were heard, and I am come for thy words** (12).

Whereas John saw the Son of Man within the candlestick, the circle of the Church, Daniel saw the "man clothed in linen" involved in a struggle with earthly governments. The same eternal Christ, who came to be revealed to and through the Church, has also through the ages concerned himself with the course of human history.

Just what was the three-week struggle with **the prince of the kingdom of Persia** (13) and what was the eventual outcome of this struggle we may not know. It must have been difficult and intense to require the aid of **Michael.** Most interpreters hold that **prince** (*sar*) used in this section refers to supernatural beings who exert special influence over the affairs of nations. Since **the prince of the kingdom of Persia** as well as **the prince of Grecia** (20) are in conflict with the glorious One and His helper, Michael, it would seem evident that some of these at least are not good angels.

One of the special responsibilities of the archangel Michael is the welfare of the people of Israel. Called in 10:13 "the first" (marg.) **of the chief princes,** he is referred to in 10:21 as **Michael your prince.** Jude 9 tells us that it was "Michael the archangel," who, "contending with the devil . . . disputed about the body of Moses." Again John tells us that it is Michael and his angelic hosts who will make war upon the dragon and cast him out of the heavenly regions (Rev. 12:7-9). This prince of the highest princes of heaven, subject to the Redeemer of Israel, is destined yet to play an important role in Israel's destiny. Daniel saw him on this occasion as "one who resembled a mortal man" (16, Moffatt).

Not only does the Angel of Jehovah confess to a struggle for the will of Cyrus, and forsee a conflict with **the prince of Grecia** (20), but He discloses that, **in the first year of Darius**

the Mede, He had **stood to confirm and to strength him** (11:1). Thus the Prince of Peace strives with the princes of earth to bring about His purposes.

In 10:2-19 we see "The Touch of God," with the text in v.19. (1) God's touch comes to us when we earnestly seek Him, 2-3; (2) It comes to us when He becomes most real to us, 5-6, 10-12; (3) God's touch brings fresh vision for our task, 14; (4) It sends us on our way with new strength, 15-19 (A. F. Harper).

2. The Conflict of the Ages (11:2—12:3)

This section of Daniel has been a bone of contention since the days of Porphyry. Its rather amazingly detailed description of events that transpired in the years following the death of Alexander the Great have led the critics to date the whole book in the times of the Seleucid kings (312-64 B.C.), particularly in the days of Antiochus Epiphanes.

a. The struggles of Persia and Greece (11:2-4). The succession of kings briefly described in this section of the message evidently reaches from the reign of Cyrus, through the climax and fall of the Persian empire, to Alexander and the breakup of his realm.

Although twelve Persian kings in all ruled (including an impostor, Pseudo-Smyrdis), **three** are singled out, before **the fourth** king of great wealth arises. This is generally identified as Xerxes I (Ahasuerus, Esther 1:1), the husband of Esther, and one of the wealthiest of Persian monarchs. It was he who stirred **up all against the realm of Grecia** (2). He marshalled an immense force of infantry, cavalry, chariots, and ships. Although an estimated five million men were engaged, this flood of might was turned back by the valiant Greeks at the crucial battles of Thermopylae and Salamis. Although other expeditions followed, none equalled this, and the power of Persia declined until its overthrow under Darius III.

The identification of Alexander, the **mighty king** (3), who stands up and rules **with great dominion,** is quite clear. Daniel foresaw that **his kingdom shall be broken, and shall be divided toward the four winds of heaven** (4) and he would leave no **posterity** to follow him. Alexander's four generals divided the kingdom and carried forward the Hellenization of the lands they governed until Greek culture prevailed everywhere.

Thus this section of the prophecy is quite clearly an enlargement of the vision of c. 8. But at this point the focus changes sharply to a close-up view of conflict in the lands encompassing the land of the covenant.

b. Israel's tribulations and the nations (11:5-35). The prophecy to this point has centered largely in the Gentile kingdoms. At this juncture the people of God come sharply into focus in a time of intense suffering. The prophecies are concerned basically with the intertestamental period between the return from exile and the birth of Jesus. At first Israel is caught in the middle between opposing forces, the kings of the south and the kings of the north (5-28). Then tragically the remnant of Israel becomes the point of concentrated attack by a vile and perfidious king (29-35).

The kings **of the south** (5) were the Ptolemies, successors of Ptolemy Soter, Alexander's general in Egypt (see map 1). From the breakup of Alexander's empire in 323 B.C. these kings were in a struggle for power and territory with their nearest neighbors. These were the kings **of the north** (6), the Seleucids, successors of Seleucus I, who ruled much of Asia Minor, Syria, and the old Babylonian and Persian territories (see map 1). For 125 years Palestine and Phoenicia were under the power of the Ptolemies. The marriage of a Seleucid, Antiochus II, **to the king's daughter of the south** (6; Berenice, daughter of a Ptolemy) led only to more war, the murder of Berenice and her son, and the bloody revenge by her brother (7-9). The subjugation of Palestine by the Seleucids came under Antiochus III (the Great) in 198 B.C. (10-19). Later **a vile person** (21), Antiochus IV Epiphanes, through a subterfuge, displaced the rightful heir to the throne and took over control for himself. Verses 21-35 are understood to refer to the plots and tyrannies of Antiochus Epiphanes. With great energy and cunning he quickly expanded his power (21-24) and launched campaigns against his neighbor, Ptolemy VI Philometor (25-28).

The persecutions and insane tyrannies which Antiochus launched against the Jews and their religion (29-35) have made him one of history's monsters. **His indignation against the holy covenant** (30), taking **away the daily sacrifice,** and placing **the abomination that maketh desolate** (31; the image of Zeus Olympus) in the Temple are examples of his profane fury. He outlawed all Jewish laws, customs, and worship. He put to the sword the mothers and crucified the fathers who had their sons circumcised. Though he burned much of Jerusalem, slaughtered many of the men, and enslaved women and children, he did not destroy the will to resist. Though many compromised and submitted to Antiochus, many more dared to resist (32-35). An army of faithful and courageous Jews rallied to Mattathias.

When Mattathias died, his son Judas took up the leadership of the rebel army. His tactics in guerrilla warfare of sudden fierce attack and flight became famous and earned him the name of "Hammer" or Maccabee. Within three years the Maccabees had divided and conquered the Syrian armies of Antiochus and recaptured Jerusalem. The Temple was restored, the altar cleansed, and worship reinstituted, December 25, 165 B.C. To this day the Feast of Dedication or *Hannukah* is observed among Jews in commemoration of the event. The house of the Maccabees, called the Hasmoneans, became the acknowledged rulers until the Romans took over Palestine under Pompey in 63 B.C.[17]

Through the darkness of the fearful prophetic picture given in this chapter a clear light of faith and heroism shines forth. **The people that do know their God shall be strong, and do exploits** (32). Here is suggested "A Program of Action for a Godly Minority." (1) They **know . . . God.** (2) They are **strong.** (3) They **do exploits.** They take action with a clear sense of direction. (4) Their battle is on the high plane of the spirit, a battle of holy ideas. **They . . . shall instruct many,** 33. (5) Their cause triumphs. **To try them . . . to purge and to make them white, even to the time of the end,** 35.

c. *The willful king—Antichrist* (11:36-45). Jerome interpreted the whole section, 11:21-45, as having a dual reference, first to Antiochus Epiphanes, second to Antichrist.[18] But many conservative commentators, including Young[19] and Seiss,[20] hold that while verses 21-35 quite properly refer to Antiochus, and secondarily to Antichrist, verses 36-45 must refer to one greater, more profane, and more godless than even Antiochus.

The king shall do according to his will . . . exalt himself, and magnify himself above every god, and shall speak marvellous things against the God of gods (36). Here the clear figure of Antiochus begins to fade in the gathering gloom, and the hulking form of Antichrist begins to loom up in the background

---

[17]The translation in *The Berkeley Version,* together with the footnotes, will be a great help in understanding 11:5-35.

[18]*Op. cit.,* pp. 129-31.

[19]*The Prophecy of Daniel,* p. 241.

[20]*Op. cit.,* pp. 279-86.

shadows. We are reminded of Paul's warnings of "the man of sin" (II Thess. 2:3-4), and of John's vision of "the beast" (Rev. 13:5-8). Clearly we see reflected the "little horn" of both Daniel 7 and 8. An interesting difference appears when we compare the two little horns with this furious king of c. 11. While the little horn of c. 8 and the fierce king of c. 11 are related to the third kingdom of Daniel's prophecy, Greece, the little horn of c. 7 springs out of the fourth kingdom, Rome. Perhaps this is to remind us that Antichrist may be expected to take unto himself all the glory and power of human achievement and seek to combine in one the culture of Greece with the glory of Rome. That the culminating genius of evil should arrogate to himself all human good as well as divine worship would not be surprising.

Yet he shall come to his end (45). The amazing power and fury of the Antichrist are destined for a quick end. The "time and times and the dividing of time" (7:25), the one-half week (9:27), the "time, times and an half" (12:7) agree with Rev. 12:14 that the days of Antichrist are numbered by the Almighty. Paul declares of that "Wicked" one that "the Lord shall consume [him] with the spirit of his mouth, and shall destroy with the brightness of his coming" (II Thess. 2:8). So even though he shall **plant the tabernacles of his palace between the seas in the glorious holy mountain,** he shall find his end in the "lake of fire burning with brimstone" (Rev. 19:20). In the very land and place where Antichrist takes his stand, there the Christ of God shall descend in His glory. "Then shall the Lord go forth, and fight against those nations, as when he fought in the day of battle. And his feet shall stand in that day upon the mount of Olives, which is before Jerusalem" (Zech. 14:3-4; Acts 1:10-12).

d. *The Great Tribulation and the Great Triumph* (12:1-3). **There shall be a time of trouble** (1). The reign of Antichrist is everywhere in Scripture pictured as a crisis of evil. Gabriel's words succinctly describe it as a time "when the transgressors are come to the full" (8:23). A recurring theme in Scripture is the teaching that a time of great trouble climaxes the age of man's defiance against God and ushers in the culmination of the kingdom of God. Jeremiah speaks of "the time of Jacob's trouble" (Jer. 30:7). Jesus in His Olivet discourse described this time of trouble as "the days of vengeance" (Luke 21:22), and "great tribulation, such as was not since the beginning of the world . . . nor ever shall be" (Matt. 24:21; Mark 13:19-20). The futuristic interpretation regards much of the Book of Revelation as given to a depicting of this period, especially cc. 6—19.

But the Great Tribulation brings far more than the climax of evil; it ushers in the triumph of God. If the Book of Daniel teaches anything, it is that the powers of the celestial world are deeply interested and engaged in the affairs of men on earth. **At that time shall Michael stand up, the great prince which standeth for the children of thy people.** This is the archangel summoned to the aid of the glorious One in 10:13. We see the dramatic climax in Rev. 12:7-8, "There was war in heaven: Michael and his angels fought against the dragon; and the dragon fought and his angels, and prevailed not."

It is clear that the people of Israel are involved in this climax of history. Again and again in Daniel the phrase appears **thy people, the children of thy people.** At the same time it is necessary to keep a perspective. God has a concern for all mankind. The events which mark the climax of the ages are cosmic; their impact, international and worldwide. Palestine is doubtless a stage of divine action. But the whole earth and the heavens are the scene of God's final doings in this age. The point toward which history is moving is the culmination of the kingdom of God.

Them that sleep in the dust of the earth shall awake (2). This is the clearest revelation of the doctrine of the resurrection in the Old Testament. It reminds us that it is *Christ* who "hath brought life and immortality to light" (II Tim. 1:10). Some interpreters believe that the resurrection mentioned here is a partial resurrection relating only to Jews who have died in the tribulation. Calvin insists that this narrowing of the scope is unjustified, if for no other reason than that it includes both evil and good—some to everlasting life, and some to shame and everlasting contempt. He insists that the word **many** means "the many" or "all" and that the general resurrection is here intended.[21]

They that be wise—that turn many to righteousness—shall shine as the brightness of the firmament . . . and as the stars for ever and ever (3). These wise ones are blessed with the "wisdom that is from above" (Jas. 3:17). The word for **wise** (*chappim*) used most frequently in Daniel (fourteen times) means those who are wise with a worldly wisdom, the Magians. But *hamaskkilim* is used here from the root *sakal*, which means

[21]*Op. cit.*, II, 374.

to be circumspect, intelligent, have understanding, to teach. So we see in the marginal reference, "they that be teachers." D. L. Moody said, "It is not the great in this world who will shine the brightest. We know of Nebuchadnezzar and the rest of them scarcely anything, except as they fill in the story about these humble men of God . . . But the man of God shines. . . . This Daniel has been gone for 2500 years; but still increasing millions read of his life and actions. And so it will be to the end. He will only get better known and better loved; he will only shine the brighter as the world grows older."[22]

3. The Conclusion of Daniel's Prophetic Mission (12:4-13)

a. Characteristics of the last days (12:4). The final message of the glorious Messenger to Daniel was, **Shut up the words, and seal the book, even to the time of the end** (4). That the words have been shut and the book sealed has been evident by the vast confusion that has characterized the interpretation of this book over the past more than two millenniums. Adam Clarke writes: "The prophecy shall not be understood, but in its accomplishment: and then the depth of the wisdom and providence of God will be clearly seen in these matters."[23]

But closing the book is not the end of the matter. There will come a time of intense activity in transportation, education, and communication. Then the very events of the end would drive those who are wise to seek greater wisdom in the revelation of the book. We can scarcely escape identifying Daniel's brief description with our day. **Many shall run to and fro, and knowledge shall be increased.** Mass transportation and speed are hallmarks of our age. Restless mobility of world peoples, almost instantaneous mass communication, insistent and universal demand for education by the masses, all these are characteristics of our times.

b. How long will it be? (12:5-13). As Daniel stood by **the bank of the river** (5, Tigris, see map 1), he received a final message concerning the mysteries he had seen. Fully conscious, he was seeing beyond the veil of human sight. The same glorious One, **clothed in linen** (7), who had appeared at the beginning of this manifestation was yet present to give comfort and under-

---

[22]*Daniel the Prophet* (New York: Fleming H. Revell Co., n.d.), p. 58.

[23]*A Commentary and Critical Notes* (Nashville: Abingdon Press, n.d.), IV, 618.

standing. Young says, "The description seems to indicate that
the Majestic Person here presented is none other than the Lord
Himself. The revelation therefore is a theophany, a pre-incarnate
appearance of the eternal Son."[24]

One angel called to the other, **How long shall it be to the
end of these wonders?** (6) The glorious One answered with His
hands lifted **unto heaven** (7) in a dramatic gesture of affirmation.
Here was the Eternal Son swearing by the true and living God
that the times were in God's hands and fixed for **a time, times,
and an half; and when he shall have accomplished to scatter
the power of the holy people, all things shall be finished.** The
RSV renders this sentence, "When the shattering of the power of
the holy people comes to an end all these things would be accomplished." When "the times of the Gentiles" is fulfilled, the treading down of Jerusalem and the shattering of God's covenant
people will terminate. This will be accomplished in the judgment
of Antichrist discussed previously.

Daniel was still puzzled, driven on by a holy curiosity that
characterized him from his youth. But God would not give to
His servant perfect knowledge—yet. The **thousand two hundred and ninety days** (11) and the forty-five days more of v. 12
are but a repetition of the **time, times, and an half** (7). They
are God's assurance that the time of desolation is limited by
God's decree. Let Daniel be content. **The words are closed up
and sealed till the time of the end** (9). God has His work among
men to do. **Many shall be purified, and made white, and tried.**
True, **the wicked shall do wickedly** . . . **but the wise shall understand** (10). Let not those who trust in God fret. "No man know-
eth the hour" (Matt. 24:36), but in God's good time, when it is
required, the meaning will come clear. **Blessed is he that wait-
eth** (12).

So to Daniel came the word, **Go thou thy way till the end
be: for thou shalt rest, and stand in thy lot at the end of the
days** (13; cf. 9).

Adam Clarke gives a comforting word: "Here is proper advice for every man. 1. Thou hast a *way*—a *walk in life,* which
God has assigned thee; *walk in that way,* it is *thy way.* 2. There
will be an *end* to thee of all earthly things. Death is at the door
and eternity is at hand; *go on to the end*—be faithful unto death.
3. There is a *rest* provided for the people of God. Thou shalt *rest;*

[24]*The Prophecy of Daniel,* pp. 225, 258.

thy body in the grave; thy soul, in the Divine favour here, and, finally in paradise. 4. As in the promised land there was a *lot* for each of God's people, so in heaven there is a *lot* for *thee*. Do not close it, do not sell it, do not let thy enemy *rob thee* of it. Be determined *to stand in thy own lot at the end of the days*. See that thou keep the faith; die in the Lord Jesus, that thou mayest rise and reign with him to all eternity."[25]

Alexander Maclaren suggests a New Year's Message with these thoughts from v. 13. (1) The Journey—Go thy way; (2) The Pilgrim's Resting Place—**Thou shalt rest**; (3) The Final Home—**Stand in thy lot at the end of the days**.[26]

Daniel received a clear confirmation of his hope of immortality. Centuries, yes, millenniums, were to pass before its full realization. But at **the end of the days**, when the consummation comes, Daniel will be there, standing with the assembled multitudes of the redeemed on earth and from heaven. Then he will be, not a spectator of visions, but a participator in the tremendous events of the ushering in of the full glory of the kingdom of God. He shall behold in rapture the glory and wisdom and honor of Him who from the beginning ordained the outcome of history in the kingdom of God. He will join in the "Hallelujah Chorus" of the ransomed from the ages. Then shall "the kingdoms of this world . . . become the kingdoms of our Lord, and of his Christ; and he shall reign for ever and ever" (Rev. 11:15).

[25]*Op. cit.*, IV, 619.

[26]*Expositions of Holy Scripture* (Grand Rapids, Michigan: Wm. B. Eerdmans Publishing Co., 1938), VI, 84-93.

Bibliography

I. COMMENTARIES

BARR, JAMES P. "Daniel," *Peake's Commentary on the Bible*. Edited by MATTHEW BLACK and H. H. ROWLEY. New York: Nelson and Sons, 1962.

CALVIN, JOHN. *Commentaries on the Book of Daniel*. 2 volumes. Translated by THOMAS MYERS. Grand Rapids: Wm. B. Eerdmans Publishing Co., 1948.

CLARKE, ADAM. "The Book of the Prophet Daniel," *A Commentary and Critical Notes*, Vol. IV. New York: Abingdon Press, n.d.

DAVIES, G. HENTON; RICHARDSON, ALAN; WALLIS, CHARLES (eds.). *The Twentieth Century Bible Commentary*. New York: Harper and Brothers, 1955.

DRIVER, S. R. *The Book of Daniel*, "Cambridge Bible for Schools and Colleges." Edited by A. F. KIRKPATRICK. Cambridge: Cambridge University Press, 1900.

FARRAR, F. W. *The Book of Daniel*, "The Expositor's Bible." Edited by W. ROBERTSON NICOLL. Ne wYork: Funk and Wagnalls, 1900.

FAUSSET, A. R. "The Book of Daniel," *Critical and Experimental Commentary*, Vol. IV, by ROBERT JAMIESON, A. R. FAUSSET, DAVID ZROWN. Grand Rapids: Wm. B. Eerdmans Publishing Co., 1948.

HEATON, E. W. "Daniel," *The Twentieth Century Bible Commentary*. Edited by G. HENTON DAVIES, ALAN RICHARDSON, CHARLES L. WALLIS. New York: Harper and Brothers, 1956.

JEFFERY, ARTHUR. "The Book of Daniel" (Introduction, Exegesis). *The Interpreter's Bible*. Edited by G. A. BUTTRICK, *et al.*, Vol. VI. New York: Abingdon Press, 1956.

JEROME. *Commentary on Daniel*. Translated by GLEASON L. ARCHER. Grand Rapids: Baker Book House, 1958.

KEIL, C. F. "The Book of the Prophet Daniel," *Biblical Commentary on the Old Testament*. By C. F. KEIL and F. DELITZSCH. Translated by M. G. EASTON. Edinburgh: T. and T. Clark, 1872.

KENNEDY, GERALD. "The Book of Daniel" (Exposition). *The Interpreter's Bible*. Edited by G. A. BUTTRICK, et al., Vol. VI. New York: Abingdon Press, 1956.

MACLAREN, ALEXANDER. *Expositions of Holy Scripture*. Grand Rapids: Wm. B. Eerdmans Publishing Co., 1938.

MONTGOMERY, JAMES A. *A Critical and Exegetical Commentary on the Book of Daniel*. "The International Critical Commentary." Edited by SAMUEL S. DRIVER, *et al*. New York: Charles Scribner's Sons, 1927.

YOUNG, EDWARD J. "Daniel," *The New Bible Commentary*. Edited by FRANCIS DAVIDSON, ALAN M. STIBBS, ERNEST F. KEVAN. Grand Rapids: Wm. B. Eerdmans Publishing Co., 1963.

YOUNG, G. DOUGLAS. "Daniel," *The Biblical Expositor*. Edited by CARL F. H. HENRY, Vol. II. Philadelphia: The Holman Co., 1960.

ZOCKLER, O. "The Prophet Daniel," *Commentary on the Holy Scriptures.* Edited by JOHN PETER LANGE. Translated and edited by PHILIP SCHAFF. New York: Charles Scribner's Sons, 1915.

II. OTHER BOOKS

BURROWS, MILLER, (ed.). *The Dead Sea Scrolls of St. Mark's Monastery.* New Haven: American Schools of Oriental Research, 1950.

————. *More Light on the Dead Sea Scrolls.* New York: Viking Press, 1958.

CHAPMAN, JAMES B. *The Second Coming of Christ.* Kansas City: Nazarene Publishing House, n.d.

DOUGHERTY, RAYMOND PHILLIP. *Nabonidus and Belshazzar.* New Haven: Yale University Press, 1929.

GAEBELEIN, ARNO C. *Gabriel and Michael the Archangel.* New York: Our Hope Publications, 1945.

————. *The Harmony of the Prophetic Word.* New York: Fleming H. Revell Co., 1907.

————. *The Prophet Daniel.* Grand Rapids: Kregel Publications, 1955.

JOSEPHUS, FLAVIUS. *The Works of Flavius Josephus.* Translated by William Whiston. Philadelphia: J. P. Lippencott and Co., 1895.

LIDDELL, HENRY GEORGE, and SCOT9, ROBERT. *A Greek-English Lexicon.* Revised, 1940. London: Oxford University Press, 1951.

MOODY, DWIGHT L. *Daniel the Prophet.* Chicago: Fleming H. Revell Co., 1884.

Oxford Annotated Bible, The. Edited by HERBERT G. MAY and BRUCE M. METZGER. New York: Oxford University Press, 1962.

PUSEY, EDWARD B. *Daniel the Prophet.* New York: Funk and Wagnalls Co., 1885.

ROWLEY, HAROLD H. *Jewish Apocalyptic and the Dead Sea Scrolls.* London: Athlone Press, 1957.

SEISS, JOSEPH A. *Voices from Babylon.* Philadelphia: The Castle Press, 1879.

STEVENS, W. C. *The Book of Daniel.* Los Angeles: Bible House of Los Angeles, 1943.

WHITCOMB, JOHN C. JR. *Darius the Mede.* Grand Rapids: Wm. B. Eerdmans Publishing Co., 1959.

YOUNG, EDWAR4 J. *The Prophecy of Daniel.* Grand Rapids: Wm. B. Eerdmans Publishing Co., 1949.

————. *The Messianic Prophecies of Daniel.* Grand Rapids: Wm. B. Eerdmans Publishing Co., 1954.

Map 1

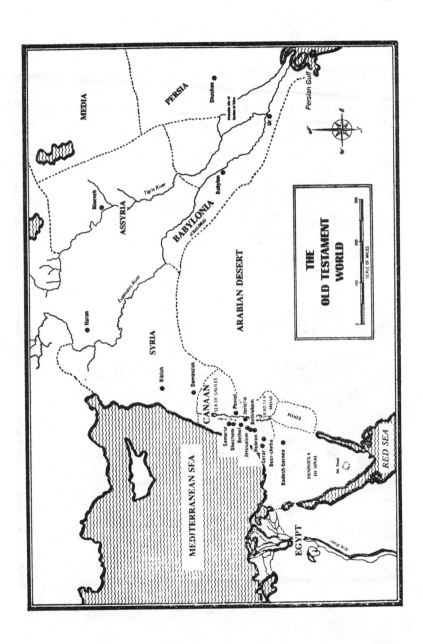

THE
OLD TESTAMENT
WORLD

SCALE OF MILES

689

Map 2

PALESTINE
in the Time of
the Divided Kingdom

0   10   20   30
SCALE OF MILES

MEDITERRANEAN SEA

PHOENICIA

Gebal

Berothai

Sidon

Zarephath

Tyre

Abel   Dan

Mt. Lebanon

Mt. Hermon

Helbon

Damascus

River Abana

River Pharpar

Chun

Zedad

Hazar-enam

Waters of Merom

Accho

Cabul

Mt. Carmel

Sea of Galilee

Ashtaroth

Dor

ISRAEL

Megiddo

Jezreel

Edrei   Nobah

Ramoth-gilead

Dothan

Tishbeh

Mahanaim

Salcah

Samaria

Shechem

Brook Cherith

River Jordan

River Jabbok

AMMON

Plain of Sharon

Joppa

Gilgal

Bethel

Gibeah   Ai   Jericho

Anathoth   Gilgal

Rabbath-ammon

Heshbon

Mt. Nebo

Medeba

Beth-peor

Jerusalem

Ashdod   Cath

Askelon

Gaza   Etam

Gerar

Lachish

Tekoa

Hebron

PHILISTIA

JUDAH

Beer-sheba

Dead Sea

Dibon

MOAB

Ar

Kir-haraseth

ARABIAN

DESERT

Kadesh-barnea

Punon

Bozrah

EDOM

Sela   Teman

Map 3

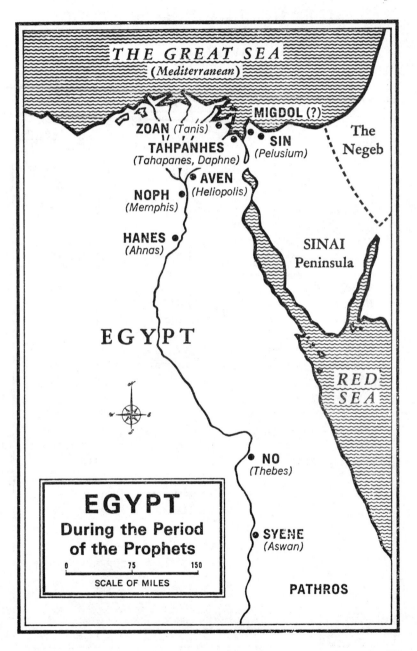

THE GREAT SEA
(Mediterranean)

MIGDOL (?)

ZOAN (Tanis)

SIN
(Pelusium)

TAHPANHES
(Tahapanes, Daphne)

The
Negeb

AVEN
(Heliopolis)

NOPH
(Memphis)

HANES
(Ahnas)

SINAI
Peninsula

E G Y P T

RED
SEA

NO
(Thebes)

EGYPT
During the Period
of the Prophets

0   75   150

SCALE OF MILES

SYENE
(Aswan)

PATHROS

Chart A

CHART OF THE KINGDOM PERIOD
FROM 1010 to 586 B.C.

DAVID (1010-971)
SOLOMON (971-931)
DIVISION (931)

ISRAEL (Northern Kingdom)   **JUDAH** (Southern Kingdom)

Reigns	Co-regencies	Reigns	Co-regencies
JEROBOAM 931-910		REHOBOAM 931-913	
NADAB 910-909		ABIJAM 913-911	
BAASHA 909-886		ASA 911-870	
ELAH 886-885			
ZIMRI 885			
TIBNI 885-880	885-880		
OMRI 885-874	885-880		
AHAB 874-853		JEHOSHAPHAT ...870-848	873-870
AHAZIAH 853-852			
JEHORAM 852-841		JEHORAM 848-841	853-848
JEHU 841-814		AHAZIAH 841	
JEHOAHAZ.........814-798		ATHALIAH 841-835	
		JOASH 835-796	
JEHOASH 798-782		AMAZIAH 796-767	
JEROBOAM II 782-753	793-782	AZARIAH 767-740	791-767
ZACHARIAH 753-752		(Uzziah)	
SHALLUM 752			
MENAHEM 752-742			
PEKAHIAH 742-740			
PEKAH 740-732		JOTHAM 740-732	750-740
HOSHEA 732-723, 722		AHAZ 732-716	
		HEZEKIAH 716-687	729-716
		MANASSEH..........687-642	696-687
		AMON 642-640	
		JOSIAH 640-608	
		JEHOAHAZ 608	
		JEHOIAKIM 608-597	
		JEHOIACHIN 597	
		ZEDEKIAH 597-586	

THE EXILE AND RETURN

POSTEXILIC PERIOD: RETURN (536-400 B.C.)

539-530	CYRUS of PERSIA (Isaiah 44:28; 45:1; II Chronicles 36:22; Ezra 1:1)
537	DECREE to RETURN (Ezra 1:1-4)
536	FIRST RETURN–ZERUBBABEL (Ezra 1:4-2:67)
	REBUILDING BEGUN (Ezra 2:68-3:13)
	HINDERED by SAMARITANS (Ezra 4:1-24)
522-486	DARIUS of PERSIA (Ezra 4:24; 6:1; Haggai 1:1; Zechariah 1:1)
520	HAGGAI and ZECHARIAH (Ezra 5; Haggai; Zechariah)
516	TEMPLE REBUILT and DEDICATED (Ezra 6)
485-465	AHASUERUS (Xerxes of Persia) (Esther 1:1)
	ESTHER and MORDECAI (Book of Esther)
458	SECOND RETURN–EZRA (Ezra 7-8)
	REFORMS at JERUSALEM (Ezra 9-10)
450-430	MALACHI'S PROPHECIES
444	THIRD RETURN–NEHEMIAH (Nehemiah 1:1-2:8)
	REBUILDING of the WALL (Nehemiah 2:9-6:19)
	INSTRUCTION in the LAW (Nehemiah 8-10)
432	NEHEMIAH BACK in JERUSALEM (Nehemiah 13)
	REFORM MEASURES
	PERIOD between the TESTAMENTS

EXILIC PERIOD: CAPTIVITY (606-536 B.C.)

605-561	NEBUCHADNEZZAR in BABYLONIA
608-597	JEHOIAKIM, KING of JUDAH (II Kings 23:34-24:6)
	VASSAL of EGYPT
	VASSAL of BABYLONIA
606	FIRST CAPTIVITY–DANIEL (II Kings 24:1; Daniel 1:1-2; 6)
600	REBELLION against BABYLONIA
597	JEHOIACHIN, KING of JUDAH (II Kings 24:8-17)
	JERUSALEM BESIEGED
	SECOND CAPTIVITY–10,000 INCLUDING JEHOIACHIN and EZEKIEL
597-586	ZEDEKIAH, KING of JUDAH (II Kings 24:18-25:21)
592-570	EZEKIEL'S PROPHECIES
588	REVOLT against BABYLONIA
586	JERUSALEM DESTROYED
	THIRD CAPTIVITY
585	OBADIAH'S PROPHECY
555	GEDALIAH SLAIN (Jeremiah 40-41)
	JEREMIAH to EGYPT (Jeremiah 42-44)
550-535	DANIEL'S PROPHECIES
538	FALL of BABYLONIA (Daniel 5)

Chart C

Stevens-Wright reconstruction of Solomon's Temple

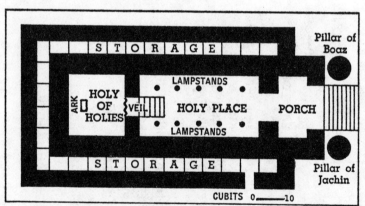

Floor plan of the Temple (*adapted from Watzinger*)